Love,
Susan

NEW

YORK

COOK

BOOK

NEW YORK

by Molly O'Neill

YORK

Photography by Howard Earl Simmons

COOK

Workman Publishing, New York

BOOK

For
Stanley W. Dry

Text copyright ©1992 by Molly O'Neill
New photographs ©1992 by Workman Publishing Company, Inc.

Library of Congress Cataloging-in-Publication Data
O'Neill, Molly.
New York Cookbook / by Molly O'Neill.
p. cm.
Includes index.
ISBN 1-56305-337-3—ISBN 0-89480-698-X (pbk.)
1. Cookery, American. 2. Cookery, International. 3. Cookery—New York (N.Y.).
4. Restaurants, lunchrooms, etc.—New York (N.Y.). I. Title.
TX715.0533 1992
641.5—dc20 92-50280
CIP

Concept: Paul Hanson
Design: Paul Hanson and Lisa Hollander
Cover and inside photographs: Howard Earl Simmons
Photo editor: Sheilah Scully
Illustrations on page 112 and 121 by Lou Carbone

Who's Who on the Front and Back Covers: see page 509.

Workman books are available at special discounts when purchased in bulk for premiums and sales promotions as well as for fund-raising or educational use. Special editions or book excerpts can also be created to specification. For details, contact the Special Sales Director at the address below.

Workman Publishing Company, Inc.
708 Broadway
New York, NY 10003

Manufactured in the United States of America
First printing November 1992
10 9 8 7 6 5 4 3 2 1

CONTENTS

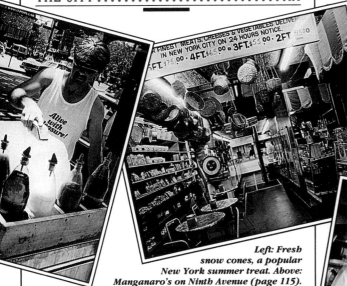

Left: Fresh snow cones, a popular New York summer treat. Above: Manganaro's on Ninth Avenue (page 115).

Meal starters, coffee breaks, street food—New York's best little bites. Falafel, Jamaican beef patties, hummus, clam fritters, savory chicken wings, and Jarlsberg squares.

Noshing with Lou Singer
Nosh Stops
A Taste of the Tropics
On Being a Hostess with the Leastest
Lox, Stock, and Bagels
To Catch a Proper Nova
Smart Cocktails by the Borough and Beyond
Many-Faced Quiche
Stone Fence
The Caviarteria and What It Knows
New York's Artesian Springs

New York bowlfuls. Chicken soup in all its ethnic varieties. Scotch broth, hot and sour soup, and Hungarian szekely. Borscht, bisque, green mine-strone, white bean soup, and snert.

Chicken Soup: A New York Panacea
Matzoh Bowl I
The Soup Man of 55th Street
Manhattan Clam Chowder

Above: Gilbert Godoy of Cammerari Bakery, Brooklyn (page 86). Right: Faicco's in the Village (page 282).

Breads with crust and breads with heft. Fresh muffins, bagels, babka, beer bread, roti, parantha, and focaccia.

The Brick Oven Brotherhood
Where to Buy a Good Loaf
Stalking the Perfect Pizza Pie
Pizza Stops
To Make a Soft Pretzel
A Bagel Is a Bagel...

FOOD WALKS 112

F ood on foot. Tours of New York's ethnic neighborhoods and food markets. Where to stop and why.

THE GREENING OF NEW YORK........126

N ew York cooks offer up Southern-style and Chinese-style greens, Caribbean callaloo, Marrakesh carrots, and artichokes with a Turkish twist. Plus baked beans, potato chips, and potato latkes. And salads. And pickles.

Right: Franks, knishes, chili dogs—quick lunch à la New York.

Above: Full-service delis abound citywide. Right: Michael Blitz at Guss' aka Essex Street Pickles (page 3).

A CHRONOLOGY OF SIGNIFICANT CULINARY EVENTS IN NEW YORK CITY 190

N ew York has always been a happening food town. From the first coffee-houses in the 1600s to soda fountains in the 1800s to hot dogs, cafeterias, Chiclets, Tootsie Rolls, and cheesecake, New Yorkers have made their mark.

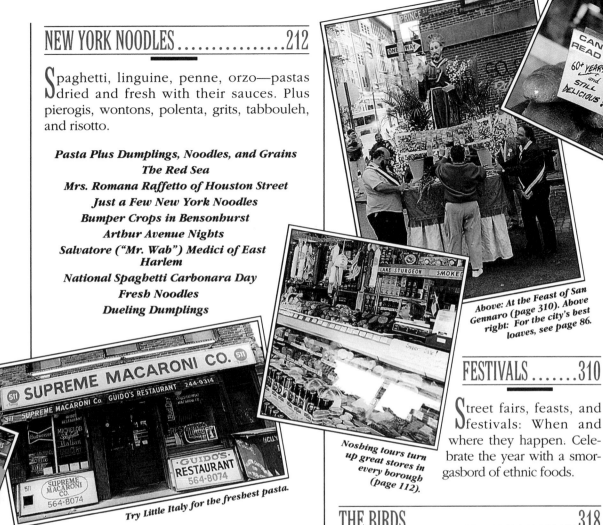

NEW YORK NOODLES 212

Spaghetti, linguine, penne, orzo—pastas dried and fresh with their sauces. Plus pierogis, wontons, polenta, grits, tabbouleh, and risotto.

Try Little Italy for the freshest pasta.

Above: At the Feast of San Gennaro (page 310). Above right: For the city's best loaves, see page 86.

Noshing tours turn up great stores in every borough (page 112).

FESTIVALS 310

Street fairs, feasts, and festivals: When and where they happen. Celebrate the year with a smorgasbord of ethnic foods.

THE MEAT OF THE MATTER 260

Great steaks, brisket, casseroles, cutlets, stews, and chops. Unbelievable barbecue, meat loaf every way, and a hamburger like no other. Plus shish kebab, leg of lamb, couscous, and South African bobotie.

THE BIRDS 318

Fragrant chickens, roasted, fried, and barbecued. Cambodian chicken salad, chicken hash, and chicken Kiev. Five ways to stuff a turkey. Poultry fricassees, grills, and stews.

A LITTLE SOMETHING SWEET 414

Desserts à la New York include chocolate cakes, carrot cakes, and six fabulous cheesecakes. Fudgy brownies, mammoth cookies, mile-high pies, Mexican flan, dense bread pudding, and crème brûlèe.

Ebinger's Blackout Cake
To Buy Fine Chocolates
A Fine and Fancy Cake
On Top of the Carrot Cake Hill
New York Cheesecake
Some Very Good Bakeries
Fox's U-Bet Chocolate Flavored Syrup

Above: At the Union Square Greenmarket (page 127). Right: Carmela Lancieri of Patsy's (page 100).

Right: Ninth Avenue offerings (page 112).

TRY OUR SPINACH, SAUSAGE or BROCCOLI ROLL

FROM RIVER, SEA, AND THE FULTON MARKET 366

New York's seafood favorites: Pan roasts and stews, stuffed lobster and a unique lobster club sandwich, scallop pie and shrimp with feta, plus shad roe, fillet of sole, tuna Rockefeller, and red snapper hash.

A Day Dawns at Fulton
Fernando Lara, Marine Muralist
Shadding on the Hudson

Above: Early morning at the Fulton Fish Market (page 367). Above right: Chinatown (page 112).

A TRIP DOWN MENU LANE................................402

New Yorkers on the town: A look at where they ate and what they ordered, from early tavern and pushcart days to Delmonico's, Luchows, and the current hot spots.

LOOKING FOR
THE HEART OF THE CITY

I came to New York City eight years ago. Like the millions before me, I was drawn to the energy, the myth, the romance of the steam that rises from the streets, at least in the movies. I was scared stiff, as they say back where I come from in central Ohio. But as they also say: "Mad dogs smell fear." I faked bravado and since false bravado and the native New York persona are difficult to distinguish, I fit in pretty well, at least I thought I did.

"Just a bailey," I informed the waiter at Dubrow's my first morning in New York. I was determined that not one

Great appetizing on the Lower East Side (page 3).

moment's hesitation would reveal the fact that I had studied guidebooks for hours before selecting this "quintessential Garment district spot." I was resolved that no fillip in my cadence would reveal that I had absolutely no clue as to what I was ordering. I was completely oblivious to the fact that, in all my nervousness, I had asked to be served a bondsman perhaps, or the cartoon character Beetle Bailey.

The waiter, who was right out of Broadway Danny Rose, greeted my request with a lev-

el and unflinching gaze. I stared back. For reasons known only to him, the waiter did not deliver the contemptuous, "A BAILEY, Miss?," that the moment called for. He smiled. He nodded. He brought a lightly toasted, oniony flattish roll on a thick plate. With a seemingly bored flick of the wrist, he skidded the plate across the Formica table. It slid to a photo-finish stop right in front of me.

"BI-A-LY," he enunciated clearly. "No butter, schmear—that would be the cream cheese—Miss, on the side."

"Thank you," I said, in equally well pronounced syllables. I must have known that this was a quintessential New York moment, one of those times when kindness, tolerance, and generosity masquerade as a crusty surliness. I left a walloping tip.

"You wouldn't believe it," I told my husband later that night.

Above: The old favorite for homemade knishes. Right: Mark Jacobowitz and Greg Pedersen (next page) at Fredricksen and Johannesen (page 122).

"The guy slings this bailey at me like its a hockey puck and I'm the goal."

"A bailey?," asked my husband.

"Bailey, bi-a-ly, whatever," I snapped. "You're as bad as the waiter."

Fate had dealt us a prototypical "starter

apartment," a cubbyhole in a former welfare hotel. When we pulled our moving truck up to the building, I noticed that some of the lights had burned out on the sign above the front door of our new home. "Hot l Wood ard," it read. We spent the next five years coming to understand what the classified ads mean when they describe a New York apartment as "charming."

There was an international students' center on the second floor, prisoners on early release on the third floor, families boarded by various state and city agencies throughout the building, as well as eight other young professional couples who, like us, paid their own rent and believed the landlord when he said that he was in the process of converting the hotel into condominiums and that we would get an insiders' price. The rest of the tenants were recent Senegalese immigrants.

When the Italians came to New York, they established produce fiefdoms; the Germans came and baked; the Irish became cops; and in the same, grand tradition of niche marketing, the Senegalese who arrived in the early '80s specialized in umbrellas. They sprouted on street corners like mushrooms whenever it rained, proffering small, black, collapsible umbrellas.

A watermelon toss at one of New York's many Korean vegetable markets.

"Humbrella, Humbrella, fie dolla, fie dolla," was the standard sales pitch. The Hot l was Humbrella headquarters. We couldn't take the elevator on rainy days because the Humbrella men were moving product. But we didn't really notice because the elevator was usually broken anyway. The Head Humbrellaman, his wife, and their infant son lived down the hall from us. He managed nearly one hundred vendors in Manhattan, supplying them with umbrellas to sell and giving them dinner every day, which his wife cooked in a battered aluminum pot the size of a trash can placed on a hot plate. The vendors brought their own bowls and spoons and ate crouched in the hallway of the Hot l, leaning on the wall between my door, and the Humbrella Man's door at the end of the hall.

"Bon jour!" some would say, as I passed. "Hell-Yo," said others. Still others, blessed with boundless zeal or in sharing my new-to-New York nervousness, would wave and say, "Humbrella, humbrella!"

I was usually on my way to a restaurant. Stanley, my husband, was working at *Food & Wine* magazine, I was the restaurant critic for *New York Newsday*. We may have slept at the Hot l but we lived in restaurants. At first, I loved it. Free-floating '80s cash had fostered an explosion of restaurants in the city. It was dizzying to keep up with them and mind-boggling to catalog and appreciate the

Above: Pete's Spice and Everything Nice (page 3). Right: What don't they have at the Party Center?

talent that swarmed here. Having cooked in restaurants for nearly a decade before we began writing about food, both Stanley and I were unsettled by the glitz and the effete fussiness of the food that appeared in the citadels of chic during the 1980s. But we were dazzled, too.

"Let's go to Astoria," (or Chinatown, or Flushing, or Atlantic Avenue, or the Lower East Side), Stanley would say every weekend. "I'm going to lose it if I don't get some real food soon."

I, on the other hand, thought I would lose it in any circumstance that echoed, however vaguely, our circumstance at the Hot l. The pungent streets of Chinatown smelled like the trash that the landlord allowed to pile up in the hall, the chatter along Atlantic Avenue sounded like the conversation outside our apartment door. "Le Cirque," I would plead. "Shun Lee, The Oyster Bar…"

Like all couples trying to bridge the un-bridgeable, we compromised. One citadel for me, one dive for him. Even after we separated, we agreed that ours had been fortuitous concessions.

The city's *haute* restaurants are its aspirations, a collective vision of how it wants to be seen and how it thinks that others (that would be auslanders, or anyone not of New York) want to see it. Dives, on the other hand, like street fairs, church suppers, and home-cooked meals, are portraits of what the city has been, a reflection of what it knows for sure about itself, and about the tastes of its patrons. The first is presumption, the second is unembellished fact. As is said, "Reality lies somewhere in between."

In the beginning, day after day, I went looking for that reality, guidebooks in hand, false bravado at the ready. My mission was to *know* New York—Bi-a-ly or Bust. But within a month I'd realized that appreciating the City, like playing tennis, takes practice. By the time that Peter Workman, Suzanne Rafer, and Paul Hanson approached me in 1987 with an idea they had for a New York City community-style cookbook, I had the confidence that comes from knowing the geography of a place. After five years of working on the book, gathering recipes and reminiscences, trying to divine the taste and the style of New York, I've learned about heart, my own and the city's.

Like every place else, I've lived—Columbus, Ohio, Vienna, Austria, Provincetown, Amherst and Boston, Massachusetts, and Paris, France—New York is at its most vulnerable in the kitchen. Unlike other people, however, New Yorkers bring the same sort of obsessive drive to their cooking that they bring to every aspect of their daily life. Riding the F train, holding a seat on the New York Stock Exchange, shopping Madison Avenue, making perfect matzoh balls—it all takes a certain kind of ornery perfectionism, a combative and indefatigable connoisseurship that is rampant in New York.

In order to collect recipes, at first I advertised in newspapers and newsletters of clubs and schools and professional organizations, asking New Yorkers to send their favorite family recipes for a forthcoming book. Soon, friends of friends of friends were sending recipes; in all I received several thousand. Most of them were hand-written and lots were of the canned-mushroom-soup-and-noodle-casserole genre that is big in my hometown. But unlike the easy accommodation of a Columbus recipe, "take some canned mushroom soup, Campbell's if you have it…" the New York recipe would call for a mushroom soup that could *only* be purchased at the exclusive Maison Glass or a particular noodle made only *one* day a week at *one* Hungarian grocery.

The part of me that went to cooking school in Paris recoiled at the mere mention of canned mushroom soup. *Quelle horreur!* But the part of me that was beginning to fall in love with New York was acquiring an instinct. I knew, for instance, that of the recipes I received calling for canned products and reading more like

Above: Italian loaves in SoHo. Right: Try Ruth Manton's Caviar Hors d'Oeuvre (page 32).

back-of-the-box gourmet than notes from the tastemaking capital of the world, former fire chief Bill Thomas' canned Tuna Rockefeller would not only taste delicious, but was also the most indisputably "New York."

The same instinct told me that only a New Yorker would dare braising her brisket in ginger ale—and be rewarded with a glorious thing. Only someone with a bit of the Big Apple somewhere in their gene pool would carry their own personal thermometer to check the temperature of dim sum before making a selection in a Chinese restaurant. Only people who grew up on the Brooklyn Dodgers and Ebinger's cakes would, at the height of their careers, in the middle of the work day, walk out of meetings in their law firms or television stations or banks where they are now CEOs to taste and appraise twelve different versions of Blackout Cake.

New Yorkers are as intense about their food as they are about their parking spaces. I know a man who carries a small folding camp chair in his Hermès briefcase, so that if he should find a parking spot near his home, he can sit and use his portable phone to alert his wife, who then moves the car out of the garage (where they pay a daily rate), and into the spot he protects (because there they can park for free, at least on alternate days). What's a dim sum thermometer to someone willing to pack a folding chair?

I'd been working on this project for a year before I realized the selflessness of the prototypical, food-loving New Yorker. John Sineno, the former fireman who wrote the *Firehouse Cookbook* had arranged for me to have dinner at a firehouse in Harlem one Sunday night. As I stood in the kitchen watching five firemen cooking, I was struck by how intently they chopped, how tenderly they stirred. The alarm rang before we sat down and I followed the trucks. As I watched the fire fighters break down doors, scale walls, and carry children out of a burning building, I noticed a similar expression, intent and tender. Dinner was delayed. But it was ebullient.

The communal sigh of relief, the celebration, the shared purpose, and the generous spirit at the Harlem firehouse epitomized the family meals I shared throughout New York City; it was present in four-star kitchens, it was the main mood among the Humbrella men outside my apartment door. Maybe the harshness of city life,

Above: Local markets sell the freshest fish. Right: Go to Brooklyn for West Indian baked goods.

like the brutality of a primordial hunt, deepens the zest for dinner. Or maybe, like the water, the food is just better in New York. In either case, food is a common language.

"Hungry?" Mrs. Head Humbrellaman would ask whenever we passed in the hall. "Very special African stew," she would say in melodic French.

"I'm testing recipes for a cookbook," I would sputter in stumbling French, offering her pierogis or matzoh balls or pho.

By then, I knew that our relationship was very New York. Lou Singer, the tour guide, epicure, and New York historian had convinced me that in the city different cultures had always exchanged habits and customs as easily as neighbors borrowing a cup of flour. I gave Mrs. Head Humbrellaman her first box of trash bags. ("Why?" she asked, as she stood by the tenth floor window with a pot full of chicken carcasses in her hands.) She'd described how one chicken can feed fifty people. ("Why so much water and vegetables and seasoning?" I had asked.)

At least when genuine questions are asked, you both have something to laugh about. Mrs. Head Humbrellaman laughed until tears rolled down her face at my idiocy. We both get the giggles when we remember how the Board of Health once staked out the Hot l in an effort to figure out who was tossing chicken carcasses directly on the sidewalk.

Coming to New York at any age insures anybody a second coming-of-age. You learn a new set of rules, new mores, new rituals, new ways. And you learn about yourself. I probably shouldn't have been surprised to find myself looking for the small town inside the city. What pulled me toward New York was the grand culture, the dazzling, urbane vision the city has of itself, its aspirations. But what keeps me in New York is the undauntable heart of the place, the small enclaves and intimate groups that remain heroically human, despite the scale, the glamour and the hassle of the city.

Again and again, I stumbled into these small towns—Sunday dinner at the Abyssinian Baptist Church and winter afternoon coffee at

the Swedish Seaman's Church; the group that cooks for the grand charity dinners and those who work shifts in soup kitchens; the group that gathers annually in Sunnyside, Queens, to sample David "The Latke King's" wares; the Fathers Who Cook night at the United Nations School; the Explorers Club dinners; the members of the Polar Bears Club who dive into the January waters off Coney Island, neutralizing the cold, one told me, by dreaming of the lemon chicken soup they slurp afterwards.

These ad hoc fraternities of shared purpose are as tightly connected as the citizenry in any small town. They are the psychic infrastructure of the city. And so often, what they share is an occasional meal.

I discovered that New York is the sum of

its small town parts and to be given its key, one needs only to ask for a family recipe. "I'm working on a book about the cooking in New York," was the ultimate pick-up line. It got me invitations to swank Park Avenue dinner parties, to banquets in the catacombs beneath Canal Street, to family dinners in dozens of non-English-speaking homes, and to charity ball suppers. I was invited into restaurant kitchens and grandmothers' kitchens, to stand near the stoves of the rich and famous, to stand at the elbow of a family cook who'd already worked a double-shift as a detective in Times Square and couldn't wait to get home to make dinner

John Sineno (page xii).

The Cyclone of Coney Island.

Ninth Avenue for unusual cuts.

for his wife and kids. I have 232 notebooks filled with jottings from these evenings.

As I amassed recipes and the stories of the people who made them, four assistants helped appraise and test each one. Since most of the recipes in the *New York Cookbook* have been passed from mother to daughter, friend to friend, we tried to find its original source, whether it was an older relative, a community cookbook, or *The Joy of Cooking*. We established a common, comprehensible style and yield and adapted each recipe to that style. We tried to resist culinary revisionism—if canned mushroom soup was called for, we used canned mushroom soup—but occasionally we substituted ingredients that are accessible throughout the country for the more arcane and exotic ingredients that can be found only in ethnic neighborhoods. Occasionally, we simplified recipes.

In all, nearly 1,000 recipes were tested and without the help of Michael Krondl, Mary-Lynn Mondich, Jane Littell and Anna Moore, I would certainly still be wandering through a maze of hand-written family secrets. In addition to testing recipes, we became detectives. We followed leads like "Angela Palladino makes the best meatballs, but I haven't seen her in years…." And we tried to crack the culinary code on some New York standbys. Orwasher's, for instance, was loath to give its recipe for pumpernickel bread, but the founder's scion was delighted to sample our versions and give a nod of approval to the

Festive food during Harlem Week (page 310).

one that came closest. The same thing happened with the prosciutto bread, whose scent has perfumed Spring Street for over a hundred years, as well as with a variety of other dishes whose taste people remembered passionately, but whose recipe they couldn't recall.

Recalcitrant cooks would say, "Come watch" and we would. We spent days in Chinese restaurants, weeks chasing the holy grail of New York's brick-oven pizza from Coney Island to Harlem. We indentured ourselves to the self-proclaimed "Bagel King," to the "King of Jerk," to the "Falafel King." After observing, an assistant and I would concoct recipes and invite in a tasting jury. The carpet between my front door and my kitchen is well worn.

We also spent months at the New-York Historical Society, the Brooklyn Historical Society, the New York Public Library, and the Museum of the City of New York, where we studied household records from the seventeenth, eighteenth, nineteenth, and twentieth centuries in an attempt to find the dishes that epitomized each era. As an auslander, I relied on the generosity of people who are passionate about eating and passionate about New York City—especially Michael and Ariane Batterberry, Ed Koch, Lydie Marshall, Richard Lord, Eileen Yin-Fei Lo, Karen Hess, John Sineno, Chira Colletti, Arthur Schwartz, and Richard Shepard as well as my colleagues, first at *New York Newsday* and now at *The New York Times,* and of course, the wonderful people at Workman. Without an initial push from Stanley Dry, I might never have abandoned a restaurant stove and tried my hand at writing; without his unflagging support and infallible judgment, I would have stopped after one borough.

And without the people whose

Left: Check page 154 for Bob Rogers' Spicy Garbanzo Pudding. Below: Eel Handrolls from Mr. Kuraoka are on page 13.

RESTAURANT nippon

recipes and stories appear in this book, there would be no *New York Cookbook*. I've heard other writers say that someone else guides their hand when they write. The people who keep New York cooking wrote this book.

I kept thinking that turning a page in *New York Cookbook* should be like turning a corner in this city. One can go from the twentieth century back to the revolutionary era by walking half a city block in Lower Manhattan, from chicken Kiev to jerked chicken and salsa in another few steps. The city is an intricate lacing of cultures and eras. I did my best to follow their threads. But in the end, I realized that no matter how many stories or recipes I collected, they were all, in some basic way, New York stories.

By the end, I had a New York story of my own.

Dubrow's had closed by the time I moved from the Hot l into the loft in Hell's Kitchen where I now live. The passing of the deli made me feel venerable and when its chairs appeared in a trendy little diner in my neighborhood I felt so venerable that I said good-bye to false bravado. Soon after, I ran into Mrs. Head Humbrellaman, shopping along Ninth Avenue. She was still swathed in traditional Senegalese prints, but in addition to the one son she'd had when we moved into the Hot l, she had a set of twins and a baby girl and when I issued a hearty, if halting, "BON JOUR!," she answered in clipped English.

"Oh, hello there," she said. "We've been wondering about you and enjoying your work immensely in the newspaper."

"You read the *Times?*" I asked, in the same bald, idiot tone I once used to order a "bailey." For five years this former neighbor had knocked softly at my door and asked me to help her translate directions for warming baby formula, for filling out government forms, for using fabric softener. Had enough time really passed for anyone to become fluent in English?

"The children speak English,

French, and Arabic. They learn so quickly that it shamed me to study harder," she said, in the same isn't-it-obvious tone she'd once used to explain making chicken for fifty. Besides, she said, her husband had moved out of umbrellas and into African art.

"He must read all the newspapers now for news of the museums and galleries," she said. We talked about the masks he'd sold to the Museum of Modern Art last year, and how he has found a piece for the Metropolitan Museum. The children, she said, love their private school, and they've moved into a larger apartment. We talked about the old neighbors and the old days at the Hot l. She asked me not to use her real name.

We talked like childhood friends. Which in a way is what we are. Like I said, when you move to New York City, you share a coming of age. You become parts of those you arrive with and they, in turn, take pages from your book.

You change. You don't even realize it's happening until you end up standing in front of a butcher who sells goat meat on Ninth Avenue, talking to a woman dressed like an African queen who carries a Gucci alligator handbag. The things that you've learned to cherish about New York lead you to ask her about African restaurants in the city. The things she's learned to cherish about New York lead her to ask you where she and her husband should go to celebrate their tenth anniversary in the City.

"Le Cirque or Lutèce?" she said. "The other French restaurants we've tried have been disappointingly ordinary, don't you think?"

Molly O'Neill

September 1992

Pandelaki Andonopulo at the Ninth Avenue Cheese Market (page 112).

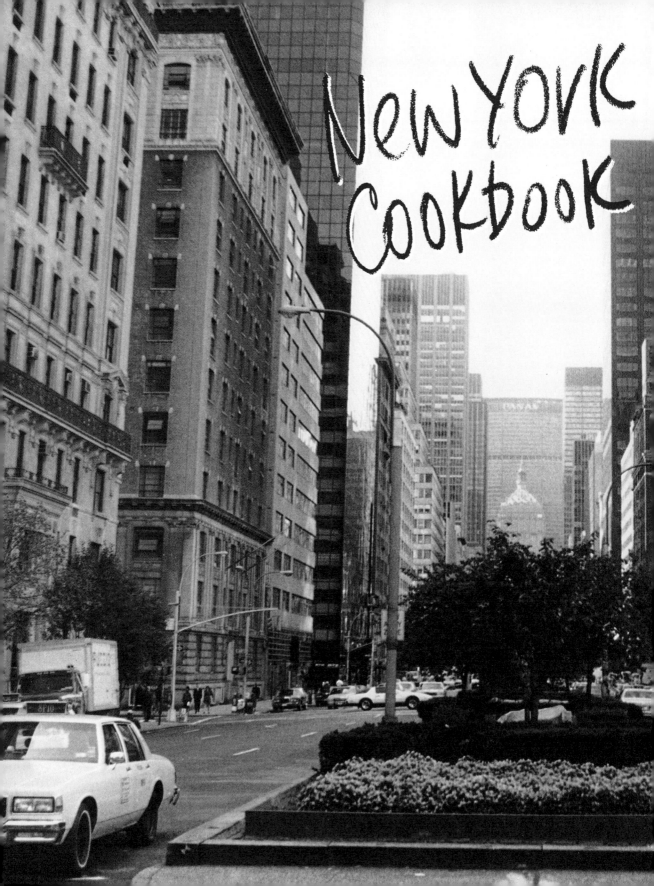

New York Cookbook

Nibbles, Noshes
and
Appetizing

NOSHING WITH
Lou Singer

Lou Singer, tour guide, has been called "The Greatest Living History Book of New York City." But on a typical business day, hunched over a Formica table at Teresa's, the Polish coffee shop on the Lower East Side, Mr. Singer looks more like a cabdriver on lunch break than a scholar. He wears a

plaid flannel shirt, a rumpled tweed jacket, and a navy blue tam-o'-shanter. He tucks into a blintz the size of a cinder block.

Mr. Singer has also been called "A Man of Tooth." To the portly, high-school drop out from Brooklyn, this sobriquet is like a Ph.D. in the cultural history of New York City. He has been studying the city, block by block, for over 60 years, and food, he said, is the thread

Abe Lebewohl, owner of the Second Avenue Kosher Deli displays a gorgeous party platter (left); tour guide Lou Singer (above) contemplating his next nosh.

3

that stitches the crazy quilt together.

"In the last 300 years, 35 million people have entered the United States. They came to this city and lived closely together. Where else can you find Irish and Italian Catholics and Eastern European Jews packed into tenements, six families to a floor. They don't share a language, they don't share a culture, they share dinner, a cup of flour, a cup of coffee, a pierogi, a knish, you name it."

THEY MAY NOT SHARE A CULTURE, SO THEY SHARE DINNER

Manhattan's Lower East Side is living history. The story of the neighborhood, like the story of the city, is "a history of disaster," he said. Wars, revolutions, persecutions, and famines abroad drove various populations to the New World, and each one displaced the previous. Mr. Singer hypothesizes that it began early: "Sometime in the seventeenth century, the Indians of Bay Ridge, Brooklyn, looked down the river, saw Verrazano's sails, and said 'there goes the neighborhood.'" The Indians fled the Dutch, the Dutch fled the English, the English fled the Irish, who arrived in the 1830s and squatted around Chatham Square. The Irish fled the Germans, who arrived in 1848. The Germans fled the Northern Italians, who came in 1850. The Northern Italians moved on in 1870 when a wave of refugees from the Austro-Hungarian empire landed in the area. Eastern European Jews came in droves in 1882." He lists the ethnic forces that shaped the city in a cadence that re-

calls "The Farmer in the Dell."

No neighborhood bears the stamp of this progression as vividly as the Lower East Side. With each wave of immigration, the neighborhood became more commercial, but it was the Eastern European Jews who elevated its food stores and lunch counters into a low-rent Café Society. "The eating places became social centers," said Mr. Singer. "People would go to kibitz—get information about relatives in the old country, find out about jobs, you name it. In one square mile, you could eat your way around the world without sitting down," says Mr. Singer.

His introductory lecture, however, is a seated affair, so Mr. Singer usually likes to begin it at Teresa's, on First Avenue between 6th and 7th Streets. Sounding as intense as an American historian

A window table at Teresa's.

addressing a detail of colonial life, he expounds on one of the icons of his beloved city. "The blintz," he said, "should be a thin, nongreasy pancake, containing an incredible amount of calories and cholesterol. The Polish pride themselves on their contributions to cellulite."

Mr. Singer always advises his students not to "even consider dieting" on tour day; he guarantees that a respectable assimilation of the neighborhood has never prompted more than a four-pound gain.

NOSH STOPS

TERESA'S COFFEE SHOP & RESTAURANT: 103 First Avenue, between 6th and 7th Streets; (212) 228-0604

RUSSO & SONS DAIRY PRODUCTS: 344 East 11th Street near First Avenue; (212) 254-7452

VENIERO'S: 342 East 11th Street, between 1st and 2nd Avenues; (212) 674-4415 or 674-7264

PETE'S SPICE AND EVERYTHING NICE: 174 First Avenue, between 10th and 11th Streets; (212) 254-8773

ECONOMY CANDY: 108 Rivington Street, between Essex and Ludlow Streets; (212) 254-1513

BLACK FOREST PASTRY SHOP: 344 East 11th Street at First Avenue; (212) 254-8181

UKRAINIAN EAST VILLAGE RESTAURANT: 140 Second Avenue, between 8th and 9th Streets; (212) 529-5024

SECOND AVENUE KOSHER DELICATESSAN AND RESTAURANT: 156 Second Avenue at 10th Street; (212) 677-0607

SCHAPIRO'S WINERY: 126 Rivington Street, between Essex and Norfolk Streets; for tour information, call (212) 674-4404

STREITS MATZOH FACTORY AND RETAIL STORE: 150 Rivington Street, between Essex and Norfolk Streets; (212) 475-7000

BEN'S CHEESE SHOP: 181 East Houston Street, between Orchard and Allen Streets; (212) 254-8290

RUSS & DAUGHTERS: 179 East Houston Street, between Orchard and Allen Streets; (212) 475-4880

GUSS PICKLES (D/B/A ESSEX STREET PICKLE CORPORATION): 35 Essex Street; (212) 254-4477

Lou Singer offers dozens of tours of New York City. To book a tour, call (718) 875-9084

Go to Pete's Spice for the plumpest dried fruit, the most fragrant spices, and a wide assortment of dried beans, grains and flours.

He defends the amount of eating required: "It's a very healthy lunch spread out over six hours." He also does his best to vary the succession of courses.

After the sweet blintzes, for instance, he herds his group toward Russo & Son Dairy Products, where, for three generations, a succession of Russos have made spectacular mozzarella five times a day. The cheese is smoked, marinated, and sold fresh. The milky fresh cheese balls—*bocconcini,* which means bite-size—draw customers from all over the city. "It is the cheese that Grandma said was the best, so generation after generation return for it," explains Mr. Singer.

This kind of loyalty isn't limited to mozzarella. Generation after generation return to Veniero's, next door, for fancy cakes and Italian biscotti. They make pilgrimages to Pete's Spice and Everything Nice shop, across the street, for the exotic spices, nuts, dried fruits, and teas that line the shelves. They travel some

Economy candy, a sweet-tooth's dream come true.

blocks south to Economy Candy to pick through barrels of penny candies and buy the figs and halvah that Grandma swore by.

As he leads his group in the footsteps of the generations that preceded them across the crumbling sidewalks, Mr. Singer explains that these stores started as pushcarts that lined the avenue during the

nineteenth century. In 1937, when the cobblestones had given way to concrete and asphalt, the vendors were moved into the public market on First Avenue between 9th and 10th Streets. Today the market is an off-Broadway theater—a perfect example of Manhattan manifest destiny, if you ask Lou Singer. Just thinking about it makes him hungry.

At Black Forest Pastry Shop, on the corner of 11th Street, a chocolate-dipped banana, wedge of Sachertorte, or slice of apple pizza make a perfect nosh, or snack eaten on the run, an eating style that is a New York City institution. "The practice was described in 1677 by two visiting French monks," said Mr. Singer. Pausing, cake in hand, a crumb clinging to his chin, he recited: "So intent are they on their business that they do not stop to dine like gentle folk elsewhere. From the multitudinous vendors of clams and corn, oysters and yams, they snatch up what they wish, munch as they march."

NOSHING: A PROTOTYPE FOR FAST FOOD

Noshing, claimed Mr. Singer, is clearly the genesis of the national fast-food industry. Mr. Singer is convinced that no other city in the United States has contributed as much to American culture as New York City. "Who do you think taught America to eat bagels and smoked fish, meatballs, pizza, hot dogs, sirloin steaks, clam chowder, you name it?" he asked.

He moved toward some sit-down activity. At the Ukrainian East Village Restaurant, Mr. Singer guided his flock toward pierogi, the meat-filled Ukranian dumplings that are judged by their heft. At the Second Avenue Kosher Delicatessen and Restaurant, bowls of mushroom barley

"Name it and claim it," at Ben's Cheese Shop.

soup were sloshed across the table, corned beef and pastrami towered high between slabs of rye bread, and chopped chicken liver was accorded the respect of foie gras.

He steered his group toward Schapiro's Winery, where 30 kinds of sacramental and fruit wines are fermented in the cellars that range beneath an entire city block. At Streits Matzoh Factory, the group watched unleavened bread being made. At Ben's Cheese Shop, a counterman mutters, "Name it and claim it," and Mr. Singer swept by the hundreds of imported and domestic cheeses to find the cheese of his childhood: farmer cheese baked with caraway or scallions, walnuts and raisins, lemon, pineapple, blueberries. You name it. "Cheesecake without the calories," said Mr. Singer. By that time, no one was counting.

At Russ & Daughters, an immaculate storefront where smoked fish has reigned since 1914, Singer debated the merits of Alaskan and Scandinavian smoked salmon. At Guss Pickles (d/b/a Essex Street Pickles), he peered into the 50-gallon barrels lined up on the sidewalk. He closed his eyes. He inhaled. The aromas of dill and garlic, pepper and horseradish unfurl above the barrels of half sours and sours, pickled green tomatoes, peppers, and sauerkraut. In a rare departure, Mr. Singer offered medical advice: "If you have sinus problems, this is the place to come," he said.

AN INSATIABLE APPETITE FOR THE CITY

Sometimes he just can't help his shtick; it fills in the gaps when his eye and mind wander up and down the blocks. Singer was born on the kitchen table of a sixth-floor walk-up at 227 Madison Street. His mother always told him: "The most delicious thing that ever was on my table was you, my Louie."

Eventually the family moved to Brooklyn. Lou started a newspaper distributorship and as he drove his delivery truck, he found Vinegar Hill, the site in Fort Greene where 12,000 American soldiers were buried after the Revolutionary War. He found a church containing the largest collection of Tiffany windows in the world. He discovered the site of the first birth control clinic in the country. He cataloged 40 different ethnic communities in Brooklyn alone. He sleuthed out the homes of Teddy Roosevelt, Aaron Burr, and Alexander Hamilton; the tryst site of Arthur Miller and Marilyn Monroe; the house where *Sophie's Choice* was filmed.

But like thousands before him, he has never been able to resist the siren's call of the Lower East Side. He returned on a tour. In the past decade, Mr. Singer has squired 25,000 people through the blocks, logging 400,000 miles in his sight-seeing van and consuming at least that many calories.

On the sidewalk, Hasidic Jews in black, Chinese pushing wire carts, young artists, and women in traditional Indian dress marched and munched. Young men in sweatshirts, jeans, and $200 sneakers wandered through the crowd advertising the availability of drugs, "*sens,* man, *sens.*" A gaggle of Mercedes with out-of-state license plates was double-parked at the curb while their owners rushed from pickles to potted pike. The Lower East Side is no Plymouth Plantation.

"That's it in a snapshot—the ethnic mix—enterprise and proof that it takes three generations for a culture to make it into the main stream and move on from the city," said Mr. Singer. "They take the city with them in some form, usually food, and invariably some kind of food draws them back."

Barrels of pickles—good and garlicky.

Lupe's EMPANADILLAS

Lupe Marti-Salgado perfected these Cuban meat pies, which she sells in her bodega at Ninth Avenue and 36th Street. Like pasties, turnovers, and egg rolls, empanadillas can be filled with guava, chopped beef, cheese, tuna or other fish, or chicken, and make a wonderful starter. This version is a chopped meat "picadillo"—a savory mixture that can make a meal in itself.

EMPANADAS
3 cups all-purpose flour
2 tablespoons sugar
1 teaspoon salt
½ cup vegetable oil
2 large eggs, beaten
⅓ cup dry white wine

PICADILLO
¼ cup vegetable oil
1 medium onion,
chopped
1 green bell pepper,
stemmed, seeded, and chopped
1 clove garlic, minced
½ pound ground beef
½ pound ground pork
¼ pound boiled ham, ground
¾ cup green olives, chopped,
or ¾ cup drained capers
1 teaspoon salt
⅛ teaspoon freshly ground black pepper
½ cup tomato sauce
¼ cup dry white wine

Vegetable oil, for deep-frying

Lupe in her chock-full bodega.

1. Make the empanadas: Sift the flour, sugar, and salt into a large bowl. Add the oil and mix. Add the eggs and wine and stir. Knead until the dough is smooth. Cover the pastry with plastic wrap and refrigerate for at least 1 hour.

2. Make the picadillo: Place the oil in a skillet over medium heat. Add the onion, bell pepper, and garlic and sauté, stirring occasionally, until soft, 5 minutes. Add all of the meats and cook, breaking up the meat with a spoon, until browned, about 5 minutes. Add the olives, salt, pepper, tomato sauce, and wine. Reduce the heat to low and simmer, partially covered, for 20 minutes. Remove from the heat and allow the mixture to cool.

3. Transfer the dough to a lightly floured board; with your hands, roll it out into a long coil. Cut the dough into 24 even pieces. Roll out each piece into a 6-inch round that is ⅛ inch thick. Spoon about 2 tablespoons of the filling onto the top half of each pastry, then fold the bottom dough up into a half moon. Crimp the edges closed with a fork.

4. Place a heavy, deep skillet over medium heat and add enough of the oil to reach a depth of 1 inch. Heat until hot enough to sizzle a scrap of dough. Add the empanadillas, a few at a time, without crowding the pan, and cook until golden brown on both sides, 5 minutes per side. Remove with a slotted spoon to drain on paper towels.

Makes 24, serves 5 to 6

Vernon's
JAMAICAN BEEF PATTIES

Beef patties are considered a "poor man's meal" on the island of Jamaica, but in New York, West Indian expatriates yearn for these savory pies, and a taste for the fiery beef patties has spread throughout the city. They make a perfect hors d'oeuvre (supply lots of napkins) or, with a small salad, an addictive first course. For more about Vernon, "The King of Jerk," see Index.

FILLING

1 large onion, minced
1 scallion, trimmed and minced
1 hot chile pepper (Scotch bonnet, if possible), seeded and minced
1 pound lean ground beef
¼ cup vegetable oil
½ teaspoon dried thyme
1 tablespoon curry powder
Salt, to taste
Freshly ground black pepper, to taste
1½ cups dried bread crumbs

PASTRY

4 cups all-purpose flour
1 tablespoon curry powder
1 teaspoon salt
1 cup (2 sticks) margarine, butter, or solid vegetable shortening
8 to 12 tablespoons ice water

Allan Vernon serves up spicy Jamaican specialties.

1. Make the filling: Mix together the onion, scallion, hot pepper, and beef in a medium bowl.

2. Heat the oil in a large skillet over medium heat. Add the meat mixture, breaking up the meat with a spoon, and cook until it is brown all over, about 5 minutes. Stir in the thyme, curry powder, salt, pepper, and ½ cup water. Cover and cook for 30 minutes.

3. Remove the pan from the heat and allow to cool. Add the bread crumbs and mix well; set aside.

4. Make the pastry: Mix the flour with the curry powder and salt in a medium bowl. Using a pastry blender or 2 forks, cut the shortening into the flour mixture until the mixture looks like small peas. Gradually add the ice water, mixing just until the pastry comes together. Gather the pastry in a ball and cover with plastic wrap. Refrigerate for 1 hour.

5. Transfer the pastry to a lightly floured board and roll out ¼ inch thick. Flour the top edge of a 2½-inch-wide drinking glass and cut out 24 circles. Roll out each circle ⅛ inch thick and about 6 inches in diameter.

NIBBLES NOSHES AND APPETIZING

6. Preheat the oven to 400°F. Grease a baking sheet.

7. Spoon about 2 tablespoons of the filling onto the upper half of each round, then fold the bottom pastry up into a half-moon shape. Crimp the edges closed with a fork. Arrange the patties on the baking sheet. Bake until golden brown, 30 minutes. Serve warm or at room temperature.

Makes 24 patties, serves 6

Moshe's
FALAFEL

In 1980, Moshe Mizarahi pushed an aluminum vending cart to the corner of 46th Street and 6th Avenue and began giving away free samples of his falafel. Within weeks, his deep-fried, cumin-scented chick-pea balls stuffed into pita and topped with chopped lettuce, tomatoes, hot sauce, and sesame sauce became a legend. Like much of the food sold from pushcarts on the streets of New York City, falafel makes a wonderful meal-on-the-run. With slight adaptations, it makes a first-rate hors d'oeuvre.

1 pound dried chick-peas, soaked overnight in
*   cold water, then drained and rinsed*
3 cloves garlic, crushed
1 large onion, finely chopped
⅓ cup finely chopped fresh parsley
1 teaspoon ground coriander seeds
1 teaspoon ground cumin
1 teaspoon salt
1 teaspoon baking soda dissolved in ½ cup water
Vegetable oil, for deep-frying
7 pita breads, tops cut off
Sesame Sauce (recipe follows)
Hot Sauce (recipe follows)
1 head lettuce, coarsely chopped
2 tomatoes, coarsely chopped
7 small sweet pickles (gherkins), sliced

1. In a food processor or blender, grind the soaked chick-peas. Add the garlic, onion, parsley, coriander, cumin, salt, and baking soda mixture. Process until smooth.

2. In a large, wide pot, heat oil to a depth of 3 inches until very hot, but not smoking. With a 1½-inch ice cream scoop, form the falafel mixture into balls the size of golf balls, using a flat knife or spatula to smooth out the scoop. Carefully slide the falafel into the oil. Continue shaping falafel and adding them to the oil, but do not crowd the pot. Cook the falafel until golden brown, about 3 minutes. Turn and continue to cook until golden brown all over, about 3 minutes more. Remove the falafel from the pot with a slotted spoon and drain on paper towels or paper bags. Keep warm while continuing to fry the falafel until all of the mixture is used.

3. To serve as a sandwich, place 4 falafel balls in the pocket of 1 pita. Drizzle 2 tablespoons of the sesame sauce and 1 tablespoon hot sauce (more or less according to taste) over the falafel. Add some of the lettuce and tomato, a drizzle more of each of the sauces, and top with a pickle. Continue assembling the remaining falafel.

To serve as an hors d'oeuvre, make a dipping sauce of two parts sesame sauce and one part hot sauce. Place a bowl of the sauce in the center of a platter lined with lettuce leaves. Fry and drain the falafel, skewer each with a toothpick, arrange around the dipping sauce, and serve.

Makes 7 falafel sandwiches, or 35 individual hors d'oeuvres

Moshe Mizarahi offers a jumbo falafel pita sandwich.

0

SESAME SAUCE

1 cup tahini paste
1 clove garlic, crushed
Juice of 1 lemon
¼ cup cold water
¼ teaspoon salt
Dash of freshly ground black pepper

Combine all of the ingredients in a bowl and whisk until smooth. Refrigerate until ready to serve.
Makes 1½ cups

HOT SAUCE

1½ cups tomato sauce
½ teaspoon dried red pepper flakes
¼ teaspoon salt
Dash of freshly ground black pepper

Combine all of the ingredients in a nonreactive small saucepan and heat over low heat, stirring occasionally, until the mixture reduces slightly and thickly coats the back of a spoon, 30 minutes. Remove from the heat and allow the sauce to cool to room temperature. Serve.
Makes 1½ cups

Millie Chan's STEAMED PORK DUMPLINGS

Millie Chan's grandfather came to the United States in the late 1800s to work on the Southern Pacific Railroad in Arizona. Chan's parents settled in San Antonio, Texas, perhaps an unlikely locale in which to learn the art of Chinese cooking, but Chan, who teaches cooking at the China Institute in Manhattan, was nourished by the strong traditions built around the Chinese home kitchen. "Chinese people carry their food heritage with them wherever they may be," she explains. Understandably, it would be impossible to leave these tender dumplings behind.

FILLING
1 pound ground pork
½ pound fresh shrimp, shelled, deveined, and
*   finely chopped*

Millie Chan keeps her pots out and at the ready.

4 dried shiitake mushrooms,
*   soaked in water to*
*   cover for 20 minutes,*
*   stems removed, and*
*   caps finely chopped*
½ cup finely chopped
*   bamboo shoots*
2 tablespoons finely
*   chopped scallions*
*   (white part only)*
1 tablespoon minced
*   fresh ginger*
½ teaspoon sugar
1 teaspoon salt
1½ tablespoons
*   light soy sauce*
1 tablespoon
*   cornstarch*

60 wonton wrappers, fresh if possible, covered
*   with a slightly damp cloth to prevent drying (if*
*   using frozen, defrost, uncovered, at room*
*   temperature)*
Hunan chili sauce, for dipping (see Note)

1. Combine all of the filling ingredients in a large mixing bowl. Stir until well mixed.

2. Place 1 wonton wrapper on a flat surface and use a pastry brush to lightly moisten the edges with cold water. Place 1 tablespoon of the filling in the center of the wrapper. Gather the edges of the wrapper up and around the filling, so it looks somewhat like a Hershey's Kiss. Gently squeeze the middle of the dumpling to be sure the wrapper adheres firmly to the filling. Press the bottom of the dumpling on a flat surface so it will stand upright. Lightly sprinkle the top edge of the wrapper with cold water as they tend to dry out during steaming. Set aside and continue making the dumplings.

3. Pour water to a depth of 2 inches into the bottom of a steamer or large saucepan. Oil the steaming rack and place it in the steamer. Place the dumplings about ½ inch apart on the rack. Bring the water to a boil, then cover and steam for 15 minutes. Serve the dumplings with the Hunan chili sauce.

Makes 60

Note: Hunan chili sauce is available in many supermarkets and specialty food stores.

Lidia Pires'
SHRIMP AND BEAN CROQUETTES

Little Brazil runs along 46th Street between Seventh and Madison Avenues, and it is an oddity in New York City: an ethnic neighborhood that ethnics go to, rather than live in.

During World War II, the Brazilian Trade Bureau was located nearby at 551 Madison, and Brazilian-run barbershops, groceries, restaurants, luncheonettes, and bookstores sprouted up. A handful remain. The Latin American Produce Company, at 142 West 46th, is still the social center. At the counter, Lidia Pires and her husband, Tony, offer travel services, translation, and general cultural counseling along with empadas de camarão (large shrimp turnovers), pastéis de carne (large beef turnovers), and acarajés (black bean croquettes)—these addictive dried shrimp and bean croquettes.

New York's Little Brazil.

CROQUETTES
3¾ cups dried black-eyed peas
1 cup dried shrimp (see Note)
1 large white onion, minced
1 teaspoon salt
1 teaspoon freshly ground black pepper
½ teaspoon hot sauce, such as Tabasco
Vegetable oil, for deep-frying

SAUCE
Juice of 4 limes
¾ cup dried shrimp
1 jalapeño chile, seeded, deveined, and coarsely chopped
1 onion, coarsely chopped
2 tablespoons vegetable oil
2 scallions, trimmed and minced

1. Make the croquettes: Soak the black-eyed peas overnight in water to cover. Drain and cook in plenty of fresh water until tender, about 1 hour. Drain and allow to cool. Place the peas in a clean dish towel and rub to remove the outer skins.

2. Mince the peas with the shrimp in a food processor or with a sharp knife. If using a processor, be careful not to purée the mixture. Add the onion and stir well to combine. Season with the salt and pepper and add the hot sauce, to taste.

3. Pour the vegetable oil into a large heavy skillet to a depth of 1 inch. Heat the oil to sizzling, but not smoking (365°F on a deep-fry thermometer). Use a tablespoon to form the batter into football shapes about 1½ inches long. Fry until deep golden on each side, about 5 minutes total. Drain well on paper towels.

4. Make the sauce: Purée the lime juice, dried

shrimp, jalapeño, and onion in a blender or food processor. Heat the oil in a nonreactive small skillet. Add the purée and cook over medium heat to blend the flavors, 5 minutes. Remove from the heat; stir in the scallions. Serve the mixture as a dipping sauce for the croquettes.

Makes 24 croquettes

Note: Dried shrimp are available in Asian, Caribbean, and other specialty food stores.

Mr. Kuraoka's
EEL HANDROLLS

Some of the best seafood in New York resides behind the sparkling glass cases of the city's sushi counters. Eel, the rich fish that is brushed with sake and soy, broiled, layered on rice, and topped with a confetti of cucumber julienne, makes a satisfying lunch or tantalizing first course. Since all of the preparation can be done ahead of time, eel handrolls from the president of Manhattan's Restaurant Nippon—are a good bet for large parties.

AWASEZU
¼ cup plus 1 tablespoon rice vinegar
2 tablespoons sugar
1 tablespoon salt

1 cup short-grain rice, rinsed
½ cup sugar
¼ cup sake
¼ cup soy sauce
5 pieces (1 to 2 inches each) eel, skin on, cut in half lengthwise, and boned
5 sheets nori seaweed (each about 8 × 7 inches), halved diagonally
2 cucumbers, peeled, halved lengthwise then crosswise, seeded, and cut into julienne
¼ cup sesame seeds

1. Make the awasezu: Combine the vinegar, sugar, and salt in a small bowl or bottle. Stir or shake to mix well and set aside.

2. In a rice cooker or medium-size saucepan, combine the rice with 2 cups of water. Bring the water to a boil over high heat, then reduce the heat, cover, and simmer until the rice is tender, 15 to 20 minutes. Mix the cooked rice with the awasezu and set aside to cool completely.

3. In a large, deep skillet or pot, bring 3 cups of water, the sugar, sake, and soy sauce to a boil. Reduce the heat and simmer until the mixture is reduced by half. Set aside.

4. Preheat the broiler.

5. Place the eel, skin side down, on a broiler pan, liberally brush with the sake-soy mixture, and broil until cooked through, about 5 minutes.

6. Place a sheet of the seaweed over a sudare (see Note). Spread about ¼ cup of the sushi rice over the seaweed. In the center of the seaweed, on top of the rice, place a piece of eel, about 2 tablespoons of the cucumber julienne, and a sprinkle of sesame seeds. Carefully roll the mixture into the shape of an ice cream cone. Serve with the remaining sake-soy sauce for dipping.

Makes 10 rolls

Note: A sudare is a bamboo mat that looks much like a bamboo window shade and is used under a sheet of nori to facilitate sushi rolling. If you don't have one, you can use a damp towel or napkin as you would for rolling up a jelly roll.

Sweet Potato
FRITTERS

Professor Jessica Harris, author of *Sky Juice & Flying Fish,* serves this West African finger food for cocktail parties and advises hosts to "make twice as many as you think people will eat."

6 medium sweet potatoes, unpeeled
1½ teaspoons salt
1 teaspoon freshly ground black pepper
1 cup all-purpose flour
2 eggs
Vegetable oil, for deep-frying
6 scallions, trimmed and minced

---

1. Place the sweet potatoes in a large pot, add 1 teaspoon of the salt, cover with cold water, and bring to a boil. Boil until the potatoes are tender, about 25 minutes. Drain and cool.

2. Combine the remaining ½ teaspoon salt with the pepper and flour in a small bowl; set aside. Beat the eggs with 2 tablespoons water. Cut the sweet potatoes into ¼-inch slices.

3. Heat the oil in a deep heavy skillet to 350°F on a deep-fry thermometer. Dip each sweet potato slice in the egg and then in the flour mixture and fry in small batches until they are golden brown, about 5 minutes on each side. Drain the slices on paper towels.

4. Serve hot, topped with the minced scallions.

Serves 6

If sweet potatoes aren't available, try yams in your fritters.

Caribbean
CODFISH PUFFS

These can be eaten as an hors d'oeuvre or layered on a sandwich roll topped with shredded lettuce and mayonnaise.

10 ounces salt cod, boned and skinned
2 tablespoons minced fresh parsley
2 tablespoons minced scallion
2 tablespoons minced white onion
1 teaspoon baking soda
1 extra-large egg
1¼ teaspoons freshly ground black pepper
1¼ teaspoons garlic powder
½ teaspoon cayenne pepper or 1 teaspoon hot
   sauce, such as Tabasco, or to taste (optional)
¼ cup evaporated milk
1 cup all-purpose flour
Vegetable oil, for deep-frying
Spicy mayonnaise (see Note) or tartar sauce, for
   serving

---

1. Soak the salt cod in cold water to cover for 2 hours. Drain and rinse well. Blanch the fish in boiling water to cover for 5 minutes. Drain well and allow to cool.

2. Use a fork to finely shred the salt cod in a large bowl. Add the parsley, scallion, onion, and baking soda and stir to combine well. In a separate bowl whisk the egg until frothy; add it to the salt cod mixture along with the black pepper, garlic powder, and cayenne, if desired. Stir in the evaporated milk and ¾ cup of water. Sprinkle the flour over the salt cod mixture and stir to combine well. Add more cayenne or hot sauce, if desired.

3. Place a heavy skillet over medium heat and fill it halfway with vegetable oil. Heat the oil until a speck of flour dropped into it sizzles and turns brown. Use a tablespoon to shape the codfish mixture into balls slightly smaller than golf balls. Gently slide them, a few at a time, into the oil and fry until golden, 5 minutes. Turn and fry the other side until golden, 5 minutes more. Use a slotted spoon to remove the fritters and drain on paper towels. Continue forming and frying the remaining puffs. The puffs can be held in a 250°F oven for up to 2 hours before serving.

4. Serve on toothpicks by themselves or accompanied by a spicy mayonnaise or tartar sauce.

Makes about 24

Note: To make mayonnaise spicy, spike it with hot sauce, a few drops at a time, until it's to your liking.

A TASTE OF THE TROPICS

This is the tale of a mother, a daughter, and codfish puffs.

The mother? She is a proper Trinidadian émigré who worked to support her three children and dreamed that her daughter might grow up to be a lawyer. The daughter? Well, she couldn't sit still long enough to study law. She became, instead, a New York City policewoman who sports disco red nails and a head full of more Senegalese twists than any other officer assigned to the Midtown South Task Force.

Oh, and the codfish puffs. They are the glue in the mother-daughter relationship. When she was off-duty, the daughter sold the codfish puffs that the mother made in a closet-size storefront called Karen's Taste of the Tropics on West 46th Street in Manhattan.

Since the mother, Urscilla O'Connor, is proud to speak careful, blue-blood English, it is surprising that she favors accra, the amorphous salt cod fritters that are considered poor man's fare in Trinidad. Since her daughter, Karen O'Connor, has never been "hepped on any kind of cooking, if you want to know the truth," it is surprising that any culinary endeavor could sustain her interest.

Karen caught the restaurant bug in 1988 when she was "walking the beat" along West 46th Street between Eighth and Ninth Avenues, and within a year, she'd laid gray linoleum in a 200-square-foot storefront on the block and painted the walls a color that resembled the last blush of a tropical sunset.

On one wall, she tacked up photographs of African art and travel, clippings from black fashion magazines, and a sign that read "Cocaine can make you blind." On another, she taped a hand-lettered menu that listed codfish puffs, beef patties, cocoa bread, and codfish sandwiches, curried chicken or beef with rice, oxtail, black cake, carrot cake, and sweet bread muffins. Prices ranged from 65 cents to six dollars.

To the steady stream of bicycle messengers and business people, neighbors and actors who stopped by for lunch, Karen offered her thoughts on the situation in South Africa and neighborhood politics along with insights into love and career dilemmas.

Basically, Karen became the Oprah Winfrey of West 46th Street. Her mother, on the other hand, continued to live life in a lower key behind the counter, carefully tending the blend of Indian, African, Chinese, and British tradition of cooking that she was raised on. Some days she made goat roti. Some days she made peas and rice. A paper-clipped arrow marked the specials on the handwritten menu.

When asked for a recipe, Urscilla O'Connor responded with the same, contemplative laugh that she uttered in response to a query about her daughter's cooking ability. "Karen? Cook?" she said, "Ah, ha. Ha. Ha. Ha."

"I tell her she doesn't know how to cook and I do," Mrs. O'Connor explained, softly. "I cook by rhythm."

Rhythm and marketing occasionally collided at Karen's Taste of the Tropics, but codfish puffs remained the model of their resolve. They agreed that, while Trinidadians will pop the fiery codfish puffs in their mouth for breakfast or lunch, dinner or snacks, Americans usually "can't take the heat." Mrs. O'Connor considered using less pepper in the fritters, "but I couldn't, uh-huh, it wouldn't be accra like that, you know."

Karen "broke customers in" by serving the peppery puffs on sweet, soft cocoa bread. "It softens the blow," she explained.

Nevertheless, she did change their name. "Nobody would know what accra is," she said. "The puff was my idea."

Boris'
KISHKA

4. Preheat the oven to 350°F.

5. In an ovenproof baking dish, combine the chicken fat and the 2 sliced onions. Arrange the kishka on top. Roast in the oven, basting frequently, for 1½ hours. Slice the kishka into 1- to 1½-inch-thick rounds.

Serves 5

Boris Pearlman is a physician by profession, but at home he is a cook extraordinaire. Providing plenty is something he learned at his mother's knee: "I never knew that I had a continuous case of heartburn until I joined the army and it disappeared." Still, he misses the good old days, and he does his best to re-create the mood for his own family by making a version of his mother's kishka, a traditional matzoh meal-stuffed sausage.

2½ cups sifted all-purpose flour
1 cup finely chopped beef fat (suet)
¾ cup matzoh meal
3 medium onions, 1 chopped and 2 sliced
2 teaspoons salt
Dash of freshly ground black pepper
1 cup beef or chicken stock, warmed
4 feet of beef casing (available from kosher butchers—you might have to order it in advance)
¼ cup rendered chicken fat

1. Mix the flour, beef fat, matzoh meal, the chopped onion, salt, and pepper in a large bowl. It will be lumpy. Stir in the stock.

2. Rinse the casing well inside and out with cold water. Stuff the casing by placing one end on a sausage horn or stuffer. Tie off the free end of the casing. Fill loosely, twisting well at regular intervals to make 4-inch links. The kishka will expand during cooking. Tie the open end of the casing, and make 2 small pricks in each sausage link to allow release of pressure.

3. Bring a large heavy pot of salted water to a boil over high heat. Reduce the heat to low and gently poach the kishka for 1 hour. Remove from the heat and drain. You can cut the kishka into individual links, if desired.

Jacques'
CHICKEN WINGS ANDALOUSE

Jacques Williams's passion for Buffalo-style chicken wings is such that it hurts him to serve the crispy, juicy treats in their original manner: from heaping platters for stand-up guests. No, to revere the flavor and wonder of these wings, guests must be comfortable. Therefore, he refined the original recipe to make it suitable for Limoges china—and properly seated guests.

2 tablespoons vegetable oil
2 pounds chicken wings, cut into drumsticks (tips and center joint reserved for another use) and lightly floured
1 red bell pepper
¼ cup dry white wine
1 tablespoon white wine vinegar
8 tablespoons (1 stick) butter, cut into tablespoons
About 1 tablespoon Tabasco sauce or
    ½ teaspoon cayenne pepper, or to taste
Salt, to taste

1. Heat the oil in a large heavy skillet over high heat. Add the chicken wings and sauté, turning frequently, until browned and cooked through, 15 to 20 minutes. Drain on paper towels.

2. Meanwhile, roast the red pepper under

the broiler or in the flames of a gas burner, turning frequently, until the skin is blackened and blistered. Place the pepper in a paper bag, close the bag, and let steam for 15 to 20 minutes. Scrape off the skin, split the pepper, and remove the seeds. Purée the pepper in a food processor or food mill.

3. In a nonreactive small saucepan over high heat, reduce the wine and wine vinegar by half, 2 minutes. Reduce the heat to medium-low and add the butter to the wine mixture, 1 tablespoon at a time, whisking to incorporate. Whisk in the red pepper purée and season with the Tabasco, a few drops at a time, and salt to taste.

4. Mound the warm wings on a platter and pour the sauce on top. Serve immediately.

Serves 8

Jacques Williams prepares his classy chicken wings.

Dhanit's CHICKEN SATE

When Dhanit Choladda, head chef at Claire, a Manhattan restaurant, left eastern Thailand at age 17, he already knew how to cook. "Grandma was always cooking at my house," he said, and of this succulent curried chicken he explains, "Everybody has a different way with saté. This is how I love to do it."

Saté and a smile from Dhanit Choladda.

MARINADE AND CHICKEN
1 can (15 ounces) unsweetened
  coconut milk
3 cloves garlic, chopped
2 tablespoons curry powder
1 tablespoon sugar (optional)
2 pounds boneless, skinless chicken
  breasts, pounded thin and cut into
  1-inch cubes

SAUCE
3½ cups (slightly less than two 15-ounce
  cans) unsweetened coconut milk
1 cup smooth peanut butter
¼ cup cider vinegar
2 tablespoons Thai fish sauce (see Note)
1½ tablespoons red curry paste
  (see Note)
1 tablespoon sugar
1 teaspoon ground cinnamon
1 teaspoon curry powder

1. Mix all of the ingredients for the marinade in a nonreactive bowl. Add the chicken, stir to coat, cover, and refrigerate overnight.

2. Combine all of the sauce ingredients in a nonreactive saucepan and whisk over medium heat until smooth. Cook until the mixture reduces by one-third, about 15 minutes. Reduce the heat to low, cover, and keep the sauce warm.

3. Preheat the broiler. Soak 10 bamboo skewers in water.

4. Thread 6 to 8 chicken pieces onto each bamboo or thin metal skewer. Place as many skewers as will fit comfortably on a rack or tray under the broiler and cook them until opaque, 3 minutes per side. Repeat with the remaining chicken.

5. Place the chicken skewers on a platter; serve at once with the sauce on the side for dipping.

Serves 5

Note: Both Thai fish sauce and red curry paste are available in Asian and other specialty food stores.

ON BEING A HOSTESS WITH THE LEASTEST

The generous of heart who entertain have a recurring fantasy: "One opens the refrigerator and inside is Zabar's," is the way that author, movie director, and Manhattanite mother of two Nora Ephron puts it.

In the dream, sides of smoked fish, mounds of caviar, and a jigsaw puzzle of wedges of different cheeses await the unannounced cocktail guest, the impromptu dinner party, the last-minute late-night buffet. Breads, crackers, dried sausages, nuts, and a four-star array of canned delicacies are also on standby.

In reality most home larders bear a closer resemblance to a fire sale than to the bounty of prepared foods and ethnic groceries available in the city. The best entertainers usually rely on a handful of staples to provide instant hospitality. For some, a single item—a can of pickled mushrooms in the cupboard or a can of inexpensive pressed caviar in the refrigerator—constitutes a pantry that can't be taken by surprise, even around the holidays.

Failing a Zabar's inventory in her own refrigerator, Ms. Ephron is content with a single jar of taramosalata, the Greek caviar spread. It gives her inner peace against unexpected knocks on the door.

To attain such a Zen-like state, Peggy Pierrepont, a realtor who entertains in her West Village apartment, needs four things: a store of scented candles, a jar of marinated Moroccan olives, hard-cooked quail eggs, and Champagne. "Quail eggs, olives, and Champagne by candlelight," she said. "How much more elegant can you get?"

Michael Aaron, chief executive of Sherry-

Lehmann, the wine and spirits company, and his wife, Christine, an interior designer, are satisfied with less. "If I have a wonderful Champagne," Mrs. Aaron said, "all I need is a bunch of cheese pastry sticks from Fraser Morris in the freezer." The cheese sticks, she says, need only a few minutes in a toaster oven to crisp and warm.

Holly Solomon, a gallery owner who regularly entertains up to 300 artists and collectors in her Sutton Place home, has perfected the minimalist pantry. "Popcorn," she said. "As long as I have vats of popcorn to pop, I am ready for company."

Others who entertain cite the comfort of canned sardines, octopus, anchovies, roasted peppers, artichoke hearts, and hearts of palm. All are available at Italian groceries and, when served on crackers, make tasty nibbles.

Green olives can be packed in olive oil, crushed garlic, and hot peppers and stored for months in the refrigerator; oil-cured black olives need only a bath of high-quality oil and lemon peel in the refrigerator. Aged hard cheeses keep better than fresh ones and many, like aged feta, can be marinated for up to a month in olive oil to make pungent cocktail fare. For reasons like these Robert Ruff, a producer at ABC News who entertains in his loft in Hell's Kitchen, wouldn't be without olive oil. "It's my security blanket," he said.

Annie Flanders, formerly the editor of *Details* magazine, is frequently host to a late-night salon in her West Village apartment and says that the vacuum-packed smoked fish and pâtés that she

buys at specialty food stores and keeps in her refrigerator give her the confidence of a latter-day Gertrude Stein.

Leslie Newman, a screenwriter, keeps Chinese pork buns in her freezer along with a selection of Chinese sausages and cold cuts for instant feasts in her apartment on the Upper West Side. The pork buns need only 10 minutes in a 350°F oven to taste as warm and fresh as the morning they were made.

A full array of sausages can be stored for unexpected guests. Ms. Newman keeps *merguez,* the spicy Moroccan sausage. W. Peter Prestcott, of *Food & Wine* magazine, favors Polish sausage, which he serves on skewers with hot mustard. He also keeps almonds and cashews in separate, tightly sealed containers in his freezer. When sprinkled with curry powder or a peppery spice blend and warmed on a tray, the nuts make an unusual appetizer.

"Condiments," Mr. Prestcott said, "keep me calm." Unusual vinegars, bottled Chinese fish sauce, black bean sauce, and hot chili oils are things that he keeps on hand to transform "prosaic ingredients" like chicken, fish, or shrimp broiled on skewers. Excellent canned salmon or trout, he pointed out, can be folded into whipped cream for an instant mousse. Frozen tortellini can be boiled, dipped in olive oil, rolled in Parmesan

cheese, and served on toothpicks.

Other hosts swear by a store of frozen spinach or meat phyllo turnovers. Phyllo pastries are available at local Greek groceries, freeze well, and require only a brush of melted butter and a few minutes in the oven to serve. For another pastry-like improvisation, Lee Bailey, a cookbook writer, keeps wrapped slices of bread and a small supply of grated Parmesan cheese in his freezer. "Unwrap the bread, sprinkle it with the Parmesan, pop it in under the toaster oven, and let the guests roll in," he says.

Not all hosts have reconciled their fantasies of a well-stocked pantry to the reality of a few standbys. Pat Buckley, a venerable "Lady Who Lunches" and doyenne of the New York City charity circuit, is confident when her home is supplied not only with the things she likes, but with a full range of items she dislikes. "Cigarettes other than my brand and root beer" bring her to a particular peace, she said.

Bill Blass, the designer who is known for his gracious entertaining, is most comfortable when his refrigerator is stocked with roasted chicken and beef, a wide range of vegetables and condiments, and plenty of different breads.

"I've always wanted to be a person like that," Ms. Ephron said. She is confident in her taramosalata but still has wistful moments thinking about the cornucopia of easy entertaining foods that is available in the city but somehow missing from her refrigerator. Mr. Blass, of course, has wistful moments of his own. "I need somebody to cook all that stuff," he said.

Shoshana's BABA GANOUSH

This makes a perfect companion dip for hummus as it should also be served with pita and vegetables for dipping.

1 large eggplant
⅓ cup tahini paste
2 cloves garlic, minced
¼ cup chopped fresh parsley
Juice of 1 lemon

1. Preheat the oven to 375°F.

2. Prick the eggplant all over with a fork; wrap in foil. Bake until fork tender, 1 hour.

3. Remove the eggplant from the oven; let cool. Peel the eggplant and mash the pulp in a medium bowl. Add all of the remaining ingredients and stir to mix well. This keeps for up to 1 week in a covered container in the refrigerator.

Makes about 2½ cups

Salsa RLX

Roedeanne Landeaux, a dress designer (Landeaux Studio X), makes this salsa in quantities so she will always have some on hand when she gets homesick for her native Dallas. This recipe makes a very, very hot sauce. For a milder version, use fewer jalapeño chiles.

1 head garlic, minced
¾ cup minced fresh cilantro
4 cups canned crushed tomatoes
6 fresh tomatoes, chopped
2 onions, chopped
⅓ cup juice from canned, bottled, or marinated jalapeño chiles
8 marinated jalapeño chiles, seeded, deveined, and minced

Combine the garlic, cilantro, canned and fresh tomatoes, onions, and jalapeño juice in a large mixing bowl. Stir in the jalapeños. Serve with chips, grilled chicken, pork, beef, or fish.

Makes 8 cups

Dress designer Roedeanne Landeaux surrounded by a cape of leaves— inspiration perhaps?

Andre Balog's KOROZOTT

"Each Hungarian housewife has her own treasured recipe for Körözött," says Andre Balog, manager of Paprikas Weiss, an Eastern European spice store. "Many add a swig of beer and a bit of anchovy paste." All Hungarians make the spicy cheese dip ahead to have on hand for entertaining or snacks. Körözött will keep in the refrigerator for up to one month.

1 large package (8 ounces) cream cheese,
    at room temperature
4 ounces Bryndza cheese, at room temperature
¼ pound (1 stick) butter, at room temperature
½ onion, finely chopped
1½ teaspoons sweet Hungarian paprika
1 teaspoon caraway seeds (optional)

———————■————————■———————

In a bowl, blend together the cream cheese, Bryndza, and butter, stirring until smooth. Stir in the onion, paprika, and caraway. Serve on crackers or rye bread.

Makes about 2 cups

Note: Bryndza cheese, an imported sheep's milk cheese, can be obtained from specialty shops; if unavailable, domestic sheep's milk cheese or blue cheese can be substituted.

Georgia's
TZATZIKI
(CUCUMBER YOGURT DIP)

Georgia Lyras, who grew up in New York and graduated from New York City Technical College, serves this zesty Greek yogurt dip with vegetables on the side or as a sauce for grilled meat or souvlaki.

2 cups plain yogurt
1 large cucumber, peeled, seeded,
    and chopped
2 cloves garlic, finely chopped
2 tablespoons olive oil
1 tablespoon white wine vinegar
Salt and freshly ground white pepper, to taste
Vegetables or pita bread, for serving

1. Line a strainer with a double thickness of dampened cheesecloth or a paper coffee filter and set it over a bowl. Spoon in the yogurt, cover with waxed paper, and place in the refrigerator overnight so that the yogurt can drain.

2. Place the drained yogurt in a mixing bowl. Fold in the cucumber, garlic, oil, and vinegar. Season with salt and white pepper to taste. Refrigerate to give the flavors time to blend, 1 hour or longer. Serve with vegetables or pita bread.

Makes about 2 cups

Jane Gol's
HUMMUS

Jane Gol got this recipe from her mother-in-law, who came from a town on the Russian-Afghan border. She has simplified the recipe. She serves the hummus drizzled with olive oil and garnished with triangles of pita bread.

2 cups (16 ounces) canned chick-peas, or 1 cup
    dried chick-peas, soaked for 4 hours, rinsed,
    and skinned (see Note below)
3 tablespoons tahini paste
1 clove garlic, minced
Juice of 2 lemons
Salt, to taste
Olive oil

———————■————————■———————

Combine all of the ingredients except the olive oil in a food processor or blender. Add ½ cup water. Process to a thick purée. Transfer to a bowl and cover with a thin film of olive oil to keep the hummus from crusting. Refrigerate until ready to use.

Makes about 2 cups

Note: To skin chick-peas, place them in a clean dish towel and rub until the skins come off.

LOX, STOCK, AND BAGELS

There are as many estimates of the amount of smoked salmon sold in New York City annually as there are varieties of the cured, smoked fish displayed in the city's appetizing counters. Buzz Billick, co-owner of Marshal Smoked Fish Company in Brooklyn, sees the city in terms of tonnage. Probably about ten thousand tons per year. Certainly more smoked fish than is sold anywhere else in the world. And certainly enough wafer-thin slices to have made New Yorkers wise in the ways of smoked salmon.

"The old-time, true-blue, traditional salmon-eater is not fooled by fancy labels or fish from other parts of the world," said Mr. Billick, whose smoked salmon house is the oldest and largest in the United States. Let the Johnny-come-lately gourmets forage through the Irish, Scottish, and Norwegian, Russian, and Baltic salmon! The best smoked salmon still comes from Brooklyn, where it has always been called Nova, and it will probably never be called *saumon fumé*.

There are six major smoking houses in Brooklyn. According to Mr. Billick, himself a true-blue, traditional-type salmon-eater, "New York has always been a lox and Nova town."

Lox is brine-cured and lightly smoked salmon. It is highly salty, and is the mainstay of older Eastern Europeans. Its saltiness triggered another New York tradition: the schmear, a swipe of cream cheese that helps balance the salt. Traditionally, Nova, a mild-cured, smoked Atlantic salmon, usually from Canada, is more expensive than lox. Lox has an affinity for bagels and cream cheese. Nova— on buttered pumpernickel or rye, or on blini with minced red onion, hard-cooked egg, and capers, or with mustard sauce on endive spears—can have enough finesse to take you right through cocktail hour.

Both Atlantic and Pacific salmon are cured in the Nova style today. Pacific, or "Western-style" salmon is the most common. After being rubbed with salt and brown sugar, and cured for three days and smoked over an 80°F hardwood fire, Western Nova is usually smooth and tastes mildly of smoke and salt.

Atlantic salmon, which is generally farm-raised, is cured for four days in brown sugar and salt and three days in a wet brine before smoking. This technique, according to Mr. Billick, "creates a very grainy, easily sliced salmon." The fish is firmer, smokier, and saltier than Western-style Nova. It is usually more expensive. Atlantic salmon cured in the Nova style is frequently called "Gaspé."

Traditional types don't buy smoked salmon by name, anyway. They look for bright flesh that glistens with natural oil. "In the trade we say 'it's alive,' when it looks like that," says Mr. Billick. Retailers agree that vacuum-packed or frozen imports appear flat and dull next to fresh sides of smoked salmon from Brooklyn. "It's never the same after it's frozen," says Murray Klein, who presides over dozens of different varieties of smoked salmon at Zabar's. In addition to brilliant color, he says, smoked salmon "has got to be soft as silk."

And then there is the flavor. "Don't ask for the name," says Mr. Klein, "ask for a taste." In fact, there is only one way a customer can circumvent sampling. "Find the best store and ask for the best they have," says Mark Russ, co-owner of Russ &

Daughters, who slices "tons, literally tons" of smoked salmon each year. In the shop, he stands under a carefully lettered sign that spells out a basic tenet of the old-time, true-blue, traditional type of New York life. "Lox *et veritas*," it says.

TO CATCH A PROPER NOVA

Marshal's, the oldest and largest salmon smoking house in America, will arrange tours of its plant. Call (718) 384-7621 to schedule a look behind the scenes. Marshal's also sells smoked salmon at near wholesale prices. The plant and store are located at 23 Anthony Street in the Greenpoint section of Brooklyn.

You can also get fine smoked salmon from the following stores:

BALDUCCI'S: 424 Avenue of the Americas (9th Street); (212) 673-2600; mail orders, (800) 247-2450 in New York, (800) 822-1444 out of state

BARNEY GREENGRASS: 541 Amsterdam Avenue (between 86th and 87th Streets); retail and mail order, (212) 724-4707

DEAN & DELUCA: 560 Broadway (Prince Street); (212) 431-8230; retail and mail order, (800) 221-7714

GRACE'S MARKETPLACE: 1237 Third Avenue (71st Street); retail and mail order, (212) 737-0600

MACY'S AT HERALD SQUARE: (212) 495-4400, ext. 2647; mail order, (800) 446-2297

RUSS & DAUGHTERS: 179 East Houston Street (Orchard Street); retail and mail order, (212) 475-4880

ZABAR'S: 2245 Broadway (80th Street); retail, (212) 787-2002; mail order, (212) 496-1234

Behind the counter at Zabar's.

Grandma Dora's
CHOPPED LIVER

Manhattan psychologist Gail Paige-Bowman inherited this recipe from her grandmother Dora. The secret to this extraordinary chopped liver is boiling the livers and chopping each ingredient by hand. Gail's grandfather insisted on using a wooden bowl for the chopping, but a chopping block works fine. "It's best served on small rye bread, but you can serve it on pumpernickel or crackers," Gail explains.

1 pound chicken livers, cleaned and rinsed
1 white onion, minced
6 hard-cooked eggs, peeled and minced
About 2 tablespoons rendered chicken fat or
*   butter, melted*
Dash of paprika
Salt and freshly ground black pepper, to taste

1. Immerse the livers in plenty of boiling water, cover, and boil gently until the livers are gray and firm, 5 to 7 minutes. Drain well. Chill in the refrigerator for 40 minutes.

2. Using a sharp knife, chop the livers to a smooth paste. Using a wooden spoon, stir together half of the liver, onion, and eggs. Add the remaining liver, onion, and eggs and stir to combine completely. Add enough of the chicken fat to moisten and hold the liver together. Add the paprika. Season with salt and pepper to taste.

Makes 3½ cups

Zabar's
SCALLION CREAM CHEESE SPREAD

The bagel, one of New York's archetypical brunch favorites, can be further enlivened by Zabar's (the venerable food emporium of Manhattan's Upper West Side) silky scallion cream cheese spread. Covered, this keeps well in the refrigerator; it's simple and addictive and can be used as a dip, a spread for croutons or crackers, or on top of baked potatoes.

1 pound cream cheese, at room temperature
½ cup sour cream
Pinch of salt
Pinch of garlic powder
½ cup chopped scallions

Combine the cream cheese, sour cream, salt, and garlic powder in a large bowl and stir until well mixed and smooth. Stir in the scallions. Serve on crackers or toasted bagel rounds.

Makes about 4 cups

Mr. Coupopoulos'
SPICY CURED OLIVES

Several years ago, when Mediterranean flavors became the rage, marinated olives became a staple of au courant refrigerators throughout New

York City. Made in two- or three-pound batches, the olives keep for months, make great nibbles, and are a fine addition to pasta sauces, or pitted and crushed, the olives can enliven simple grilled fish or chicken. But the merits of marinated olives are not an invention of the 1990s. In 1932, when Helen Worden wrote *The Real New York* the largest Greek settlement wasn't Astoria, Queens, it was "Little Athens," the dense blocks radiating from 40th Street and Eighth Avenue in Manhattan.

There, in the grocery run by one Mr. Coupopoulos, Ms. Worden found "Greek hors d'oeuvre, dainties that make a hit at cocktail parties, delicious ripe olives seasoned with a garlic clove, fragrant spices and tiny strips of lemon rind." Here is the recipe.

1 lemon
1 pound oil-cured black olives
2 cloves garlic, crushed
2 teaspoons dried red pepper flakes
2 tablespoons olive oil

Endless spicy black olives to nibble on—bet you can't eat just one.

Use a sharp knife to remove the zest from the lemon in thin sheets. Mince the zest very fine. Toss the zest with the olives, garlic, pepper flakes, and olive oil. Store in a glass container for at least 1 day; refrigerate before serving. The olives will keep for 1 month.

Serves 10 to 15

Eileen's
HONEY WALNUTS

In China, honey walnuts are served with cold platters or sometimes as complementary nibbles for cocktails," says Eileen Yin-Fei Lo, author of four cookbooks and a cooking instructor at the China Institute in New York City. "Many people enjoy them with their afternoon tea."

¾ pound freshly shelled walnut halves
2 tablespoons sugar
3 to 4 cups peanut oil

1. Bring 4 to 5 cups of water to a boil in a wok or medium-size saucepan over high heat. Add the walnuts and boil for 5 minutes (to remove the bitter taste). Strain out the walnuts and then run cold water over them. Strain again, then return the nuts to the wok.

2. Add 4 cups of fresh water and bring to a boil. Cook for 5 minutes. Repeat the straining process. Set the nuts aside to drain.

3. Wash the wok. Then add ⅓ cup of cold water. Bring to a boil over medium-high heat. Add the sugar and boil, constantly stirring, for 1 minute. Add the walnuts. Stir and cook until the walnuts are coated with sugar and the remaining liquid has evaporated.

4. Remove the walnuts and set aside on a well-greased cookie sheet. Wash the wok with extremely hot water to remove the sugar. Dry thoroughly.

5. Heat 3 to 4 cups of peanut oil in the wok over high heat until very hot (you will see a wisp of white smoke). Carefully add the walnuts and fry until golden brown, 2 to 3 minutes.

Makes 4 cups

SMART COCKTAILS
BY THE BOROUGH AND BEYOND

New Yorkers have long appreciated a smart cocktail. New Yorker writer, H. L. Mencken, who wrote for *The New Yorker* magazine, once called the martini, "The only American invention as perfect as a sonnet." The cocktail may have been invented by a bartender at the Occidental Hotel in San Francisco, or it may have been coined by the Martini vermouth company. But it was in New York that it reached its apogee. The iced martini glass became synonymous with sophistication.

Perhaps it was poetic whim that led bartenders to immortalize both Manhattan and the Bronx in cocktail form. The Bronx is a less well-known and certainly less popular drink than the Manhattan, and in that sense its fortunes imitate those of the borough itself. The creation of the Bronx cocktail is credited to a bartender named Johnnie Solon at the Waldorf Hotel, early in the twentieth century.

RAINBOW ROOM'S BRONX

This recipe is from the Rainbow Room, which is in Manhattan, but on a clear day you can see the Bronx from its vantage point 65 stories above ground at Rockefeller Center.

1½ ounces gin
2 dashes sweet vermouth
2 dashes dry vermouth
2 ounces orange juice
1 burnt orange peel twist (see Note),
   for garnish

Combine the gin, sweet and dry vermouths, and orange juice in a shaker with ice. Shake well. Strain into a large cocktail glass and garnish by giving the burnt orange peel a twist and placing it atop the cocktail.
Serves 1

Note: To make a burnt orange peel twist, take a strip of orange peel, hold it over a flaming match, and twist the peel slightly. The oil released from the peel will flare up briefly.

RAINBOW ROOM'S "MANHATTAN"

The Manhattan cocktail goes back to before the turn of the century. It is thought that the drink was invented by a bartender at the Manhattan Club and named after the club rather than the borough. Recipes for the drink vary somewhat, but it is usually made with bourbon or blended whiskey and sweet vermouth. A dry Manhattan is made with dry vermouth in place of the sweet, and a "perfect" Manhattan is made with half sweet and half dry vermouth.

This recipe is also from the Rainbow Room, where the Manhattan is one of the specialties.

1½ ounces blended whiskey
½ ounce sweet vermouth
Dash of Angostura bitters
1 maraschino cherry

Stir the whiskey, vermouth, and bitters with ice in a mixing glass. Strain into a martini glass and garnish with the cherry.
Serves 1

Grandma Kate's STUFFED PEPPERS

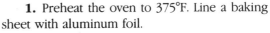

Remembers Margot Greenbaum Mustich, "When my husband and I first started dating, it surprised me that he, who is a second-generation Italian-American, did not enjoy eating out in Italian restaurants. After I had tasted his mother and grandmother's cooking, I understood." And though Margot wanted to duplicate the dishes, she feared that "nice Jewish girl that I am, I would never be able to turn out food that would measure up to the familial standard." With some time in the kitchen with her grandmother-in-law, Catherine Di Stasio, however, she mastered this superb dish.

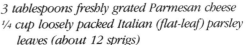

*12 green or red
    Italian frying peppers*
*6 to 8 slices (about ½
    pound) European-
    style white peasant
    bread, crusts re-
    moved*
6 flat anchovy fillets
*3 cloves garlic,
    peeled*
3 tablespoons freshly grated Parmesan cheese
*¼ cup loosely packed Italian (flat-leaf) parsley
    leaves (about 12 sprigs)*
½ cup plus 2 tablespoons extra-virgin olive oil

1. Preheat the oven to 375°F. Line a baking sheet with aluminum foil.

2. Cut the tops off the peppers and reserve for another use. Clean the insides of the peppers with a paring knife and rinse thoroughly to eliminate seeds; set aside.

*The Rainbow Room(left). Photo courtesy of The Rainbow Room.
Grandma Kate (above) with granddaughter Margot and great-
granddaughter Emma.*

3. Tear the bread into smaller pieces. In a food processor, combine the bread with the anchovies, garlic, Parmesan, and parsley. Turn the machine on and, with the motor running, slowly pour in ½ cup of the olive oil. Stop the machine and check the mixture; the bread should be the texture of coarse bread crumbs and should be fairly moist. Add 1 to 2 tablespoons water to moisten if needed.

4. Loosely stuff the peppers with the bread mixture just short of the edge of the open end; do not pack too tightly. Arrange the stuffed peppers on the baking sheet, and tuck any leftover stuffing around the peppers (you can use it to garnish the serving dish).

5. Moisten the peppers by sprinkling with the remaining 2 tablespoons olive oil. Bake, basting twice with the pan juices, until the peppers are nicely browned and have begun to collapse, 35 to 45 minutes. Add more water, if necessary, to keep the bottom of the pan wet.

Serves 4 to 6

Gail Vogel's
ROASTED PEPPERS

Gail Vogel, a model, always has a supply of these peppers for guests. If well-covered, they last for up to a month and are delicious served with mozzarella cheese, bread, or crackers.

10 to 12 bell peppers (in assorted colors)
3 to 4 cloves garlic, chopped
Olive oil

1. Preheat the broiler. Place the broiler tray as close to the heat source as possible.

2. Place the peppers in a single layer on a baking sheet or shallow roasting pan. Broil, turning with tongs, until the peppers are charred on all sides, 10 minutes. Place the peppers in a paper bag, close the bag, and allow the peppers to cool.

3. When cool, remove one pepper at a time from the bag. Cut it in half, remove the seeds, and peel off the skin with a paper towel. Do not rinse under cold water or you will lose the smoky taste. Cut each pepper into 1-inch strips.

4. In a wide-mouthed jar, layer the peppers with the garlic until the jar is almost full. Pour olive oil over the mixture until the oil reaches the top of the jar. Cover and refrigerate for 24 hours before eating.

Makes about 3 cups

Mrs. Simpson's
BACON TOAST POINTS

These hors d'oeuvres were a favorite of the Duchess of Windsor and remain a standby of the Upper East Side cocktail circuit.

½ pound bacon
½ cup mayonnaise
½ cup chopped scallions
25 buttered crustless toast rounds or triangles

1. Preheat the oven to 350°F.

2. Fry the bacon in a skillet over medium heat until crisp. Drain, cool, and crumble.

3. In a small bowl, combine the bacon with the mayonnaise and scallions. Spread 1 tablespoon of the mixture on each toast round or triangle. Place on a baking sheet and warm in the oven for 5 to 7 minutes.

Makes 25 appetizers

MANY-FACED QUICHE

Quiche, the once beloved, now much-maligned savory pie, still makes a delightful first course and a handy appetizer. Like most things in New York, quiche comes in many permutations. Following are representatives from upper Madison Avenue and Italy, the West Indies, Japan, and Provence.

3. In a large bowl, combine the eggs, cheese, and chives. Stir in the cooled mushrooms. Add the white pepper, nutmeg, and tarragon and mix well. Taste and correct the seasonings.

4. Spread the mixture evenly in the prepared pan. Bake until a knife inserted in the center comes out clean, about 25 minutes. Let cool in the pan on a rack for 5 to 7 minutes before cutting into squares and serving.

Makes about 24 squares

Janeen's JARLSBERG SQUARES

Janeen Sarlin serves this dish as an alternative to cheese at cocktail parties or with a green salad for lunch. The squares are best hot from the oven.

1 tablespoon butter
½ cup chopped mushrooms
4 eggs, lightly beaten
4 cups shredded Jarlsberg cheese (1½ pounds)
¼ cup snipped chives
½ teaspoon freshly ground white pepper
¼ to ½ teaspoon freshly grated nutmeg
1 teaspoon chopped fresh tarragon,
*   or ½ teaspoon dried*

1. Preheat the oven to 350°F. Grease and flour an 8-inch-square cake pan to make thick squares or a 13 × 9-inch cake pan to make thin squares.

2. Melt the butter in a sauté pan over medium-high heat. Add the mushrooms and sauté until all of the liquid evaporates, about 3 minutes. Remove from the heat; set aside to cool.

Guy's ONION AND OLIVE PIE

Local French folklore has it that when the French liners still docked on the West Side around 45th Street, huge numbers of sailors jumped ship and opened the modest little restaurants that still dot the blocks. The recipe for this pie was dear and passed along often. It is anyone's guess who the original Guy was. But it's a pie that would please any guy.

CRUST
2 cups all-
*   purpose*
*   flour*
½ pound (2
*   sticks) butter,*
*   sliced*
½ teaspoon
*   salt*
1 egg yolk
3 tablespoons ice water

Ready for the slicing.

FILLING
2 tablespoons butter
3 pounds white onions, thinly sliced
Salt and freshly ground black pepper, to taste
12 anchovy fillets
1 cup oil-cured black olives, pitted and halved

1. Make the crust: Using your fingertips, quickly work the flour into the butter until the mixture has the consistency of coarse cornmeal. Add the salt. Beat the egg yolk into the ice water. Form a well in the flour mixture, add the yolk mixture, and combine swiftly with a fork. Add more flour, if necessary, to keep the dough from sticking. Shape the dough into a ball, wrap in plastic, and chill for 1 hour.

2. Make the filling: Melt the butter in a large skillet over high heat. Reduce the heat to low and add the onions. Cook, stirring, until the onions are soft and gold in color, about 10 minutes. Season with salt and pepper to taste; remove from the heat.

3. Preheat the oven to 375°F.

4. Roll out the dough on a lightly floured surface into a round about 11 inches in diameter and ¼ inch thick. Use as much extra flour as necessary to keep it from sticking. Press the dough into a large tart pan. Prick the bottom and sides evenly with a fork. Trim and crimp the edges.

5. Arrange the anchovies in a starburst pattern from the center of the pie. Sprinkle on half of the black olives. Layer on half of the onions, then the remaining black olives, and then top with the remaining onions. Bake the tart until the crust is golden and the onions are caramelized and brown, 40 to 50 minutes.

Serves 8

Andrea Girard's
SPINACH PIE

This spinach pie is a terrific do-ahead appetizer. Andrea Girard, a native New Yorker, publicist, and self-proclaimed "great party giver," prefers this pie for her buffet table because it slices neatly and draws rave reviews.

1 pound spinach, well rinsed, dried, and chopped
⅔ cup dried bread crumbs
¾ cup freshly grated Parmesan cheese
5 tablespoons butter, at room temperature
1 pound ricotta cheese
3 tablespoons sour cream
2 large eggs
1 tablespoon dried basil
1½ teaspoons salt,
  or to taste
½ teaspoon freshly
  ground black pepper,
  or to taste

Andrea Girard offers up a hot-from-the-oven spinach pie.

STONE FENCE

In his **1809** *History of New York*, Diedrich Knickerbocker (aka Washington Irving), told how the Dutch "lay claim to be the first inventors of the recondite beverages, cock-tail, stone-fence, and sherry-cobbler." The first Stone Fence appears to have been made with sweet cider and applejack; this recipe is based on one that appeared in *The American Heritage Cookbook and Illustrated History of American Eating and Drinking.*

2 ounces bourbon
2 to 3 ice cubes
Sweet apple cider

Pour the bourbon into a highball glass, add the ice cubes, and fill the glass with sweet cider.

Serves 1

1. Preheat the oven to 350°F.

2. Steam the spinach, covered, in a heavy pot until it is tender but not falling apart, 2 minutes. Remove from the pot; set aside to cool.

3. Meanwhile, make the crust: Combine the bread crumbs, ¼ cup of the Parmesan, and the butter in a bowl. Press evenly into a 9-inch pie plate; set aside.

4. In a large bowl, combine the ricotta, sour cream, eggs, basil, salt, pepper, and the remaining ½ cup Parmesan. Beat until smooth. Stir in the spinach.

5. Pour the filling into the pie crust. Top with more pepper. Bake until a knife inserted in the center comes out clean, 45 minutes. Cool to room temperature and serve.

Serves 6

Ismay Samuels'
SPINACH PIE

Savory pies are favored by party givers, since they can be made and baked in advance and served at room temperature or reheated in the microwave. Ismay Samuels' spinach pie is so easy, she says she could make it with her eyes closed. It offers a wonderful variety of colors, textures, and flavors.

2½ cups grated Cheddar cheese
1 prebaked pie shell
3 cups fresh spinach, well rinsed, dried, and
*   chopped*
6 large eggs, beaten
½ cup chopped mushrooms
½ cup chopped onion
1 cup milk
¼ cup vegetable oil
1 tablespoon diced red bell pepper or pimiento
¼ teaspoon salt
¼ teaspoon freshly ground black pepper

1. Preheat the oven to 375°F.

2. Sprinkle ¼ cup of the Cheddar on the bottom of the pie shell. Reserve ¼ cup of the Cheddar for the top of the pie.

3. In a large mixing bowl, stir together all of the remaining ingredients. Pour the filling into the pie shell. Sprinkle the reserved cheese on top. Bake until a knife inserted in the center comes out clean, 45 minutes. Serve hot or at room temperature.

Serves 6 to 8

Nippon's
JAPANESE PANCAKE

This light, omelet-like pie, from Manhattan's four-star Japanese restaurant, makes a marvelous first course for two on a hot day or before a heavy meal. Cooked pork, shrimp, squid, or octopus can be substituted for the beef and the pie is best served immediately from the skillet.

2 tablespoons bonito flakes (see Note)
2 tablespoons tonkatsu sauce (a soy and fruit
*   based sauce usually used with pork;*
*   see Note)*
2 tablespoons ketchup
2 tablespoons mayonnaise (optional)
⅔ cup New York Penicillin (page 47),
*   canned chicken broth, or water*
1 egg, beaten
2 tablespoons mashed cooked yam
⅔ cup all-purpose flour
1 tablespoon vegetable oil
¼ cup shredded cabbage
¼ cup fine carrot julienne
1 scallion, trimmed and minced
¼ cup bean sprouts
2 shiitake mushrooms, chopped
¼ cup minced cooked beef
Aonori (seaweed), shredded, for garnish
*   (see Note)*

1. Mix together the bonito flakes, tonkatsu sauce, ketchup, and mayonnaise in a small bowl. Set the sauce aside.

2. In a bowl, stir together the chicken broth, egg, and yam. Add the flour and mix well. Heat the oil in a medium skillet over medium heat. When the pan is hot but not smoking, pour two-thirds of the batter into the pan and spread it out like a pancake. Sprinkle the cabbage, carrot, scallion, bean sprouts, mushrooms, and meat on top. Drizzle the remaining batter over the top. Cook until the pancake is golden brown on the bottom, about 4 minutes. Use a spatula to carefully turn and brown the other side, about 4 minutes more. Remove the pancake from the skillet, trim the edges, and top with the sauce and the seaweed. Serve immediately.

Serves 2

Note: Bonito flakes, tonkatsu sauce, and aonori can be found in Japanese groceries and other specialty food stores.

Caviar
HORS D'OEUVRE

Ruth Manton, who heads her own firm that licenses the use of fashion designers' names on ancillary products (like perfume), says she "inherited this recipe somewhere along the line. I wish I could remember where." Serve this with "fairly bland little English water biscuits."

6 hard-cooked eggs, yolks and whites separated,
yolks mashed, whites diced
4 tablespoons (½ stick) unsalted butter, at room
temperature
¼ cup mayonnaise
3 tablespoons minced fresh chives
⅓ cup minced scallions
Salt and freshly ground black pepper, to taste
1 cup sour cream
3½ ounces black lumpfish caviar, drained

1. In a large bowl, mix the egg yolks, butter, mayonnaise, chives, and scallions until smooth. Gently mix in the egg whites; season with salt and pepper to taste.

2. Press the mixture into a small (8½ × 4½ × 2½-inch) bread pan; cover with plastic wrap pressed directly on the surface. Refrigerate until cold and firm.

3. To serve, turn the loaf out onto a serving dish. Cover the top with the sour cream; spoon the caviar on top, being careful not to mash the eggs.

Serves 8

Starburst
OF CAVIAR

Katherine Melchoir Ray.

Katherine Melchoir Ray, a New York–based correspondent for Japanese television serves friends this simple, but elegant hors d'oeuvre.

½ cup sour cream
2 tablespoons cream
cheese, at room temperature
3 endives, spears separated, rinsed, and dried
5 ounces caviar

1. Mix the sour cream and the cream cheese until smooth.

2. Spoon ½ teaspoon of the cheese mixture on the stem end of each endive spear. Top with ½ teaspoon of the caviar. Repeat with the remaining endive, cheese mixture, and caviar.

3. Fan the filled endive spears in a circle on a round tray. They may be covered and refrigerated for 45 minutes before serving.

Serves 20

Marika's
BLINI

These light, half-dollar-size buckwheat pancakes are a staple of weddings, funerals, and holidays in Russia. In New York's Brighton Beach, platters of blini, with melted butter, or fresh farmer's cheese or sour cream, caviar and smoked fish toppings are served at the Russian nightclubs that crowd the area. They make a wonderful hors d'oeuvre or first course.

2 cups buckwheat flour
1 cup all-purpose flour
2 envelopes active dry yeast
½ cup lukewarm water (105° to 115°F)
⅓ cup sugar
5 large eggs, beaten
¼ pound (1 stick) butter, melted and cooled
4 cups milk
½ teaspoon salt
Vegetable oil, for frying

1. Sift together the buckwheat and all-purpose flours in a small bowl. Set aside.

2. In a medium bowl, dissolve the yeast in the lukewarm water. Add half of the sugar and ⅓ cup of the flour mixture. Cover the bowl with a towel, set aside, and let rise in a warm place until doubled, 30 minutes to 1 hour.

3. In a large bowl, mix together the eggs, melted butter, and 2 cups of the milk mixed with 1½ cups water, the remaining sugar, and the salt. Stir in the yeast mixture. Stir in enough of the remaining flour mixture so that the dough has the consistency of sour cream. Cover the bowl with a towel; set aside to rise for 30 minutes.

4. Bring the remaining 2 cups milk to a boil in a small saucepan. Remove from the heat. Pour the milk over the dough and stir gently.

5. In a 10-inch skillet over medium heat, add enough oil to just coat the bottom. When the pan is hot, drop 1 tablespoon of the blini batter onto the pan. Spread it out to about 3 inches in diameter. When the blini bubbles break, after about 10 seconds, turn the blini over with a spatula and cook for 15 seconds more. Repeat with the remaining batter. Keep the blini warm in a low oven.

6. Serve the blini with sour cream, melted butter, farmer's cheese, honey, jam, sugar, red or black caviar, salmon, or herring.

Makes 50 blini

Martha Burr's
SMOKED WHITEFISH
PATÉ

Martha Burr, a graduate student at New York University, updated one of her family's Middle European recipes and came up with this pâté. She makes it whenever she can get good fresh fish and prefers to serve the pâté at room temperature with drinks.

¾ pound smoked whitefish, skinned, boned, and
  flaked (to yield ½ pound flaked fish)
1 large package (8 ounces) cream cheese, at room
  temperature
2 tablespoons unsalted butter, at room
  temperature
1 tablespoon grated onion
2 to 3 tablespoons prepared horseradish, drained
Dash of hot Hungarian paprika
¼ teaspoon dill seeds
Fresh dill sprigs, for garnish (optional)

1. With a fork, mash together the flaked fish, cream cheese, and butter until creamy. Beat in the grated onion, then season with the horseradish, to taste. Turn the pâté into a shallow serving bowl. Sprinkle with the paprika and dill

seeds. Cover and refrigerate for 1 hour.

2. Serve the pâté chilled or at room temperature, garnished with the fresh dill sprigs. Spread on plain crackers or dark bread.

Makes 6 generous servings

BAKED POTATOES STUFFED

with Caviar + Cream

During the 80s, this dish was de rigueur on restaurant menus. It remains an easy, festive hors d'oeuvre, and it is nearly impossible to eat just one.

12 very small potatoes, such as red Bliss or new
  potatoes
2 tablespoons butter, softened
1 cup crème fraîche or sour cream
1 ounce caviar
6 fresh chives, minced

1. Preheat the oven to 350°F.

2. Scrub the potatoes well, then dry with a towel. Rub the skins well with the butter; arrange the potatoes on a baking sheet.

3. Bake the potatoes until soft, about 40 minutes.

4. Remove the potatoes from the oven. Wrap each in a towel to prevent burning your hands and press gently to open. Place a spoonful of the crème fraîche in each, add a dollop of the caviar, sprinkle with the chives, and serve immediately.

Serves 6 well-mannered people, otherwise, many less

THE CAVIARTERIA AND WHAT IT KNOWS

Since 1955, Louis Sobel and his family have been importing and selling caviar. Their tendrils stretch from a tiny storefront deep into the James Bond world of Russian and Iranian caviar, pulling the best into New York. During the holiday season, Zabar's and Macy's bellow their prices; but year-round, Caviarteria, which is packed with caviar accoutrements like bone spoons and sterling caviar cradles with crystal liners, quietly sells low. Mr. Sobel, who says that beluga *malossol* is his biggest seller and that his store's "Kamchatka Caviar," broken eggs from the bottom of the 200-pound barrels of beluga, is the best value.

Traditionally, he said, caviar is the processed and salted roe of the sturgeon. Historically, Russia and Iran were the principal sources of the imported delicacy, producing beluga, osetra, and sevruga. Each type bears the name of a species of Caspian sea sturgeon from which the roe are harvested. Today, Russia is the principal source of all imported caviar. There are many other varieties of caviar, and prices vary enormously. Here are the major types:

Beluga caviar is the name linked inextricably with status and luxury. With sturgeon eggs ranging in color from dark to light gray, it is the largest-grained, most delicately flavored, and most expensive variety.

Osetra caviar is the designation for smaller sturgeon eggs that are covered with a distinctive golden-brown coating of fat. It is not as mild as beluga, and some prefer it for its stronger flavor.

Sevruga caviar is composed of the smallest sturgeon eggs, whose color varies from dark gray to black. The most robust-flavored of the three, it's generally the least expensive type of sturgeon caviar.

Pressed caviar is made from broken sturgeon eggs packed together into a thick, marmalade-like consistency; it may contain beluga, osetra, and sevruga eggs, and it is preferred by some caviar aficionados for its intense flavor.

American sturgeon caviar varies considerably in taste and texture. Some has a deliciously nutty flavor; others can be extremely salty and bitter. The black eggs are generally small and not as firm in texture as Russian sturgeon caviar.

Salmon caviar, either imported or domestic, is characterized by medium to large eggs, ranging in color from light to reddish orange. The eggs normally have a somewhat gooey consistency, with a characteristic crunch and intense flavor.

Whitefish caviar varies in color from pale yellow to black and comes from several species found in the Great Lakes and Canada. The pale yellow or "golden" variety is the most prized. The eggs are very small, with a low oil content and a mild taste.

Lumpfish caviar, imported primarily from Iceland, is the most inexpensive and widely available type on the market. The eggs are small, dyed black or red, and heavily salted. Usually seen in pasteurized form, it is sometimes available fresh.

Malossol is a term you will see frequently on caviar labels or in advertisements. It is Russian for "little salt," so, in theory, the caviar should not be heavily salted. But it is not a guarantee of quality, nor does the term indicate a type of caviar.

Caviarteria at 29 East 60th Street, between Park and Madison, also offers mail-order service. Out of state, dial (800) 4-CAVIAR. In New York the number is (212) 759-7410.

NEW YORK'S
ARTESIAN SPRINGS

In the world according to seltzer connoisseurs, this is about the year 20 A.P.

Two decades have elapsed since plastic bottles with screw tops began to replace the blue or green glass siphon bottles with hand-operated valves that are to a lively seltzer what a flared cork is to a bottle of proper Champagne. In the years B.P. (Before Plastic), sales held their own. After Plastic (A.P.), sales of sparkling water geysered. There are now high-priced imports. There is orange, lemon, lime, and raspberry seltzer.

But there isn't the same sparkle—at least not for seltzer cognoscenti, who grew up at a table set with a siphon bottle as certainly as it was set with napkins.

"Before plastic you could rely on a fresh seltzer—by that I mean good bubble activity," said Sam Steinberg, past president of the Good Health Seltzer Association, a trade group in New York that was founded in the 1930s and grew to 501 members, B.P. "There's one guy left," said Mr. Steinberg, who is now retired.

That would be George Howell, owner of Havana Dry Beverages in the Bronx. Mr. Howell, who is called "Sweet George," because,

he says "maybe people appreciate that somebody still delivers real seltzer," began working for Havana Dry when he was 17 years old. Forty-two years later, he still runs his business "like Avon," delivering fresh seltzer to about 400 customers.

His career was more like a calling. "It wouldn't let me go," he said. His product starts with the city's own artesian spring—tap water. It is filtered through charcoal and paper to remove salt and additives, then is infused with carbon dioxide, hosed into glass bottles and fitted with a siphon and valve that customers cannot remove. "You can never open him, he can never go flat," Sweet George said.

Like the mineral water from bucolic sources that lines grocery store shelves today, the local elixir has a venerable past. Named for Niederselters, a German village that began producing carbonated tonics in the sixteenth century, the elixir was introduced to New York "by a Frenchman after the revolution," Mr. Steinberg said. But it wasn't until 1809 that Joseph Hawkins patented the machinery for carbonating water, and the glass bottles became a part of the well-set table.

"Every block had a milkman, a laundry man, a seltzer man," Mr. Steinberg recalled.

But by the late 1960s, imported waters started to make a dent in the local market, though seltzer connoisseurs aren't sure why. "It's just seltzer that bubbles up from the ground and is expensive," Mr. Steinberg said.

When New York seltzer purists vary their own beverage intake, they tend to stay local.

Dr. Brown's Cel-Ray Soda is one respectable alternative. The tonic—an infusion of celery seeds, sugar, and, of course, seltzer—is said to have been invented in 1869 by a doctor treating immigrant children. Dr. Brown's is now owned by Canada Dry Bottling Company of New York and is made in College Point, Queens.

"We are no threat to Pepsi," said Harry Gold, marketing director of Dr. Brown's, "but people who grew up in New York never lose a taste for Cel-Ray."

About a million bottles and cans of Dr. Brown's Cel-Ray are sold a year. About that many bottles of another local seltzer derivative, Manhattan Special, are also sold annually. That beverage, a blend of espresso, cane sugar, and a splash of seltzer was invented by Dr. Theresa Cimino in 1895.

"It's a low-carbonated drink," said the inventor's great-granddaughter, Aurora Passaro, now the president of the Brooklyn company, "but the fizz is essential to the refreshment."

The fizz is equally indispensible to a classic New York egg cream, a mix of milk and chocolate syrup that is spritzed to a fine foam with seltzer. "I don't know how it got its name because it has no egg, no cream," said Mr. Steinberg. "But I know it's nothing without fresh seltzer." (For a recipe, see Index.)

People like to make lamps out of the bottles, said Sweet George Howell. More than increased imports or changes in the marketplace, he battles the flea-market value of his container. The bottles, which were recycled by seltzer companies, are not made anymore, and the best of the hand-blown Czechoslovakian ones can fetch up to $10. He has "bottle locators" in Philadelphia and New Jersey who search out and snatch up cases of 10 for $3.20 to $3.50.

But he can't deliver these valuables to just anyone. "We can't go lugging 50-pound cases up walk-ups for people to make lamps," Mr. Howell said. Only the thirsty need apply.

George Howell shows bow to beft a case of seltzer.

Grandma Simon's
PICKLED HERRING

Margot Greenbaum Mustich doesn't remember when she first tasted her grandmother's pickled herring, but like honoring her father and mother, loving her grandmother's pickled herring is a fact of life. Being a devoted granddaughter, she adopted the view that the versions of pickled herring in sour cream sauce that line supermarket shelves are "sloppy excuses for a dish that can be subtle, elegant, and just plain addictive." In this recipe, the saltiness of the herring is held in check by a marvelous sweet and sour combination of apple, onion, and lemon.

It is best made a day or two before serving and can be stored in the conventional manner—refrigerated in a tightly sealed jar—or in more eccentric ways. According to her granddaughter, Mildred Simon, who is now in her 90s and lives in Florida, makes her pickled herring at home, puts it in jars, and then places the jars inside Cornish game hens (for insulation). She packs them in her suitcase for the trips north for family Thanksgivings.

1 jar (12 ounces) herring fillets in wine sauce
1 Bermuda onion, thinly sliced
1 large or 2 small McIntosh apples, peeled, cored, and thinly sliced
1 cup sour cream
½ teaspoon sugar
Splash of distilled white vinegar
½ lemon, thinly sliced
1 fresh dill or parsley sprig, for garnish

1. Remove the herring from the jar and drain, reserving the sauce. Scrape any black skin and membranes off the herring pieces with a knife.

2. In a medium bowl, combine the herring, onion, apple, sour cream, sugar, and vinegar. Cut the lemon slices into quarters and add to the herring mixture. Add the reserved herring sauce and stir to coat all of the ingredients evenly. Cover and refrigerate for at least 24 hours.

3. Before serving, taste for seasonings and add more vinegar or sugar, to taste. Garnish with the dill or parsley sprig. Serve cold, with a good dark pumpernickel or rye bread cut into small squares.

Serves 4 to 6

James O'Shea's
IRISH SMOKED COD ROE

James O'Shea, an Irish émigré, advises serving this marvelous appetizer with or on tiny Irish oatmeal buttermilk pancakes. Irish smoked cod roe is available at Petrossian and Zabar's (in New York) and other gourmet food outlets. There is no substitute.

1 pound Irish smoked cod roe, at room
  temperature, membrane removed
2 tablespoons crème fraîche
2½ tablespoons unsalted butter
2 tablespoons vegetable oil, for the ramekins

1. Combine all of the ingredients except the vegetable oil in a food processor. Process until well mixed and smooth, being careful not to over-process.

2. Oil 4 to 6 ramekins. Pack the mixture into the ramekins; chill overnight. Turn out onto plates to serve.

Serves 4 to 6

The Pool Room at The Four Seasons was designed by architect Phillip Johnson. Photo courtesy of The Four Seasons

The Four Seasons' SALMON RILLETTES

This rich, smooth appetizer epitomizes the understated elegance of the restaurant where it was created. It is worth all the effort it takes to prepare. Serve with warm toast fingers.

COURT BOUILLON
1 onion, sliced
1 carrot, sliced
1 celery rib, sliced
1 leek, cleaned and sliced
3 stalks fresh fennel,
    coarsely chopped (optional)
1 fresh thyme sprig, or ¼ teaspoon dried
4 fresh dill stems, or 1 teaspoon dried
½ teaspoon salt
4 white peppercorns

RILLETTES
¾ pound fresh salmon fillets, skin on
½ pound (2 sticks) unsalted butter, softened
    slightly
1 tablespoon Armagnac, cognac, or Calvados
Pinch of salt
Pinch of freshly ground white pepper
Pinch of cayenne pepper
¾ pound smoked salmon, trimmed and coarsely
    shredded
4 ounces salmon caviar

1. Make the court bouillon: Combine the onion, carrot, celery, leek, fennel, thyme, dill, salt, peppercorns, and 2½ cups cold water in a saucepan. Bring to a boil over high heat. Cover and simmer for 25 minutes. Strain, discarding the solids; reserve the court bouillon. (You may make the court bouillon ahead. Cover tightly and freeze until ready to prepare the rillettes.)
2. Make the rillettes: Bring the court bouillon

to a boil in a nonreactive skillet large enough to hold the fish snugly in one layer. Add the fresh salmon fillets, reduce the heat, and cover the pan. Simmer until the salmon is opaque in the center, about 8 minutes per inch of thickness. Remove from the heat; set aside to allow the salmon to cool completely in the broth.

3. Drain the poached salmon, remove the skin and any bones, and break up the meat. Place the salmon meat, butter, Armagnac, salt, white pepper, and cayenne in a food processor. Add the smoked salmon. Pulse on and off until the mixture is smooth.

4. Gently fold in the salmon caviar. Adjust the seasonings with additional salt and pepper to taste. Spoon the mixture into a 1-quart decorative mold or serving dish. Tap the mold lightly on a towel-lined surface to eliminate air bubbles. Cover with plastic wrap and chill until set, 8 hours or over-night. The rillettes will keep well for up to 2 days in the refrigerator.

5. Remove the rillettes from the refrigerator 20 minutes prior to serving. Chill a serving spoon under cold water and scoop the salmon onto cold plates.

Makes 8 servings

Robert Motherwell's
BRANDADE DE MORUE

Robert Motherwell, the late artist who coined the term "The New York School" for the group of abstract expressionists that began to make waves in the art world in the 1940s, first tasted this dish when he was a young artist in Paris. After a few lessons from the late Cordon Bleu chef Dione Lucas, he prepared this (and many other dishes) for the likes of Willem de Kooning and Jackson Pollock in his Greenwich Village apartment. The purée can be served warm with toast points as an appetizer or spooned into puff pastry shells for a first course.

1 pound dried salt cod
3 large baking potatoes
6 cups fish broth or bottled clam juice
2 cloves garlic, crushed
½ cup extra-virgin olive oil
½ cup heavy (whipping) cream
Sea salt and freshly ground black pepper, to taste

———————————————

1. Soak the cod for 8 hours or overnight in cold water, changing the water every few hours.

2. Preheat the oven to 450°F.

3. Bake the potatoes until soft, about 1 hour. Cool and scoop the potato pulp from the skins into a bowl.

4. Drain the cod and discard any skin, bones, or tough parts. Cut the fish into small bits. Combine the fish and the broth in a nonreactive small saucepan over medium heat. Bring to a simmer and cook for 20 minutes; drain.

5. Place the fish in a bowl or mortar. Use a wooden spoon or pestle to pound it to a fine paste. (You may also use a food mill to do this, but not a food processor.) Add the potato and garlic and pound to combine. Still pounding, drizzle in the olive oil and then the cream. Season with the sea salt and pepper, to taste.

Serves 8 as an appetizer, 4 as a first course

Mimi Bochco's
GEFILTE FISH

Steven Bochco, the television producer, has no words for the perfection of his mother's gefilte fish. Had she not finally moved to Los Angeles, he would have tried to move the center of the television world to Brooklyn to be closer to her delicate ground fish dumplings.

If desired, a fishmonger can grind the fish for you, making the dish all the more easy to prepare.

3 slices white bread, crusts removed
1¾ pounds whitefish, ground
1¾ pounds yellow pike, ground
½ pounds carp, ground
3 large onions, 2 grated and 1 sliced
3 large eggs
Heads and bones of 3 fish, preferably whitefish,
    pike, and carp
2 teaspoons salt
⅛ teaspoon saffron threads, for color (optional)
½ teaspoon freshly ground black pepper
Horseradish, for serving

1. Soak the bread in cold water to cover. In a wooden bowl, combine the ground fish and grated onions and mix with the eggs. Drain the bread and add it to mixture. Chop the mixture until the fish gets fluffy and pasty and sticks to the chopper, 20 to 30 minutes. This makes the fish light and airy.

2. Put the fish heads and bones in a large pot. Add the sliced onion on top, cover with cold water, and add 1 teaspoon of the salt.

3. Gently shape the fish mixture into egg-shaped dumplings, each about 3 × 2 inches. Put the gefilte fish in the pot on top of the onions. Bring the water to a boil, reduce the heat, and partially cover the pot. Boil slowly for 2 hours. Dissolve some saffron in a little hot water and add to the pot for color, if desired, as the fish may have a slightly gray color without it.

4. Remove the pot from heat and let cool for 10 to 15 minutes. Transfer the gefilte fish to a platter or deep dish. Strain the cooking liquid; discard the solids. Add the pepper and remaining salt and pour the liquid over the fish. Refrigerate to chill (the liquid will gel). Serve cold with plenty of horseradish.

Makes about 2 dozen

Jerome Alden's
ARGENTINIAN CEVICHE

Playwright Jerome Alden says he "has almost always done all the cooking" in his family. His easy Argentinian ceviche is perfect for a hot summer day. Since the lime juice "cooks" the scallops, you don't have to stand over a hot stove. All you have to do is mix, marinate overnight, and enjoy the results in front of a fan, or better yet, in an air-conditioned room.

Waiting for the ceviche to chill, Jerome Alden takes a break.

1 pound sea or bay scallops, rinsed (if using sea scallops, cut into bite-size pieces)
Juice of 8 limes
1¼ cups chopped onion
½ cup Spanish olives, pits removed and sliced into quarters
2 tablespoons olive brine from jar
3 tomatoes, peeled and chopped, with juice reserved
1 bottle (14 ounces) Heinz Hot Ketchup, or 1¾ cups plain ketchup mixed with 1 tablespoon dried red pepper flakes
1 tablespoon crumbled dried oregano

1. In a glass or ceramic bowl, cover the scallops with the lime juice. Cover and refrigerate for 3 hours.

2. Meanwhile, combine all of the remaining ingredients in a separate nonreactive bowl. Cover the sauce and keep at room temperature.

3. When the scallops are "cooked," drain in a colander. Rinse under cold running water and pat dry with paper towels. Add the scallops to the sauce; mix well. Cover and refrigerate overnight until ready to serve.

Serves 4 to 6

Thomas Keller's
EGGPLANT CAVIAR

When he was the chef of New York's now departed Chez Louis—the restaurant that elevated bistro food to an art form—Thomas Keller made vats of this dip and served it with bread sticks. It is one of the world's perfect snacks or first courses, and it is so addictive that a second course may remain untouched.

4 large eggplants
1 tablespoon kosher salt
1 cup extra-virgin olive oil
4 cloves garlic, chopped
1 tablespoon Dijon mustard
Salt and freshly ground black pepper, to taste

1. Halve the eggplants lengthwise, score with a knife, and sprinkle lightly with the kosher salt. Cover with a heavy plate and weigh down the plate to press out the moisture for 1 hour.

2. Preheat the oven to 375° F. Oil a baking sheet.

3. Squeeze out any excess water from the eggplants. Place the eggplant halves, skin sides up, on the baking sheet. Bake until the meat is completely soft, 35 to 45 minutes. Set aside to cool.

4. When cool enough to handle, skin the eggplants. Chop the pulp and tie in a large square of dampened cheesecloth. Let hang above the sink or a bowl until most of the liquid has drained off, about 15 minutes.

5. In a medium bowl, whisk together the olive oil, garlic, mustard, and salt and pepper. Add the eggplant pulp and stir to mix. Cover and refrigerate for 1 day before serving.

Makes about 5 cups

City Island
CLAM FRITTERS

Paper boats of clam fritters are still pushed across fast-food counters on City Island, the subdued Bronx cousin of Coney Island, but most vendors agree that it would be difficult to top this recipe. It is adapted from one that appeared in the *Ford Treasury of Favorite Recipes from Famous Eating Places*, edited by N. Kennedy.

1 cup sifted all-purpose flour
¼ teaspoon salt
½ teaspoon sugar
1 teaspoon baking powder
1 cup drained, chopped clams (about 2 dozen littlenecks)
1 egg, beaten
¼ cup milk
1 tablespoon butter, melted
Peanut oil, for deep-frying

1. In a large bowl, stir together the flour, salt, sugar, and baking powder. In a small bowl, stir together the clams, egg, milk, and butter. Add the wet ingredients to the dry and stir just to mix.

2. In a 10-inch skillet, pour the oil to a depth of 1 inch. Heat until very hot but not smoking. Drop the batter from a spoon into the oil and fry, turning once until golden brown, 4 minutes total. Remove with a slotted spoon and drain on paper bags. Continue frying more batches until all of the clams are cooked.

Makes 12

Chicken Soup
A NEW YORK PANACEA

Chicken soup is synonymous with New York City. It is a curative, a panacea, a culinary medium. Its aroma rushes from the doors of Jewish delis and waves like steamy ribbons behind the bicycles that deliver Chinese food throughout the city. The scent of chicken soup lingers over kitchen stoops in the Italian section of Cobble Hill and above the homes of Greek families in Astoria. It seeps from the thermoses of the Senegalese who peddle umbrellas on the street corners of Manhattan. An epicurean archeologist could piece together a social history of the city, simply by studying the permutations of its chicken soup.

Sharing a taste for chicken soup is about as close as the city comes to communion. So, of course, each nuance, every variation is fervently debated. This is New York.

Since the nineteenth century, bowls of the golden broth, shimmering with a slick of rich fat and laden with kreplach or golf-ball-size matzoh balls, have linked suc-

Soups for Sipping, Slurping, Supper

At left, Lawrence Gordon stirs a cauldron of Lord & Taylor's Scotch Broth (see page 55), while above, Garth Vaughn shows the proper New York soup slurping technique.

cessive generations of the city's Eastern European immigrants. Louis Auerbach, the retired owner of the Stage Deli in Manhattan refers to chicken soup as a "bowl of well-being" and claims that New Yorkers who travel often, such as Kareem Abdul-Jabbar, Cher, and Woody Allen, have grown misty-eyed just inhaling its steam.

JEWISH PENICILLIN IS CULTURED

Historians are divided as to exactly which Catskill comedian first uttered the words "Jewish penicillin." But from that unidentified mouth to God's ears: In a 1984 newsletter, the Mayo Clinic endorsed the use of chicken soup in soothing cold symptoms. This didn't surprise Lydia and Joan Wilen, who grew up in Brooklyn and wrote the book *Chicken Soup and Other Home Remedies*. "Traditions don't thrive if they don't work," said Joan Wilen.

At the very least, chicken soup stirs up memories of feeling good. And though they baptized the broth, Jewish and Eastern European immigrants are not the only ones who swear by and swoon for it.

The Dutch, who originally settled New York, may have used chicken in addition to ham bones in *snert,* their pea porridge. The British and Irish settlers who followed may have added chicken to the mutton they stewed for soup. But it wasn't until the Germans arrived in the late nineteenth century, says Meryle

Evans, a culinary historian, that clear chicken soup (garnished with liver balls and egg noodles) appeared. Later that century, Eastern Europeans arrived with their kreplach and matzoh.

By the early twentieth century, Greeks were whisking egg and lemon into the soup, and Chinese immigrants in lower Manhattan were transforming the broth into rice noodle soups and hot and sour soups. The Latin American and Caribbean cooks who moved to the city in the 1930s advocated mashing carrots, onions, and garlic into the soup. Brazilians added peppers, onions, and rice to make their soothing *canja.* In the past decade, Indo-Chinese refugees have added noodles and subtle seasonings to make a meal soup similar to the Vietnamese *pho* out of the vats of chicken soup that simmer in tiny Su Chow-style kitchens in Chinatown today.

A PANOPLY OF FLAVORS

But while diverse aromatics and add-ins give the city as many different bowls of chicken soup as there are neighborhoods, the pot of basic broth remains much the same. A four- to five-pound chicken covered with four quarts of cold water and simmered for four hours with carrots (for color and sweetness), onions and celery (for salt and depth), parsley, bay leaf, and

Matzoh ball soup, a New York specialty.

black peppercorns makes a sturdy rich medium.

Like a good cup of coffee, a good chicken soup begins with cold water. To extract the most flavor, it should be brought slowly to a simmer and skimmed frequently. A heavy hand with herbs or vegetables can overpower the chicken flavor. The older and fatter the bird, the richer the broth.

Leonore Fleischer, who grew up eating chicken soup in the Washington Heights section of Manhattan and wrote *The Chicken Soup Book,* says that chicken feet make the difference between good chicken soup and a religious experience. Two small chicken feet add body to a soup; a turkey wing, four chicken wings, or two additional legs and thighs are close substitutes.

Like patriots defending their country's honor, the pan-cultural maestros of chicken soup argue bitterly over the nuance of perfume (some add dill, others add thyme, others add a clove of garlic). They debate the proper cooking time (the longer the bird simmers, the higher the gelatin content and marrow-essence of the soup).

But whether they come from Asia, Africa, or Atlantic Avenue in Brooklyn, chicken soup experts agree about one thing. It's a dirty little chicken soup secret that's passed from mother to daughter. "If you tell anybody, I will deny knowing you," threatened a prominent Manhattan soup-maker.

(Add a quarter of a chicken bouillon cube, a dash of chicken base, or a splash of commercially made chicken soup to the pot for perfect chicken soup.)

Shhh.

New York PENICILLIN

Guardian Angel Curtis Sliwa's 89-year-old Aunt Marie Stacey still makes this chicken soup in her Howard Beach home and takes it to revive ailing Angels on the New York City subways. Mrs. Stacey maintains that after cooking, the chicken meat should be shredded and vegetables mashed into the soup to release their curative powers. But if the vegetables and meat are strained out, this recipe makes a wonderful base for the chicken soup variations that follow. The broth can be frozen in small containers for future soups or in ice cube trays to use in sauces.

4 quarts cold water
1 chicken (4 to 5 pounds), quartered
2 chicken feet, or 4 chicken wings, or 1 turkey wing
1 clove garlic, peeled and bruised
1 onion, peeled
2 carrots, peeled and cut into 1-inch pieces
2 ribs celery, cut into 1-inch pieces
½ bunch fresh parsley, tied together with string and rinsed
1 bay leaf
1½ teaspoons salt
½ teaspoon black peppercorns

1. Pour the cold water into a large pot. Add the chicken, garlic, onion, carrots, celery, parsley, bay leaf, salt, and peppercorns and slowly bring to a boil. Reduce the heat and simmer for 4 hours, skimming frequently. (The soup can be strained at this point to use in the recipes that follow, both in this chapter and throughout the book. Mrs. Stacey proceeds with the next two steps.)

2. Strain the soup. Discard the onion, parsley, bay leaf, and peppercorns but reserve the other vegetables. Remove the chicken, skin and debone it, and reserve the meat. Return the chicken stock, chicken meat, carrots, celery, and garlic to the pot and bring back to a simmer; season with additional salt or pepper, to taste.

3. Serve the soup in big bowls over pastina, rice, or spaghettini. The soup's curative powers are released only when the vegetables are mashed together in the bowl. Use a fork for mashing. Use a big spoon for eating. You'll feel better soon.

Makes 3 quarts (12 cups) broth

Katherine Polyzo's
AVGOLEMONO

This is a rich, clean-tasting version of the Greek classic. The recipe comes from Ms. Polyzo's grandmother.

6 cups New York Pencillin (page 47) or canned
    chicken broth
1 cup long-grain rice
4 egg yolks
½ cup freshly squeezed lemon juice
Salt and freshly ground black pepper,
    to taste

1. Quickly bring the chicken broth to a boil in a nonreactive large pot. Add the rice, reduce the heat, and simmer until tender, 15 to 20 minutes.

2. Meanwhile, in a large mixing bowl, beat the egg yolks until frothy. Continue to whisk the egg yolks while drizzling in the fresh lemon juice.

3. When the rice is tender, ladle the chicken broth and rice into the egg and lemon mixture and whisk constantly until all of the soup has been added. Season with salt and pepper. Serve immediately.

Serves 4

Ermina Apolinario's
CANJA

Ermina Apolinario, who works as a babysitter in New York, moved to the city from Brazil. She makes this spicy chicken and rice soup to chase away the winter blues and blahs.

8 cups New York Penicillin (page 47) or
    canned chicken broth
1 tablespoon vegetable oil
1 onion, thinly sliced
4 cloves garlic, thinly sliced
2 green bell peppers, stemmed, seeded,
    and thinly sliced
1 teaspoon minced jalapeño chile or
    other chile
3 tomatoes, peeled, seeded, and
    chopped
1½ cups long-grain rice
1 teaspoon salt
1 cup minced fresh parsley leaves
        Dash of hot pepper sauce, to taste

Fresh chiles spice up a bowl of canja.

1. Pour the chicken broth in a nonreactive large pot and set over low heat.

2. Meanwhile, warm the oil in a nonreactive large skillet over medium heat. Add the onion, garlic, and bell peppers and sauté until very soft, about 10 minutes. Stir in the chile and tomatoes and sauté for 3 minutes more; set aside.

3. Add the rice and salt to the chicken soup, partially cover the pot, and simmer for 30 minutes. Add the sautéed vegetables and parsley and simmer, uncovered, for 10 minutes more. Season with additional salt and a dash of hot pepper sauce. Serve.

Serves 6

In New York's Chinatown shops, there's always plenty to see.

Su Chow
SOUP

I developed this recipe, along with two Chinese cooks, after many meals spent gazing at the master soupmakers at Bo Ky Restaurant in Chinatown.

SOUP
6 cups New York Penicillin (page 47) or canned
chicken broth
1 large onion, studded with 4 whole cloves
1 piece (2 inches) fresh ginger
4 whole star anise
1 cinnamon stick
4 parsnips, peeled and cut into 2-inch cubes
1 teaspoon salt
2 tablespoons Vietnamese hot chile paste (tuong ot
tuoi, preferably Huy Fong brand)
3 tablespoons Vietnamese fish sauce (nuoc mam)
1 pound wide rice sticks (noodles) (banh pho)
2 pounds boneless beef sirloin

GARNISH
2 cups fresh mung bean sprouts
2 fresh red chiles, minced
2 scallions, trimmed and minced
½ cup loosely packed fresh cilantro leaves, rinsed
½ cup loosely packed mint leaves, rinsed
½ cup loosely packed basil leaves, rinsed
1 lime, thinly sliced

1. Pour the broth into a large pot and set over low heat.

2. Skewer the clove-studded onion and the ginger and char them over a gas burner or under the broiler (4 inches from the heat source) until their outsides are blackened, 15 minutes. Tie the onion, ginger, star anise, and cinnamon stick in dampened cheesecloth. Place the cheesecloth parcel in the soup along with the parsnips and salt. Simmer for 1 hour. Remove and discard the spice bag; stir in the chile paste and fish sauce.

3. Meanwhile, soak the rice sticks in warm water to cover for 30 minutes. Bring 4 quarts of water to a boil in a large pot. Drain the rice sticks and drop them into the boiling water. Use chopsticks to lift and separate the noodles and prevent clumping. As soon as the water returns to a boil, drain the rice sticks in a colander. Refresh under cold running water and drain again. Set aside.

4. Use a very sharp knife to slice the sirloin against the grain into paper-thin slices; set aside.

5. Divide the mung bean sprouts and minced chiles evenly among 6 very large bowls. Divide the cooked noodles over the sprouts. Top each bowl with an equal portion of the sliced raw beef. Bring the soup to a rapid boil; ladle over the noodles and meat, which will cook immediately. Garnish each bowl with the scallions, cilantro, mint, basil, and a slice of lime. Serve immediately.

Serves 6

Mai Loan's
VIETNAMESE
SWEET AND SOUR SOUP

When Mai Loan Bass and her family left Vietnam in 1968, they brought generations of recipes with them to New York City. This southern Vietnamese soup would be an everyday kind of dish, but the addition of shrimp makes it a special occasion treat.

2 cloves garlic, unpeeled
1 teaspoon olive oil
3½ cups New York Penicillin (page 47) or canned chicken broth
2½ tablespoons distilled white vinegar (or lemon or lime juice)
2 tablespoons sugar
1 tablespoon plus 1 teaspoon Vietnamese or Thai fish sauce
1 small onion, thinly sliced
1 carrot, peeled and thinly sliced
¾ cup drained, canned sliced bamboo shoots
1 small zucchini, cleaned and thinly sliced
¼ pound medium shrimp, peeled, deveined, sliced lengthwise in half
1 cup fresh bean sprouts
6 to 8 fresh mint leaves, rinsed and minced
1 green chile, seeded and thinly sliced
Freshly ground black pepper, to taste

■──────────────■

1. Preheat the oven to 400°F.

2. Place the garlic cloves on a piece of aluminum foil. Drizzle with the oil and seal the foil closed. Place the foil packet in a shallow pan and roast in the oven until the garlic is soft and golden, about 15 minutes. Allow to cool, then peel. Mince the garlic and set aside.

3. In a nonreactive saucepan, heat the chicken broth with the vinegar, sugar, and fish sauce until it almost reaches the boiling point. Add the onion, carrot, bamboo shoots, zucchini, and shrimp; simmer until the shrimp turn pink and are cooked through, 3 to 5 minutes.

4. Divide the bean sprouts among 4 warm soup bowls. Add the hot soup. Garnish with the mint leaves, sliced chile, and roasted garlic. Season with black pepper.

Serves 4

Lydia and Joan Wilen still practice the art of kreplach-making.

Lily's Luscious
KREPLACH FOR CHICKEN SOUP

Joan Wilen and Lydia Wilen grew up in Brooklyn eating chicken soup laden with their mother Lily's savory dumplings. The sisters still whip up batches of chicken soup on Jewish holidays and whenever they feel the twinge of a cold coming on.

¾ pound boneless trimmed chuck steak
1½ tablespoons peanut oil
1 onion, chopped
¼ pound beef liver
2 large eggs
Salt and freshly ground black pepper, to taste
2 cups unbleached all-purpose flour
4 quarts New York Penicillin (page 47) or other favorite homemade chicken broth

1. Cook the chuck in water to cover over medium heat until tender, about 45 minutes. Drain the meat; set aside to cool to room temperature.

2. Heat the oil in a heavy skillet over medium heat. Add the onion and liver and sauté until the onions are soft and the liver is cooked through, 3 to 4 minutes per side. Drain off any excess oil from the liver and onions; set aside to cool to room temperature.

3. With a meat grinder or in a food processor, grind the liver and chuck. Add 1 of the eggs, season with salt and pepper, and process until well mixed.

4. In a large mixing bowl, combine the flour and ¼ teaspoon salt and make a well in the center. In a small bowl, whisk the remaining egg with ¼ cup water. Pour the egg mixture into the well of dry ingredients and mix with a spoon until smooth. Turn out the dough onto a floured board and knead until soft and silky, about 6 minutes. If the dough is too dry, add a few drops of water. If the dough is too wet, dust with flour and knead it in. Divide the dough into 2 even balls. Let the dough rest for 1 to 2 hours.

5. Roll out the dough, 1 ball at a time, ¼ inch thick. Cut the dough into 3- to 3½-inch squares. Arranging each square of dough with 1 corner pointing toward you, take 1 tablespoon of the meat mixture and put it on the top half of the dough. Moisten 2 sides of the dough with cool water and fold the bottom half up over the top, forming a triangle. Fold the 2 opposite edges together, pinching the dough so that the kreplach resembles a tortellini. Repeat with the remaining dough squares and filling. (You can freeze the kreplach at this point in freezer bags. They keep 2 to 3 months. Defrost in the refrigerator on a rack, so the bottoms don't get soggy.)

6. Bring the broth to a boil in a large pot. Slide the kreplach into the boiling chicken broth and cook them through, about 5 minutes. Serve immediately.

Makes 25 to 30 kreplach, or serves 8

Carolyn's Aziz
SPINACH SOUP

When her husband was a foreign correspondent in India, Carolyn Lelyveld fell for the country's cooking, especially its pungent soups. As long as the garlic, ginger, onion, and spices are very fresh, almost any green vegetable, lightly cooked and puréed, can be stirred into the base of this soup and will take on its wonderful perfume. The spinach used here is particularly addictive.

1 tablespoon butter
½ white onion, sliced
¼ teaspoon minced fresh ginger
1 large clove garlic, minced
6 whole cloves
2 cinnamon sticks
1 teaspoon all-purpose flour
4 cups New York Penicillin (page 47) or canned
    chicken broth, heated
1 pound spinach, well rinsed
Salt and freshly ground black pepper, to taste
1 cup milk

1. Melt the butter in a large skillet over medium heat. Add the onion and sauté until golden, 5 minutes. Add the ginger, garlic, whole cloves, and cinnamon; stir and continue to cook for 5 minutes. Stir in the flour. Whisk in the warm chicken broth and simmer for 40 minutes.

2. Meanwhile, in a separate nonreactive pan, steam the spinach until just wilted, 2 minutes. Drain, squeeze out the water, and purée. Set the purée aside.

3. Strain the soup, discarding the solids. Return the broth to a nonreactive large saucepan over medium heat. Stir in the spinach purée; season with salt and pepper. Stir in the milk and warm through. Serve at once.

Serves 4

MATZOH BOWL I

The air was full of pastrami and spring-time as contestants in New York's First Annual Matzoh Bowl gathered at the Stage Deli. Each of the 20 contestants, flanked by family and fans, carried his or her recipe as well as eight to ten representative matzoh balls to compete for the title of "Mr. or Mrs. Matzoh Ball."

Until then, matzoh supremacy had been a matter of speculation. In New York homes and restaurants, "light and fluffy" texture is weighed against a ball's flavor, while shape and size are balanced against its capacity as a "sinker" or "floater." The matzoh-gourmet cooks in a minefield of opinion and relies on family tradition, innate ability, or extensive practice to produce a proper ball.

"Matzoh balls are like people," said Jimi Levy Stein, a contestant from Queens. "Each one's got a personality and each one's different." At Matzoh Bowl I, the competing balls ranged in shape from perfectly round to polymorphous. Elizabeth Neuman, whose entry was perfectly round, confided that she beats her egg whites before adding them to the batter.

Contestant Burton Berinsky cringed. "I'm not making a soufflé," snorted the free-lance hat designer who submitted softball-size matzoh balls. "These should be heavy with flavor." Mr. Berinsky used chicken fat to ensure his desired result.

Carol Wolk of Brooklyn uses vodka to moisten and flavor her matzoh meal. "I am not sure if my grandmother or great-grand-mother started it," she said. Marilyn Somach of Staten Island had a similar difficulty in tracing the lineage of her secret technique: "the instinctual knowledge of how much egg to add." She is not sure whether this innate knowledge is "genetic or environmental."

"My earlier ones were cannon fodder," admitted Brooklynite Ruthy Rosen. Her daughter, Jody, a young aspiring songwriter, commemorated this in the ditty she performed: "Out of the shtetl, into the mouth of a judge. We hope it tastes like matzoh balls and not like matzoh sludge."

"Ladies and gentlemen," rasped Paul Zolenge, co-owner of the sponsoring deli, "We are gathered here today for the most prestigious of culinary Olympics." The contestants nodded gravely. "Once and for all," continued Zolenge, "who makes the best matzoh balls?"

"Taste," according to judge Louis Auerbach, Zolenge's partner, "is all that matters."

Judge Ernie Grunfeld of the New York Knicks put a finer point on his critical parameters. "I am comparing everything to my mother's," he said.

Judge Antoinette D'Amato, whose son is the senator, Alphonse, found the range of matzoh ball flavors remarkable. Along with her co-judges, she found it difficult to choose between the two recipes on pages 53 and 54.

Italian
EASTER SOUP

In her Italian neighborhood in Brooklyn, Maria Rosa is famous for the soup she serves at the beginning of the feast traditionally eaten to break Lent's 40-day fast. Although she follows the soup with delicious Easter pies stuffed with sausage, lamb and salami, mozzarella and ricotta, it is the soup, light, filling, and full of surprises, that keeps the neighbors talking.

8 cups New York Penicillin (page 47) or canned chicken broth
1 carrot, peeled and minced
1 onion, minced
1 rib celery, scraped and minced
1 clove garlic, minced
1 cup shredded cooked chicken
1 pound lean ground beef
Salt and freshly ground black pepper
4 tablespoons finely chopped parsley leaves
1 pound ricotta cheese
1 egg

1. Pour the chicken broth in a wide pot and set over low heat. Add the carrot, onion, celery, and garlic and simmer over very low heat for 40 minutes. Add the shredded chicken.

2. In a bowl, combine the ground beef with ½ teaspoon salt, 1¼ teaspoons pepper, and 1 tablespoon of the minced parsley. Form the mixture into meatballs that are about 1 inch in diameter. After the chicken has been added, use a spoon to gently slide the meatballs into the broth and cook for 20 minutes. Do not raise the heat or stir, but use a spoon to gently turn each meatball so that they cook evenly.

3. In a bowl, combine the ricotta, egg, 1 teaspoon salt, ½ teaspoon black pepper, and 1 tablespoon of the minced parsley. Stir well. After the meatballs are cooked, use a teaspoon to form ricotta dumplings. Carefully slide the dumplings into the broth and cook until they are set, about 7 minutes. Do not raise the heat or touch the dumplings.

4. Adjust the seasonings with additional salt and pepper to taste. Carefully ladle the soup into warmed bowls. Garnish each serving with some of the remaining 2 tablespoons minced parsley and serve.

Serves 8 to 10

Carol Wolk's
MARVELOUS MATZOH BALLS FOR CHICKEN SOUP

1 cup matzoh meal
5 large eggs
1 tablespoon plus 2 teaspoons salt
1 tablespoon Russian vodka
2 tablespoons club soda or seltzer
1 tablespoon chicken broth
¼ cup vegetable oil
4 quarts New York Penicillin (page 47) or other favorite homemade chicken broth

1. In a mixing bowl, combine the matzoh meal and eggs. Add the salt, vodka, club soda, chicken broth, and oil and mix well. Cover and put in the freezer for 20 minutes.

2. Meanwhile, bring a deep pot of water to a boil. Reduce the heat to a simmer. Slowly lower 2-tablespoon-size scoops of the matzoh mixture into the water, one at a time, until all is used up. It's okay to crowd the matzoh balls. Cover the pot and cook for 40 minutes. Drain the matzoh balls in a colander.

3. Bring the chicken broth to a boil in a large pot. Add the matzoh balls and serve, figuring 2 to 3 matzoh balls per eater.

Makes 18 large matzoh balls, serves 6 to 9

Sheila Rosenbaum's
NO-FAIL FLOATERS

6 large eggs, separated
Pinch of kosher salt
1½ cups matzoh meal
4 quarts New York Penicillin
  (page 47) or other
  favorite homemade
  chicken broth

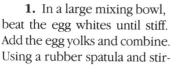

It's hard to beat Sheila Rosenbaum's matzoh balls.

1. In a large mixing bowl, beat the egg whites until stiff. Add the egg yolks and combine. Using a rubber spatula and stirring quickly, add the salt and the matzoh meal. Let the mixture stand at room temperature for 10 minutes.

2. Meanwhile, bring a large pot of salted water to a boil. Using your hands, roll the matzoh mixture into golf ball-size balls. Drop each into the boiling water and simmer for 20 minutes.

3. Bring the chicken broth to a boil in a large pot. Add the matzoh balls and serve, figuring 2 to 3 matzoh balls per eater.

Makes 15 to 20 large matzoh balls, serves 6 to 10

Adriana's
AJIACO

Adriana P. Lemos, an art historian, makes this dish from her native Colombia for special occasions. It takes some time to prepare but can be served like a meal in a pot, and the ritual adding of condiments makes it an excellent, guest-participation dish.

STOCK
1 chicken (3 to 4 pounds),
  with liver and neck,
  well rinsed
2 ribs celery, chopped
1 white onion, chopped
1 red onion, chopped
1 head garlic, unpeeled,
  separated into cloves
1 bunch fresh parsley, rinsed
½ bunch fresh cilantro,
  rinsed
4 scallions, trimmed

CHICKEN
1 tablespoon olive oil
1 white onion, minced
4 tomatoes, seeded and
  chopped
2 scallions, trimmed and chopped
¼ bunch fresh cilantro, finely
  chopped
Salt and freshly ground black pepper,
  to taste

AJI
1 tomato, seeded and minced
1 white onion, minced
1 scallion, trimmed and minced
¼ bunch fresh cilantro, minced
1 chile, seeded and minced
2 teaspoons cider vinegar
2 tablespoons olive oil
Salt and freshly ground black pepper,
  to taste

ASSEMBLY

*4 small white potatoes, peeled and
    cubed*
*6 small red potatoes, peeled and
    cubed*
*Salt and freshly ground pepper,
    to taste*
*1 avocado, peeled, pitted, and
    cubed*
½ cup drained small capers
1 cup sour cream
6 ears fresh corn, husked and halved

---

1. Make the stock: Combine all the stock ingredients in a stockpot or large saucepan. Add cold water to cover. Bring to a boil over medium heat. Reduce the heat and simmer for 1½ hours. Carefully remove the chicken and set aside. Strain the broth and discard the vegetables.

2. Make the chicken: Skin and bone the reserved poached chicken; shred the meat. Warm 1 tablespoon olive oil in a nonreactive sauté pan over medium heat. Add the minced onion and sauté until translucent, 5 minutes. Add the shredded chicken and toss to warm through; remove from the heat. Stir in the chopped tomatoes, scallions, and cilantro. Season with salt and pepper to taste. Cover and refrigerate.

3. Make the *aji:* In a bowl, combine the tomato, onion, scallion, cilantro, chile, vinegar, and oil; stir to combine well. Season with salt and pepper to taste. Cover and refrigerate.

4. To assemble the *ajiaco:* Bring the chicken stock to a boil in a large pot. Add half of both kinds of potatoes to the stock, reduce the heat, and simmer until the potatoes are soft, about 15 minutes.

5. Using a whisk or potato masher, thicken the soup by mashing the cooked potatoes into the stock. Add the remaining potatoes and simmer for 10 minutes. Season with salt and pepper to taste.

6. To serve, place small bowls of the chopped avocado, capers, and sour cream on the table along with platters of the chilled chicken and the *aji* sauce. Ladle the soup with the potatoes into individual bowls. Add the raw corn and let each guest garnish to taste.

Serves 8 to 12

Lord & Taylor's
SCOTCH BROTH

Since 1955, Lord & Taylor department store in New York City has simmered 25 to 30 gallons of this meaty broth daily in huge copper kettles in its 10th floor Soup Bar. For shoppers, it's always been a heady restorative.

*3 pounds breast of lamb with bone, or stewing
    lamb*
8 cups cold water
½ cup pearl barley
2 tablespoons butter
2 carrots, peeled and diced
1 white turnip, peeled and diced
2 ribs celery, diced
1 onion, diced
Salt and freshly ground black pepper, to taste

---

1. In a large stockpot, cover the lamb with the cold water; bring to a boil. Add the barley, partially cover the pot, and simmer until the meat and the barley are tender, 1½ hours. Add more water to adjust for evaporation; skim the surface of the soup as necessary.

2. Remove the meat from the broth. Cut the meat away from the bone, discard the bones, and return the meat to the soup. Continue simmering the soup.

3. In a skillet, melt the butter over medium heat. Add the carrots, turnip, celery, and onion and cook, stirring often, for 10 minutes.

4. Add the vegetables to the soup. Simmer until the vegetables are tender, 10 minutes more. Season with salt and pepper to taste. Serve.

Serves 8

*Making
a Scotch Broth
the Lord &
Taylor way.*

Pierre's FOUR-ONION SOUP

Pierre Moulin makes this soup whenever he is homesick for his native France, even though the scallions, leeks, and shallots crept into his recipe after he moved here and opened Pierre Deux Antiques in Greenwich Village nearly 30 years ago. He serves the soup with a platter of cold sliced beef, parslied potatoes, mustard, and horseradish.

3 tablespoons olive oil
1 pound yellow onions, sliced
½ cup well-rinsed, sliced white part of leeks
½ cup sliced light green part of scallions
½ cup sliced shallots
1 teaspoon sugar
1 teaspoon salt
¾ pound Swiss cheese, grated
6 cups Savory Beef Stock (page 61)
Sourdough bread, sliced into 6 thick rounds

Pierre Deux Antiques of Bleecker Street in Manhattan's Greenwich Village.

1. Preheat the oven to 350°F.

2. Heat the oil in a large heavy skillet or Dutch oven over medium-low heat. Add the onions, leeks, scallions, and shallots and stir constantly until the onions are translucent, 5 minutes.

3. Add the sugar and salt, increase the heat to medium-high, and continue stirring until the onions caramelize, 15 minutes. They will be golden brown but still moist.

4. Divide the onions among 6 ovenproof soup bowls. Sprinkle some of the cheese over the onions, reserving some for the tops. Ladle in the beef stock. Place a slice of bread on top of each serving and sprinkle with the remaining cheese. Bake in the oven until golden, 20 to 30 minutes. Let sit for 10 minutes before serving.

Serves 6

Colonial BEEF TEA

Hot "beef tea" was frequently mentioned as a restorative in accounts of colonial life in New York. This recipe is adapted from *Mrs. Mary Wells' Receipt Book,* a handwritten collection housed at the New-York Historical Society.

1 pound lean stew beef, cubed
Lightly toasted toast points (optional)
Freshly ground black pepper

1. Combine the beef and 5 cups cold water in a large heavy pot over low heat. When the water boils, cover the pan and cook for 2 hours.

2. Remove from the heat and skim off the fat. Strain the broth through a sieve or napkin; let it stand and settle for 10 minutes. Pour off the clear "tea." Serve with lightly toasted bread and/or a few grinds of black pepper.

Serves 4

Estée Lauder's
BEEF AND BARLEY SOUP

This hearty soup is the Lauder family's favored call for dinners at home.

2 pounds small beef ribs
4 beef marrow bones
½ cup pearl barley
1 teaspoon salt
1 onion, minced
4 carrots, peeled and diced
1 potato, peeled and diced
1½ pounds fresh peas
¼ pound fresh string beans, tipped
¼ cup chopped fresh dill
½ cup minced fresh parsley leaves
2 cloves garlic, minced
Salt and freshly ground black pepper,
    to taste

1. In a large stockpot, combine the beef ribs, marrow bones, and barley. Add 4 quarts cold water and the salt and bring to a boil. Reduce the heat and simmer, skimming frequently, for 1 hour.

2. Add the onion, carrots, and potato; simmer for 1 hour more.

3. Remove the bones from the soup. When they are cool enough to handle, scrape off the meat and marrow, return it to the soup, and discard the bones. Stir in the peas and beans and simmer for 30 minutes.

4. Add the dill, parsley, and garlic; season with salt and pepper to taste. Serve.

Serves 6 to 8

Mrs. Biderman's
POZOLE

Beth Biderman learned to make this Mexican fiesta soup from a friend on Martha's Vineyard who, in turn, learned it in the Taxco region of Mexico. The original recipe called for a hog's head, but Mrs. Biderman uses fresh ham or pork loin and still comes up with a rich meal-in-a-pot that guests ask for again and again.

SOUP
1 fresh ham or pork loin (4 to 5 pounds)
2 cloves garlic, minced or crushed
2 tablespoons kosher salt
4 cans (14 ounces each)
    whole hominy, drained

GARNISHES
4 limes, cut into eighths
4 avocados, peeled, pitted,
    and diced
1 large Spanish onion, diced
2 packages unflavored tortilla
    chips
2 packages fried pork rinds
¼ cup dried red pepper flakes
Chopped fresh oregano

Beth Biderman brings a touch of Mexico to her New York kitchen with this hearty Pozole.

1. In a large stockpot, combine the meat, garlic, salt, and 4 quarts water. Bring to a boil. Reduce the heat and simmer until the meat is tender or until the internal temperature registers 175°F on a meat thermometer, about 2 hours. Remove the meat and allow it to cool. Skim the fat from the broth.

2. Shred the meat and place it in a large shallow baking dish. Add a ladle or two of the broth to keep the pork moist. Cover with aluminum foil and set aside. (The recipe can be prepared ahead up to this point.)

3. Preheat the oven to 250°F.

4. Place the pork in the oven to warm.

5. Meanwhile, bring the broth to a boil again. Add the drained hominy and simmer for 20 minutes.

6. To serve, divide the pork and hominy among 6 to 8 large soup bowls. Add enough of the broth to fill the bowl halfway. Pass the garnishes at the table.

Serves 6 to 8

John's
HOT AND SOUR SOUP

J ohn Cioffi, a financial manager, got this recipe from a friend and says that he has yet to taste a better version. It can make a whole meal or a snappy beginning to a winter roast.

¼ *cup cider vinegar*
1 tablespoon plus 1 teaspoon light soy sauce
2 tablespoons cornstarch
6 cups New York Penicillin (page 47) or canned chicken broth
¼ *cup shredded turnip*
½ *cup shredded Chinese roast pork*
½ *cup drained, canned shredded bamboo shoots*
2 to 3 dried Chinese mushrooms, soaked in cold water for 30 minutes, sliced, stems discarded
2 tofu cakes, thinly sliced
1 teaspoon dried red pepper flakes

1. In a small bowl, stir together the vinegar, soy sauce, and cornstarch until smooth; set aside.

2. In a nonreactive large pot, combine the chicken broth, turnip, and 1 cup water. Bring to a boil. Reduce the heat and simmer for 5 minutes. Add the pork, bamboo shoots, and mushrooms and cook for 5 minutes. Add the tofu and red

pepper flakes, and bring to a boil. Add the reserved cornstarch mixture and stir until the soup thickens slightly, 2 minutes. Cook until the vegetables are tender, 15 to 20 minutes.

Serves 4

Tina's
HUNGARIAN SZEKELY

T here are probably as many ways to make this hearty Hungarian dish as there are cooks who have it in their repertoire. Tina Ujlaki learned this growing up in a Hungarian neighborhood on Manhattan's Upper East Side and says that this stew is one that improves each time you heat it. The recipe, she says, depends on two things— good, fresh, Hungarian paprika (which is now available in supermarkets) and good sauerkraut. She warns not to let the stew boil after adding the sour cream and recommends serving steamed or boiled parslied potatoes on the side.

Tina Ujlaki, pictured here with her son Nicholas, redefines Hungarian goulash.

*¾ pound Hungarian sausage, such as gyulai,
csabai, or hunier, cut into ½-inch slices
(any spicy Eastern European sausage
can be used)*

*1½ pounds stewing beef, trimmed and cut in
¾-inch cubes*

*1½ pounds boneless fresh ham or lean pork,
trimmed and cut into ¾-inch cubes*

⅓ cup bacon fat or vegetable oil

4 onions, finely chopped

⅓ cup sweet Hungarian paprika

*½ pound sauerkraut (not canned), drained (if
flavor is overwhelming, rinse and blanch in
boiling water before using)*

*3 to 4 cups New York Penicillin (page 47), canned
chicken broth, or water*

4 bay leaves

½ teaspoon dried thyme

Salt and freshly ground black pepper, to taste

1 to 2 cups sour cream

---

1. In a large skillet, sauté the sausage slices over medium-high heat, tossing, until lightly browned on both sides. Drain on paper towels. Add the beef and pork cubes to the fat remaining in the skillet and brown over high heat. Work in batches, if necessary. Set aside.

2. In a large casserole, heat the bacon fat. Add the onions and sauté over medium heat until translucent, 10 to 15 minutes.

3. Sprinkle the paprika over the onions and cook, stirring, until the ingredients form a thick paste and the scent of raw paprika disappears, about 5 minutes. Add the beef and pork cubes, sauerkraut, chicken broth, bay leaves, and thyme and stir well to combine all of the ingredients. Add more broth, if necessary, to cover the contents of the pot.

4. Bring to a boil. Reduce the heat to a simmer, cover, and cook for 45 minutes. Add the sausage slices and continue cooking until the meats are very tender, about 45 minutes longer. Season with salt and pepper to taste. Let cool, then cover and refrigerate overnight.

5. The next day, reheat over medium heat until piping hot. Stir in sour cream to taste and cook until just heated through.

Serves 8 to 10

Artistic
FISH SOUP

Rich fish soups are no strangers to the city that is roped with rivers and rimmed by the Atlantic. This version is adapted from a recipe that appeared in *A Culinary Collection from the Metropolitan Museum of Art.*

2 tablespoons butter

1 onion, chopped

1 clove garlic, minced

1 tomato, seeded and chopped

*Salt and freshly ground black pepper,
to taste*

½ teaspoon hot paprika

*1 pound shrimp, peeled and
deveined*

¾ pound halibut fillets

*3 medium squid, cleaned and sliced
into rings*

5 lobster tails or other shellfish

*18 clams, well scrubbed and
rinsed*

2 bay leaves

*1 tablespoon chopped fresh parsley
leaves*

---

1. In a nonreactive large, heavy pot, melt the butter over medium heat. Add the onion and garlic and cook, stirring frequently, until the vegetables soften, 5 minutes. Add the tomato and cook for a few minutes longer, being careful not to brown the onion and garlic. Stir in salt, pepper, and paprika to taste.

2. Arrange the seafood on top of the vegetables, adding the clams last. Add just enough water to cover the seafood but not the clams. Sprinkle on the bay leaves and parsley, cover the pot, and boil gently until the clams open and the fish is cooked through, 30 minutes. Serve at once.

Serves 5

Wintry UKRAINIAN BORSCHT

Nancy Arum, who lives in lower Manhattan with her artist husband and young son, learned to make this soup from a Ukrainian friend. She has adapted the recipe over the years, and this is the version that her family and friends lobby for on cold winter nights.

2 pounds beef marrow
    bones
1 tablespoon salt
3 pounds beef brisket
1 small can (17 ounces)
    whole plum
    tomatoes with liquid
2 onions, 1 quartered
    and 1 chopped
2/3 cup chopped celery
4 fresh parsley sprigs, rinsed
4 whole black peppercorns
1 bay leaf
3 cups coarsely shredded cabbage
1/4 cup chopped fresh dill
1/2 cup cider vinegar
3 tablespoons sugar
1 1/2 cups sliced carrots
1 can (16 ounces) beets, cut into
    julienne with liquid reserved (or
    2 cups cooked fresh beet julienne
    with 1 cup of the cooking liquid)
Sour cream, for serving
Fresh dill sprigs, for serving
Kosher salt, for serving

1. In a nonreactive stockpot, combine the marrow bones, salt, and 8 cups water. Cover and bring to a boil. Skim the surface, reduce the heat, and simmer, covered, for 1 hour.

2. Add the brisket, tomatoes with their liquid, and the quartered onion. Stir in the celery, pars-

ley, peppercorns, and bay leaf; cover and simmer until the meat is tender, about 2 1/2 hours. Remove the meat; set aside to cool. Let the soup cool. Cover and refrigerate the meat and the soup separately until cool, about 2 hours.

3. Skim the fat off the chilled soup. Add the cabbage, the chopped onion, the dill, vinegar, and sugar. Return to medium heat and bring to a boil. Reduce the heat, cover, and simmer until the vegetables are tender, about 20 minutes. Add the carrots and beets and simmer for 15 minutes more.

4. Slice the beef; put several slices in each individual soup bowl. Ladle some of the soup over the meat. Top with spoonfuls of sour cream and fresh dill sprigs. Serve with kosher salt.

Serves 8 to 12

When plum tomatoes look as fresh as these, it's tempting to substitute them for the canned variety.

Mrs. Ratner's RUSSIAN CABBAGE SOUP

Cecile Ratner, who grew up in the Bronx, learned to make this soulful soup from her Russian mother-in-law. "It's never been served to anyone famous," she says, "but everyone who tastes it loves it."

1 head green cabbage, shredded
2 onions, thinly sliced
1 tart apple, peeled, cored, and thinly sliced
1 cup tomato sauce
2 1/2 pounds beef flanken or short ribs
2 beef soup bones (about 1 1/2 pounds)
1 tablespoon salt
1/4 teaspoon freshly ground white pepper
1/2 teaspoon paprika
3/4 teaspoon sour salt (also called citric salt)

1. In a stockpot, combine the cabbage, onions, apple, tomato sauce, beef, beef bones, salt, pepper, paprika, and 10 cups cold water. Bring to a boil over medium heat, cover, and simmer for 1 hour, skimming occasionally.

2. Add an additional 1 cup cold water and the sour salt. Simmer, uncovered, for 30 minutes.

3. Remove the soup bones and skim off the fat. Adjust the seasonings. Serve hot.

Serves 6 to 8

gently scrape the caramelized juices off the sides and the bottom of the pan. Boil to reduce the liquid slightly. Add the cooking juices to the stockpot along with all of the remaining ingredients and 4 quarts of cold water.

4. Bring the liquids to a boil, reduce the heat, and simmer the stock, partially covered for 4 to 5 hours, skimming it about every 15 minutes.

5. Remove the stock from the heat; set aside to cool. Strain the stock until it runs clear. Refrigerate overnight and skim off any excess fat.

Makes 3 quarts

Savory BEEF STOCK

This is my favorite beef stock, a perfect base for rich meaty soups.

1 beef shank, beef marrow bones, or beef ribs (4 to 5 pounds)
3 carrots, peeled and coarsely chopped
3 onions, coarsely chopped
3 ribs celery, tops included, coarsely chopped
1 cup boiling water
1 tablespoon fresh thyme leaves, or 1 teaspoon dried
1 large bay leaf
2 fresh parsley sprigs, rinsed
6 black peppercorns, crushed
Salt, to taste

1. Preheat the broiler.

2. Spread the meaty bones out in a roasting pan and broil, turning occasionally, for 10 minutes. Add the carrots, onions, and celery and continue broiling until the vegetables are browned, about 15 minutes more.

3. Transfer the bones and vegetables to a large stockpot. Pour off the fat remaining in the roasting pan and add the boiling water. Over low heat,

Hearty MUSHROOM SOUP

Steve Goldfinger, a psychologist who was once the weekend chef for former mayor Koch of New York, loves this soup and loved to serve it to the mayor because it is simple and versatile. At different times, he has used chopped winter vegetables or beans, lentils, split peas, or barley to add variety to the basic recipe and to make a more robust soup. The soup, he said, also freezes well.

Steve Goldfinger, one-time chef for Ed Koch.

4 tablespoons melted butter or peanut oil

2 tablespoons all-purpose flour

6 shallots, chopped

1 pound white mushrooms, cleaned, trimmed,
    and sliced

¾ pound shiitake mushrooms, cleaned, trimmed,
    and sliced

6 cups New York Penicillin (page 47) or canned
    chicken broth

½ teaspoon salt

¼ teaspoon freshly ground black pepper

1 tablespoon fresh thyme, or 1 teaspoon dried

1. In a heavy skillet, heat 2 tablespoons of the butter over low heat until bubbling. Whisk in the flour. Stir and cook until the mixture is pale gold. Remove from the heat and set aside.

2. In a stockpot, heat the remaining 2 tablespoons butter over medium heat. Add the shallots and sauté until soft, about 5 minutes. Add all of the mushrooms and cook until soft, about 5 minutes. Add the chicken broth, salt, pepper, and thyme and simmer for 10 minutes.

3. Skim the soup. Whisk 1 cup of the broth into the butter and flour mixture. Continue to whisk until thick, creamy, and smooth, 2 minutes. Stir the mixture back into the soup and simmer until thickened, 5 minutes more. Serve hot. Or, add additional sautéed vegetables, grains, or beans to the syrup and allow to simmer over low heat, adding more chicken broth, if necessary, until cooked.

Serves 6

Teresa's
MUSHROOM CONSOMME

Throughout the year, Teresa Thompson wraps leftover mushroom stems and chicken scraps and saves them in her freezer to make this deep,

Teresa Thompson with husband Lenny Lopate.

woodsy broth, which she serves to guests as an apéritif on cold winter nights. The broth is a warm "hello," and it makes a wonderful first course as well.

3 pounds mushrooms or mushroom stems
    (domestic and/or wild mushrooms), cleaned,
    trimmed, and quartered

½ pound fresh white mushrooms, cleaned,
    trimmed, and quartered

5 pounds chicken scraps, including backs, necks,
    and gizzards (no livers)

1 white onion, coarsely chopped

2 carrots, peeled and coarsely chopped

1 rib celery, chopped

12 black peppercorns

¼ teaspoon whole allspice berries

2 bay leaves

½ bunch fresh parsley, rinsed

½ teaspoon dried thyme

½ teaspoon salt

Aquavit or vodka, for garnish

1. Combine all of the ingredients except the aquavit or vodka in a large stockpot over low heat. Cover with 2 to 3 gallons of cold water and slowly bring to a boil. Reduce the heat and simmer for at least 6 hours, skimming frequently. The broth can simmer for up to 24 hours. It should reduce by half and turn black.

2. Strain the broth, discarding the solids. Adjust the seasonings with additional salt or pepper to taste. Serve the mushroom consommé in a cup and splash each serving with aquavit or vodka.

Serves 8

Autumn
BAKED SQUASH SOUP

Sheila Lukins, who co-founded the Silver Palate and is the co-author of the *Silver Palate Cookbook, Silver Palate Good Times Cookbook,* and the *New Basics Cookbook,* devised this soup for fall meals. It is a soulful porridge that can be served as a starter, or with bread as a whole meal.

2 butternut squash (2 pounds each), peeled,
    seeded, and cut into ½-inch cubes
2 carrots, peeled and cut into ½-inch lengths
1 onion, thinly sliced
4 tablespoons (½ stick) unsalted butter
5 cups New York Penicillin (page 47) or canned
    chicken broth
2 tablespoons dark brown sugar
½ teaspoon ground mace
½ teaspoon ground ginger
Pinch of cayenne pepper
Salt, to taste
2 tablespoons fresh lemon juice
Sour cream, for garnish
Minced fresh chives, for garnish

1. Preheat the oven to 400°F.

2. Place the squash, carrots, and onion in a nonreactive roasting pan. Dot the vegetables with the butter. Pour 1½ cups of the broth over the vegetables and sprinkle evenly with the brown sugar. Cover the pan tightly with foil and bake until the vegetables are tender, 35 minutes.

3. Remove the pan from the oven and place the vegetables and any cooking liquid in a stockpot. Stir in the remaining 3½ cups broth, the mace, ginger, cayenne, and salt. Bring to a boil. Reduce the heat and simmer, uncovered, for 10 minutes. Stir in the lemon juice.

4. In a food processor or blender, purée the soup in small batches until smooth. Return the purée to the pot, adjust the seasonings, and heat through. Ladle into bowls and garnish each with a dollop of sour cream and a sprinkling of chives.

Serves 6

Over the years Sheila Lukins has shared hundreds of terrific recipes with millions of her fans.

Oscar de la Renta's
PUMPKIN AND CRAB SOUP

Hearty in flavor and texture, this soup won the prize for Oscar de la Renta at a gourmet gala. It remains a delicate starter because of the addition of crabmeat and sweet corn. Out of season, canned corn kernels and canned pumpkin purée are fine substitutes and make this an easy soup to prepare. For those who wish to remain svelte enough for haute couture ensembles, the soup should be the meal, with perhaps a green salad. For others, it is an excellent prologue to a light second course.

1 pumpkin (4 to 6 pounds) rinsed, top cut
   off, strings and seeds scooped out,
   or 2 to 4 cups pumpkin purée
Salt and freshly ground black pepper,
   to taste
1 teaspoon dry mustard
Vegetable oil, for brushing on pumpkin
2 tablespoons olive oil
2 scallions, minced
2 tablespoons curry powder
½ teaspoon ground coriander
½ teaspoon ground cinnamon
½ teaspoon brown sugar
6 cups New York Penicillin (page 47)
   or canned chicken broth
1 cup corn kernels
1 pound lump crabmeat
1 cup plain yogurt

---

1. If using fresh pumpkin, preheat the oven to 375°F. If using pumpkin purée, skip ahead to step 3.

2. Cut the pumpkin into large pieces. Season with the salt, pepper, and dry mustard. Brush the outside with the vegetable oil, put the chunks in a large baking pan, and bake until tender, 45 minutes. When cool enough to handle, scoop out the flesh. Purée in a food processor.

3. If using canned pumpkin, stir in the dry mustard and season with salt and pepper. Warm the olive oil in a large saucepan over medium heat. Add the scallions and sauté for 1 minute. Add the curry powder, coriander, cinnamon, and brown sugar, and cook for 1 minute. Stir in the chicken broth and pumpkin purée, then add salt and pepper to taste. Simmer gently for 30 minutes.

4. Add the corn kernels and crabmeat. Cook to heat through, 3 to 4 minutes. Stir in the yogurt and serve.

Serves 6 to 8

Loretta's
ITALIAN ZUCCHINI SOUP

Says Loretta Butler, "Italians use a lot of vegetables. My mother used to make this all the time during the Depression years. I think Americans have now become acquainted with this very healthful and inexpensive vegetable, and in the summertime, there is a lot of it around."

2 tablespoons olive oil
1 onion, diced
2 cups (one 16-ounce can) plum
   tomatoes
1 pound small, firm zucchini, well rinsed
   and sliced
1 large potato, peeled and diced
1½ to 2 teaspoons salt, or to taste
¼ to ½ teaspoon freshly ground black
   pepper, or to taste
1 large egg, beaten
½ cup freshly grated Parmesan or
   Romano cheese
6 fresh basil leaves, torn into tiny
   pieces

---

1. Heat the olive oil in a nonreactive medium saucepan over medium heat. Add the onion and sauté until translucent, 5 minutes. Add the tomatoes, crush against the side of the pan, and cook until the water evaporates and the tomatoes are thickened, about 15 minutes.

Loretta Butler knows that a garden can never produce too much zucchini. Zucchini soup is just one of many delicious ways to use them.

2. Add the zucchini and potatoes and enough water to cover the mixture by about 2 inches. Bring to a boil. Reduce the heat to a simmer, season with the salt and pepper, and continue cooking until the vegetables are tender, about 20 minutes.

3. Add the beaten egg in a thin stream, stirring all the while with a wooden spoon, and cook for about 2 minutes longer.

4. Turn off the heat and stir in the cheese and then the basil. Serve immediately with crusty Italian bread.

Serves 6 to 8

Luncheonette signs, once so common in New York, are now a rarity. Coffee shops have taken over.

Luigi Scappini's
GREEN MINESTRONE

Said printer and poet Luigi Scappini, "During the beat years, green minestrone soup was a standby at Greenwich Village luncheonettes." Poets extolled its wholesomeness, and immigrants from northern Italy fiercely debated the proper formula, which, of course, is an oxymoron because this is a soup made for bumper crops or leftovers. This version weighs in heavily on the peasant side of the debate, since it's more rustic than the delicate versions that are simply greened with pesto.

SOUP

½ cup dried white beans, picked over, rinsed, and
    soaked overnight in water to cover
2 tablespoons olive oil
1 clove garlic, sliced
1 onion, minced
1 small bulb fennel, trimmed and minced
4 ribs celery, sliced
2 cups shredded kale, rinsed
2 cups shredded collard greens, rinsed
2 cups shredded green cabbage, rinsed
2 cups cut green beans (about ¾ pound)
2 baking potatoes, peeled and cubed
3 quarts New York Penicillin (page 47) or other
    favorite homemade chicken broth
    ¼ cup chopped Italian parsley leaves
    ½ cup chopped fresh basil leaves
    1 tablespoon salt
    2 teaspoons freshly ground black pepper

PESTO

¼ cup lard
¼ cup chopped Italian parsley leaves
¼ cup freshly grated Parmesan cheese
2 tablespoons minced fresh rosemary
2 tablespoons minced fresh sage
1 small clove garlic, minced

1. Drain the beans, put them in a medium-size saucepan with plenty of water to cover, and bring to a boil over high heat. Reduce the heat to medium and cook, partially covered, until the beans are tender, about 45 minutes. Drain.

2. Heat the olive oil in a stockpot over low heat. Add the garlic, onion, and fennel and sauté until soft, about 10 minutes. Add the celery, kale, collard greens, cabbage, green beans, white beans, potatoes, and chicken broth, and bring to a boil. Reduce the heat and simmer for 1 hour.

3. Stir in the parsley, basil, salt, and pepper, and simmer for 30 to 40 minutes more.

4. Make the pesto: In a blender or food processor, combine the lard, parsley, Parmesan, rosemary, sage, and garlic. Purée until smooth.

5. To serve, ladle the soup into bowls. Garnish with a dollop of the pesto; drizzle with additional olive oil, if desired.

Serves 8

Marco's PASTA E FAGIOLI SOUP

Marco Fregonesco, who grew up near Milan, brought this recipe with him when he moved to New York early in 1985. It remains more pungent, perhaps more old-world than new-world, than other versions that have had more time to acclimate to the city. It is a wonderful dish on a cold day.

¼ pound dried cannellini beans, picked over, rinsed, and soaked overnight in water to cover

2 potatoes, peeled and cut into quarters

2 tablespoons olive oil

½ onion, chopped

1 rib celery, chopped

½ carrot, peeled and chopped

1 teaspoon dried sage

1 teaspoon dried rosemary

1 cup dried pasta (any small macaroni shape), cooked and drained

Salt and freshly ground black pepper, to taste

1. Bring a large pot of water to a boil. Add the beans and potatoes and cook until tender, 1½ to 2 hours. Set aside to cool. Purée the mixture in a blender with enough of the cooking water to make a smooth, thin purée.

2. Heat the olive oil in a saucepan over medium heat. Add the onion, celery, carrot, and herbs, and sauté until soft, about 10 minutes. Purée the mixture in a blender or food processor.

3. Combine both purées with the cooked pasta. Bring to a boil over medium heat. Season with salt and pepper and serve.

Serves 6

Thursday's WHITE BEAN SOUP

Rafael Feliciano makes this hearty soup on Thursdays at La Taza de Oro, a Spanish luncheonette in Manhattan's Chelsea neighborhood. The soup is the perfect solution for leftover sausage and pork.

6 pieces oxtail (2½ pounds)

2 cups dried navy beans, picked over, rinsed, and soaked overnight in water to cover

Salt, to taste

4 links chorizo sausage (1½ to 2 pounds), cooked and diced

6 pieces pork spareribs (1½ pounds), cooked

4 pork chops (2 pounds), cooked and diced

4 slices Virginia ham (1 pound), diced

1 piece (2 to 3 ounces) fatback

1 clove garlic, smashed

1 onion, chopped

1 green bell pepper, stemmed, seeded, and chopped

1½ teaspoons dried oregano

Freshly ground black pepper, to taste

2 small potatoes, peeled and diced

8 leaves collard greens, rinsed and chopped

½ cup chopped cilantro leaves

1. Place the oxtails in a large heavy pot and cover with water. Bring to a boil. Reduce the heat and simmer for 4 hours. Remove the oxtails from the pot and reserve the broth.

2. Meanwhile, drain the beans and place in a large heavy pot. Cover with fresh, cold water and add 1 teaspoon salt. Bring to a boil. Reduce the heat and simmer, partially covered, until the beans are almost tender, about 45 minutes. Skim.

3. Add the chorizo, spareribs, oxtails, pork chops, ham, fatback, garlic, onion, bell pepper, and oregano. Add the oxtail broth to cover (add water if there isn't enough broth) and bring to a boil. Reduce the heat and simmer for 30 minutes. Season with salt and pepper to taste.

4. Stir in the potatoes, collard greens, and cilantro and cook for 5 minutes. Remove the fatback. Serve.

Serves 8

2 to 3 large onions, chopped
4 large garlic cloves, minced
3 to 4 small Indian green chiles, chopped,
*   or 4 jalapeño chiles, chopped*
*   (including the seeds), or*
*   3 tablespoons extra-hot ground*
*   dried chiles*
3 tablespoons peanut oil
3 pounds lean chopped sirloin
Kosher salt and freshly ground black pepper, to
*   taste*
1 tablespoon ground coriander
3 tablespoons ground cumin
1 teaspoon dried thyme leaves
1 teaspoon dried Greek
*   oregano*
2 cans (28 ounces each)
*   imported Italian*
*   whole plum tomatoes*
4 bay leaves
2 cans (16 ounces each) pinto
*   beans, rinsed and drained*
1 bunch cilantro or Italian
*   (flat-leaf) parsley, rinsed*
*   and chopped*

At Pete's Spice on Second Avenue in the East Village, the selection of dried beans and grains is wide and varied.

Confessional CHILI

David Durk, whose career in law enforcement has spanned 23 years and included a stint as the partner of the famous Frank Serpico, purports to have served this atomic chili to tight-lipped prisoners and potential informers, many of whom he claims "would never talk to a New York cop." How soon after consumption did they start gabbing? "Immediately," he laughs.

1. In a large heavy pot or Dutch oven over medium heat, sauté the onions, garlic, and chiles in the oil until the onions are translucent, 5 minutes.

2. Crumble the chopped sirloin over the top of the vegetables. Season with the salt and pepper; stir in the coriander, cumin, thyme, and oregano. Cover and cook until the meat is cooked through, about 7 minutes.

3. Pour the tomatoes into a small bowl and coarsely crush with your hands. Pour the tomatoes and juice on top of the chili mixture. Stir in the bay leaves. Cover or leave uncovered, depending on the consistency you prefer (a covered pot will yield a thicker chili), and simmer until the flavors are well married, about 30 minutes.

4. Stir in the pinto beans and simmer, covered, for 15 minutes. Stir in the cilantro and simmer for another 5 minutes. Serve at once.

Serves 8 to 10

Barbara's
BLACK BEAN SOUP

arbara Scott-Goodman, a book designer, loves this soup "because it's heavy-duty, yet elegant." She most often serves it as an appetizer for a fish dish but says it's also terrific with bread and cheese on a lazy Sunday afternoon.

1 onion, finely chopped
2 ribs celery with leaves, finely chopped
3 tablespoons olive oil
1½ cups black beans, picked over, rinsed, and
*   soaked overnight in water to cover*
6 cups New York Penicillin (page 47) or canned
*   chicken broth*
2 teaspoons celery seeds
Salt and freshly ground black pepper, to taste
Juice of ½ lemon
Dry sherry, to taste
Lemon slices, for garnish
Chopped fresh parsley, for garnish

1. In a large heavy pot, sauté the onion and celery in the olive oil until softened, 5 minutes. Drain the beans and add them along with the chicken broth. Bring to a boil. Reduce the heat, cover, and simmer until the beans are tender, 2½ to 3 hours. Set aside to cool.

2. In a blender or food processor, purée the soup in batches with the celery seeds.

3. Return the puréed soup to the pot and reheat, stirring frequently. Season with salt and pepper. Stir in the lemon juice and sherry. If the soup is too thick, adjust with additional broth or water. Serve topped with the lemon slices and parsley.

Serves 6

Meet Barbara Scott-Goodman with daughters
Alexandria (left) and Isabelle (center).

Ouidad's
LENTIL AND SPINACH SOUP

uidad Wise, a hair stylist whose coifs appear regularly in the pages of fashion magazines, says that she is not as versatile in the kitchen as she is in the salon. "This hearty recipe from my grandmother is one of the few things I cook well," she said.

1½ cups brown or green lentils, picked over,
*   rinsed, and drained*
½ cup olive oil
1 onion, chopped
2 cloves garlic, finely minced
10 spinach leaves, well rinsed and
*   finely chopped*
1 rib celery, finely chopped
½ cup fresh lemon juice
1½ teaspoons salt
Freshly ground black pepper,
*   to taste*

Search out loose lentils; it's worth the effort.

1. Place the lentils and 7 cups cold water in a nonreactive pot and bring to a boil over high heat. Reduce the heat, partially cover, and simmer until the lentils are tender, about 35 minutes.

2. Meanwhile, heat the olive oil in a skillet over medium heat. Add the onion and sauté until lightly browned, about 8 minutes. Stir in the garlic, spinach, and celery and cook until the vegetables are softened, about 5 minutes.

3. Remove about one-fourth of the lentils; purée in a blender or food processor. Return the puréed lentils to the pot.

4. Bring the lentils back to a boil. Add the mixture from the skillet, reduce the heat, and simmer for 5 minutes. Add the lemon juice, salt, and pepper. Simmer to soften the lemon flavor, a few additional minutes.

Serves 4 to 6

Netherland Club's
SNERT

The Dutch, who originally settled Manhattan Island in the seventeenth century, brought with them the recipe for this rib-sticking pea porridge. Today, it still is served at the Nether-land Club in Manhattan. Other split pea soups pale in comparison.

1 pound split peas, picked over and rinsed
1 large pig's knuckle, or 2 pig's feet
¼ pound smoked slab bacon or salt pork, diced
3 leeks, white and green parts separated, well rinsed, and coarsely chopped
1 large onion, coarsely chopped
2 large carrots, peeled, 1 cut into large chunks and 1 diced
1 celeriac, peeled and cut in half
Bouquet garni: 2 whole cloves, 1 bay leaf, 6 peppercorns, 1 blade of mace, tied in cheesecloth
1 rib celery with leaves, diced
1 pound cooked smoked sausage, such as kielbasa, cut into ¼-inch rounds
Salt and freshly ground black pepper, to taste
½ bunch parsley, rinsed and chopped

1. In a nonreactive, large heavy stockpot over medium heat, combine the split peas, 3 quarts cold water, the pig's knuckle, bacon, leek greens, onion, and the chunked carrot. Cut half of the celeriac into large chunks and add along with the bouquet garni. Bring to a boil over medium-high heat. Reduce the heat, partially cover, and simmer, stirring occasionally, until the peas are very soft, about 2 hours.

2. Remove the pig's knuckle; set aside to cool. Remove and discard the bouquet garni. Purée the remaining contents of the pot in batches in a food mill or processor until smooth. Return to the pot.

3. Cut the meat from the pig's knuckle and add to the pot along with the white part of the leek, the chopped carrot, and the celery. Finely chop the remaining celeriac and add it to the pot. Simmer, stirring occasionally, until all of the vegetables are soft, about 30 minutes.

4. Stir in the kielbasa and cook until heated through, about 5 minutes. Season with salt and pepper to taste. Serve hot in soup bowls, with the chopped parsley on top.

Serves 6 to 8

THE SOUP MAN OF 55TH STREET

By 11:45 A.M., Monday through Friday, people have already begun to line up on West 55th Street to wait for Al Yeganeh to slide open his glass window and begin passing out soup in pint-size cardboard containers. Mr. Yeganeh is a very precise person. If he says his soup is good, it's good. And when he tapes a sign to his door that says "OPEN AT NOON," it means he won't ladle a drop until then.

But customers line up anyway—sometimes all the way to Eighth Avenue. "Can't you read?" Al Yeganeh yells through his closed door. Customers who might be expecting a question like "Can I help you?" appear surprised by the 40-year-old proprietor who wears a white chef's jacket and a frown. But regulars, and most of the 400 people that Mr. Yeganeh serves daily are regulars, have long since decided to take the attitude to get the soup.

Al Yeganeh makes serious soup. He makes vegetable soup, watercress soup, lentil soup, and pea soup. He makes hamburger soup, buffalo meat soup, and African peanut soup. Since the containers of soup he sells are meant to be a meal, he frequently evokes a main-course concept in soups, such as his Greek moussaka soup, eggplant Parmesan soup, or steak and potatoes soup. On St. Patrick's Day he makes corned beef and cabbage soup; at Jewish holidays he makes matzoh ball soup; around Thanksgiving he makes turkey soup. "New York does strange things to people," he says.

Since he opened in 1984, Mr. Yeganeh has filled each one of 10 black cauldrons in his shop with a different soup every day. Sometimes, if he needs inspiration, he leafs through the cookbooks, newspapers, and menus that are stored in a cardboard box under the counter. When he can't take one more customer asking one more question, Al Yeganeh puts up a sign that says "CLOSED." He goes to Europe, Africa, or Asia and soothes himself with solitary soup research.

"Everything is answered by the menu, but they ask anyway and slow down the line," he says. In addition to the menu, he posted a sign that reads: "For most efficient and fastest service, the line must be kept moving. Please have money ready, pick up the soup of your choice, and move to the extreme left." Soup selling should be as fast as soup making should be slow, says Al Yeganeh, who came to the city from the Middle East in 1968 to study physics.

In less than 100 minutes, he can ladle 75 gallons of soup into pint-size containers and pass them, along with a paper napkin and a plastic spoon, to the customers outside his store. He maintains a marathon pace and he fumes when it is disrupted. "You talk too much, dear," he told

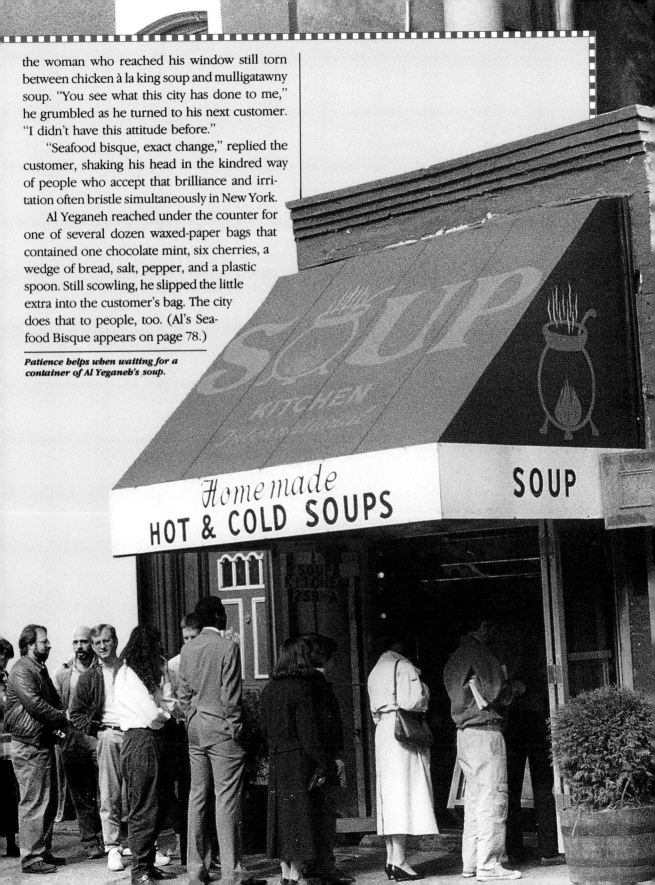

the woman who reached his window still torn between chicken à la king soup and mulligatawny soup. "You see what this city has done to me," he grumbled as he turned to his next customer. "I didn't have this attitude before."

"Seafood bisque, exact change," replied the customer, shaking his head in the kindred way of people who accept that brilliance and irritation often bristle simultaneously in New York.

Al Yeganeh reached under the counter for one of several dozen waxed-paper bags that contained one chocolate mint, six cherries, a wedge of bread, salt, pepper, and a plastic spoon. Still scowling, he slipped the little extra into the customer's bag. The city does that to people, too. (Al's Seafood Bisque appears on page 78.)

Patience helps when waiting for a container of Al Yeganeh's soup.

Beets for borschok.

Grandma's
CHILLED SHCHI

Valentina Novikov was a housewife and mother in Russia and maintained the same career after emigrating to New York with her children and grandchildren. This cold sorrel soup cooled many of their steamy summer evenings in the city.

2 tablespoons butter
1 onion, finely chopped
6 white potatoes, peeled and quartered
10 cups Savory Beef Stock (page 61) or other
    favorite homemade beef stock
2 bunches (about 3 pounds) fresh sorrel,
    rinsed and dried, tough
    stems removed
1 cup sour cream or buttermilk
Salt and freshly ground white pepper, to taste

1. Melt the butter in a nonreactive large stockpot over medium heat. Add the onion and sauté until translucent, 5 minutes. Add the potatoes and beef stock, and bring to a boil. Simmer over low heat until the potatoes are positively falling apart, about 40 minutes.

2. Stir in the sorrel and simmer until tender, about 30 minutes. Let the soup cool slightly.

3. Purée the soup in batches in a blender or food processor. Transfer to a bowl, cover, and refrigerate until chilled, 2 to 3 hours. Whisk in the sour cream; season with salt and white pepper to taste. Serve.

Serves 6

Alex's
BORSCHOK

Alex Getmanov, a Russian scholar and translator, grew up on Manhattan's Upper West Side in a colony of white Russians. At a young age, he realized that cold borscht is a "lightweight" version of the traditional, heavy warm soup, hence *Borschok*—its diminutive name. But the cold soup is a refreshing one that remains a standby of his summer kitchen.

4 carrots, peeled and minced
2 onions, minced
2 beets, scrubbed and minced
2 tablespoons butter
3 quarts Savory Beef Stock (page 61) or other
    favorite homemade beef stock
8 whole beets with beet greens attached,
    scrubbed
6 chives, minced
¼ cup minced fresh dill
Salt and freshly ground black pepper,
    to taste
1 cup sour cream

Alex Getmanov's borschok uses a beet purée rather than small beet chunks or strips.

1. In a heavy stockpot over low heat, combine the carrots, onions, minced beets, and butter and cook until softened, about 10 minutes.

2. Add the broth and simmer until reduced by one-third, about 30 to 45 minutes.

3. Strain the broth, discarding the vegetables. Return the broth to the pot.

4. Trim off and reserve the beet greens. Coarsely chop the beets. Add the beets to the broth and simmer over very low heat for 45 minutes.

5. Meanwhile, rinse and dry the beet greens. Use a very sharp knife to slice them into a fine julienne; set aside.

6. Purée the beets and broth in a blender or a food processor. Return the purée to the pot. Stir in the chives, dill, and beet greens. Season with salt and pepper to taste. Cover and chill until the soup is nearly cold. Whisk in the sour cream. Serve.

Serves 4

Grandma Wimmer's
POTATO SOUP

At the turn of the century, Frances Wimmer Grayson came to New York from Germany with her parents. This recipe (a version of which was made by her great-uncle at the old Luchow's restaurant on 14th Street) was a mainstay of their Yorkville home. Her family learned to wait until the soup had cooked and had a chance to sit before adjusting the seasoning. As an appetizer or a whole meal, the soup is a fine way to warm a cold and windy New York night.

NOODLES
3 cups all-purpose flour
1 large egg
1 tablespoon salt
½ cup cold water

SOUP
6 large potatoes, peeled and diced (about 3½ pounds)
1 onion, diced
1 tablespoon vegetable oil
1 tablespoon sweet paprika
2 cups sour cream, at room temperature
Salt, to taste

1. Make the noodles: Mound the flour on a flat surface and make a well in the middle. Add the egg, salt, and a little of the water. Mix very well, gradually adding all of the water. Cover and set aside for 15 minutes.

2. Roll out the dough ⅛ inch thick on a floured board. Cut into 3-inch-long strips that are ⅛ inch wide. Sprinkle the noodles with flour and spread out to dry, about 1 hour.

3. Make the soup: Put the potatoes in a 10-quart stockpot and fill with 7½ quarts cold water. Bring to a boil over high heat. Reduce the heat and simmer for 15 minutes. Add the noodles and simmer for 10 minutes, stirring often.

4. Meanwhile, in a small skillet over medium heat, sauté the onion in the oil until dark brown, about 15 minutes. Allow to cool slightly. Stir in the paprika; add the mixture to the soup.

5. Stir a little of the soup broth into the sour cream and stir until smooth. Add the sour cream to the soup, stirring until smooth. Set the soup aside to allow the flavors to meld. The soup will thicken as it sits, and you can add water to achieve the consistency you like. Season with salt to taste and serve.

Serves about 16

Vichyssoise
A LA RITZ

Louis Diat came to New York City in 1910 as chef of the Ritz-Carlton Hotel. For decades,

The Roof Garden of the Ritz-Carlton.

simmer until the potatoes are soft, 40 minutes.

2. Purée the soup in a blender or food processor. Stir in the milk and light cream; season with salt and white pepper to taste. Cover and chill until cold, at least 4 hours.

3. Stir in the heavy cream; adjust the season-ings, if needed. Ladle into soup bowls. Garnish with the minced chives.

Serves 8 to 10

he ruled the kitchens, developing a battery of recipes that became Manhattan standards. The recipe for his renowned vichyssoise was origi-nally published in 1941 in his cookbook, *Cooking à la Ritz,* and remains a mainstay of New York home kitchens.

2 tablespoons unsalted butter
4 leeks, white and pale green parts, thinly sliced
    and rinsed several times
1 onion, minced
5 medium potatoes, peeled and diced
4 cups New York Penicillin (page 47) or canned
    chicken broth
1 tablespoon salt
2 cups milk
2 cups light cream or half-and-half
Freshly ground white pepper, to taste
1 cup heavy (whipping) cream
1 bunch chives, minced, for garnish

1. Melt the butter in a heavy stockpot over medium heat. Add the leeks and onion and cook until translucent, 5 minutes. Add the potatoes, broth, and salt, and bring to a boil. Reduce the heat and

Persian CARROT SOUP

Susan Knightly adapted this from the old per-sonal recipe archives of an Iranian woman who now lives in New Jersey. With a tabbouleh salad on the side, this soup makes a terrific and easy vegetarian dinner.

2 tablespoons vegetable oil
4 onions, chopped
3 garlic cloves, minced
1 eggplant, peeled, seeded, and diced
2 tablespoons chopped fresh parsley
1 rib celery, chopped
8 large carrots, peeled and chopped
2 potatoes, peeled and chopped
1½ teaspoons salt
2 teaspoons freshly ground black pepper
2 cups cooked kidney beans
Chopped fresh mint, for garnish

1. Heat the oil in a nonreactive, heavy stock-pot over medium heat. Add the onions and garlic and sauté until the onions are translucent, 5 minutes. Stir in the eggplant and parsley and cook to soften the eggplant, 10 minutes.

2. Add 8 cups water, along with the celery, carrots, and potatoes. Bring to a boil, then reduce the heat and simmer until the potatoes are tender, 15 minutes. Add the salt, pepper, and beans and cook for 30 minutes. Remove from the heat; set aside to cool.

3. Purée the soup in batches in a blender or food processor. Transfer to a bowl, cover, and refrigerate until chilled, 2 to 3 hours. Adjust the seasonings; garnish with the mint. Serve.

Serves 4

Greenwich Village
GUMBO

When covering the 1988 Republican convention, Joe Conason, now an editor of the *New York Observer,* fell for the cooking in New Orleans. Over the next two years, he perfected this recipe to defend himself against pale imitations in New York City. "If you want a decent gumbo up here," he says, "you have to cook it yourself."

8 live blue crabs
1 cup plus 3 tablespoons safflower oil
5 pounds chicken legs, drumsticks and thighs
*   separated, knob at drumstick tip trimmed away*
½ cup all-purpose flour
4 large yellow onions, finely chopped
4 large green bell peppers, stemmed, seeded, and
*   finely chopped*
1 pound andouille sausage, tasso, or other
*   smoked sausage*
2 pounds okra, trimmed and sliced
2 bay leaves
Cayenne pepper, to taste
Salt and freshly ground black pepper, to taste
Chopped scallions, for garnish

1. Half-fill a large heavy pot with water and bring to a boil over high heat. Add the crabs and cook until their color brightens, about 5 minutes. Drain and set aside to cool.

2. Heat the 3 tablespoons oil in a large skillet over high heat. Add the chicken and sauté until browned all over, 3 minutes per side. Remove the chicken to a nonreactive, large heavy pot.

3. Heat the remaining 1 cup oil in the skillet. Sprinkle on the flour and make a paste, stirring constantly, over medium-low heat. Cook, stirring constantly, until the paste is the color of light milk chocolate, about 30 minutes.

4. Remove the skillet from the heat. Mix in half of the chopped onions and half of the chopped bell peppers; set aside.

5. Clean the crabs by removing the large shell and the gills inside. Add the cleaned crabs to the pot containing the chicken. Stir in the sausage, okra, the remaining onion and bell pepper, and the bay leaves. Add water to cover and bring to a boil. Reduce the heat and simmer, covered, for 1 hour.

6. Slowly stir about ½ cup of the hot gumbo broth into the skillet containing the paste and vegetables. Stir well to eliminate any lumps. Pour the mixture back into the gumbo pot, stirring constantly. Season with cayenne pepper and salt and pepper to taste. Simmer until the vegetables dissolve into a thick stew, about 3 hours.

7. Remove the chicken from the pot and discard the skin and bones; return the meat to the pot. Remove the crabs and break them up with a wooden mallet; return the pieces to the pot. Skim off the fat. Serve the gumbo in individual bowls; garnish with the scallions.

Serves 10 to 12

Joe Conason shares his perfected gumbo recipe.

MANHATTAN CLAM CHOWDER

On December 25th, 1978, Mr. Austin Phelps Winters sat down at his typewriter and set about straightening out the facts as they pertained to his grandfather, William H. Winters and Manhattan Clam Chowder.

It was a difficult moment for Mr. Winters, who was born in New York City in 1906 and ran a successful rubber stamp company in Midtown before retiring to Marco Island, Florida. There were things that he wanted to write to his daughters, things that his grandchildren, in turn, should know. Yet he hesitated. How do you tell your children that they are the progeny of the self-proclaimed inventor of Manhattan clam chowder?

Mr. Winters believed that his grandfather's was a heinous act. And for generations, public opinion concurred. Tomatoes were an anathema to chowder. Chowder, from *chaudière,* the French word for a large cauldron, meant cream. According to John F. Mariani's *Dictionary of American Food & Drink,* Breton seamen who sailed to Newfoundland, Nova Scotia, and New England in the seventeenth and eighteenth centuries invented the dish, and if French sailors were minding the pot, it probably contained cream.

By the late eighteenth century, chowder was a staple of the Eastern seaboard. Mr. Mariani claims that Rhode Island cooks began adding tomatoes to their chowder: "A practice that brought down unremitting scorn from chowder fanciers in Massachusetts and Maine," he writes. The public, he concludes, decided that only people who lived in New York were crazy enough to add tomatoes to chowder and named the dish accordingly.

Richard J. Hooker, who wrote *The Book of Chowder,* found contradictory evidence in the form of recipes. Manhattan clam chowder, he wrote "may have descended from the chowders served during the late nineteenth century at Coney Island stands. In 1894, Charles Ranhofer, famed chef of Delmonico's restaurant, published a recipe for 'Chowder de Lucines.' "

Nevertheless, Manhattan clam chowder remained "a notable heresy." In 1939, a Maine legislator introduced a bill outlawing the use of tomatoes in chowder. In 1940, Eleanor Early, lambasted the "terrible pink mixture" in her book *New England Sampler.* Manhattan clam chowder, she wrote "is only a vegetable soup, and not to be confused with New England Clam Chowder, nor spoken of in the same breath."

"Tomatoes and clams," she wrote, "have no more affinity than ice cream and horseradish."

No wonder cooks didn't rush to claim the invention. It may have been an economizing move, a flight of fancy, or even an innocent substitution: Short on cream, a cook reached for tomatoes. But the occurrence of Manhattan clam chowder reverberated like an act of sabotage against the New England clam chowder tradition. Mr. Winters suffered the stigma of the claim he was about to reveal. "Dear Girls:" he typed.

"Papa's father, William H. Winters, was born in East Marion, Long Island, and had one bachelor brother, James. After the Civil War, in which he ran a blockade runner, he was run out of town (I was told by an old old lady from East Marion) and he and his brother went to Brooklyn and opened a fish store on Fulton Street. After the Brooklyn Bridge was built, they moved across to Manhattan, but kept the name, Fulton Fish Market, which became a fairly big operation, including running clambakes for political clubs, like Tammany Hall."

Long before contemporary health concerns and regional chauvinism bestowed a chic on the dish, William Winters bragged about his invention. He told his grandson he and his brother made vats of Manhattan clam chowder that were served on the vote-buying cruises that Tammany

Hall sponsored. "He was proud of it!" recalled his grandson with horror. "I can't stand the stuff."

In the letter, which Austin Winter's daughters donated to the archives at the South Street Seaport Museum, he laments, "Isn't it awful, to be the grandson of the inventor and not liking it at all?"

PIERRE BLOT'S CLAM CHOWDER

"**It is generally admitted** that boatmen prepare it [chowder] better than others," wrote Pierre Blot in his *Handbook of Practical Cookery,* published in 1877. "The receipts we give below came from the most experienced chowder-men of the Harlem River. Potatoes and crackers were used in different proportions, the more used, the thicker the chowder will be.

"Put in a pot (technical name) some small slices of fat salt pork, enough to line the bottom of it; on it, potatoes; on the potatoes, a layer of chopped onions; on the onions, a layer of tomatoes, in slices, or canned tomatoes; on the latter a layer of clams, whole or chopped (they are generally chopped), then a layer of crackers.

"Then repeat the process, that is, another layer of potatoes on that of clams; on this, one of onions, etc., till the pot is nearly full. Every layer is seasoned with salt and pepper. Other spices are sometimes added according to taste; such as thyme, cloves, bay-leaves, and tarragon.

"When the whole is in, cover with water, set on a slow fire, and when nearly done, stir gently, finish cooking, and serve."

Manhattan Island CLAM CHOWDER

¼ cup diced pork fatback
1 onion, minced
24 littleneck clams, well scrubbed
4 potatoes, peeled and cut into ½-inch cubes
6 fresh tomatoes, peeled, seeded, and chopped, with their juice
1 cup dry white wine
1 teaspoon dried thyme
¼ cup minced fresh parsley
¼ teaspoon freshly ground black pepper
1 cup cracker crumbs from pilot biscuits, sea toast, or crackers
1 tablespoon butter

1. Sauté the fatback in a nonreactive stockpot over medium heat for 5 minutes. Add the onion and sauté until tender, about 10 minutes.

2. Add the clams, cover the pot, and steam until the clams open, 7 minutes. Remove the clams, discard the shells, and set the clam-meat aside. Discard any that do not open.

3. Add the potatoes, tomatoes, wine, and 3 cups water to the stockpot. Bring to a boil, then reduce the heat and simmer for 5 minutes. Stir in the thyme, parsley, black pepper, and cracker crumbs, and simmer for 5 minutes. Add the clams and simmer for 3 minutes. Whisk in the butter; adjust the seasonings. Serve hot.

Serves 6

AL'S
SEAFOOD BISQUE

For years soup impressario Al Yeganeh has dished out hundreds of containers of freshly made creative offerings to his daily line up of patient take-out customers. For more about Al and his unique business, see page 70.

2 cups dry white wine
1 bay leaf
1 onion, roughly chopped
1 clove garlic
2 ribs celery
1 lobster (1 to 1½ pounds)
12 medium shrimp in the shell
24 mussels, well scrubbed
12 sea scallops
4 cups heavy (whipping) cream
1 cup milk
1 teaspoon dried thyme
1 tablespoon minced fresh parsley
  leaves
¼ teaspoon dried rosemary
1 cup fresh spinach, well rinsed and
  chopped
½ cup grated carrot
Salt and freshly ground black pepper,
  to taste
½ teaspoon fresh lemon juice

1. Combine the white wine, bay leaf, onion, garlic, and celery in a nonreactive, large stockpot over medium heat. Bring to a boil. Add the lobster, cover the pot, and steam for 10 minutes. Remove the lobster.

2. Add the shrimp, cover the pot, and steam for 5 minutes. Remove the shrimp with tongs.

3. Add the mussels, cover the pot, and steam until they open, about 5 minutes. Remove the mussels with tongs, extract the meat, and discard the shells. Discard any that do not open.

"Fine clams: choice clams; Here's your Rock-a-way beach clams: Here's Your fine young, sand Clams."

"This young man sings round the city from morning till night, 'clams' as above. These, though not equal in taste to the oyster, yet are a hearty and well tasted food. They are taken in most of the bays and harbors along the coast; but they are found in the greatest plenty along the south side of Long Island. Those which live in the sand are generally better than those in the mud. A place called Rockaway, on the south side of the island, is famed for the best clams; but there are other places, such as Flushing, and Cow-Bay...."

—*Cries of New York,* 1808–1814,
Samuel Woods

4. Add 2 cups water to the liquid in the pot, bring to a boil, then add the scallops. Cover the pot and steam for 3 minutes. Remove the scallops with tongs.

5. Extract the lobster meat, reserving the shells. Peel and devein the shrimp, reserving the shells. Chop the meats into bite-size pieces; cover and set aside.

6. Return the seafood shells to the pot of broth and add 2 cups water. Bring to a boil, then reduce the heat and simmer for 30 minutes. Strain the broth and return it to the pan.

7. Bring the broth to a simmer over low heat. Add the cream, milk, thyme, parsley, and rosemary and simmer until the mixture thickens slightly, 5 minutes. Add the lobster, shrimp, mussels, and scallops and simmer for 2 minutes. Stir in the spinach and carrots and simmer another 2 minutes to just wilt the spinach. Season with salt and pepper, and stir in the lemon juice. Serve hot.

Serves 6

German
SOUR CHERRY SOUP

Erika Freiman explains that this recipe comes from her mother, Minna Börsch, who brought it when she emigrated from northern Germany to the Bronx 60 years ago. It's a common Middle European dish and was served as a main course in her family. It's rich in protein because of the tapioca. It makes an excellent summer dish.

1 pound fresh or canned or jarred
  sour cherries
2 whole cloves
1 cinnamon stick (about 1 inch long)
1 piece lemon zest (a 1-inch-wide strip
  from around the middle)
1/8 teaspoon salt
2/3 cup (or more) sugar
1/4 cup quick-cooking tapioca
3 to 4 tablespoons sour cream

1. Pit the cherries. Save 10 of the pits and tie them in cheesecloth.

2. In a nonreactive medium-large saucepan, combine the pitted cherries, the parcel of pits, the cloves, cinnamon stick, lemon zest, and 4 cups water. Bring to a boil, partially cover, and boil until the cherries soften, about 8 minutes.

3. Meanwhile, in a bowl, combine the salt, sugar, and tapioca. Slowly add to the cooked cherries, stirring to combine. Bring the mixture back to a boil. Reduce the heat and simmer for about 8 minutes more. Add more water, if needed.

4. Set the mixture aside to cool. Remove the cloves, cinnamon stick, lemon zest, and cherry pits. Cover and chill thoroughly.

5. Serve chilled, with a dollop of sour cream on top and cinnamon toast on the side.

Serves 3 to 4

To Bake an Honest Loaf

THE BRICK OVEN
Brotherhood

For over 70 years, Louis Orwasher, the patriarch of Orwasher's Bakery in the Yorkville section of Manhattan, has charted the relationship between the quality of bread and the quality of life in his hometown. The bread has gotten better lately in New York, and Mr. Orwasher wouldn't be surprised if the city follows suit.

History sides with his hunch. As Mr. Orwasher says, "New York wasn't always a white-bread town." The city was always a collection of neighborhoods, each with a bakery at its heart. There were dozens of Eastern European bakeries like Orwasher's as well as Italian, Greek, Scandinavian, and French bakeries. Each made bread from slow-rising sourdough starters, kneading the bread by hand, and firing it in kiln-hot, subterranean brick ovens.

In the days when there was a bakery on every block, there was two-way traffic on the side streets, Mr. Orwasher says, and the biggest danger on most was walking through a stickball game. But the blocks and the breads

Louis Orwasher, front and center, in the old-style bakery that bears his name. (Inset) Fragrant loaves at Ecce Panis on Manhattan's Upper East Side.

changed. To him, the connection between the two is clear.

"Starting in 1950, you had your big corporations swallowing the little guys and consolidating them all under one label," he says. "They did everything by machine. A machine doesn't understand the individuality of a loaf of bread."

There was also the less apparent quality-of-life connection: When a neighborhood loses its bakery, it loses its keeper of the night and a strand of the tether that connects the city to the world of nature and weather and changing seasons.

At Eli Zabar's E.A.T. Cafe, the instructional tableware wisely advises hungry customers.

But as ill-bred loaves invaded the city, Mr. Orwasher never let his starter stop bubbling, never let the fire die in his oven. Baking bread is his life. He began to develop the bread instinct at the age of seven when, with the aid of a cream-cheese crate, he could reach the kneading bench in the basement of his family's bakery. He learned to bank the oven's fire, to know its hot and cold spots and the hisses of steam that make a bread crust form slowly.

SOURDOUGH SHAPES A WORLD VIEW

In the floury, hot world beneath the sidewalk on East 78th Street, he learned to mind the vat of fermenting water, sugar, and flour that had been used to leaven the bread before commercial yeast was reliable. The slow action of the starter, which he would not give up, gave his family's 12 different breads their distinct flavors and chewy, unpredictable textures.

Sourdough also shaped Mr. Orwasher's world view. He dreads the rainy mornings when bread turns limp. He favors autumn and its yeast-loving, temperate days. These are the basic facts of his life and for the most part they go unexamined.

Yet his bakerly bias and his appreciation of the power that nature wields over every loaf are contagious. In a world where cobblestone has been replaced by asphalt, his quiet sensibility is a balm.

Slowly, new members of the unofficial fraternal order of brick-oven bakers were initiated in the last few years. Some say the health-food mentality of the 1960s and 70s created a taste for honest bread. Others contend that fine loaves are a natural consequence of the gourmet food rage of the 80s. Mr. Orwasher simply says, "Nature corrects its own imbalances." By 1987, crusty sourdough bread, well-made pumpernickel, and chewy whole-grain bread began to reappear in New York.

Some of its makers were elected by fate. Eli Zabar, who began baking tart, sourdough wands in 1987, was remodeling the basement of E.A.T., his food store on upper Madison Avenue, when he discovered a brick oven. It was an omen.

The wood-fire oven, which he heats as high as 700 degrees was just the beginning. Mr. Zabar learned to use hard winter wheat, unbleached. "Anything else has that Clorox-y taste," he says. He also came to know the moods of his sourdough starter.

LEAVENING AS A WAY OF LIFE

On cold days, the starter works slowly. On hot days, it's like a hyperactive child. Rain means cutting back on the liquid added to the dough, shortening the rising time, lessening the steam in the oven. Sourdough is a superb leavener, and a capricious one. That's part of its spell.

"Consider the vagaries of modern life,"

> "totoot—totoot—too-too—East! Here's East!"
> With two pails suspended from his yoke, this man, in pursuit of a livelihood, takes his daily rounds.... Yeast, which he measures in a small tin measure, at 1 cent per measure, by the help of which, being added to the meal and kneaded into dough, the experienced housewife is enabled to furnish us with good, light and wholesome bread and cakes."
>
> —*Cries of New York*, 1808 and 1814, Samuel Woods

says Mr. Zabar, who sells some 100,000 loaves of bread weekly. "This is one you can learn to direct."

Living by the leavening can create some very odd people. "Bakers are known for being socially maladjusted," says Noel Comess, who nevertheless chose the life. In 1987 he opened Tom Cat Bakery in Long Island City, Queens, and began life as a microfarmer.

Hot rolls fresh from Tom Cat's oven.

"I tend this vat of fermenting sourdough culture, and all I ever talk about is the weather and how it affects my crop."

His concern places him "in a separate world" within New York City. Some days, the world is almost biblical. "The starter is like Abraham and from it comes all these generations and you guide them, but you are still surprised by every loaf," he says.

Other days, the bread baker is less Jehovah and more a guardian of the tradition that has always softened the hard edges of the city. Stoking the ovens that glow 24 hours a day, Mr. Comess and his bread-baking brothers and sisters are keepers of an urban flame.

They perform their alchemy in the middle of the night, and none claim to work difficult magic. "The traditional bread baker," says Mr. Orwasher, "is simply a man who pays attention to the important things."

Yorkville
RAISIN PUMPERNICKEL

STARTER
2 cups warm (105° to 110°F) water
4 cups rye flour
1½ teaspoons malt syrup or brown sugar
1 teaspoon cake or active dry yeast, softened in
*   1 tablespoon warm water*

BREAD
½ cup coarse-ground cornmeal
¾ cup dark molasses
1 tablespoon butter
1 tablespoon salt
2 teaspoons packed brown sugar
½ ounce unsweetened baking chocolate, finely
*   chopped*
2 potatoes, peeled, boiled, mashed, and cooled
3½ cups rye flour
½ cup whole wheat flour
1 cup raisins

1. Begin the starter 3 days before baking the bread: Combine the water, rye flour, malt syrup, and yeast mixture in a bowl. Cover and set aside at room temperature for 1 day. Then refrigerate for 2 days. The starter will double in size and develop a thick layer of bubbles on its surface as it ferments. Let come to room temperature before beginning to make the bread.

2. Prepare the bread: In a saucepan over medium heat, combine the cornmeal with 1½ cups water and cook, stirring, until thick, about 5 minutes. Remove the pan from the heat and stir in the molasses, butter, salt, brown sugar, and chocolate. Set aside to cool.

3. In a large bowl, combine the starter with the cooled cornmeal mixture. Stir in the mashed potatoes, then the rye flour and whole wheat flour.

4. Dust a board with coarse cornmeal and whole wheat flour. Turn out the dough and knead

until it is stiff and pulls cleanly away from the board, 15 minutes. Add the raisins and knead to evenly distribute them, 3 minutes more.

5. Place the dough in a bowl, cover loosely, and set aside to rise in a warm place until doubled in size, about 1 hour.

6. Butter 2 baking sheets and dust them with cornmeal. Punch down the dough, knead for 1 minute, and divide in half. Shape each half into a round loaf. Place each loaf on a prepared baking sheet, cover loosely, and set aside to rise for 30 minutes.

7. Meanwhile, preheat the oven to 400°F.

8. Bake the bread for 45 to 50 minutes. When tapped on the bottom, the bread should sound hollow. Cool on a wire rack.

Makes 2 loaves

Tom Cat's
WHOLE WHEAT
BREAD

STARTER
¾ teaspoon active dry
*   yeast*
1 cup warm (105° to
*   110°F) water*
1 cup bread flour
1 cup fine or medium
*   stone-ground*
*   whole wheat flour*

Weighing out the dough under pristine conditions at Tom Cat's.

BREAD
1¼ teaspoons active dry yeast
2 tablespoons warm (105° to 110°F) water
1¾ cups plus 2 tablespoons cold water
4 cups bread flour
4 cups stone-ground whole wheat flour
1 tablespoon plus 2 teaspoons salt

1. Prepare the starter: In a large bowl, dissolve the yeast in the warm water and set aside to rest for 15 minutes. Stir in the bread flour and whole wheat flour until the mixture becomes batter-like in consistency. Cover the bowl with plastic wrap and set aside at room temperature for 6 to 8 hours. The starter will double in size and develop a thick layer of bubbles on its surface as it ferments.

2. Prepare the bread: In a large bowl, dissolve the yeast in the warm water. Set aside to rest for 15 minutes.

3. Add the starter, cold water, and both types of flour. Slowly mix the dough with a wooden spoon for 3 minutes so that it becomes easier to handle. Add the salt and knead the dough with your hands until smooth, about 9 minutes. Place the dough in a clean, lightly greased bowl, cover with plastic, and set aside to rise at room temperature until it doubles in size, 1½ to 2 hours. *Do not punch down.*

4. Remove the dough from the bowl and divide into 4 equal pieces. Shape each portion into a long or round loaf, cover loosely with plastic wrap, and set aside to rise at room temperature, until doubled in size, 1½ to 2 hours.

5. Place clay tiles on 2 racks of the oven and preheat it to 425°F. Allow the tiles to get hot.

6. Place 2 loaves on each of 2 baking sheets. Place the sheets on top of the hot tiles. Bake until the loaves are dark brown, 20 to 30 minutes.

Makes 4 loaves

Cousin Jane's
POLISH BABKA BREAD

J oe Pinto, a banker in Yonkers, and his family look forward to the Christmas season for the cheer and the babka. The traditional Polish babka bread is almost as delicious toasted and buttered as it is fresh.

2 packages active dry yeast
¾ cup plus ½ teaspoon sugar
2 cups warm (105° to 110°F) milk
12 tablespoons (1½ sticks) salted butter, cut into small pieces and softened
½ teaspoon salt
8 cups all-purpose flour
3 eggs, lightly beaten
1½ cups golden raisins

1. In a bowl, combine the yeast and the ½ teaspoon sugar with ½ cup of the warm milk. Stir with a wooden spoon until dissolved. Set aside until the yeast mixture bubbles and froths, about 5 minutes. (If the yeast doesn't bubble up, discard the mixture and start again with fresh ingredients.)

Fresh and fragrant breads make for an attractive display.

2. In a large mixing bowl, combine the remaining 1½ cups warm milk with the butter, salt, and remaining ¾ cup sugar. Stirring well after each addition, add 5 cups of the flour, the eggs, and the yeast mixture. Add the remaining 3 cups flour and knead until the flour is incorporated and the dough is smooth.

3. Transfer the dough to a large, clean bowl, cover with a towel, and set aside to rise in a warm place until doubled in size, about 1 hour.

4. Punch down the dough. Cover and let rise again in a warm place until doubled, 1 hour.

5. Preheat the oven to 350°F. Butter a baking sheet.

6. Punch down the dough. Knead in the raisins until well blended. Form the dough into a large oval or round loaf. Place on the prepared baking sheet. Bake until golden and the bottom sounds hollow when tapped, 50 to 60 minutes. Cool on a wire rack.

Makes 1 loaf

WHERE TO BUY A GOOD LOAF

BALDUCCI'S: 424 Avenue of the Americas at 9th Street; (212) 973-2600. A wide selection of breads; the focaccia and olive bread are delicious and most unusual.

BLOOMINGDALE'S: 1000 Third Avenue at 59th Street; (212) 705-2954. The breads and muffins are expensive here, but the peasant-style Italian bread and sourdough baguette are worth the price.

BONTÉ PATISSERIE: 1316 Third Avenue, between 75th and 76th Streets; (212) 535-2360. Excellent croissants and brioches.

CAMMARERI: 502 Henry Street, Carroll Gardens, Brooklyn; (718) 852-3606. Wonderful brick oven–baked Italian bread.

DAMASCUS BAKERY: 195 Atlantic Avenue, near Court Street, Brooklyn; (718) 625-7070. Half a dozen varieties of pita including an addictive herbed pita.

D & G BAKERY: 45 Spring Street, between Mulberry and Mott Streets; (212) 226-6688. For brick oven–baked prosciutto bread.

DEAN & DELUCA: 560 Broadway at Prince Street; (212) 431-1691. Stocks an amazing selection of breads from around New York—and the world.

D & T SHMURA: 460 Albany Avenue in the Crown Heights section of Brooklyn; no telephone. Like a handful of storefronts along this street, D & T makes *shmura,* religiously correct matzoh. The round wafers, which are made in less than 18 minutes, sell for 3 to 4 times the price of grocery store matzoh. Browsing through the unmarked storefront is a trip into another world.

E.A.T.: 1064 Madison Avenue, between 80th and 81st Streets; (212) 772-0022. The mother lode for Eli's bread and changing array of other loaves, all of which are excellent.

ECCE PANIS: 1120 Third Avenue between 65th and 66th Streets; (212) 535-2099. Fabulous quality, country-style breads; the olive and onion focaccia is superb.

MOISHE'S KOSHER BAKE SHOP: 115 Second Avenue, between 6th and 7th Streets; (212) 505-8555. Makes excellent Russian pumpernickel and whole wheat challah.

ORWASHER'S BAKERY: 308 East 78th Street, between First and Second Avenues; (212) 288-6569. Raisin pumpernickel, corn sticks, and Hungarian potato bread are the stars of this old-world bakery.

POSEIDON BAKERY: 629 Ninth Avenue, between 44th and 45th Streets; (212) 757-6173. Makes a wonderful Greek egg bread and, in season, Greek Easter bread.

SPICE & SWEET MAHAL: 135 Lexington Avenue at 29th Street; (212) 683-0900. For Indian and Mediterranean breads, such as pita and roghani and messi nan.

STREITS MATZOH COMPANY: 150 Rivington, between Clinton and Suffolk Streets; (212) 475-7000. Fresh matzoh and bargain bags of matzoh chips. On some days, tours of the venerable matzoh factory are also given; call ahead.

TRIO FRENCH BAKERY: 476 9th Avenue, between 36th and 37th Streets; (212) 695-4296. Supplies many New York restaurants with bread; their breadsticks are well worth traveling for.

ZABAR'S: 2245 Broadway, between 80th and 81st Streets; (212) 797-2000. Stocks everything from sourdough baguettes to a wonderful 7-grain health bread, all at good prices.

ZITO'S BAKERY: 259 Bleecker Street, between Sixth and Seventh Avenues; (212) 929-6139. On Saturdays and the day before any holiday, people begin to line up before 8 A.M. to buy a loaf of what may be the best Italian bread in the city.

Polish
CORN BREAD

Terry Kornick says of this recipe, "Although the ingredients for this corn bread are the same as most standard corn breads, the way the bread is handled makes it very different. My mother learned to make this from her brother, Izzy, who emigrated to New York from Poland, where he had been in the shoe business."

SOURDOUGH STARTER
2 cups cold water
6 cups rye flour
1 teaspoon active dry yeast

BREAD
4 cups warm (105° to 110°F) water
5½ cups rye flour
5½ cups all-purpose flour
4 packages active dry yeast, dissolved in ¼ cup
  warm (105° to 110°F) water
2 tablespoons salt
¼ cup coarse-ground cornmeal
2 teaspoons caraway seeds

1. Start the sourdough starter at least 3 days before baking: Combine the cold water, rye flour, and yeast in a bowl. Mix well; it will be lumpy. Pour the mixture in a clean bowl, cover with a cloth, and refrigerate for 3 days.

2. Remove the starter from the refrigerator 2 hours before beginning to make the bread.

3. Transfer the starter to a large bowl and add the warm water, rye and all-purpose flours, yeast, salt, cornmeal, and caraway seeds, and mix until smooth, 5 minutes.

4. Divide the dough in half. Shape into 2 even rounds. Place each round in a lightly greased large bowl, cover with a clean cloth, and set aside to rise in a warm place until doubled in size, 1 to 2 hours.

5. Place a roasting pan on the bottom of the oven and fill it with hot water. Preheat the oven to 400°F. Sprinkle a baking sheet with cornmeal.

6. Dampen your hands and reshape the bread into even round mounds. Place the loaves on the prepared baking sheet. Bake the bread until crusty, about 2 hours. If the water in the roasting pan runs low during the baking, replenish it to provide the bread with steam heat. Cool on a rack if you wish, but it's more fun to eat this bread hot.

Makes 2 large loaves

Eli's
BREAD

It takes two days to make the sourdough starter for Eli Zabar's bread, but once it is made, it can be renewed again and again. Which is a good thing because once you've tried this bread, you may not be able to settle for less.

SOURDOUGH STARTER
4 cups all-purpose flour
2 cups rye flour
1½ teaspoons malt syrup, or 1 teaspoon packed
  brown sugar
¼ teaspoon salt
1½ cups warm (105° to 110°F) water

BREAD
4 cups all-purpose flour
1½ cups water
2 tablespoons salt

1. Prepare the starter: In a bowl, combine 2 cups of the all-purpose flour with the rye flour, malt syrup or brown sugar, salt, and 1 cup of the warm water. Mix well. Cover with plastic wrap, and set aside in a warm place for 24 hours.

Eli Zabar takes a short break.

2. Discard half of the day-old starter. Place the remaining starter in a large bowl and add the remaining 2 cups of all-purpose flour and the remaining ½ cup of warm water. Knead to combine. Cover with plastic wrap and set aside in a warm place for 24 hours more. This makes the "chef."

3. Prepare the bread: In a large bowl, combine the all-purpose flour, water, and salt. Add half of the chef and mix (see Note). If using a mixer with a dough hook, beat for 8 minutes on low speed to combine well. If using your hands, knead for 10 minutes. Cover the dough with plastic wrap and set aside to rise in a warm place until it doubles in size, 8 hours.

4. Preheat the oven to 500°F.

5. Cut the dough into 12 equal pieces. Flatten (don't punch) each piece of dough into a long stick about 12 inches long. Place 6 of the sticks on each of 2 baking sheets and dust lightly with all-purpose flour. Using a sharp knife, cut 4 diagonal slashes on each stick.

6. Place the loaves in the hot oven. Using a plant mister, spray the inside of the oven every 5 minutes, and bake until the loaves are golden brown, 10 to 15 minutes. Eat these ficelles while they are still warm.

Makes 12 ficelles, which will serve 6 who have had a chance to smell the bread baking

Note: To reserve the starter for future use, add to the remaining "chef" 2 cups all-purpose flour, 1 cup rye flour, ½ teaspoon brown sugar, a pinch of salt, and ¾ cup warm (105° to 110°F) water. Mix well. Store in a clean container in the refrigerator, where it will keep indefinitely. Be sure to refresh it as above after each use. The starter may be frozen; just be sure to let it come back to room temperature before proceeding.

New World RYE BREAD

The Dutch, Manhattan's original immigrant settlers, brought with them a yen for the dense, whole-grained breads of their homeland. The New World offered a coarse-ground cornmeal in addition to Old World rye and wheat, and the cornmeal became a staple of the city's most popular loaf. This particular recipe appeared in *Holland Cookbook,* a collection of traditional New York Dutch recipes that was published in 1887 by the First Reformed Protestant Dutch Church in Kingston, New York. Peter Rose, a culinary historian who specializes in Dutch culture, recommends using Philipsburg cornmeal, made at Philipsburg Manor, in Tarrytown, New York. The cornmeal can be mail-ordered (New York area only) by calling (914) 631-3992. Stone-ground cornmeal can also be used.

1 cup coarse yellow cornmeal
2 cups rye flour
2 teaspoons baking powder
2 teaspoons sugar
¼ teaspoon salt
1 egg
1½ cups milk
2 tablespoons butter, melted

Miller Charles Howell at the grist mill at Philipsburg Manor. Courtesy of Historic Hudson Valley, Tarrytown, NY.

1. Preheat the oven to 350°F.

2. In a large bowl, stir together the cornmeal, rye flour, baking powder, sugar, and salt.

3. In a small bowl, mix the egg, milk, and butter. Make a well in the dry ingredients and pour the wet ingredients into the well. Mix until well blended. Pour the batter into a lightly greased 10-inch cast-iron skillet. Bake until golden and airy, about 1 hour.

Serves 6

3. Return the dough to the bowl, cover loosely, and set aside to rise in a warm place until doubled, about 1 hour.

4. Preheat the oven to 400°F. Butter a baking sheet.

5. Knead the dough for 2 minutes. Shape it into an oblong loaf, place on the prepared baking sheet, cover loosely, and set aside to rise in a warm place until it doubles in size, another 30 minutes.

6. Use a sharp knife to cut 4 slashes in the top of the loaf. Bake until golden brown, about 45 minutes.

Makes 1 loaf

Julia Hedrik's
POTATO BREAD

Julia Hedrik, whose family is from Budapest, is the premier cook at the Hungarian Reformed Church on the Upper East Side. In her family, potato bread was made by feel rather than measure, but there is one thing that Mrs. Hedrik is very specific about: "The potatoes must be riced, none of that mashing machine stuff."

1 envelope active dry yeast
2 cups warm (105° to 110°F) water
6 cups all-purpose flour
1½ tablespoons salt
1½ teaspoons caraway seeds
3 medium potatoes, peeled, boiled, riced, and
* cooled*

1. In a large bowl, dissolve the yeast in ½ cup of the warm water. Add ½ cup of the flour and allow the mixture to bubble up for 1 hour.

2. Stir in the remaining 1½ cups warm water, the salt, and the caraway seeds until combined. Add the riced potatoes and the remaining 5½ cups flour. Turn out the dough onto a lightly floured board and knead until the dough is elastic enough to pull cleanly away from the surface, about 15 minutes.

Pat Burns'
IRISH SODA BREAD

After nearly half a decade of making traditional soda bread, Pat Burns, who lives in Brooklyn, has discovered the secret of serving the unwieldy loaves: Cut each loaf in half, stand them cut side down, and slice. "This," she says, "gives a more even distribution to size and number of slices."

4 cups all-purpose flour
1 teaspoon salt
1 teaspoon baking soda
1 tablespoon baking powder
¼ cup sugar
1 to 2 tablespoons caraway seeds
1 cup raisins, softened in warm water and
* drained*
1 egg, beaten
2 cups sour milk, buttermilk, or sour cream (see
* Note)*
6 teaspoons butter, softened

1. Preheat the oven to 350°F.

2. In a bowl, sift together the flour, salt, baking soda, baking powder, and sugar. Combine the caraway seeds and softened raisins and add to the flour. Add the egg and sour milk to the mixture; combine with a fork until all of the dry ingredients are well moistened.

3. Use 2 teaspoons of the butter to grease two 8-inch cake pans or pie plates, then dust them with flour. Divide the batter evenly between the 2 pans. Bake until golden and cooked through, 40 to 45 minutes.

4. Turn the bread out on a rack immediately. Butter the top of each loaf with 2 teaspoons of the remaining butter. Serve immediately.

Makes 2 loaves

Note: To sour regular milk or cream, add 1 tablespoon distilled white vinegar to each cup.

SAVVY COOK

It is impossible to duplicate a brick oven at home, but it can be simulated by lining the bottom of a home oven with baker's clay tiles, which are available at most kitchen supply stores. Preheat the oven to its highest possible temperature for 1 hour. Spray the interior using a plant mister at regular 5- to 10-minute intervals through the first half of the baking to create the steam that allows the crust to form slowly.

The Swedish Seaman's Church.

Swedish SAFFRONS BROD

At the Swedish Seaman's Church in Manhattan, these buns are made for Saint Lucia Day (December 13) and are served with coffee in the church's reading room. They should be eaten the same day they are baked, and they should never be refrigerated.

1½ cups milk
1 tablespoon butter
1 teaspoon saffron threads
1¾ ounces cake yeast
¾ cup plus 2 tablespoons sugar
6 cups all-purpose flour
Raisins, for garnish
1 egg, beaten, for glaze

1. Combine the milk and butter in a small pan and bring to a boil over medium heat. Stir in the saffron, remove from the heat, and set aside to cool until just tepid.

2. Pour the saffron mixture into a mixing bowl. Add the yeast and stir to dissolve. Add the sugar and continue stirring while adding 5 cups of the flour. The dough should be smooth. Cover the bowl with a clean towel and set aside to rest for 30 to 40 minutes.

3. Sprinkle the remaining 1 cup flour on a board and knead it into the dough for 10 minutes. Divide the dough into 4 equal pieces. Set aside to rest for 30 minutes.

4. Meanwhile, preheat the oven to 475°F. Butter 2 baking sheets.

5. Divide and shape each of the 4 pieces of dough into 8 buns. Place on the baking sheets. Dot each bun with 2 raisins. Brush the buns with the egg glaze. Bake until golden, 10 to 12 minutes. Cool slightly; you don't want to lose the saffron scent. Serve with coffee.

Makes 32 buns

Eliska's
CZECH CHRISTMAS BREAD

Eliska Jelinek moved to New York from Czechoslovakia shortly after the Second World War. She worked as a housekeeper and a nurse for a number of families and gave one charge this, the recipe for her masterpiece bread. Traditionally, it is a Christmas bread, but in at least one of the homes where Eliska worked her magic, the bread has become synonymous with any festive occasion.

2 packages active dry yeast
¾ cup sugar
2 cups warm (105° to 110°F) milk
1 large egg
3 large eggs, separated
½ pound (2 sticks) unsalted butter, softened
½ teaspoon vanilla extract
8 cups all-purpose flour
1½ teaspoons salt
½ teaspoon ground mace
½ teaspoon ground fennel
1 teaspoon grated lemon zest
1 cup golden raisins or black currants
¾ cup slivered almonds
½ cup finely chopped citron

1. In a small bowl, dissolve the yeast and 1 tablespoon of the sugar in the warm milk. Set aside until the mixture froths and bubbles, about 15 minutes. (If the mixture doesn't bubble up, start over with fresh ingredients.)

2. In a large bowl, combine the remaining ½ cup plus 3 tablespoons sugar, the whole egg, the egg yolks, butter, and vanilla. Mix until smooth.

3. In another bowl, combine the flour, salt, mace, fennel, and lemon zest. Add the sugar mixture to the flour mixture and combine well.

4. Add the yeast mixture and beat with a wooden spoon to mix well. Knead until the dough blisters, 10 to 15 minutes by hand or about 5 minutes with a dough hook on an electric mixer. Add the raisins, almonds, and citron and knead again, adding more flour, if necessary, until the dough does not stick to your hands or the bowl.

5. Place the dough in a clean bowl, cover loosely, and set aside to rise in a warm place until doubled in size, about 1 hour.

6. Meanwhile, butter 3 loaf pans.

7. Divide the dough into 3 equal parts. Shape each piece into a loaf and place it in one of the buttered loaf pans. Set the loaves aside to rise for 1 hour.

8. Preheat the oven to 400°F.

9. In a bowl, whisk the egg whites with 1 tablespoon water until just frothy. After the loaves have risen a second time, brush the tops with the egg whites.

10. Place the loaves in the oven and bake for 5 minutes. Reduce the oven to 350°F and bake the bread until golden, about 1 hour. Cool on a wire rack.

Makes 3 loaves

Shonna Valeska's
CHALLAH

Shonna Valeska, a photographer, made her first challah when she was in high school in Gary, Indiana. The recipe came from her cousin E. G. Enbar, and Valeska remembers how her bread brought people together. As she says, "Isn't that what cooking is all about?"

Shonna Valeska's kitchen walls take the boredom out of waiting for the dough to rise.

3 packages active dry yeast
¼ cup warm (105° to 110°F) water
¾ cup corn oil
¾ cup sugar
2 cups hot water
1 teaspoon salt
5 large eggs
9 cups all-purpose flour
½ cup sesame or poppy seeds (optional)

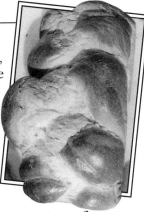

1. In a large bowl, dissolve the yeast in the warm water. Add the oil, sugar, hot water, and salt and stir well. Mix in 4 of the eggs and gradually stir in 4 cups of the flour. Gradually stir in 4 cups more flour and mix until smooth.

2. Sprinkle the remaining 1 cup flour on a work surface. Vigorously knead it into the dough until smooth, 10 minutes.

3. Return the dough to the bowl, cover with a damp cloth, and set aside to rise in a warm place until slightly risen, 30 to 40 minutes.

4. Punch down the dough. Knead for 3 more minutes. Return the bread to the bowl, cover, and set aside to rise until doubled in size, 1 hour.

5. Punch down the dough. Knead for 1 minute. Divide the dough in half. Shape each half into a ball; set aside to rise for 10 minutes.

6. Meanwhile, preheat the oven to 350°F. Butter 2 baking sheets.

7. Separate each ball of dough into 3 smaller balls. Roll out each ball into a 10- to 12-inch rope of dough. Braid 3 strands into a loaf, pressing the ends together very firmly. Repeat with the second large ball of dough. Place each loaf on a prepared baking sheet.

8. In a small bowl, beat the remaining egg. Using a pastry brush, paint the loaves with the egg. Bake for 30 minutes.

9. Sprinkle the loaves with the sesame or poppy seeds, if desired. Continue baking until golden brown, 15 to 25 minutes more. Cool on a rack before serving.

Makes 2 loaves

Artemesia's
GREEK EASTER BREAD

Julie Athas, who grew up in the Astoria section of Queens, can still remember the game her mother, Artemesia, made of concocting this traditional bread for Greek Easter. "She'd let us dye the eggs and place them into the bread. Sometimes she would slip a few coins into the batter and whoever ate those slices of bread were sure to have good luck in the following year. Our family and close relatives all loved the bread, but the children probably loved it the most. We wanted those quarters!"

½ cup warm (105° to 110°F) water
3 packages active dry yeast
1 cup sugar
6¼ cups all-purpose flour, sifted
½ cup milk
¼ pound (1 stick) unsalted butter
1 teaspoon salt
4 large eggs, beaten
1 tablespoon mahlepi (cherry seeds, available at Greek groceries), pulverized in a blender or food processor
2 hard-cooked eggs, dyed red
1 egg, beaten, for glaze
2 tablespoons sesame seeds

1. Pour the warm water into a large bowl. Stir in the yeast, ¼ cup of the sugar, and ¼ cup of the flour. Cover with a towel and set aside until bubbly.

2. In a small saucepan over medium heat, scald the milk until it starts to bubble around the edges. Remove from the heat and stir in the butter, the remaining ¾ cup sugar, and the salt. Mix well. Set aside to cool.

3. Add the milk mixture to the yeast mixture and mix well. Stir in the beaten eggs. Slowly mix in 3 cups of the flour, 1 cup at a time, using your hands to blend well. Sprinkle on the *mahlepi* and work into the mixture. Work in the remaining 3 cups flour, slowly kneading and mixing until the dough pulls away from the sides of the bowl.

4. Turn out the dough onto a floured board and knead for 15 minutes. Place the dough in a greased bowl and cover with a clean towel. Wrap bath towels around the bowl, and set aside in a warm place to rise until doubled in size, about 1 hour.

5. Punch down the dough. Cover and let rise again until almost doubled in size, about 1 hour.

6. Punch down the dough. Divide the dough in half. Cut each half into 3 equal parts, each the size of an orange. Cover with a towel and let rest for 15 minutes.

7. Grease two 9-inch cake pans. Roll out each piece of dough into a 12-inch-long rope. Press 3 of the ropes together at one end and braid them loosely; press the ends together. Arrange the braided dough in a cake pan, forming a circle with the dough. Lightly press the dyed egg upright into the center of the braided dough. Repeat the process for the second loaf of bread. Cover the breads and set aside to rise until doubled in size, 1 hour.

8. Preheat the oven to 350°F.

9. Brush the tops of the loaves with the beaten egg glaze. Sprinkle with the sesame seeds. Bake until golden brown, about 30 minutes. Cool slightly on a rack.

Makes 2 loaves

Grandma Dooley's
WASHTUB
BREAD

Martin Yerdon, a New York artist, has lots of memories about growing up in New York and about this bread: "My grandmother made this recipe during the hot summer months. It alleviated the problem of having to constantly watch the dough rising in hot and humid weather. When clothes weren't being washed in the wooden washtub and my grandfather wasn't making beer, Grandma Dooley filled the tub with clean, cool water and allowed bread to rise overnight. She would slip the dough into an old, clean pillowcase and submerge it overnight."

5 cups unbleached all-
   purpose flour
1 cup stone-ground
   whole wheat flour
1½ tablespoons
   salt
1 cup warm (105° to
   110°F) water
2 tablespoons sugar
1 package active dry
   yeast

Martin Yerdon shares a childhood favorite.

1. Mix both flours and the salt in a large microwave-safe bowl. Place the bowl in a microwave oven and cook on LOW for 2 minutes. Remove from the microwave and stir to make sure there are no hot spots. (If you don't have a microwave, place the flour in a metal bowl in a preheated 200°F oven for 4 minutes, then stir.)

2. In a small bowl, mix together the warm water, sugar, and yeast. Set aside until the mixture froths, about 5 minutes. (If the mixture does not bubble up, discard and start again with fresh ingredients.)

3. Make a well in the flour and pour in the yeast mixture. Stir to incorporate. Add 1 cup water and stir until a dough forms. Pick up the dough in the bowl and knead to incorporate any visible flour. Turn out the dough onto a lightly floured surface and knead until smooth, 6 to 8 minutes.

4. Wrap the dough in a clean cloth that is big enough to go around it at least 6 times. Place the wrapped dough in a large bowl and fill with enough water to cover the dough. Set aside for 2 hours. The dough will float to the surface; just turn it occasionally, and make sure the cloth covers the dough completely.

5. Place a shallow pan half-filled with water on the bottom rack of the oven. Preheat the oven to 450°F.

6. Dust the work surface with flour. Remove the dough from the water and unwrap it. Shape into a round loaf. With a sharp knife, cut 3 slashes across the top.

7. Bake on a baking sheet until golden and the bread sounds hollow when tapped, 35 to 40 minutes.

Makes 1 loaf

Spring Street
PROSCIUTTO BREAD

For over 100 years, the brick oven beneath D & G Bakery on Spring Street in Manhattan has been turning out vaguely smoky loaves of prosciutto bread with slightly charred undersides and buttery tops. And for nearly that long, the formula for the famed bread has been locked in the minds of the bakers, who measure by the five-gallon pail and fine-tune by touch. After requesting the recipe, I was offered, instead, a look at the bakery, and after watching, I devised this version for the home cook.

2½ teaspoons active dry yeast
1 cup warm (105° to 110°F) water
2 eggs
2 tablespoons olive oil
About 3¾ cups all-purpose flour
1½ teaspoons salt
½ teaspoon freshly coarse-ground
   black pepper
1 cup freshly grated Parmesan
   cheese
2 cups minced prosciutto
Cornmeal, for dusting

1. Dissolve the yeast in the warm water in a large mixing bowl and set aside for 15 minutes.

2. Stir in the eggs and oil. Combine 3 cups of the flour with the salt and pepper and stir into the yeast mixture. Knead to combine, adding more flour, a little at a time, to make a firm dough.

3. Combine the Parmesan and the prosciutto and lightly dust with flour. Work the mixture into the dough. Turn the dough out onto a floured board and knead until smooth, 10 minutes. Return the dough to a well-oiled bowl, cover, and set aside to rise in a warm place until doubled in size, 2 hours.

4. Punch down the dough and knead for 3 minutes. Divide the dough in half. Form each half into an oblong loaf. Sprinkle 2 baking sheets with cornmeal and place a loaf on each. Set aside to rise until doubled in size, about 1 hour.

5. Line the oven with wet baking tiles, stones, or trays of terra-cotta chips and preheat to 425°F.

6. Using a razor, make 6 slashes diagonally across the top of each loaf. Bake until golden, about 40 minutes, spraying with a plant mister every 5 minutes for the first 15 minutes of the baking. Cool on a wire rack.

Makes 2 loaves

Jennifer Hardy outside D&G Bakery, owned by her mother Mary Jackson.

Virginia Vernon Littell's
BEER BREAD

Mrs. Littell learned to make this German beer bread from her mother. It is simple and satisfying.

8 slices bacon
2 packages active dry yeast
3¾ to 4 cups sifted all-purpose flour
¼ cup dry onion soup mix
1¾ cups German beer
¼ cup milk
1 tablespoon sugar
2 tablespoons cornmeal

---

1. Fry the bacon until crisp. Drain on paper towels; coarsely chop. Reserve 3 tablespoons of the bacon fat.

2. In a large bowl, mix together the yeast, 1¾ cups of the flour, and the onion soup mix; set aside.

3. In a nonreactive saucepan, heat the beer, milk, sugar, and 2 tablespoons of the bacon fat until warm. The mixture will look curdled; remove it from the heat.

4. Stirring constantly, add the wet ingredients to the yeast and flour mixture. Stir in the bacon and enough of the remaining 2 to 2¼ cups flour to make a stiff dough. Turn out onto a floured board and knead until smooth. Place the dough in an oiled bowl, cover, and set aside to rise until doubled in size, about 45 minutes.

5. Meanwhile, generously butter 2 baking sheets.

6. Punch down the dough, then divide and shape it into 16 equal-sized balls. Place 2 inches apart on the prepared baking sheets, brush the tops of the dough with the remaining 1 tablespoon bacon fat, and sprinkle with the cornmeal. Cover the pans and set aside to rise slightly, 30 minutes.

7. Meanwhile, preheat the oven to 375°F.

8. Bake the rolls until golden brown, 20 minutes. Serve piping hot, with butter.

Makes 16 rolls

June Bobb turns out plenty of fresh, hot roti in her home kitchen.

June Bobb's ROTI

This West Indian bread is suddenly all over New York City, but few versions can compete with this heirloom recipe from Mrs. Bobb, who lives in Brooklyn.

2 cups all-purpose flour
¼ teaspoon baking powder
¼ teaspoon salt
Corn oil, for grilling

---

1. Sift together the flour, baking powder, and salt in a large bowl. Add enough water to make a stiff dough, adding more flour if the dough is too sticky. Divide the dough and shape into 4 to 6 balls. Flatten each ball into a disk with a rolling pin.

2. Brush each roti with corn oil and dust with flour. Fold the roti back into a ball by turning the ends in on each other. Let the roti rest, uncovered, for 30 to 45 minutes.

3. Heat a griddle. Meanwhile, roll out the roti into flat, crêpe-like circles. Cook, turning frequently, until lightly browned all over, about 3 minutes on each side. Drizzle a little corn oil on the roti to keep them from sticking. As you remove each roti from the griddle, place it in the palm of your hand, and "clap" your hands together 2 or 3 times, taking care not to burn yourself. This will puff breads up in the center. Eat immediately.

Makes 4 to 6

Subhir's
ALOO PARANTHA

Subhir Seth learned to make this bread in the Khyber Pass on the border of West Afghanistan and North Pakistan. He recommends serving it as a first course with cumin-flavored yogurt for dipping.

BREAD
3½ cups whole wheat flour
1 tablespoon vegetable oil
½ teaspoon salt

STUFFING
1 pound potatoes
⅓ cup minced fresh cilantro
¼ teaspoon fresh minced chile
½ teaspoon ground cumin
1 tablespoon minced fresh
*   ginger*
¼ teaspoon salt

COOKING
About 1 cup vegetable oil

1. To make the bread: Combine the flour, vegetable oil, salt, and 1½ cups water in a large bowl. Knead to make a smooth dough, about 5 minutes. Divide the dough into 10 equal balls. Place the dough on a tray and set aside to rest in a cool place while you make the stuffing.

2. To make the stuffing: Boil the potatoes in salted water until soft, 30 minutes. Drain and allow to cool slightly.

3. Peel the potatoes, then rice or mash them by hand in a bowl. Stir in the cilantro, chile, cumin, ginger, and salt. Divide the mixture into 10 equal balls.

4. Use your finger to make a deep indentation in each of the dough balls. Place some of the stuffing in each and seal the dough over the stuff-

ing. On a lightly floured board, use a rolling pin to gently flatten each stuffed dough into an 8-inch disk.

5. To cook: Place a griddle or cast-iron skillet over medium heat and coat with 1 tablespoon of the oil. When the oil is hot, place 1 bread in the pan and fry for 1 minute on each side. Sprinkle the bread with additional oil and fry for another minute on each side. Continue frying the breads, one at a time, with additional oil. Serve immediately.
Makes 10 paranthas

*Focaccia topped with
fresh tomatoes.*

Grandma's
POTATO
FOCACCIA

Maria Behr's recipe for potato pizza or focaccia combines the recipes of her grandmothers, who came from different parts of Bari, Italy. Mrs. Behr, who lives in Jackson Heights in Queens, often makes this recipe for a simple supper, teamed up with some cheese and a glass of wine. Try it with Giorgio's Shaved Artichoke and Parmesan Salad (see Index).

2 all-purpose potatoes
1 package active dry yeast
1½ cups warm (105° to 110°F) water
4 cups all-purpose flour
2¼ teaspoons salt
2 tablespoons olive oil
1 large, very ripe tomato, cut into 10 to 12
*   wedges*
½ teaspoon dried oregano

1. Boil the potatoes in water to cover until tender. Drain and peel; mash the potatoes while they are still hot.

2. Dissolve the yeast in the warm water.

3. In a large bowl, mix the potatoes, flour, 2 teaspoons of the salt, the dissolved yeast, and 1 tablespoon of the olive oil until blended. Cover with a cloth and set aside to rise until doubled in size, 1 hour.

4. Preheat the oven to 350°F.

5. Coat an 8-inch-square baking pan with the remaining 1 tablespoon olive oil. Flour your hands, place the dough in the pan, and turn to coat the dough with the oil. Push down slightly to fill the pan with the dough. Arrange the tomato wedges on top of the dough and press in slightly. Sprinkle the oregano and the remaining ¼ teaspoon salt over the top.

6. Bake until golden brown, 1 hour. Serve hot.

Serves 4

Mohammed's
FLAT BREAD

Mohammed K. Rohzyi moved to New York City from Afghanistan in 1979. Within weeks, he set up a pushcart on the corner of 47th Street and Sixth Avenue and began serving hunks of flat bread topped with Afghan kebabs. Eventually, he began baking the bread and wholesaling it throughout the city. Today, he owns two restaurants and a bakery. And he still dotes on this flat bread recipe.

1 package active dry yeast
1 teaspoon sugar
2 cups warm (105° to 110°F) water
4½ cups chick-pea flour
1 teaspoon salt
1 tablespoon black cumin seeds
    or poppy seeds

1. Combine the yeast, sugar, and warm water in a small bowl; set aside until foamy, 5 to 15 minutes. (If the yeast doesn't bubble up, discard the mixture and start again with fresh ingredients.)

2. In a large bowl, combine the chick-pea flour and salt and add the yeast mixture. Gradually sprinkle in cold water 1 tablespoon at a time to make a soft dough that easily pulls away from the sides of the bowl.

3. Knead the bread for 10 minutes on a lightly floured work surface. Return the dough to the bowl, cover, and set aside to rise in a warm place until doubled, 1 hour.

4. Place 2 baking sheets in the oven. Preheat the oven to 425°F.

5. Divide the dough into 4 balls. Roll out each ball on a lightly floured surface into an 18-inch-long oblong, between ¼ and ½ inch thick. Divide the cumin seeds among the 4 breads.

6. When the baking sheets are very hot, remove, sprinkle each lightly with chick-pea flour, and place 1 loaf on each tray. Bake each bread until golden, 8 to 10 minutes. Repeat with the remaining 2 loaves. Serve warm or at room temperature.

Makes 4 loaves

"The pushcarts on Mott Street from Canal to Broome, a block east of Mulberry Street, are relics of a thriving market that once embraced the four streets west of the Bowery. They sell ripe and green olives, artichokes, goats' cheeses, finochio [sic] (sweet fennel), and ready-to-eat pizza, an unsweetened pastry filled with tomatoes and cheese, meat, or fish."

—*The WPA Guide to New York City*, 1939

At John's Pizzeria on Bleecker Street, the toppings are carefully added to the dough.

Evelyne Slomon's
PERFECT PIZZA PIE

Pizzas can be topped with almost anything your heart desires: olive oil and coarsely ground garlic; fresh tomatoes and basil; tomato sauce and mozzarella, crumbled sausage, sautéed peppers; or any personal variation. Go ahead and be adventurous.

1 cup warm (105° to 110°F) water
1 package active dry yeast
3 to 3¼ cups all-purpose flour
½ teaspoon salt

1. Pour the water into a mixing bowl and sprinkle in the yeast. Stir gently with a fork until the yeast dissolves and the liquid turns light beige in color.

2. Add 1 cup of the flour and the salt; mix well. Stirring with a wooden spoon, add a second cup of flour. The dough should pull away from the sides of the bowl and begin to form a soft, sticky mass.

3. Sprinkle some of the remaining cup of flour over a work surface and your hands. Remove the dough from the bowl and knead in the ad-

ditional flour a bit at a time, until the dough no longer feels sticky. Push the heel of your hand down into it and hold it there for 10 seconds. If your hand comes up clean, the dough is done; if it sticks, a bit more kneading is necessary.

4. Lightly oil a 2-quart bowl with vegetable oil. Roll the ball of dough around in the bowl to coat it with the oil. Tightly seal the bowl with plastic wrap and set aside in a warm, draft-free place, preferably in a gas oven with a pilot light. For electric ovens, set the thermostat at 200°F for 10 minutes, turn the oven off, and place the bowl inside. Let the dough rise until doubled in size, 30 to 45 minutes.

5. Punch down the dough, remove it from the bowl, and knead for about 1 minute. Set aside to rise a second time until doubled in size, 1 hour.

6. After the second rising, the dough is ready to be shaped, topped, and baked. Preheat the oven to 500°F.

7. Roll into two 18-inch pies or into four 10-inch individual pies. Add the toppings of your choice now. Bake on clay baking tiles for even baking if possible (if not, use a baking sheet) until the crust is golden, 20 to 25 minutes for a large pie, 15 to 20 minutes for small pies.

Serves 2 pizza fanatics or 4 polite people

Louise Ciminieri and her uncle Joel Ciminieri with a fresh Totonno's pizza (see page 100).

STALKING THE PERFECT PIZZA PIE

New York's coal-oven, pizza-parlor pie has suffered compromise over the past four decades. There was the assault of the gas-fired oven and the arrival of commercially made mozzarella; Wonder bread-style crust began appearing, so did canned tomato sauce—quality concessions to the burgeoning call for New York's favorite fast food: "A slice-a."

Yet hope springs eternal in the hearts and mouths of New York pizza fanatics like Evelyne Slomon. A chef and author of the *Pizza Book,* Slomon is sure that "a pie can still attain perfection."

Slomon was working toward her Ph.D. in art history when bitten by the pizza-bug and she applied her researching skills to the social history

of pizza.
"New York invented pizza parlor–style pizza," she claimed as she headed up First Avenue to Patsy's Pizzeria and Restaurant. In the 1890s, according to Slomon, Italian bakeries and groceries installed coal ovens and began making tomato and mozzarella pies in the Neapolitan tradition.

Patsy's, four dark, adjoining storefronts that house a bar, dining room, kitchen, and pizza counter, was opened by Pascale and Carmela Lancieri in 1933. Now in her 90s, Mrs. Lancieri wears widow's black and presides from a table in the rear of her restaurant. She peels roasted peppers and remembers the time, in

the '40s and '50s, when Patsy's was the center of the Manhattan after-hours world. Next door, in front of the old coal-fired oven, Patsy's pie-men still stretch the dough with both

PIZZA STOPS

PATSY'S PIZZERIA AND RESTAURANT: 2287 First Avenue, between 117th and 118th Streets; (212) 534-9783; open Tuesday through Sunday, noon to 4 A.M.

TOTONNO PIZZERIA NAPOLETANO: 1524 Neptune Avenue, off 16th Street; (718) 372-8606 (call first); open Friday through Sunday, 12:30 P.M. to 9 P.M.

JOHN'S PIZZERIA: 278 Bleecker Street, between 6th and 7th Avenues; (212) 243-1680; open 7 days a week, 11:30 A.M. to 11:30 P.M. weekdays and until 12:30 A.M. on Fridays and Saturdays.

Another perfect pizza goes into the oven at Totonno's.

hands to form the restaurant's old-fashioned pie.

This earns Slomon's approval. "Nobody twirled dough on their fingertips until the '60s," she snorted. "When people started selling slices instead of the whole pie, they moved the pizza-maker from the back of the store to the front window and started the dough-twirling show-manship." Patsy's pie has the tender crust that comes from careful stretching, it is nicely charred on the bottom and has blackened blisters. "In the industry those are called 'New York Blisters,'" according to Slomon. "You need a coal oven to get that kind of bake."

After sampling the crust, Slomon inspected the tomato and mozzarella. Patsy's topping is "world class," she said, though Slomon only nibbles. "If you think this is good," she said, "wait till we get to Totonno's."

In Coney Island, next door to a tire repair shop, is Totonno Pizzeria Napoletano, where the hours as well as the number of available pies are determined by the mood of pizza-maker/proprietor, Jerry Piro. His mood soars when Slomon walks through the door.

Like Tibetan abbots in a snowstorm, they put their heads together in the flurry of white flour that rises from the marble slab in front of Piro's coal kiln. "Watch his thumb," Slomon whispered, as the master effortlessly turned a white, firm ball of dough into a pliant pie. He dabbed crushed Italian tomatoes onto the disk. He dealt slices of fresh mozzarella, scattered chopped garlic, and drizzled top-grade olive oil over the pie. Using a long, wood-handled paddle, he slid the pizza into the oven and, for the next six minutes, jostled it mindlessly as he and Slomon continued chatting.

Piro takes the puffed, gold, brown, and black-crusted pie for granted. Slomon takes it as a sign: "Heaven," she said, "is at hand."

At John's Pizzeria in Greenwich Village, the pizza is saltier and thinner-crusted than at Totonno's. It is crispier, brown, and blistered, almost perfection. Decades of Woody Allenesque reality emanate from the worn booths of the 30-year-old landmark pulling patrons back to what Slomon describes as "a time when everybody had their favorite pie and every pie-maker had his secret."

TO MAKE A SOFT PRETZEL

Close genealogical study has revealed that the soft pretzels that are warmed over coarse hot salt and sold from carts on New York Streets all descended from bagel dough. The current generations of street pretzels bear little resemblance to their ancestors, but it is possible to recall the faded generation of pretzels at home.

Make the basic bagel dough from Bagel Oasis' Very Good Bagel (page 105). Cut the dough into strips, and roll out each like a rope. Cut the rope into 6-inch lengths. Take each piece of dough and form it into a horseshoe shape, with the bottom of the horseshoe closest to you. Pull the ends towards each other, as if you were making a circle, but instead cross, then wrap one piece around the other, placing each end on opposite sides of the pretzel loop. Boil the pretzels according to the instructions for bagels. Dust the pretzels with kosher salt (optional). Bake at 425°F until golden brown, 20 minutes. Serve warm.

Makes 6 large pretzels

Andrea's BREADSTICKS

Andrea Hellrigl learned to make these breadsticks in the lake country of Italy and prepares them daily for the bread basket at Palio Restaurant in Manhattan, where he is the chef. Whether nibbled with cocktails or along with appetizers, these breadsticks are addictive and have garnered a cult following in New York. They are simple to make, handy to have on hand for last-minute guests, and keep well in a covered container.

8 cups all-purpose flour
2 tablespoons salt
1½ teaspoons freshly ground white pepper
½ cup olive oil
3 tablespoons minced fresh rosemary
3 tablespoons minced fresh sage
⅛ cup fresh yeast

1. Sift the flour with the salt and pepper in a large bowl. Make a well in the flour and pour in the olive oil. Mix the oil into the flour, then add the rosemary and sage and blend.

2. Place the yeast and ¼ cup water in a small bowl. Mix until creamy. Thoroughly blend the yeast into the flour mixture, then blend in 1¾ cups more water. Turn the dough out onto a lightly floured surface and knead lightly. Let the dough rest, covered, in a warm place until it rises slightly, 30 minutes.

3. Knead the dough until smooth, 5 to 10 minutes. Return it to the bowl, cover, and refrigerate for at least 12 hours.

4. Preheat the oven to 400°F. Lightly oil 2 large baking sheets with olive oil.

5. Roll out the dough into a rectangle just under ¼ inch thick. Cut the dough into 12-inch-long strips that are narrower than a pencil.

6. Transfer the strips to the prepared baking sheets and

Andrea Hellrigl at Palio with a tempting platter of his crispy breadsticks.

bake until golden brown, about 15 minutes. Cool slightly.

Makes about 36 breadsticks

Broomstick
ONION ROUNDS

Elaine Hoffman, who grew up in Brooklyn, remembers that her grandmother used a broomstick to roll out the dough for these savory treats, but a rolling pin will do the job. These are delicious served with thinly sliced ham or salami.

2 cups all-purpose flour
2 teaspoons baking powder
1 teaspoon salt
Dash of freshly ground black pepper
¼ cup poppy seeds
2 large or 3 small onions, chopped
¼ cup vegetable oil
2 eggs, lightly beaten

1. Preheat the oven to 375°F. Grease a baking sheet.

2. In a mixing bowl, combine the flour, baking powder, salt, pepper, and poppy seeds. Stir in the onions, oil, eggs, and ¼ cup water. Quickly mix together.

3. Turn out the dough onto a well-floured surface and knead until glossy and no longer sticky, 5 to 10 minutes. Roll out the dough about ¼ inch thick. Cut the dough into about forty 1½-inch rounds. Re-roll the remaining dough and cut more rounds.

4. Place the rounds on the prepared baking sheet. Bake until golden, 20 to 25 minutes. Serve warm.

Makes about 40

Freddy's
BAKING POWDER
BISCUITS

Fred Ferretti, *Gourmet* magazine's "Gourmet at Large," has tried varying the ingredients for baking powder biscuits, but he's found his mother's recipe to be the best. These are "the biscuits I grew up on in New York," says Ferretti, "and in my house we eat them on Sunday mornings with butter and preserves or with scrambled eggs and bacon or sausage."

¼ cup melted butter
2 cups sifted all-purpose flour
1 teaspoon salt
1 tablespoon baking powder
¼ pound (1 stick) butter, or ⅓ cup solid vegetable shortening
¾ cup milk

1. Preheat the oven to 425°F. Use some of the melted butter to grease a 12-cup muffin tin.

2. Combine the flour, salt, and baking powder in a mixing bowl. Cut the stick butter or shortening into small pieces, and cut into the flour mixture with a knife or pastry blender until the mixture resembles coarse meal. Add the milk, a little at a time, until the dough becomes a bit elastic.

3. Place 2 heaping tablespoonfuls of the batter in each muffin cup. Bake for 6 minutes. Brush a bit of the melted butter on the tops of the biscuits. Return to the oven and bake until browned, 6 to 9 minutes more. Serve immediately.

Makes 12 biscuits

A BAGEL IS A BAGEL. . .

Like many things in New York City, bagel making has changed a lot in the 20 years since Abe Moskowitz bought Bagel Oasis in the Jamaica section of Queens. Back then, every neighborhood had a bagel bakery and every bagel was handmade and chewy. "Today bagel joints open up as fast as pizza parlors," said Mr. Moskowitz. "They use sugar instead of malt, they use one machine to mix the dough, another one to shape it, and then they bake their bagels without boiling them."

But not at Bagel Oasis. In a steamy preserve behind the storefront shop, bagels are still shaped by hand, sunk into boiling water, and baked in hot ovens 24 hours a day, 365 days a year.

Bagels, you see, are tender things. They flourish under what Mr. Moskowitz describes as "the taste of the hand." When

At Bagel Oasis (above), José Rosso (left) readys bagels for the oven.

bagel dough is mixed by machines and "extruded" into doughnut-like shapes, it toughens. When a bagel is baked factory-style (without the prelude of a hot bath and without being turned during the baking), it develops bumps on its bottom side as well as an uneven crust-to-chew ratio.

This is not fair to the bagel! It defies bagel tradition! Standing in his yeasty domaine, Mr. Moskowitz closes his eyes and shakes his head. The crew of five bagel-makers and bagel-bakers look up from their mountains of dough, their vats of boiling water, and their hot ovens and shake their heads, too.

In Moskowitz's preserve, bagel dough is made by combining flour, yeast, salt, water, and malt in a six-by-six-foot hopper. It is then placed on a cornmeal-dusted counter, where veteran bagel-shapers like Stuart Palefsky cut 2-inch strips from the dough mountain. He rolls the strip with his palms until it resembles a coil. With a flick of his right wrist, he loops the line into a bagel shape. He stretches it. He breaks it off between his hands. With his right hand he pinches the ends to close the circle. He averages 21 bagels a minute.

A bagel-boiler dunks each into boiling water. A bagel-baker minds them in the oven. A bagel-lover would be bereft without the ritual. Nevertheless, it is a fading one. Bagel Oasis is one of the last havens for the practice of this traditional art. Facing an invasion of bagel mixing, shaping, and baking machines, Mr. Moskowitz advises home-bageling. "You can use brown sugar instead of malt in the dough," he said. "Just make sure you keep your oven near 500°F, oil your baking sheets well, and learn to use your hands."

Bagel Oasis
VERY GOOD BAGEL

1 package active dry yeast
3 teaspoons dark brown sugar
1½ cups warm (105° to 110°F) water
1 tablespoon salt
4 cups all-purpose flour
About ½ cup cornmeal, for dusting
Sesame seeds, poppy seeds, kosher salt, crushed
garlic, or minced onion, for toppings
(optional)

A sign in the window at the Bagel Oasis proudly announces the bagels are made by hand.

1. Proof the yeast by placing it in a large bowl and adding 1½ teaspoons of the brown sugar and the warm water. Stir well and set aside until the mixture bubbles and a slight foam forms on top, about 5 minutes.

2. Add the remaining 1½ teaspoons sugar and the salt; stir well. Gradually add the flour, 1 cup at a time. Using your hands, mix the dough until the flour is well incorporated. Knead the dough in the bowl until smooth, about 7 minutes. The dough should retain a sheen and not appear too floury. Cover the bowl and set aside to rest in a warm place for 40 minutes.

3. Lightly dust half a large cutting board with flour and half with cornmeal. Turn out the dough onto the floured side of the board. With a sharp knife, cut a thick 2-inch strip from the dough. On the cornmeal-dusted board, roll out the strip with the palms of your hands until it resembles a rope as thick as 2 fingers. Grip the right end of the strip with your right hand and loosely hold the middle of the coil with your left hand. Bring the right end to the middle of the coil, stretching the dough slightly as you work. Break off the bagel with your left hand. Use the thumb of your right hand to pinch the bagel together. If it fails to hold together, squeeze the seal in your hand for a few seconds, then reshape the bagel, stretching and

squeezing it with your hands. Continue making the rest of the bagels.

4. Lightly dust a baking sheet with cornmeal. Place each bagel on the prepared baking sheet and set aside in a warm place, uncovered, for 30 minutes.

5. Preheat the oven to 425°F. Heavily dust another baking sheet with cornmeal.

6. Fill a large, wide pot two-thirds full of water and bring to a boil. Using a wide, slotted spoon, drop the bagels in batches into the water; they must not touch. Boil on one side for 2 minutes. Turn the bagels and boil on the second side for 1½ minutes. They should firm and puff up. Carefully remove from the water and drain for 1 minute on a rack.

7. Place the bagels on the prepared baking sheet and sprinkle with the desired topping(s). Immediately place the sheet in the oven and bake for 12 minutes. Turn the bagels and bake until deep golden brown all over, about 7 minutes. Remove from the baking sheets to cool on paper towels.

Makes 10 to 12 bagels

The breads at D&G Bakery on Spring Street in Manhattan are off-set by some New York street art.

Astor House
ROLLS

This is New York's version of the Boston "Parker House roll," soft, chewy dinner rolls that, according to nineteenth-century guidebooks and diaries, were served warm, wrapped in a white napkin in restaurants from the beginning of the Delmonico era to the roaring Nineties. This recipe is adapted from *Grandmother in the Kitchen: A Cook's Tour of American Household Recipes from the Early 1800s to the Late 1890s,* by Helen Lyon Adamson.

1 package active dry yeast
½ cup warm (105° to 110°F) water
1½ teaspoons plus 1 pinch sugar
4 cups all-purpose flour
1 teaspoon salt
14 tablespoons (1¾ sticks) butter
1 cup milk, scalded and cooled until just warm

1. Dissolve the yeast in the warm water in a small bowl. Stir in the pinch of sugar. Set aside to proof until foamy, 3 minutes. (If the yeast doesn't bubble up, discard the mixture and start again with fresh ingredients.)

2. Combine the remaining 1½ teaspoons sugar, the flour, and salt in a large bowl. Stir. With a pastry blender or 2 forks, cut 6 tablespoons of the butter into the flour mixture until it resembles coarse meal. Stir in the milk and yeast mixture, and mix until the dough forms a coarse ball and pulls away from the sides of the bowl.

3. Turn out the dough onto a lightly floured board and knead until smooth, about 10 minutes. Place in a lightly oiled bowl, cover with plastic wrap, and set aside to rise in a warm place until doubled in size, about 1 hour.

4. Butter 2 baking sheets. Turn out the dough onto a floured board and roll out ½ inch thick. Using a floured glass or biscuit cutter, cut out 24 rolls. Place on the prepared baking sheets, cover with plastic wrap, and set aside to rise for 30 minutes.

5. Meanwhile, preheat the oven to 400°F.

6. Cut the remaining 8 tablespoons butter in 24 pieces. Flatten each roll with the palm of your hand. Place a piece of butter on one side, fold the roll over into a half-moon shape, and pinch to seal. Repeat with the remaining rolls.

7. Place the rolls 2 inches apart on the prepared baking sheets. Bake until golden, about 18 minutes. Cool slightly on a wire rack.

Makes 2 dozen

Scottish
Housekeeper's
SCONES

These rich, flaky scones were originally made by a Scottish housekeeper who worked for Teddy Burlingame's grandmother in her Fifth Avenue apartment. Mr. Burlingame, an investment banker who now lives in London, says that the smell of these baking is his version of Proust's madeleine, and he regrets that the name of the original baker has long since faded from memory, though her recipe has now been passed through four generations.

4 cups all-purpose flour

1 cup sugar

2 teaspoons baking powder

1 teaspoon salt

¾ pound (3 sticks) unsalted butter,
    cut into small pieces

1 cup raisins

1 egg

¾ cup milk

—————————◼————————

1. Preheat the oven to 400°F. Grease a large baking sheet.

2. In a mixing bowl, combine the flour, sugar, baking powder, and salt. Using a pastry blender or 2 knives, cut in the butter. Stir in the raisins. Add the egg and milk and stir to combine. Knead the dough in the mixing bowl until smooth, 5 to 10 minutes.

3. Pat out the dough on the prepared baking sheet until it is a large square, 1 inch thick. Cut into twelve to fifteen 3-inch squares. Bake until golden, 30 to 40 minutes. Cool slightly before serving.

Makes 12 to 15 scones

At Tom Cat, bins of rolls, ready to be bought and buttered.

Sara Shankman's
CORN BREAD

A transplant from West Monroe, Louisiana, Sarah Shankman has firm opinions about corn bread. The following recipe, she says, can be used for muffins, corn sticks, or corn bread. The bread, however, must be made in a black skillet: "A nine-inch one is about right. If you don't have a seasoned cast-iron skillet, you should. Nothing else will do." Preheating the oil in the skillet gives a wonderfully crusty bottom.

¼ cup corn oil

1 cup yellow cornmeal

1 cup all-purpose flour

½ teaspoon salt

¾ teaspoon baking powder

1 egg

1 cup buttermilk

—————————◼————————

1. Preheat the oven to 425°F.

2. Pour the oil in the skillet, taking care that the oil coats the sides to about halfway up. Place the skillet in the oven to preheat for 5 to 10 minutes while you make the batter.

3. Combine the cornmeal, flour, salt, and baking powder in a medium bowl.

4. In a small bowl, beat together the egg and buttermilk. Add the wet mixture to the dry and combine with a few swift strokes.

5. Remove the skillet from the oven, pour the corn oil into the batter, and stir. The batter will be very thick, but you may add a little more buttermilk if the mixture will not pour.

6. Pour the batter into the oiled skillet. Bake until golden, 20 to 25 minutes. Serve warm.

Serves 4

Fruit BREAD

When Marie Lyons attended City High School in the 1930s, her class developed many recipes that she recorded and still cooks from today. Of the fruit bread, she says, "For delicious sandwiches, cut in thin slices and spread with butter or cream cheese."

2 cups sifted all-purpose flour
1 tablespoon plus 1 teaspoon
*   baking powder*
1½ teaspoons salt
¾ cup sugar
2 cups graham (whole-wheat) flour
¾ cup candied orange peel,
*   thinly sliced*
¾ cup mixed nuts, such as cashews,
*   walnuts, and almonds*
*   (peanuts won't work)*
2 eggs, well beaten
1⅔ cups milk
¼ cup melted butter, cooled

1. Preheat the oven to 350°F. Grease two 8 × 4-inch loaf pans.

2. In a large bowl, combine the sifted all-purpose flour, baking powder, salt, and sugar. Sift the ingredients together.

3. In a separate bowl, combine the graham flour, orange peel, and nuts. Add to the flour mixture and mix.

4. Combine the eggs, milk, and melted butter. Add to the flour mixture and mix to make a batter.

5. Divide the batter between the 2 prepared pans. Bake until golden brown, about 1 hour.

6. Remove the loaves from the pans and cool thoroughly on a wire rack. Store overnight, unwrapped, before slicing.

Makes 2 loaves

Fill your house with the inviting fragrance of coconut bread from Sharifa Burnett.

Sharifa's WEST INDIAN COCO BREAD

Sharifa Burnett, a travel agent, occasionally does the cooking for West Indian or Jamaican weddings and other social events. The "essence" called for is a liquid blend of spices that can be found in specialty stores. Vanilla extract makes a fine substitute.

1 cup sugar
1 cup warm (105° to 110°F) water
4 packages active dry yeast
8 cups all-purpose flour
¾ pound (3 sticks) butter or margarine, at room
*   temperature*
4 large eggs, beaten
Grated meat of 1 coconut
¼ teaspoon vanilla essence or vanilla extract
2 teaspoons salt

1. In a large bowl, dissolve the sugar in the warm water. Add the yeast, mix, and set aside for a few minutes, until foamy. (If the yeast doesn't bubble up, discard the mixture and start again with fresh ingredients.)

2. Stir 3 cups of the flour into the yeast mixture and mix until smooth.

3. In a medium bowl, cream together the butter, eggs, coconut, essence, and salt until smooth. Add to the yeast and flour mixture and beat until the dough is smooth. One cup at a time, add the remaining 5 cups flour, and mix until the dough is stiff and pulls away from the bowl.

4. Begin kneading the dough in the bowl, then turn out onto a lightly floured board. Knead until the dough is elastic and smooth, 5 to 10 minutes, adding more flour if necessary. Place the dough in a lightly greased bowl, cover with a towel, and set aside to rise until double in size, 1 hour.

5. Remove the dough from the bowl and divide in half. Shape into 2 loaf shapes. Cover the loaves with a towel and set aside to rise a bit, 30 minutes.

6. Meanwhile, preheat the oven to 350°F.

7. Place the loaves on a baking sheet or baking tiles and bake until golden brown, about 1 hour. Cool on a wire rack.

Makes 2 loaves

Elizabeth Bonwich's
MORNIN' TIME MUFFINS

This recipe won first place in the 1987 City Harvest Fair. Be sure to eat the muffins warm from the oven.

½ cup melted butter
1 cup sugar
2 eggs
½ cup plain yogurt
1 teaspoon baking soda
2 cups sifted all-purpose flour
Grated zest of 1 lemon
1 cup fresh blueberries, dusted with flour

1. Preheat the oven to 375°F. Butter a 12-cup muffin tin, or place a paper liner in each cup.

2. Combine the melted butter, sugar, and eggs in a large mixing bowl. Stir in the yogurt. Combine the baking soda, flour, and lemon zest and stir into the mixture. Finally, using a few swift strokes, add the blueberries.

3. Divide the batter among the 12 cups, filling each to the top. Bake until golden, 30 minutes.

Makes 12 large muffins

Whole Wheat
BANANA BREAD

Bette Duke, art director and designer, makes this satisfying, dense bread often at the studio for breakfast and finds that clients always ask for the recipe.

¼ pound (1 stick) unsalted butter, at room
temperature
1⅓ cups dark brown sugar
3 large eggs, lightly
beaten
1 teaspoon vanilla
extract
1 teaspoon baking
soda
¼ cup sour cream
¾ cup whole wheat
flour
¾ cup all-purpose
flour
¼ teaspoon salt
1 cup mashed ripe
bananas (about
2 medium)

Bette Duke offers a recipe for a New York favorite—homemade banana bread.

1. Preheat the oven to 350°F. Grease a 9 × 5 × 3½-inch loaf pan.

2. In a mixing bowl, cream the butter and brown sugar together. Add the eggs and vanilla and beat until the mixture is light. Stir the baking soda into the sour cream. Beat the mixture into the batter.

3. Sift together the whole wheat flour, all-purpose flour, and salt. Alternately add the flour mixture and the mashed bananas to the batter and mix until combined.

4. Turn the batter into the prepared loaf pan. Bake until a tester inserted in the center comes out clean, about 1 hour. Cool on a wire rack.

Makes 1 loaf

Bubbie's
PASSOVER MUFFINS

These muffins, which taste similar to Yorkshire pudding, are a good accompaniment to brisket and gravy.

1 pound matzoh farfel (8 cups)
6 eggs
1 teaspoon salt
½ teaspoon freshly ground white pepper
1 tablespoon peanut oil

1. Preheat the oven to 350°F. Grease two 12-cup muffin tins. Place them in the oven to warm.

2. Soak the farfel in water to cover for 1 minute; drain.

3. In a large mixing bowl, beat the eggs with the salt and pepper. Stir in the farfel and mix well.

4. Spoon the mixture into the muffin tins, filling each cup. Bake until the tops become golden, 30 to 35 minutes. Serve immediately.

Makes 24 muffins

Golden Fidler's
MATZOH BREI

Golden Fidler remembers her Austrian-born mother making fried matzohs when she was a child; now Golden's daughter and granddaughter make it. "Although it is a traditional Passover dish, we love it so much we eat it throughout the year as a breakfast meal," Fidler explains. This peasant-type dish is served like an omelette.

4 plain, unsalted matzohs (6-inch square)
1 cup milk
4 large eggs, beaten
1 small onion, finely diced
Salt and freshly ground pepper
2 tablespoons butter

1. Soak the matzohs in the milk for 1 minute; remove.

2. Beat the eggs in a mixing bowl. Add the onion, and season with the salt and pepper. Crumble the soaked matzohs into the egg mixture.

3. Melt the butter in a large skillet over medium heat. When it is very hot, add the matzoh mixture. Brown on one side, then turn and brown the other, 2 to 3 minutes per side. Serve immediately.

Serves 4

Sheets of matzoh ready for brei-ing.

At Moishe's Kosher Bakery on Second Avenue, the rugelach and other traditional pastries are New York favorites.

Sophie Minkoff's
SPICED PUMPKIN BREAD

This recipe won first place in the 1985 City Harvest Fair. It makes a comforting snack for autumn walks through the woods.

1 cup raisins
2 large eggs
½ cup vegetable oil
1 cup unsweetened pumpkin purée
2 cups all-purpose flour
¾ cup sugar
1 teaspoon baking soda
¾ teaspoon ground cinnamon
½ teaspoon freshly grated nutmeg
½ teaspoon salt
½ cup coarsely chopped walnuts

1. Preheat the oven to 350°F. Grease a 9 × 5 × 3½-inch loaf pan.

2. Combine the raisins and ⅓ cup water in a saucepan. Bring to a boil over high heat. Remove from the heat, and set aside to cool.

3. Meanwhile, in a mixing bowl, whisk together the eggs, oil, and ¼ cup water. Add the pumpkin purée and stir to combine.

4. In a large mixing bowl, combine the flour, sugar, baking soda, cinnamon, nutmeg, and salt. Stir the pumpkin mixture into the dry ingredients. Stir in the undrained raisins and the walnuts.

5. Transfer the batter to the prepared loaf pan. Bake until a wooden skewer or toothpick inserted in the center comes out clean, 1 to 1¼ hours. Cool on a wire rack.

Makes 1 loaf

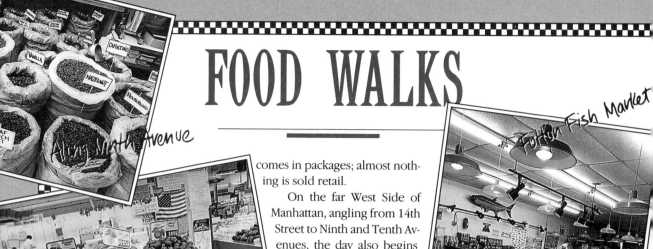

FOOD WALKS

Along Ninth Avenue

Along Arthur Avenue

Fulton Fish Market

Fourteenth Street Meat Market

comes in packages; almost nothing is sold retail.

On the far West Side of Manhattan, angling from 14th Street to Ninth and Tenth Avenues, the day also begins before dawn in the city's meat district. Refrigerated trucks purr outside the low-lying buildings. Meat

T he food day begins shortly before midnight in the **Hunts Point Terminal Market** in the Bronx. It is a militaristic-looking complex in a wasteland of auto wreckers and junkyards. Convoys of semitrailers pass through a tollgate opening in the barbed-wire and corrugated-tin wall that surrounds the compound. They unload, they load. In recent years, up to five million pounds of fresh fruits and vegetables were sold from the gargantuan warehouses here, primarily to grocery chains and huge wholesale buyers. Meat, packaged fish, dairy goods, canned and frozen food are also sold, about $7 billion worth a year. Almost everything

cutters in splattered white coats and hard hats push racks of swinging lamb and sides of beef across the uneven sidewalks. The aromas of game and diesel fuel hang over the blocks.

At 3:30 A.M., as trucks begin to pull away from the Hunts Point Market, a different fleet idles around the **Fulton Fish Market,** the 158-year-old fish exchange under the East River Drive, near the tip of Manhattan. In shin-high rubber boots, workers push handcarts loaded with

mussels and clams, baskets of small flatfish, and loose dinosaurian halibut across the wet cobblestones.

Commerce has etched New York City's topography as irrevocably as any natural force. And commerce began with the buying and selling of food. Today, New York can be seen as a long food chain. From the wholesale markets, on the city's fringes, it spirals through the shops in each borough's ethnic neighborhoods and on to the large grocery stores and boutiques that dot the city.

You can still buy and sell almost any kind of food in New

York City. But the nature of that buying and selling is changing. Centralization and bulk buying are nibbling away at the old-time wholesalers, and the effect can be felt in the sense of erosion that now pervades the outer ends of the food chain.

When it opened in 1967, the Hunts Point Market, with its modern, efficient, bulk-buying mentality, eclipsed the nearby **Bronx Terminal Market**. Today, the older

W. Nassau Meat Market

market is a quieter shopping area, still running under the Major Deegan Expressway, still harkening back to a time when produce was chosen by touch and aroma. The three-block stretch smells of cilantro and garlic. Hunts Point has pallets of canned tuna; its predecessor still has dollies loaded with fresh sugar cane, bits of watermelons, mounds of mangos. Although no longer a major source for large supermarkets, the Bronx

Terminal Market is still a mecca for Hispanic grocery stores.

Before dawn, the owners of New York's small bodegas and corner shops pull their battered vans into the market. There is something fragile in the crumpled greenbacks they exchange. There is something endangered about the peculiar odor that comes when parsley stems and fruit peels and cigarettes are paced into the diesel fuel-drenched pavement. But the market perseveres.

So does **La Marqueta,** the string of shedlike buildings that stretches beneath the Metro North tracks along Park Avenue from East 111th Street to East 116th Street. Needed renova-

North Avenue Cheese Market

tions have been at a standstill for the past two years, and more than half of the market's 150 food stalls have been abandoned. But La Marqueta remains the place for chayote squash and fresh tamarind pods, for smoked turkey necks, fresh farm eggs, and sorrel syrup—still sold at some of the best prices in town.

The downtown meat district pushes anyone who walks here back to the time before meat was portioned and wrapped in plastic. Tons of meat are shipped from here each week. And yet that number diminishes each year, according to Edward Seh, Jr., of Pacific Seh Wholesaling, who has been selling meat from the area for 40 years. "The big chains buy boxed meat directly from the slaughterhouses," he explains, which cuts out some of the middlemen of Manhattan.

And so, the Bronx Terminal Market and La Marqueta grow quieter. In the meat district, established wholesalers

Along Arthur Avenue

Trunza in Brooklyn

worry about their sales. Will they crumble like the piers that stretch their ghostly tentacles into New York Harbor?

Not long ago, small parcels of food were landed on those narrow piers, everything from local fish to bananas from Panama. Then small parcels gave way to semitrailer-size containers, and they could only be landed and stored in sprawling ports like Red Hook, in Brooklyn, and Elizabeth, in New Jersey.

New York is still the most active harbor in the country. And despite some decay, its wholesale markets continue to feed some fundamental need. Maybe the sense of adventure it takes to embrace the city's wildly varied foodstuffs is predicated on the assurance that somewhere two people shook hands over the ingredients.

No market portrays the abiding importance of this exchange better than the Fulton Fish Market. More than 450 varieties of fish—90 million pounds annually—are sold from the sagging tables that line the stalls of the largest fish market in North America. And in an era of computerized accounting and bulk buying, every deal at the Fulton Fish Market is person-to-person, handshake-by-handshake, cash-to-pocket.

By 6 A.M., the local bakeries begin to issue yeasty smells. The city's ethnic enclaves rouse. The second link in the New York food chain wakes up.

Not far from the East River, in the former German and Hungarian enclave on the Upper East Side, the aromas of baking rye and raisin and pumpernickel

bread wafts from **Orwasher's Bakery** on East 78th Street. At the same time, the smell of sourdough creeps up to the sidewalk from the subterranean bakery at nearby **E.A.T.**

By 7 A.M., there is bread-truck gridlock outside **Trio** on Ninth Avenue. Bread for hotels, restaurants, and food stores is loaded, pushcart vendors stock up on sandwich rolls, and neighbors wander in to buy still-warm rolls. Ninth Avenue, one of the oldest ethnic enclaves in the city, has begun to stir.

In the back of **Diluca Dairy and Deli,** a closet-size storefront on Ninth Avenue between 37th and 38th Streets, a man whose hands are used to the feel of boiling milk begins making some of the best fresh mozzarella in town. Behind the double windows of **Manganaro Grosseria Italiana** (488 Ninth Avenue, between 37th and 38th), where jars   of im-

ported pasta, olive oil, and cheese are displayed with a couple of gilt Venuses, Sal Dell'Orto dons his blue grocer's jacket and sips the morning's first espresso.

Back in 1890, when his mother's family opened the grocery, recalls Mr. Dell'Orto, the neighborhood was called "Paddy's Market," and pushcarts lined Ninth Avenue from 31st Street to the low 50s. Today, much of the best shopping is compressed between 36th and 40th Streets. "It's a tough time," said Mr.

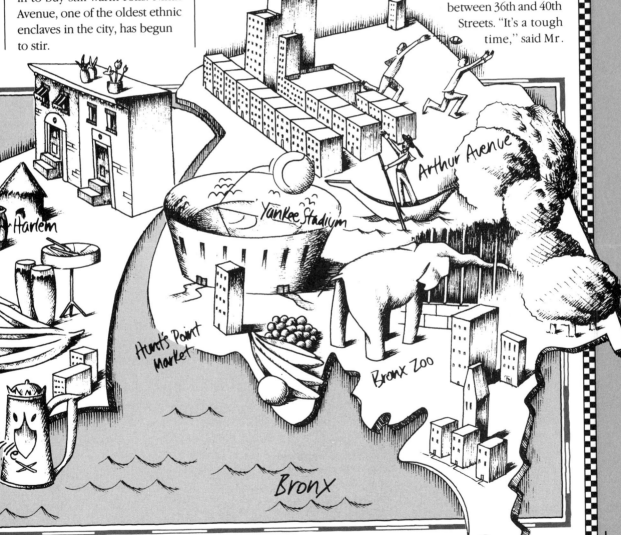

Arthur Avenue, The Bronx

The Belmont neighborhood of the Bronx, a handkerchief-size Italian enclave, is at its best on Saturday mornings when neighborhood alumni who have moved to other sections of the city return, like homing pigeons, to shop for comestibles.

ARTHUR AVENUE RETAIL MARKET: 2344 Arthur Avenue; (718) 764-2800; no mail order. A rambling covered market that is open Monday through Saturday from 8 A.M. to 5 P.M. It has stalls with high-quality cheese and vegetables (the Marchese family stall sells some of the best olive oil in the city) and, with its small-town atmosphere, is a pleasure to shop.

BORGATTIS RAVIOLI & NOODLE COMPANY: 632 East 187th; (718) 367-3799. This is an old-time shop that makes old-time, delicious, handmade pasta.

THE PASTA FACTORY: 686 East 187th Street; (718) 842-6066. This store makes delicate pastas and a wonderful fresh ricotta ravioli.

TERRANOVA BAKERY: 691 East 187th Street; (718) 367-1237. Turns out a terrific olive bread.

MADONIA BAKERY: 238 Arthur Avenue; (718) 295-5573. Makes simple cookies and stout semolina bread.

CALANDRA CHEESE SHOP: 2314 Arthur Avenue; (718) 365-7572. Stocks a respectable line of imported cheeses.

TINO'S SALUMERIA: 609 East 187th Street; (718) 733-9879; no mail order. Stocks difficult-to-find sausages and bacons.

CALABRIA PORK STORE: 2338 Arthur Avenue; (718) 367-5145. Here you'll find heavy sausages and obscure cuts of meat.

TIM'S MEAT MARKET: 600 East 187th Street; (718) 733-3637. This is the place to go for baby lamb and goat.

Dell'Orto, noting the scheduled razing of a nearby block of tenements and the high-rise (and meaning high-rent also) apartment complex that has been proposed for the site.

But until that development materializes, these four blocks of Ninth Avenue offer food of an astounding ethnic diversity.

Manganaro's sells a wide range of Italian staples, and **Giovanni Esposito and Sons Pork Shop** (500 Ninth Avenue at the corner of 38th) has delicious Italian parsley sausage. At the **Ninth Avenue Cheese**

At Manganaro's

Madonia Bakery on Arthur Avenue

Along Arthur A[venue]

Arthur Avenue

Market (525 Ninth Avenue between 39th and 40th), **Karen and Pando Andonopulo** sell more than 300 kinds of cheeses, in addition to dried fruits, olives, Russian sausage and yogurt, Iranian caviar, and Turkish groceries. **Central Fish Company** (527 Ninth Avenue between 39th and 49th), a wholesale and retail store, stocks species to ease the worst case of homesickness, whether the longing is for Greece or Italy or Southeast Asia. With its bins of dried spices and beans and tubs of fresh feta, **International Groceries and Meat Market** (529 Ninth Avenue between 39th and 40th) is an important Greek grocery. And the **West African Grocery** (535 Ninth Avenue, between 39th and 40th) in the shadow of the Port Authority Bus Terminal, offers white corn, pigeon beans, ground yams, palm wine, and Nigerian beer.

By 7 A.M., the ethnic enclaves on the fringes of Manhattan, Brooklyn, and Queens are also awakening. In tiny shops on Canal Street, bundles of long green beans, fresh lemongrass, hairy melons, bok choy, rice stalks, and duck eggs covered in ash are arranged for display. Swimming in cloudy aquariums, carp and black bass turn a lazy eye to the tourists and Chinese housewives who drag their wire carts along the crowded sidewalk.

The area around Mott, Pell, and Doyers is like an alley in Hong Kong, offering such treasures as fresh water chestnuts, taro root, or snow pea shoots. **Kam-Man Food Products** (200 Canal Street, between Mott and Mulberry) is an excellent overall market, as is **Kam Kuo,** (7 Mott,

A Few Essential Ingredients in Italian Cooking

BALSAMIC VINEGAR: Aged vinegar from Modena, Italy

BISCOTTI: crisp cookies, often with nuts, that are usually dunked in espresso or dessert wine

CHEESES:
  FONTINA: a semi-soft cheese used in cooking and desserts

  GORGONZOLA: a blue-veined cheese, pungent, but not as salty as blue cheese

  MASCARPONE: a thick cheese, like clotted cream, used mostly in desserts

  PARMESAN: a hard, gratable cow's milk cheese, used most as a topping

  PROVOLONE: a spicy, firm cheese, a deli sandwich favorite

  RICOTTA: creamy and cottage cheese-like

  ROMANO: sheep's milk cheese, sharper in flavor than Parmesan

FOCACCIA: flat, thin, chewy bread

MEATS:
  MORTADELLA: finely ground cuts of pork flavored with anise and garlic, salami-shaped

PANCETTA: cured pork, the same cut as bacon, but it is not smoked

PROSCIUTTO: cured salted ham

SOPRESSATA: (hot or sweet) coarse pork sausage flavored with black peppercorns

PORCINI: Italian mushrooms with a meaty texture, they have tan to dark brown caps, thick stems

near Chatham Square) where English-speaking clerks offer a huge selection of Chinese produce, dried goods, and groceries, as well as the pots to cook them in. Other interesting shops include **Tai Pei** (53 Mott Street, between Canal and Bayard) for Chinese alcohol and the **Han May Company** (69 Mulberry Street at Bayard) for meat. The **Chinese American Trading Company** (91 Mulberry Street, between Canal and Bayard) stocks an array of dried mushrooms, soy sauces, and

Chinese canned goods.

Along Mulberry Street, the smell of ginger gives way to that of garlic as Chinatown ends and Little Italy begins. For the most part, food stores have been eclipsed by tourist restaurants here, but a few fine shops remain. **Alleva Dairy** (188 Grand Street at Mulberry) continues to sell fresh and smoked ricotta, along with a huge selection of other fresh and aged cheeses. **Milan Home Wine and Beers** (57 Spring Street, between Lafayette and Mulberry) offers spices and home-brewing equipment. The **Italian Food Center** (186 Grand at Mulberry) stocks pasta, canned goods, sausages, and oils.

Farther north, **Faicco's Pork Store** specializes in pork braciola. And although glitzy pasta shops have covered New York City like locusts, not one of them turns out a more tender fresh ravioli than **Raffetto's** (144 West Houston Street, between Mac-Dougal and Sullivan).

The East Village (a real estate term that promises clean supermarkets filled with tightly wrapped,

Kam Man in Chinatown

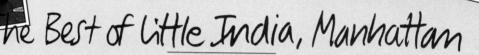

K. Kalustyan in Little India

The Best of Little India, Manhattan

K. KALUSTYAN: 123 Lexington Avenue, between 28th and 29th Streets; (212) 683-8458; mail orders accepted. This widely stocked store is supplemented by a take-out counter and tempting trays of freshly made hummus, baba ganoush, marinated olives, goat's milk yogurt, and falafel in addition to a wide variety of Indian comestibles. On the shelves you'll find bulgur, whole wheat, jasmine rice, dried seeds and fruits, fresh pita, and Afghan flat bread. The staff is glad to offer you a taste of a crisp falafel ball dipped in cumin-scented tahini sauce, or advise how to make the most of creamy goat's milk yogurt.

SPICE AND SWEET MAHAL: 135 Lexington Avenue at 29th Street; (212) 683-0900; mail orders accepted. Spice and Sweet Mahal is a small store full

from floor to ceiling with everything the name promises: from sugary and savory treats like *punjabi wadian,* and cooked cheese *chamcham* to small fiery peppers and pungent spice blends including the traditional garam masala. Brightly packaged fruit syrups, teas, pickles, and chutneys call for your attention while the smells of dals, jasmine, and fresh produce including curry leaves, okra, and lychees mingle.

LITTLE INDIA STORE: 128 East 28th Street, between Lexington and Park Avenues; (212) 683-1691; mail order (800) 244-4634. The largest of the neighborhood's Indian stores, Little India supplies Indian movies on video, pots, pans, and utensils, as well as a great variety of packaged goods and fresh fruits and vegetables. This is a good stop.

A Few Essential Ingredients in Indian Cooking

AMCHOOR: seasoning made of dried slices or powder of unripe mangos

ASAFETIDA: brown resin substance, with truffle-like flavor

BASMATI RICE: long-grain rice

CHAPATI FLOUR: finely ground whole wheat flour

CORIANDER, FRESH/CILANTRO/CHINESE PARSLEY: an herb resembling parsley, but with lighter green leaves. It is also often used in Mexican cooking.

CORIANDER, DRIED: dried seeds of the coriander plant. Their flavor is deeper than fresh coriander.

CURRY LEAVES: available fresh or dried, they look like and are used like bay leaves

DALS: dried split peas and beans

FENNEL: a spice with an intense anise flavor, available in seed or powder

FENUGREEK: a slightly bitter spice often used as a digestive aid

GARAM MASALA: a mixture of different spices, but most commonly combining cloves, cinnamon, cardamom, cumin, and peppercorns

GHEE: clarified butter (NOTE: the makers of high quality ghee have completely removed all of the butter's milk solids. Therefore, it is common, and perfectly acceptable, to store ghee at room temperature.)

GRAM FLOUR/BESAN: chick-pea flour

LYCHEE: small fruit with a brownish rose-colored shell; fruits smell and taste flowery

MUSTARD SEEDS: black or yellow seeds used in pickling, as digestives, and seasonings. Yellow seeds are milder and less bitter than black.

NIGELLA: small black seeds used in pickling and bread baking

PANCHPHORAN: Bengali spice mixture of cumin seeds, fennel seeds, nigella seeds, fenugreek seeds, and radhuni

RADHUNI: tiny aromatic seeds; an adequate substitute is black mustard seeds

SAFFRON: intense yellow spice collected from crocus stigmas

TAMARIND: fruit encased in bean-like pod

TURMERIC: bright yellow spice powder

---

mass-produced groceries) is encroaching on the Lower East Side. But family-run specialty stores that are crowded with bins of unpacked foods still open early in the morning. (For a listing, see the appetizer chapter, pages 2 to 43.)

Today, some of the most authentic ethnic strongholds are outside of Manhattan. In Brooklyn, waves of Russian émigrés have been revitalizing the food-shopping center under the elevated subway on Brighton Beach Avenue. On Sundays, every Russian within a hundred-mile radius seems to be packed into **M & I International** (249 Brighton Beach Avenue), known as the Zabar's of Brighton Beach. And there are plenty of other seductive shops: **Stolichny Deli** (239 Brighton Beach Avenue) and **Fish Town Appetizing and Deli** (414 Brighton Beach Avenue) both sell whitefish and caviar; **Melrose Take Home Foods** (268 Brighton Beach Avenue) has sweet-potato

M & I International on Brighton Beach

kugel and homemade gefilte fish; **Israel's Take Home Foods** (409 Brighton Beach Avenue) has delicious pierogi, and outside the **Continental Grocery** (303 Brighton Beach Avenue), a young woman sells cabbage-filled knishes.

On Brooklyn's Atlantic Avenue, Middle Eastern groceries abound. The gentrification of Cobble Hill and Brooklyn Heights may have spurred renovations at the **Sahadi Importing Company** (187-189 Atlantic Avenue), but it didn't change the quality of the store's olives, fresh dates, cracked wheat, or spices. **The Oriental Pastry and Grocery Company** (170-172 Atlantic Avenue) offers lamb sausage as well as *zata* (pita with spices and olive oil), along with a dozen types of olives and six different kinds of preserved lemons. **Damascus Bakery** (195 Atlantic Avenue) specializes in pita bread; **El-**

Asmar International Delights (197 Atlantic Avenue) is the place for feta cheese.

In the West Indian and Caribbean neighborhood of Crown Heights, the narrow sidewalks are crowded with women wrapped in vivid African dresses, and the early-morning air is dense with Rastafarian incense and the aroma of frying meat patties. **Ultrafine Meats** (529 Nostrand Avenue) may be the most exotic butcher in New York, regularly offering fresh goat, oxtail, hog's head, and smoked turkey, in addition to more ordinary fare. **El Caribe Market** (849 Nostrand Avenue) stocks a wide selection of island vegetables.

Brooklyn is not without its Italian strongholds. Along the trim streets of Carroll Gardens, you can still find deep-fried chickpea balls and rice balls, fresh biscotti (at **Caputo's,** 329 Court Street), and potato pizza (at

Monte Leone's, 355 Court Street). Most importantly, the neighborhood is home to the premier branch of **G. Esposito Jersey Pork Store** (357 Court Street), which offers cuts of meat from Manhattan's meat district as well as sausage, prosciutto balls, and fresh pasta. (For shops in Bensonhurst, see the listing below.)

When the early morning light dances across the Aegean-blue facades of the shops along 30th Avenue in Astoria, Queens, baklava and spinach pies are already cooling on bakery counters. Astoria has been called the third-largest Greek city (after Athens and Salonika) in the world. It is a place where bouzouki music plays against the rumble of trains on the El, where dill and oregano, mint and sage grow in window boxes. At **Titan Foods** (25-50 31st Street), the A & P of Astoria, lines of people

Bensonhurst, Brooklyn

TRUNZO BROTHERS, INC.: 6802 18th Avenue, Brooklyn; (718) 331-2111; no mail order. A mecca for Italian food, Trunzo Brothers is a large store with fresh meats, sausages, cheeses, canned goods, and fresh and frozen pastas.

PICCOLO MONDELLO: 6824 18th Avenue, Brooklyn; (718) 236-3930; no mail order. A step inside this Pescheria Italiana is a step into the heart of the Italian community who shop here for squid, and gossip among fresh fish and sawdust-strewn floors.

ALBA: 7001 18th Avenue, Brooklyn; (718) 232-2122; no mail order. This Italian pastry shop has provided four generations of "community service." It's a neighborhood hangout with a pot of free espresso to welcome you, and a large selection of fresh pastries and sorbets.

QUEEN ANN RAVIOLI: 7207 18th Street, Brooklyn; (718) 256-1061. Queen Ann offers a vast selection of fresh and dried pastas and canned goods.

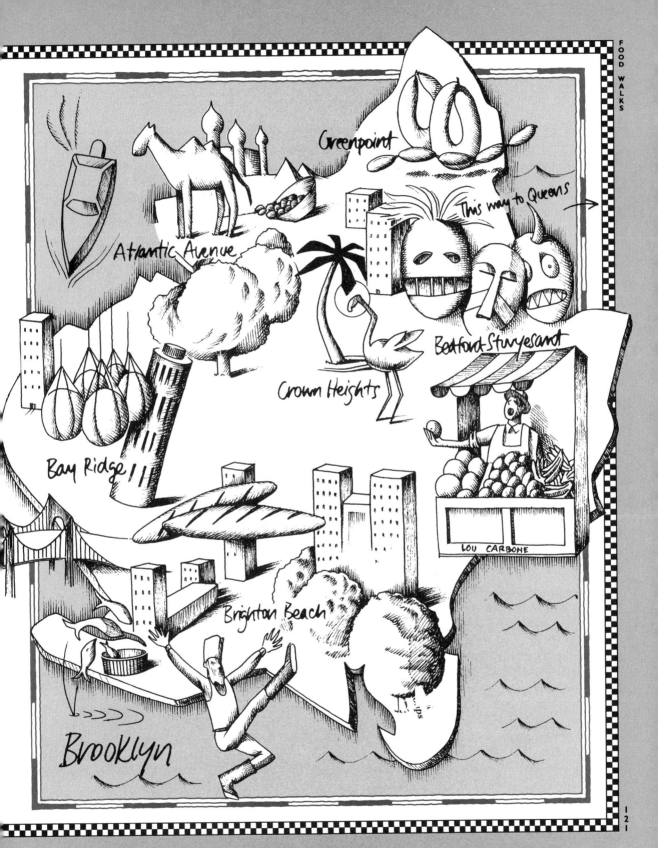

Greenpoint

This way to Queens →

Atlantic Avenue

Bedford-Stuyvesant

Crown Heights

Bay Ridge

LOU CARBONE

Brighton Beach

Brooklyn

Bay Ridge, Brooklyn

Bay Ridge was flooded with Scandinavians when the shipping industry moved to Brooklyn. Fifth Avenue has a Scandinavian enclave in the mostly Italian neighborhood of Bay Ridge, the beautiful area near the Verrazano Narrows bridge.

FREDRICKSEN AND JOHANNSEN: 7719 Fifth Avenue, Brooklyn; (718) 745-5980; mail orders accepted. Here you'll find high-quality Scandinavian sausages, condiments, smoked fish, cheese, crackers, jams, breads, candy, and baking equipment.

LESKE'S DANISH BAKERY: 7612 Fifth Avenue, Brooklyn; (718) 680-2323. You won't be able to call another pastry a Danish ever again after you've let one of Leske's real cheese and fruit pastries melt in your mouth. Leske's also makes great coffee and sponge cakes, breads, and cookies.

PETZINGER'S DELI: 7802 Fifth Avenue, Brooklyn; (718) 833-8883. A small deli with canned goods, syrups, meats.

PIERROT ICE CREAM AND DESSERT: 75-15 Third Avenue, Brooklyn; (718) 748-5840. This quaint, bakery with a few small tables is a perfect spot for breakfast or a snack. When there, enjoy delicious pastries, and homemade sorbets in exotic flavors.

Greenpoint

debate the qualities of the store's nine different kinds of feta, and they can buy sheep's milk yogurt, olive oil, and canned and preserved Greek groceries. **Mediterranean Foods** (33-20 30th Avenue) also stocks an extensive array of Greek groceries. And the **Ocean Number 11 Fish Market** (35-08 30th Avenue) stocks the fresh octopus and thumb-size squid that Greeks dote on.

Flushing is New York's second Chinatown, where prices are lower than in Manhattan, and Korean, Japanese, and Southeast Asian goods are often piled in profusion among the goods from mainland China. The shelves of **Daido/Main Street Foods** (137-80 Northern Boulevard) are an amazing panoply.

Like Manhattan's Ninth Avenue, Jackson Heights has a great variety of storefront groceries. The aroma of Indian spices surrounds **Patel Brothers** (37-40 74th Street), while the clean perfume of fresh lemongrass emanates from the **Thai Grocery** (37-60 90th Street), and the sweet molasses smell of Latin American pastries envelops **Las Americas** (93-09 37th Avenue).

By 8 A.M., Manhattan has begun to stir. Gray suits and briefcases scurry along the sidewalks toward midtown offices, the farmers in greenmarkets around the city are finishing setting up their stalls, and the third link in the New York food chain—the city's specialty stores and carriage-trade grocers—are unfurling their tidy awnings. Unlike the wholesalers, but, indeed, like the farmers, the small, ethnic providers count on presentation and service as much as they do on quality.

Thai Grocery in Queens

Specialty emporiums—like **Zabar's** (2245 Broadway at 80th Street) for smoked fish, cheese, condiments, and coffee, **Fairway** (2127 Broadway between 74th and 75th) for cheese and produce, **Murray's Sturgeon Shop** (2429 Broadway between 89th and 90th) for smoked fish, **Todaro Brothers** (555 Second Avenue) for Italian groceries, and **Jefferson Market** (455 Avenue of the Americas at 10th) for exquisite personal service and general groceries—haven't moved very far from the days when they had their saw-dust on their floors. Each store is a loud circus where assertive shopping is the key.

But the rising generation of carriage-trade stores sometimes seems to be moving away from the idea of groceries as comestibles and toward the notion of food as art. At the ever-enlarging **Balducci's** (424 Avenue of the Americas at 9th) for instance, the huge and arcane selection of produce is always impeccably polished. At **Dean & DeLuca** (560 Broadway at Prince) every sprig of mountain-grown wild thyme, every scallop with its bright orange roe intact, every bottle of green olive oil has been selected for its perfection. And, even if buying a basket of these groceries can run the price of a piece of museum-quality art, it's impossible not to be grateful.

Stores such as Balducci's and Dean & DeLuca have been designed to soothe the ever-escalating concerns of food shoppers.

Greenpoint, Brooklyn

Greenpoint is often called Little Poland, and as soon as you get off the subway you'll understand why: You hear Polish on the streets, read it on the store signs, and taste it in the stores. The Polish Way is to cook everything until it's falling off the bone or turning to mush. So although Polish restaurants, or obidays, offer mounds of food for little money, you might want to consider choosing from the many inexpensive ingredients and taking them home to cook.

JASLOWICZANKA BAKERY: 163 Nassau Avenue, Brooklyn; (718) 389-0263. This small bakery prepares fresh Polish sweets and bread. Typical offerings include custardy cakes topped with glazed apples, plums, or chocolate, and bright-colored gelatin squares.

STEVE'S MEAT MARKET: 104 Nassau Avenue, Brooklyn; (718) 383-1780. Their awning brags "best kiska/kielbasa in the U.S." The store is small but stuffed with meat products. You can try the dried spicy, jerky-like sausage or the fresh, soft sausage, or the varieties of coiled kielbasa. They also have fresh pierogis.

W. NASSAU MEAT MARKET: 915 Manhattan Avenue, Brooklyn; (718) 389-6149. This is one of the best markets in Greenpoint; you can tell by the smell of the place—spicy and savory. Freshly baked Silver Bell Lithuanian rye is piled in the window; inside there are imported gooseberries, Scandinavian candies and cookies, bottled fruit syrups, and German chocolates, as well.

Bedford-Stuyvesant, Brooklyn

According to Lou Singer (page 3), Bed-Stuy has the highest percentage of black-owned homes in the world. Fulton Avenue is the place if you're hankering for West Indian coconut bread or gospel records or yams or fresh aloe or anything else Caribbean or African.

THE BREAD BASKET: 1309 Fulton Avenue, Brooklyn; (718) 789-9296. Offered here, among typical bakery fare, is the devastatingly delicious coconut bread.

NEW KIM'S FRUIT AND VEGETABLE MARKET: 1228 Fulton Avenue, Brooklyn; (718) 636-6192. Featured are fresh aloe, six kinds of yams, raw sugar, fresh fish, many canned goods and spices.

MOONS FRUIT AND VEGETABLES: 1307 Fulton Avenue, Brooklyn; (718) 638-1773. They carry many spices, including a variety of curries; mango achar, a kind of chutney; Jamaican Scotch bonnet peppers, among the world's fiercest; and many sparkling bunches of greens.

The gleaming glass cases promise precious ingredients that have been protected from dirty hands and tainted environments. The marble counters don't give up splinters or salmonella. Every ingredient carries a pedigree of its origin, picking time, shipping time, and possible use in the kitchen.

The flavors—of wild strawberries at Dean & DeLuca, caviar at Caviarteria, cheese at Cheese of All Nations, chocolate at Teuscher—are often astounding. And along with these well-groomed groceries, the food products that were bought before dawn on the fringes of New York reach another apogee in dishes prepared to be sold like groceries in carry-out food stores.

Though the city's hundreds of carry-out gourmet food stores are generally located far from the rough edges of the city, their pristine, white tile floors are not bedrock. They are stages supported by an economy that began hundreds of years ago.

"What's the gourmet going to be without me?" asked a rubber-booted lumper at the Fulton Fish Market one recent dawn. Like the previous generations of men who pushed dollies loaded with seafood, he had stopped to warm his hands over a fire built in a metal trash drum. He was scowling.

French Culinary Institute

Recipes from Balducci's

Dean & DeLuca

Residents of a near-by co-op, it seems, had called the fire department to complain.

There are 95 ethnic neighborhoods in New York City, 35 of them in Brooklyn, and these are simply the shopping walks I like the best.

To locate the best sources for specific ingredients, check the shoppers guides in the pertinent chapters.

For more complete listings of the city's ethnic shopping spots, the best books I know of are: *Zagat Survey of Food Sources,*

Passport's Guide to Ethnic New York by Mark Leeds, *A Cook's Guide to New York, The New York Ethnic Food Market Guide and Cookbook* by Velma Liacouras Chantiles, and *New York Eats* by Ed Levine.

New York Cooking Schools

What to do with all the wonderful ingredients that New York offers? Consider taking a class at one of the city's notable cooking schools. A listing of some of the better schools follows.

PROFESSIONAL

THE FRENCH CULINARY INSTITUTE: 462 Broadway, New York, NY 10013; (212) 219-8890.

NEW YORK FOOD AND HOTEL MANAGEMENT SCHOOL: 154 West 14th Street, New York, NY 10011; (212) 675-6655.

NEW YORK RESTAURANT SCHOOL: 27 West 34th Street, New York, NY 10001; (212) 947-7097.

PROFESSIONAL AND AVOCATIONAL

A LA BONNE COCOTTE (LYDIE MARSHALL): 23 Eighth Avenue, New York, NY 10014; (212) 675-7736.

THE CHOCOLATE GALLERY: 34 West 22nd Street, New York, NY 10010; (212) 675-2253.

THE CULINARY INSTITUTE OF AMERICA (CIA): North Road, P.O. Box 53, Hyde Park, NY 12538; (914) 452-9430. (Not really New York City, but close enough.)

CULINARY ARTS AT THE NEW SCHOOL: 100 Greenwich Avenue, New York, NY 10011; (212) 255-4141.

THE NATURAL GOURMET COOKERY SCHOOL: 48 West 21st Street, 2nd Floor, New York, NY 10010; (212) 645-5170.

PETER KUMP'S NEW YORK COOKING SCHOOL: 307 East 92nd Street, New York, NY 10128; (212) 410-4601.

AVOCATIONAL

CAROL'S CUISINE, INC.: 1571 Richmond Road, Staten Island, NY 10304; (718) 979-5600.

THE CHINA INSTITUTE: 125 East 65th Street, New York, NY; (212) 744-8181.

CLUB CUISINE: 244 Madison Avenue, New York, NY 10016; (212) 286-0214.

DE GUSTIBUS AT MACY'S: 343 East 74st Street, Suite 9G, New York, NY 10021; (212) 439-1714.

GIULIANO BUGIALLI'S COOKING SCHOOL IN FLORENCE: 53 Wooster Street, New York, NY 10013; (212) 334-6430.

RICHARD GRAUSMAN: 155 West 68th Street, New York, NY 10023; (212) 873-2434.

The Greening of New York

*BEEFSTAKE TOMATOES
1.00 lb.*

THE GREENING OF
New York

At 7 A.M. on Saturday morning you can still hear the caw-caw of crows above the traffic of East 14th Street. You can hear pigeons ohh-coo over crusts of bread on the sidewalk at Union Square. Pickup trucks putter into the north end of the square.

Farmers pull out folding tables, the kind you see at church suppers, and set them up in front of their trucks. They hang scales. They spill their harvest. The sun rises like an iridescent marigold beyond the east end of the square.

"When I moved to New York, we never had anything like this," whispers Edna Lewis. A stately woman with a grandma-white bun of hair, Lewis is a cookbook author (*The Edna Lewis Cookbook* and *In Pursuit of Flavor*) and the chef of Gage & Tollner in Brooklyn. She is also the doyenne of the Union Square Greenmarket.

On a late summer Saturday morning, Edna Lewis carefully chooses her greens (inset) and Christopher Tomford sells the most flavorful tomatoes (left), at the Union Square Greenmarket.

La Marqueta at 111th Street in East Harlem, is the oldest market in the city.

NOT EVERYTHING NEEDS SOIL TO FLOWER

Over 50 years of New York living have taught the Virginia-born woman that life is a perennial, one that's timed by decades rather than seasons. The market at Union Square is a perfect example. To Lewis, it is a plot of Manhattan that took 50 years to flower.

"I came to New York when Orson Welles gave that big scare. People were running and screaming that the world was going to end. . . ." Lewis gives a ladylike shake of the head. "I couldn't find a market like this. I waited for food packages from home."

Her gait is swaying and careful, as if the asphalt underfoot were the carefully tended furrows of a family garden. But the Greenmarket is inescapably New York.

Lewis continues to whisper. She bends over pots of chives, parsley, and rosemary. She pauses in front of a profusion of goldenrod and bittersweet, dahlias, cosmos, and bunches of epazote, the Mexican mint. "We had to take epazote for worms when we were kids," she says. "It was horrible."

That was back in Freetown, Virginia, a village founded by her grandfather after Emancipation. Growing up on a farm there, Lewis learned to wait—for wild greens to sprout, berries to ripen, and potatoes to swell underfoot. She decided, among other things, that "a vegetable grown in an open field never tastes as good as one grown in a small garden."

Her view was at odds with the pre-war Manhattan she moved to. Back when Bloomingdale's had a wooden floor, she recalls, life was limited to the cultivated: "All we had were the supermarkets."

In her early years in the city, Lewis was a prop stylist for fashion magazines. "Marilyn Monroe was a model for one cover," she recalls. "At that time I shopped the Italian greengrocers on 59th between Second and Third."

CHEF TO THE STARS

After the war, Lewis became chef at the eccentric Cafe Nicholson. "Everybody came. Rita Hayworth, Tennessee Williams. Howard Hughes gave us a check one day, so we knew who he was. . . ."

Her voice fades. Names embarrass as well as impress. She switches to groceries: "At that time, the shopping was best on

Ninth Avenue." In the '70s, she found flavorful produce at La Marqueta uptown. In the late '70s, the Greenmarket opened at Union Square.

"There was something familiar about it right away," says Lewis. At the square the pigeons' coos have been eclipsed by the click-click-click of 10-speed bicycles and the jingle of dog tags. Lewis has reached Chip Kent's fruit stand. Speaking softly and slowly, she names the fruits he grows: "white peaches, mulberries, quince, gooseberries, opalescent apple. . . ."

Gently, as a crowd of Saturday shoppers surge by her, she picks up an antique variety of pear. She marvels at the patience of the fruit. "You can't find these old-fashioned varieties in supermarkets. It's amazing how they held out until this time came. . . ."

Edna Lewis' GREENS

Edna Lewis observes that "Greens were one of the most important vegetables in the South. They were considered to have great nutritional value. We hunted the lowland during the winter for wild watercress and early spring for wild mustard, shoots of poke plants, and such greens as lamb's quarters or pigweed; then we'd harvest the cultivated greens such as rape, turnip greens, mustard, and wild purslane. All of these greens were cooked with pork as a seasoning.

"We used cured pork or a cut of pork known as streak of lean. I prefer cured or smoked pork, whichever is on hand, for seasoning. Many of the wild greens have been wiped out because of farmers using weed killers; many of these greens are weeds. However, you can still find many of the wild greens at the greenmarkets from farmers who do not use chemicals. If you do not see the greens, ask—the farmers will happily bring them in for you."

2 pounds cured pork shoulder or slab bacon
3 pounds turnip greens or mixed mustard, poke, collards, and lamb's quarters or pigweed, stems removed, well rinsed

Greenmarkets provide fresh-produce-starved New Yorkers with the real McCoy.

1. In a heavy pot over low heat, simmer the pork in 3 quarts cold water for 1 hour. Remove and discard the pork and skim the broth. This stock can be prepared 1 day ahead of time and refrigerated until needed.

2. In a nonreactive large pot, warm the broth. Add the greens, cover the pot, and simmer for 20 minutes. Check a few leaves to see if they are tender: Young greens may be nice and soft after 30 minutes; older ones can require up to 2 hours of simmering. When the greens are soft, taste. Add salt if needed.

3. Serve the greens hot with relish or fresh sliced onions and vinegar.

Serves 8

NEW YORK'S GREENMARKETS

The greenmarkets provide some of the best produce shopping in the city. Following is a list of those markets, including their approximate dates of operation. Most markets open around 7:30 A.M. and disband by noon; some stay open through the afternoon. Locations and times change year to year so for further information, telephone the Council on the Environment of New York (212) 566-0990.

Manhattan/Bronx

CITY HALL (Park Row): Tuesdays and Fridays; year round

WORLD TRADE CENTER (Church and Fulton Streets): Tuesdays and Thursdays; June–December

FEDERAL PLAZA (Broadway and Thomas Streets): Fridays; year round

WASHINGTON MARKET PLAZA (Greenwich and Reade Streets): Wednesdays and Saturdays; June–November

ST. MARK'S CHURCH (10th Street and Second Avenue): Tuesdays; June–November

WEST VILLAGE (Gansevoort and Hudson Streets): Saturdays; June–November

UNION SQUARE (17th Street and Broadway): Wednesdays, Fridays, and Saturdays; year round

ROOSEVELT ISLAND (Bridge Plaza): Saturdays; year round

SHEFFIELD PLAZA (57th Street and Ninth Avenue): Wednesdays and Saturdays; year round

IS 44 (77th Street and Columbus Avenue): Sundays; year round

WEST 102ND STREET (102nd Street and Amsterdam): Fridays; June–November

WEST 125TH STREET (Adam Clayton Powell Boulevard): Tuesdays; July–November

WEST 175TH STREET (Broadway): Thursdays; June–December

IS 52 INWOOD (Broadway and Cummings Street): Saturdays; July–November

POE PARK (Grand Concourse and East 192nd Street): Tuesdays; June–November

Brooklyn

CADMAN PLAZA WEST (Montague Street): Tuesdays and Saturdays; year round

GRAND ARMY PLAZA: Saturdays; July–November

ALBEE SQUARE (Fulton Street and Dekalb Avenue): Wednesdays; July–November

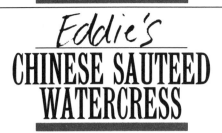

Eddie's
CHINESE SAUTEED
WATERCRESS

This standby of Chinese restaurants is simple to make at home and is a satisfying side dish with fish or roasted meat.

2 tablespoons vegetable oil
1 to 2 cloves garlic, finely minced
2 bunches watercress, well rinsed and drained
½ teaspoon salt, plus more to taste
1 tablespoon Chinese rice wine
(preferably Shao Hsing) or dry sherry

1. Warm a large wok or skillet over high heat until it smokes. Add the oil and garlic and stir for 3 seconds. Add the watercress and salt and stir-fry for 5 seconds. Add the wine and stir constantly until the watercress wilts, about 20 seconds. Remove from the heat.

2. Using a wooden spoon or spatula, quickly gather the watercress together on one side of the wok. Press the watercress with the back of a spoon, forcing as much liquid as possible out of the leaves. Remove the watercress and set aside.

3. Return the wok with the liquid to high heat. When the liquid boils, dip in the cooked and drained watercress for 30 seconds, as if blanching. This will turn the watercress bright green. Drain immediately in a colander. Serve immediately, with additional salt to taste.

Serves 4 to 6

Because only local produce is sold at the Greenmarkets, what's in season is what's for sale.

Suki's
KOREAN SPINACH

Suki Chon, who owns a dry cleaning store on Manhattan's West Side, grew up in South Korea, where this spinach dish was served cold as a condiment with most meals. If the spinach leaves are cooked until tender but not limp and are chilled immediately, this dish will keep, well covered in the refrigerator, for up to 5 days. The spinach can be served warm with rice or stir-fried tofu, shrimp, or chicken to make a meal.

1 tablespoon safflower oil
1 tablespoon Oriental sesame oil
2 pounds young, tender spinach leaves, well
    rinsed and dried
1 teaspoon rice wine vinegar
½ teaspoon fresh lemon juice
1 teaspoon light soy sauce
1 teaspoon salt
¼ teaspoon freshly ground white pepper

1. Warm the safflower and sesame oils in a wok or large skillet over medium-high heat. Add the spinach in batches and toss until wilted. Add more spinach as it fits into the wok. When all the spinach has been added, sprinkle on the vinegar, lemon juice, and soy sauce and continue stir-frying for 1 minute. Remove from the heat.

2. Using a wooden spoon or spatula, gather the greens to one side of the pan. Press to remove as much moisture as possible. Remove the spinach and set aside.

3. Return the wok with the liquid to high heat. Boil until the volume of liquid is reduced by half, about 3 minutes. Add the spinach and cook for a quick 30 seconds; drain immediately. Season with the salt and white pepper to taste. Serve warm or chilled.

Serves 4 as an appetizer, or 2 as a side dish

Longchamps'
CREAMED SPINACH

The original Longchamps, a legendary chain of French restaurants, opened in 1920 on upper Madison Avenue, and by 1954, when *The Longchamps Cookbook* by Max Winkler was published, it had grown into a string of 10 restaurants with locations throughout New York as well as in Philadelphia and Washington, D.C. Vintage New York guidebooks are in accord about one aspect of the restaurants' repertoire: the vegetables.

" 'Fresh' has but one meaning for this fastidious restauranteur—it's a clean-cut description of vegetables that are so recently removed from the ground that they will arrive upon your plate still damp from the soil," writes George Ross in *Tips on Tables.*

In his book *Dining, Wining and Dancing in New York,* Scudder Middleton offers a simple explanation for the restaurant's prowess with produce. Longchamps, he wrote, is "owned and operated by Henry and Allen Lustig who were at one time—and may still be—wholesale dealers in vegetables."

This creamed spinach dish epitomizes Longchamps, and this recipe was passed on from Louis McAlister, a cook who moved from Longchamps to the "21" Club in the 1940s.

2 pounds fresh spinach, well rinsed
1½ teaspoons salt
1 cup heavy (whipping) cream
2 tablespoons unsalted butter
½ teaspoon freshly ground pepper
⅛ teaspoon ground nutmeg

1. Remove the spinach stems and ribs. Place 2 cups water in a nonreactive large pot over high heat. Add 1 teaspoon of the salt and bring to a boil. Add the spinach, cover, and steam until the leaves are wilted, 3 minutes. Drain the spinach, cool completely under cold water, and gently squeeze out the excess moisture.

2. Place half of the spinach in a blender. Add 1 tablespoon of the heavy cream and purée. Repeat with the remaining spinach and 1 tablespoon more cream.

3. In a nonreactive large skillet, melt the but- ter over medium heat. Add the spinach, the remaining ½ teaspoon salt, the pepper, and nutmeg and stir well. Cook, stirring and beating in the remaining cream, tablespoon by tablespoon, until the spinach is thick, about 5 minutes. Adjust the seasoning with more salt and pepper to taste. Serve immediately.

Serves 4

THE SAVVY SHOPPER

PRODUCE PARADISE

Most residential neighborhoods have at least one "Korean-on-the-corner" jam-packed vegetable stand that sells everything from apples to zucchini. The Korean Produce Association estimates that there are now 3,500 Korean greengrocers in metropolitan New York. The association, which was formed in 1974, when Koreans supplanted Italians as kings of corner produce, says that the number of produce stands has tripled in the last 10 years. During that time, the standard inventory has grown as well—fresh herbs, pricey lettuces, wild mushrooms, and fragile berries are sold by many Korean vegetablemongers now. Still, some specialty items can be stalked only in some of the city's pricier produce boutiques. For variety and quality, these are some of the city's best choices:

BALDUCCI'S: 424 Sixth Avenue, between 9th and 10th Streets; (212) 673-2600)

COMMODITIES: 117 Hudson Street at North Moore Street; (212) 334-8330

DEAN & DELUCA: 560 Broadway at Prince Street; (212) 431-1691

FAIRWAY: 2127 Broadway, between 74th and 75th Streets; (212) 595-1888

GRACE'S MARKETPLACE: 1237 Third Avenue, between 71st and 72nd Streets; (212) 737-0600

PARADISE MARKET: 1100 Madison Avenue at 83rd Street; (212) 732-0049

A gorgeous abundance at Fairway.

Leona Singer's
SPINACH BALLS

Leona Singer, who lives in the Fort Greene section of Brooklyn, learned this recipe from her mother and she swears by it. "Every time I look at the recipe, I think it's too easy to be true, but this dish is delicious, and whenever I serve it, my friends ask for the recipe."

2 packages frozen chopped spinach, thawed and drained
2 cups plain Pepperidge Farm stuffing
1 onion, chopped
4 eggs, beaten
8 tablespoons (1 stick) unsalted butter, melted
½ cup freshly grated Parmesan cheese

1. Preheat the oven to 375°F.
2. Combine all the ingredients in a large bowl. Form the mixture into bite-size balls and place on a baking sheet. Bake until heated through, about 20 minutes. Serve either as an appetizer or side dish. (The spinach balls can be frozen on the baking sheet. Defrost for 20 minutes before baking as above.)
Makes about 36, serves 6

Fern's
BACON AND CABBAGE

Fern Mallis, who grew up in Brooklyn and is currently director of the Council of Fashion Designers of America, created this side dish from "found food" in her refrigerator. She serves

it with winter roasts, goose, or chicken. With good bread and dessert, it can make a meal.

1 head red cabbage, shredded
1 pound thick-sliced bacon, rind removed, bacon cut into 1½-inch chunks

1. In a steamer or large pot, steam the cabbage until slightly soft, 10 minutes. Remove from the heat.
2. In a large skillet, cook the bacon over medium heat until soft and light brown, but not crunchy. Remove the bacon from the skillet and keep covered. Add the cabbage to the skillet, cover, and cook until the cabbage is very soft and has absorbed the bacon flavor, 5 to 10 minutes. Add the bacon pieces and stir until heated through, 1 to 2 minutes.
Serves 4

Abyssinian Baptist Church's
SLOW-COOKED GREEN BEANS

Since it was built in Harlem in 1923, the Abyssinian Baptist Church (132 West 138th Street), the oldest black church in the city, has served Sunday dinner after the 11 A.M. service.

Regardless of how they got hungry, most parishioner's were (and still are) hungry for good home cooking and the spirit of a country supper that lingers at the church. Most Sundays about 250 people pay $4 to eat baked chicken, lamb or veal, old-fashioned stuffed fish, baked macaroni, and slow-cooked green beans.

The cooks change decade to decade at the church, but Martha Dunn Hatcher, whose husband, James L. Hatcher, is a deacon of the church, has spent Saturdays snapping ends from green beans for Sunday dinner for as long as she can remember. Kentucky Wonder or other long, thick green beans work best for the dish because they like the long cooking and can remain in a warm oven for several hours after cooking.

1½ pounds slab bacon, unsliced
8 cups cold water
3 pounds green beans, ends and strings removed
½ teaspoon salt (if necessary)
¼ teaspoon freshly ground black pepper

The Abyssinian Baptist Church.

1. Combine the bacon and cold water in a large heavy pot over medium heat. Bring to a boil, reduce the heat, and simmer for 1 hour.

2. Remove and discard the bacon. Skim the liquid. Add the green beans and simmer for 2 hours.

3. Taste and add the salt, if the bacon hasn't made the beans salty enough. Add the black pepper and serve.

Serves 8

New Amsterdam ASPARAGUS

Household manuals and "receipt" books from the pre-revolutionary era often described "asparagus with good Holland butter and grated nutmeg." About 20 years ago, the Netherlands Consulate General in New York printed instructions for "How to Eat Asparagus the Dutch Way":

"Neatly stack drained and piping hot, fresh asparagus on an oval, napkin-covered serving dish. Surround them with halved, hard boiled eggs (hot). Pass with salt, pepper and ground nutmeg and a creamy butter sauce.

"With a fork, mash a half egg on the dinner plate and, with seasoning and a helping of butter sauce, make a paste. Holding the fork in the right hand and an asparagus stalk in the left, dip the tip in the egg mixture; bring it to the mouth with the aid of the fork. Repeat this with the next section of the stalk. Leave the end of the stalk on the side of the plate, and continue with the next stalk. With some trial and error this can be done gracefully. According to Dutch etiquette, the use of a knife is taboo."

8 tablespoons (1 stick) unsalted butter, softened
¼ cup tepid water
4 eggs, hard-cooked and cooled
2 pounds asparagus, ends trimmed and stalks peeled
Salt and freshly ground black pepper
Freshly grated nutmeg

1. In a mixing bowl, beat the butter until creamy. Slowly add the water, drop by drop, beating as if making a mayonnaise. When the sauce becomes thick and creamy, set aside. Peel the eggs; set aside.

2. Use butcher's twine to tie the asparagus in a bundle. Bring 1 inch of water to a rapid boil in a tall pot. Stand the asparagus in the water, tips up, and cover the pot. Steam until tender, 2 to 5 minutes, depending on the size of the asparagus.

3. Place the asparagus on a serving platter, cut the twine, and discard. Halve the eggs and place around the asparagus. Serve with the butter sauce and salt, as well as a pepper mill and a nutmeg grater and follow the instructions above for a New Amsterdam rite of spring.

Serves 4

"... a girl with a dish on her head passes along the streets, crying 'Hot corn, hot corn.' In the fall of the year, this cry is abundantly heard from children whose business it is to gather cents, by distributing corn to those who are disposed to regale themselves with an ear. It is boiled in the husks while green, and, with the addition of a little salt, which the children carry with them, is very pleasant eating."

—*CRIES OF NEW YORK*, 1808–1814
SAMUEL WOODS

Greenmarket
LIMA AND EARLY CORN RAGOUT

Wednesdays and Fridays are chefs' days at the Union Square Market. In an effort to avoid tourists (and amateurs), the city's professionals converge at the market before 8 A.M. with blue paper cups of coffee from a nearby Greek coffee shop in hand and the first stirrings of a menu in mind.

After a few sips, they begin ruminating, talking to each other, free associating with the ingredients they see to create their restaurants' specials. Anyone can pick up good recipes, and this simple and irresistible dish is based on a conversation between Bernard Leroy (an itinerant French chef who specializes in organic cooking), Michael Romano (chef at Union Square Cafe), and a farmer from Windfall Farms.

The dish can be served as a first course (it makes a wonderful foil for slices of prosciutto or smoked fish) or as a side dish to meat or fish. If cooked lobster meat is added in the last five minutes of cooking, the ragout makes a marvelous dinner for two.

2 tablespoons unsalted butter
2 cups shelled fresh lima beans
2 cups fresh sweet corn kernels
¼ cup heavy (whipping) cream
½ teaspoon salt
¼ teaspoon freshly ground black pepper

1. Melt the butter in a heavy skillet over medium heat. Add the lima beans and corn, toss, and cook for 3 minutes. Stir in the heavy cream, salt, and pepper. Reduce the heat to low and simmer for 7 to 10 minutes, until the vegetables are tender.

2. Adjust the seasonings with additional salt and pepper to taste. Serve immediately.

Serves 4 as a first course or side dish, or 2 as a main course

Daisann's
CALLALOO

Serve as a side dish with rice or a starchy vegetable. Daisann McLane, a calypso dancer and cook who lives in Brooklyn, learned this recipe by watching her Trinidadian friends make it for a traditional Sunday feast. Sunday lunch was an event that lasted all day, and callaloo was often served as a side dish that the guests would eat with rice from pots on the stove.

Fresh cooked corn—an early New York street food (left).
Courtesy of The New York Public Library Picture Collection

Daisann McLane's love of island culture stretches from dance to food.

1 tablespoon vegetable oil
1 large onion, chopped
4 cloves garlic, crushed
1¼ to 1½ pounds spinach, well rinsed, stems trimmed, and chopped
1½ cups sliced okra
1 Scotch bonnet chile
2½ to 3 cups unsweetened coconut milk
1 medium crab (about 1 pound), cleaned but left whole
Salt and freshly ground black pepper, to taste

1. Warm the oil in a nonreactive large pot over medium heat. Add the onion and garlic and sauté until the onion is translucent, about 5 minutes. Add the spinach, a handful at a time, and stir to blend. Add the okra and chile. Pour the coconut milk over the mixture and stir once. Add the crab, cover the pot, and simmer over low heat until the callaloo is the consistency of creamed spinach, 35 minutes.

2. Remove and discard the chile. Remove and discard the crab or hack into bite-size pieces and set aside. Purée 1 to 2 cups of the callaloo in a blender or food processor. Return the purée to the pot, stir, and cook until heated through and some of the liquid has evaporated, 5 to 10 minutes longer.

3. If using, return the crab to the pot. Season the callaloo with salt and pepper to taste.

Serves 6

MRS. BEAUSOJOUR'S SHORT GUIDE
TO CARIBBEAN VEGETABLES

For over a quarter of a century, Ellie Beausojour has reigned over wicker baskets and wooden crates in a 10-foot stall at La Marqueta, the city's oldest food market. When she arrived in New York from Haiti, the rambling shed-like buildings under the Metro North train tracks from East 111th Street to 116th Street were a vivid exchange fueled by low prices and unbeatable variety.

These days La Marqueta is so quiet that you can hear the shed vibrate when trains pass above. And you no longer have to strain to catch Beausojour's advice on the tropical produce she sells. In a battered green felt hat and billowing windbreaker, she cuts wedges of West Indian pumpkin (calabaza) and slices yautia (malanga) as she holds forth on the curative and culinary properties of her stock:

"Breadfruit is green and the size of a giant softball. It is starchy when hard and young. Ripe, it has an eggplant-like texture and is excellent stuffed with some ground meat and roasted in the skin.

"Boniato are light colored and look (and taste) like a cross between a sweet and a baking potato. With their creamy texture and subtle sweetness, they can be prepared like either.

"Cilantro, also called fresh coriander, is the parsley look-alike with thin, lacy leaves and a rough wild aroma that Latin cooks use much like parsley.

"Calabaza, also called West Indian pumpkin or Cuban squash, is the size of a large melon and has mottled skin that ranges from green to buff. It is less watery than most squash, and it makes a tasty alternative to pumpkin or butternut squash in soups and stews.

"Chayote, also called mirliton, are white or green pear-shaped gourds with thick, bumpy skin. They taste like a cross between cucumber and zucchini and can be puréed in soups or halved and stuffed with raisins and pork."

Beausojour recommends steaming green chayote with lemon and cilantro. The white ones she says are "For the blood pressure."

"Jícama looks like a giant beet with tan skin. It is crunchy, juicy, and mildly sweet. It can be peeled and sliced in salads, stir-fried, or tossed with onions and peppers or with exotic fruits to make slaw.

"Ñame (pronounced "Na-ah-may") is the log-shaped yam with a tan shaggy coat that West Indians broil or bake to serve alongside strong-flavored dishes.

"Plantains are the vegetable banana of the Caribbean. Green, they are starchy and can be used like a potato, especially for chips.

"Ripe plantains, which range from gold to black, are banana-sweet and are wonderful as fritters, or sliced and grilled.

"Tamarillo are the egg-shaped tomato-like fruit with apricot flavor tones. They range from yellow to red, and a little goes a long way in flavoring sweet and savory sauces or chutney for pork, ham, or chicken.

"There are about 600 varieties of yams, and although they are often used interchangeably with sweet potatoes, the two vegetables are in different botanical families. Yams can have skin ranging from tan to black-brown, and the flesh varies from white to yellow.

"Yautia, also called malanga, is yam-shaped with shaggy brown skin, a crisp texture, and a nutty, musty flavor. It makes great chips. Peeled and boiled, it becomes silky.

"What'll it be?" asks Ellie Beausojour.

An Ethnic
FUSION PLATTER

Dr. Barbara Kirshenblatt-Gimblett, a professor of performance studies at the Tisch School at New York University, lives in a sprawling loft on the Bowery with her husband, the painter Max Gimblett. In the winter, she says, she likes to wander from their loft "like from the hub of a great wheel, following the spokes to Chinatown, Little Italy, the Lower East Side, the East Village, and Soho," plucking produce as she wanders through the incredible array.

This giant mixed ethnic platter (dressed with Thai Garden Vinegar, page 187) is a dish that Dr. Kirshenblatt-Gimblett has developed over the years to chase away winter blahs and celebrate the diversity of her weekend walks.

There is no specific recipe; the cook must buy what looks good and arrange it to please oneself, she says. But she offers the following blueprint.

The Fusion Platter can serve any number of people depending on the amount of ingredients you buy. It is perfect for a party of 6 to 8 seated at a big table. Adjust the amount of Thai Garden Vinegar according to the amount of ingredients.

1. Lay a bed of Napa cabbage and watercress on the biggest platter you can find.

2. Parboil lotus root for 3 to 4 minutes in water and lemon juice. Drain, cool, peel, and cut into ¼-inch-thick slices. Smear with *uméboshi* (Japanese pickled plum).

3. Roast whole, unpeeled beets with a little water in a covered cast-iron pan in the oven. Peel and cut into eighths. Dress with Thai Garden Vinegar and toss with garlic chives or cilantro.

4. Boil fresh or frozen fava or soybeans for 5 minutes, then drain. Toss with thinly sliced scal-

La Marqueta, the place for Puerto Rican and Cuban favorites.

lions, a little finely sliced leafy Chinese celery tops, salt, and lemon juice to taste.

5. Peel and slice jícama; dress with lime juice and a dash of cayenne pepper.

6. Peel and thickly slice carrots. Dress with Thai Garden Vinegar. Toss with chopped fresh mint or Thai basil.

7. Peel and slice daikon radish or kohlrabi.

8. Hard-cook a dozen quail eggs.

9. Boil little purple pearl onions. Drain, peel, and halve lengthwise. Dress with balsamic vinegar.

10. Slice fennel through the root. Dress with Thai Garden Vinegar.

11. Quarter and steam kabocha squash, then slice.

12. Steam small blue, Red Bliss, or Yukon Gold potatoes, then halve.

13. Assemble all of the food on the platter.

Millie Chan's DRY-FRIED STRING BEANS

Cookbook author Millie Chan, who lives on Manhattan's Upper West Side, makes these addictive green beans as a side dish for family meals. With some rice, they make a fine meal.

2 cups corn or peanut oil, for deep-frying
1½ pounds fresh string beans, well rinsed, ends trimmed
4 to 6 dried hot chiles, to taste
¼ pound ground pork
1 tablespoon dark soy sauce
1 tablespoon rice wine
1 tablespoon red wine vinegar
½ teaspoon salt
1½ teaspoons sugar

---

1. Set a large strainer over a metal mixing bowl. Have all of the ingredients ready to use and near the cooking area.

2. Heat a wok over high heat until very hot. Add the oil, and when very hot but not smoking, turn off the heat. Add the beans, turn the heat to high, and cook, stirring constantly, until the beans are slightly wrinkled, 3 to 5 minutes. Remove the wok from the heat. Pour the beans into the strainer, allowing the oil to drain into the bowl. Reserve the used oil.

3. Return the wok to medium heat. Add 2 tablespoons of the reserved oil and the chiles. Stir-fry over medium heat until the peppers turn dark brown, 5 to 7 minutes. Turn the heat to high, add the ground pork, and stir-fry until the pork browns, about 3 minutes. Stir in the soy sauce, rice wine, vinegar, and salt. Add the sugar and beans, stir to combine, and serve.

Serves 4 to 6

Sephardic
GREEN BEANS

Emily Russo grew up in Egypt, where she learned to prepare *fasulia,* or green beans—along with a battery of other delicacies prepared by Sephardic Jews to celebrate Jewish holidays.

1 tablespoon olive oil
3 cloves garlic, minced
3 small shallots, minced
1 beefsteak tomato, peeled, seeded, and chopped
1 pound haricots verts (thin, tiny green beans),
   ends trimmed
2 teaspoons fresh lemon juice
1 tablespoon dry red wine
½ teaspoon salt
¼ teaspoon freshly ground black pepper

1. Warm the olive oil in a nonreactive sauté pan over medium heat. Add the garlic and shallots, lower the heat, and sauté until soft, about 3 minutes.

2. Add the tomato, haricots verts, lemon juice, wine, salt, and pepper. Simmer until tender, 3 to 5 minutes. Serve immediately.

Serves 4

Mohamed's Marvelous
MARRAKESH CARROTS

Mohamed Jennah, who grew up in Marrakesh, Morocco, is an extraordinary cook. He now works as a private cook in a Park Avenue home, where his way with vegetables is the subject of the very best dinner parties. This and the Amazing Arabic Okra (page 145) can be made ahead and eaten cool or at room temperature as an appetizer or, on a hot summer night, as the main event with a little couscous. Both are delicious (and improve for two days after they are made), so it is advisable to double or triple the recipes.

1 pound whole carrots, peeled and
   trimmed
1 tablespoon fresh lemon juice
3 tablespoons olive oil
1 teaspoon sweet paprika
½ teaspoon ground cumin
1 teaspoon salt
¼ teaspoon ground cinnamon
2 tablespoons minced fresh parsley

1. Place the carrots in a pot of cold water over medium heat and bring to a boil. Cook until soft but not mushy, 10 to 15 minutes. Drain and cool under cold water.

LEXICON OF ASIAN VEGETABLES

The Asian vegetable markets in Chinatown and Flushing offer a dizzying array of exotic produce—though uninitiated shoppers rarely know what is indispensable to the well-stocked Asian pantry. Here, then, is a mini-guide:

Bitter melon: not a melon at all, this vegetable looks like a shriveled fat cucumber with bumps and ridges. It has the cool, bitter taste of quinine. Used in Indian cooking.

Black fungus (cloud ears, tree ear mushrooms, wood ear mushrooms): pungent mushrooms native to the Szechuan province of China. Sold dried and used in soups and stir-fries.

Bok choy (Chinese white cabbage): loose-leaf cabbage, a pale green with slightly frilled edges. Used in Thai and Chinese cooking and stir-frying.

Chinese broccoli: a member of the cabbage family, it tastes of broccoli. Used in Thai and Chinese cooking.

Galangal: like ginger, galangal is a rhizome. It is most often available dried, either sliced or ground into a powder. Used in Thai cooking as a spice, it tastes gingery.

Heart of banana: eaten like heart of palm, the tender inside of a banana plant is often used in salads. Used in Indian cooking.

Holy basil (*bai kaprow*): a variety of basil with a sharper flavor than the common sweet basil. Leafy and green, holy basil is used as an herb in Thai cooking.

Kohlrabi: a member of the cabbage family, this often rutabaga-size vegetable is white or purple. The leaves, which have a vague collard green taste, as well as the root, mildly cabbage-like, are eaten. Used in Indian cooking.

Krachai (lesser ginger): from the same family as ginger and galangal, but with fiercer flavor. Krachai is shaped like gingerroot, with brown skin and yellow flesh. Used in Thai cooking, where it is sometimes eaten whole as a vegetable, but more usually dried and ground for use as a spice.

Long beans (asparagus beans, yard-long beans): up to 3 feet long, they taste and are used like string beans. Used in Thai and Chinese cooking.

Lotus root: a potato-like tuber, the lotus root is the stem of the water lily. Bought dried, canned, or occasionally fresh, the interior of the lotus root is made up of a symmetrical pattern of holes and flesh. Lotus root is crunchy and slightly sweet. Used in Indian and Chinese cooking.

Napa cabbage (Peking cabbage): a head cabbage with long, pale leaves and a subtle flavor. Used in Chinese cooking.

Nori: seaweed, sold in flat, dried sheets, used in Japanese and Korean soups and sushi.

Sheem: a hard-skinned flat bean used in Indian cooking.

Straw mushrooms: small meaty mushrooms. Used in Thai and Chinese stir-fried dishes.

Water spinach: this green with arrowhead-shaped leaves has a high water content and tastes slightly like spinach. It is found in markets in spring and is used in Chinese and Thai cooking.

White radish (daikon): a long radish that looks like an albino carrot. Mildly pungent, it is used in Indian and Japanese cooking.

In an Asian market, where the vegetables look beautiful and the variety is overwhelming.

2. Meanwhile, place the lemon juice in a medium bowl. Whisk in the olive oil to make a vinaigrette. Whisk in the paprika, cumin, salt, and cinnamon.

3. Cut the carrots into bite-sized dice. Add to the vinaigrette and toss. Stir in the parsley. Season with additional salt or spices to taste. Serve.

Serves 4

Takis'
ARTICHOKES A LA POLITA

Takis Anoussis, who has managed hotels in New York for several decades, is a home cook extraordinaire. Growing up in Athens, he helped his father run a restaurant. "Polita" refers to the Turkish origin of the dish, which Anoussis favors served with lamb as a main course (for his wife's recipe, Rina's Lamb, see Index). For a lighter meal or appetizer, feta cheese can be served with the artichokes.

6 large artichokes
2 lemons, halved
⅓ cup olive oil
1 yellow onion, grated
1 pound new potatoes (about 10), peeled and cut into ½-inch cubes
½ pound carrots (about 4), peeled and cut into 2-inch lengths
½ pound white pearl onions, peeled
1 teaspoon minced fresh dill
Salt and freshly ground black pepper, to taste

1. Clean the artichokes by removing the stems, discolored leaves, and prickly chokes. Rub with a lemon half and place in a large bowl of cold water.

2. Warm the olive oil in a large pot over low heat. Add the grated onions and sauté until translucent, 5 minutes.

3. Add the artichokes, stem ends up. Sprinkle on the juice of 1 lemon and cover with plenty of cold water. Bring to a boil over high heat. Lower the heat to a simmer, cover the pot, and cook the artichokes for 15 minutes.

4. Add the potatoes, carrots, and pearl onions. Continue to simmer until the potatoes and carrots are tender but not soft, 15 to 20 minutes. Sprinkle with the dill and season with salt and pepper.

5. Divide among 4 plates and serve with some of the cooking juices. It also can be served cold.

Serves 6

Union Square Cafe's
MASHED TURNIPS WITH CRISPY SHALLOTS

From the time that Union Square Cafe opened in 1985, this rich dish has been converting even avid turnip-haters. It can be served as a vegetable with meat or game. But it is so rich that it is often eaten as a main course, with a little salad before and some dessert to follow.

1½ pounds turnips or rutabagas, peeled and
*   coarsely diced (about 2 cups)*
1 cup shallots (about 6 large shallots),
*   peeled and thinly sliced*
2 tablespoons butter, melted
1 cup heavy (whipping) cream
1 tablespoon unsalted butter
Salt and freshly ground black pepper,
*   to taste*
Pinch of freshly grated nutmeg
Pinch of minced fresh parsley,
*   for garnish*

1. Place the turnips in a large pot of cold water and bring to a boil. Cook until they are fork-tender, about 15 minutes. Drain.

2. Put the turnips through a ricer or purée in a food processor; set aside.

3. Meanwhile, in a deep saucepan over medium heat, sauté the shallots in the butter until they turn golden brown, about 15 minutes. With a slotted spoon, remove the shallots and drain on paper towels.

4. Set a heavy saucepan over medium heat. Add the cream and 1 tablespoon butter and bring to a simmer. Add the turnips, stir briskly, and season with the salt, pepper, and nutmeg.

5. Spoon the purée onto serving plates and garnish liberally with the shallots and lightly with the parsley. Serve immediately.

Serves 8

Fresh shallots at the Union Square Greenmarket.

Mrs. Verdillo's
BROCCOLI RABE

Thomas "Tomasso" Verdillo, an opera singer who owns Tomasso Restaurant in Brooklyn, said that this southern Italian recipe came from his mother, Ida. It was an ordinary dish and part of many evening meals when he was growing up. Now he serves it as a hot first course or as an accompaniment to grilled or baked sweet Italian sausage on a sandwich.

2 tablespoons extra-virgin olive oil (preferably
   from Tuscany)
4 cloves garlic, peeled
Pinch of dried red pepper flakes
2 pounds broccoli rabe, tough ends
   trimmed, well rinsed but not
   dried
Pinch of salt
¼ cup chicken broth (optional)

1. In a heavy pot with a cover, combine the olive oil and garlic over medium heat. Add the red pepper flakes and sauté until the garlic is lightly golden, 5 minutes.

2. Add the damp rabe and the salt, cover, and steam until cooked, 5 to 7 minutes. If the pan gets too dry, add a little chicken broth or water. Serve immediately.

Serves 4

Mr. Jennah's
AMAZING ARABIC OKRA

A nother splendid recipe from Mohamed Jennah (see page 141 for his Marvelous Marrakesh Carrots).

1 tablespoon olive oil
2 cloves garlic, peeled
1 can (32 ounces) whole Italian plum tomatoes
½ teaspoon freshly ground white pepper
1 tablespoon sweet paprika
2 teaspoons salt
1 teaspoon ground cinnamon
¼ teaspoon cayenne pepper (optional)
Juice of 1 lemon
2 pounds okra, stems removed, each piece cut
   crosswise into thirds

1. Warm the olive oil in a nonreactive saucepan over medium heat. Add the garlic and cook until golden, 3 to 5 minutes. Remove the garlic.

2. In a food processor, roughly purée the tomatoes. Add to the saucepan along with the white pepper, paprika, salt, cinnamon, cayenne, and lemon juice. Stir well. Simmer the sauce over low heat for 30 minutes.

3. Meanwhile, bring a pot of water to a boil. Add the okra and simmer until tender, about 20 minutes. Drain well.

4. Add the okra to the tomato sauce and simmer together for an additional 10 minutes. Serve.

Serves 4

Angela Carter of Irish Books.

2. Add the watercress to the pot. Steam for 5 minutes. Remove and set aside.

3. Meanwhile, in a skillet over low heat, cook the shallots and garlic in the butter until limp. Remove from the heat and set aside to cool.

4. Preheat the oven to 350°F.

5. Combine the parsnips, watercress, shallots, garlic, and salt and pepper to taste in a food processor. Process until smooth, 20 seconds. Spoon the mixture into a 9-inch casserole.

6. Bake, uncovered, until heated through, 10 to 20 minutes.

7. Remove the casserole from the oven and sprinkle on the Cheddar cheese. Place under the broiler until the cheese bubbles and browns, about 5 minutes.

Serves 4

Angela's PARSNIPS WITH WATERCRESS

Angela Carter, who manages Irish Books in SoHo, recommends this flavorful dish as a partner with pork chops or pork sausage. Leftovers, she says, are great on toast.

4 parsnips, peeled and cut into ½-inch slices
1 bunch watercress, well rinsed, tough stems removed
6 shallots, finely chopped
2 cloves garlic, finely chopped
1 tablespoon butter
Salt and freshly ground black pepper, to taste
½ cup grated Cheddar cheese (optional)

1. Bring 1 cup of water to a boil in a heavy pot over medium heat. Place the parsnips in a colander or steamer, place in the pot, cover, and steam until tender, about 15 minutes. Remove the parsnips from the heat and set aside.

CAULIFLOWER CASSEROLE à la Astoria

Daka Tikasis, an elementary school teacher who lives in Astoria, Queens, learned to make this dish from her grandmother while growing up in Athens. She recently taught her granddaughter to make it and still serves it as a side dish with family meals.

1 head cauliflower, cut into florets
1½ cups New York Penicillin (page 47) or canned chicken broth
1 tomato, minced
1 tablespoon fresh oregano, or 1½ teaspoons dried
1 teaspoon salt
½ teaspoon freshly ground black pepper
1 cup crumbled feta cheese
1½ cups fine, dried bread crumbs
2 tablespoons olive oil

■———————————————■

1. Preheat the oven to 350°F.

2. Place the cauliflower florets in an 11 × 9-inch baking pan. Pour on the broth. Sprinkle the minced tomato, oregano, salt, and pepper over the cauliflower. Add the feta cheese and toss well.

3. Cover the pan with foil. Bake for 45 minutes. Remove the foil and continue baking until the cauliflower is very tender, 30 minutes longer.

4. Toss the bread crumbs with the olive oil. Sprinkle the crumbs over the cauliflower. Bake until the crumbs are golden brown, an additional 30 minutes.

Serves 4

James O'Shea's
TURNIP PANCAKES

What James O'Shea remembers most vividly about growing up in County Cork, Ireland, is the turnip pancakes that his Grandma O'Neill made. After he moved to New York, Mr. O'Shea couldn't resist "taking a little of this and a bit of that" from the ingredients that he found here.

He believes that Grandma O'Neill would bless the ginger and sesame oil that he's added to her turnip cakes. These can be served as an appetizer or as a side dish to any hearty winter meal.

4 medium turnips, peeled and cut into 1½-inch cubes
2 nickel-size slices fresh ginger, peeled and lightly smashed
1 teaspoon Oriental sesame oil
8 tablespoons (1 stick) butter, cut up
Pinch of coarse sea salt
Freshly ground black pepper, to taste
¼ cup plus 2 tablespoons heavy (whipping) cream
¼ cup all-purpose flour
Cornmeal, for dusting
2 tablespoons olive oil, for sautéing

■———————————————■

1. Place the turnips and ginger in cold water to cover in a large pot. Add the sesame oil and bring to a boil over medium-high heat. Cook until the turnips are fork-tender, 25 minutes. Remove from the heat and drain. Return the turnips to the pot and set over low heat until dry, 7 to 8 minutes. Watch closely and stir occasionally to prevent sticking.

2. Remove the turnips from the heat, add the butter, and mash with a hand masher until the turnips are slightly lumpy. Add the salt, pepper, cream, and flour. Stir well and set the mixture aside to cool.

3. Shape the turnips into patties, each about 2 inches thick; dust with cornmeal. Cover with a

When choosing ginger, look for plump "fingers" and tight-fitting skin.

towel and refrigerate to set, 1 to 2 hours. Bring to room temperature before cooking.

4. Warm the olive oil in a skillet over medium heat. When hot, add a few of the pancakes at a time, making sure not to crowd them, and cook, covered, until browned on both sides, 5 minutes per side. Transfer to a heated serving platter and keep warm until all of the pancakes are cooked.

Serves 4

Mr. Berger in front of the Famous Dairy Restaurant.

Famous ORIGINAL VEGETABLE CUTLET

Kosher dairy restaurants in New York City have always faced the problem of giving a meat-like experience without violating dietary laws. "Your vegetable cutlet is more or less the archetypal response," said Mr. Berger, owner of the venerable Famous Dairy restaurant in the Borough Park section of Brooklyn. "It's not dairy, it's not meat, it's vegetable-based, and you feel like you've eaten a steak afterwards."

CUTLET

1 pound carrots, peeled and grated

½ pound turnips, peeled and grated

1 head cauliflower, cut into small florets

1 small onion, grated

2 cloves garlic, minced

1 package (10 ounces) frozen green peas

½ pound fresh green beans, ends trimmed, cut into bite-size pieces, and blanched

2 eggs

1 cup matzob meal

½ cup unseasoned dried bread crumbs

1 teaspoon freshly ground black pepper

1 teaspoon kosher salt

3 tablespoons powdered vegetable bouillon concentrate, dissolved in 1 cup water

GRAVY

2 tablespoons butter

1 medium onion, minced

2 pounds white mushrooms, thinly sliced

3 tablespoons powdered vegetable bouillon concentrate dissolved in 4 cups water

¼ teaspoon freshly ground black pepper

2 teaspoons arrowroot, dissolved in ¼ cup cold water

1. Preheat the oven to 350°F. Lightly grease a baking sheet.

2. Combine all of the cutlet ingredients in a large bowl and mix well with your hands. Form the mixture into eight 1-inch-thick patties. Place the cutlets 1 inch apart on the prepared baking sheet. Bake until lightly browned and heated through, 1 hour.

3. Meanwhile, make the gravy: Warm the butter in a large skillet over medium heat. Add the onion and cook until deep gold in color, about 5 minutes. Add the mushrooms, partially cover, and cook, stirring occasionally, until the mushrooms are soft, about 10 minutes.

4. Add the dissolved bouillon mixture and the pepper and stir well. Simmer until reduced by half, 20 to 30 minutes.

5. Remove from the heat and whisk in the dissolved arrowroot. Return to very low heat and cook until thickened, about 3 minutes. Do not allow to boil.

6. Serve the cutlets with the gravy.
Serves 8

marinade and grill on the foil for 15 minutes. Then remove the foil from the grill, return the eggplants and cook, turning them, until lightly browned, about 1 minute more. Watch that the eggplants don't burn.

If using the broiler, move the broiling rack 6 inches from the heat. Broil the eggplants, turning frequently, until soft, 5 to 10 minutes. There is no need for the second cooking.

4. Slice the eggplants into ½-inch pieces before serving.
Serves 2

Barbecued EGGPLANT

Sonja Chong, a pianist, grills these eggplants on her terrace on the Upper West Side of Manhattan. They are just as delicious when cooked under the broiler.

3 tablespoons Szechuan chili paste
1 tablespoon dark soy sauce
2 tablespoons dry sherry or Chinese rice wine
3 tablespoons red wine vinegar
2 tablespoons sugar
¼ cup plus 2 tablespoons Oriental sesame oil
1 tablespoon chopped garlic
Salt, to taste
4 small eggplants (½ to 1 pound total weight), ends trimmed, halved lengthwise

1. Combine all the ingredients except the eggplants in a nonreactive bowl and mix well. Add the eggplants, toss well, and set aside to marinate for at least 1 hour and up to 4 hours.

2. Prepare a charcoal grill or preheat the broiler. Cover the grill rack with aluminum foil.

3. If using a grill, when the coals are white, remove the eggplants from the

Charles Street ZUCCHINI

I tasted this intriguing zucchini dish at a block party in the West Village several years ago and, when I asked for the recipe, I was given a battered copy of a neighborhood cookbook. This recipe is adapted from that book, *The Charles Street Association Cookbook*.

2 to 3 medium zucchini
½ cup walnuts, finely chopped
½ cup raisins, chopped
½ cup dried apricots, finely chopped
Pinch of freshly grated nutmeg
Pinch of ground cinnamon
¼ cup honey
4 tablespoons (½ stick) butter
Pinch of crushed dried rosemary

1. Preheat the oven to 400°F.
2. Trim the zucchini and halve each one lengthwise. Cut each half

crosswise into 3 pieces. Scoop out some of the flesh so that each piece resembles a cup.

3. In a small bowl, mix together the walnuts, raisins, apricots, nutmeg, cinnamon, and honey. Spoon the mixture into the zucchini cups and then arrange the zucchini in a baking dish. Top each piece with a bit of the butter and a sprinkle of the rosemary.

4. Cover the pan with aluminum foil. Bake until tender but firm, 20 to 30 minutes. Serve hot.

Serves 4

Gail Vogel's
GRILLED VEGETABLE MELANGE

Gail Vogel, a former model who now conducts parties for single people on Manhattan's Upper West Side, regularly grills sweet bell peppers, which she keeps covered with olive oil in the refrigerator and serves, along with olives or mozzarella cheese, to guests (see page 28 for her recipe). Her hors d'oeuvre takes on dinner dimensions when she adds eggplants and other summer vegetables and serves the grilled vegetables as an accompaniment to fish or chicken, or on a hot summer night, by themselves.

1 cup olive oil
3 large eggplants, cut lengthwise into ½-inch-thick slices
3 zucchini, trimmed and halved lengthwise
3 yellow squash, trimmed and halved lengthwise
2 cups fresh basil leaves, rinsed and patted dry
2 teaspoons salt
1 teaspoon freshly ground black pepper
3 red bell peppers
3 green bell peppers

1. Prepare a charcoal grill.

2. Place ½ cup of the olive oil in a small bowl and, using a pastry brush, lightly brush the eggplant, zucchini, and squash slices with the oil.

3. Combine the remaining olive oil and the basil leaves in a large bowl and stir to coat the basil well. Add the salt and pepper and set aside.

4. When the grill is hot, roast the peppers, using tongs to turn frequently to avoid burning. When the peppers are soft and charred all over, place them in a large paper bag. Close the bag and allow the peppers to steam. Grill the eggplant, zucchini, and squash slices until lightly browned on each side. Let the slices cool on a tray.

5. Remove the peppers from the bag and gently rub off their skins. Remove the stems and seeds from the peppers. Cut the peppers into ¼-inch slices; add to the basil and oil mixture. When the eggplant, zucchini, and squash are cool, cut each into ½-inch chunks. Add to the peppers and toss to combine. Cover and refrigerate.

Serves 8

La Côte Basque's
STUFFED VEGETABLES

The dining room at La Côte Basque in a quiet moment. Photo courtesy of La Côte Basque

In "La Côte Basque," an intimate sketch that appears in the book *Unanswered Prayers,* the late Truman Capote describes the long-favored watering hole of some of the "ladies who lunch."

"Côte Basque is on East 55th Street, directly across from the St. Regis. It was the site of the original Le Pavillon, founded in 1940 by the honorable restaurateur Henri Soulé." M. Soulé, Mr. Capote relates, relocated Le Pavillon after a feud with the landlord, returning a few years later to establish La Côte Basque, for three decades the center stage for *TOUT* New York.

In the early 1970s, wrote Mr. Capote, the restaurant was still an arbiter of social standing. "Preferred clients, selected by the proprietor with unerring *snobbisme,* were placed in the banquette-lined entrance area—a practice pursued by every New York restaurant of established chic. . . ." The daily lunch conversation drifted from fashion commentary to sexual intrigue, but one thing never changed: the showy platter of stuffed vegetables that was served to every table.

"There is at least one respect in which the rich, the really very rich, *are* different from . . . other people. They understand —vegetables," Lady Ina Coolbirth confides to Jonsey in the story.

Following are a variety of the stuffed vegetables that are still served in the restaurant.

STUFFED ONIONS

4 onions
3 tablespoons butter
2 tablespoons crème fraîche
¼ cup shredded Swiss cheese
½ teaspoon salt
¼ teaspoon freshly grated nutmeg
1 egg yolk, beaten
½ cup fine, dried, homemade bread crumbs
2 cups New York Penicillin (page 47) or canned chicken broth

1. Bring water to a boil in a large saucepan. Add the onions and blanch the onions for 5 minutes. Drain and set aside to cool.

2. Keeping the 3 outermost layers of the onions intact, use a sharp knife or spoon to remove the inner core of onion, leaving a solid base at the bottom of the onion cup.

3. Arrange the onion cups in a baking dish. Mince the inner onion layers.

4. Preheat the oven to 350°F.

5. Heat 2 tablespoons of the butter in a nonreactive skillet. Add the minced onion and cook slowly, stirring constantly, until nearly golden, about 10 minutes.

6. Off the heat, stir in the crème fraîche, Swiss cheese, salt, nutmeg, and egg yolk. Stir in half of the bread crumbs.

7. Divide the mixture among the onion cups. Sprinkle on the remaining bread crumbs and dot with the remaining 1 tablespoon butter. Pour the chicken broth into the baking dish and cover with aluminum foil. Bake until tender and hot throughout, 30 minutes.
Serves 4

STUFFED ARTICHOKES

Juice of 1 lemon
8 large artichokes, trimmed
½ lemon
1 tablespoon minced shallot
1 tablespoon olive oil
4 cups fresh spinach (2 pounds), rinsed and minced
¼ cup finely minced smoked ham
1½ tablespoons fine, dried, homemade bread crumbs
⅓ cup crème fraîche
¼ to ½ teaspoon salt
Dash of freshly ground black pepper
2 egg yolks

1. Combine the lemon juice and water in a large steamer. Add the artichokes and steam until tender, 30 to 40 minutes. Set aside to cool completely. Remove the stems, all of the outer leaves, and the chokes. Rub the hearts with the lemon and place them in the refrigerator.

2. Preheat the oven to 350°F.

3. In a nonreactive large skillet, sauté the shallot in the olive oil until soft, about 3 minutes. Add the spinach, toss, cover, and cook until wilted, about 2 minutes. Remove the lid and cook until all of the liquid evaporates, about 5 minutes.

4. Stir in the ham, bread crumbs, and crème fraîche; season to taste with the salt and pepper. Beat the egg yolks into the mixture and cook over very low heat until the eggs are cooked but not scrambled, about 3 minutes.

5. Spoon the mixture into the artichoke hearts. Place them on a baking sheet. Bake until heated through, 10 minutes. Serve hot.

Serves 4

mushrooms and cook slowly until soft, about 10 minutes.

3. Stir in the anchovies and parsley and about half of the bread crumbs to make a moist but pliable mixture. Season with the salt and pepper.

4. Preheat the oven to 350°F.

5. Divide the mixture among the mushroom caps. Sprinkle on the remaining bread crumbs; dot each with a small piece of the remaining 1 tablespoon butter.

6. Pour the white wine and sherry into a nonreactive small saucepan and set over medium-high heat until the alcohol burns off, 5 minutes. Carefully pour the wine into the baking dish.

7. Bake until the mushrooms are warmed through and the crumbs are golden, 15 to 20 minutes.

Serves 4

STUFFED MUSHROOMS

24 white mushrooms
1 lemon, halved
3 tablespoons butter
2 shallots, minced
½ clove garlic, minced
1 slice bacon, minced
2 anchovy fillets, minced
2 tablespoons minced fresh parsley
¼ cup fine, dried, homemade bread crumbs
¼ teaspoon salt
¼ teaspoon freshly ground black pepper
1 cup dry white wine
1 tablespoon dry sherry, red wine, or port

1. Remove the stems from 16 of the mushrooms. Rub the caps with a lemon half and place in a nonreactive baking dish; set aside. Mince the mushroom stems with the 8 remaining whole mushrooms.

2. Warm 2 tablespoons of the butter in a nonreactive large skillet. Add the shallots, garlic, and bacon and sauté for 3 minutes. Add the minced

Fresh white mushrooms with perfect tight caps ready to stuff.

STUFFED TOMATOES

4 ripe tomatoes, tops removed
¼ cup olive oil
2 small onions, chopped
2 cloves garlic, minced
2 sweet Italian sausage links, chopped
1 ripe tomato, peeled, seeded, and chopped
2 tablespoons fresh thyme leaves

1. Preheat the oven to 250°F. Lightly grease a shallow baking pan.

2. With a small spoon, scoop out the insides of the whole tomatoes. Do the best you can to save the pulp without the seeds. Set the tomato "cases" aside.

3. Warm the olive oil in a skillet over medium heat. Add the onions and garlic and sauté until the onion is translucent, 5 minutes. Add the sausages, tomato pulp, chopped tomato, and thyme and sauté until no longer pink, about 5 minutes. Remove from the heat and set aside to cool.

4. Divide the filling equally among the tomato cases. Stand the tomatoes in the prepared baking pan and cover with aluminum foil. Bake until soft and hot throughout, 30 to 40 minutes, depending on the size of the tomatoes.

Serves 4

Vegetable CHOW MEIN

Jimmy Chin was six years old and his brother Wally was eight in the 1940s when their family moved from the Canton province of China to the Jewish section of Brownsville in Brooklyn. They lived in the back of their grandfather's hand laundry, learning to adapt their mother's dishes to the tastes of neighborhood friends, tastes that were sometimes kosher and always honed on carry-out Chinese food.

Chow mein—a dish that was invented in America—was "the main call of my main friends," said Jimmy Chin. Here is his Brooklyn version of the dish.

¼ cup vegetable oil
Pinch of minced garlic
1½ cups New York Penicillin (page 47) or
*   homemade or canned chicken or vegetable*
*   broth*
¼ cup dry sherry
½ large white onion, sliced
1 cup fresh bean sprouts
1 cup shredded bok choy or Chinese cabbage,
*   rinsed*
½ cup shredded celery
¼ cup shredded bamboo shoots
1 scallion, trimmed and minced
1 teaspoon salt
½ teaspoon sugar
Pinch of freshly ground black pepper
5 drops Oriental sesame oil
2 tablespoons cornstarch, dissolved in
*   2 tablespoons cold water*
4 wonton skins or egg roll wrappers,
*   deep-fried in vegetable oil*
*   until crispy, and shredded,*
*   for garnish*

1. Warm a seasoned wok over high heat until almost smoking. Standing back a bit from the stove, add the vegetable oil and garlic and stir-fry for a few seconds. Add the broth and sherry and cook for 1 minute. Add the onion, sprouts, bok choy, celery, bamboo shoots, and scallions and bring to a boil. Cook for 4 minutes.

2. Stir in the salt, sugar, pepper, and sesame oil and bring to a boil again. Add the cornstarch mixture and stir until thickened. Top with the fried wonton skins.

Serves 2

Spicy
GARBANZO PUDDING

Bob Rogers is a Manhattan designer who has worked in theater, fashion, and textiles. He created this recipe as part of a diet regimen, intending it to be a meat substitute with plenty of spice and flavor. He serves it as a main course, but it is also delicious as an appetizer dip accompanied by pita bread.

*2 cans (15 to 16 ounces each) garbanzo beans
    (chick-peas)*
2 tablespoons safflower oil
1 large egg
1 clove garlic, minced
1 tablespoon all-purpose flour
1 tablespoon chili powder
1½ teaspoons ground cumin
½ teaspoon sweet paprika
½ cup minced scallions, for garnish
Steamed brown rice, for serving

1. Preheat the oven to 350°F. Grease a 9 × 5-inch loaf pan.

2. Combine the garbanzo beans and their liquid, the oil, egg, garlic, flour, chili powder, cumin, and paprika in a food processor. Purée the mixture until smooth.

3. Pour the mixture into the prepared pan. Bake until loosely set and golden brown, 1¼ to 1½ hours.

4. Serve the pudding hot, garnished with the minced scallions and accompanied by steamed brown rice.

Serves 8 as a main course

Hamburger Mary's
YAMS SOUFFLE

At the height of its popularity in the late 1930s, Hamburger Mary's, a joint at 17 West 51st Street, featured hamburgers and fried chicken. "Mary herself is a character who weighs a light 200 pounds, has sung on Major Bowes' program, and counts the big-wigs as her friends," wrote Diana Ashley in her book, *Where to Dine*

in '39, where this recipe originally appeared. The savory soufflé remains a staple of many old-time New York tables. Sweet potatoes can be substituted for the yams.

3 large yams
¼ cup plus 1 teaspoon sugar
3 extra-large eggs, separated
3 tablespoons plus ½ teaspoon butter
⅛ teaspoon ground cinnamon
⅛ teaspoon freshly grated nutmeg
Pinch of salt, or more to taste
2 tablespoons milk

■────────────────■

1. Preheat the oven to 400°F. Lightly grease a 1-quart soufflé dish.

2. Place the yams in a large pot, cover with water, and bring to a boil. Cook until tender, 20 to 30 minutes. Drain and set aside to cool.

3. Peel the yams. In a bowl, mash the yams. Add 1 teaspoon sugar, the egg yolks, 2 tablespoons of the butter, the cinnamon, nutmeg, salt, and milk; beat well.

4. In a large, preferably copper, bowl, whisk the egg whites until stiff peaks form. Fold the whites into the yam mixture.

5. Pour the yam mixture into the prepared soufflé dish. Dot the top with the remaining butter and sprinkle with ¼ cup sugar. Bake until golden brown, 30 minutes. Serve hot.

Serves 6

Horn & Hardart's BAKED BEANS

At the height of its glory, and it was a glorious thing, Horn & Hardart, the "Automat" that opened with the promise "Less work for Mother," had 34 restaurants in New York City and 15 retail stores. The magic of the little glass-windowed machines that showed each dish and dispensed it when the right amount of nickels was inserted, as well as the gleaming industrial-deco interiors of the stores, are fundamental to a certain New York childhood. So are the flavors of Horn & Hardart's Baked Beans and their Macaroni and Cheese (see Index).

The first New York City Automat opened at Broadway and 13th Street in 1903. Although the New York flagship and last remaining Automat at 42nd Street and Third Avenue closed for good in 1991, their recipes remain some of the best in the class: They are easy, designed to be cooked ahead, get better with age—and make lifelong friends of nostalgic New Yorkers.

1 pound great Northern or navy beans, soaked overnight in cold water
1 cup chopped onions
4 slices bacon, diced
2 tablespoons sugar
1 tablespoon dry mustard
½ teaspoon cayenne pepper
⅔ cup molasses
2 tablespoons cider vinegar
1½ cups tomato juice
Salt, to taste

Working the food-vending windows at Horn & Hardart's. Photo: UPI/Bettmann

■────────────────■

1. Drain the beans and place them in a large saucepan. Add fresh water to cover the beans. Bring to a boil over medium heat. Reduce the heat and simmer, uncovered, until the beans are almost tender, 45 minutes to 1 hour. Drain.

2. Meanwhile, preheat the oven to 250°F.

3. Place the beans in a baking pot or casserole. Stir in the onions, bacon, sugar, dry mustard, cayenne, molasses, vinegar, tomato juice, and 1 cup water.

4. Bake the beans, uncovered, until very tender, about 4 hours. Check the beans occasionally while baking and add more water, if necessary to prevent the mixture from drying out. Season with salt to taste.

Serves 8

Sophie's FAVA

Nick Malekos, who owns a tour guide business, loves the simplicity of this dish. "You just have to be careful the peas don't stick to the pan, adding more stock if necessary," he explains. Malekos's sister, Sophie Pavlos, learned to make fava from their mother, Bessie, who was born in Greece.

Nick Malekos keeps alive the family's fava-making tradition.

1 large onion, chopped
2 to 3 tablespoons olive oil
1 pound yellow split peas, rinsed and picked over
5¾ cups New York Penicillin (page 47) or canned chicken broth
1 teaspoon dried marjoram
1 teaspoon dried thyme
Salt and freshly ground black pepper, to taste
Chopped scallions, for garnish

1. In a large heavy skillet, sauté the onion in the olive oil over medium heat until the onion is light brown, 8 minutes.

2. Add the split peas, half of the chicken broth, and the dried herbs, and reduce the heat to a simmer. Cook, stirring occasionally and adding more broth as the mixture simmers, until it is the consistency of mashed potatoes. When the peas have absorbed all of the broth, they are done. It will take 30 to 40 minutes. Season the fava with salt and pepper.

3. Serve hot or cold, with the scallions sprinkled on top.

Judy Rundel's FAMOUS CHIPS

Judy Rundel, advertising manager at St. Martin's Press, lives in the Cobble Hill section of Brooklyn. When she makes these potatoes, she slices some thin and some thick in order to preserve domestic tranquility. She likes the thickly sliced potatoes, and her husband likes them thin and crispy. Either way, they are easy to make and tasty.

8 tablespoons (1 stick) unsalted butter
8 medium baking potatoes, scrubbed and sliced ⅛ inch thick
½ teaspoon dry mustard
½ teaspoon hot paprika
¼ teaspoon chili powder
1 small onion, minced
2 teaspoons salt

1. Preheat the oven to 425°F. Generously butter 2 jelly roll pans or baking sheets.

2. Overlap the potato slices in single rows on the buttered baking sheets.

3. Melt the butter in a small saucepan over medium heat. Remove from the heat, and stir in the dry mustard, paprika, chili powder, and onion. Using a ladle or spoon, generously drizzle the seasoned butter over the rows of potatoes.

4. Sprinkle the buttered potatoes with salt. Bake until the potatoes are golden and the whole house smells good, about 45 minutes.

Serves 8 to 10

MICKEYS AND CHIPS

Shortly after the Irish potato famine and ensuing emigration in the mid-nineteenth century, potatoes began to climb the social ladder in New York. It was an arduous haul, beginning with "mickeys," the potatoes that young boys roasted over open fires and sold to passersby on street corners throughout Manhattan and Brooklyn. As a chic eat, potatoes received a giant push in 1853 when a chef, George Crum, exasperated by a demanding customer, sliced potatoes wafer thin and deep-fried them. There are conflicting versions about whether this occurred at the Cary Moon's Lake Lodge or at the Montgomery Hall Hotel, but both places were in Saratoga, New York, hence the "Saratoga Chip" (for recipe, see Index). Shortly after, paper cones full of warm potato chips were sold from push-carts in New York City.

Latkes and hash browns followed, probably in that order, the first coming from Eastern European immigrants and the latter from German immigrants. French fries appeared toward the end of the century, and various vendors along the Coney Island Boardwalk continue to claim that their great-grandfathers invented the dish. Nathan's Famous makes a convincing case; on the other hand, Nathan's fries are cut in a spiral shape, not the thin or "frenched" cut that gave the fry its name.

In any case, spuds reached an apogee in New York 1980s, when miniature versions appeared baked and topped with crème fraîche and a dab of caviar or, as at The Four Seasons restaurant, baked and slathered with olive oil and truffles and served up as a "Power Lunch."

KP duty and a smoke break for this young Irish lad.

David (The Latke King) Firestone's
LATKES
(IN HIS OWN WORDS)

Every year around Chanukah, David "The Latke King" Firestone, a journalist, gives a party in honor of the latke in his home in Sunnyside, Queens.

"The country tosses nervously in its bed each night, moaning vaguely for potatoes, fried potatoes, throw in a little onion, please. It wakes up instead to cold cereal and baked beans, a corroded economy and a failed national promise," read the announcement of one year's party.

"The Latke King knows what you need. The Latke King knows what this country needs. Sadly only a portion of the country can fit into our home in Queens," the invitation continued. For those who can't fit into his home, The Latke King offers this formula.

2½ pounds Idaho baking potatoes, unpeeled
1 large yellow onion, quartered
2 eggs, lightly beaten
¼ cup matzoh meal
4 to 5 teaspoons chopped fresh parsley
1 teaspoon salt
¼ teaspoon freshly ground black pepper
2 to 3 cups olive oil
1 large jar (16 ounces) unsweetened applesauce

1. Pick up the potatoes and admire their heft, their pure starchiness. Then scrub them with a brush.

2. Place the onion in a food processor. Pulse the blade a few times until the onion is diced into crunchy bits. Remove the blade and scrape the onion bits into a small bowl. Return the food processor bowl to the machine. No need to wash it yet.

3. Cut the potatoes lengthwise to fit in the food processor feed tube. Find the medium-coarse food processor shredding disk, which you've never used. Put it into the machine and turn it on. Begin feeding the potato slices into the machine.

The Latke King with Prince Daniel (left) and Prince Jonathan (right).

FOR THOSE WHO DON'T KNOW DAVID "THE LATKE KING," THERE IS SOME HOPE

Since 1984, the Lower East Side has also sponsored a Latke Festival. Originally, the downtown festival was undertaken as a challenge to The World Series of Latkes, which was then held on the West Side of Manhattan. Roger Mummert and David Starr, latke organizers, firmly believed that "the Lower East Side is latke territory." Period. They resented Johnny-come-lately, uptown latke pretensions.

Nevertheless, to encourage latke creativity, they created Nouvelle/New American and New Wave categories of latke cookery, in addition to the Traditional. As a result, there have been sweet potato latkes, latkes marinara, Mexi-latkes, potato and apple latkes with mascarpone and macadamia nuts, and mixed vegetable latkes with shiitake mushrooms and crème fraîche. In all categories, potatoes must be the main ingredient, the latkes must be vegetarian, and they must be fried in vegetable oil.

Roger Mummert with winning sisters Prilly (left) and Susan (right) Cobb. Photo: Tony Mangia

Latkes of every stripe are judged on a 20-point scale on the basis of presentation, aroma, relative weight, crunchability, and the "return factor" (were they so good you wanted to return for more?).

The festival is held on a Monday or Tuesday night during Chanukah, and the location is different each year. For further information about the Lower East Side Latke Festival, contact Roger Mummert at (516) 367-3072.

---

4. When the potatoes are shredded, put them in a colander over a large bowl. Dump in the onion bits and mix everything around with your hands, squeezing the potato moisture out as you work. Let the mixture drip for a few minutes while you put on a recording of Kitty Carlisle singing "Beat Out That Rhythm on a Drum."

5. Pour out the potato liquid from the bowl, but leave the starch that clings to the bowl. This is good for you. Dump in the shredded potato and onion mix. Add the eggs, the matzoh meal, the parsley, the salt, and the pepper. Stir the mixture eagerly. Then let it sit for about 10 minutes.

6. In a large cast-iron skillet, pour in ¼ inch of oil. Over high heat, get the oil very hot, but don't set off the smoke detector. Using a ¼-cup measure or a long-handled serving spoon, start spooning the batter into the skillet. Flatten each with a metal spatula to a diameter of 4 to 5 inches. Do not try to make the latkes uniformly round. Reduce the heat to medium and cook the latkes until golden brown on one side. Then turn over and fry them some more. When crispy on the outside and moist inside, about 5 minutes per side, remove and place on several thicknesses of paper towels. Keep doing this until you run out of batter.

7. Remove from the room anyone who prefers latkes with sour cream. Serve the latkes immediately. With applesauce.

Makes about 16 latkes, which is all you should eat the first night. By the end of Chanukah, you should be able to eat twice that many.

Dorio's
MASHED POTATOES AND TURNIPS

In the kitchen with Dorio Cario.

Fire fighter Dorio Cario was still in grammar school when his parents, who owned an Italian greengrocery in Richmond Hill, Queens, were given this recipe by a German customer. Fifty years later, both at home in Richmond Hill and at work in Brooklyn's Engine Company 280, Cario always serves roast turkey with a side of these creamy mashed potatoes and turnips.

2½ pounds Idaho potatoes, peeled and cut into 2½-inch chunks
1 pound turnips, peeled and cut into 1½-inch pieces
¼ pound (1 stick) butter
1½ cups milk or heavy (whipping) cream
Salt and freshly ground black pepper, to taste

1. Cover the potatoes with cold water and bring to a boil in a large pot. Cook until tender, about 40 minutes. Drain.

2. Meanwhile, cover the turnips with cold water and bring to a boil in a medium pot. Cook until tender, about 30 minutes. Drain.

3. Preheat the oven to 375°F. Lightly grease a 13 × 9-inch baking pan or casserole.

4. In a large bowl, combine the potatoes and turnips. Mash together, using a potato masher or an electric mixer. Add the butter and milk and continue mashing until smooth. Season with salt and pepper to taste.

5. Transfer the mixture into the prepared pan. Bake until lightly browned on top, about 45 minutes. Serve at once.
Serves 10 to 12

Louis'
POTATO PIE

David Liederman, founder of David's Specialty Foods, created this pie for Chez Louis, the restaurant that he owned on Manhattan's East Side. The restaurant is gone, but the craving for this potato pie hasn't abated.

4½ to 5 pounds large Idaho baking potatoes, peeled
4 cloves garlic, peeled
3 tablespoons unsalted butter
3 tablespoons mild olive oil
Salt and freshly ground black pepper, to taste

1. In a large pot, boil the potatoes in salted water with 2 of the garlic cloves until the potatoes are tender, 20 to 25 minutes. Drain the potatoes; set aside to cool.

2. Meanwhile, melt the butter with the oil in a large heavy skillet. Add the remaining 2 garlic cloves and sauté gently until they turn golden brown, 5 minutes. Do not allow to burn. Remove from the heat and set the skillet aside.

3. When the potatoes are cool, cut them into ¼-inch slices.

4. Preheat the oven to 450°F.

5. Add enough potato slices to the skillet of garlic, oil, and butter to fit comfortably without crowding. Set over medium heat and sauté the potatoes until lightly browned, 15 to 20 minutes. Add salt and pepper to taste. Repeat with the remaining potatoes. If the garlic gets too browned, discard it.

6. Arrange the potatoes in a heavy, ovenproof, 9-inch skillet. Press down firmly on the slices with the back of a spoon so they hold together in a "pie."

7. Bake until the potatoes are crispy on the outside, 20 to 25 minutes. You can bake them for a few minutes longer, or until the pie is brown, for an especially crisp exterior.

8. Remove the skillet from the oven. Slide a spatula under the pie and transfer it to a serving plate. Serve immediately.

Serves 6

VEGETABLE WISDOM
Wise Words from *The Charles Street Association Cookbook*

■ If you want to peel potatoes in advance, keep them from turning brown by covering them with water and adding a few drops of vinegar and placing them in the refrigerator. They will keep for days this way.

■ It is wise to cover vegetables that grow underground while cooking. Those that grow above the ground may be cooked uncovered.

■ Carrots cut best if you've had them at room temperature for an hour beforehand.

■ To remove vegetable stains from your fingers, rub with a slice of raw potato or lemon.

Frank Bolz's POTATO CASSEROLE

Before his retirement from the New York City Police Department after more than 27 years of service, Frank A. Bolz was Commanding Officer of the NYPD Hostage Negotiating Team and the department's chief negotiator. He personally negotiated more than 285 incidents that resulted in the release of more than 850 hostages, without loss of life, before retiring to start his own consulting firm. He attributes much of his success to the preparing ("a Zen-like experience") and eating ("heaven") of this dish, which he frequently prepared for colleagues after a "hostage situation."

6 potatoes, peeled and thinly sliced
1 onion, thinly sliced
4 slices boiled ham, cut into long strips
(see Note)
1 cup ricotta cheese
Salt and freshly ground black pepper, to taste
2 tablespoons unsalted butter
3 cups milk
4 slices Swiss cheese, cut into long strips
1 tablespoon chopped fresh parsley

1. Preheat the oven to 375°F.

2. Alternately layer the potatoes, onion, ham, and ricotta in a 2-quart casserole. Season each layer with salt and pepper to taste. Dot the top layer with the butter and pour the milk over the top. Bake until the potatoes are tender, 1¼ hours.

3. Arrange a lattice of Swiss cheese strips on top of the casserole. Continue baking until the top browns slightly, 20 minutes. Sprinkle with the parsley before serving.

Serves 8 to 10

Note: For a main course dish, double the amount of ham.

BRIGHTON BEACH MEMORIES

A knish, the Eastern European variation on the crêpe, is a thin dough, traditionally stuffed with mashed potatoes and caramelized onions. The tasty, hefty snack became an icon at Mrs. Stahl's, a stand on the Brooklyn Boardwalk. According to *The Brooklyn Cookbook,* by Lyn Stallworth and Rod Kennedy, Jr., "There really was a Mrs. Stahl, who made knishes in her home in the early 1930s and sold them on the boardwalk."

Mrs. Stahl opened her stand in 1935 and, according to *The Brooklyn Cookbook,* "was known for her generosity." The business she began has been sold and knish aficionados claim that Mrs. Stahl's name has never been sullied with regard to the quality of the knishes made under her label.

Other aspects of the business have changed, however. When asked for his recipe, Les Green, the current owner, shrieked into the telephone: "Are you crazy?" We assured him that we had no major mental disorders, though we certainly are wild about the knishes, which he now sells in miniature versions that make perfect cocktail fare.

"Is this a joke?" screeched Mr. Green. No way, we said, knishes are to us almost holy,

and certainly no laughing matter. In fact, since knish recipes attributed to Mrs. Stahl can be found in manuscripts at the Brooklyn Historical Society and the Museum of the City of New York, we said, we know that this particular knish is a weighty thing, indeed. And that is why we called Mr. Green. We saw it as a courtesy, like the scholars who still bother to call the Dead Sea Scroll cartel in Israel instead of whipping off to California where they can study copies of the scrolls.

"Would you call Hershey's and ask them for the recipe for their chocolate bar?" bellowed Mr. Green. We didn't have the heart to tell him that the chocolate company likes to give recipes, besides we've never liked mixing chocolate with potatoes and onions. So we gathered a small band of knish connoisseurs, chugged over to Brooklyn, and ate a dozen or so in an effort to unravel the mystery of Mrs. Stahl.

Tasted in a midtown kitchen some weeks later, the version here is close enough to summon the sound of pigeon wings, the screech of gulls, and the nasal twang of those who wander the boardwalk along the subway Riviera.

Mrs. Stahl's for potato, apple, cabbage, vegetable, and kasha knishes.

Memorable
KNISHES

DOUGH
2 cups all-purpose flour
1 teaspoon baking powder
½ teaspoon salt
2 tablespoons vegetable oil
2 eggs, lightly beaten

FILLING
2 tablespoons melted chicken fat (Schmatz, page 342) or vegetable oil
2 cups finely chopped onions
2 cups plain mashed potatoes
Salt and freshly ground black pepper, to taste

1. To make the dough: Combine the flour, baking powder, and salt in a large bowl. Make a well in the center and add the oil, eggs, and 2 tablespoons water. Gradually mix the wet ingredients with the flour. Add up to 2 tablespoons more water if necessary. Knead the dough until it forms a rough ball.

2. Knead the dough on a lightly floured surface until the dough is smooth, about 6 minutes. Place the dough in a lightly oiled bowl, cover, and refrigerate for 1 hour.

3. Preheat the oven to 350°F.

4. To make the filling: Combine the chicken fat, onions, potatoes, and salt and pepper to taste in a bowl.

5. Remove the dough from the refrigerator and divide it into thirds. On a floured surface, roll out one piece of the dough into a thin rectangle about 10 inches long. Spread about ⅔ cup of the filling along one long end, about 1 inch from the edge. Roll up like a jelly roll and pinch the edges closed. Repeat with the remaining pieces of dough and filling.

6. Arrange the rolls on baking sheets. Bake until browned, about 40 minutes.

7. Slice the knishes and serve.
Makes about 2 dozen

Ginny's
WARM POTATO SALAD

This potato salad is descended from good German stock; it has been updated to an American standard with the addition of a chicken stock roux. Without the mayonnaise found in many potato salads, it is filling yet zesty and light and a wonderful accompaniment to fall or winter dishes.

2 pounds Red Bliss potatoes, unpeeled and
quartered (6 cups)
1¾ teaspoons salt
¼ pound thick-sliced bacon, cut into
½-inch pieces (¾ cup)
3 tablespoons all-purpose flour
2 cups New York Penicillin (page 47)
or canned chicken broth, warmed
2 teaspoons dry mustard
2 tablespoons sugar
1 teaspoon celery seeds
⅓ cup cider vinegar
½ cup finely chopped scallions
⅛ teaspoon freshly ground black
pepper

1. Place the potatoes in a medium pot and add 5 cups cold water and 1½ teaspoons of the salt. Bring to a boil over high heat. Reduce the heat and simmer gently 8 to 10 minutes. Drain.

2. Meanwhile, fry the bacon in a skillet over medium heat until crispy. Drain on paper towels. Reserve the bacon fat.

3. In a medium saucepan, heat 1½ tablespoons of the bacon fat. Sprinkle on the flour and whisk the fat and flour together to form a paste (the roux). Cook, whisking continually, to cook the flour, 2 to 3 minutes.

4. Slowly whisk the chicken broth into the roux and continue to whisk until smooth and thickened, about 2 minutes.

5. In a small bowl, mix together the dry mustard, sugar, celery seeds, and vinegar. Add the mixture to the sauce and bring to a boil. Reduce the heat and simmer until slightly thick, 5 to 10 minutes.

6. Pour the sauce over the potatoes. Add the bacon, scallions, the remaining ¼ teaspoon salt, and the pepper. Toss and serve warm.

Serves 6

Mary Henderson's
SARATOGA POTATOES

Mary F. Henderson originally presented this recipe in her *Practical Cooking and Dinner Giving*, which was published in 1878 and is in the collection at The New-York Historical Society. The recipe is consistent with most early documents on the legendary Saratoga chip.

4 large potatoes
½ pound lard
Salt, to taste

1. Fill a large bowl with ice water and set aside. Using a mandoline or a sharp knife, cut the potatoes wafer-thin. Place the slices in the ice water.

2. Melt the lard in a deep heavy pot over medium heat until hot enough to sizzle and bubble a potato crumb vigorously. Carefully lower 5 to 6 potato slices into the pot and fry until they are a delicate yellow color, 3 to 5 minutes. With a slotted spoon, remove them to a cooling rack set over paper towels. Sprinkle with salt. Continue until all of the potatoes are fried.

Makes about 75 chips, serves 6 to 8

Romanian
EGGPLANT SALAD

Alex Goren, an investor who lives on Park Avenue, was born in Romania and grew up in Italy. This recipe came down to him from his paternal grandmother. The original specified using all wooden utensils so the eggplant would not acquire a metallic taste. Stainless steel, ceramic, or glass serve the same purpose.

Alex Goren's eggplant dish makes a delicious appetizer or side dish.

2 eggplants (1 pound each)
1½ teaspoons sea salt, or more to taste
⅓ cup safflower oil
¼ cup extra-virgin olive oil
1 tablespoon milk
1 fresh tomato, sliced
15 Greek black olives
¼ cup chopped onion

---

1. Roast each eggplant, turning frequently, over a flame or under a broiler, until the skin is charred all over, 20 to 25 minutes.

2. Using a sharp knife, peel the eggplants and rinse thoroughly under cold water. Quarter the eggplants lengthwise and discard as many seeds as possible. Toss with 1 teaspoon sea salt, then place the eggplants in a stainless-steel or other non-aluminum colander and squeeze out as much water as possible. Allow to drain in the colander for 30 minutes. Blot up any excess moisture with paper towels.

3. Cut the eggplant flesh into 1½-inch cubes. Place the cut eggplant in a glass or ceramic bowl

and, stirring continuously with a wooden spoon, slowly add the safflower and olive oils and remaining ½ teaspoon sea salt. Stirring, add the milk.

4. Spread out the eggplant on a large plate, and using a fork, score parallel lines on the surface. Garnish with the tomato slices and olives. Serve the chopped onion on the side.

Makes about 2½ cups, serves 4 to 6

Michael's
COLD CHINESE
EGGPLANT

Michael Tong, who owns the Shun Lee Palace and Shun Lee West restaurants, learned to make this dish from his mother in China. As an appetizer or side dish, it is wonderful year-round.

¼ cup peanut oil
4 small, firm eggplants (1 pound total weight), ends trimmed, flesh cut into bite-size pieces
½ tablespoon minced fresh ginger
1 teaspoon minced garlic
1 tablespoon hot bean paste
½ cup vegetable or chicken stock or canned broth
2 tablespoons soy sauce
1 teaspoon sugar
½ teaspoon salt, or to taste
½ tablespoon brown rice wine vinegar
½ tablespoon Oriental sesame oil
1 tablespoon minced scallion

---

1. Warm a nonreactive skillet or wok over medium heat until hot. Add the peanut oil and eggplant and stir-fry until soft, about 3 minutes. Remove from the heat. Use a large spoon to press the eggplant against the side of the skillet to squeeze out the excess oil. Remove from the skillet and set aside.

2. Return the skillet to medium heat and add the ginger, garlic, and bean paste. Cook until softened and aromatic, about 1 minute. Add the stock, soy sauce, sugar, and salt and bring to a boil. Return the eggplant to the skillet and cook to blend the flavors, 3 minutes. Add the vinegar and sesame oil, stir, and remove from the heat. Set aside to cool to room temperature or cover and chill in the refrigerator.

3. Sprinkle with the scallions before serving.
Serves 2

Michael Tong's recipe for Shun Lee's BBQ Pork is also included in New York Cookbook. *Check the index.*

Mrs. D'Angelo's
EGGPLANT CAPONATA

Mrs. Francis D'Angelo, a milliner whose son once owned a bakery called D'Angelo & Latucca in Brooklyn, taught her son's friends to make this holiday dish when they were teenagers. It is wonderful.

Salt
2 pounds baby Italian eggplants, ends
*   trimmed, flesh cut into bite-size*
*   chunks*
3 tablespoons olive oil
1 cup diced Vidalia or other sweet
*   onions*
2 cloves garlic, chopped
4 anchovy fillets
Dried red pepper flakes, to taste
*   (optional)*
1 can (6 ounces) tomato paste
½ cup currants
½ cup sliced celery
½ cup sliced fennel
3 tablespoons drained capers
½ cup white wine vinegar
¼ cup dry white wine
5 fresh basil leaves
¼ cup chopped fresh parsley
½ cup good-quality black or green olives
*   (optional)*
Freshly ground black pepper,
*   to taste*

1. Salt the eggplant chunks, place in a nonreactive colander or on a plate, cover with a plate, and weigh down to force the water and bitterness from the eggplant. Let sit for 20 minutes.

2. Warm the oil in a nonreactive large saucepan over medium heat. Add the onions, garlic, anchovies, and pepper flakes (if using). Cook, stirring frequently, until the onions are translucent. Add the tomato paste, currants, celery, fennel, capers, vinegar, wine, basil, parsley, and olives (if using). Cover the pan and bring the mixture to a boil. Reduce the heat to medium-low and cook until thickened, about 30 minutes, adding a little water if the mixture gets too thick.

3. Rinse the eggplants and drain thoroughly. Add the eggplant to the mixture in the pan, cover, and cook until the eggplant is tender, about 40 minutes.

4. Season the caponata with pepper and additional salt to taste. Remove from the heat. Cover and refrigerate for 24 hours before eating.

Serves 4 as a side dish, or 2 as a main course

Dilled
GREEN BEAN AND PEPPER SALAD

A great picnic could pop up at any time, and this salad is perfect for just such an occasion. According to Barbara Scott-Goodman, who lives in Soho, green beans and peppers are almost always available at the greenmarkets or at your corner vegetable stand. And this tasty side dish is versatile and takes very little time to prepare.

1½ pounds green beans, ends trimmed
1 red bell pepper, stemmed, seeded, and cut into strips
1 yellow bell pepper, stemmed, seeded, and cut into strips
2 tablespoons Dijon mustard
2 tablespoons balsamic vinegar
2 tablespoons soy sauce
½ cup olive oil
Salt and freshly ground black pepper, to taste
¼ cup chopped fresh dill

1. Cook the beans in boiling salted water to cover until tender, about 7 minutes. Drain in a colander and refresh under cold running water.

2. Place the peppers in a colander and pour a kettle of boiling water over them to blanch. Refresh under cold running water and drain well.

3. Combine the beans and peppers in a large bowl and set aside.

4. Combine the mustard, vinegar, and soy sauce in a small bowl. Whisk in the oil until emulsified and season with the salt and pepper.

5. Pour the sauce over the vegetables, toss well, and sprinkle with the dill. Toss again. Serve chilled or at room temperature.

Serves 4

Pickled mushrooms, a savory side dish.

Parsley
PICKLED MUSHROOMS

R osemary Duggan, a retired nurse, learned to make these sprightly mushrooms from an Italian colleague she once worked with at St. Luke's Hospital. They make a delicious first course, or, served with toothpicks, a good hors d'oeuvre. The trick, said the late denizen of Yorkville, is "blanching the mushrooms for less than 10 seconds in boiling water and then dunking them in the pickle. This cleans the little buggers and softens them for the marinade."

1 teaspoon salt
¼ cup fresh lemon juice
½ teaspoon freshly ground black pepper
¾ cup olive oil
1 cup minced Italian (flat-leaf) parsley leaves
2 pounds white mushrooms, stemmed, caps quartered
1 pound shiitake mushrooms, stemmed, caps quartered

1. Fill a large pot half full with water and bring it to a boil.

2. Meanwhile, in a large bowl, dissolve the salt in the lemon juice. Add the black pepper. Using a wire whisk, slowly drizzle in the olive oil, whisking constantly, until all of the oil has been added. Stir in the parsley. Cover and refrigerate.

3. When the water is boiling, add the white and shiitake mushrooms and blanch for 10 seconds. Immediately drain the mushrooms in a colander and refresh under cold water. Continue rinsing until the mushrooms have cooled. Drain well and pat dry with paper towels.

4. Stir the mushrooms into the lemon-parsley vinaigrette. Cover and chill for 1 hour before serving. Refrigerated, this dish will keep for up to 3 days.

Serves 8

Peter Rose's
DUTCH CABBAGE SALAD

The Germans didn't introduce 'slaw' to New York, according to Peter Rose, author of *The Sensible Cook: Dutch Foodways in The Old and New World,* the Dutch had their own version of cabbage salad in New Amsterdam. This pungent, satisfying slaw is adapted from a recipe that appeared in her book.

⅓ cup red wine vinegar
¼ cup vegetable oil
Salt and freshly ground black pepper, to taste
2 cups shredded green cabbage
2 cups shredded red cabbage

Combine the vinegar, oil, salt, and pepper in a nonreactive medium-size bowl and whisk until smooth. Add the cabbages and stir well to coat. Cover with plastic wrap and refrigerate until chilled, at least 4 hours.

Serves 4

Ted's
HUNGARIAN CUCUMBER SALAD

Ted Koryn, apron at the ready.

Ted Koryn, a business consultant who lives on the East Side, brags that his Hungarian Cucumber Salad will be "the best leftover you'll ever have in your life, which is convenient, since this salad keeps a long time." Koryn urges that the salad be served after the main course, in the European manner.

6 medium to large cucumbers, peeled,
seeded and cut into julienne or grated
¼ cup salt
½ cup sugar
¼ cup plus 2 tablespoons red wine vinegar
1 tablespoon Dijon mustard
¼ cup plus 2 tablespoons vegetable oil
1 large red onion, diced
2 tablespoons minced fresh dill
2 teaspoons sweet paprika

1. Place the cucumbers in a nonreactive colander and sprinkle the salt over, mixing well with your hands. Let stand for 2 hours.

2. Gently squeeze the water out of the cucumbers by hand. Return the cucumbers to the colander.

3. In a large bowl, whisk together the sugar, vinegar, mustard, and oil. Add the cucumbers and mix with your hands. Mix in the onion. Cover and refrigerate for 2 hours.

4. Add the dill and paprika and mix well. Serve. The salad can be kept in the refrigerator for as long as 1 week, and it improves with age.

Serves 6

Cool and Crunchy COLESLAW

1 head green cabbage (about 2 pounds), finely sliced

1 large green bell pepper, stemmed, seeded, and finely sliced

1 large or 2 medium Spanish onions (about ½ pound total weight), thinly sliced

1 carrot, peeled and grated

1 cup sugar

1 cup distilled white vinegar

¾ cup vegetable oil

1 tablespoon salt

1 teaspoon dry mustard

A winning recipe from the 1986 City Gardeners Harvest Fair, this coleslaw is the creation of Marlene Licciardello, at the time an N.Y.U. student who worked part-time at the Brooklyn Botanical Garden. Licciardello makes coleslaw during the summer, when her heat-stricken family cries out for "something cool to pick at."

1. In a nonreactive, large mixing bowl, combine the cabbage, bell pepper, onions, and carrot. Sprinkle on ¾ cup of the sugar and toss.

2. In a nonreactive small saucepan over medium heat, combine the remaining ¼ cup sugar with the vinegar, oil, salt, and dry mustard. Bring to a boil, stirring often. Pour the boiling sauce over the cabbage mixture and toss well. Cover and refrigerate for at least 1 hour before serving.

Serves 8

Marlene Licciardello with her dad Alfred and mom Marie.

THE CAESAR SALAD SONG

Caesar salad was created as a main course on July 4th, 1924, by Caesar Cardini, an Italian immigrant who owned restaurants in Tijuana, Mexico. It was popular with movie stars and became the darling of Hollywood. It also became the showpiece of Manhattan dining rooms, where New York waiters perfected the showmanship of tableside Caesaring. One of the earliest maestros of Caesar Salad was Nicola Paone, a former tenor and Broadway soloist, who opened his namesake restaurant 50 years ago. He composed this song to accompany and elucidate the tableside preparations of his fine version of Caesar Salad.

I

With the salt be avaricious
Quarter teaspoon, even less
With the pepper use your judgment
It's the flavor you'll assess

Use the vinegar with prudence
Just two tablespoons will do
And then crush one clove of garlic
Which is always good for you

A half cup of crumbled pieces
Of the Parmigiano cheese
One half cup of olive oil
Use the extra virgin, please

Caesar . . . Caesar . . .
Gonna gonna make it good
Gonna gonna make it right
Gonna gonna make it so
My love will love me more tonight

II

Make a paste of two anchovies
One egg yolk, room temperature
Lemon juice: One tablespoonful
Make sure that it is fresh and pure

Have one romaine lettuce ready
Trim it to bite size, washed and
  dried
One half cup of bacon pieces
Not too fat, but crisply fried

One teaspoon of Worcestershire
  sauce
Half teaspoon of mustard, too
And then get half cup of croutons
So the preparation's through

Caesar . . . Caesar . . .
Gonna gonna make it good
Gonna gonna make it right
Gonna gonna make it so
My love will love me more tonight

III

Take your time, be ever patient
So you'll never lose control
Now, let's put these things together
In a spacious salad bowl

Put the salt and put the pepper,
And the vinegar just thus
Put the oil and the garlic
Garlic is salubrious

Lemon juice and Worcestershire
  sauce
Place the yolk of egg right in
Use the mustard, leave the rest out
And you're ready to begin

IV

Now it's time to beat the dressing
Beat it creamy-smooth and then
In the bowl put in the lettuce

And with vigor go again
In good spirit you will toss it
Toss it well and you are bound
To get praise for all your talent
If the leaves are coated round

Take the garlic out, discard it
Make your dishes nicely cold
Place the salads in the platters
Before serving them behold

V

Take the croutons and the bacon
With good care and neatly done
Sprinkle them atop the salads
And my wish is: LOTS OF FUN
California, I adore you
Giving me this precious dish
I can taste and feel your sunshine
Nothing better one could wish

Sense the breeze from the Pacific
Hear your waves from every shore
With closed eyes I see your magic
Things I never dreamt before

Caesar . . . Caesar . . .
Gonna gonna make it good
Gonna gonna make it right
Gonna gonna make it so
My love will love me more tonight

Accompanying himself on the guitar, Nicola Paone gives a full-fledged performance of his Caesar Salad Song.

© 1989

Caesar Salad
SONG TRANSLATION

¼ teaspoon salt

¼ teaspoon freshly ground black pepper, or more to taste

2 tablespoons white wine vinegar

2 tablespoons fresh lemon juice

1 clove garlic, peeled and smashed

½ teaspoon Dijon mustard

1 teaspoon Worcestershire sauce

2 anchovies, minced

1 egg yolk

½ cup extra-virgin olive oil

1 head romaine lettuce, rinsed, dried, and torn into bite-size pieces

½ cup crisply fried chopped bacon

½ cup freshly grated Parmesan cheese

1 cup croutons (see Note)

1. In a large bowl, combine the salt, pepper, vinegar, lemon juice, garlic, mustard, Worcestershire sauce, anchovies, and egg yolk. Whisk until frothy. Continue whisking while drizzling in the olive oil.

2. Add the lettuce, bacon, cheese, and croutons, toss quickly, and serve.

Serves 4

Note: For the croutons, place a slice of garlic in 2 tablespoons of extra-virgin olive oil and let sit for an hour or so. Cut enough crusty white bread into ½-inch cubes to equal 1 cup. Sauté the bread over medium heat in the fragrant oil until toasty brown.

Georgio's
SHAVED ARTICHOKE AND PARMESAN SALAD

This cool artichoke salad comes from Georgio Cozzi, who grew up in Parma and now is a pattern-maker on Seventh Avenue. The salad can be served as a first course, or, accompanied by cold lamb, beef, or seafood, it makes a fine summer supper.

3 tablespoons fresh lemon juice
½ teaspoon salt
¼ teaspoon freshly ground black pepper
¼ cup plus 2 tablespoons extra-virgin
    olive oil
1 tablespoon minced fresh mint leaves
1 wedge (4 ounces, not grated)
    top-quality Parmesan cheese
4 large fresh artichokes
Additional fresh mint leaves,
    for garnish

1. Combine 2 tablespoons of the lemon juice with the salt and pepper in a glass or ceramic bowl. Whisking vigorously, drizzle in the olive oil to make a vinaigrette. Add the minced mint; set aside.

2. Slice the Parmesan into wafer-thin sheets and set aside.

3. Using a sharp knife, cut away all of the outer leaves from the artichokes; peel the stems and remove the hairy chokes. Cut each artichoke heart crosswise into thin slices. Toss immediately with the remaining 1 tablespoon lemon juice so that the artichokes do not discolor. Add the lemon-mint vinaigrette and toss gently.

4. Divide the salad among 4 chilled salad plates. Place the Parmesan on top and garnish with additional mint or black pepper. Serve.

Serves 4

Oranges for Sarah Elmaleh's unusual salad.

Sarah Elmaleh's
ORANGE AND OLIVE SALAD

Sarah Elmaleh, the daughter of a rabbi, was born in 1898 in the seaport village of Essaouira in Morocco, and learned many of her cooking techniques from the family's Arab servants. She came to Brooklyn in 1939 with her husband, a businessman, their children, and an exotic repertoire of recipes that combined Moroccan and Sephardic cuisines. This recipe comes from her granddaughter, Lisa Craig Kuhr. It makes an alluring first course and is wonderful followed by lamb, grilled chicken, or a fish stew.

5 navel oranges, peeled and diced
¾ cup black salt-cured (shriveled) olives, halved
    and pitted
2 cloves garlic, minced
¼ teaspoon coarse (kosher) salt, or to taste
1 teaspoon sweet paprika
½ cup minced fresh parsley
½ teaspoon ground cumin
Dash of cayenne pepper
2 tablespoons olive oil

Combine all the ingredients in a bowl and toss well. Refrigerate to chill, then serve.

Serves 4 to 6

Wally's
CHOPPED SALAD

This salad is said to have originated at the Palm restaurant, where it's called the Monday Night Salad. About 20 years ago, when one of the owners of Palm opened Wally's, now Wally's and Joseph's, in the theater district, he brought with him most of the Palm's dishes, including this one, which, by the way, is now part of the standard New York steakhouse menu.

1 large, ripe tomato, chopped and
    drained
1 head lettuce (such as oak leaf, salad bowl,
    Boston, or iceberg), rinsed, dried,
    and chopped
1 cucumber, peeled, seeded, and
    coarsely chopped
2 ribs celery, finely chopped
1 Spanish onion, diced
3 whole red pimientos, diced
1 tablespoon capers, rinsed and
    drained
2 tablespoons coarsely chopped green
    or imported black olives (or a
    combination of both)
4 or 5 flat, oil-packed anchovy fillets, coarsely
    chopped
2 tablespoons olive oil
Salt, to taste
1 tablespoon red wine or balsamic
    vinegar
Freshly ground black pepper,
    to taste

1. Drain the chopped tomato in a colander, pressing down with a wooden spoon to squeeze out any excess water.

2. In a large bowl, combine the chopped lettuce, cucumber, celery, onion, pimientos, capers, olives, and anchovies. Add the drained tomatoes. Using a sharp knife, give the mixture an extra chopping right in the bowl.

3. Add the oil and mix thoroughly. Add the salt to taste, then the vinegar. Taste again. The salad should have a fairly lively flavor at this point. If not, carefully add a little more salt and season with the pepper.

Serves 4

Jane's
TOMATILLO
SALSA

Inspired by Mexican salsas, Jane Littell's version is wonderful with grilled meat or as a dip with vegetables or corn chips.

1 pound tomatillos, husked
⅔ cup fresh cilantro leaves
Juice of 2½ limes
1½ teaspoons salt
2 tablespoons minced chipotle chile (you can use
    canned), or 1 teaspoon minced fresh jalapeño
    chile (optional)

1. Rinse the tomatillos under cool water. Place them in a nonreactive pot, cover with water, and bring to a boil. Reduce the heat and cook until the tomatillos are softened and dull green in color, about 5 minutes. Remove the tomatillos with a slotted spoon and set aside until cool enough to handle.

2. In a blender or food processor, combine the cilantro, lime juice, salt, and chipotle and process until smooth. Halve each tomatillo, add them to the food processor, and process to the desired consistency. Serve cool or at room temperature.

Makes about 1½ cups

Belmont Avenue
GIARDINIERA

These pickled Italian vegetables are as indispensable to the tables in restaurants along Arthur Avenue as ketchup is at a hamburger joint. They can stave off hunger, soothe the nibbling impulse, and also make a good condiment alongside heavy roasted meats.

4 carrots, peeled
3 ribs celery
½ pound green beans, ends trimmed
1 large turnip, peeled
1 red bell pepper, stemmed and seeded
1 yellow bell pepper, stemmed and seeded
½ pound white button mushrooms
½ pound pearl onions, skins removed
1½ cups cauliflower florets
4 bay leaves
4 teaspoons yellow mustard seeds
4 whole cloves
4 dried chiles
4 teaspoons black peppercorns
4 cloves garlic, peeled
1 teaspoon salt, or to taste
2 quarts white wine vinegar
1 teaspoon sugar
2 quarts olive oil

1. Cut the carrots, celery, green beans, turnip, and red and yellow bell peppers into ½-inch chunks. Clean the mushrooms but leave them whole.

2. Bring a pot of well-salted water to a boil. Add the carrots, celery, green beans, turnips, red and yellow bell peppers, pearl onions, and cauliflower and blanch for 1 minute. Drain immediately and chill completely under cold running water. Transfer the vegetables to a large bowl, add

the mushrooms, and toss to combine.

3. Sterilize four 1-quart Mason jars (see instructions, this page). Into each jar place: 1 bay leaf, 1 teaspoon mustard seeds, 1 whole clove, 1 dried chile, 1 teaspoon black peppercorns, 1 garlic clove, and salt to taste. Divide the mixed vegetables among the jars.

4. Bring the vinegar and sugar to a boil in a nonreactive saucepan. Pour the vinegar over the vegetables to cover completely. Seal the jars and set aside to marinate for at least 2 days and up to 1 week.

5. After marinating, drain the vinegar and replace it with the olive oil. Refrigerated, the vegetables will keep for up to 1 month.

Makes 4 quarts

Minatchee Arjune's
MANGO ACHAR

6 green mangos (see Note) or large green
    tomatoes, or 12 very sour crab apples
20 fresh Scotch bonnet chiles
½ cup sea salt or coarse (kosher) salt
1 teaspoon fenugreek seeds
1¼ cups malt vinegar
6 cloves garlic, peeled
¼ cup chopped fresh ginger
¼ cup ground cumin
¼ cup ground coriander
2 cups grapeseed oil, mustard oil, or peanut oil
1 tablespoon black mustard seeds
1 tablespoon fennel seeds
1 teaspoon ground turmeric
1 teaspoon chili powder
1 tablespoon fine salt

1. Mangos have a hard center stone. Slice the fruit from the stone in 2 large pieces. Remove the flesh from the skin of each piece, then slice each piece into fourths. Repeat with the remaining mangos. If using green tomatoes, remove the stems and slice into eighths. If using crab apples, remove the stems, quarter, peel, and remove the seeds. Cut the chiles lengthwise in half. Place the fruit and the chiles on a tray, sprinkle with the sea salt, and place in a sunny spot to dry for 2 days.

2. Soak the fenugreek seeds in the vinegar overnight. Place the vinegar, garlic, ginger, cumin, and coriander in a food processor or blender and purée to make a paste.

3. Heat the oil in a large nonreactive saucepan. Add the mustard seeds, fennel seeds, turmeric, and chili powder and remove from the heat for 3 minutes. Add the puréed mixture, return the pan to the heat, and simmer, stirring constantly, for 2 minutes. Add the salted fruit and chiles, bring the mixture to a boil, and simmer for 30 minutes. (If using crab apples, simmer for only 10 minutes.)

4. Stir in the fine salt and set aside to cool. Spoon into two sterilized pint jars (see instructions, this page). The oil should cover the top of the pickle. If it does not, add more oil to each jar. Tightly cover and store in the refrigerator for up to 1 year.

Makes 1 quart

Note: Mango skins contain a chemical that can cause a poison-ivy-like rash in people sensitive to it. Therefore, it is a good idea to wear rubber gloves when peeling the fruit.

STERILIZING

Pickles are best stored in sterilized jars. To sterilize, carefully place the clean glass canning jars and closures on a rack in a large pot. Add hot water to cover by 2 inches and bring to a full, rolling boil. Cover the pot and boil for 10 minutes. Leave the jars in the hot water until they are needed. Use tongs to remove the jars and caps. Place each on a clean towel and fill immediately.

NEW YORK IN A PICKLE

Pickles may be synonymous with bumper crops, their precise formulation fueling competition for ribbons at state fairs and occasional internecine battles in late-summer kitchens.

But the pickling impulse isn't limited to the great rural outdoors. City Picklers get the urge, too. And while their country cousins may be content with variations on the cucumber, City Picklers see any ingredient as fair game and any preserving technique as possible.

One of the earliest indications of this is in the *Echo Cook Book,* which was published in 1886 and is in the collection of the Brooklyn Historical Society. It features recipes for chow-chow, cauliflower and peppers lightly brined with ginger and curry, as well as for piccalilli, green tomatoes, cabbage, and peppers.

In New York, picklers continue to snatch carrots, celery, cabbage, onions, and beans, tomatoes of every hue from pale green to deepest red, broccoli, cauliflower, and eggplant. Watermelon rind is fine, but unripe mangos are even more intriguing. In the wide range of exotic preserving blends they deploy, they are celebrating the waves of immigrants who are to a city what fields of grain are to the countryside: the lifeblood, the allure, the romance.

THE URGE TO PICKLE

It is not easy to be a City Pickler. The aftereffects of simmering strong spices and vinegar in a smal' apartment can be daunting. Minatchee Arjune, who is known for the Indian green mango pickles she makes in her family's apartment in Brooklyn, admits that the searing steam that rises from the roasting herbs, chile peppers, and vinegar in her recipe have caused her family to flee coughing and eyes streaming.

But Mrs. Arjune is undeterred. "I must pickle," she says. "I have no control over that."

Jung Sook Kim, who puts up vats of kimchi in the cellar of a Korean grocery in Flushing, Queens, has encountered a different problem in the urban jungle.

"The cabbage must be dried in the sun to make the best kimchi," she said on a recent afternoon. She watched over the trays of sliced Chinese cabbage that she had propped on milk crates on the sidewalk bordering her store, perpetually in the shade of neighboring high-rise apartment buildings.

"Very little sun makes a job hard," she said.

A PICKLER'S GOT TO DO WHAT A PICKLER'S GOT TO DO

Yet sun and space and occasional supply constraints don't faze determined City Picklers. Faced with a dearth of underripe mangos, Mrs. Kim turned to green tomatoes and immature crab apples. Mrs. Kim has kimchi-ed yellow and red cabbage and savoy cabbage; on very shady days, she has even used a slow oven to dry her cabbage. Are these accommodations much to ask of the ardent pickler?

City Picklers don't think so. It helps them contribute to the urban panoply of Indian and Korean, Italian and Indonesian, American and Eastern European pickles. In each category, there are hundreds of variations.

"I have green tomatoes and red tomatoes, sours, half sours, three-quarter sours, hot pickles, sweet pickles, sauerkraut, and pickled peppers," said Tim Baker, owner of the Essex Street Pickle Company, pacing through the

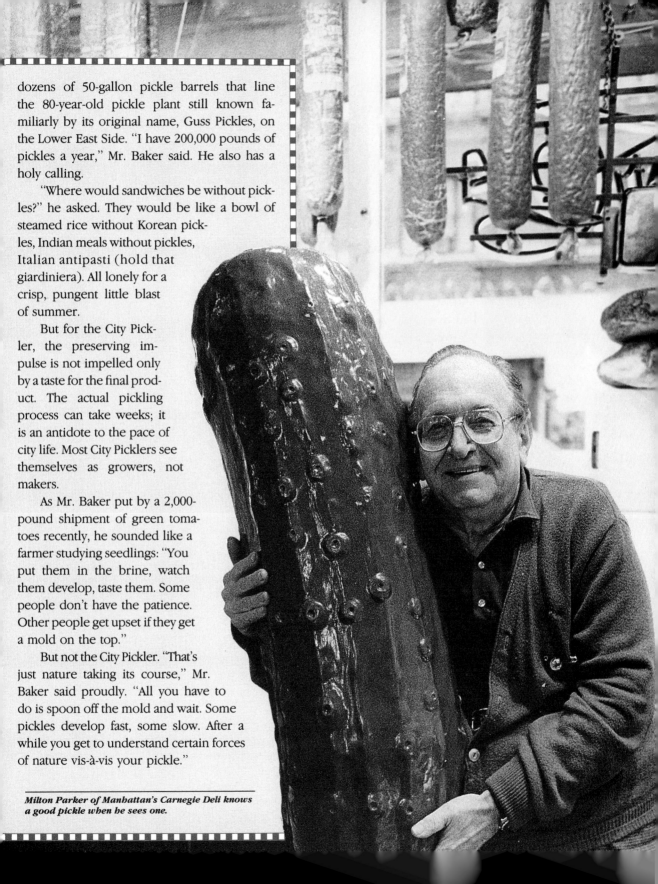

dozens of 50-gallon pickle barrels that line the 80-year-old pickle plant still known familiarly by its original name, Guss Pickles, on the Lower East Side. "I have 200,000 pounds of pickles a year," Mr. Baker said. He also has a holy calling.

"Where would sandwiches be without pickles?" he asked. They would be like a bowl of steamed rice without Korean pickles, Indian meals without pickles, Italian antipasti (hold that giardiniera). All lonely for a crisp, pungent little blast of summer.

But for the City Pickler, the preserving impulse is not impelled only by a taste for the final product. The actual pickling process can take weeks; it is an antidote to the pace of city life. Most City Picklers see themselves as growers, not makers.

As Mr. Baker put by a 2,000-pound shipment of green tomatoes recently, he sounded like a farmer studying seedlings: "You put them in the brine, watch them develop, taste them. Some people don't have the patience. Other people get upset if they get a mold on the top."

But not the City Pickler. "That's just nature taking its course," Mr. Baker said proudly. "All you have to do is spoon off the mold and wait. Some pickles develop fast, some slow. After a while you get to understand certain forces of nature vis-à-vis your pickle."

Milton Parker of Manhattan's Carnegie Deli knows a good pickle when he sees one.

Sri Lankan EGGPLANT PICKLE

It would be difficult to find a better condiment for summer's grilled foods. But this spicy eggplant condiment is also wonderful on steamed rice or spooned inside a baked potato.

2 large eggplants
2 teaspoons coarse (kosher) salt
1 tablespoon ground turmeric
¼ to 1 cup peanut oil
1 tablespoon black mustard seeds
½ cup rice wine vinegar
1 onion, minced
4 cloves garlic, sliced
1 tablespoon minced fresh ginger
½ cup tamarind pulp, dissolved in ¾ cup hot
  water
2 tablespoons good-quality curry powder
1 tablespoon minced fresh chile
1 cinnamon stick (2 inches long)
2 teaspoons sugar

1. Cut the eggplant crosswise into ¼-inch-thick rounds. Combine the salt and the turmeric, sprinkle over the eggplant slices, and allow to sit for 1 hour. Drain off the liquid and use paper towels to pat the slices dry.

2. Heat 2 tablespoons of the oil in a large skillet over low heat. Add the eggplant slices in batches and fry on each side until brown, about 4 minutes each side. Add more oil as needed. Remove the eggplant slices to a large bowl.

3. Combine the mustard seeds, vinegar, onion, garlic, and ginger in a food processor or blender. Process to a smooth purée and set aside.

4. Strain the tamarind mixture and reserve the liquid.

5. Heat the remaining oil (you should have 2 tablespoons left) in a nonreactive large skillet. Add the vinegar purée and simmer for 5 minutes.

Add the curry powder, chile, cinnamon stick, sugar, and tamarind liquid and simmer for 5 minutes.

6. Gently stir in the eggplant, along with all of the liquid that has accumulated in the bowl. Cover the skillet and simmer for 15 minutes.

7. Remove the pan from the heat and set aside to cool. Spoon the pickle into sterilized pint jars (see instructions, page 175). Stored in the refrigerator, the eggplant pickle will keep for up to 1 month.

Makes 1½ quarts

Paul Zolenge's GREEN TOMATO PICKLE

Paul Zolenge, co-owner of New York's Stage Delicatessen.

25 firm green tomatoes
1 teaspoon yellow mustard seeds
1 tablespoon celery seeds
1 tablespoon coriander seeds
1 tablespoon black peppercorns
1½ teaspoons whole cloves
1½ teaspoons whole allspice
1 bay leaf
¼ cup cider vinegar
1 cup salt
1 rib celery, halved
2 cloves garlic, peeled

1. Soak the tomatoes overnight in a large pot of cold water. Drain and place them in a large pottery crock.

2. Combine the mustard seeds, celery seeds, coriander seeds, peppercorns, cloves, allspice, bay leaf, vinegar, and salt in a large bowl. Add 4 cups water and stir well. Pour the mixture over the tomatoes and add the celery and garlic. Make sure that the tomatoes are completely covered with the pickling liquid and that there is at least 2 inches of headspace in the bowl so that when the tomatoes ferment the liquid won't ooze all over.

3. Place a plate or wooden lid over the tomatoes and place a 3- to 5-pound weight on the lid. Let the tomatoes sit in a cool place, undisturbed, until the fermenting stops, 2 to 3 weeks.

4. Transfer the pickled tomatoes to sterilized glass jars (see instructions, page 175). Cover with the pickling liquid, seal, and store in a cool place.

Makes 4 quarts

of a glazed ceramic bowl or crock. Sprinkle liberally with some of the salt and dust with some of the cayenne. Add another layer of cabbage, salt, and cayenne and continue layering until all of the cabbage is salted. Cover the bowl or crock with a ceramic plate just large enough to fit inside and weigh down with a heavy jar. Refrigerate for 1 week.

3. Drain the cabbage and rinse completely under cold water. Use a clean cloth to squeeze out the excess moisture. Slice each segment into 1-inch sections. In a shallow glass casserole layer the cabbage, onion, garlic, chiles, and ginger until all of the ingredients are used. Combine the soy sauce with 2 cups water and pour over the cabbage. Cover with a lid and refrigerate, undisturbed, for 5 days. The kimchi is excellent eaten cold with warm rice or as an accompaniment to grilled fatty meats or fish. Covered, it will keep in the refrigerator for 1 month.

Makes 1 quart

Jung Sook Kim's
KOREAN KIMCHI

1 head Chinese cabbage
1 cup coarse (kosher) salt
½ teaspoon cayenne pepper
1 white onion, thinly sliced
4 cloves garlic, minced
2 fresh chiles, minced
1 tablespoon minced fresh ginger
2 teaspoons soy sauce

1. Core the cabbage. Cut the cabbage lengthwise into 6 segments. Cut each segment crosswise in half. Spread out the cabbage on a baking sheet and place it in a sunny spot to dry for 4 hours.

2. Place a layer of the cabbage on the bottom

Shopping for kimchi ingredients.

Astoria GREEN OLIVE CHUTNEY

Tekki Dimitrus, a cabdriver, makes this chutney to slather on the lamb, chicken, or fish that he cooks on his grill in Sunnyside, Queens.

1 pound cracked green olives, pitted and minced
4 cloves garlic, minced
½ fresh chile, minced
Minced zest of 1 lemon
2 tablespoons capers, rinsed and minced
2 tablespoons olive oil
1 teaspoon freshly ground black pepper

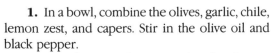

1. In a bowl, combine the olives, garlic, chile, lemon zest, and capers. Stir in the olive oil and black pepper.

2. Transfer to a glass jar and seal tight. Refrigerate for at least 2 days before using. The chutney will last for 3 weeks and can be used as a garnish or sauce for chicken, fish, beef, or lamb. Spread on croutons or crackers, it can be instant cocktail fare.

Makes 1 quart

Mardee's YOGURT CHUTNEY

Kitchen equipment maven Mardee Haidin Regan perfected her version of a standard Indian condiment for her husband, who is British and has an insatiable desire for Indian food.

Mardee Regan shares the spotlight with sphinx-like friend, Nancy.

The chutney makes a great dip for crudités, topping for rice or baked potatoes, or condiment for grilled meat or fish.

1½ cups plain yogurt
2 tablespoons minced white onion
1 tablespoon minced scallion
1 tablespoon minced fresh ginger
1 clove garlic, minced
2 tablespoons minced fresh cilantro
2 tablespoons minced fresh mint
½ teaspoon ground cumin
Cardamom seeds from 6 pods
½ teaspoon coarse (kosher) salt
¼ teaspoon freshly ground black pepper
¼ teaspoon cayenne pepper

1. Whisk the yogurt in a bowl until smooth. Stir in all of the rest of the ingredients, adding more of any to suit your personal taste. Cover and chill for at least 1 hour to let the flavors develop.

2. Serve the chutney with grilled fish, chicken, or lamb, as a topping for potatoes or rice, or as a spread inside a pita pocket. The chutney keeps for up to 2 weeks if covered tightly and stored in the refrigerator.

Serves 6

Paula's
MACEDONIAN RELISH

Although she lived in Europe for 15 years, cookbook author Paula Wolfert never lost her New York accent. She uses this irresistible condiment with grilled or broiled meats. It's also delicious with rice or grilled vegetables.

1 head garlic, cloves separated, 3 peeled and
*   minced, the rest left whole and unpeeled*
3 large eggplants, halved lengthwise
6 green bell peppers
6 green tomatoes, halved lengthwise
½ chile pepper, minced
¼ cup olive oil
1 tablespoon distilled white vinegar
2 teaspoons salt
1 teaspoon freshly ground black pepper

1. Prepare a grill or preheat the oven to 400°F.
2. If using a grill, grill the vegetables until soft when the coals are covered with ash. Place the whole garlic cloves on a piece of aluminum foil; it will take about 20 minutes; the eggplants, about 30 minutes; the bell peppers, about 20 minutes; and the tomatoes, about 15 minutes.

If using an oven, place the whole garlic cloves and eggplants in a nonreactive large baking dish and roast for 10 minutes. Then add the bell peppers and roast for 10 minutes more. Add the tomatoes and roast for 10 to 15 minutes more.
3. Peel the garlic and stem, seed, and peel the bell peppers and place in a seasoned wooden bowl. Discard the liquid from the eggplant; peel and place the pulp in the bowl. Carefully peel the tomatoes and place them in the bowl. Use a fork to mash the vegetables into a smooth paste. It will be very loose and juicy.
4. Whisk the oil into the vegetable paste. Combine the minced garlic, chile, and vinegar, and add the mixture to the vegetable paste. Season with the salt and pepper. Cover and allow the mixture to rest overnight in the refrigerator.
5. The relish can be served as a dip with bread or slathered on grilled pork, lamb, beef, chicken, or fish. After several days, the "pindzur" gets watery and makes a good marinade for meat or fish. It will keep up to 1 week if covered well and refrigerated.
Serves 12

Scott Campbell's
FRIED SQUID DIPPING SAUCE

Scott Campbell, a chef in New York City, said he got the idea for this recipe from lemonade. He wanted a sauce that was refreshing and simple. It is a terrific foil for fried squid—or just about any fried or grilled seafood.

⅓ cup mixed fresh lemon and lime juices
2 tablespoons sugar
½ teaspoon salt
¼ teaspoon freshly ground black pepper
1 jalapeño chile, thinly sliced
2 tablespoons finely chopped shallots
¼ cup roughly chopped fresh cilantro

1. Pour the lemon and lime juices in a bowl and stir in the sugar, salt, pepper, jalapeño, shallots, and ¼ cup water. Stir to dissolve the sugar and salt. Cover and refrigerate for 1 hour.
2. Add the cilantro 15 minutes before ready to serve.
Serves 4

WILDMAN LOOKS FOR DINNER

There are vegetable stands on most street corners in the city, and the typical New Yorker stops by on a daily basis, buys a little of this and a little of that, and carries it home in a white plastic sack that cuts creases into the hand.

Steve Brill is not a typical New Yorker. When he shops for dinner, he ferrets around Central Park in Manhattan, or Alley Pond Marsh in Queens, or Pelham Bay in the Bronx, or Prospect Park in Brooklyn. There are hundreds of acres of city parks and they are his produce store. Mr. Brill, who is in his 40s, is a forager.

When foraging, he wears camouflage fatigues and carries a very large backpack for toting his booty. He answers his telephone "Wildman" and signs the books that he has written and published privately as "Wildman" Steve Brill. He wrote *Shoots and Greens of Early Spring in Eastern North America.*

FOOD FOR THE FORAGING

In 1982, Wildman, self-taught naturalist and an ecologist and vegetarian by political persuasion, began offering foraging tours of New York City parks. He was determined to teach the difference between "picking weeds and uprooting rare flowers," to show people "the earth beneath the asphalt and teach respect."

But even as he led small bands crashing through underbrush in search of wild mushrooms, wild spinach and sorrel, water mint, and wild leeks, he expected trouble. "I knew the city government would imagine swarms of foragers descending like locusts on the parks, eating every flower, root, bush, and tree. Plus, they would think that if foragers got indigestion, they could sue the city," he said. "I knew they'd try to get me."

In fact, Wildman was arrested in 1986 for allegedly foraging without a permit, reported *The New York Times*. According to Wildman, he was also charged with carrying concealed gardening tools, a charge he denied. "I pick by hand," he said. The arresting officers did not find gardening tools in Wildman's backpack, though they did find sassafras tree saplings ("it makes a good tea," said Wildman), wild carrots ("incomparable flavor," he said), winter cress and cattails ("you can peel them and stir-fry them like bamboo shoots; they are nutritious and very tasty," he said). Wildman admits that he ate the evidence.

Eventually the city hired Wildman to give his field

In the field with Wildman Steve Brill.

tours. Four years later, the Parks Department fired Wildman because, he said, he wouldn't punch a time clock or fill out appropriate bureaucratic forms. He said that he was "too wild" for the Parks Department and began giving his tours privately again.

"The parks are the people's grocery store," said Wildman, who has messianic moments. "I will not stop until the people are free to forage."

Betsy Gottbaum, then the Parks Commissioner, said that parks are also for dogs and she feared that dog "activity" on potential ingredients could pose a health risk. Wildman answered that in New York's parks, people have a greater chance of being killed by a mugger than by a dandelion. He's led thousands of people through the parks, he said. And nobody's gotten sick. He always washes his greens.

"They are afraid of me," said Wildman, who sees himself as nature's liberator in New York. "They are afraid that if people find out how delicious and nutritious this wild food is, they won't shop in rip-off stores anymore." Indeed, dozens of chefs have toured with Wildman. One, the French chef Michel Bras, was "jealous," he said, because "you can't find this good vegetables and mushrooms in Paris, at least not in the parks in Paris."

STEALTHY OF FOOT

In his walks now, Wildman tends to creep through underbrush more quietly and stand behind trees when park rangers are in the vicinity. "I hope they don't arrest me," he says often in a loud whisper.

He finds things like chickweed, which he steams and serves with whole wheat noodles, and young chicory, which he adds to salads. Curled dock, he combines with mushrooms to make soup; dandelion greens he uses in a homemade wine. He uses garlic mustard leaves to make horse-radish, and nettles, he steams with wild carrots. Sorrel and purslane, he combines with potatoes and yogurt to make soup, and wild asparagus, well "everybody has their favorite recipe," he said.

In addition to recipes, Wildman knows the lore of medicinal herbs. And while others extol the ethnic meld of the city, he sings odes to the plethora of "non-native plant species. We have gingkos right in the middle of the city!" he exclaimed, standing on a small knoll in Central Park, waving his arms toward the skyscrapers.

"Look at this! Wild garlic!" he said, tramping down the knoll, crouching through some underbrush and arriving, triumphantly, clutching a fistful of wild garlic.

He approached a group of young boys who were throwing spitballs to the accompaniment of rap from the boom box they had brought into the park. "Do you know what this is?" asked Wildman, who believes that if young people can be educated, they can save the planet, possibly avoid drugs, and certainly eat better and cheaper.

Like most New York kids, the ones who were pitching to rap music had seen a lot. But for a good three beats, they stared wordlessly. Finally, one said, "That's a weed, mister."

"An edible weed!" said Wildman and as they watched in horror, he took a big triumphant bite.

Harvesting a park find.

For information on foraging tours or to order books, contact Wildman Steve Brill, (718) 291-6825.

Wildman Brill and group gently shake a tree in order to collect its fruity offering.

Wildman's
WILD ONION SAUCE

This pungent sauce has been adapted so that domesticated onions and garlic can be used, and it makes a wonderful condiment for any robust grilled food. Wildman likes the sauce over brown rice or whole wheat noodles.

2 tablespoons olive oil
4 small onions, preferably wild, minced
4 cloves garlic, minced
2 tablespoons all-purpose flour
½ cup dry white wine
1¼ cups New York Penicillin (page 47) or other favorite homemade chicken broth
¼ teaspoon freshly ground white pepper
¼ teaspoon ground allspice
1 bunch wild chives (Allium vineale), *minced*

1. Warm the oil in a nonreactive skillet over low heat. Gently sauté the onions and garlic until golden brown, about 12 minutes.

2. Add the flour gradually and continue cooking, stirring constantly, until the flour begins to turn gold.

3. Add the wine and bring to a boil. Cook until the wine is totally absorbed by the vegetables. Stir in the broth, pepper, and allspice and simmer for 5 minutes. Add the chives and serve.

Makes 1½ cups

Yoko's
JAPANESE SALAD DRESSING

Housewife Yoko Meinhardt-Leye learned to make this delicious dressing from a family cook at her home in Japan. It is wonderful over lettuce or assorted lightly steamed vegetables.

3 tablespoons rice wine vinegar
1 teaspoon soy sauce
1 teaspoon dark Oriental sesame oil
½ teaspoon wasabi (Japanese horseradish paste)
½ teaspoon toasted sesame seeds, smashed in a mortar with a pestle
¼ teaspoon sugar
¼ teaspoon dried red pepper flakes
½ teaspoon white miso paste
½ teaspoon grated fresh ginger
1 tablespoon grated carrot
1 tablespoon minced fresh chives

Combine all of the ingredients except the chives in a blender and purée until smooth. Stir in the chives.

Makes ¼ cup

THE SMART COOK

More and more cooks are stocking a selection of infused vinegars and oils in their pantries. These modern cooks' helpers can give zest to salads, marinades, or dressings as well as nuance to grilled or poached fish, chicken, or meat.

In general, the infusions are easy to make and have a long shelf life. Stored at room temperature, vinegars last almost indefinitely, though the aromatic herbs, fruits, garlic, or onions should be removed after 10 days so that they don't leave an acrid taste.

Simple infused oils—ones in which peppers, garlic, or herbs have been steeped— will keep for up to 6 months, though, as with the vinegar, the aromatics should be strained out after 10 days. Oils that are flavored through an emulsification, such as the ones made by chef Jean-Georges Vongerichten, owner of Jo-Jo on Manhattan's Upper East Side, should be stored in the refrigerator. They will last for up to 2 weeks, though the freshness of the flavor begins to fade after the first week. For simple oil infusions, a good grade of olive oil is best; the emulsifications need a less assertive oil, such as grapeseed or canola.

Chef Jean-Georges Vongerichten with a display of infused oils at Jo-Jo's.

USING INFUSED AND SYRUP-FLAVORED OILS

Chef Jean-Georges Vongerichten keeps a rainbow of infused oils in the kitchen of Jo-Jo, his Upper East Side restaurant, using them whimsically in lieu of heavy sauces to give nuance to his dishes.

Some of the oils are simply infused with aromatics; others get a more intense flavor by being emulsified with fruit or vegetable syrups. All the oils can be used in endless combinations. But in an interview that appeared in *Cook's* magazine, Chef Vongerichten made the following specific suggestions for winning combinations:

- Sauté shrimp in cinnamon oil and drizzle the cooked seafood with carrot-cinnamon oil.

- Sauté steak in paprika oil.

- Marinate a butterflied leg of lamb or lamb chops in curry oil before grilling them outdoors or broiling them in the kitchen.

- Sauté cod in ginger oil and drizzle the finished fish with ginger-beet oil.

- Dip chicken breasts in beaten egg, dredge them in dehydrated potato flakes, then sauté them. Drizzle the crisp-cooked chicken breasts with tomato-chili oil.

- Make a curry mayonnaise by gradually whisking ¾ cup curry oil into 1 egg yolk until thickened. Stir in a minced garlic clove. Serve this mayonnaise with steamed mussels.

- Marinate tuna steaks in wasabi oil before grilling them.

- Toss your favorite type of pasta with lemon oil and sliced black olives.

- Toss pasta with saffron oil and some chopped fresh tomato.

- Drizzle slices of roast pork loin with cranberry-orange oil.

- Marinate chicken breasts in cardamom oil for 15 minutes before grilling or sautéing them. Drizzle the cooked chicken with cardamom-pineapple oil.

- Flavor lean ground lamb with cumin oil. Form the ground lamb into thick patties, stuffing each patty with a piece of goat cheese. Then grill, broil, or sauté the patties.

- Flavor a Middle Eastern tabbouleh-style salad with ginger oil.

- Toss cooked shrimp in a vinaigrette made with curry oil and place the shrimp on a bed of mixed greens for a curried shrimp salad.

Barbara's
THAI GARDEN VINEGAR

Chinese rice vinegar and Italian white wine vinegar are milder and fruitier than their French counterparts and make a mellower medium for this infusion that Professor Barbara Kirshenblatt-Gimblett makes for her giant salads (page 139).

1 quart Chinese rice vinegar or Italian
    white wine vinegar
6 stalks fresh lemongrass
1 kaffir lime or regular lime
6 kaffir lime leaves
3 slices galangal
1 tablespoon sliced and peeled fresh
    ginger

1. Pour the vinegar in a tall glass jar. Cut the bottom ends off the lemongrass stalks to release the perfume and add the stalks to the jar. Peel the lime and add the peel to the jar (use the lime for something else). Add the kaffir lime leaves, galangal, and ginger. Cover and let the vinegar stand in a dark place for 1 week.

2. Strain the vinegar, discard the aromatics, and sprinkle the vinegar over roasted beets, boiled potatoes, steamed carrots, raw fennel, boiled fava beans, or boiled taro.

Makes 1 quart

Versatile
INFUSED VINEGARS

Jane Littell grew up savoring her mother's potato salad and other favorites of her German family that were often seasoned strongly with a tangy splash of vinegar. Back then there was just one bottle of vinegar in the pantry, she recalls. Later she and her mother experimented with infused vinegars, moving from simple white wine vinegars to the sherry, Champagne, and rice wine vinegars that line the shelves of New York groceries. These are a few of the mother and daughter team's favorite recipes. All are simple to make and, since they frequently can take the place of fattier dressings or marinades, are endlessly versatile in the kitchen.

BARBECUE VINEGAR

Try marinating beef kebabs or steak in 1 cup of this vinegar for 1 to 2 hours, then grill over aromatic wood chips.

2 tablespoons dried green peppercorns
5 large cloves garlic, peeled
5 pearl onions, peeled
5 cherry tomatoes
5 jalapeño or other small, hot chiles
5 cups cider vinegar or red wine vinegar

1. Preheat the broiler. Soak 5 bamboo skewers in water.

2. Place the peppercorns in a 42-ounce widemouthed glass jar.

3. Thread each skewer with a garlic clove, onion, tomato, and chile. Broil, turning as necessary, until charred all over, about 10 minutes.

With tongs, remove the skewers from the broiler and place them in the jar.

4. In a nonreactive saucepan over medium heat, warm the vinegar until hot but not boiling. Pour immediately through a funnel into the jar, leaving just enough room for a lid. Close and store in a cool, dark place for 2 days. Remove and discard only the garlic.

Makes 5¼ cups

SPICY PEACH VINEGAR

Marinate chicken or fish in 1 cup of this infused vinegar for 1 hour, then grill or broil. This vinegar also makes a delicate vinaigrette for greens, or you can splash a few tablespoons over ice and seltzer for a refreshing drink.

4 peaches, peeled and sliced
2 cinnamon sticks (each 1 to 2 inches long)
1¼ cups rice wine vinegar

1. Place the peach slices and cinnamon sticks in a 16-ounce bottle or jar.

2. In a nonreactive saucepan over low heat, warm the vinegar until hot but not boiling. Immediately pour through a funnel into the bottle, leaving just enough room for a cork stopper or lid. Close and store in a cool, dark place for 10 days before using.

Makes 2 cups

Peaches for a wonderful vinegar with the flavor of summer.

TUSCAN VINEGAR

A few teaspoons of this vinegar will liven up soups, stews, and tomato sauce. Mixed with Dijon mustard and olive oil, it also makes a wonderful vinaigrette.

4 sprigs fresh rosemary
4 sprigs fresh thyme
4 sprigs fresh oregano
1 branch fresh basil
1 tablespoon black peppercorns
1¾ cups plus 2 tablespoons red wine vinegar

1. Insert the herb sprigs, cut ends first, into a 16-ounce glass jar or bottle. Add the peppercorns.

2. In a nonreactive small saucepan over low heat, warm the vinegar until hot but not boiling. Pour immediately through a funnel into the bottle, leaving just enough room for a cork stopper or lid. Close and store in a cool, dark place for 10 days before using.

Makes 2 cups

Herb or Spice INFUSED OILS

½ cup dried herb or spice of choice, such as paprika, chili, curry, wasabi (Japanese horseradish paste), ground ginger, mustard, cardamom, nutmeg, cinnamon, saffron, clove, or cumin
1 cup canola, grapeseed, safflower, or corn oil

1. Mix the herb or spice of choice with ½ cup water in a wide-mouth jar with a lid. Stir well to make a paste. Add the oil, cap the jar, and shake to distribute the ingredients. Let stand at room temperature to allow the flavor of the herb or spice to infuse the oil, about 3 days. After the first day, the herb or spice paste will settle at the bottom of the jar.

2. After 3 days, carefully ladle the infused oil into an 8-ounce jar; discard the paste at the bottom. The infused oil can be covered and stored in a cool, dark place for up to 6 months.

Makes 1 cup

Admire your infused oils and vinegars on the windowsill, if you must, but store them in a cool dark place.

Citrus
INFUSED OIL

2 tablespoons grated citrus zest of choice, such as grapefruit, lemon, lime, or orange
1 cup canola, grapeseed, safflower, or corn oil

1. Combine the citrus zest and oil in an 8-ounce bottle. Cover and let stand at room temperature for about 3 days.

2. Strain the oil, discarding the zest. Return the oil to the bottle and cover. The oil can be stored in a cool, dark place for up to 6 months.

Makes 1 cup

Vegetable or Fruit
INFUSED OILS

VEGETABLE OR FRUIT SYRUP
3 pounds vegetable or fruit of choice, such as beets, cranberries, carrots, tomatoes, pineapples, and/or yellow or red bell peppers

1 teaspoon sherry vinegar
½ cup herb- or spice-infused oil of choice (see facing page), or plain canola, grapeseed, safflower, or corn oil

1. To make the syrup, mix and match ingredients for color and flavor or use just 1 ingredient at a time. Each ingredient calls for slightly different handling: Carrots, bell peppers, or beets should be grated and puréed in the food processor until very fine. Tomatoes or pineapples should be cut into 2-inch pieces and puréed. Cranberries should be finely ground.

2. Transfer the processed vegetable or fruit pulp of choice to a large sieve lined with a double thickness of dampened cheesecloth and squeeze to release 2 cups of liquid. Discard the solids.

3. Transfer the juice to a nonreactive saucepan and bring to a boil over medium heat. Simmer until reduced to ½ cup, 25 to 30 minutes.

4. Strain this syrup through a fine sieve, and discard the solids. You should have ½ cup. Store the syrup in the refrigerator.

5. To make the oil, combine the syrup and vinegar in a nonreactive bowl.

6. For a vegetable- or fruit-flavored infused oil, gentle stir an herb- or spice-infused oil into the syrup mixture; do not emulsify.

To make a vegetable- or fruit-flavored plain oil, add one of the bland oils to the syrup mixture in a slow steady stream and whisk until well-combined.

7. Cover and refrigerate either type of oil for up to 2 weeks.

Makes 1 cup

A CHRONOLOGY OF SIGNIFICANT CULINARY EVENTS IN NEW YORK CITY

Certain foods say New York City. Deli sandwiches and sour pickles, oyster stew and sirloin steaks, blintzes and cheesecake. The city is the place for pristine sushi, for Cantonese dim sum, for Italian food that would make mama weep with joy, for state-of-the-art French cooking.

The streets of New York are head-turning: One pushcart fries falafel; across the street, Afghan kebabs sizzle; a Greek spiro turns slowly on its spit; pizza is slapped out by the slice; sausages and peppers smolder; Polish pierogi simmer; and the sweet aroma of honey-roasted cashews rises above all the sultry, ethnic scents.

Some New Yorkers live by their egg creams, some covet bagels, some can't imagine life away from hot dogs with the proper bite. This is an eating town. In the seventeenth century, Oliver Wendell Holmes, Sr., described

the town as "a tongue that is licking up the cream of commerce and finance of a continent."

But contrary to popular myth, New Yorkers are not insatiable individualists who consume solely for personal gain. They are serious arbiters who share the burden of shaping the tastes of the nation. We take our responsibility seriously.

Since 1626, when Peter Minuit purchased Manhattan Island from the Indians for 60 Dutch guilders ($24), the city has been a port of entry for far-flung ingredients and cooks. Due to the diligence of local diners and the

unflagging commitment of cooks who have plied their magic at home, on pushcarts, and in the city's citadels of chic, the city is a laboratory of foods and drinks that have gone on to become national symbols.

Like the Statue of Liberty or the Empire State Building, these edible icons are no bit players in New York City's zeitgeist. Following is a brief compendium of the culinary achievements credited to the city of New York.

THE BIRTH OF AMERICAN BAR FOOD 1642 The first two taverns were opened in Manhattan. According to I. N. Phelps Stokes, in his *Iconography of Manhattan Island,* Philip Gerard, a French soldier in the West India Company's service, opened a public house on the north side of Stone Street near Whitehall

Street. Within months, "Gerard was prosecuted by the treasury for selling beer at a higher rate than the local ordinance allowed." He was also prosecuted for being absent from guard duty without leave. As a humiliating punishment, he was sentenced to ride the Wooden Horse during parade, with a pitcher in one hand and a drawn sword in the other." Legend has it that he named his tavern The Wooden Horse in "sheer defiance."

Willem the Tasty opened on Coenties Slip. Exactly how the saloonkeeper earned his title is not known. It is known that plates piled high with hot home-cooked food were routinely dispensed for free to paying drinkers. Dutch dishes such as Snert, a pea porridge (recipe appears on page 69), accompanied by a slab of New World Rye Bread (see recipe, page 89), are in keeping with the era and could certainly have won Mr. Tasty his moniker.

What is known for sure is that the giveaway food concept that shaped the taverns of North America for the next 250 years began in New York City. By 1776, there was a tavern for every 45 residents in New York City.

————

Pushcarts at the ice skating rink at Rockefeller Center (facing page).

THE AMERICAN UNION BREWED OVER NYC COFFEE? 1670 The New York Merchant's Coffeehouse opened and, like the coffeehouses that opened afterwards, was considered "more civilized than taverns for gentlemen to meet in," according to *America Eats Out* by John F. Mariani. He adds that the New York Merchant's Coffeehouse later earned a reputation for being the "birthplace of the American Union." It may have at least set the stage for serious doings over coffee. The Tortine Coffee House, which

GOVERNOR MINUIT BUYS MANHATTAN ISLAND

The Old Brewery in 1852.

THE CRADLE OF AMERICAN BREWING

Anthony Rutgers of Albany, New York, opened a brewery on the north side of Stone Street between William and Nassau Streets in lower Manhattan and became a symbol of the beer brewers who were colonizing the city. The listing of Freedmen of New York, between 1695 and 1786, gives 17 names of brewers and maltsters. It is unlikely that they all had private businesses; probably most worked for larger companies, such as the Rutgers Brothers, according to *Brewed in America* by Stanley Baron.

By 1898, most brewers had moved to Brooklyn, where the more than 45 breweries made it the brewing capital of the United States. Piels, Trommers, Schaefer, and Rhinegold were all founded in either the Williamsburg or Bushwick sections of Brooklyn.

was built at the corner of Water and Wall Streets in 1794, housed the stock exchange.

BARBECUE BEFORE THERE WAS A TEXAS MID-1700S Dr. Alexander Hamilton, of Annapolis, Maryland, was an obscure gentleman who kept an anecdotal diary of his travels along the Eastern seaboard. In *Hamilton's Itinerarium,* he describes Turtle Barbecue as an established New York City amusement: "They have a diversion here [that is] very common, which is the barbecuing of a turtle, to which sport the chief gentry in town commonly go once or twice a week." For contemporary barbecue recipes, see pages 267 to 273.

OYSTER CAPITAL, USA 1748 Peter Kalm, the Swedish naturalist, describes how the oysters that were so plentiful in New York's harbors and bays were preserved.

According to his book, *The America of 1750*:

"As soon as the oysters are caught, their shells are opened and the fish washed clean; some water is then poured into a pot, the oysters are put into it, and they are boiled for a while; the pot is then taken off the fire again and the oysters taken out and put upon a dish till they are almost dry. Then some nutmeg, allspice and black pepper are added, and as much vinegar as is thought sufficient to give a sourish taste. All this is mixed with half the liquor in which oysters are boiled, and put over the fire again. While boiling great care should be taken to skim off the thick scum. At last the whole pickling liquid is poured into a glass or earthen vessel, the oysters are put into it, and the vessel is well stopped to keep out the air. In this manner, oysters will keep for years, and may be sent to the most distant parts of the world."

After the railroad and the Erie Canal were built, New York became the capital of barreled oysters. Locally caught bivalves were packed with salt in barrels to ship west, where people hungered for the elegance and epicurean refinement that the bivalves from the East Coast epitomized.

By 1850, over $6 million worth of oysters were sold in New York City, according to *On the Town in New York* by Michael and Ariane Batterberry. Cape Cod, Chesapeake, Blue Points, Lynnhavens, Mattitucks, and Peconics were all available, and Canal Street was "catacombed" with oyster cellars. The "Canal Street Plan" was a deal by which a diner could consume all the oysters he wanted for six cents. Oyster stew (see recipe, page 370) was a staple of saloons. Champagne was the haute accompaniment to oysters.

So powerful was the lure of the mythical Manhattan oyster that by 1880, the average American consumer was eating 660 oysters a year and the local oyster beds were exhausted.

An oyster stand on Canal Street.

·1·7·7·7·

FIRST SCREAMS FOR ICE CREAM SOUNDED IN NYC

On May 12, Philip Lenzi's confectionery shop advertised in the *New York Gazette* that ice cream "may be had almost every day." This is among the earliest evidence of the semi-frozen confection being served outside private homes. During the summer of 1790, George Washington ran up a $200 ice cream tab according to "the records of an ice cream merchant on Chatham Street in New York," writes Paul Dickson in *The Great American Ice Cream Book*.

The love of ice cream continued and gathered strength. By July 10, 1812, the *New York Morning Post* advertised that pineapple, strawberry, and raspberry were available at the Columbia Garden, an ice cream parlor. In 1934, Thomas Andreas Carvelas of Yonkers invented a machine for making "frozen custard," and began selling up and down the streets of New York from a battered truck. He later shortened his name to Tom Carvel and the rest of the story was presumably a piece of cake.

In 1960, Reuben Mattus, a Polish immigrant who lived in the Bronx, invented Häagen-Dazs ice cream. Making a frozen confection with high butterfat content and very little air, he started the super-premium ice cream trend with only three flavors: vanilla, chocolate, and coffee.

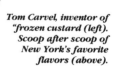

Tom Carvel, inventor of "frozen custard (left). Scoop after scoop of New York's favorite flavors (above).

YES, WE HAVE SOME BANANAS 1804

Bananas are first recorded in New York City as having entered the United States from Cuba. The rise of the once exotic fruit from oddity to part of the national diet is the produce version of the American dream.

In 1850, according to *Empire in Green and Gold* by Charles Morrow Wilson, both red and yellow bananas were priced at 10 to 25 cents a "finger." So dazzled were New Yorkers with the fruit that in 1864 C. Augustus Frank, a ship's steward, ventured into the malarial hinterlands of Colón, Panama, bought six dozen bunches of green bananas, loaded them on his ship, and, after an 11-day voyage, unloaded the fruit and sold it on New York piers at a net profit of approximately 1,000 percent. Frank continued to import bananas from Colón to New York and eventually returned there to supervise the clearing and planting of one of the first banana farms.

Bananas got their big theatrical break in the middle 1920s when jazz-band drummer Frank Silver heard a Greek produce peddler responding to a customer's request for the fruit by yelling up to a tenement window: "Yes, We Have No Bananas!" Silver described it to Sam Cohn, a fellow musician, and the two young men joined in a first venture as popular song writers with an upbeat song of the same name.

Said the Batterberry's in *On the Town in New York,* "Within a year the sheet music was selling at the rate of 25,000 copies a day. In New York and London nightclubs, drummers were beating away with bananas, band men were sitting on bunches of bananas, dance floors were being strewn with banana peels." New Yorkers still have a soft spot for the fruit (see recipes, pages 463 and 465).

Tropical fruits landing at Burling Slip in Manhattan.

SELTZER, SODA, AND THE SODA FOUNTAIN Since the 1790s, "tea water" (fresh spring water) had been sold from the horsedrawn carts that plied the streets of New York. But in 1809 Joseph Hawkins patented the machinery for carbonating fizzy water water, and by 1811, the

The root beer seller.

seltzer business had become one worth defending: According to the *Iconography of Manhattan Island* by I. N. Phelps Stokes, Sophia Usher, who claimed that her late husband was the original distiller of mineral water, was granted the right to sell the libation by City Hall on March 25, 1812, and may have spawned the local industry of bottling and delivering "pure, good health water" that endures today. (For local seltzer lore, see page 36).

New York's bubbling water,

however, soon became the basis of two other national institutions: the soda fountain and, eventually, the soft drink industry. In 1832 John Matthews began supplying carbonated water to New York stores and, according to Paul Dickson in *The Great American Ice Cream Book,* "he began manufacturing a compact dog-house-sized apparatus for carbonating water which was soon widely known as the fountain."

Matthews' high-level advertising helped to make carbonated water a rage,

and opened the door to flavored soda, now a billion dollar industry. "Youth as it sips its first soda experiences the sensations, which, like the sensations of love, cannot be forgotten," read one ad.

"The Evolution of the Soda Fountain," an article by Mary Gay Humphreys in the *Harper's Weekly* of November 21, 1891, suggests that Mr. Matthews' advertising was, at the very least, a self-fulfilling prophecy:

"It is a suggestive fact that no natural food or drink has appealed so widely to the imagination as this purely artificial compound. There are hundreds of thousands of people to whom the soda-water fountain has given

In the 1800s, peddlers delivered tea water right to the door.

·1·8·1·9·

CAN THAT FOOD

Two Englishmen, William Underwood of Boston and Thomas Kensett, who settled in New York, each started canning food, originally using glass containers.

Some suggest that it was Thomas Kensett and his uncle Ezra Dagett who first canned salmon, oysters, and lobsters in New York City. At the very least, it was Kensett who took out the original patent on the tin can in 1825, thus opening the gates to the single largest category on America's grocery shelves today. Both Underwood and Kensett switched from glass to tin in 1839.

their first realizing sense of the beauties of art and the glories of architecture.... The alliance of the fragrant fruit (syrups) with the 'sylph-like draught' was as ideally perfect as moonlight, music, love, and flowers or any other of those unions that evolve the muse.... But the crowning merit of soda water, and that which fits it to be the national drink, is its democracy. The millionaire may drink champagne while the poor man drinks beer, but they both drink soda-water. There is no quarter of this great town so poor that the soda-water fountain, cheaply but ostentatiously erected in marble and plate, does not adorn the street corners.... For him who drinks, it is small cost to see the bubbles winking on the brim, to feel the aromatic flavors among the roots of his hair and exploring the crannies of his brain, and to

realize each fragrant drop as it goes dancing down his throat."

By 1891, there were more soda fountains than bars in New York according to *On the Town in New York* by Michael and Ariane Batterberry. In the 1920s, the "egg cream," an eggless, creamless libation was invented in a New York soda fountain (for a recipe, see page 451). The annals of time have obscured the name of the egg cream inventor and the rational and philosophical underpinnings of the drink's name. And today, there are only half a dozen "soda fountain shops" in New York City.

The man who started it all still has a local monument. According to *The Great American Ice Cream Book,* "A fountainlike granite monument rises above the mortal remains of John Matthews in Greenwood Cemetery, Brooklyn."

Before the advent of screw-top plastic bottles, New Yorkers got weekly deliveries of seltzer syphons.

HOME OF THE WORLD'S FIRST A LA CARTE MENU CIRCA 1838 Delmonico's on South William Street introduced an à la carte menu, allowing guests to choose their own courses rather than simply order "table d'hotel." The restaurant, note Michael and Ariane Batterberry in *On the Town in New York,* was "the crucible of fine dining in America," but it wasn't until 30 years later that its finesse was publicly heralded by a culinary ambassador from the Old World. At a dinner at Delmonico's in 1868, Charles Dickens amended his earlier and rather dyspeptic remarks about American dining, noting that at Del's, he had been treated with "unsurpassable politeness, delicacy, sweet temper, hospitality and consideration." Service was not the only area in which Delmonico's was king. In 1898, in his *History of Old New York Life and the House of Delmonico's,* Leopold Rimmer noted: "There is hardly one hotel in New York today whose chef did not learn his cooking at Delmonico's."

AMERICA'S FIRST COOKING SCHOOL EARLY 1860S

At least a decade before the famed Boston Cooking School opened, a French chef named Pierre Blot began writing cookbooks in which he described himself as "a Professor of Gastronomy and founder of the New York Cooking Academy." Such an institution did not exist, according to the New York Directory, but its absence there may be semantics: Something named The New York Cooking School did stand at 35 East 17th Street until 1880 when it moved to 22 East 17th Street.

In their book, *The Story of Man and His Food,* C. C. Furnas and S. M. Furnas suggest that Pierre Blot "gave a tour of lectures in the East and wound up by starting the New York Cooking Academy." When Mr. Blot returned to France, Juliet Corson continued to train homemakers and professional cooks in the school.

Mr. Blot's first book published in the United States, *What to Eat . . . and How to Cook It,* "containing over one thousand recipes systematically and practically arranged, to enable the Housekeeper to prepare the most difficult or simple dishes in the best manner" was published by D. Appleton and Co., New York, in 1863. The book seemed a forerunner to those of Fannie Farmer et al. and was reviewed by *The New York Times* on July 14 of that year:

"The tempting bill of fare, set forth in Mr. Blot's title page, will be found realized in his work. More business-like than Soyer, his little manual is plain and precise in its directions, bringing American practice to test the theories of French science. If it is true, as most travelers assert, that the profusion of the good gifts of nature in the United States is as remarkable as the waste and neglect that too often accompanies the process of their conversion into the food of man, the multiplication of the works of this nature is a positive service to the economic inter-

A ladies' luncheon at Delmonico's, 1902 (above). The Modern School of Cookery in New York in 1916 (right). The wall signs include one demanding a commission to insure sanitary food conditions, one explaining refrigeration as a way to keep foods fit, one describing food composition, and one showing edible and poisonous mushrooms.

Students at a New York vocational cooking school.

The Great American Tea Company, which later became the A & P supermarket chain, opened at 31 Vesey Street. "By cutting out middlemen, by buying tea in quantity and by importing it themselves from China and Japan, they offered tea at the spectacularly low price of 30 cents a pound when others were charging $1.00," wrote Daniel J. Boorstin in *The Americans: The Colonial Experience.*

He continues, "They attracted customers by Barnum-esque showmanship: premiums for lucky customers, cashier's cages in the shape of Chinese pagodas, a green parrot in the center of the main floor, and band music on Saturdays. They sent eight dapple-grey horses pulling a great red wagon through the city and offered $20,000 to anyone who could guess the combined weight of the wagon and team."

By constantly increasing its line of groceries, the company grew to 29 stores by 1880 and to more than 200 stores in the 1890s. A & P used the transcontinental railroad to bring California oranges, Georgia peaches, and Texas grapefruits to middle-class American tables. In the 1890s, according to Stuart Berg Flexner in *Listening to America,* "the stores introduced the cash-and-carry policy, bringing a no-deliveries and no-charge-accounts mentality to the grocery business."

ests of the country. 'French Cookery' is often used as if the term implied luxury and extravagance, but so far is this from the truth, that its most noticeable feature is the elegant simplicity of its methods, based on enlightened experience, and equally adapted to the cottage home as to the gilded salons of the capital."

Mr. Blot also wrote *The Handbook of Practical Cookery for Ladies and Professional Cooks,* published in 1877.

BIRTHPLACE OF CHICKEN A LA KING CIRCA 1860 Chicken à la King, the rich creamed chicken and vegetables that was served in puff pastry shells, became a mainstay of a generation of Gibson girls. Odds favor New York as the birthplace, though history remains divided as to its inventor. Three people claim the dish.

Delmonico's chef Charles Ranhofer suggests that Foxhall P. Keene and James R. Keene created it at Delmonico's restaurant; chef George Greenwald said he made it for the proprietors, Mr. and Mrs. E. Clark King III, at New York's Brighton Beach Hotel; and James R. Keene claims that he made it up at Claridge's restaurant in London after his horse won the 1881 Grand Prix.

A & P MENUS week of DEC. 31st 1934

Prepared and proven in the A & P Kitchen

A&P TESTED

May your ship make port this coming year

It's A&P's job to go on year after year, in good times and in bad, making it easier for more and more Americans to get an abundance and variety of good food at prices they can afford to pay.

You may rest assured that A&P will do everything humanly possible to make 1935 a happy New Year to our customers.

Menus for four—$11 to $13 a week

	BREAKFAST	LUNCH OR SUPPER	DINNER
MONDAY DEC. 31	Grapefruit Pettijohn's Popovers Butter Preserves Coffee Milk	Dried Lima Beans with Onions Raisin Bread and Butter Apple Sauce Tea Milk	Meat Balls with Italian Spaghetti Green Salad, French Dressing Bread and Butter Crackers Cheese Coffee
TUESDAY JAN. 1	Orange Juice Soft-cooked Eggs Whole Wheat Toast Butter Coffee Milk	NEW YEAR'S SUPPER Clam Chowder Crackers Fruit Fruit Cake Tea Milk	Consommé Julienne [1] Roast Duck with Danish Stuffing and Sauce Bigarade Mashed Potatoes Brussels Sprouts Pickled Crabapples Lettuce, Chicory and Watercress Salad Rolls and Butter [2] Georgia Holiday Pudding Coffee
WEDNESDAY JAN. 2	Tangerines Shredded Wheat with Hot Milk Crisp Bacon Cinnamon Toast Coffee Milk	Duck Hash Cole Slaw Bread and Butter Baked Apple Tea Milk	Lamb Chops Baked Potatoes Green Peas (canned) Rolls and Butter Cottage Pudding, Chocolate Sauce Coffee
THURSDAY JAN. 3	Orange Juice Mello-Wheat Whole Wheat Toast Butter Preserves Coffee Milk	Cream of Potato and Onion Soup Melba Toast Butter Fruit Salad Cottage Pudding Tea Milk	Liver and Bacon Mashed Potatoes Kale Bread and Butter Chocolate Pudding Coffee
FRIDAY JAN. 4	Sliced Bananas Rice Crispies Creamed Salt Codfish Toast Butter Coffee Milk	Scalloped Salmon Shredded Cabbage and Green Pepper Salad Bread and Butter Stewed Prunes Tea Milk	Baked Stuffed Potatoes au gratin Creamed Turnips Buttered Beets Spinach with Chopped Egg Bread and Butter Rice Custard with Raisins Coffee
SATURDAY JAN. 5	Orange Juice Cereal for Children Crisp Bacon Fried Mush Syrup Butter Coffee Milk	Spinach Timbales Cheese Biscuits Butter Prune Whip Tea Milk	Veal Pot Pie Cole Slaw Buttered Carrots Bread and Butter Apple Betty Coffee
SUNDAY JAN. 6	Grapefruit Rolled Oats Canadian Bacon Muffins Butter Preserves Coffee Milk	Tomato Cheese Toasted Crackers Grapefruit Salad Honey French Dressing Tea Milk	Celery Boiled Ham Mashed Sweet Potatoes Creamed Cabbage Bread and Butter Quince Jelly Floating Island Coffee

These numbered recipes are designed to serve 4 to 6 persons

(1) ROAST DUCK WITH DANISH STUFFING AND SAUCE BIGARADE

Clean and dress duck, cut off neck. Sprinkle inside with salt, fill with stuffing, sew up opening, and truss. Rub duck with salt and pepper, place on its back in an open roasting pan, preferably on a rack. Do not add water. Start roasting in a hot oven, 500° F., for 15 to 20 minutes. Reduce heat to 350° F. Allow 25 minutes per pound. Cook neck and giblets in seasoned water until tender. Use broth for gravy.

Danish Stuffing

1 slice onion, minced
2 tablespoons butter
¼ teaspoon salt
1 cup chopped celery
1½ cups dry bread crumbs
1 cup cooked prune pulp
1 cup tart apple, chopped

Brown onion in butter, add salt, celery, and bread crumbs. When mixture is hot, add prunes which have been cut in small pieces, and apple. Mix thoroughly and stuff duck.

Sauce Bigarade

1 pint broth
3 tablespoons fat
3 tablespoons flour
Salt and pepper
¼ cup orange juice
Finely shredded rind of 1 orange

Pour off the liquid in pan in which duck has been roasted. Skim off fat. To the liquid add enough broth from neck and giblets to make 1 pint. Re-

(Recipe continued on page 2)

HOT DOG! GET YOUR HOT DOG HERE! CIRCA 1900 Two New Yorkers take credit for putting the sausage in a bun: Charles Feltman at Feltman's in Coney Island and Harry Magely Stevens who was the director of catering at the New York City Polo Grounds. Solid cases have been built for each man; neither patented the concept. In either case, hot dogs were part of the New York zeitgeist by 1900.

T. A. Dorgan, a local sports cartoonist, eventually lampooned the sandwich with a drawing of a dachshund between two slices of bread and the "hot dog" became a street corner institution. By the turn of the century, locals started to take the name literally, and in a 1913 effort to erase all canine associations with the tasty treat, the Coney Island Chamber of Commerce banned the use of the term *hot dog* from all advertisements and signs, according to John F. Mariani in *The Dictionary of American Food and Drink*.

It took several more years before hot dogs strayed to ball parks and mainstream America.

According to John Spayde, a third man actually made this happen. In his article, "Nathan's Famous: In This Dog-Eat-Dog Town, It's the Real Wiener," which appeared in *Travel & Leisure* magazine, Spayde writes that Nathan Handwerker, the originator of Nathan's Famous,

worked at Feltman's until 1916, when he left to found his own stand with a $300 stake.

Mr. Handwerker cut his price per dog from the going rate of 10 cents to a proletarian nickel. The marketing move backfired when the cheap dog raised questions of quality.

1·8·8·2

SIPPING SODA THROUGH A STRAW

Harry M. Stevens, a recent émigré from Great Britain, began serving bottles of soda pop with a straw at Ebbets Field, so that Dodgers fans could keep their eye on the ball, instead of the bottom of the bottle.

THIS IS THE ORIGINAL

Nathan's
FAMOUS FRANKFURTER & SOFT DRINK STAND

FRANKFURTER
ROAST BEEF
HAMBURGER
WITH FRIED ONIONS
5¢

PURE
MILK
SHAKE **6¢**

ICE COLD
SODA PURE FRUIT SYRUP **5¢**

HORTON'S
ICE CREAM SODA **10¢**

ICE COLD
ORANGE, PINEAPPLE
GRAPE or LEMON DRINK

ROOT BEER **5¢**

HOT ROAST BEEF **5¢**

HAMBURGER **5¢**

ROAST FRIED POTATO CHIPS

REILLY'S HOMEMADE
RESTAURANT

RESTAURANT

Nathan responded to the public's fear of his cheap dogs with the move that made him famous. He offered free hot dogs to the interns at nearby Coney Island Hospital on the condition that they come to his stand in their white lab coats. Soon Nathan's was being pointed out as "the stand where the doctors eat." The nickel frank was home free. Nathan, though deceased, is still famous. His son, Murray Handwerker, runs the family business.

LOBSTER NEWBURG MAKES DEBUT 1876 Lobster Newburg, a rich blend of lobster with a shellfish cream sauce, was invented at Delmonico's.

The Handwerker family behind the counter at Nathan's of Coney Island in 1922. Second from left is Nathan Handwerker holding his son Murray.

THOMAS'S PROMISES 1880
Samuel Bath Thomas opened a bakery on 20th Street in New York City. Using his mother's recipe that he brought from England, Mr. Thomas created the "English muffin," which he marketed through the S. B. Thomas Company, which later was shortened to Thomas's.

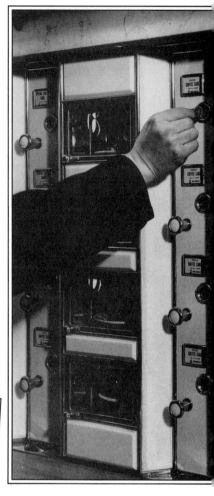

MANHATTAN CLAM CHOWDER

Like most of the city's namesake dishes, many folks claim to have first put the tomato in the chowder. In *The Handbook of Practical Cookery for Ladies and Professional Cooks,* published in 1867, Pierre Blot offered several recipes for this heretic stew and noted that it was frequently made by "the experienced chowder men of the Harlem River."

But of the many claims, the one that seems most compelling can be found in a leaf of family correspondence housed at the South Street Seaport Museum, in which the grandson of a fish vendor who catered political fund-raisers in lower Manhattan, tells his children that his grandfather, in fact, invented the tomatoey version of the stew (see page 76).

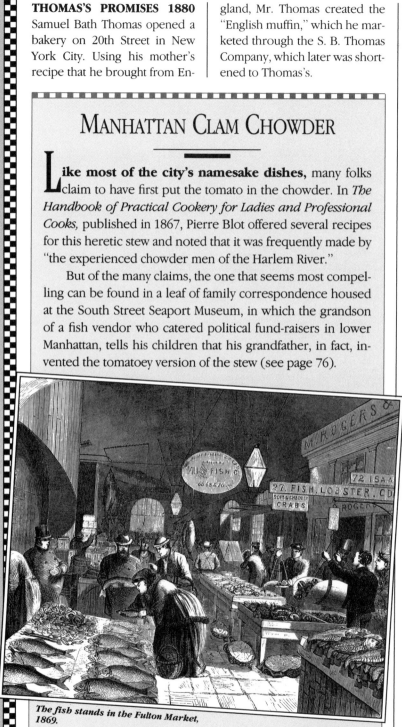

The fish stands in the Fulton Market, 1869.

THE MOTHER LODE OF CAFETERIA FOOD? The Exchange Buffet, the first American cafeteria, opened in Manhattan's commercial district in 1885. With its self-service and its polished look, it was hailed as an ultra-modern dining concept—except for their admissions policy: Women were not served. The Automat, the first egalitarian modern cafeteria, originally opened in Philadelphia in 1902. On July 7, 1912, according to Philip Langdon in

Put another nickel in—Horn & Hardart's Automat.

COOKING FOR THE NEEDIEST 1877

Juliet Corson, then the superintendent of The New York Cooking School, issued her book *Fifteen Cent Dinners for Families of Sin*. Soon after, The St. Andrews Society began operating one-cent coffee stands on the streets of New York. In the first three weeks of operation, five of these stands fed 1,500 people and became, in fact, one of the earliest known soup kitchens in America.

Food and Hunger Hotline at 252 Seventh Avenue says there are 650 food programs in NYC today. Food programs include both soup kitchens and food pantries. Ms. Sander at the hotline said that the number of soup kitchens is not indicative of need because they do not service families. There are also shelters that provide assistance but are not included in this total.

Dr. Kennion (the distinguished-looking gentleman on the left) offered coffee as an alternative drink to the drunks of Brooklyn in the 1880s.

Orange Roofs and Golden Arches, Mr. Horn and Mr. Hardart opened their first New York Automat at Broadway and 13th Street. By 1939, there were 40 Automats in New York City.

In 1990, New York City lost the Automat. But the recipe for Horn and Hardart's popular macaroni and cheese appears on page 248, and the one for incomparable baked beans can be found on page 155.

1·8·7·4
THE MANHATTAN COCKTAIL IS BORN

To celebrate the election of Governor Samuel Tilden, a bartender at the Manhattan Club invented the Manhattan, a mixture of bourbon or blended whiskey, sweet vermouth, and bitters with crushed ice (see recipe, page 26).

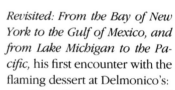

ADAM'S NEW YORK GUM— SNAPPING AND STRETCHING 1870

Thomas Adams of Staten Island, a part-time photographer and part-time inventor, tried and failed to make a synthetic rubber out of *Chicle-the,* the milky juice or latex of a tropical evergreen, according to *Listening to America* by Stuart Berg Flexner.

But in a perfect example of New Yorkers' ability to turn lemons into lemonade, Mr. Adams remembered that his son Horatio liked to chew the tasteless substance, and to facilitate that, Adams Sr. mixed the gum with hot water and rolled it into balls. Another son, Thomas Adams, Jr., a traveling salesman, sold it all the way to the Mississippi.

Later, Adams Sr. packaged his gum as "Adams' New York Gum—Snapping and Stretching." Since chicle can also be flavored, he introduced the first flavored gum: sassafras. Like his earlier experiments with synthetics, sassafras was a flop. Undeterred, Mr. Adams introduced "Black Jack," the licorice-flavored gum that is still beloved and still produced.

In the 1880s, Adams Sr. introduced the term "vending machine," using a device that he called a "gumball machine"

to sell his tutti-fruitti spheres on elevated train platforms throughout New York.

Inspired by candy-coated almonds, Henry Fleer, a candy salesman, invented Chiclets, America's first candy-coated gum, in 1914 for the Adams Chewing Gum Company, which had relocated to Long Island City. Chiclets are now manufactured by the Warner-Lambert Company of New Jersey and pull in over $100 million annual revenue worldwide. The company claims to have the first Chiclet that came out of the first production safely stowed away in the corporate vault.

JUST DESSERTS Chef Charles Ranhofer, of Delmonico's, gave the Baked Alaska its name to commemorate the American purchase of Alaska in 1867, according to *American Gourmet* by Jane and Michael Stern.

Several years later an Englishman, George Augustus Sala, recorded in his book *America*

Revisited: From the Bay of New York to the Gulf of Mexico, and from Lake Michigan to the Pacific, his first encounter with the flaming dessert at Delmonico's:

"The 'Alaska' is a baked ice... The nucleus or core of the entremet is an ice cream. This is surrounded by an envelope of carefully whipped cream, which, just before the dainty dish is served, is popped into the oven, or is brought under the scorching influence of a red hot salamander; so that its surface is covered with a light brown crust. So you go on discussing the warm cream soufflé till you come, with somewhat painful suddenness, on a row of ice. E'en so did the Shepherd Virgil grow acquainted with love and find him a native of the rocks."

A century later, the dessert was brought out of partial retirement and became one of the stars of the menu at the Rainbow Room.

Gumballs, a small but important offering.

ADAMS ®

Chiclets ®

ppermint Gum 12 PIECES
ARTIFICIALLY FLAVORED

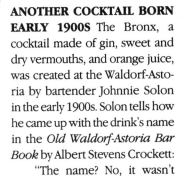

The familiar Chiclet's box with it's peek-a-boo window revealing the much loved candy-coated gum (above). The stern-looking J.H. Kellogg (right).

THE BEST TO YOU EACH MORNING MID-1800S The breakfast food idea may have dawned in the mid-1800s at a little third-story room on the corner of 28th Street and Third Avenue, where J. H. Kellogg, then a medical student at Bellevue, lived.

"My cooking facilities were very limited, [making it] very difficult to prepare cereals," he wrote in his journal. "It often occurred to me that it should be possible to purchase cereals at groceries already cooked and ready to eat, and I considered different ways in which this might be done."

ANOTHER COCKTAIL BORN EARLY 1900S The Bronx, a cocktail made of gin, sweet and dry vermouths, and orange juice, was created at the Waldorf-Astoria by bartender Johnnie Solon in the early 1900s. Solon tells how he came up with the drink's name in the *Old Waldorf-Astoria Bar Book* by Albert Stevens Crockett:

"The name? No, it wasn't really named directly after the borough or the river so-called. I had been at the Bronx Zoo a day or two before, and I saw, of course, a lot of beasts I had never known. Customers used to tell me of the strange animals they saw after a lot of mixed drinks. So when Traverson said to me, as he started to take the drink in to the customer, 'What'll I tell him is the name of this drink?' I thought of those animals and said: Oh, you can tell him it is a 'Bronx.'" (See page 26 for the recipe).

WHERE ELSE BUT THE WALDORF? 1893 Waldorf Salad, originally a mix of apples, celery, and mayonnaise, was invented in 1893 by Oscar Tschirky, a maître d'hôtel at the Waldorf Hotel. In the next decade, chopped walnuts were added to the recipe, and the dish became *de rigueur* on the ladies' luncheon circuit throughout the United States.

TOOTSIE ON A ROLL 1896 New Yorker Leo Hirschfield invented the Tootsie Roll, a chewy chocolate treat that he named for his daughter Clara, whose nickname was, what else, Tootsie.

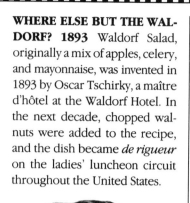

Dining at the Waldorf Astoria.

1·9·0·5

NEW YORK PIZZA

G.**Lombardi's,** the self-professed "first American pizzeria," opened on Spring Street and continued to sell pizzas for 80 years. Brick oven pizzas became a symbol of New York (for a more complete treatment of this phenomenon, see page 100), and the city's pizza pie became the standard by which all others are judged. Except in Chicago. Or San Francisco. Or Rome. . . .

A REUBEN, EXTRA PICKLES, PLEASE EARLY 1900S The Reuben, a grilled sandwich made of corned beef, Swiss cheese, sauerkraut, and creamy dressing on rye bread, may have been invented in Atlantic City in

NEW YORK DELI FOODS GO NATIONAL 1905 Boars Head brand deli products was founded in Brooklyn.

VICHYSSOISE, S'IL VOUS PLAIT 1910 Vichyssoise, the chilled potato and leek soup, was invented by Louis Diat at the Ritz-Carlton Hotel (for a recipe, see page 73).

NEW YORK CHEESECAKE Using the Eastern European combination of cream cheese and pot cheese, Jewish immigrants baked the cheesecakes that, near the turn of the century, began to take the New York appellation. In *Bronx Primitive,* her memoir, Kate Simon referred to her mother's Polish version as "cement block." But by 1940, a similar rich, dense cake became the star of the show at Lindy's, the theater district restaurant that is credited with immortalizing New York cheesecake (a selection of local recipes begins on page 435).

WHERE WOULD BAGELS BE WITHOUT IT? 1920 The Breakstone Company formulated Breakstone's Downsville Cream Cheese, which author

the early 1900s, or by Reuben Kulakofsky at the Blackstone Hotel in Omaha, Nebraska, or at Reuben's Delicatessen on 58th Street in Manhattan. In any case, the sandwich rapidly made its way out of the city and into the repertoire of sandwich shops across the United States.

John F. Mariani suggests was named after the New York community where it was made. It was upsville from there. What was once a homemade specialty of New York delicatessens became part of the standard larder in groceries throughout the country.

AND YET ANOTHER COCKTAIL IS BORN 1930S The Gibson, a dry martini with a garnish of a small white onion rather than the usual olive, was first made by bartender Charles Connolly of The Players Club in the 1930s. He was out of olives. *The Dictionary of American Food and Drink* by John F. Mariani says that the libation was served to and named for Charles Dana Gibson, the illustrator famous for his drawings of the Gibson Girl.

A REAL SQUARE 1930S Local confectioner Philip Silverstein formulated the Chunky candy bar, a square chunk of chocolate with brazil nuts, cashews, and raisins, in the 1930s. According to *The Dictionary of American Food and Drink* by John F. Mariani, he named the candy after his "chunky" daughter.

EGGS ON HER PLATE 1920S

When Mrs. LeGrand Benedict complained that there was nothing new on the Delmonico's menu in the 1920s, the chef responded with Eggs Benedict, an English muffin, split and topped with a slice of ham or Canadian bacon, poached eggs, and hollandaise sauce. It is still a brunch staple across the United States.

BROOKLYN SON GOES INTO DEEP FREEZE 1924

Using, as he said, "Eskimos' knowledge and the scientists' theories" and adapting them to mass production, Clarence Frank Birdseye, who was born in Brooklyn on December 9, 1886, became the father of modern frozen food. He was one of the founders of General Foods, which is now Kraft General Foods and is still one of the largest producers of frozen foods in America.

IN A CITY THAT LOVES TO EAT 1961

When Jean Nidetch, then a plump resident of Queens, was given a diet from the Department of Health Obesity Clinic, she had an idea: Calorie counting should be shared with friends.

Beginning as meetings in her basement, Weight Watchers International was incorporated in 1963. Today Weight Watchers, which is headquartered on Long Island, holds 32,000 meetings a week in 24 countries.

THE CARIBBEAN IN A CAN 1936

Seeing the influx of Caribbean émigrés, Don Prudencio Unanue and his wife, Doña Carolina Casal, founded the Goya Company at 173-175 Duane Street in downtown Manhattan in 1936. The company moved to Brooklyn and then New Jersey, where it remains today, the largest family-owned Hispanic food company in America.

THE WORLD'S FAIR 1964

Belgian waffles, the puffy, yeasted models that are still served at street fairs and state fairs across the county, were introduced in this country at the 1964 World's Fair at Flushing Meadows.

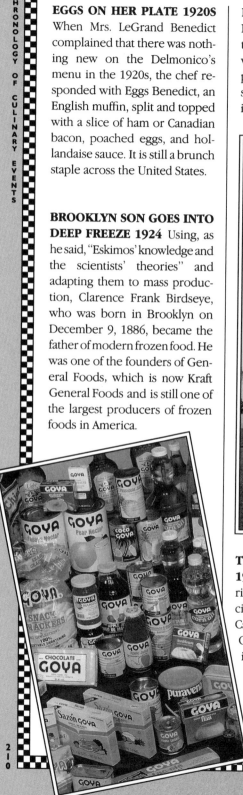

An array of Goya Products (left). The prominent unisphere stood at the center of the 1964 World's Fair.

THE SEMINAL PASTA PRIMAVERA 1974

In May, Sirio Maccioni, the owner of Le Cirque, was sampling restaurants in Canada, and after a few days of venison and lobster, "I had to eat pasta," he said. So much so, that he set out to make two sauces, an Alfredo sauce and a simple butter sauce with asparagus, zucchini, and tomatoes. At the last minute, he mixed the two together, *et voilà,* a star was born.

Mr. Maccioni listed the dish on his menu until it attracted 50 percent of the orders. Concerned that Le Cirque would become known as a "spaghetti house," he took it off the menu 15 years ago. Since then, Pasta Primavera (see page 226) has become a mainstay of spaghetti houses and tony dining rooms across the country. Mr. Maccioni is quite disturbed by the "appropriation and misrepresentation" of his dish.

HOW SWEET IT IS 1979

David's Cookies were invented by David Liederman, a lawyer and chef. His rich, often chocolate-laden confections heralded the era of fresh-baked premium cookies. Today Liederman sells about 1 million pounds of cookies from 10,000 outlets nationwide. During test marketing, there was one cookie that New Yorkers loved and no one else did. For the recipe, see page 447.

"Ah, what artists they were!" wrote Edith Wharton, recalling in her autobiography, *A Backward Glance,* the cooks who worked for her family.

"How simple yet sure were their methods —the mere perfection of broiling, roasting and basting—and what an unexampled wealth of material, vegetable and animal, their genius had to draw upon! Who will ever again taste anything in the whole range of gastronomy to equal their corned beef, their boiled turkeys with stewed celery and oyster sauce, their fried chickens, broiled red-heads, corn fritters, stewed tomatoes, rice griddle cakes, strawberry short cake and vanilla ices? I am now enumerating only our daily fare, that from which even my tender years did not exclude me; but when my parents 'gave a dinner,' and terrapin and canvas-back ducks or (in their season) broiled Spanish mackerel, soft-shelled crabs with a mayonnaise of celery and peach-fed Virginia hams cooked in champagne (I am no doubt confusing all the seasons in this allegoric evocation of their riches), lima-beans in cream, corn souffles and salads of oystercrabs, poured in varied succulence from Mary Johnson's lifted cornucopia—ah, then, the *gourmet* of that long lost day, when cream was cream and butter butter and coffee coffee, and meat fresh every day and game hung just for the proper number of hours, might lean back in his chair and murmur 'Fate cannot harm me' over his cup of Moka and his glass of authentic Chartreuse."

The Brent family at Christmas dinner in the early 1900s.

Pasta Plus
DUMPLINGS, NOODLES, AND GRAINS

The story of Italians in New York City stretches like a long strand of pasta across nearly five centuries. Sometimes a satin ribbon, other times a rough staple, the quality and social standing of the noodle rises and falls along with the fortunes of the successive immigrant waves.

In the annals of local pasta lore, we see the noodle as gauntlet: US (*Mangia, Mangia, belle pasta*) and THEM (They eat potatoes, what do they know?).

We see the noodle in a tug-of-war between immigrants from the north of Italy and those from the south. Beginning with Giovanni da Verrazano, who discovered the city's harbor in 1524, the earliest émigrés were aristocratic Tuscans and other northern Italians, who favored fine olive oil, aged cheese, and fresh herbs on

Sirio Maccioni of Le Cirque prepares Pasta Primavera (see page 226), at table (left). Photographer Howard Simmons happily digs into the results (above).

their pasta. Beginning in the 1880s, the city became a magnet for Italians from the south where tomatoes are synonymous with spaghetti.

You don't need insider information to figure out that the majority of New York Italians are of southern extraction today. There is so much tomato sauce here that one comedian says there is a central pipeline that supplies all Italian restaurants.

There are, and always have been, more people from Italy living in New York City than from any other European country. Over a million residents are either Italian or Italian-American.

The number has been relatively stable since 1932 when Helen Worden wrote in *The Real New York*: "Residence in this country does not disturb the Italians' foreign way of living. Their neighborhoods are more picturesque, their people more colorful, and their customs more interesting than other nationalities."

The city's Italian neighborhoods are still more eloquent than statistics. At the center of each is a pasta-master, whose daily rolling and cutting, saucing and tossing etches a strand in the rope of Italian culture that weaves through the city.

To Tony Morante, who grew up in the Belmont section of the Bronx and now works in the ticket office of the New York Yankees, this explains why the long curling fusilli, so representative of twists and turns, remains the number one Sunday dinner choice among Italian families in New York.

Nora Ephron's
SAUCE SEGRETTO

A nice, mellow, all-purpose pasta sauce. It perfectly suits a pound of good, old-fashioned spaghetti.

Nora Ephron—author, screenwriter, and creator of a smooth, rich tomato sauce. Photo: Michele Singer

½ pound (2 sticks) butter
1 onion, diced
1 carrot, diced
1 rib celery, diced
1 can (35 ounces) peeled
*   tomatoes*
½ teaspoon salt
¼ teaspoon freshly ground
*   black pepper*
¼ to ½ teaspoon dried red
*   pepper flakes*
1 pound spaghetti
About ½ cup freshly grated
*   Parmesan cheese*

1. In a nonreactive large sauté pan, melt 1 stick (8 tablespoons) of the butter over medium heat. Add the onion, carrot, and celery and cook until the onion is translucent but not browned, about 10 minutes.

2. Dump the can of tomatoes into the pan and mash with a spoon. Cook over medium-low heat until the sauce starts to thicken slightly and picks up the slightly orange color of the carrots, 30 to 40 minutes.

3. Cut the remaining 1 stick butter into slices and stir it into the sauce. Season with the salt, pepper, and red pepper flakes—the more hot pepper flakes the better.

4. Meanwhile, cook the spaghetti in boiling salted water until tender; drain.

5. In a large bowl, toss the cooked spaghetti with the sauce. Add the Parmesan cheese and toss before serving.

Serves 4

THE RED SEA

L et them laugh. All those who sneer at the prodigious quantities of red sauce that wash over New York City. Sure, restaurant versions can be heavy and dull. But the variety of sprightly tomato sauces concocted by home cooks in this town is dizzying. And so is the loyalty of its makers.

"You can put up a sun-dried tomato front for only so long," said the writer Nora Ephron, referring to the trendy ingredient that, for a while, eclipsed the old-fashioned sauce. Like other red sauce aficionados, she maintains that the nostalgia value of the sauce is equaled only by its versatility.

The sauce can be made in quantity and frozen to use on pasta, in lasagne, or on pizza. It can be spooned between layers of a vegetable casserole, baked with chicken, fish, or veal, or drizzled over grilled or steamed food.

"My sauce segretto is as close as I could come to my grandmother's sauce," said Ms. Ephron. "She always said it was a secret. The secret turned out to be a can of Campbell's tomato soup."

After a lengthy investigation, Robert B. Hodes, an attorney, found that the secret to the vibrance of a low-calorie sauce served in an East Side Italian restaurant is the addition of a red pepper.

Nach Waxman, who owns Kitchen Arts & Letters, a cookbook store on the Upper East Side, found that using both plum and beefsteak tomatoes makes a dense sauce with a juicy flavor. To revive frozen sauce, he adds a swirl of fresh herbs or a squeeze of lemon juice.

Anyone who grew up on traditional red sauce can identify with Jerry Della Femina of advertising fame, who wrote in his memoir *An Italian Grows in Brooklyn:* My grandmother would start making her meat sauce at seven in the morning on Sunday and within five or six hours that smell would be all through the house, covering everything—clothing, furniture, appliances—and then it would go out the front door and into the streets, to mix with the aroma of neighboring meat sauces."

Each sauce had its own little *je ne sais quoi,* something that Angelo Pernicone, a fire fighter for 30 years and the chef of choice at Brooklyn's Ladder 132, found in prosciutto. "It adds a nice something extra," he says, to the sauce that he uses as a marinara. "You know how you can look at the river every day and every day it looks different?"

"Well, red sauce is the same, just one little change and you have a whole new picture."

FEATURING OUR FRESH HOMEMADE! SAUCES!

POMODORO
ITALIAN TOMATOES, ONION, GARLIC, PURE OLIVE OIL, SALT, PEPPER & OREGANO.
½ $2.25 ½ PT ½ $3.98 PT

MARINARA
ITALIAN TOMATOES, ONION, GARLIC, OREGANO, PARSLEY, ANCHOVIES.
½ $2.50 ½ PT ½ $4.69 PT

MALA FEMMINA
ITALIAN TOMATOES, ONION, GARLIC, BLACK & GREEN OLIVES, CAPERS, ANCHOVIES, OREGANO, HOT PEPPER & BAY LEAF.
½ $2.75 ½ PT ½ $4.98 PT

TOMATO & CREAM
ITALIAN TOMATOES, CREAM, BUTTER ONION, CARROT, CELERY & SALT.
½ $2.75 ½ PT ½ $4.98 PT

PESTO
PURE OLIVE OIL, FRESH BASIL, PARMIGIANO ROMANO, PINENUTS, WALNUTS, GARLIC, SALT & PEPPER.
½ $4.98 ½ PT ½ $7.98 PT

SUGOLOSO
SUNDRIED TOMATOES, PARMIGIANO, OLIVE OIL, PINENUTS, GARLIC, SALT & PEPPER.
½ $4.98 ½ PT ½ $8.98 PT

Nach Waxman's
SIMPLE FRESH TOMATO SAUCE

Created by the owner of Kitchen Arts & Letters, a specialty bookstore in Manhattan, this intense tomato sauce is delicious over pasta or can be used in constructing lasagne, Parmesans, or other casseroles.

HERB PUREE
1 cup loosely packed fresh basil leaves
¼ cup olive oil
⅓ cup pine nuts

RED SAUCE
5 pounds beefsteak tomatoes (or other juicy
*   tomatoes), as ripe as possible*
1½ pounds fresh, ripe plum tomatoes
¾ cup fruity Italian olive oil
3 leafy ribs celery, coarsely chopped
2 large onions, coarsely chopped
3 cloves garlic, coarsely chopped
¼ cup plus 2 tablespoons tomato paste
1 sprig fresh oregano
½ cup packed fresh basil leaves
2 sprigs fresh Italian (flat-leaf) parsley
1 dried red chile, crumbled
1 teaspoon red wine vinegar
½ teaspoon brown sugar
Freshly ground black pepper, to taste
Salt, to taste

1. Make the herb purée: Place the basil in a colander, rinse with boiling water, and drain.

2. In a blender or food processor, combine the drained basil, olive oil, pine nuts, and ¼ cup water. Purée at medium speed until smooth; set aside.

On Arthur Avenue in the Bronx, the variety of ingredients is legendary.

Nach Waxman, owner of New York's popular specialty bookstore, Kitchen Arts & Letters.

3. Make the red sauce: Dip both types of to-matoes in boiling water and place in a colander to cool. Slip off the skins, then squeeze the tomatoes over a bowl; reserve the juice. Cut the tomatoes into quarters and scoop out the seeds (or if you like a more astringent sauce, leave the seeds in). Coarsely chop the tomatoes; add to the bowl of reserved juice.

4. In a nonreactive, large Dutch oven or other ovenproof heavy pot, warm ¼ cup of the olive oil over medium heat. Add the celery, onions, and garlic and sauté until the onions are translucent, 5 minutes. Add the tomatoes with their juice and the tomato paste and bring to a boil. Reduce the heat to low, partially cover the pot, and simmer for 2 hours, stirring every 15 minutes. At each stirring, drizzle in 1 tablespoon olive oil.

5. Preheat the oven to 350° F.

6. After the sauce has cooked for 2 hours, stir in the oregano sprig, whole basil leaves, and pars-ley sprigs. Add the dried chile, vinegar, brown sugar, and black pepper. Transfer the pot to the oven. Cover and cook until the sauce is dense and thick, 1 to 1½ hours. Correct the seasonings, add salt to taste, and remove the herb sprigs.

7. Just before serving, swirl in 1 tablespoon of the herb purée per portion.

Serves 10

Easy-on-your-Diet
SPAGHETTI SAUCE

Created by attorney Robert B. Hodes to be easy to make as well.

1 can (35 ounces) peeled Italian plum tomatoes
1 red bell pepper, stemmed, seeded, and diced
1 onion, diced
2 cloves garlic, minced
2 cups New York Penicillin (page 47) or canned chicken broth
2 teaspoons sugar
2 tablespoons dried basil, or ¼ cup fresh basil leaves
Salt and freshly ground black pepper, to taste

1. Combine all of the ingredients in a non-reactive large saucepan over medium heat. Sim-mer until thickened, 30 minutes.

2. Remove the sauce from the heat. Purée in a blender or food processor.

3. Return the sauce to the pan, season with salt and pepper to taste, and simmer until reduced to 2½ cups, about 1½ hours. This sauce freezes very well.

Makes 2½ cups, serves 4 to 6

Robert Hodes with his daughter Paz.

Angelo Pernicone preparing Prosciutto Sauce, a firehouse favorite.

the prosciutto and cook for 5 minutes. Add the juice from the tomatoes. Using your hands or a fork, break up the whole tomatoes and add to the pot. Simmer, uncovered, for 30 minutes.

2. Stir in the basil, parsley, wine, and pepper flakes, season with salt and pepper to taste, and simmer for 1 hour.

3. Remove the sauce from the heat. Whisk in the butter until melted.

Makes 3½ cups, serves 4

Angelo Pernicone's
PROSCIUTTO SAUCE

F ellow fire fighters beg Mr. Pernicone to make his full-bodied prosciutto sauce. Serve it over a pound or so of your favorite macaroni.

2 tablespoons olive oil
3 cloves garlic, minced
1 onion, minced
¼ pound prosciutto, thinly sliced and cut into strips
2 cans (35 ounces each) peeled Italian plum tomatoes
1 cup loosely packed fresh basil leaves, chopped
¾ cup loosely packed Italian flat-leaf parsley leaves, chopped
1 cup dry white wine
¼ teaspoon dried red pepper flakes
Salt and freshly ground black pepper, to taste
2 tablespoons butter

1. Warm the oil in a nonreactive large pot over medium heat. Add the garlic and onion and cook until the onion is translucent, 5 minutes. Add

Filthy Rich
ALL-PURPOSE PASTA SAUCE

P eter Prestcott, the impresario of *Food & Wine* magazine, serves this simple, creamy pasta dish at post-theater or -opera buffets in his Greenwich Village home.

2 cups heavy (whipping) cream
6 shallots, chopped
2 large cloves garlic, chopped
1 cup dry white wine
1 pound dried pasta, preferably spaghetti or linguine
1 tablespoon butter
1 tablespoon olive oil
2 large tomatoes, peeled, seeded, and chopped
Pinch of sugar
1 teaspoon salt
½ teaspoon freshly ground white pepper
1 cup loosely packed fresh basil leaves, shredded
½ cup freshly grated Parmesan cheese

1. In a nonreactive heavy saucepan over medium-low heat, combine the cream, shallots, garlic, and wine. Simmer gently until the mixture thickens, 20 to 25 minutes. Purée the mixture in a blender or food processor. Set aside and keep warm.

2. Cook the pasta in a large pot filled with plenty of boiling water until tender.

3. Meanwhile, in a nonreactive sauté pan over medium-high heat, heat the butter and olive oil. Add the tomatoes, sugar, salt, and pepper and toss briefly to just warm the tomatoes.

4. In a large warm bowl, combine the cream sauce and the tomato mixture. Drain the pasta and add it to the sauce. Toss well. Add the basil and Parmesan and toss again. Serve.

Serves 4

Allesandro's
MELANZANA PASTA SAUCE

Allesandro Gualandi, a Greenwich Village grocer, was born in Florence and was originally served this creamy eggplant sauce by friends of his family there. "I really liked the idea of sauces with cream added at the end," he said. "I guess it reminded me of ice cream."

1 can (28 ounces) peeled Italian plum tomatoes
8 tablespoons extra-virgin olive oil
2 tablespoons rinsed, drained capers
3 cloves garlic, chopped
2 small eggplants, peeled and cut into 1-inch cubes
Salt and freshly ground black pepper, to taste
Dried red pepper flakes, to taste
3 tablespoons heavy (whipping) cream
1 pound pasta, such as fusilli, cooked

1. Empty the tomatoes into a large bowl. With your hands, crush the tomatoes, letting the juice run back into the bowl.

2. In a nonreactive large saucepan, heat 3 tablespoons of the olive oil over medium heat for 1 minute. Add the tomatoes and juice and cook until the excess water cooks out, 7 to 8 minutes. Remove from the heat.

3. In a nonreactive heavy skillet, warm 3 tablespoons of the oil over medium heat for 1 minute. Add the capers and garlic and cook for 1 minute. Add the eggplant, salt, pepper, and pepper flakes, and cook until the eggplant softens, 5 minutes. Add the remaining 2 tablespoons oil (or more if needed) and the tomatoes and cook for 3 minutes. Remove from the heat. Stir in the heavy cream. Serve the sauce immediately over freshly drained, cooked pasta.

Serves 4

Pasta bowls and plates at the ready.

MRS. ROMANA RAFFETTO OF HOUSTON STREET

Life used to be simple at Raffetto's. In 1906, when the storefront opened on Houston Street in Manhattan, it offered handmade "ravioli Genoa style" (with meat and cheese) and "ravioli Naples style" (with cheese). Houston Street was called the Mason-Dixon line back then, the boundary between the southern Italians, who had fled poverty and packed the tenements of Mulberry Bend, and those from the north, who generally left Italy with more money and education than their southern cousins, and whose neat homes lined the crooked sidewalks of the West Village.

NEUTRAL TERRITORY

Perched between the two worlds, Raffetto's was like the country of Switzerland, selling ravioli by the pound. "My father-in-law had something for the Genovese and something for the Neapolitans, he didn't need anything else," said Romana Raffetto, who helps her husband, Gino, and their two sons, Andrew and Richard, run the store. "Then America discovered pasta and things got complicated," she said.

"They wanted ravioli with seafood, ravioli with wild mushrooms, ravioli with pesto, ravioli with pumpkin, ravioli with spinach and cheese, vegetable ravioli with no eggs or cheese." She looked at the assorted ravioli boxes stacked in the store's refrigerator and shook her head.

"Saffron pasta. Squid ink pasta. Black pepper pasta. Pasta with herbs. Pasta with chile peppers. Pasta with lemon," she recited, nodding to the sheets of fresh noodles that were folded and stacked as tenderly as fresh linen on the tables behind the store's front counter.

"Personally, I'm not for it," she said. But as she buttoned a white chef's jacket over her flowered house dress and headed toward the store's front counter, Mrs. Raffetto was EveryMother, patiently indulging a cultural adolescent phase.

The store, she figures, is a stabilizing influence in a pasta-crazed world. Bottles of olive oil stretch from gold to green along one wall and are flanked by jars of olives, bottled clams, sacks of polenta, and rice. There are cans of good Italian tomatoes and bottles of real Italian fruit syrups. There are chubby links of sausages, wheels of provolone and Parmesan, vats of ricotta. The same good, basic foods that have carried Raffetto's going onto 90 years.

The store was in the right place when it opened, but within two decades, well-heeled Italians moved on up, first to Italian Harlem, then to Arthur Avenue in the Bronx, then, and still, to Westchester and New Jersey, Bensonhurst and Long Island. By 1932 the Italian West Village had shrunk to a small patch of butchers along Bleecker Street, a handful of social clubs, latticini, and salumeria along both Sullivan and Bleecker Streets.

"Little Italy" was already a tourist theme park of "red wine and plaster saints," wrote Helen Worden in *The Real New York*.

But something pulled people back,

back to the ravioli store where their mothers shopped, back to double-parking in front of Raffetto's. When pasta detonated in mainstream America, the family that still lived above their store on Houston Street was ready.

They had more than pasta. The Raffettos had been intimate with strangers in a strange land for over five decades. As Americans sailed from the world of meat and potatoes toward the shores of pasta, the store was a local lodestar, its matriarch, the needle on the compass.

"In a way, nothing changes," said Mrs. Raffetto. Her sons make about 5,000 pounds of pasta a week. Like their grandfather they are diplomats, although the Mason-Dixon line they straddle today lies between the trendy and the traditional.

"Each side affects the other. That's the nature of people living together," said Mrs. Raffetto, philosophically.

Occasionally, a strand of mod-pasta catches even her eye. "It's not that I don't like the flavor in the pasta," she said. Lowering her voice as if to whisper across the backyard fences that are no longer on these blocks, she did wonder, however, "If they have all that flavor in the pasta, what in the world do you think they put in their sauce?"

...ana Raffetto and the shop that bears the family name.

Raffetto's · FRESH PASTA PRODUCTS · Est. 1906

Romana Raffetto's
LASAGNE

Romana Raffetto adapted her lasagne to suit American tastes.

Says Romana Raffetto, "There isn't *one way* to cook. You start cooking what you know personally, what you like. Along the way, you accommodate your family, your friends, other peope's tastes and dislikes."

"I'm from Asolo, the north of Italy, where they use the cheese and cream sauce in lasagne. But I raise my children here, their friends eat tomatoes, I try tomatoes, pretty soon I am making my cheese lasagne with tomato sauce."

1 pound ricotta cheese
1 large egg
2 tablespoons minced fresh
    parsley leaves
5 cups Romana's Red Sauce
    (recipe follows), at room
    temperature
1 pound fresh lasagne noodles
    (see Note)
1 pound mozzarella cheese, cut into
    ¼-inch-thick slices
1 cup freshly grated Parmesan cheese

---

1. Preheat the oven to 350°F.

2. In a large mixing bowl, beat together the ricotta and the egg. Stir in the parsley.

3. Spread 1 cup of the red sauce over the bottom of a 13 × 9-inch baking dish to cover. Top with a layer of lasagne noodles. Using a rubber spatula, spread a ½-inch-thick layer of the ricotta mixture over the noodles. Evenly place the slices of mozzarella, sprinkle with the Parmesan, and drizzle with more red sauce. Add another layer of noodles and continue layering until 4 tiers have been assembled. End with a generous layer of sauce and a hefty sprinkling of Parmesan.

4. Bake until the top is lightly browned, about 1½ hours. Cool the pan on a rack for 15 minutes before cutting and serving.

Serves 6

Note: If fresh lasagne noodles are not available in your area, cook 1 pound of dried noodles until cooked but not soft in plenty of salted water mixed with 1 tablespoon vegetable oil. Immediately drain into a colander and rinse the noodles in cold running water until chilled. Drain and pat the noodles dry before using.

ROMANA'S RED SAUCE

This all-purpose ragout sauce can be used in the lasagne recipe above or on any favorite pasta shape.

¼ cup good-quality olive oil
2 white onions, chopped
1 clove garlic, chopped
2 ounces pancetta or double-smoked bacon, diced
1 carrot, peeled and diced
1 rib celery, diced
1 pound lean ground beef
1 cup dry white wine
1 can (35 ounces) imported peeled Italian plum
    tomatoes, puréed
¼ cup chopped fresh basil leaves
Salt and freshly ground black pepper, to taste

1. Warm the oil in a nonreactive, heavy saucepan over medium heat. Add the onions, garlic, and pancetta and sauté until the onions are translucent, 5 minutes, stirring often. Add the carrot and celery and cook for 5 minutes, stirring so that the mixture does not brown.

2. Add the ground beef and stir, using a fork to crumble and combine it with the vegetables. Add the wine and cook until the wine evaporates, about 5 minutes.

3. Stir in the tomatoes and bring the sauce to a boil. Reduce the heat and simmer for about 1 hour, stirring frequently so that the sauce does not stick to the pan and burn. Add the basil and season with salt and pepper to taste. This will keep, covered, in the refrigerator for 2 days.

Makes 8 cups

Mike Gordon's LASAGNE

The foundation of Mike Gordon's lasagne is traditional, but his addition of tarragon and Marsala wine gives it a sophisticated, intriguing flavor. Mr. Gordon encourages making large quantities of his lasagne, since "it always tastes better the next day."

SAUCE AND NOODLES
1 pound lean ground beef
2 cloves garlic, minced
3 tablespoons minced fresh tarragon
⅓ cup dry Marsala wine
8 fresh tomatoes, peeled and chopped, or *4 cups canned crushed Italian plum tomatoes*
½ cup tomato paste
1 teaspoon salt
1 teaspoon freshly ground black pepper
1 pound lasagne noodles

FILLING
1 pound ricotta cheese
2 eggs, lightly beaten
¼ cup unflavored seltzer
⅓ cup freshly grated Parmesan cheese
⅓ cup freshly grated Romano cheese

ASSEMBLY
¼ pound Parmesan cheese, thinly sliced
¼ pound Romano cheese, thinly sliced

■———————————■

1. Prepare the sauce and noodles: In a nonreactive large pot over medium heat, brown the ground beef, breaking it up with a spoon, 5 to 10 minutes. Pour off any excess fat. Add the garlic to the pan and sauté for 1 minute. Add the tarragon and Marsala, and cook for 2 minutes, stirring to scrape up any bits stuck to the bottom of the pan. Stir in the tomatoes, tomato paste, salt, pepper, and 1 cup water. Partially cover and simmer over low heat, stirring occasionally, for up to 8 hours (the longer the better).

2. Meanwhile, bring a large pot of water to a boil. Add the lasagne noodles and cook until al dente. Drain and rinse under cold water. Set aside in a large bowl of cold water to prevent the noodles from sticking together.

3. Preheat the oven to 350°F.

4. Make the filling: In a large bowl, stir together the ricotta and eggs. Whisk in the seltzer; the mixture should be fluffy. Fold in the grated Parmesan and Romano cheeses.

5. Assemble the lasagne: Butter a large baking dish or lasagne pan. Remove a few noodles from the water and pat them dry. Arrange a layer of noodles over the bottom of the pan. Ladle 1 cup of the sauce over the noodles; top with a layer of the sliced Parmesan and Romano cheeses. Spread 1 cup of the cheese filling on top. Repeat the layering process, using the remaining noodles, sauce, sliced cheese, and cheese filling, until you reach the top of the pan. End with a final layer of noodles. Top with any remaining sliced Parmesan and Romano cheeses.

6. Bake the lasagne until the top is golden brown, 1 hour. The lasagne is best if you let it rest overnight and reheat it the next day.

Serves 8

JUST A FEW NEW YORK NOODLES

An eclectic guide to some noodle shapes and preparations—and some international noodle dishes—that can be found in New York.

ITALY

Acini di pepe (little peppercorns): Very small pasta for soups and broths

Agnolotti: Half-moon shaped, filled pasta

Bucatini: Thick, hollow, long, spaghetti-sized tubes

Cannelloni: Wide medium-length tubes, usually stuffed and baked

Capelli d'angelo (angel's hair): The thinnest long pasta

Cappelletti (little hats): Stuffed pasta

Cavatelli: Small curled shells

Conchiglie: Small shells

Conchiglioni: Large shells

Ditali (thimbles): Small short tubes

Farfalle: Bow tie or butterfly shape

Fettuccine: Long flat noodles, wider than spaghetti, narrower than tagliatelle

Fusilli: Loose corkscrew-shaped pasta

Gnocchi: Italian potato dumplings

Lasagne: The widest flat pasta, used mostly in casseroles

Linguine: Flat long noodles, about the same size as spaghetti

Manicotti: Large tubes, usually filled with cheese, vegetables, or meat

Orecchiette (little ears): Small, roundish disks, shaped like bowls and perfect for catching sauce

Plenty of New York pasta.

Orzo: Rice-shaped pasta, most often used in soups

Pappardelle: 1-inch-wide flat noodles

Penne: Short, quill-shaped tapered tubes

Penne rigati: Ridged penne

Ravioli: Stuffed square pillows

Rigatoni: Ridged tubes

Rotelle: Wagon wheel–shaped pasta

Rotini: Little corkscrews

Ruote, also wheels: Wheel shapes with hubs

Spaghetti: Long thin round noodles or strings

Spaghettini: Very thin spaghetti

Tagliatelle: Long, narrow, flat pasta ribbons

Tortellini: Small pasta rings stuffed with meat, cheese, or vegetables

Tortelloni: Larger tortellini

Vermicelli: Very fine spaghetti

Ziti: Medium length large tubes

THAILAND

Pad thai: Thai fried noodle dish using egg noodles

CHINA

Fen ssu/cellophane noodles/bean thread/ Chinese vermicelli: Translucent noodles made from mung bean starch

Mai fun: Rice vermicelli

Wonton: Chinese dumplings

JAPAN

Harusame/Sai fun: Japanese potato starch noodles

Soba: Japanese buckwheat noodles

Udon: Japanese wheat noodles

VIETNAM

Banh hoi: Extra- thin banh pho

Banh pho: Rice sticks or dried rice sticks, made from water and rice flour, used in soups and stir-fries

Bun: Thin rice vermicelli, used in soups and noodle salads

Mi: Fresh egg noodles

Mien/bun tau: Bean threads, or mung bean vermicelli (see *fen ssu*)

Somen: Vietnamese thin wheat-flour noodles

THE PHILIPPINES

Lug-lug: Thick rice-stick noodles

KOREA

Mo mil kook so: Acorn starch noodles

GERMANY

Dampfnudeln: Steamed dumplings

Hefeklosse: Yeast dumplings

Kloss, Klotz, Kartoffelk- losse: Potato dumplings

Spaetzle ("little sparrow"): Small egg pasta dumplings, dropped into boiling water

HUNGARY

Strapachka: Hungarian po- tato dumplings

UKRAINE

Vareniki: Stuffed Ukrainian dumplings

POLAND

Pierogi: Stuffed Polish dump- lings, served fried or boiled

Le Cirque's SPAGHETTI PRIMAVERA

Sirio Maccioni, the impresario of the restaurant, Le Cirque, in Manhattan, is credited with creating this dish, variations of which have become a standby in restaurants across the country—mostly as the retitled Pasta Primavera. This is the original recipe.

1 bunch broccoli, trimmed and cut into bite-size florets
2 small zucchinis, quartered lengthwise and cut into 1-inch lengths
4 asparagus spears (about 5 inches long), peeled, trimmed, and cut into thirds
1½ cups green beans, trimmed and cut into 1-inch pieces
½ cup fresh or frozen peas
4 tablespoons olive oil
2 cups thinly sliced mushrooms
1 teaspoon finely chopped fresh red or green chile, or about ½ teaspoon dried red pepper flakes
1 teaspoon finely chopped garlic
3 cups seeded, diced ripe tomatoes, reserve the juice separately
¼ cup finely chopped fresh parsley
6 fresh basil leaves, chopped
1 pound spaghetti or spaghettini
4 tablespoons (½ stick) butter
½ cup heavy (whipping) cream, or more if needed
⅔ cup freshly grated Parmesan cheese
Salt and freshly ground black pepper, to taste
⅔ cup toasted pine nuts

1. Cook the broccoli, zucchini, asparagus, and green beans in boiling salted water until crisp but tender, about 4 minutes. Add the peas and cook for 1 minute more. Drain and refresh the vegetables in cold water. Drain and set aside in a mixing bowl.

2. Heat 1 tablespoon of the olive oil in a nonreactive large skillet over medium heat. When hot, add the mushrooms and chile and sauté for about 2 minutes. Add the remaining 3 tablespoons olive oil, the garlic, and tomatoes and cook, stirring gently so as not to break up the tomatoes, for about 4 minutes. Add the parsley and basil; stir and set aside.

3. Cook the spaghetti in boiling salted water until just al dente; the spaghetti must retain just a slight resilience in the center. Drain.

4. Meanwhile, in a nonreactive pot large enough to hold the drained spaghetti and all of the vegetables, melt the butter over medium heat. Add the cream and Parmesan and stir constantly until heated through. When hot, reduce the heat and cook gently on and off the heat until smooth. Add the spaghetti and toss quickly to blend. Add half of the vegetables and pour in the reserved juice from the tomatoes. Toss and stir over very

Sirio Maccioni presents the original Pasta Primavera.

low heat until the mixture is heated through, 5 minutes. Season with salt and pepper.

5. Add the remaining vegetables and toss gently. If the sauce seems too dry, add additional cream, but the sauce should not be soupy. Adjust the seasonings. Add the pine nuts and give the mixture one final toss. Serve in heated soup or spaghetti bowls. Spoon some of the tomato mixture over each serving. Serve immediately.

Serves 4 as a main course, or 6 to 8 as an appetizer

Borgattini's
LEMON AND OLIVE ORZO

Daphne Borgattini, a retired operator with the New York Telephone Company, serves this tangy pasta dish with roasted lamb or chicken for Sunday dinner at her home in Astoria. It also makes a good main course.

1 pound orzo
Finely minced zest of 1 lemon
1 cup oil-cured olives, pitted and chopped
2 cups loosely packed arugula or watercress, well rinsed, patted dry, and chopped
½ cup olive oil
1 cup freshly grated ricotta salata or feta cheese
Salt and freshly ground black pepper, to taste

1. Boil the orzo in a large pot filled with plenty of boiling salted water until tender.

2. Meanwhile, place the lemon zest, olives, arugula, oil, and grated cheese in a large bowl and stir well. Set aside.

3. Drain the pasta. Add the orzo to the bowl

and toss immediately with the olive mixture. Season to taste with salt and freshly ground black pepper. Serve immediately.

Serves 4

Tommaso's
PENNE WITH ZUCCHINI

1 clove garlic, peeled and smashed
¼ cup extra-virgin olive oil
1 onion, minced
¼ teaspoon dried red pepper flakes
¼ cup minced thinly sliced prosciutto
3 zucchini, scrubbed and cut into julienne
2 tomatoes, chopped
1 pound penne
1 tablespoon unsalted butter
¼ cup minced fresh Italian (flat-leaf) parsley
½ cup loosely packed fresh basil leaves, torn
1 teaspoon salt
½ teaspoon freshly ground black pepper
1 cup freshly grated pecorino cheese

1. Warm the garlic in the oil in a nonreactive large sauté pan over medium heat until the garlic is golden, 5 minutes. Remove and discard. Add the onion and pepper flakes and cook until the onion is soft, 7 minutes. Add the prosciutto and zucchini, partly cover the pan, and cook until barely soft, about 5 minutes. Stir in the tomatoes and cover the pan. Reduce the heat to very low.

2. Boil the penne in plenty of well-salted water until tender; drain.

3. Meanwhile, add the butter, parsley, basil, salt, and pepper to the sauce and stir well.

4. Place the sauce in a large pasta bowl. Add the penne and toss. Add the pecorino cheese and additional salt and pepper to taste and serve.

Serves 4

BUMPER CROPS IN BENSONHURST

A bumper crop of zucchini isn't something you'd expect in Bensonhurst. The patch of asphalt that stretches from 17th Avenue to Avenue U, between the water and 60th Street in Brooklyn, appears to be sown only with row upon row of brick and stone houses. But just as there is a stoop and a well-polished car out front, there is a zucchini patch behind most of the homes in the Italian enclave.

In late summer, harvesters roam the blocks on a primordial neighborly mission: giving away the squash. They are unswayed by gushing fire hydrants, the skateboarders who careen by them, or by the hard rock that booms from the cars that cruise the blocks.

"You'd expect this in some little paisani village in Italy," said Thomas Verdillo, chef, tenor, and owner of Tommaso's Restaurant on 86th Street. "You do not expect to open the door of your restaurant in Brooklyn and find somebody there with an armload of home-grown zucchini and a smile that says, 'Take this, I grew it for you.'"

But Mr. Verdillo understands. He has lived his entire life in the neighborhood. Zucchini in the summer, bathtub red wine in the fall, the local custom of hanging prosciutto to cure over the washing machine, and first communion celebrations that cost a year's rent—"These are little reminders that Bensonhurst is a living Italian neighborhood, not some museum," he said.

ONCE ITALIAN, ALWAYS ITALIAN

A ccording to Frank Vardy, a demographer with the City of New York, over 95,000 Italian people live in Bensonhurst, making it the largest Italian neighborhood in the city, and one that continues to absorb newcomers. Other Italian neighborhoods become shrines to the past when Italians move on to wider streets and bigger backyards and are replaced by other ethnic groups. But in Bensonhurst, Italians are replaced by other Italians, and backyard zucchini production remains more or less stable.

"You have to understand that the Italian who moves to this neighborhood from Italy does not go out to a restaurant to eat zucchini," Mr. Verdillo said. "He grows zucchini in Brooklyn because he grew it in Italy. He eats zucchini at home because he grows zucchini. He gives you zucchini because you are his friend. But he comes to a restaurant to eat steak, not zucchini." Mr. Verdillo has cooked many steaks in his time.

On the other hand, Mr. Verdillo has his own zucchini response. He grew up the youngest of 10 children in a home where the nightly dinner table was set for Bacchus, and Puccini played on the hi-fi, and the zucchini vines engulfed the backyard. He must cook zucchini. "You have to understand where I come from," he said.

For steak-seeking patrons, Mr. Verdillo adds zucchini to the antipasto assortment. He slices, breads, and deep-fries it. He shreds the squash with onion, adds Parmesan and black pepper, beats it into eggs, and makes a Neapolitan frittata. He minces the squash and their blossoms for fritters and makes minted zucchini pickles.

He has cut zucchini in half and stuffed it with wild mushrooms and veal, though this recipe is "rather obvious. The Italian from Italy may eat around it and in any case the recipe doesn't use that much zucchini," said the impresario, adding that he regularly faces "blight quantities" of the vegetable.

"You have to understand that when you are dealing with Italians, you are dealing with a lot," he said, philosophically. "It just happens that at zucchini time in this neighborhood, you deal with a lot of a lot."

ROMANCING THE ZUCCHINI

Second-, third-, and fourth-generation Italians, he said, are more likely to romance the vegetable. For them, he concocts entire zucchini menus. He adds to the antipasti assortment zucchini blossoms stuffed with three cheeses, dipped in frothy egg whites, and gently pan-fried. He uses zucchini slices as lasagne noodles, layering them with fresh, nutmeg-scented ricotta and a light tomato sauce. He tosses penne with pecorino, fresh basil, and slivered zucchini, a recipe he calls "classic, it uses lots of zucchini and it tastes great."

On a summer night, when there is zucchini in some guise on each of his 35 tables, Mr. Verdillo, a tenor who trained at Juilliard and can sing nine full operas, is prone to song. If, in addition, a customer requests a favored Verdi score, a Broadway show tune, or a rare vintage from his 20,000-bottle wine

cellar, his eyes actually fill with tears behind his wire-rimmed glasses. He inhales until his abdomen puffs like a well-stuffed zucchini blossom over the waistband of his trousers. He opens his arms to the room full of regulars, and begins his serenade.

Buy zucchini by the bagful if the neighborhood crop is slim.

Michael Harvey's PASTA

Recalls Michael Harvey, an artist, "A friend of mine got this recipe from a magazine, and when we went shopping for the ingredients, we couldn't find everything the recipe specified. We improvised and the pasta turned out great. Then when I made it myself, I improvised again, and this is the result."

Michael Harvey's pasta is the result of improvising on the improvisation.

1 pound tomatoes,
   coarsely chopped
¼ pound Gorgonzola cheese, crumbled
¼ pound mascarpone cheese, diced
¼ cup oil-cured black olives,
   pitted and chopped
4 anchovy fillets, chopped
1 tablespoon plus 1 teaspoon minced
   Italian (flat-leaf) parsley,
   coarsely chopped
1 clove garlic, minced
¼ teaspoon dried red pepper flakes
¼ teaspoon salt
¼ teaspoon freshly ground black pepper
2 tablespoons olive oil
1 pound linguine

1. Preheat the oven to 400°F.
2. Cover the bottom of a 14 × 10-inch baking pan with half of the tomatoes. Dot with half of the Gorgonzola and half the mascarpone. Add half each of the olives, anchovies, parsley, garlic, red pepper flakes, salt, and black pepper. Repeat, using the remaining tomatoes and cheeses and topping them with the remaining half of the other ingredients. Drizzle the olive oil over the top. Bake for 20 minutes.
3. Meanwhile, cook the linguine in a large pot of boiling salted water until tender. Drain.
4. Place the cooked linguine in a large bowl. Add the baked tomato mixture and combine thoroughly.
Serves 4

FARFALLE IMPATIATE
Tony's of the Bronx

Evidence of Neil Simon's second law of the universe (see box, facing page) as offered up by Tony Morante's favorite restaurant, Tony's, which shares his name, but which he doesn't own.

1 yellow bell pepper, stemmed, seeded, and
   coarsely chopped
2 red bell peppers, stemmed, seeded, and coarsely
   chopped
1 large white onion, roughly chopped
2 tablespoons unsalted butter
¼ teaspoon salt
½ teaspoon freshly ground black pepper
½ cup loosely packed fresh basil leaves
2 cups packed whole spinach leaves, stems
   discarded, leaves well rinsed and minced
1 clove garlic
⅛ teaspoon dried oregano
⅛ teaspoon dried thyme
⅛ teaspoon dried red pepper flakes
⅓ cup dry white wine
10 fresh plum tomatoes, seeded and minced
1 cup heavy (whipping) cream
Pinch of freshly grated nutmeg
⅔ cup freshly grated Parmesan cheese
1 pound farfalle pasta

ARTHUR AVENUE NIGHTS

Tony Morante grew up in the Belmont section of the Bronx. From his front porch, you look one way toward Yankee Stadium, the other way toward the Bronx Botanical Gardens. Straight ahead is Arthur Avenue.

He started working as an usher at the stadium when he was 12 years old; 30 years later, he does community relations for the Bronx Bombers, gives tours of the Botanical Gardens, and is ombudsman for Arthur Avenue.

"You can go in the day if you want to shop," he says when he calls me. "For theater, you can come at night. We have a little pasta at Tony's and we go up to the theater."

Nobody is prouder than Morante of the neighborhood's reper-

tory theater. Over farfalle at Tony's, he mentions quite often that the theater is "legitimate, the only one off-Broadway and this far north."

Tony takes a deep satisfaction from never having left these blocks, and feels a nearly mystical connection with the generations of Italian masons and shopkeepers who have kept the sidewalks smooth and clean. When he runs out of words to describe the allure of his neighborhood, he recites Neil Simon, who said, "There are two laws of the universe: The law of gravity and everybody likes Italian food."

1. In a food processor, combine the yellow and red bell peppers and half of the chopped onion and pulse until the vegetables are finely chopped but not puréed.

2. Melt 1 tablespoon of the butter in a nonreactive large sauté pan over low heat. Add the bell pepper mixture and season with ⅛ teaspoon of the salt and ¼ teaspoon of the black pepper. Cook until tender, about 7 minutes. Remove from the heat. Stir in the basil and spinach; cover and set aside.

3. Melt the remaining 1 tablespoon butter in a nonreactive sauté pan. Add the remaining chopped onion, the garlic, oregano, thyme, red pepper flakes, and the remaining ¼ teaspoon black pepper. Sauté until the onions are translucent, 5 minutes. Add the wine and reduce until it is nearly evaporated, 3 to 5 minutes.

4. Stir in three-fourths of the tomatoes and simmer for 3 minutes. Add the cream and nutmeg, season with the remaining ⅛ teaspoon salt, and

Tony Morante can look to all that's important from his porch: Yankee Stadium, Arthur Avenue, and the Botanical Gardens.

simmer until reduced by half, 15 to 20 minutes. Reduce the heat to very low.

5. Boil the farfalle in plenty of salted water until tender; drain.

6. Combine the bell pepper mixture with the cream mixture in a large bowl. Add the pasta, Parmesan cheese, and the remaining tomatoes. Toss and serve.

Serves 4

SALVATORE ("MR. WAB") MEDICI OF EAST HARLEM

"I was born on East 114th Street. I never left. I never want to. I close the place couple weeks in summer, but I don't leave. Ah, maybe up to Arthur Avenue, walk around, do a little shopping. You gotta get outta this place once in a while. This neighborhood is a disaster area."

Salvatore Medici the gruff sucked scotch and soda from a half-moon wine glass. He smoothed a splattered cook's apron over his short-sleeved, yellow tee shirt. His eyes wandered down the leg of his tattersall polyester leisure pants to the dark linoleum floor of Andy's Colonial Tavern, the bar/restaurant that he owns on First Avenue near 116th Street.

The only things "colonial" about the place are the ersatz wheel chandeliers and maybe the wood paneling that's tacked on the walls. But then, Andy's Colonial Tavern isn't an outpost on a frontier, it's a remnant of a time when families left their doors unlocked and went to mass every day. A leftover.

ITALY ON THE EAST RIVER

Mr. Medici looked up to the three dinner customers he'd joined. "In them days it was mostly Italians. From 100th Street to 116th, from the River to Third Avenue," he said, pulling on a Pall Mall.

"This was a family neighborhood. My father was born here, went back to Italy, don't ask why, came back and raised ten children here, on 114th Street. Our house was like a restaurant. My mother, Rose, when I cook, I think of her. Them days, nobody locked a door. Our Lady of Mount Carmel around the corner there, that was the biggest Italian parish in the world outside Rome.

"*We* elected Fiorello La Guardia."

"*We* cheered for Joe DiMaggio."

Mr. Medici tippled his scotch. "Call me 'Mr. Wab,' " he said. "Everybody in this neighborhood has a nickname, don't ask why."

EARL OF TUSCANY

Lite rock dappled over the eight gold-clothed tables that are topped with a protective piece of glass and set to the right of the eight-stool bar at Andy's Colonial Tavern. Five diners tucked into bushel basket–size portions of macaroni. The perfume of the red and green—garlic and tomato, basil, oregano—lingers with all the other memories in the East Harlem joint. So does the scent of olive oil, or "earl," as Mr. Wab says, which is the secret of his cooking, "The very best Tuscan earl."

Outside, shots and occasional sirens strike the refrain in the interminable dirge of urban decay. "Safe as the bank in here, don't ask," said Mr. Wab.

Most folks left, that's true. Moved up to bigger houses and backyards. "The city ripped down beautiful family homes to put up those eyesore projects. I saw it happen.

"After the '40s, the elite start meeting to eat in East Harlem. They don't live here. They come here. To be dangerous. To be trendy. They go to Rao's to see each other. I used to cook there. You're not missing anything. The people that want to look go to Rao's. The people that want to eat come to Andy's.

"Let me show you a picture. See, that guy there standing in front of the bar looking like Teddy Roosevelt. That's the original Andy, don't ask his real name. This place has been here over 100 years. Used to be me, my wife, my son Giuseppe, named for his grandfather. I lost my wife last year. Giuseppe—Giuseppe, bring these people some coffee over here—he's my right hand, my son, the bachelor. It's just us. We live over on 114th Street.

"It's a madhouse at lunch with all the neighborhood businessmen, don't ask. I cook what I want, which is what the people want. Puttanesca, marinara, garlic and earl. People want to eat, they come here. I'm always here. I close on Sunday but I cook for my family, a few friends. This is important, Sunday dinner. Some macaroni, some fish, some veal."

He put down the empty glass, eased himself out of the chair, minding the creaks and resistance in his legs as a good clam man with a knife would listen for the give inside a particularly obstinate bivalve.

Giuseppe set down the glasses he was polishing near the bar and moved toward his father. His black mustache seemed at military attention to the old man's moves, his neatly manicured hands a ready net.

"I'll be 75 years old next month. I'm not going anywhere," said Mr. Wab, pushing his feet toward the kitchen.

"I might go down the East Side after we close tonight. My friends have restaurants down the 80s and 70s. Tomorrow I might go up Arthur Avenue for a walk."

PUTTANESCA A LA
Andy's Colonial Tavern

This is a sassy, fiery version of a classic Italian dish. And, it takes surprisingly little time to prepare.

¼ cup olive oil
3 cloves garlic, minced
1 can (35 ounces) peeled Italian plum tomatoes, seeded, drained, and roughly chopped
1 tablespoon capers, well rinsed
⅔ cup oil-cured black olives, pitted and roughly chopped
½ teaspoon dried red pepper flakes
1 teaspoon dried basil
1 teaspoon dried oregano
⅛ teaspoon freshly ground black pepper
Salt, to taste
1 pound spaghetti
2 tablespoons minced fresh parsley leaves

1. Heat the oil in a nonreactive large saucepan over medium heat. Add the garlic, stir, remove the pan from the heat, and allow the hot oil to turn the garlic pale gold, 5 to 10 minutes. Stir in the tomatoes, capers, olives, red pepper flakes, basil, oregano, and black pepper, return to medium-low heat, and simmer for 10 minutes. Taste the sauce and add salt and pepper if needed. Reduce the heat to very low.

2. Cook the spaghetti in plenty of well-salted, boiling water until al dente; drain.

3. Toss the spaghetti with the sauce, sprinkle on the fresh parsley, and serve.

Serves 4

Out in front of Andy's Colonial Tavern with Salvatore Medici.

Bill Liberman's
LINGUINE WITH SWISS CHARD

Bill Liberman's quick pasta dish is perfect for a late-night post-theater dinner.

Bill Liberman, a theater manager, created this very rich, special-occasion dish for after-theater suppers. He makes his own linguine, adding very finely chopped Swiss chard to the dough, but the dish is also delicious made with a good store-bought linguine.

3 tablespoons olive oil
¼ cup pine nuts
1 tablespoon finely chopped garlic
⅓ cup chopped shallots
2 cups chopped red or green Swiss chard
1 cup heavy (whipping) cream
Large pinch of saffron, dissolved in 2 tablespoons water
1 pound linguine
½ cup freshly grated Parmesan cheese
Salt and freshly ground black pepper, to taste
Finely minced zest of ½ lemon

---

1. Heat 1 tablespoon of the olive oil in a small skillet over medium-low heat. Add the pine nuts and stir to coat with the oil. Sauté the nuts, stirring often, until lightly browned, 5 minutes. Set aside.

2. In a nonreactive skillet large enough to hold all of the cooked pasta, sauté the garlic and shallots in the remaining 2 tablespoons olive oil over medium heat until softened. Increase the heat, add the chard, and cook until softened, 1 to 2 minutes. Add the cream and saffron infusion and cook over low heat until thickened, about 5 minutes. Remove from the heat and set aside.

3. Meanwhile, cook the linguine until tender in a large pot of boiling salted water. Drain but do not rinse.

4. Bring the sauce back to a simmer over medium heat. Add the linguine and toss to coat well. Add the Parmesan, salt and pepper to taste, and the minced lemon zest and toss well. Serve immediately, garnished with the toasted pine nuts.

Serves 4

SanClementi's
BROCCOLI RABE WITH PENNE

In the kitchen with Charles SanClementi, Jr.

This recipe has been in the SanClementi family for generations. Mr. SanClementi has been known to use this dish to lure hungry Italian art dealers to his studio. Unlike more "refined" broccoli rabe recipes, SanClementi uses the entire vegetable in this dish. The garlic should be sautéed until golden. In fact, it is better to overcook the garlic rather than undercook it, because the broccoli rabe will "heal" any slightly burned cloves.

1 bunch broccoli rabe (1 to 1½ pounds), well rinsed, tough skin peeled, and chopped (keep flowers whole)
⅓ cup extra-virgin olive oil
5 large cloves garlic, minced
1 teaspoon dried oregano
Salt and freshly ground black pepper, to taste
1 pound dried penne

Jeanette Bartetti offers her grandmother's recipe for pasta with cauliflower.

1. In a large pot or steamer, steam the broccoli rabe until tender, 10 to 15 minutes. Remove from the heat and drain, reserving the cooking water.

2. Warm the olive oil in a nonreactive large skillet over medium-low heat. Add the garlic and sauté until golden, 3 minutes. Add the broccoli rabe, ¾ cup of the reserved cooking water, the oregano, and salt and pepper to taste. Cover and simmer for 20 minutes.

3. Meanwhile, warm a serving bowl in a 200°F oven. Bring a large pot of water to a boil (using as much of the reserved broccoli water as remains). Add the penne and cook until al dente, 8 to 10 minutes. Drain the pasta.

4. Remove the bowl from the oven, place the pasta in the bowl, and top with the broccoli mixture. Mix well and serve hot.

Serves 4

Giovannina's
PASTA RIMINATA

Jeanette Bartetti of Staten Island says that this recipe was passed down from her grandmother, Giovannina, who was born in Palermo, Sicily. It's a wonderful dish, a family favorite, and can be made with any shape pasta that catches your eye.

1 head cauliflower, cut into florets
½ teaspoon salt
1 large onion, chopped
3 tablespoons olive oil
2 tablespoons pine nuts
2 tablespoons raisins
¼ teaspoon freshly ground black pepper
1 pound ziti or rigatoni
Freshly grated Parmesan cheese

1. Combine the cauliflower, 1½ cups water, and ¼ teaspoon of the salt in a saucepan over medium heat. Cover and cook until tender, about 10 minutes. Drain, reserving the cooking liquid. Mash the cauliflower and set aside.

2. In a sauté pan, sauté the onion in the oil until softened, about 6 minutes. Stir in the pine nuts, raisins, the remaining ¼ teaspoon salt, and the pepper, and cook until the nuts start to turn golden, about 2 minutes. Add ¼ cup of the reserved cauliflower water and the mashed cauliflower and simmer until thick, about 15 minutes, adding cauliflower water as needed to prevent sticking.

3. Meanwhile, cook the pasta in a large pot of boiling salted water until al dente, or as you like it; drain.

4. In a large serving bowl, mix one-fourth of the cauliflower sauce with the pasta. Pour the remaining sauce over the top, sprinkle with the Parmesan cheese, and serve hot.

Serves 4 to 6

NATIONAL SPAGHETTI CARBONARA DAY

In 1983, Calvin Trillin, who writes for *The New Yorker*, initiated a campaign to have Thanksgiving changed to Spaghetti Carbonara Day. "It was at other people's Thanksgiving tables that I first began to articulate my spaghetti carbonara campaign," he wrote in his book *Third Helpings.*

At various Thanksgiving tables, he began dropping hints about "the esthetic advantages of replacing turkey with spaghetti carbonara—in fact, for instance, that the President would not be photographed every year receiving a large platter of spaghetti carbonara from the Eastern Association of Spaghetti Carbonara Growers. . . . I spoke of my interest in seeing what the floatmakers at Macy's might come up with as a 300-square-foot depiction of a plate of spaghetti carbonara. I reminded everyone how refreshing it would be to hear sports announcers call some annual tussle the Spaghetti Carbonara Day Classic."

SPAGHETTI IN EVERY POT

I figured that the Trillins would be the ones to ask for a recipe, so I called their Greenwich Village home.

"Yes, it is definitely time to discuss Spaghetti Carbonara Day!" he said. In the background his wife, Alice, uttered a wounded-animal sound.

"Did you hear that?" asked Mr. Trillin. "That wasn't even her not-this-old-chestnut-again sigh. Of all my jokes, Alice hates Spaghetti Carbonara Day the most. For years, I would go on Channel 13 every year and tell the real story of Thanksgiving. Sort of like the Queen's Christmas Address. I think Alice got tired of listening."

The truth of Thanksgiving, according to Mr. Trillin runs like this:

"In England, a long time ago, there were people called Pilgrims who were very strict about making sure everyone observed the Sabbath and cooked food without any flavor and that sort of thing, and they decided to go to America, where they could enjoy Freedom to Nag. In America, the Pilgrims tried farming, but they couldn't get much done because they were always putting their best farmers in the stocks for crimes like Suspicion of Cheerfulness. The Indians took pity on the Pilgrims and helped them with their farming, even though the Indians thought the Pilgrims were about as much fun as teenage circumcision. The Pilgrims were so grateful that at the end of their first year in America, they invited the Indians over for a Thanksgiving meal. The Indians, having had some experience with Pilgrim cuisine during the year, took the precaution of taking along one dish of their own. They brought a dish that their ancestors had learned many generations before from none other than Christopher Columbus, who was known to the Indians as 'the big Italian fellow.' The dish was spaghetti carbonara. The Pilgrims hated it. They said it was 'heretically tasty' and 'the work of the devil.'

COINING A PHRASE

"The Indians were so disgusted that on the way back to their village after dinner one of them made a remark about the Pilgrims that has unfortunately caused confusion among historians about the first Thanksgiving meal. He said, 'What a bunch of turkeys!'"

One year, the Trillin family had spaghetti carbonara for Thanksgiving dinner. As a sort of bonus, Channel 13 had given them a spaghetti carbonara recipe from a cookbook and Alice cooked it. Usually, the Trillins go to other peo-

ple's houses for Thanksgiving. However, the invitations, said Mr. Trillin, have slowed down in the past few years.

THE PROGRESS SO FAR

"Alice thinks it is because of my outspoken position on spaghetti carbonara," he said.

"That's a shame," I said, adding that it was also a shame that the spaghetti carbonara campaign had never really taken off.

"I wouldn't say that," said Mr. Trillin. "The government retraining of turkey farmers, to turn them into spaghetti carbonara farmers, well, I guess that's gone a little slow. It depends on which administration is in the White House...."

"Well, I guess the President has not yet been photographed receiving a platter of spaghetti carbonara from the Eastern Association of Spaghetti Carbonara Growers," he covered the telephone: ("Alice have you seen any pictures of the president with a platter of spaghetti carbonara, yet?").

"Um, no. Well, I'm not sure about the Macy's Thanksgiving Parade.... (Alice, have you noticed a Spaghetti Carbonara float in the parade?)"

"Um, well, you'd have to talk to sportswriters to get a count of the Spaghetti Carbonara Day Classics around the country. I don't keep up with that sort of thing.

"But, um, well, I wouldn't say that the Spaghetti Carbonara Campaign didn't take off. I'd say the turkey enforcer thugs have been out. About this time of year, I get a lot of letters from Spaghetti Carbonara Day supporters."

"Gee," I said, "how many?"

"Oh, I dunno. (Would you say in the thousands, Alice?) Um. Well. I'd say a lot."

"I guess that's why Channel 13 asks you back every year," I said.

"Uh, actually, they didn't call this year."

"Oh, I'm sorry."

"No, no, don't be sorry. I bet the Queen doesn't give her address either. I think we'll probably go to Chinatown on Thanksgiving. We did last year. You want to come along?"

Turkey Day
SPAGHETTI CARBONARA

Calvin Trillin, a man who's obviously serious about serving carbonara for Thanksgiving (see page 236).

The Trillins "don't cook carbonara," but they gave a thumbs-up (or was that a gobble?) to this rich version.

8 thick slices bacon or pancetta, chopped (to equal 1 cup)
2 tablespoons butter
4 egg yolks
1 cup heavy (whipping) cream
½ cup freshly grated Parmesan cheese
1 teaspoon coarsely ground black pepper
½ teaspoon salt
1 pound spaghetti
1 tablespoon minced fresh parsley leaves

1. Cook the bacon in a skillet over medium heat until it begins to crisp. Add the butter and remove from the heat.

2. In a nonreactive bowl, whisk together the egg yolks, cream, Parmesan, black pepper, and salt and set aside.

3. Boil the spaghetti in a large pot of well-salted water until tender; drain.

4. Return the skillet and bacon to medium heat. Add the spaghetti and toss well to coat. Pour the cream mixture over the noodles and toss quickly with a fork. Remove from the heat to avoid scrambling the egg and continue to toss; the hot noodles will cook the eggs to a custard consistency.

5. Serve at once, garnished with the parsley and additional black pepper or grated Parmesan.
Serves 4

GARLIC
PARSLEY
3.98 POUND

GNOCCHI
2.39 POUND

CHEESE
TORTELLINI

PUMPKIN
TORTELLONI

SPINACH
TORTELLONI

Baskets of pasta at Todaro's.

FRESH NOODLES

Bronx

BORGATTI'S RAVIOLI & NOODLE COMPANY: 632 East 187th Street; (212) 367-3799. Arcane shapes and flavored noodles (whole wheat, carrot, spinach, black pepper, and tomato noodles are all in stock) as well as finely made durum wheat noodles.

THE PASTA FACTORY: 686 East 187th Street; (212) 295-4857. A huge variety of fresh noodles and the cheese ravioli alone make the trek to this Bronx outpost worthwhile.

Brooklyn

PASTA FRESCA: 6518 11th Avenue in Bensonhurst; (718) 680-7193. Very close to the corner

of Borough Park, this storefront closet turns out tender ravioli and tortellini that both Dom DeLuise and Sophia Loren rhapsodize about.

PASTOSA RAVIOLI COMPANY: 370 Court Street in Carroll Gardens; (718) 635-0482. Makes excellent fresh tortellini, ravioli, and manicotti.

QUEEN ANN RAVIOLI & MACARONI INC: 7205 18th Avenue in Bensonhurst; (718) 256-1061. Fresh and dried homemade pasta, shells stuffed with spinach and ricotta, the ravioli, and the manicotti are all excellent.

Manhattan

PIEMONTE HOMEMADE RAVIOLI COMPANY: 190 Grand Street at Mulberry Street; (212) 226-1033. A wide range of novelty dried pastas, such as spinach fettuccine and angel hair with squid ink, as well as meat- and cheese-filled ravioli.

RAFFETTO RAVIOLI: 144 West Houston Street, between Sullivan and MacDougal Streets; (212) 777-1261. A large selection of fresh pasta, including spinach, egg, tomato, black pepper, squid ink, saffron, and mushroom.

At Queen Ann Ravioli & Macaroni Company in Bensonhurst, Brooklyn.

Silvala's
PIZZOCCHERI VALTELLINESE

Silvala Conterno, a native of Piedmont, is an itinerant pastamaker who rolls out her buckwheat noodle dough for health food stores and high-fashion Italian restaurants throughout the city. With a quick cabbage and potato sauce, the noodles make a wonderful winter meal.

NOODLES
1½ cups stone-ground whole wheat flour
1½ cups buckwheat flour
3 eggs
2 tablespoons milk
1 teaspoon salt
Semolina flour, for dusting

PIZZOCCHERI VALTELLINESE
2 potatoes, peeled and diced
½ cup julienned cabbage
2 teaspoons minced fresh sage
3 tablespoons freshly grated Parmesan cheese
½ cup freshly grated Taleggio cheese
Fresh sage leaves, for garnish

1. Make the noodles: On a work surface, combine both flours with your hands and form them into a mound. Make a well in the center and break the eggs into it. Add the milk, salt, and 2 tablespoons water and mix with your fingertips, gradually bringing in the flour from the edges of the well. When the dough begins to form a ball, knead it, using a pastry scraper to retrieve any dough that sticks to the board and adding more flour if the dough is too sticky, until smooth and satiny, about 3 minutes. Dust the dough with the semolina flour, cover with a towel, and let rest for 20 minutes.

2. Dust a work surface with semolina flour.

Break off half of the dough and roll out with a pasta roller or a rolling pin to a uniform ⅛-inch thickness. With a small sharp knife, slice into noodles ½ inch wide by 6 inches long. Place in layers on sheets of waxed paper, cover with a towel, and refrigerate until ready to use. Repeat with the remaining half of the dough.

3. Make the pizzoccheri: Pour 2 cups of water into a medium saucepan. Add the potatoes and cook until just tender, 20 minutes. Remove the potatoes from the pan with a slotted spoon and set aside. Add the cabbage to the remaining boiling water and blanch for 45 seconds. Remove and drain, reserving the cooking liquid.

4. In a saucepan, combine the potatoes, cabbage, minced sage, cheeses, and ⅓ cup of the cooking water. Cook over medium heat until the mixture begins to thicken, about 3 minutes. Reduce the heat to low and keep warm without burning.

5. Bring a large pot of salted water to a boil. Add the noodles and cook until just al dente, about 3 minutes. Remove from the heat and drain.

6. Add the pasta to the sauce and stir to combine. Remove from the heat and serve immediately, garnished with fresh sage leaves.

Serves 4

Now, that's a pasta machine.

Staten Island
PASTA WITH CHICKEN

Tony Tung, a former landmark's commissioner, is a legendary cook who combines his Chinese heritage with his love of Italian food to create dishes like this one.

Remove from the heat and keep covered.

2. Cook the pasta in plenty of salted boiling water until tender; drain.

3. In a warm bowl, combine half of the chicken mixture, 1 cup of the cheese, and ¼ cup of the bread crumbs. Add the pasta, toss, and season with fresh black pepper. Crown with the remaining chicken, cheese, and bread crumbs and serve.

Serves 8

Tony Tung of Montelbano's on Staten Island presents his pasta with chicken.

¼ cup olive oil
1 clove garlic, minced
3 skinless, boneless chicken breasts (1¼ to 1½ pounds), cut into bite-size chunks
2 tablespoons fresh oregano
2 tablespoons soy sauce
1 cup dry white wine
1 bunch broccoli, cut into florets, stems discarded
1 jar (16 ounces) marinated Italian mushrooms, drained and quartered
8 tablespoons (1 stick) butter
2 pounds fresh spaghetti
2 cups freshly grated Romano cheese
½ cup Italian-style dried bread crumbs
Freshly ground black pepper, to taste

1. Heat the olive oil in a nonreactive large skillet over medium-high heat. Add the garlic and cook to soften slightly. Add the chicken and cook until browned lightly on all sides. Add the oregano, soy sauce, and wine and simmer, uncovered, for 2 minutes. Add the broccoli, cover the pan tightly, and steam until the broccoli begins to soften, 3 to 5 minutes. Add the mushrooms, cover the pan and heat the mushrooms, 2 minutes. Whisk in the butter, 1 tablespoon at a time, thoroughly incorporating each before adding the next.

Starr's PASTA

Starr Ockenga, a photographer known for her lush still lifes, is "basically a minimalist" when it comes to cooking. "This is one of my basic 10-ingredient dishes," she says. She serves this simple, luscious dish for family dinners or as a first course for the company meals she serves in her TriBeCa loft.

2 cups fresh ricotta cheese
½ cup oil-cured olives, pitted and minced
4 scallions, trimmed and chopped
½ cup packed basil leaves
2 tomatoes, chopped
¼ cup olive oil
1 pound fusilli or rigatoni
Salt and freshly ground black pepper, to taste
Freshly grated Parmesan cheese, for serving

1. Place the ricotta cheese in a large bowl and beat with a fork until smooth. Stir in the olives, scallions, basil, tomatoes, and olive oil. Set aside.

2. Cook the pasta in a large pot of well-salted boiling water until tender; drain.

3. Add the pasta to the sauce mixture and toss. Season with salt and pepper to taste. Serve immediately with grated Parmesan cheese.

Serves 4

Alex Goren's EMERGENCY SPAGHETTI

When guests show up unannounced, Alex Goren, a businessman, always has the makings on hand to concoct this dish. He explains, "Originally created out of desperation, Emergency Spaghetti has become a regular sort of thing. All my friends love it."

¼ teaspoon coarse sea salt
½ cup plus 1 teaspoon extra-virgin
   olive oil
1 pound spaghetti
4 tablespoons (½ stick) butter
1 pound yellow onions, coarsely chopped and
   drained of excess liquid
2 tablespoons chopped fresh oregano
2 tablespoons chopped fresh basil
1 teaspoon freshly ground black pepper
1 teaspoon fine sea salt

1. Fill a large pot with 5 quarts of water. Add the coarse sea salt and 1 teaspoon of the olive oil. Cover and bring to a boil over high heat. Add the spaghetti and cook until tender; drain. Allow some water to remain clinging to the spaghetti; it will enhance the sauce.

2. Meanwhile, in a large skillet, melt the butter with the remaining ½ cup olive oil over medium heat. Add the onions and stir. Add the oregano, basil, black pepper, and fine sea salt and mix with a wooden spoon. Sauté until the onions are translucent, about 8 minutes.

3. Put half of the onion sauce in a bowl. Add the spaghetti and cover with the remaining onion sauce. Mix very thoroughly and serve to the astounded guests who just "happened to be in the neighborhood."

Serves 4

TORTELLONI Howard

Howard Levitt is a commercial real estate consultant who lives on Sutton Place. His antennae are as attuned to "good and easy" pasta as they are to property value, and this is a dish he's been known to prepare when closing a big deal.

½ ounce dried porcini mushrooms,
   soaked in water to cover for 2 hours
   or until soft
2 tablespoons plus 1 teaspoon olive oil
2 cloves garlic, minced
1 tablespoon fresh thyme leaves
½ cup dry vermouth
1 cup half-and-half
Salt and freshly ground black pepper,
   to taste
1 pound fresh tortelloni

1. Drain the mushrooms. Warm 2 tablespoons of the olive oil in a nonreactive large saucepan over very low heat. Add the mushrooms, garlic, and thyme and cook, stirring frequently, until the garlic turns a light straw color, about 4 minutes. Add the vermouth and simmer until it reduces slightly, about 5 minutes. Reduce the heat to very low and slowly add the half-and-half, a little at a time, stirring to combine. Season the sauce with salt and pepper. Increase the heat to medium, stir, and simmer the sauce until it thickens, 10 minutes.

2. Meanwhile, fill a large, heavy pot with water; add a pinch of salt and the remaining 1 teaspoon olive oil. Bring to a boil. Add the tortelloni and cook until they rise to the top and are tender, about 4 minutes. Drain well.

3. Stir the tortelloni into the cream sauce. Reduce the heat to low, cover, and cook for 5 minutes. Serve.

Serves 4

Gino Cammarata's
SICILIAN PASTA WITH SARDINES

Imported sardines work best in this Sicilian standby that seems to taste best on cool, rainy nights.

5 tablespoons olive oil
2 small onions, chopped
1 can (6 ounces) tomato paste, dissolved in 1½ cups water
12 fresh sardines, imported from Portugal or Sicily, heads and bones removed
¾ cup cooked cauliflower florets
¼ cup fresh dill, rinsed, dried, and chopped
3 tablespoons pine nuts
3 tablespoons golden raisins
1 pound bucatini, spaghetti, or linguine
½ cup fine, dried bread crumbs

1. Warm 2 tablespoons of the olive oil in a nonreactive large skillet. Add the onions and sauté until softened, 5 minutes. Add the diluted tomato paste and sardines and stir until the fish flake and turn white on the inside, 3 minutes more. Add the cauliflower, dill, pine nuts, and raisins and sauté until the mixture turns pinkish and begins to boil around the edges, 1 to 2 minutes. Reduce the heat to low.

2. Bring a large pot of well-salted water to a boil. Add the pasta and cook until al dente.

3. Meanwhile, toss the bread crumbs with the remaining 3 tablespoons oil and sauté in a skillet over high heat until brown. Stir frequently to prevent burning.

4. Remove the sardine mixture from the heat and place in a large bowl. Drain the pasta. Add it to the bowl and toss. Divide the pasta among 4 bowls and top with the toasted bread crumbs.
Serves 4

Gino Cammarata at Siracusa restaurant in Manhattan.

Dinner Party
RIGATONI ALLA PANNA

This pasta recipe originally appeared in *A Culinary Collection from the Metropolitan Museum of Art,* and it is still a mainstay of art circle dinner parties in Manhattan.

1 pound dried rigatoni
1 bay leaf
2 tablespoons butter
¼ teaspoon dry English mustard
1 cup heavy (whipping) cream
2 egg yolks
½ cup freshly grated Parmesan cheese
Salt and freshly ground black pepper, to taste

1. Bring a large pot of salted water to a boil. Add the rigatoni and bay leaf and cook until al dente, about 10 minutes.

2. Meanwhile, make the sauce: Melt the butter in a skillet over medium heat. Whisk in the mustard and then the cream. Reduce the heat to medium-low, then, one at a time, whisk in the egg yolks. Slowly add the cheese and whisk constantly until the sauce thickens enough to coat the side of the pan. Do not let the sauce boil. Add salt and pepper to taste.

3. Drain the pasta. Place it in a warm serving dish and pour the hot sauce over it. Serve immediately.

Serves 4 to 6

1. Bring a large pot of water to a boil. Add the linguine and cook until al dente, about 10 minutes. Drain.

2. Meanwhile, warm the olive oil in a nonreactive large skillet over medium heat. Add the garlic and pepper flakes and stir until the garlic is soft and light golden, 3 to 5 minutes. Add the clams, wine, and lemon juice, cover, and steam until the clams open, about 7 minutes. Shuck the clams, dropping them back into the skillet. Discard any that do not open.

3. Toss the pasta with the clam sauce, garnish with parsley, and serve piping hot.

Serves 8

Tommy's
LINGUINE WITH CLAM SAUCE

Linguine with clam sauce is a standby of Italian restaurants around the city, but too often, canned clams and garlic powder give the dish an acrid taste. Made with fresh clams and very little else, this is one of the best versions ever. The Tommy of this recipe is the uncle of Thomas Verdillo of Tommaso's Restaurant (see page 228).

1 pound dried linguine
5 tablespoons extra-virgin olive oil
5 cloves garlic, smashed
About ½ teaspoon dried red pepper flakes, or to taste (no seeds)
32 littleneck clams (smallest you can find), scrubbed and rinsed well
1 cup dry white wine
Juice of ¼ lemon
¼ cup chopped fresh Italian (flat-leaf) parsley

Mario R. Daniele's
PASTA FRITTATA

Mario Daniele, a wine importer who lives in East Harlem says, "This was originally designed to make use of leftover pasta, but the frittata is so versatile, so delicious served with ratatouille, mushrooms, pesto, or meat sauce —that it's become a favorite family meal."

Mario R. Daniele's frittata is a perfect use for leftover pasta.

2 eggs
¼ cup milk
½ cup shredded mozzarella cheese
2 tablespoons freshly grated Parmesan
*   cheese*
Salt and freshly ground black pepper,
*   to taste*
½ pound thin pasta, such as spaghettini
*   or vermicelli*
3 tablespoons unsalted butter
1 cup julienned red bell pepper
1 cup julienned green bell pepper
1 onion, cut in half and thinly
*   sliced*

1. In a mixing bowl, beat the eggs with the milk. Add the mozzarella and Parmesan and beat to combine. Season with dashes of salt and pepper; set the mixture aside.

2. Cook the pasta in a large pot filled with salted boiling water until al dente. Drain the pasta in a colander. Return the pasta to the pot in which it was cooked, add the egg mixture, and, using a kitchen fork, toss to coat well. Set aside.

3. Melt 1 tablespoon of the butter in a skillet over medium heat. Add the bell pepper julienne and the onion and season with salt and pepper to taste. Cook until the vegetables are soft, about 8 minutes. Set aside.

4. Meanwhile, melt 1 tablespoon of the butter in a 10-inch skillet over medium heat. Swirl the pan to coat it with the butter and add the pasta and egg mixture, distributing evenly. It should be 1 to 1½ inches thick and flat on the top. Cook for 3 minutes. Reduce the heat to low and cook until a brown crust forms, about 15 minutes. Loosen the crust with a spatula and cook until the crust is crisp, 3 to 5 minutes more.

5. Place a plate over the skillet and invert the frittata onto the plate. Scrape the skillet, add the remaining 1 tablespoon butter, and return the pan to medium heat. Slip the frittata, crust side up, into the pan and cook the second side following the same procedure as before.

6. When crusty, turn the spaghetti cake out on a warm serving plate. Garnish with the sautéed onions and peppers and serve.

Serves 4

Stu Ewen's
SPECIAL PASTA

City College Professor Stuart Ewen's "culinary collage" is a combination of recipes that have lingered on his taste buds over the years. "The foundation is an 'authentic Italian' sauce recipe I got from my Italian mother-in-law," Ewen explains, "and I've built this sauce up from there." He usually serves the sauce over rigatoni.

2 pounds hot Italian sausages, each halved
*   crosswise*
3 tablespoons olive oil
1 ounce dried porcini mushrooms
1 can (2 ounces) rolled anchovy fillets with capers
1 medium-large onion, chopped
1 fat carrot, peeled and chopped
4 plump cloves garlic, minced
Zest of 1 lemon, minced
8 to 10 oil-marinated sun-dried tomatoes,
*   chopped*
20 green olives, pitted and chopped
1 teaspoon salt
1 tablespoon dried basil
1 tablespoon chopped fresh parsley
12 black peppercorns
1½ cups dry red wine (preferably Nebbiolo)
1 can (6 ounces) tomato paste
1 can (28 ounces) whole peeled tomatoes
*   (preferably imported Italian), chopped*
1½ pounds rigatoni

1. Place the sausages and olive oil in a nonreactive Dutch oven or deep casserole and add water to cover. Cook over medium-high heat, stirring occasionally, until the water evaporates and the sausages are browned all over, 15 minutes.

2. Meanwhile, soak the porcini in 1 cup of warm water until softened, about 10 minutes.

3. Add the can of anchovies (and their oil) to the sausages and stir well. Reduce the heat to medium, add the onion, carrot, and garlic, and cook, stirring, until the onion turns translucent, 5 minutes. Drain the porcini, cut them into thin slices, and add them to the sauce, along with the lemon zest, sun-dried tomatoes, olives, salt, basil, parsley, and peppercorns. Stir for about 1 minute. Stir in the wine, tomato paste, and tomatoes and bring to a boil. Reduce the heat to low and simmer until the sauce thickens, 1 hour.

4. Meanwhile, cook the pasta in a large pot of salted boiling water until al dente; drain.

5. Serve the pasta with the sauce spooned over the top.

Serves 6 to 8

Stu Ewen added his own special touch to a recipe he originally got from his mother-in-law.

The DiStacci Family's
AMAZING PESTO

100 fresh basil leaves, well rinsed and
    patted dry
1 clove garlic, minced
1 tablespoon pine nuts
1 tablespoon freshly grated pecorino cheese
1 tablespoon freshly grated Parmesan cheese
⅔ cup olive oil

In a blender or food processor, combine the basil, garlic, pine nuts, and both cheeses. With the machine running, drizzle in the olive oil. Process until smooth.

Makes about 1 cup

Nilda's
PANSIT

Nilda Jaynal, who grew up in the Philippines and now organizes the annual Philippine Independence Day festivities in New York, says that pansit, or pancit, is a symbolic dish to Filipinos. "Traditionally, each bowl of pansit was made with very long noodles," she says. "Each noodle was supposed to be endless and symbolize long life." Noodles are still popular at celebrations and festive meals.

½ cup shredded Chinese cabbage
½ cup carrot julienne
½ cup snow peas
½ cup sliced water chestnuts
½ cup straw mushrooms
2 whole chicken breasts (1 to 1½ pounds), split
10 medium shrimp, peeled and deveined
1 tablespoon vegetable oil
1 onion, chopped
1 clove garlic, minced
½ cup mushroom soy sauce
1 package (14 ounces) rice vermicelli or rice sticks
Salt and freshly ground black pepper, to taste
2 scallions, trimmed and minced
2 hard-cooked eggs, peeled and sliced

1. Bring 6 cups water to a boil in a nonreactive large pot over high heat. Add the cabbage, carrot, snow peas, water chestnuts, and mushrooms and boil for 2 minutes. With a slotted spoon or skimmer, remove the vegetables to a colander and immediately rinse under cold water. Set aside.

2. Bring the water back to a boil, if necessary, and add the chicken. Simmer until the chicken is just cooked through, 15 minutes.

3. Remove the chicken with a slotted spoon and set aside until cool enough to handle. Remove the pot from the heat. Add the shrimp to the hot liquid in the pot. When the shrimp turn pink, remove from the pot and set aside. Strain and reserve 3 cups of the cooking liquid.

4. When the chicken is cool enough to handle, remove the skin and bones and slice the meat into bite-size pieces. Set aside with the shrimp.

5. Warm the oil in a nonreactive large sauté pan over medium heat. Add the onion and sauté until translucent, 3 minutes. Add the garlic and cook for 1 minute more. Stir in the soy sauce and 2½ cups of the reserved cooking liquid. Add the pasta and half of the blanched vegetables and cooked chicken and shrimp. Cook until the pasta is al dente, about 3 minutes. If the pansit becomes too dry, add the remaining ½ cup reserved cooking liquid.

6. Season the dish with salt and pepper to taste. Divide among 2 to 4 deep bowls. Garnish with the remaining chicken, shrimp, and vegetables, and the scallions and hard-cooked eggs.

Serves 2 as a main course, or 4 as an appetizer

Marion Gold's CABBAGE AND NOODLES

Rozanne Gold, a restaurant consultant, remembers that when she was growing up in New York, her mother served this hearty pasta dish with corned beef on winter nights. Her father, Bill Gold, who played football for the Washington Redskins, swears by the concoction, as does anyone who tastes it.

8 tablespoons (1 stick) unsalted butter
1 large green cabbage, cored and sliced
1 onion, thinly sliced
½ pound egg noodles
Freshly ground black pepper, to taste
Salt, to taste

1. Melt the butter in a large heavy skillet over medium heat. Add the cabbage and onion and cook slowly, stirring occasionally, until the mixture is very soft, 30 to 40 minutes.

2. Meanwhile, cook the noodles in a large pot of boiling salted water until tender; drain.

3. Add the noodles to the cabbage mixture and toss, adding lots of freshly ground black pepper. Season with salt to taste and serve.

Serves 4 as a main dish, or 8 as a side dish

Dhanit's PAD THAI

Dhanit Choladda, who lives in Manhattan, learned this dish from his grandmother. Unlike many of its cousins around the city, this Thai pasta isn't greasy, and it is full of fresh, sprightly flavor.

½ pound Thai rice noodles
1½ teaspoons vegetable oil
1 teaspoon minced garlic
1 onion, diced
12 medium shrimp, shelled and deveined
1 tablespoon ketchup
1 tablespoon fish sauce
1 tablespoon sugar
1 tablespoon freshly squeezed lemon juice
1 tablespoon white wine vinegar
2 eggs, slightly beaten
¼ pound bean sprouts
½ cup unsalted peanuts, coarsely ground

GARNISH
¼ pound bean sprouts
1 lemon, cut into wedges
½ cup unsalted peanuts, coarsely ground
Chopped cilantro leaves

1. In a medium bowl, cover the noodles with cold water and set aside to soak for 15 minutes. Drain.

2. Return the noodles to the bowl, pour hot water over the noodles, and soak for 15 minutes more. Drain, rinse in cold water, and drain again. Set aside.

3. Heat the oil in a wok or large skillet over medium heat. Add the garlic and onion and stir-fry until the onions are translucent, 5 minutes. Add the shrimp and stir-fry until they turn pink, 2 to 3 minutes. Add the ketchup, fish sauce, sugar, lemon juice, and vinegar and stir well. Pour in the beaten eggs and let them set slightly, about 3 minutes. Add the noodles, bean sprouts, and peanuts and mix well.

4. Transfer the noodles to a large serving platter and place a heap of bean sprouts and lemon wedges to one side. Sprinkle the peanuts and cilantro over the noodles and serve.

Serves 4

Horn & Hardart's
BAKED MACARONI AND CHEESE

Photo: The Bettmann Archive

As Mr. Horn and Mr. Hardart discovered, this is a great do-ahead dish for a crowd, keeps well, and reheats like a dream. It certainly was an Automat favorite.

1 tablespoon butter
1 tablespoon all-purpose flour
3 cups milk
1 teaspoon salt
Dash of freshly ground white pepper
Dash of cayenne pepper
2 cups shredded Cheddar cheese
½ pound elbow macaroni, fully cooked and drained
½ cup canned tomatoes, drained and chopped
1 teaspoon sugar

1. Preheat the oven to 350°F. Grease a 1½-quart baking dish.

2. Melt the butter in a saucepan over medium-low heat. Whisk in the flour, then add the milk, salt, and both peppers. Stir almost constantly until the mixture thickens and is smooth, 8 to 10 minutes. Add the cheese and cook, stirring, until it melts. Remove from the heat.

3. In a mixing bowl, combine the macaroni and the sauce. Stir in the tomatoes and sugar. Transfer the macaroni mixture to the greased baking dish. Bake until the surface browns, 30 to 40 minutes.

Serves 4 to 6

Tessie's
PASTITSIO
(GREEK BAKED MACARONI)

Tessie Chrissotimos, who lives on Staten Island, says, "All Greeks have different versions of pastitsio, but basically they're the same thing. My mother taught me to make it. At our house we eat it on big holidays—with leg of lamb at Easter and with roast pork or chicken at Christmas."

MEAT SAUCE

1 large onion, finely chopped
2 tablespoons butter or corn oil
2 pounds lean ground beef
1 cup tomato sauce
1 teaspoon freshly grated nutmeg
½ teaspoon ground cinnamon
2 teaspoons salt
Dash of freshly ground black pepper

CREAM SAUCE

3 cups milk
8 tablespoons (1 stick) butter, melted
¼ cup all-purpose flour
Dash of freshly grated nutmeg
Dash of ground cinnamon
3 eggs, beaten well
¼ cup freshly grated Parmesan cheese

ASSEMBLY

1 tablespoon corn oil
1 pound ziti
1½ cups freshly grated Parmesan cheese
2 tablespoons butter

Next Easter or Christmas, serve up hearty portions of Tessie Chrissotimos' pastitsio.

1. Make the meat sauce: In a nonreactive large skillet over low heat, sauté the onion in the butter (don't brown) until translucent, 5 minutes. Add the beef and cook, breaking it up with a spoon, until browned, 5 to 10 minutes. Add the tomato sauce, nutmeg, cinnamon, salt, and pepper. Partially cover and simmer over low heat until thickened, 1 hour.

2. Make the cream sauce: Scald the milk in a saucepan over medium heat. Remove from the heat and set aside.

3. Melt the butter in another saucepan over low heat. Add the flour and cook, whisking constantly, for 5 minutes. Slowly whisk in the hot milk and whisk constantly until the mixture thickens slightly, 5 to 10 minutes. Stir in the nutmeg and cinnamon; remove from the heat.

4. Gradually blend 1 cup of cream sauce into the beaten eggs. Stir the mixture into the cream sauce, then add the Parmesan and mix well.

5. Assemble the dish: Bring a large pot of salted water to a boil over high heat. Add the oil and ziti and cook until the pasta is al dente. Drain and rinse with cold water.

6. Preheat the oven to 350°F. Place a sheet of aluminum foil on the bottom rack of the oven to catch any possible spills. Grease a $14 \times 10 \times 2$-inch baking dish.

7. Place half the cooked macaroni evenly in the bottom of the dish. Sprinkle ½ cup of the grated Parmesan over the macaroni. Spread all the meat sauce over the cheese. Cover with half of the cream sauce. Add the remaining macaroni, sprinkling ½ cup of the cheese over it. Pour the remaining cream sauce over the top, spreading it with a spatula to cover evenly. Sprinkle with the remaining ½ cup cheese. Dot with butter and bake until golden brown, about 45 minutes. Let sit for 15 minutes before cutting.

Serves 12

Casmiro Spagnoli's
LA BOMBA

Accccording to his grandson, Dick Cattani, the late Casmiro Spagnoli left his native Parma 50 years ago and came to New York. His first job was at the Plaza Hotel, where he peeled potatoes for 65 cents a day. Eventually he rose to be executive chef in a local restaurant. But this mold of risotto stuffed with chicken was the special dish he saved for his family, making it every Christmas.

CHICKEN FILLING
4 tablespoons (½ stick) unsalted butter
4 skinless, boneless chicken breasts
(1½ to 2 pounds), cut into
½-inch slices
1 large onion, minced
1 clove garlic, minced
½ ounce dried mushrooms, such as
porcini, soaked in warm water for
20 minutes, drained, rinsed, and
chopped
1 teaspoon dried rosemary
1 tablespoon minced fresh parsley
1½ cups Savory Beef Stock (page 61)
or canned broth
1 can (16 ounces) stewed tomatoes

RICE CRUST
8 tablespoons (1 stick) unsalted butter
1 large onion, minced
4 cups New York Penicillin (page 47)
or canned chicken broth
1 pound arborio rice
¼ cup fine, dried bread crumbs
½ cup freshly grated Parmesan cheese

1. Make the filling: Melt the butter in a non-reactive large skillet over medium heat. Add the chicken and brown lightly all over, 3 to 5 minutes. Add the onion and sauté until translucent, 5 minutes. Add the garlic, chopped mushrooms, rosemary, parsley, beef stock, and tomatoes. Simmer gently, uncovered, until the mixture reduces and thickens, 20 minutes.

2. Make the crust: Melt 8 tablespoons of the butter. Add the onion and sauté until translucent, 5 minutes. Add the broth and bring to a boil. Reduce the heat to medium, stir in the rice, cover the pot, and simmer until the rice is cooked yet still firm, 15 minutes. Add additional broth, if necessary, to keep the rice moist.

3. Preheat the oven to 400°F. Generously butter a 2-quart casserole and dust with the bread crumbs.

4. Spoon some of the rice into the casserole, spreading it to form a 1-inch layer on the bottom and sides. Spoon in the chicken mixture. Top with the remaining rice and pat down. Sprinkle evenly with the Parmesan. Bake, uncovered, until golden and bubbly, 30 minutes.

5. To remove from the pan, loosen on all sides with a spatula. Invert a large platter over the casserole and quickly turn it over, tapping gently until the rice loosens.

Serves 6 to 8

Lee's
COLD SESAME NOODLES

The recipe for these addictive noodles, shown to me by a cook in Chinatown, can be tripled and made ahead of time, refrigerated, and served to a crowd. They are delicious.

½ pound fresh Chinese egg noodles
(spaghetti-like long strands)
¼ cup Oriental sesame oil
2 teaspoons tahini (sesame seed paste)
⅓ cup peanut butter
1½ tablespoons distilled white vinegar
2 teaspoons Hunan pepper sauce
1 teaspoon minced fresh red chile
2 tablespoons sugar
1 cup New York Penicillin (page 47)
or canned chicken broth
½ teaspoon freshly ground white
pepper
2 cucumbers, peeled, seeded, and cut
into fine julienne
2 scallions, trimmed and minced
¼ cup minced cilantro

1. Boil the noodles in a large pot of well-salted water until tender. Drain, cool thoroughly in cold water, and drain again. Toss the noodles with the sesame oil. Cover and refrigerate for 1 hour.

2. In a large bowl, combine the tahini, peanut butter, vinegar, Hunan pepper sauce, chile, sugar, chicken broth, and white pepper. Add the cold noodles and toss well. Add the cucumbers, scallions, and cilantro, toss well, and serve.

Serves 4 to 6

Gus' MEAT PIEROGI

DUMMLINGS
DUMPLINGS

3 eggs, lightly beaten
½ cup milk
1 teaspoon salt
¼ cup vegetable oil
2¼ cups all-purpose flour

FILLING

1 onion, finely chopped
2 cloves garlic, finely chopped
½ teaspoon salt
1 teaspoon pepper
Pinch of ground cumin
Pinch of ground allspice
2 eggs, lightly beaten
1¼ pounds lean ground beef
2 tablespoons vegetable or safflower oil
Fried onions, applesauce, or sour cream, for serving

1. Make the dumplings: Gently beat together the eggs, milk, salt, and oil with an electric mixer. Slowly add the flour. Add water, a tablespoon at a time, if needed to bring the dough together.

2. Knead the dough on a floured surface until smooth. Shape the dough into a ball, wrap it in a towel, and let stand at room temperature for 2 hours. Refrigerate for 30 minutes.

3. On a floured surface, roll out the dough ⅛ inch thick. Cut out 2- to 3-inch circles with a cookie cutter; cover with plastic wrap and set aside.

4. Make the filling: In a large bowl, mix the onion, garlic, and all of the spices with the eggs. Add the ground beef and mix well with your hands.

5. Heat the oil in a large skillet. Add the meat mixture and sauté, breaking up the meat with a wooden spoon, until it is no longer pink, 3 to 5 minutes. Put the meat in a clean bowl and set aside. Taste and correct the seasonings.

6. Meanwhile, bring a large pot of water to a rolling boil.

7. Place about 1 teaspoon of the meat filling on one side of each round. Fold the other half over in the shape of a half moon. Seal the pierogi with your thumb and index finger.

8. Lower the heat so the boiling water simmers gently. One by one add the pierogis to the water and cook them in batches of 4 to 6 until cooked through, about 8 minutes. Take them out with a slotted spoon and drain on paper towels. Keep warm until all of the pierogis are cooked. Serve with fried onions, applesauce, or sour cream.

Makes over 30 pierogis, serves 6

Faina Merzlyak's POTATO AND MUSHROOM PIEROGI

Faina Merzlyak, a Russian-born nurse now living in Brooklyn, uses yogurt in the dough to give her potato pierogi a clean, tart finish. The flavor is so addictive that the recipe placed second in the 1991 Dumpling Derby (see page 254).

DUMPLINGS

*2 cups fresh, full-fat, plain yogurt, preferably
    homemade*
1 egg, lightly beaten
1 teaspoon salt
2¼ cups all-purpose flour

FILLING

1 very large potato (½ to ¾ pound)
4 tablespoons (½ stick) unsalted butter
1 onion, chopped
1 pound white mushrooms, trimmed and minced
Salt and freshly ground black pepper, to taste
Fried onions or sour cream, for serving

---

1. Make the dumpling dough: Lightly beat the yogurt, egg, and salt together with an electric mixer. Slowly add the flour and continue beating until smooth. Knead the dough on a floured surface until smooth. Add water, a teaspoon at a time, only if needed to smooth out the dough; it should feel like pizza dough. Form the dough into a ball, wrap it in a kitchen towel, and set aside in a cool place for 2 hours.

2. Meanwhile, make the filling: Peel and quarter the potato. Cover with cold water, bring to a boil, lower the heat, and simmer until it offers no resistance when pricked with a fork, 15 to 20 minutes. Drain and set aside.

3. Melt 2 tablespoons of the butter in a skillet over very low heat. Whip the potato with the butter until it is fluffy and creamy. Set aside.

4. Melt the remaining 2 tablespoons butter in the skillet over medium heat. Add the onion and sauté until translucent, 5 minutes. Add the mushrooms, salt, and pepper and sauté until the mushrooms are tender and any liquid exuded by the vegetables evaporates, about 5 minutes. Remove the mixture from the skillet and set aside to cool slightly. Mix the vegetables into the mashed potatoes.

5. Bring a large pot of salted water to a boil.

6. Meanwhile, roll out the dough ⅛ inch thick. Cut into 3-inch rounds with a cookie cutter or the rim of a glass. Put about 1 heaping teaspoon of the mashed potato filling on one side of the circle. Fold the other side over the filling so the pierogi looks like a half moon. Press the edges together

Faina Merzylak with a plate of freshly made pierogis.

with your thumb and index finger, sealing the pierogi.

7. Lower the heat so the boiling water simmers gently. One at a time, add the pierogis to the water in batches of 4 to 6. Simmer until cooked through, 5 to 7 minutes. Remove with a slotted spoon and drain on paper towels. Keep warm while cooking the remaining pierogis. Serve with fried onions or sour cream.

Makes 25 to 30 pierogis, serves 5 to 6

Janny Leung's
WINNING WONTONS

J anny Leung is a young pharmacist from Flushing, Queens. Her wonton recipe won the Dumpling Derby held in New York City in September, 1991 (see page 254). They are tender and delicious either steamed or in soup. Wontons freeze well in plastic freezer bags.

75 wonton skins, fresh or frozen
*1¼ pounds fresh medium shrimp, peeled and
    deveined*
1 egg, separated
2 scallions, trimmed and chopped
1 tablespoon Oriental sesame oil
1 teaspoon salt
½ teaspoon freshly ground black pepper
¾ pound lean ground beef

5 dried Chinese mushrooms or cèpes, soaked in
water to cover for 20 minutes, drained,
squeezed dry, and chopped
½ cup loosely packed fresh cilantro leaves,
minced
New York Penicillin (page 47), Savory Beef Stock
(page 61), or other favorite homemade chicken
or beef broth, for serving soup wontons
Mr. Yip's Szechuan Wonton Sauce (recipe follows),
for serving steamed wontons

1. If you are using frozen wonton wrappers, stack them in a colander and defrost in the open air for about 1 hour. Carefully peel them off the stack one by one as they soften. Restack the wrappers and refrigerate until ready to use them. Discard any skins that are waterlogged.

2. Very finely chop the shrimp by hand.

3. In a large bowl, lightly beat the egg yolk. Add the scallions, sesame oil, salt, and pepper and mix well. Add the shrimp, beef, mushrooms, and cilantro and mix together well with your hands.

4. To make wontons for soup: Lay out a wonton skin on a flat surface and lightly brush the edges with the egg white. Place about 1 teaspoon of the filling in the middle. Fold into a triangle shape. Seal the edges with the tines of a fork, pressing down around the border. Brush the edges with a little more egg white and refrigerate, covered. Continue until all the wontons are filled and wrapped.

5. To cook the wontons: Bring a large pot of salted water to a boil. Reduce the heat so the water simmers and gently add the wontons. Simmer until they are cooked through, 5 to 7 minutes. Drain on paper towels. Add the wontons to bubbling broth to serve.

6. To make wontons to serve as a first course: Lay out a skin on a flat surface and lightly brush the edges with egg white. Place about 1 teaspoon of the filling in the middle. Bring up opposite corners to meet in the middle over the filling and pinch firmly to seal, brushing the edges with a little more egg white, if needed.

7. Steam the dumplings over high heat in a tightly covered wok or pot for 15 minutes. Serve immediately with soy sauce, or add a Szechuan touch to this Cantonese dumpling and serve with Mr. Yip's Sauce.

Makes 75 wontons

Mr. Yip's
SZECHUAN WONTON SAUCE

S picy-hot and perfect for adding punch to a wonton.

3 tablespoons soy sauce
3 tablespoons distilled white vinegar
1 tablespoon sugar
2 tablespoons dry sherry
½ teaspoon cornstarch
3 tablespoons chicken broth
3 tablespoons vegetable oil
1 clove garlic, minced
½ teaspoon chopped fresh ginger
1 scallion, trimmed and chopped
¼ teaspoon ground Szechuan
peppercorns
1 tablespoon chili paste
2 tablespoons Oriental sesame
oil
1 tablespoon chopped cilantro

1. In a bowl, combine the soy sauce, vinegar, sugar, sherry, cornstarch, and chicken broth. Whisk well to combine the cornstarch and set aside.

2. In a nonreactive skillet or wok over medium heat, warm the vegetable oil. Add the garlic, ginger, scallion, peppercorns, and chili paste and stir-fry for 15 seconds. Remove from the heat. Add the soy mixture, then add the sesame oil and cilantro. Serve in a small bowl for pouring over or dipping in wontons, dumplings, or noodles.

Makes about 1 cup of sauce, enough for 25 wontons

DUELING DUMPLINGS

The term "multiculturalism" had been deployed with such abandon that Joseph Ben-Moha, the owner of the Roxy Deli, began to take a more philosophical view of dumplings.

"I look at my kreplach and I say, 'What makes you different from my pierogi?'" he said. "And then I must think what makes a wonton not a kreplach, a kreplach not a pierogi, a pierogi not a wonton?"

He decided to pursue these questions by sponsoring a dumpling derby in his Times Square deli. One fall day in the early '90s, nine cooks and four celebrity judges met to cook and compete and appraise. Supplied with a 50-pound array of Chinese wontons, Polish pierogi, and Eastern European kreplach, they also debated if a dumpling is a dumpling is a dumpling.

IT'S ALL IN THE FILLING

"They're all dough," reasoned Mr. Ben-Moha. "The only difference is the insides. If people in my restaurant ask me what is a kreplach, I tell them it's like a wonton," he said.

Janny Leung, a pharmacist who lives in Flushing, smiled politely. A fourth-generation wonton-maker, she doesn't recall ever having used the term kreplach. Tony Yip, a dim sum chef from the restaurant Shun Lee West, crinkled his brow until it resembled the top of a steamed dumpling. "Wonton are spicy," he said. "Szechuan wonton are very spicy."

"Small wrapped food is a universal concept," said Dan Lenchner, who owns Manna, a kosher catering company in Manhattan's TriBeCa section. His Mexican fried beef and chile wonton was a beacon of pluralism. "I tend to stay away from traditional kosher forms," he said.

His decision resonated with one judge, Michael Klefner, a record industry executive. "I grew up in Brighton Beach, Brooklyn, Little Odessa on the Atlantic, where every restaurant had pierogi, which they called vareniki, and they all had kreplach," he said. "But everybody went to the New Deal Chinese Restaurant to eat dumplings."

THIN-SKINNED

The wonton contingent quietly chalked this preference up to the paper-thin wonton skins that are premade and sold in packages of 100. In China, wontons are considered a noodle, not a dumpling. Stuffed with pork, chicken, or shrimp, the packet can be fried, steamed, or boiled and is generally served in broth.

In the U.S., however, the line between wontons (of which there are Peking, Cantonese, Shanghai, and Szechuan versions) and Cantonese dumplings has been slightly blurred. Dumplings are shaped like fat Hershey's Kisses are served steamed or fried, and as dim sum. There is speculation that wontons slipped into the dumpling category before parchment-thin wonton skins were available in New York, when Chinese cooks used the heavier eggroll skins to wrap their dumplings. Both Ms. Leung and Mr. Yip wave aside the semantics. They consider themselves dumpling makers.

Kreplach competitors, on the other hand, are shy of the dumpling nomenclature. To most, kreplach is kreplach, heavy dumplings that are shaped like lumpy round pillows, stuffed with meat, then boiled, and usually served in chicken soup.

"Kreplach is a religious symbol more than a dumpling," said Olga Gurwitz, a 70-year-old retired businesswoman who lives in Manhattan. The dough enveloping her amorphous beef pillows has to be thicker than a wonton skin. "It is handmade and the dough symbolizes the protection we have from a harsh world," she said.

Considering the paucity of cross-cultural influence in kreplach as compared to the variations on wontons and Cantonese dumplings, Mrs. Gurwitz said, "It's easier to improvise when you don't feel you are meddling with something sacred."

A FAMILY AFFAIR

Ms. Leung acknowledged the communal tradition surrounding her family's dumplings. "On Saturdays, it takes the five of us two hours to make 100 dumplings," she said.

The communal aspect of dumpling making seems to remain stable across shifting ethnic lines. "This is the way you maintain your past," said *Newsday*'s Bea Lewis, another judge who says that she is a kreplach expert by dint of having recently become a grandmother. "A Jewish grandmother has to know everything about kreplach so she can teach her grandchildren," she said. "This is the way your past becomes your future."

Bosena Mcaward, a pierogi contestant who was born in Poland and recently moved to Brooklyn, agreed. "I need my family to make pierogi," she said. Polish pierogi are generally half moon–shaped dumplings stuffed with either meat, potatoes, mushrooms, or farmer's cheese. They can be boiled and served in soup, or with sour cream, caramelized onions, or applesauce as a first course. Pierogi can also be deep-fried.

Gus Kavis, another pierogi contestant and the owner of Odessa Restaurant on Avenue A in Manhattan, told Ms. Mcaward that few American pierogi-philes still make their own. "They come to me in cars from New Jersey and Connecticut and buy them," he said.

Ms. Mcaward shook her head. The purity of pierogi, she suggested, is best preserved by making one's own. This opinion seemed to be shared by all contestants.

When asked whether he could envision using kreplach dough to wrap a Hong Kong–style dumpling, Mr. Yip replied that this would be tantamount to placing a hamburger in a hot dog roll. Improvisation, like the kosher caterer's Mexican wonton, seemed too ephemeral. "Interesting to taste," said Ms. Mcaward in a tone of voice that said "not destined for the family recipe box."

Considering their dumplings, the contestants voiced a "separate but equal" point of view. Dumpling making, they said, is a time-honored tradition, whose essence is repetition: the grandchild who best mimics the matriarch's dumpling stands to become the next dumpling queen.

The dignity of any dumpling is difficult to capture in a recipe. "It's a touch," said Mrs. Gurwitz, and the other contestants agreed. "It is something you are born with," she said. Which may explain why, when she was awarded first prize in the kreplach category, Mrs. Gurwitz cried.

Like a latter-day Miss America, she accepted her $100 cash prize and a dozen roses, waved to the audience, and said: "I've waited for this my whole life."

Dorothy Desir's
RICE A COCO

Coconut and rice make a soothing, rich combination. Dorothy adds cumin, basil, and paprika to enliven this dish. Serve with spicy eggplant pickle.

2 cups unsweetened coconut milk
1 teaspoon ground cumin
½ teaspoon dried basil
¼ teaspoon freshly ground black pepper
½ teaspoon sweet paprika
Dash of garlic powder
1½ cups long-grain rice
2 cups flaked coconut
2 tablespoons minced fresh parsley
¼ cup minced scallions
¼ cup raisins

1. In a nonreactive large saucepan, combine the coconut milk, cumin, basil, pepper, paprika, garlic powder, and 2½ cups water and bring to a boil. Reduce the heat and simmer for 3 minutes. Add the rice and flaked coconut and bring back to a boil. Reduce the heat to low, cover, and simmer until the rice is tender, 20 to 25 minutes.

2. Stir in the parsley, scallions, and raisins and serve.

Serves 8 to 10

Francesco Antonucci at Remi.

Francesco's
POLENTA WITH WILD MUSHROOMS

When wild mushrooms hit the local greenmarkets, Francesco Antonucci, the chef of Remi in Manhattan, turns out this sensational dish. He serves it as a first course. I call it dinner.

MUSHROOM RAGOUT
1½ ounces dried cèpes
¾ pound fresh oyster mushrooms, trimmed and thinly sliced
¾ pound fresh shiitake mushrooms, trimmed and thinly sliced
2 tablespoons olive oil
4 cloves garlic, finely chopped
1 tablespoon fresh rosemary leaves, finely chopped
1 teaspoon salt
2 teaspoons freshly ground black pepper
6 sprigs Italian (flat-leaf) parsley, heavy stems trimmed, leaves finely chopped

POLENTA
1 teaspoon salt
1 tablespoon extra-virgin olive oil
1½ cups coarse yellow cornmeal

1. Make the ragout: Place the cèpes in a small saucepan and add 3½ cups water. Bring to a boil, then lower the heat and simmer until the cèpes are tender, about 20 minutes. Line a fine-mesh sieve with cheesecloth and strain the mushrooms, reserving the liquid. Roughly chop the cèpes and toss them together with the fresh mushrooms.

2. Heat 1 tablespoon olive oil in a large cast-iron skillet until it gets very hot and starts to smoke. Add enough mushrooms to cover the bottom of the skillet in an even layer. Sauté until golden brown, 10 minutes. Transfer the mushrooms to a bowl. Add the remaining 1 tablespoon olive oil to the skillet; sauté the remaining mushrooms.

3. Return all of the mushrooms to the skillet. Add the reserved cèpe liquid, the garlic, rosemary, salt, and pepper and simmer over medium-high heat until the liquid is reduced by half, about 5 minutes. Stir in the parsley and set aside.

4. Make the polenta: Bring 7 cups of water to a boil in a large pot. Add the salt and the olive oil, then lower the heat and slowly add the cornmeal. Stir continuously, making sure that no lumps form as you add the cornmeal. Lower the heat to medium-low and continue to stir the polenta for 30 minutes. The polenta should have a creamy consistency. Add more boiling water, a few tablespoons at a time, if the polenta gets too thick before it is cooked.

5. Warm the mushrooms over low heat until heated through, about 5 minutes. Spread the polenta on a large serving plate and spoon the mushroom ragout in the center. Serve immediately.

Serves 4

Nipa's
SHRIMP FRIED RICE

In several decades of preparing fried rice, Nipa Kitpanichvises, who grew up in Thailand and is now chef/owner of Siam Grill in Manhattan,

Enjoy Nipa Kitpanichvises' Thai-style fried rice.

has learned five basic tenets for perfect results: 1) The pan should be hot at all times. 2) The rice should be perfectly cooked—not too soft, not too firm. 3) All of the ingredients must be added at the right time. 4) If the rice starts to stick to the pan, add a little oil. 5) Cook two servings at a time.

2 tablespoons vegetable oil
1 teaspoon minced garlic
1 egg, lightly beaten
6 shrimp, peeled and deveined
2 tablespoons chopped onion
2 teaspoons Thai fish sauce
½ teaspoon sugar
1½ cups cooked long-grain rice
1 tablespoon fresh peas
¼ tomato, peeled, seeded, chopped
1 tablespoon thinly sliced scallion
¼ cucumber, thinly sliced
2 lemon wedges, for serving

1. Heat the oil in a nonreactive skillet over medium heat. Add the garlic and sauté until light golden, 5 minutes. Add the egg and stir-fry for 10 seconds. Add the shrimp, onion, fish sauce, and sugar and stir until the shrimp turns pink, 3 minutes. Add the rice, peas, tomato, and scallion, and stir-fry a few more seconds to blend the flavors.

2. Remove from the heat. Serve with sliced cucumbers and a wedge of lemon.

Serves 2

Greene's
GREEN RISOTTO

Gael Greene, *New York* magazine's restaurant critic, has also added strips of young spinach to this delectable rice dish, and sometimes watercress or arugula, depending on what is around.

3 stalks broccoli, florets removed from the stems
 and divided into small blossoms, stems peeled
 and cut into tiny cubes
6 cups homemade meat or chicken broth (see
 Savory Beef Stock, page 61, and New York
 Penicillin, page 47), or low-sodium broth
4 tablespoons extra-virgin olive oil
½ cup chopped shallots or onion
1 tablespoon minced garlic
2 cups Italian short-grain rice, such as arborio
1 cup chopped fresh parsley
1 cup chopped fresh cilantro
½ pound snow peas or sugar snap peas, trimmed
 and cut in half at an angle
½ cup freshly grated Parmesan cheese
Juice of ½ lemon
Salt and lots of freshly ground black pepper
Freshly grated Parmesan cheese, for serving

1. Cook the broccoli florets in a small pot of boiling water until tender. Drain and reserve.

2. Meanwhile, in a small pot, bring the broth to a simmer.

3. In a large heavy saucepan, warm 2 tablespoons of the olive oil over medium heat. Add the shallots, garlic, and cubed broccoli stems and cook until the onions soften, 5 minutes. Add the rice and stir to coat the grains thoroughly. Increase the heat to medium-high and add a ladle of the simmering broth. Stir continuously until the broth is absorbed. Add another ladle of broth, and one-third of the chopped parsley and chopped cilantro. Again, stir continuously until the broth

is absorbed. Keep on adding broth a ladleful at a time, stirring to make sure the rice doesn't stick to the bottom, until the rice is tender but firm (without a hard, chalky core) and the mix is soupy. If you run out of broth, use warmed white wine or water.

4. Meanwhile, in a sauté pan, warm the remaining 2 tablespoons oil over medium heat. As you see the risotto reaching its grand finale, add the broccoli florets and snow peas and toss until warmed through.

5. Add the vegetables to the risotto and toss. Add half of the remaining chopped parsley and cilantro, the Parmesan, and lemon juice and mix well. Season with salt and freshly ground black pepper to taste. Sprinkle the remaining chopped parsley and cilantro over the top and serve with extra grated Parmesan on the side.

Serves 4 as a main course, or 6 to 8 as an appetizer

Barbara's
CHEESE GRITS

Barbara Braddock, who was born in Shreveport, Louisiana, serves grits with small sausages and eggs at brunch in her East Side apartment.

1 cup grits
8 tablespoons (1 stick) butter, cut into pieces
8 ounces Cheddar cheese, grated
½ cup milk
2 eggs, well beaten

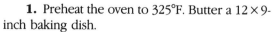

1. Preheat the oven to 325°F. Butter a 12 × 9-inch baking dish.

2. Bring 3 cups of salted water to a boil. Add the grits in a thin, steady stream, stirring constantly. Return to a boil. Cook, stirring, until the mixture thickens slightly, 2 to 3 minutes. Add the butter and cheese and cook, stirring, until the butter and cheese melt. Remove from the heat. Stir in the milk and eggs.

3. Pour the mixture into the prepared baking dish and smooth the top. Bake until golden on top, about 30 minutes.

Serves 4 to 6

about 15 minutes. Remove from the heat.

4. In a large bowl, mix together the kasha, pasta, and onion. Add salt and pepper to taste and serve immediately.

Serves 8 as a side dish

Mother's
KASHA VARNISHKAS

Frances Edelstein is the grand dame of the Polish Tearoom at the Hotel Edison, a rumpled coffee shop where Broadway musicians, journalists, and tourists share herculean portions of food. Her mother's recipe for kasha varnishkas remains the hands-down favorite.

*1 cup buckwheat
  kasha (groats)
½ pound farfalle
  (bow-tie) pasta
2 tablespoons
  vegetable oil
1 large yellow
  onion, chopped
Salt and freshly
  ground black
  pepper, to taste*

Frances Edelstein at the counter of the Polish Tearoom.

1. Combine the kasha and 1½ cups water in a large heavy pot. Cover and simmer over low heat until the kasha has absorbed the water and is tender, 30 minutes. Remove from the heat.

2. Meanwhile, bring a large pot of water to a boil; salt it lightly. Add the pasta and cook until al dente. Drain and set aside.

3. Warm the oil in a heavy saucepan over low heat. Add the onion and cook until golden brown,

Selina's
TABBOULEH

The Middle Eastern cracked wheat salad is ubiquitous throughout the city. However, few versions come close to this zippy aromatic one.

*1 cup bulgur
3 ripe tomatoes, finely chopped
2 small cucumbers, preferably
  Kirbys, finely chopped
½ onion, finely chopped
½ cup finely chopped fresh mint
¼ cup finely chopped fresh parsley
Juice of 2 lemons
½ cup olive oil
Salt, to taste
1 head romaine lettuce leaves*

1. Place the bulgur in a medium-size bowl with cold water to cover and leave undisturbed until softened, 2 to 2½ hours for 1 cup. Squeeze the excess water from the bulgur.

2. Drain any excess liquid from the tomatoes and cucumbers. In a large bowl, combine the bulgur, tomatoes, cucumbers, onion, mint, and parsley. Add the lemon juice, olive oil, and salt and mix well. Cover with plastic wrap and refrigerate for at least 1 hour—the longer, the better. Tabbouleh is traditionally served spooned onto romaine leaves and eaten with the hands.

Serves 6

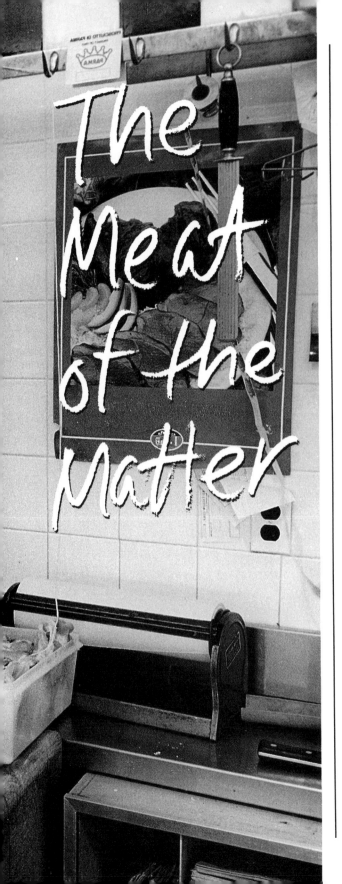

The Meat of the Matter

THE NEW YORK
Barbecue Summit

For those who live by barbecue, Kansas City's brisket and "burnt ends" sound one siren's call, the ribs and shredded pork of Memphis another. From the pits of Greensboro, North Carolina, vinegar-basted pork issues a hickory-scented invitation. Lubbock, Texas, where the fuel is mesquite or oak and the meat is again brisket of beef, has an allure of a different *eau*.

New York City, on the other hand, lacks barbecue mystique. Among connoisseurs, the term "New York barbecue" will more likely elicit a guffaw than an anticipatory licking of the chops.

This lack of respect appalls the maestros of the city's terrace-based grills and sidewalk smokers; it is downright loathsome to

Onofrio Ottomanelli, of Ottoman-elli's on Bleecker Street, prepares an order (left). Barbecued ribs, corn bread, and plenty of napkins. Now dig in (right).

the pioneers who have bravely brought a barbecue mosaic to the restaurants in this urban frontier.

Enough already! A New York Barbecue summit was called.

Sylvia Woods' daughters learned the trick of massaging the ribs from their mother.

Representatives from eight disparate schools of barbecue gathered in a midtown loft to address the politics and public image of their hometown barbecue.

Sylvia Woods, the 65-year-old grand dame of South Carolina–style oven barbecue, delegated her daughters, Crizette Fireson and Bedelia Woods. Bedelia arrived wearing a red silk blouse that nicely complemented the sauce on the 20 pounds of ribs she carried.

Rusty Staub, the former New York Met who owns Rusty's on 5th, represented a Louisiana-style oven barbecue. He wore the sort of chalk-striped gray suit that one sees a lot of at Hall of Fame dinners and exuded a pre-game "we're gonna win this one, guys," attitude. Robert Pearson, owner of Stick to Your Ribs, a restaurant in Long

Island City, Queens, was the Texas-style, cool-smoke delegate and he wore acid-washed jeans with a white, cowboy-cut shirt. Simon Oren, co-owner of Brothers Barbecue in Lower Manhattan, was the deputy of a Kentucky-style smoked barbecue and a prototype of downtown fashion.

Martin Yerdon and Eileen Weinberg, co-owners of Good & Plenty To Go in midtown Manhattan, represented the North Carolina style, though the brisket they brought had been cooked in a closed, rather than open pit, using the post oak and apple wood that are indigenous to New York, rather than the hickory that is used in the Low Country. This revelation brought a slight lift of the collective brow. Mr. Yerdon waved it aside.

"We have to address the issue of modifications and the limits of the urban setting," he said in the tone of a presidential advisor suggesting full disclosure of classified material. With furrowed brow, the group nodded.

"But look at this," said Mr. Yerdon, waving to the group and toward the platters of barbecue that already crowded the summit table. "How can anybody say that we can't barbecue! This city has more transplanted sons and daughters of Dixie than the entire city of Atlanta!"

GLOBAL BARBECUE

Mr. Oren, who grew up in Israel, shifted slightly in his tee shirt and loose-fitting linen jacket. His reaction was mitigated by the arrival of Yon Suk Choi, who owns the Woo Chon Korean restaurants in Manhattan and Queens and who looked like an exotic travel poster come-to-life in her floor-length, Korean ceremonial dress. "Famous Barbecue Beef," she said, offering both a platter of her specialty and the approximate extent of her English. She had also brought a translator.

Michael Tong, who owns Shun Lee Palace, Shun Lee West, and Shun Lee Café, followed. He wore a well-tailored business suit and assured the crowd that he would "call and have some barbecued ribs and duck delivered. We, uh, have gotten the delivery thing down." While Mr. Tong called his restaurant, Allan Vernon entered. He sported a blue blazer, a baseball cap that read "Vernon: Number One Jerk in America," and carried 20 pounds of Jamaican barbecue.

The demographics of the assembled delegates were emblematic of a basic pathos of New York Barbecue. The city's repertoire is so diverse that it lacks a single identifying flavor. Barbecue fanatics tend toward monolithic passion and are therefore confounded by the New York barbecue scene. In addition, what one master reverently calls barbecue, another calls the anti-Christ. In the past, this has limited conversations among New York's barbecue experts. It was no coincidence that the first items on the summit agenda emphasized commonality.

"We all live outside the barbecue belts," said the British-born Mr. Pearson. A former hairdresser, he was reborn a " 'cue master" after studying the craft from the Carolinas to Texas.

Like most aficionados, when Mr. Pearson looks at a map of the United States, he sees one great barbecue belt that stretches from the Carolinas and the American South to Kentucky and Tennessee and features marinated pork cooked slowly in an open pit. The other barbecue belt stretches from Texas and the American Southwest to Kansas and most of the Midwest and features beef cooked slowly in an open pit and basted with a myriad of dry and wet "mops," or tenderizing sauces.

COUNTRY COOKING ON URBAN SIDEWALKS

These two wide-ranging appellations are credited with taking the Spanish *barbacoa,* a grill made from green wood that was employed to prop meat over an open fire, and using it to create an All-American art form—and eventually All-American fanaticism. Barbecue freaks won't be swayed by anything other than the precise form they were raised on and resist all attempts at expanding their definition of barbecue.

That is bad news for New Yorkers, who live and 'cue in the epicenter of innovation and cross-cultural culinary exchange. Despite their varying approaches, the delegates felt united.

"I call this barbecue," said Mr. Staub, sinking his teeth into one of the Chinese barbecued ribs that Mr. Tong had supplied. Mr. Tong said that his ribs, like Mrs. Choi's sliced beef, are cooked over a slow fire (or grilled), rather than surrounded by slow smoke (as in traditional barbecue).

Mr. Staub paused, appeared to gulp, and then continued. "Good meat to bone ratio," he said, approvingly.

Secretly, representatives of the traditional strands of American barbecue wouldn't go so far as to use rice wine, hoisin sauce, or sesame oil in their sauces, but they have an abiding empathy for non-traditional flavor boosts. "Traditionally, it was the flavor of your fuel that permeated your 'cue," said Mr. Yerdon. "Not many people in this city are set up to cook a hunk of meat for 12 hours over a load of oak."

The barbecue delegates agreed that open-pit options are limited in New York City, though Mr. Vernon did refer to one particular pothole on lower Park Avenue and Mr. Oren nodded enthusiastically. "I could do a whole pig in that one," he said.

Others waxed about their attempts to simulate pit-cooking. Mr. Yerdon and Ms. Weinberg began experimenting with barbecue during the winter of 1982, using a grill on the terrace of their East Side apartment. "We had flare-ups and the thing caught on fire, so I ended up serving 35 firemen," recalled Mr. Yerdon, who later spent $18,000 to build his first steel and

brick smoker. "It burned down, too," said Mr. Yerdon. "I rebuilt in '83."

The other delegates shook their heads sympathetically. "Flare-ups are a real problem," said Mr. Pearson, who places a pan of water on the floor of his smoker-type oven to catch the dripping grease that can lead to flare-ups. It's not the fires he minds so much, it's charring the meat or— *quelle horreur*—"raising the internal meat temperature above 210°F and boiling the juice in the meat." Long, slow, moist heat breaks down the fat and the tough membranes in the inexpensive cuts of meat typically barbecued.

Slow smoking can be simulated on a backyard (or terrace or sidewalk) grill by waiting until the coals turn white, placing the meat on the grill and placing the lid over the grill with the vents open to promote the flow of smoke. The fire should be stoked gradually so that the cooking temperature never goes above 200°F. "Then you just have to allow sufficient time to achieve desired results," said Mr. Pearson. "Say, 15 hours for briskets, 10 hours for pork shoulders, 5 hours for pork ribs, chicken, and beef ribs."

"That's about right," said Mr. Oren, who uses electric smokers at Brother's Barbecue. Along with the other 'cue masters, he acknowledged that taking 15 hours to cook a brisket is somewhat at odds with the spirit of a town where that cut of meat is usually purchased already cured and called corned beef, a favored feast with cabbage on St. Patrick's Day.

No use just staring at the window of Brothers Bar-B-Q. The ribs and chicken are great—better to go in and order up a plate.

GOOD HELP IS HARD TO FIND

Just as the outside world doesn't understand the effect of the city on barbecue, the city doesn't fully appreciate what the finer points of the craft require of a New Yorker. In addition to building Rube Goldberg-style smokers and having the patience to stoke them, skilled labor is a problem. "A good pitman is about as easy to find as an unemployed sheepherder in this town," said Mr. Yerdon.

Which may be why some of the local 'cue masters turned from the pit to the oven. "My daddy used half a tin drum in the backyard and I get the same result in the oven," said Mr. Staub, who says that careful marinating and saucing and long, slow braising can perform magic on meat, though it is no less time-consuming. "We hire people just to massage the meat every night before we cook it," said Bedelia Woods, of Sylvia's. "That's the only way you can get that falling-off-the-bone effect."

"I can get that with peppers, baby," said Mr. Vernon, adjusting the bill of his hat. "The philosophy of jerk is to use your jerk sauce to tenderize the meat and then just add a little smoke at the end," he said, noting that after marination, he oven-braises and finishes his meat, chicken, or fish on a low grill.

Both Mr. Tong and Mrs. Choi use similar methods. "We don't have much of a history of open-pit cooking in China," said Mr. Tong. "Waste of fuel," said Mrs. Choi through her interpreter. She held one of

Mr. Staub's baby back ribs at arm's length and, in an effort to save her costume a splatter, leaned forward for a nibble. "Ummm," she said.

The other delegates followed suit. Flushed with sampling over 100 pounds of barbecue and comforted by the smoking grill on the terrace near the conference table, they began sharing cooking techniques and pondering the quandary of 'cue. It was a brotherhood of barbecue. A rare moment. The first steps, said each delegate loudly, toward building a positive, local 'cue image.

Quietly, however, they said other things. "Look at the gristle on his ribs," whispered one. "He uses liquid smoke," hissed another. You can take barbecue out of the country, but you can't take the Hatfield & McCoy tone away from the pursuit of barbecue perfection.

Walking away from the table, two delegates noted that another had not been particularly forthcoming on his cooking technique. "I bet he uses a hair dryer," said one, noting that the delegate under discussion was a former hairdresser. "Um," said the other, wiping his barbecue slathered hands on his silk ascot, "gives a good flavor, doesn't it?"

THE SAVVY SHOPPER

NEW YORK'S BEST BARBECUE

BROTHER'S BAR-B-Q: 228 West Houston Street, between Sixth Avenue and Varick Street; (212) 727-2775. Specializes in smoked pork butt and pork ribs.

COPELANDS: 547 West 145th Street, between Broadway and Amsterdam Avenue; (212) 234-2356. Pricey barbecued ribs in a posh Harlem setting.

RUSTY STAUB'S ON 5TH: 575 Fifth Avenue at 47th Street; 682-1000. Louisiana home-run barbecue.

SHUN LEE CAFE: 43 West 65th Street, between Central Park West and Columbus Avenue; (212) 595-8895. Chinese barbecued ribs and duck.

STICK-TO-YOUR RIBS: 5-16 51st Avenue, near the junction of Vernon Boulevard and Jackson Avenue, Long Island City, Queens; (718) 937-3030. Sliced brisket, chopped pork, meaty ribs; Texas-style barbecue.

SYLVIA'S RESTAURANT: 328 Lenox Avenue, between 126th and 127th Streets; (212) 996-0660. Barbecued pork ribs.

VERNON'S JERK PARADISE: 254 West 29th Street, between Seventh and Eighth Avenues; (212) 268-7020. Jamaican-style jerked meat, fish, and chicken.

WOO CHON: 8-10 West 36th Street, between Fifth and Sixth Avenues; (212) 695-0676. Barbecued beef, chicken, fish, seafood, and vegetables done at the table.

Martin's
SMOKY BRISKET

Eileen Weinberg and Martin Yerdon at their former restaurant, Carolina.

Martin Yerdon, co-owner of Good & Plenty To Go, who caught the barbecue bug when an art student at the University of Kentucky, believes that the proper succession of dry and wet mopping and long, slow smoking can "take your basic brisket into realms that a sirloin never dreamed of." He warns that properly cooked barbecue will always be pink at the bone. This recipe was a favorite at Martin's former restaurant, Carolina's.

DRY MOP AND BRISKET
½ cup sweet paprika
3 tablespoons salt
2 tablespoons freshly ground black
    pepper
1 first-cut beef brisket (4 pounds)

WET MOP
1½ tablespoons instant coffee crystals
2 cups ketchup
¾ cup Worcestershire sauce
8 tablespoons (1 stick) butter

BBQ SAUCE
1 onion, grated
¼ cup olive oil
1 large can (35 ounces) Italian plum
    tomato purée
¾ cup (packed) dark brown sugar
2 bay leaves
2 beef bouillon cubes
3 tablespoons Frank's hot sauce
2 tablespoons chili powder
1 tablespoon cayenne pepper
1 tablespoon freshly squeezed
    lemon juice
¾ teaspoon freshly ground black
    pepper
¼ teaspoon salt
⅓ cup cider vinegar

1. Prepare the dry mop: In a small bowl, combine the paprika, salt, and pepper. Rub the dry mop all over the brisket, then set aside for 1 to 2 hours at room temperature.

2. Prepare the wet mop: In a nonreactive saucepan, dissolve the instant coffee in ⅔ cup hot water. Add the ketchup and Worcestershire sauce and bring to a boil. Reduce the heat and simmer for 20 minutes. Remove from the heat and whisk in the butter 1 tablespoon at a time.

3. Prepare the grill: Place the charcoal in the bottom of the grill opposite the air vent, then light the coals. After the coals turn a powdery gray-red, put a pan of water next to the coals. Place the brisket on a grill over the water and opposite the air vent. Place the cover on the grill so that the cover vent is opposite the brisket. This will draw smoke and heat through the brisket. Keep the air vents open just enough to keep the charcoal burning. Baste the brisket with the wet mop every 30 minutes for the first 2 hours of cooking.

4. After that, baste the brisket once every hour with the wet mop. Cook for at least 15 hours. Replenish the charcoal and water regularly. The brisket is cooked when the meat registers 150°F on a meat thermometer, although the longer you cook it, the better the texture.

5. While the meat is cooking, make the barbecue sauce: In a nonreactive large skillet or saucepan over medium heat, cook the onion in the olive oil until translucent. Add all of the remaining ingredients except the vinegar. Stir in 2 cups water and bring to a boil. Reduce the heat and simmer for 20 minutes.

6. Remove the sauce from the heat and stir in the vinegar. When the brisket is cooked, slice it thin and serve with the barbecue sauce.

Serves 6

ROBERT PEARSON'S STICK TO YOUR RIBS

Robert Pearson, owner of Stick to Your Ribs, is a former hairdresser who learned barbecue while teaching in Texas. "I had a good rapport with Texan hairdressers." He believes that sauces vary (his, of course, is the best) but that the invariable in barbecue is that the cooking temperature should never go above 210°F. (For his Barbecued Chopped Chicken recipe, see Index).

Sylvia's BARBECUED RIBS

Sylvia Woods grew up in South Carolina, became a beautician, and moved to Harlem over 40 years ago. She opened an 18-stool ribs and chicken joint in 1962; the restaurant now covers most of a city block. Ms. Woods says her success is due to "massaging the ribs and the crushed red pepper has a lot to do with it, too." She uses an oven rather than a smoker: "I was raised on oven barbecue and you don't miss what you never had."

RIBS
1 tablespoon salt
1 tablespoon freshly ground black pepper
2 slabs pork ribs (about 6 pounds total)
1 tablespoon dried red pepper flakes
2 cups distilled white vinegar

BARBECUE SAUCE
1 celery rib, finely chopped
1 green bell pepper, stemmed, seeded, and finely chopped
½ large onion, finely chopped
2 cups hot sauce, preferably Red Devil
2 cups Italian plum tomato purée
1½ cups sugar
2 large lemons, squeezed and sliced

1. Prepare the ribs: Mix the salt and black pepper in a small bowl. Rub the mixture all over the ribs in a massage-like motion; repeat with the red pepper. Place the ribs in a nonreactive 12 × 6-inch baking pan, add the vinegar, cover, and let sit in the refrigerator overnight.

2. Preheat the oven to 375°F.

3. Roast the ribs in the oven for 1½ hours. Remove the ribs to a clean jelly roll pan, turning them in the process. Increase the oven temperature to 400°F. Roast the ribs for 30 minutes more.

4. In the meantime, make the sauce: In a food processor or blender, purée the celery, bell pepper, and onion. Scrape the mixture into a nonreactive saucepan and add all of the remaining ingredients. Simmer over low heat until the sauce thickens, 15 to 20 minutes. Do not allow the sauce to boil. Serve the ribs with the sauce.

Serves 8 to 10

Rusty's BBQ

Rusty Staub grew up "on backyard barbecue" in New Orleans. He sought to replicate the flavor within the bounds of a restaurant (or home) kitchen with grand success.

4¾ cups of your favorite hickory-smoked
  barbecue sauce
¾ cup good dry sherry
¾ cup dry red wine
½ fresh, ripe pineapple, peeled and finely puréed
6 large cloves garlic, crushed through a press
1 tablespoon packed dark brown sugar
Juice of 1 lemon
½ teaspoon minced jalapeño chile
Dash of liquid hickory seasoning or
  liquid smoke (optional)
1 teaspoon salt, or to taste
½ teaspoon freshly ground black pepper, or to
  taste
⅓ cup finely chopped cilantro leaves
1 sirloin or porterhouse steak (12 to 16 ounces),
  1 inch thick

Baseball great Rusty Staub is currently a Mets
sportscaster, owner of Rusty Staub's on 5th, and
a serious barbecue maven.

1. In a nonreactive large pot, combine the
barbecue sauce with the sherry, wine, pineapple,
garlic, brown sugar, lemon juice, jalapeño, hickory seasoning, salt, and pepper. Bring to a boil
over medium heat. Reduce the heat to a simmer
and stir in the cilantro. Cook to thicken the sauce
slightly, 10 minutes; remove from the heat.
2. Preheat the grill. Slather the barbecue sauce
over the meat and grill over medium-hot coals
for about 7 minutes on each side for medium rare.
Serves 4

Yon Suk Choi's
FAMOUS BEEF BBQ

Yon Suk Choi grew up in northern Korea where
every respectable dinner table is equipped
with a hot plate for barbecue. She has the most
pride in "secret sauce using fruit and little something spicy," and says that the sauce can be used
to marinate chicken or pork, too.

2 racks short ribs of beef with bone (14 ounces
  each), or 2 rib-eye steaks (9 ounces each), sliced
  very thin
1 piece (3 inches) fresh ginger, peeled
1 papaya, peeled, seeded, and puréed
1 tablespoon Korean (clear) honey
3 tablespoons soy sauce
2 tablespoons minced fresh pear
2 tablespoons minced fresh pineapple
½ small onion, chopped
1 tablespoon rice wine (sake)
1 teaspoon minced garlic
½ teaspoon freshly ground black pepper
2 scallions, trimmed and coarsely chopped
½ teaspoon sugar, or to taste (optional)
½ teaspoon sesame seeds
2 tablespoons Oriental sesame oil

FOR SERVING
Sliced white mushrooms
Sliced onions
Trimmed broccoli spears
Kimchi (see Index)

1. In a large bowl or pot, cover the meat with
cold water. Soak overnight in the refrigerator. Remove the meat from the water, pat dry, and set
aside. Strain the soaking water and reserve ⅓ cup.
2. Grate the fresh ginger against the finest
side of the grater, keeping a bowl beneath to catch
the juices. Measure out 1 tablespoon of a mixture
of the ginger pulp and juice.

3. In a nonreactive small saucepan, combine the reserved ⅓ cup soaking water, the ginger and juice, the papaya purée, honey, and soy sauce. Cook over very low heat for 10 minutes; do not allow to boil. Remove and set aside to cool slightly.

4. In a blender or food processor, combine ¼ cup plus 2 tablespoons of the cooked sauce, the pear, pineapple, onion, rice wine, garlic, pepper, scallions, and sugar. Purée until smooth. Stir in the sesame seeds. Pour into a nonreactive small saucepan and cook the marinade over low heat, stirring occasionally, until it thickens, 30 minutes.

5. Place the beef on a plate. Pour ¼ cup plus 2 tablespoons of the marinade onto the plate and rub it into the beef. Rub the sesame oil into the beef. Set aside for 10 minutes.

6. Preheat the grill. Grill the ribs for 7 minutes per side; grill the steak for 1 minute per side for medium beef. Serve with sliced mushrooms, onions, and broccoli that have been slushed through the marinade and grilled briefly. Serve kimchi on the side.

Serves 2 to 4

THE KING OF JERK

Allan Vernon, the self-proclaimed "King of Jerk," moved to New York from Jamaica (via England) in 1971. He worked in construction until the day he gazed over the city from a roof top and noticed "a distinct lack of jerk." He opened a fast jerk store in the Bronx in 1982, followed by Vernon's Jerk Paradise in 1989. The King says that the secret of good jerk is the sauce (for Vernon's Jerk-Style Jamaican Chicken, see Index).

Allan Vernon, seen here in a low-key moment, has a jerk sauce that packs a wallop.

Shun Lee's BBQ RIBS

Michael Tong moved to the United States from Hong Kong in 1963 and proceeded to meld the Cantonese style of barbecuing pork, ribs, duck, and suckling pig with techniques from northern Mongolia where open-pit barbecue is practiced. "Americans like the more intense flavor." Chinese people, he said, "eat barbecue like convenience food, shredded over rice for a meal or snack."

It's Shun Lee for Michael Tong's barbecued ribs and pork.

¼ *cup sugar*
2 tablespoons honey
2 tablespoons rice wine or dry sherry
2 tablespoons hoisin sauce
½ *teaspoon salt*
1½ pounds beef ribs

1. In a small bowl, combine the sugar, honey, rice wine, hoisin sauce, and salt. Stir to mix well. Place the ribs in a nonreactive shallow bowl and brush the sauce all over the ribs. Cover with plastic wrap and refrigerate for 3 hours, turning occasionally.

2. Cover the grill with aluminum foil and heat to medium. Grill the ribs, covered, for 35 minutes. Turn over and grill for 40 minutes more. Carefully peel back the foil and set the ribs directly on the grill. Cook, uncovered, just until they are sizzling and browned, about 5 minutes. Remove from the grill, cut into strips, and serve.

Serves 2

Shun Lee's BBQ PORK

2½ *tablespoons sugar*
2 tablespoons honey
2 tablespoons rice wine or dry sherry
¼ *teaspoon salt*
1 pound pork tenderloin

1. In a small shallow bowl, mix the sugar, honey, rice wine, and salt. Place the tenderloin in a nonreactive shallow bowl and brush the sauce all over the meat. Cover with plastic wrap and refrigerate for 3 hours, turning once or twice.

2. Cover the grill with foil. Preheat the grill to hot. Grill the pork, covered, over medium-low heat for 30 minutes, turning occasionally.

3. Carefully peel off the foil from the grill and set the pork directly on the grill. Cook, uncovered, just until meat is sizzling and browned, about 5 minutes. Remove from the grill, cut into ¼-inch-thick pieces, and serve.

Serves 2

Brothers' BAR-B-Q

Simon Oren, co-owner of Brothers Bar-B-Q, grew up in Israel, where there is "no barbecue tradition, per se, but grilling is everywhere."

Simon Oren takes a break at Brothers, the popular West Houston Street barbecue source.

Convinced that New York was hungry for 'cue, Mr. Oren sought advice from 350 different Chambers of Commerce in American towns known for barbecue and found, "New Yorkers are faithful to the Texas-style tomato barbecue." He says, however, that sauce is secondary to actual smoke.

PIG SAUCE AND RIBS
1 quart distilled white vinegar
2 tablespoons dried red pepper flakes
2 tablespoons freshly ground black pepper
2 tablespoons salt
2 cloves garlic, minced
1 slab of pork ribs (2½ to 3 pounds)

BBQ SAUCE
1 tablespoon vegetable oil
1 onion, chopped
2 cups tomato sauce
1 cup red wine vinegar

1 tablespoon garlic powder
¼ teaspoon freshly ground black pepper, or more to taste
¼ teaspoon cayenne pepper, or more to taste
¼ teaspoon sweet paprika, or more to taste
1 tablespoon salt
½ cup packed dark brown sugar
2 tablespoons Worcestershire sauce

BLUE GRASS BOURBON SAUCE
¾ cup BBQ Sauce (see above)
2 tablespoons orange marmalade or other fruit preserves
1 tablespoon bourbon

---

1. Prepare the pig sauce: In a medium bowl, combine the vinegar, pepper flakes, pepper, salt, and garlic. Place the ribs in a nonreactive shallow pan and pour on the pig sauce. Turn the ribs to coat thoroughly. Marinate for 1 to 2 hours at room temperature. Remove from the sauce and set aside to drain.

2. Make the bbq sauce: In a nonreactive large saucepan, warm the oil over medium heat. Add the onion and cook until lightly browned, 5 to 10 minutes. Stir in all of the remaining sauce ingredients and bring to a boil. Reduce the heat and simmer, uncovered, for about 45 minutes. You should have about ¾ cup sauce. Remove from the heat.

3. Make the bourbon sauce: In a small bowl, mix together the ¾ cup barbecue sauce, the marmalade, and bourbon. Set aside.

4. Preheat a grill (or ideally, a smoker, to 170°F). Place the ribs over indirect heat, cover the grill, and cook until tender, 3 to 3½ hours. Smother with the bourbon sauce and serve.
Serves 4

The love of ribs is by no means the sole province of the professional sphere in New York City. Dozens of home cooks sent in their preferred versions and here are three winners.

Brenda Manning's
SHORT RIBS

Brenda Manning's short ribs are honest, straightforward, easy to make, and wonderful with collard greens or baked macaroni.

1 tablespoon all-purpose flour
Salt, to taste
Freshly ground black pepper, to taste
Paprika, to taste
Pinch of garlic powder
1 to 2 pounds beef short ribs
1 onion, chopped

1. Preheat the oven to 350°F.

2. In a small bowl, combine the flour, salt, pepper, paprika, and garlic powder. Rub the spices all over the ribs to coat thoroughly. Place the ribs in a nonreactive baking pan. Add the onions and about 1½ cups water or just enough to cover the bottom of the pan.

3. Cover the pan with aluminum foil. Bake until the meat is tender, about 1 hour.

Serves 2 to 3

Shanghai
SPARERIBS

Shanghai émigré Choi Fung Woo has nine grandchildren who clamor for these ribs on Chinese New Year and for Thanksgiving dinner.

1 rack (3 to 3½ pounds) spareribs
½ cup hoisin sauce
3 tablespoons oyster sauce
3 tablespoons light soy sauce
3 tablespoons dark soy sauce
½ teaspoon freshly ground black pepper
1 clove garlic, minced
2 tablespoons honey

1. Trim the spareribs of excess fat. Score with a knife and make slits into the thick part between each rib.

2. Mix together the hoisin sauce, oyster sauce, soy sauces, pepper, and garlic. Place the spareribs in a roasting pan. Slather the mixture on the spareribs, coating them thoroughly. Set aside to marinate for at least 3 hours in the refrigerator, turning once or twice during this time.

3. Preheat the oven to 400°F.

4. Place the spareribs in a roasting pan or jelly roll pan. Roast for 20 minutes, basting frequently with the marinade. Turn the ribs over and roast, basting frequently, until tender, another 20 minutes.

5. Preheat the broiler

6. Remove the pan from the oven. Brush 1 tablespoon of the honey on each side of the ribs. Finish under the broiler until the ribs are glazed, about 1 minute on each side.

Serves 4

Jacqueline's
SPARERIBS

In the summer, the Newman family cooks these ribs on a backyard grill; in the winter, the oven does just fine. Serve these ribs with fresh corn, a Caesar Salad, or Edna Lewis' Greens (see Index for both recipes).

1 rack (about 3½ pounds) pork spareribs
1 cup dark soy sauce
1 cup fresh orange juice
½ cup sugar
3 cloves garlic, minced
3 tablespoons solid vegetable shortening

1. Trim any excess fat from the ribs and cut into three 4- or 5-rib sections.

2. In a bowl, mix the soy sauce, orange juice, sugar, and garlic until the sugar dissolves.

3. Place the ribs in a nonreactive pan or container. Add the marinade and turn the ribs to coat thoroughly. Cover and refrigerate overnight, turning once or twice in the evening and again in the morning. (The ribs can be kept in the marinade for up to 3 days.) Drain the ribs.

4. In the summer, prepare a charcoal grill until hot. Grill until tender, 35 to 45 minutes, turning often.

In the winter, preheat the oven to 350°F. Bake until tender, turning often, 40 to 50 minutes.

Serves 4

Cleavers make easier work of separating ribs.

San Wong's
BEEF AND BROCCOLI

San Yan Wong is a chef, teacher, and calligrapher who lives in Queens. "In this recipe," he says, "you may substitute other vegetables such as snow peas, peppers, and onions for the broccoli." Serve over rice.

MARINADE AND MEAT
1 egg
1 tablespoon dry white wine
1 teaspoon soy sauce
1 teaspoon cornstarch
1 tablespoon vegetable oil
¼ teaspoon salt
⅛ teaspoon freshly ground black
    pepper
¾ pound flank steak, thinly sliced across
    the grain

SAUCE
3 tablespoons soy sauce
1 tablespoon dry white wine
1 teaspoon Oriental sesame oil
½ teaspoon sugar
¼ cup chicken broth

ASSEMBLY
2 to 3 cups vegetable oil, for frying
3 cups bite-size broccoli pieces
    (florets and tender stems)
1½ teaspoons cornstarch mixed with
    1 tablespoon cold water

1. Combine all of the marinade ingredients through the black pepper. Add the steak and marinate for 30 minutes.

2. Combine all of the sauce ingredients and set aside.

3. Assemble the dish: In a wok or deep skillet over high heat, heat 2 cups of the vegetable oil. When very hot, add the beef and marinade and stir-fry until the beef changes color, about 30 seconds. Remove the beef and drain well.

4. Make sure the oil in the wok is still hot; add more if necessary. Add the broccoli and stir-fry for about 20 seconds. Remove from the heat and drain well.

5. Drain the oil from the wok. Reheat the wok and add the sauce ingredients. Bring the sauce to a boil over high heat. Add the beef and broccoli, stirring, for about 10 seconds to warm the ingredients. Add the cornstarch paste and stir until the sauce is thick. Serve with steamed rice.

Serves 2

Queen's
SHISH KEBABS

Shish kebabs are a fixture of James Kunreuther's annual backyard barbecue in Jamaica, Queens. Kunreuther learned about Oriental and Indian cooking from his friends and decided to combine the influences of Eastern cuisine with his all-American love of barbecue. Serve these with Dilled Green Bean and Pepper Salad (see Index).

MARINADE
⅓ cup honey
2 tablespoons packed light brown sugar
Juice of 2 lemons
Juice of 1 lime
1 tablespoon grated fresh ginger
⅓ cup distilled white vinegar
¼ cup vegetable oil
1 green bell pepper, stemmed, seeded, and finely diced
1 teaspoon Tabasco sauce
1 clove garlic, minced
⅓ cup of your favorite barbecue sauce, preferably with strong hickory flavor
¼ teaspoon ground cinnamon
¼ teaspoon ground cumin

KEBABS
3 pounds boneless lamb and/or top round steak, cut into 1-inch cubes
1 pound sweet Italian sausage, cut into 1-inch slices
12 ounces fresh white mushroom caps (1¼ pounds with stems)
2 red bell peppers, stemmed, seeded, and cut into 1-inch squares
2 zucchinis (¾ pound), halved lengthwise and cut into ½-inch-thick half-moons
2 onions, cut into wedges (5 per onion)
1 pint cherry tomatoes

1. Make the marinade: Mix all of the marinade ingredients together in a nonreactive bowl.

2. Assemble the kebabs: Thread the meat and vegetables onto ten 12-inch-long metal skewers, alternating the ingredients.

3. Lay the skewers side by side in a nonreactive shallow baking pan. Pour the marinade over the kebabs and turn to coat thoroughly. Marinate at room temperature for 1 hour. Turn the kebabs and marinate for 1 hour more.

4. Prepare a charcoal grill and cook the kebabs over medium to medium-high heat for 10 to 15 minutes, basting liberally with the marinade and turning occasionally as needed.

Makes 10 skewers, serves 5

The Ritz's
CARPETBAG STEAK

Before "New York Steak" was a part of our vernacular, carpetbag steak was the rage in the city. The recipe for this version comes from the hotel's legendary chef, Louis Diat, and originally appeared in his 1941 book, *Cooking à la Ritz*. Serve Italian Broccoli Rabe (see Index) alongside.

1 boneless sirloin steak (3 pounds), 2 inches thick
1 tablespoon Worcestershire sauce
Salt, to taste
Freshly ground black pepper, to taste
1 dozen oysters, shucked

1. Lie the steak flat and split it in half through its thickness to make a pocket. Leave it attached at one end. Rub the Worcestershire sauce, salt, and pepper all over the steak, including inside the pocket. Cover with plastic wrap and refrigerate for 1 hour.

2. Preheat the broiler.

The Old Homestead, one of New York's famous steakhouses.

3. Stuff the oysters into the pocket of the steak, then sew shut with thick thread. Broil for 15 minutes. Turn and broil for 15 minutes more. Cut the steak into ½-inch-thick slices and serve.

Serves 6 to 8

Elaine's
BEEF TERIYAKI

Few Japanese New Yorkers are impressed by "The New York Steak" myth and would choose $100 Kobe beef steaks at the Old Homestead restaurant over a porterhouse at Peter Luger's any day. Faced with a sirloin, skirt, or flank steak, however, this particular teriyaki could make even the most die-hard Kobe fanatic smile. Serve the teriyaki with Chinese Sautéed Watercress (see Index).

3 tablespoons soy sauce
3 tablespoons dry sherry
1½ tablespoons sugar
4 cloves garlic, minced
6 thin slices fresh ginger, smashed
¼ teaspoon freshly ground black pepper, or more to taste
1½ pounds flank steak

1. In a small bowl, mix together the soy sauce, sherry, sugar, garlic, ginger, and pepper. In a nonreactive shallow pan, combine the steak and the sauce. Cover and refrigerate overnight.

2. Preheat the broiler.

3. Broil the steak, turning once, until medium-rare, 3 to 4 minutes per side. Slice across the grain, as you would a London broil.

Serves 4

BRISKET WITH
Sweet Potatoes and Prunes
(PRESSURE COOKER METHOD)

Says pressure cooker expert Lorna Sass of her brisket recipe, "This is an especially hearty version of the Jewish *tsimmes*. Ideally, the brisket is made the day before and refrigerated so that the congealed fat can be easily removed from the gravy. Just before serving, the gravy is cooked with apple cider, prunes, sweet potatoes, and parsnips and poured over the sliced reheated meat."

2 to 3 tablespoons oil or rendered chicken fat
1 first-cut beef brisket (3⅓ pounds)
2 ribs celery, finely chopped
2 large carrots, finely chopped
1 large onion, finely chopped
2 cups Savory Beef Stock (page 61), canned broth, or bouillon
1¼ teaspoons ground cinnamon
¼ teaspoon freshly grated nutmeg
⅛ teaspoon ground allspice
½ to 1 cup apple cider (optional; see Note)
2 pounds sweet potatoes, peeled and cut into ½-inch-thick slices
1½ pounds parsnips, peeled and cut into 1-inch cubes
1 cup pitted prunes, coarsely chopped
Salt and freshly ground black pepper, to taste

1. In a 6-quart pressure cooker, heat 2 tablespoons of the oil or fat over high heat. Add the brisket and brown well on both sides, lifting it frequently with tongs or a spatula to prevent sticking. Add the additional 1 tablespoon oil or fat, if needed. Set the browned brisket aside.

2. Add the celery, carrots, and onion to the oil remaining in the pressure cooker. Sauté for 3 minutes, scraping up any browned bits of meat or vegetables that stick to the bottom of the pot. Add the beef stock, cinnamon, nutmeg, allspice, and 1 cup water. Submerge the pressure cooker's rack or trivet into this mixture, place the meat on it, fat side facing up, and lock the lid in place. Bring the cooker to high pressure over high heat. Adjust the heat to maintain high pressure and cook for 55 minutes.

3. Let the pressure drop naturally, 10 to 15 minutes. Remove the lid, tilting it away from you to allow any excess steam to escape. If the brisket is done, you should be able to easily pry a small chunk of meat from one end with a fork. If it is not sufficiently tender, lock the lid back into place and return to high pressure for another 5 to 10 minutes. Again, let the pressure drop naturally.

4. When done, remove the brisket from the pot. If time permits, allow to cool to room temperature, then refrigerate the brisket and gravy overnight in a covered container. Remove any congealed fat the next day, and return the gravy to the cooker before proceeding with the recipe.

5. About 20 minutes before serving, stir enough of the cider into the gravy to equal about 2 cups. Add the sweet potatoes, parsnips, and prunes and lock the pressure cooker lid in place. Bring to high pressure over high heat. Adjust the heat to maintain high pressure and cook for 3 minutes. Quick-release the pressure. Remove the lid, tilting it away from you to allow any excess steam to escape. Adjust the seasonings, adding salt and pepper to taste.

6. Slice the brisket, cutting on the diagonal. Place the slices in the cooker and spoon the gravy and vegetables on top. Set the cover in place (but do not lock it) and cook over medium heat just until the meat is warmed through, 10 minutes. Arrange the slices of brisket on a platter and surround

Lorna Sass, Queen of the Pressure Cooker. Photo: Charmian Reading

with the vegetables. Pour the gravy on top.

Serves 4 to 6

Note: The amount of liquid that remains after cooking is quite variable, and it may not be necessary to add any cider at all. Then again, you may opt for more than 2 cups of delicious gravy.

Curried
BRISKET

This irresistible dish is a specialty of the Malaysia Restaurant in Chinatown. It is wonderful served with rice or even noodles and tastes better the second day.

1 first-cut beef brisket (1½ pounds), rinsed and
  excess fat trimmed away
6 shallots, peeled
4 cloves garlic, peeled
1 piece (1 inch) peeled fresh ginger
¼ cup plus 1 tablespoon curry powder
½ cup vegetable oil
1 cinnamon stick, broken into 3 pieces
3 cups unsweetened coconut milk
½ pound potatoes, cut into ½-inch cubes
Salt, to taste
1 teaspoon sugar, or to taste

1. Cut the brisket into 2-inch chunks. In a mortar and pestle, or in a blender, mash the shallots, garlic, and ginger. In a small cup, dissolve the curry powder in ½ cup water.

2. In a nonreactive, large, deep skillet or pot, heat the oil over medium heat. Add the shallot mixture and stir-fry until softened and fragrant, 5 minutes. Add the curry water and cook for 10 minutes. Add the beef and cinnamon pieces and stir-fry for 3 minutes. If the pan is too dry, add ¼ cup water.

3. Slowly stir in the coconut milk, potatoes, salt, and sugar. Cook over medium-low heat until the meat is tender, about 35 to 45 minutes.

Serves 4

Haina's
SUREFIRE BRISKET

Haina Just's mother, Jean, has been making this brisket for so long she can't remember how it came to be. She does know that it's a versatile and easy staple of her kitchen. "I usually cook it, let it cool, and slice it ahead of time, then heat it as I need it, with the sauce separate," Just says. Boiling the potatoes with the brisket infuses them with a wonderful meaty flavor.

1 first-cut beef brisket (3 to 4 pounds)
2 tablespoons sweet paprika
1 teaspoon peanut oil
3 cups ginger ale
1 packet Goodman's or Lipton's Onion Soup Mix
6 potatoes, quartered

1. Preheat the oven to 350°F.

2. Coat both sides of the brisket with the paprika. In a Dutch oven over high heat, heat the peanut oil until smoking. Add the brisket and sear on all sides. Remove from the heat.

3. Stir in the ginger ale and onion soup mix. Cover the pot. Roast in the oven for 1 hour.

4. Turn the meat over. Cover and cook for 1 additional hour. Add the potatoes and cook for 45 minutes more.

5. When the brisket is tender, remove it to a cutting board and allow to cool slightly. Slice the brisket across the grain. Drizzle the pan juices over the meat. Serve with the potatoes.

Serves 6

DELI SPOKEN HERE

In his book *When Brooklyn Was the World: 1920–1957,* Elliot Willensky recalls the delis that dotted the blocks of his childhood. Walking inside, he said, customers immediately faced a "teaser": "Atop the meat case stood a teaser, an open display of small knobs of a thickly sliced *knublvoorsht*—garlic wurst—ornamented by a hand-lettered sign, A NICKEL A SHTICKL, or a nickel apiece. They were sachets of the delicatessen, redolent of garlic and placed at adult nose level; gravity took care of us shorter kids. The owners really knew how to get your juices flowing."

In addition, New York delis have contributed handsomely to deli-speak, the ineffable language of short-order cooking everywhere. These examples were gleaned from the Carnegie Deli, the Second Avenue Deli, Juniors, the *American Dictionary of Slang,* and *The Great American Ice Cream Book,* both by Paul Dickson.

A pistol on rye and a regular, perhaps, at the Carnegie Deli.

Whiskey down: rye bread, toasted

Schmear: light spread of cream cheese on bagel

Regular: coffee with milk and sugar

Wing ding setup: plastic cup with ice

Grade a: glass of milk

Double l: rolled beef

Full house: bacon, lettuce, tomato, and turkey

CB: corned beef

Pistol: pastrami

Dutch: anything with American cheese

Jack: American cheese and tomato

Jack hammer: American cheese, tomato, and ham

Combo: ham and swiss

One off: plain frankfurter

One with: frankfurter with sauerkraut

Combination: any sandwich with two meats

21 or 211: two items on one plate

Adam's ale: water

Baby: glass of milk

Break it and shake it: put eggs in a drink or whatever

Burn: a malted milkshake, chocolate unless otherwise specified

Burn it and let it swim: float

Clean up the kitchen: hamburger or hash

Eighty-seven and a half: attractive female approaching

First lady: spareribs

In the hay: strawberry milkshake

Make it virtue: cherry coke

Nervous pudding: Jell-O

Twist it, choke it, and make it crackle: chocolate malted with egg.

IN SEARCH OF NEW YORK STEAK?
ASK ANYWHERE BUT NEW YORK

Some aspects of New York mythology are easier to read at a distance. Take the famous New York steak. The term, according to Pat Cetta, who owns Sparks Steak House in Manhattan, means one thing to people from out of town, but it means so many different things locally that it ends up meaning nothing.

"Someone from out of town comes in and orders a New York Steak and they want a prime shell steak with a crust on the outside, rare on the inside, and they get it," he said. "With a local, it can mean a strip or a sirloin or a shell, or . . ."

Stanley Lobel, co-owner of Morris Lobel & Sons, a Madison Avenue butcher shop, said that the confusion over the steak that bears the city's name prompted him and his brother Leon to write their treatise, *Meat.* "The variations on the same cut were getting out of hand," he said.

In general, the brothers decreed, New York steak is 1 to 1¼ inches thick and is cut from the center portion of the steer, behind the short rib, where muscle development (and hence toughness) is low and fat content (and hence rich marbling) is high. "Take a porterhouse, remove the fillet and the tail and the bone, and you are left with a strip steak, or a shell steak, or a New York steak, or whatever you want to call it," Mr. Lobel said. "I just call it steak."

Which is part of the problem. Many New Yorkers think that whatever they call "steak" is automatically a New York steak. Dorothy Casey of the venerable Peter Luger Steak House in Brooklyn, said, "I'm prejudiced. When I think about a New York steak, I think about our steak, which is aged, prime porterhouse. The thing other people call New York steak is only part of the New York steak I know." Stan Zimmerman, owner

of Sammy's Famous Roumanian Steak House, considers his garlic-rubbed beef tenderloin for two "the quintessential New York steak, tender, tender, tender." Cooks in the storefront Argentinian steak houses that dot Roosevelt Avenue in Brooklyn have one response when asked to define New York steak. They heave over a pound of bone-in sirloin onto a plate, shake their heads, and say: "Steak. New York. New York Steak."

An out-of-towner, having traveled to the source of the mythic slab of beef, might take such responses as typical New York Attitude. In fact, it is a rare instance of parochialism. "The only place in the world that a steak isn't called a New York steak is in New York," Mr. Cetta said.

WHAT'S IN A NAME?

Meat mavens concerned with the etymology of New York steak have tried to divine the cut of meat, the grade of meat, and the precise cooking methods that can render the steak that thrills carnivores nationwide. "It's a connotation, not a real term," said Marc Sherry, co-owner of the Old Homestead, the 122-year-old restaurant that borders the meat-packing area on the West Side of Manhattan near 14th Street. "New York Steak means good steak."

"Before refrigeration, the best cuts of beef were sent to New York City," said Marc Sarrazin, owner of DeBragga & Spitler, a New York butcher who supplies meat to more than 300 restaurants in the city. Ellis Simberloff, who grew up the son of a meat purveyor in New York City, is more specific. "Historically, there was a huge kosher butchery in the city," he said. "In order to get a two-inch brisket, butchers needed hind quarters from 'strong,' or well-developed cattle that tend to be well marbled and well fatted." Mr. Simberloff remembers when the "entire 14th Street meat industry hinged on hind quarter breaking," and says that "the first time I was ever served something called a New York Steak was when I went to college in Iowa."

In the end, Mr. Simberloff's definition is not at odds with Mr. Sarrazin's: "The New York steak meant the best steak," he said. "It can be a sirloin steak, it can be a shell steak, but it has to be a good steak."

Today, only a handful of packing houses actually cut beef in New York. For ease of transportation, beef is cut and "boxed" near the feed lots and slaughterhouses in Chicago, sealed in vacuum packs, and shipped nationwide. Nevertheless, the New York steak mystique endures. New York still means "the best there is."

SO WHAT'S THE BEST?

If that's what you want, say local meat mavens, and then they launch into a detailed step-by-step: The best New York steak is generally well-marbled, prime grade. The best New York steak is generally a 1- to 1½-inch-thick shell steak. The apron of fat that rims the meat should be scored to keep the steak from curling and cooking unevenly. Lightly rub the steak with butter or olive oil to encourage a crisp crust, season it with pepper only; salting too far ahead of time can pull the juice from the meat. Broil it as close to the heat as possible. For a rare steak, broil for about 3 minutes on each side. For a medium steak, broil for about 4 minutes on each side.

So assume that "New York" means good steak. Just don't ask anyone to be specific about the cut.

"Some people call it a strip, some people call it a sirloin," said Mr. Sherry of the Old Homestead.

At Nevada Meat Market, where the beef is prime.

"A shell steak, a sirloin steak, a strip steak," said Mr. Lobel.

"It's a, how do I say it?" asked Mr. Sarrazin, who originally came from France where steak vernacular is simpler, though the steak is rarely as good. "You cut the filet and the butt from the sirloin and then you have the New York steak. Or else you ask somebody who lives out of the city; they can tell you better, dear."

WHERE'S THE BEEF?

AKRON PRIME MEATS: 1174 Lexington Avenue at 80th Street; (212) 744-1559. Sells dry-aged prime beef as well as game.

ALBERTS PRIME MEATS: 836 Lexington Avenue, between 63rd and 64th Streets; (212) 751-3169. Stocks well-aged beef, a wonderful crown roast of lamb, and spring lamb.

BALDUCCI'S: 424 Sixth Avenue at 9th Street; (212) 673-2600. Has a huge selection of prime meats, game, and sausage.

ESPOSITO'S PORK STORE: 500 Ninth Avenue at 38th Street; (212) 279-3292. May have the largest variety of meat in town and is undaunted by requests for suckling pigs, game, baby lamb, and chittlings—if ordered a day ahead.

FAICCO'S PORK STORE: In Manhattan: 260 Bleecker Street, between Sixth and Seventh Avenues; (212) 243-1974; in Brooklyn: 6511 Eleventh Avenue, between 65th and 66th Streets; (718) 236-0119. Shops are charming throwbacks to an earlier era. Hand-rolled sausage is the store's strong suit.

FITZ & SONS: 944 First Avenue at 52nd Street; (212) 753-3465. Offers prime beef that can be smoked to order, fresh game, and almost any specialty meat imaginable.

JEFFERSON MARKET: 455 Sixth Avenue, between 10th and 11th Streets; (212) 675-2277. Has top quality meat, especially the prime beef, venison, and spring lamb.

KUROWYCKY MEAT PRODUCTS: 124 First Avenue, between 7th Street and St. Marks Place; (212) 477-0344. A vintage Ukrainian meat market with its own smokehouse, this is a sure bet for sausages and fresh-smoked hams.

MORRIS LOBEL & SONS: 1096 Madison Avenue at 82nd Street; (212) 737-1372.

High-quality butcher, whose beef and lamb can't be topped in the city.

NEVADA MEAT MARKET: 2012 Broadway, between 68th and 69th Streets; (212) 362-0443. Has wonderful aged beef as well as veal and lamb, and game in season.

OPPENHEIMER CO. MEATS: 2606 Broadway at 99th Street; (212) 662-0246. Offers a wide selection of excellent meat and game.

OTTOMANELLI'S MEAT MARKET: 285 Bleecker Street, between Seventh Avenue and Jones Street; (212) 675-4217. An old-time Italian butcher who has the best selection of game— wild boar, buffalo, and hare—in town.

SCHALLER & WEBER: 1654 Second Avenue, between 85th and 86th Streets; (212) 879-3047. An old-time German shop where sausages, hams, and cutlets reign; steak is house-aged and delicious. Reasonable prices.

TOM'S MEAT MARKET: 214 Third Avenue at 20th Street; (212) 475-0395. An old-fashioned market with a wide selection of excellent meats— and repartee.

UNITED MEAT MARKETS: 84 Mulberry Street, between Canal and Bayard Streets; (212) 962-6440. Has baby back ribs, suckling pigs, and wonderful Chinese sausage.

Luchow's
SAUERBRATEN

For decades, Luchow's epitomized haute German New York, and sauerbraten was one of the favored dishes. A version of this recipe originally appeared in *Luchow's German Cookbook,* by Jan Mitchell, but Peter Aschkenasy, the final owner of Luchow's, revised it slightly. In the restaurant, the dish was served with potato pancakes (David Firestone's Latkes, see Index, would make a nice accompaniment) and red cabbage (see the Index for Fern's Bacon and Cabbage).

1 beef round roast (3 pounds)
1 tablespoon salt
½ teaspoon freshly ground black pepper
2 onions, sliced
1 carrot, sliced
1 rib celery, chopped
4 whole cloves
4 black peppercorns
2 bay leaves
2 cups red wine vinegar
2 tablespoons beef fat or lard
6 tablespoons (¾ stick) butter
¼ cup plus 1 tablespoon all-purpose flour
1 tablespoon sugar
8 gingersnaps, crushed

1. Wipe the roast with a damp cloth and then season with salt and pepper. Place in a large nonreactive bowl. In a medium bowl, combine the onions, carrot, celery, cloves, peppercorns, bay leaves, vinegar, and 5 cups water. Pour the mixture over the meat, adding more water if the mixture doesn't cover it completely. Cover the bowl with plastic wrap or a lid and refrigerate for 4 days, turning daily. On the fifth day, remove the bowl from the refrigerator. With slotted spoons, remove the meat from the bowl; reserve the marinade.

2. In a nonreactive heavy pot over medium heat, melt the beef fat and 1 tablespoon of the butter. When melted, add the meat and brown on all sides. Add the reserved marinade and bring the mixture to a boil. Reduce the heat to a simmer and cook, partially covered, for 3 hours.

3. Melt the remaining 5 tablespoons butter over low heat in a small saucepan. Add the flour and sugar and stir until dark brown, about 5 minutes. Scrape into the simmering meat mixture and stir well. Cover and continue cooking until the meat is tender, about 1 hour longer.

4. Remove the meat to a warmed serving platter. Stir the crushed gingersnaps into the sauce and cook until the mixture thickens, about 10 minutes. Pour the gravy over the sauerbraten and serve.

Serves 6 to 8

Luchow's on 14th Street. Photo: UPI/Bettmann.

Carbonnade
FLAMANDE

Marsha Palanci spent her childhood in Belgium and France, where flamande was the soul of many winter nights. Today she makes this Belgian beef stew 2 or 3 days in advance to allow the flavors to mature before serving it in her downtown apartment.

2 cups cold water

2 ounces salt pork, cut into ¼-inch
    cubes

½ cup all-purpose flour

¼ teaspoon salt

¼ teaspoon freshly ground black pepper

4 pounds lean beef stew meat (such as chuck),
    cut into 1½-inch cubes

3 tablespoons vegetable oil

2 cloves garlic, halved

3 bottles (12 ounces each) dark beer

¼ cup red wine vinegar

3 tablespoons Dijon mustard

3 bay leaves

½ teaspoon dried thyme

2 tablespoons unsalted butter

4 large onions, cut into ¼-inch-thick rings

8 carrots, cut into ½-inch pieces

1. In a medium saucepan, bring the cold water to a boil with the salt pork. Reduce the heat and simmer for 5 minutes. Drain and rinse the salt pork under cold water. Dry on paper towels. Place the salt pork in a heavy casserole and set aside.

2. Season the flour with the salt and pepper. Dredge the beef cubes in the seasoned flour.

3. Heat the oil in a nonreactive, large, heavy skillet over medium heat. Add the garlic and cook until golden brown, stirring occasionally, 3 minutes. Discard the garlic. Add only enough of the beef to the skillet to fit comfortably without crowding. Cook, turning occasionally, until well browned. Transfer the beef to the casserole. Repeat the browning process until all of the beef has been browned.

4. Pour off the oil from the skillet. Over medium-high heat, add the beer to the skillet and cook, scraping up any browned particles. Stir in the vinegar, mustard, bay leaves, and thyme. Pour the beer mixture into the casserole.

5. Add the butter to the same skillet and melt over medium-high heat. Add the onions and cook until golden brown, about 7 minutes. Transfer the onions to the casserole.

6. Bring the stew in the casserole to a simmer over medium heat. Reduce the heat to low, cover, and cook for 1 hour, skimming the fat as necessary.

7. Add the carrots to the stew and cook until the meat is tender, 30 to 45 minutes.

8. If the stew is too dry, add water. If it is too liquid, remove the beef and vegetables and boil, uncovered, to reduce the liquid to the desired consistency. Return the meat and vegetables to the pot and heat through.

Serves 8

Gary Regan's
STEAK IN ALE AND PORT WINE GRAVY

Gary Regan grew up in England eating this dish. The meat slowly cooks with caramelized vegetables, earthy ale, and sweet port and makes a hearty dish, perfect for the fall or winter. Cooked on a Friday night, it gets better as the weekend progresses.

¼ pound slab bacon, cut into ½-inch cubes

3 carrots, thinly sliced

2 large onions, chopped

⅓ cup all-purpose flour

¾ cup strong dark ale (Thomas Hardy, if
    available)

½ cup tawny port

2 tablespoons vegetable oil

2 pounds stewing beef, trimmed and cut
    into 1-inch cubes

1 teaspoon salt

½ teaspoon freshly ground black pepper

½ teaspoon dried marjoram

1 pound button mushrooms, stems trimmed

About 1¼ cups beef stock or canned broth

1. In a nonreactive, large, deep saucepan or Dutch oven, render the bacon over medium-low

Gary Regan offers up a hearty beef stew, English-style.

heat until soft and browned but not crisp, about 10 minutes. Add the carrots and onions, and cook until soft, 5 to 8 minutes. Sprinkle the flour over the vegetables and stir thoroughly. Cook, stirring frequently, for 5 minutes. Stir in the ale and port, and bring to a boil over medium-high heat. Reduce the heat to low and simmer while you brown the beef.

2. Place the oil in a large skillet over medium-high heat and brown the beef on all sides. Remove from the pan and drain on paper towels.

3. Add the beef to the saucepan. Stir in the salt, pepper, marjoram, and mushrooms. If the mixture seems too thick, add just enough beef broth to make the stew somewhat liquid. Cover and simmer until the beef is tender, 2 to 3 hours. Check occasionally, adding more beef broth, if necessary.

4. Serve the stew in bowls with crusty French bread, sweet butter, and British ale.

Serves 4 to 6

Wintry CHOLENT

Cookbook author Copeland Marks on this soul-satisfying one-pot dish: "Cholent was one of my favorite winter dishes back home in Ver-

mont. It's a poor man's dish of Eastern European Jewish origin—filling, fattening, and delicious when the snow is on the ground. It was put in a coal oven late Friday afternoon, and the fire was banked so that the very low heat cooked the cholent slowly. The dish was served after synagogue at noon on Saturday, having baked all night and most of the morning. I prepare it once or twice during the New York winter for friends who have a strong case of nostalgia."

1 cup dried navy beans
1½ pounds boneless beef chuck, cut into
    4 equal pieces
4 potatoes, peeled
1 onion, quartered
1 teaspoon salt
⅛ teaspoon freshly ground black pepper
3 cups New York Penicillin (page 47) or canned
    chicken broth (optional)

1. Soak the beans in water to cover overnight.

2. Preheat the oven to 350°F.

3. Drain the beans and place them in a large clay bean pot with the meat, potatoes, onion, salt, and pepper. Add enough water to just reach the top of the ingredients, about 1½ cups. Cover the pot tightly, first with a piece of aluminum foil, then with the lid of the pot. Bake for 30 minutes.

4. Reduce the heat to 200°F. Bake for 10 hours or more. Do not stir or disturb in any way.

5. Serve the cholent in soup plates, adding a little hot chicken broth, if you wish. Season with salt and pepper to taste.

Serves 4

Copeland Marks' recipe repertoire is vast and reflective of years of extensive travel.

Trimming the meat at Lobel's on Madison Avenue.

and pepper to taste. Simmer until the vegetables are tender, about 45 minutes, adding water as necessary to barely cover the stew.

4. In a bowl, combine the remaining ¼ cup flour with ½ cup of the cooking liquid and whisk to a smooth paste. Whisk or stir the mixture into the stew. Simmer for an additional 10 minutes. Serve.

Serves 8

Mulligan's
MULLIGAN STEW

This hearty recipe comes from retired Fire Commissioner John Mulligan.

4 pounds stewing beef, cut into 1½-inch cubes
2 teaspoons salt
1 teaspoon freshly ground black pepper
¾ cup all-purpose flour
2 to 3 tablespoons vegetable oil
3 large carrots, cubed
1 cup turnips, peeled and cubed
1 small onion, thinly sliced
4 large baking potatoes, cut into ½-inch slices

1. Sprinkle the beef with the salt and pepper. Using ½ cup of the flour, dredge the meat in the flour, coating well. Heat 1 tablespoon of the oil in a 6-quart flameproof casserole. Brown the meat on all sides, in batches, over medium-high heat. Use more oil as needed. Set the meat aside.

2. Pour ½ cup water into the casserole and scrape well to loosen the bits of meat that adhered to the casserole. Return the meat to the casserole. Add enough water to cover the meat by 1 inch. Bring to a boil and boil for 5 minutes. Reduce the heat and simmer for 2 hours.

3. Skim the stew. Add the carrots, turnips, onion, and potatoes; season with additional salt

Hugh's
MONGOLIAN HOT POT

Hugh O'Neill, who lives on the Upper East Side, is co-owner of a grill that was built to his specifications in Saigon nearly 30 years ago. This grill, which currently resides in its co-owner's garden, is used when Hugh visits with a hankering for Chinese barbecue. But when loath to fire up the grill, O'Neill and his friends make do with their Mongolian hot pot, a doughnut-shaped pot with a cone in the center for burning charcoal. The pot is used to make a traditional Oriental fondue-type dish in which thin slices of beef or lamb are cooked with vegetables in a broth at the table. If you are unable to find a traditional Mongolian hot pot, which, because it burns charcoal, must be used outdoors, or if you are an indoor eater, a fondue pot or electric skillet makes an adequate pinch hitter.

BROTH
Boiling water, for mushrooms and bean thread noodles
1 ounce dried Chinese mushrooms
1 bundle (2 ounces) bean threads (cellophane noodles)
6 cups Savory Beef Stock (page 61) or canned beef broth
2 cakes fresh firm tofu (bean curd), diced
1 teaspoon minced garlic
1 teaspoon minced fresh ginger

DIPPING SAUCE

3 cups rice wine

¾ cup soy sauce

¾ cup Oriental sesame oil

¾ cup rice vinegar

¾ cup sesame paste

¼ cup hot pepper sauce, such as Tabasco

1 cup chopped scallions

HOT POT

2 pounds beef or lamb, sliced paper-thin
(Ask your butcher to cut meat for sukiyaki.
If you are cutting the meat yourself,
place it in the freezer until nearly frozen
before slicing.)

1 small head Chinese cabbage, rinsed and
trimmed, cut into bite-size pieces

1 pound fresh spinach, rinsed, tough stems
removed, torn into bite-size pieces

1 large head broccoli, stems removed and
discarded, florets cut into bite-size pieces

12 large or 18 small pita breads, halved, wrapped
in aluminum foil, and warmed in the oven

---

1. Make the broth: In a small bowl, pour enough boiling water over the dried mushrooms to cover. Let sit for 20 minutes. In a bowl, pour enough boiling water over the bean thread noodles to cover. Let sit for 20 minutes.

2. Strain the mushroom liquid into a large casserole. Rinse the mushrooms, cut into small pieces, and add to the casserole. Drain the noodles, discard the liquid, and cut the noodles in half. Add to the casserole. Add the beef broth, bean curd, garlic, and ginger and place the casserole over medium-low heat.

3. Each diner should have a bowl for dipping sauce, chopsticks or a fondue fork, a soup spoon, a small soup bowl, and a plate. Place the ingredients for the dipping sauce in separate bowls on the table. Arrange the meat and vegetables on platters and place on the table with the pita breads. Place the Mongolian hot pot (or fondue pot or electric skillet) in the center of the table.

Pour the broth into the pot, and if you're using the Mongolian hot pot, carefully place white-hot charcoal pieces into the cone. If you're using a fondue or other pot, light or turn on that pot.

4. As the broth comes to a boil, have the diners combine the ingredients for the dipping sauce to their liking in the smallest bowls. When the broth boils, place a slice or two of meat and a few vegetables into the pot. After about 30 seconds, remove the meat and/or vegetables with a fondue fork or chopsticks, check for desired doneness, and if cooked to your liking, dip into the sauce and place in a pita bread. Continue with the remaining ingredients, filling the pitas with the desired amounts of meat and vegetables. When all of the meat and vegetables are eaten, ladle the remaining broth from the hot pot into the soup bowls.

Serves 6

Hugh O'Neill and his Mongolian hot pot.

Paul's MEAT LOAF

Paul Schwarz, the director of the Brooklyn New School in Red Hook, says that this meat loaf is much better the second day. He speaks highly of a meat loaf sandwich with rye bread and ketchup.

1½ pounds lean ground chuck
½ pound hot Italian sausage, removed from its casing and crumbled
1 cup coarse bread crumbs, preferably from toasted rye bread
2 eggs, lightly beaten
1 teaspoon salt
½ teaspoon freshly grated nutmeg
Pinch of freshly ground black pepper
Pesto (recipe follows)
1½ cups grated Cheddar cheese
6 slices bacon, cooked until crisp, drained, and crumbled
2 hard-cooked eggs, chopped

1. Preheat the oven to 350°F. Cover the inside of a 13 × 9-inch baking pan with aluminum foil.

2. In a mixing bowl, thoroughly combine the ground chuck, sausage, bread crumbs, beaten eggs, salt, nutmeg, and pepper.

3. In a separate bowl, combine the pesto, 1 cup of the Cheddar cheese, the crumbled bacon, and the hard-cooked eggs.

4. Place the meat mixture between 2 sheets of waxed paper and roll into a rectangular shape about ⅓ inch thick.

5. Remove the top sheet of waxed paper and spread the pesto mixture all over the top of the flattened meat. Roll up the meat like a jelly roll, peeling back the remaining waxed paper as you go. Shape the ends of the roll, as needed, with your hands to form a neat cylindrical shape, entirely enclosing the pesto.

6. Place the meat loaf, seam side down, in the prepared baking pan. Sprinkle the meat loaf with the remaining ½ cup Cheddar cheese. Bake until cooked through and browned, 1 hour. Serve hot.

Makes 6 to 8 servings

PESTO

2 cloves garlic
⅓ cup olive oil
2 cups tightly packed fresh basil leaves
¼ cup pine nuts
¾ cup freshly grated Parmesan cheese

1. Place the garlic and half of the olive oil in a food processor. Process until the garlic is puréed. Add the remaining oil, the basil, pine nuts, and Parmesan. Process to a smooth paste.

2. The pesto should be fairly dry for the meat loaf. If the purée is too wet, blot it with paper towels to remove excess oil.

Makes 1½ cups

Bill Blass' MEAT LOAF

Bill Blass says his meat loaf was developed by trial and error. He considers it a success, saying, "I haven't lost any friends yet." When Mr. Blass cooks for friends at his country house, this is bound to be on the menu, usually served with red pepper jelly, baked potato skins, and corn pudding. It's as good cold as it is hot from the oven.

1 cup chopped celery
1 onion, chopped
3 tablespoons butter
2 pounds ground beef sirloin
½ pound ground veal
½ pound ground pork
½ cup chopped fresh parsley
⅓ cup sour cream
½ cup soft bread crumbs
Pinch of dried thyme
Pinch of dried marjoram
Salt and freshly ground black pepper, to taste
1 egg
1 tablespoon Worcestershire sauce
1½ cups Heinz chili sauce
3 slices bacon

---

1. Preheat the oven to 350°F. Oil an 8 × 4-inch loaf pan.

2. In a heavy skillet over medium heat, sauté the celery and onion in the butter until soft. Remove from the heat and set aside to cool for 5 minutes.

3. Add the meats, parsley, sour cream, bread crumbs, thyme, marjoram, and salt and pepper to the skillet. Whisk the egg with the Worcestershire sauce and add to the mixture. Using a wooden spoon or your hands, combine the mixture and mold into a loaf shape.

4. Place the meat loaf in the prepared loaf pan. Top with the chili sauce and bacon slices. Place in the oven on a jelly roll pan to catch any drips. Bake until cooked through and nicely browned, 1 hour.

Serves 6 to 8

Barbara Walters and Bill Blass out for a non-meat-loaf evening.
Photo: Reuters/Bettmann Newsphotos

Ann Getty's
MEAT LOAF

This winning meat loaf has been a standby of the charity dinner circuit in New York and has been passed from caterer to caterer. It has a wonderful, woodsy character because of the mushrooms.

2 tablespoons dried porcini or cêpe
    mushrooms
6 tablespoons (¾ stick) butter
1 pound fresh mushroom caps (1½ pounds
    with stems), chopped
½ teaspoon salt
¼ teaspoon freshly ground black pepper
1 tablespoon vegetable oil
2 cups chopped onions
2 garlic cloves, minced
1½ cups coarse dried bread crumbs
1 cup New York Penicillin (page 47) or
    canned chicken broth
3 pounds ground beef round
3 eggs
½ cup chopped fresh parsley
2 tablespoons Dijon mustard
1 teaspoon minced fresh thyme leaves

---

1. Preheat the oven to 350°F.

2. Cover the dried mushrooms with warm water and set aside to soak for 5 minutes. Drain and chop.

3. Melt 4 tablespoons of the butter in a heavy skillet. Add the dried and fresh mushrooms and sauté over medium heat until all of the liquid evaporates, 10 to 15 minutes. Season with the salt and pepper and set aside.

4. Add the remaining 2 tablespoons butter and the oil to the skillet and set over medium heat. Fry the onions, stirring often, until golden brown, 5 to 10 minutes. Stir in the garlic and cook to soften, 1 minute more.

5. Soak the bread crumbs in the chicken broth to moisten them. In a large bowl, combine the beef, mushrooms, bread crumbs, onion mixture, eggs, parsley, mustard, and thyme. Mix well and form the mixture into a loaf shape. Place in an 8 × 4-inch loaf pan. Bake until cooked through and golden brown, 1½ hours.

Serves 8

Suzanne's
MEAT LOAF

Meat loaf is one of the most comforting foods around. Suzanne Rafer, an editor at Workman Publishing, makes hers with pickling spice. The combination of black pepper, mustard seed, coriander seed, and ginger lends an intriguing complexity to this "everyday" dish.

2 pounds ground beef round
1 large egg plus 1 egg white
1 large clove garlic, minced
⅓ cup fine dry bread crumbs
¼ teaspoon salt
1 tablespoon olive oil
½ cup ketchup, preferably Heinz
2 cups Savory Beef Stock (page 61) or canned broth
¼ cup whole mixed pickling spices, tied in cheesecloth
2 imported bay leaves

1. Preheat the oven to 350°F.
2. Place the meat in a large mixing bowl. Flatten it slightly. Beat the egg and the egg white in a small bowl. Add the garlic, bread crumbs, and salt and stir to combine. Pour the egg mixture over the meat, then use your hands to knead the meat until the mixture is well blended. Form the meat into a loaf shape, about 8 × 4 × 2½ inches.

3. Heat the oil in a large heavy pot over medium heat. Add the meat loaf and brown for 3 to 4 minutes. Gently turn to brown the other side, an additional 3 to 4 minutes. Once browned, slide a spatula under the loaf to make sure it hasn't stuck to the bottom of the pan. If it has, loosen it and scrape up any bits of meat that are stuck.

4. Pour the ketchup over the top and down the sides of the meat loaf. Pour the stock around the meat loaf and stir to combine with the ketchup. Add the pickling spices, and place 1 bay leaf on each side of the loaf. Bring the stock to a boil. Cover the pot and place it in the oven. Bake the meat loaf until firm and cooked through, 1 hour.

5. Remove the meat loaf from the oven. It tastes best if allowed to cool down and then sit for several hours or overnight in the refrigerator (first remove the bay leaves and the bag of pickling spices, pressing the juices out of the cheesecloth with the side of a spoon).

6. Close to serving time, remove the meat loaf from the refrigerator, and cut into 1-inch-thick slices. Discard the hardened layer of fat from the top of the gravy. Add up to ½ cup water if the gravy seems too skimpy. Remember you're going to want to spoon it all over your creamy mashed potatoes—the only appropriate accompaniment besides string beans. Return the meat loaf slices to the pot and reheat over medium-low heat until the gravy is lightly boiling and the meat is heated through, about 12 minutes. Dig in.

Serves 4 to 6

Turkish
KARNIYARIK

There is nothing like the combination of beef and eggplant. Unlike many cooks, Lauri Saxe Sila does not scoop out the eggplant meat. Instead, the ground beef is mixed with tomatoes, peppers, and parsley, and placed on top of the vegetable. The juxtaposition of brown, purple, red, and green makes a very attractive dish.

3 tablespoons vegetable oil
1 pound ground beef round
2 large onions, minced
2 cups whole Italian plum tomatoes (16 ounce can)
1½ green bell peppers, stemmed, seeded, and chopped
½ bunch fresh parsley, stemmed and chopped
Salt and freshly ground black pepper, to taste
4 small eggplants

1. Warm 1 tablespoon of the vegetable oil in a skillet over medium heat. Add the ground beef and onions and cook, breaking up the meat with a large spoon, until the meat is lightly browned, 15 to 20 minutes.

2. Meanwhile, drain the tomatoes, reserving the juice and 2 whole tomatoes. Chop the rest of the tomatoes and add them to the meat mixture. Cook, stirring to combine, for 1 minute.

3. Reserve 2 tablespoons of the bell pepper. Add the remaining bell pepper to the meat mixture and cook until the peppers are softened, 15 minutes.

4. Stir in the parsley, season to taste with salt and pepper, and cook for 10 minutes.

5. Preheat the broiler.

6. Wash and dry the eggplants. Using a sharp knife, peel off ½-inch-wide lengthwise strips of skin from the eggplants to make a striated pattern. Cut each eggplant in half lengthwise. Without piercing the skin, diagonally slash the inside pulp of each eggplant several times. Rub all sides of the eggplants with oil.

7. Arrange the eggplants on a baking sheet. Broil the eggplants as far from the heat as possible, turning as necessary, until light brown on both sides, 10 minutes total.

8. Preheat the oven to 350°F.

9. Arrange the eggplant halves, skin sides down, in a nonreactive, shallow baking pan. Divide the meat mixture evenly among them and spread over each half. Decorate each with slices of the reserved tomatoes and a sprinkle of the reserved bell pepper. Drizzle the reserved tomato juice over the eggplants. Cover the baking pan with foil. Bake until warm and soft, 45 minutes.

Serves 4

Mrs. Mallis'
MINA
(TURKISH MEAT PIE)

Vera Mallis, whose parents were born in Istanbul, recommends Mina—a Turkish meat pie with a matzoh crust—for Passover. Mrs. Mallis,

The Mallis women (left to right): Brooke, Stephanie, Vera, Fern, Joanne, and Victoria.

a Brooklyn housewife, eats Mina with Turkish Eggs: "Save your onion skins for a week or so. In a large heavy pot, put onion skins, coffee grounds, and 1 dozen eggs. Fill pot with cold water and cook on low heat for 3 or 4 hours. The taste of these eggs is out of this world. Just don't tell anyone how you cooked them."

3 tablespoons vegetable oil
5 onions, chopped
½ teaspoon salt
¼ teaspoon freshly ground black pepper
1 teaspoon ground cinnamon
2 pounds ground beef round
3 eggs, beaten
About 6 sheets of matzoh
1 egg, beaten, for glaze

1. Heat the oil in a large skillet over medium heat. Add the onions and cook until translucent, 5 minutes. Add the salt, pepper, cinnamon, and meat and cook, breaking up the meat with a large spoon, only until lightly browned, 15 to 20 minutes. Stir in ½ cup water. Remove the pan from the heat and let cool, uncovered, in the refrigerator, 30 minutes.

2. Add the eggs to the meat mixture and mix well; set aside.

3. Preheat the oven to 350°F.

4. Fill a large wide bowl with cool water and add the matzohs. Soak until they are wet through but not falling apart. Remove and lay on several layers of paper towels. Place another couple of paper towels on top of them to soak up any extra moisture. Line the bottom and sides of a 13 × 9-inch baking pan with some of the matzohs. Cover with the meat mixture. Top with the remaining matzohs. Brush the top with the beaten egg. Bake until golden brown, 45 minutes.

Serves 8

The famous jockeys outside the "21" Club.

"21" Club
BURGER

Huge and juicy—this updated version of a New York Classic is tough to beat.

HERB BUTTER
¼ pound (1 stick) butter, at room temperature
2 tablespoons finely chopped fresh basil
1 tablespoon finely chopped fresh thyme
1 tablespoon finely chopped fresh parsley
¼ teaspoon salt, or to taste
Pinch of freshly ground black pepper, or to taste

SALAD GARNISH
24 slices ripe, red tomatoes
16 thin slices red onion
1½ cups olive oil
1 cup freshly squeezed lemon juice

BURGERS
6 pounds ground chuck
Salt and freshly ground black pepper,
    to taste
16 slices Italian country
    bread, about 5 inches
    in diameter and cut
    ½ inch thick
½ cup olive oil

1. Make the herb butter: Place all of the ingredients in a food processor and process until smooth. Then place on plastic wrap, roll into a log, and freeze in the wrap.

2. Make the salad: Combine all the ingredients in a nonreactive bowl. Stir to coat and set aside.

3. Preheat a grill or broiler.

4. Make the burgers: Remove the butter from the plastic wrap and cut into 8 pieces. Divide the meat into 8 equal balls. Make an indentation in each ball with your thumb, press 1 piece of butter in each, then close the meat over the butter. Shape each ball into a 1-inch-thick patty. Sprinkle salt and pepper over the burgers.

5. Grill the burgers for 4 minutes per side for medium-rare.

6. Meanwhile, brush the bread with the olive oil. Grill until toasted on both sides. Place each burger on 2 slices of Italian toast and top with the salad garnish.

Serves 8

Madison Square
MARINATED HAMBURGERS

When most people hear Madison Square, the next word that comes to mind is Garden. But there is a Madison Square Park, just north of the Flatiron Building. Around the park, hungry workers lunch on hamburgers like these, marinated in wine and garlic and sold from a street cart.

2 pounds ground beef round
8 cloves garlic, minced
3 cups dry white wine
Salt and freshly ground black pepper, to taste

1. Form the ground beef into 6 hamburgers. Place in a flat nonreactive bowl or baking dish. Sprinkle the garlic over the hamburgers, pour the white wine over them, and season with salt and pepper. Cover with plastic wrap and refrigerate for at least 3 hours, turning the hamburgers every hour. Remove from the refrigerator 30 minutes before cooking.

2. Preheat a grill or broiler or heat a seasoned cast-iron skillet over medium-high heat until almost smoking.

3. Grill, broil, or pan-fry the burgers for 3 to 4 minutes per side for rare. Serve on kaiser rolls.

Serves 6

Angela Palladino's
MEATBALLS

Angela Fodele Palladino, painter and sculptor, grew up in Sicily. When she cooks, friends and family line up, plates in hand. These meatballs can be eaten as an appetizer or a main course, with pasta or stuffed inside a sandwich roll.

1 pound ground beef round
2 eggs, lightly beaten
⅓ cup chopped Italian (flat-leaf) parsley
3 slices American white bread (crusts removed), soaked in 2 cups milk
2 tablespoons freshly grated Romano cheese
2 tablespoons freshly grated Parmesan cheese
Freshly ground black pepper, to taste
1 cup safflower oil, for frying

Angela Palladino's meatballs are great plain or sauced.

1. In a large bowl, mix together the beef, eggs, and parsley. Gently squeeze the milk from the bread and shred it as you add it to the meat mixture. Add the cheeses and pepper. Form the meat mixture into 12 balls. Place on a baking sheet and refrigerate for 15 minutes.

2. Heat a large heavy skillet over medium heat. Add the oil. When hot, add the meatballs and cook, turning, until browned on all sides, about 10 minutes. If you plan to eat them right away, cook until cooked through, 10 minutes more. If you plan to add the meatballs to a sauce, remove them from the pan with a slotted spoon and add to the saucepot. Cook for 15 minutes more before serving.

Makes 12 meatballs

Friday Night STUFFED CABBAGE

Friday night dinner meant stuffed cabbage, challah, and chicken when artist Brenda Miller was growing up in New York. Her mother, Florence, who came to America in 1932 from Moldavia, "made the whole house smell like cabbage," Brenda remembers. "We ate this as an appetizer, with plenty of challah to sop up the juice."

1 Savoy cabbage
1 pound ground beef round
1 egg
Salt and freshly ground black pepper, to taste
Juice of 1 small lemon
1 onion, chopped
1 tablespoon raw white rice
6 fresh tomatoes, cored, seeded, and chopped
1 can (8 ounces) tomato sauce
¾ cup raisins
1 tablespoon plus 2 teaspoons sugar
1 teaspoon dried oregano
1 teaspoon sweet paprika

1. Cut the cabbage across the base and separate the leaves. Any leaves that are not large enough to roll should be chopped.

2. Bring a large pot of water to a boil. Blanch the cabbage leaves until they are soft. Drain in a colander and cool under cold running water. Drain and pat dry. Lay the leaves flat on a cutting board and cut out any thick ends, in the shape of a small triangle, at the bottom of the leaves.

3. In a mixing bowl, combine the ground beef, egg, salt, pepper, half of the lemon juice, 2 teaspoons of the chopped onion, and the raw rice.

4. In a nonreactive large pot, combine the remaining chopped onion and the chopped cabbage.

5. Place 1 tablespoon of the meat mixture on the lower third of a cabbage leaf. Fold the base of the leaf over the meat mixture and then fold each side toward the center. Roll up the leaf to form a cylinder. Repeat with each leaf until all of the meat mixture is used up, placing each cylinder on the onion and cabbage in the pot as you finish it.

6. Pour the tomatoes, tomato sauce, raisins, remaining lemon juice, the sugar, oregano, and paprika over the cabbage rolls. Season with salt and pepper. Cook, covered, over low heat for about 2 hours to get all the flavors mingled.

Serves 4 to 6

Pat Riley's CREAMY CHIPPED BEEF

Remembers Pat Riley, "When I was a child, I ate a less sophisticated version of this dish. I think it remains easy and successful for light suppers or brunches in particular." If the dried beef is very salty, cover it with cold water for a few minutes and then drain.

4 tablespoons (½ stick) butter or margarine
¼ pound chipped beef, torn into bite-size
   pieces
2 tablespoons finely chopped onion
3 tablespoons all-purpose flour
2½ cups milk
1 cup sour cream
2 tablespoons finely chopped parsley
4 English muffins, split

1. Melt the butter in a skillet over medium heat. Add the beef and onion and sauté until the onion is soft, 5 to 10 minutes. Add the flour, stir for 1 minute, and then gradually add the milk. Cook, stirring, until the sauce is smooth and thick, 5 to 10 minutes more.

2. Stir in the sour cream and parsley and cook until heated through, 1 minute.

3. Serve on toasted English muffin halves.

Serves 4

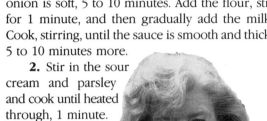

Kenny Galura's
VENISON ROAST

This is a favored dish of the Bad News Bears gentleman's eating club in Yonkers. A beef roast can be substituted for venison without changing the cooking time. Preceded by a salad, accompanied by noodles and string beans, and followed by apple pie (see Index for pie recipes), it makes a he-man's meal.

1 boneless venison or beef roast
   (5 to 7 pounds)
4 cloves garlic, halved
¾ cup green peppercorn mustard
1½ cups ketchup
¾ teaspoon salt
½ teaspoon freshly ground black pepper
3 cups minced fried bell peppers, with their oil
   and juice

1. Preheat the oven to 350°F.

2. Place the venison or beef in a roasting pan. Make 8 evenly spaced ½-inch-deep slits in the roast and insert the halved garlic cloves.

3. Combine the mustard and ketchup in a mixing bowl. Slather the mixture all over the roast and sprinkle with the salt and pepper.

4. Smother the roast with the peppers. Drizzle the pepper juice over the meat. Cover the pan with aluminum foil and bake until tender, 2 to 2½ hours. While it is cooking, baste the roast 3 times with the pan juices. Let the roast rest for 15 minutes before slicing.

Serves 10

Pat Riley at the Union Square Greenmarket.

Detective Hayward's
VENISON STEW

This is a scaled-down version of Walter "Bud" Hayward's original recipe. A detective with the midtown north homicide unit, Mr. Haywood usually cooks enough to feed 15 to 30 people.

¼ cup all-purpose flour
1 teaspoon salt
½ teaspoon freshly ground black pepper
3 pounds venison or beef chuck, cut into 1-inch cubes
¼ cup vegetable oil
2 cups canned crushed tomatoes
1 large onion, diced
3 carrots, diced
4 ribs celery, diced
2½ pounds potatoes, peeled and cut into ½-inch cubes
1 cup fresh or frozen peas
1 tablespoon chopped fresh parsley

1. Season the flour with salt and pepper. Dredge the venison in the seasoned flour.

2. Place the oil in a nonreactive heavy casserole over medium-high heat. Add the meat and brown on all sides. Add the tomatoes, onion, carrots, and celery. Pour in enough water to cover the ingredients by 1 inch. Bring to a boil. Reduce the heat to a simmer and cook for 45 minutes, adding more water, if necessary, to keep the meat well covered.

3. Add the potatoes and simmer for 35 minutes.

4. Add the peas and simmer for 10 minutes. Adjust the seasonings. Ladle the stew into bowls and sprinkle with the chopped parsley.

Serves 6 to 8

Firehouse
VEAL AND EGGPLANT PARMIGIANA

Fire fighter Frank Gambino tries a lot of different things in the kitchen, and both his family and his fellow fire fighters think they all turn out great. One of his specialties is this dish, which he serves with ziti or rice with mushrooms, and peas on the side. You could also serve it with Giorgio's Shaved Artichoke and Parmesan Salad (see Index).

1 egg
½ cup milk
1 pound veal cutlets, pounded thin
2 cups seasoned (Italian) fine, dried bread crumbs
1 cup olive oil
1 eggplant, cut lengthwise in ¼-inch-thick slices
1 can (32 ounces) tomato sauce
¼ pound prosciutto, trimmed of fat and very thinly sliced
¼ cup chopped fresh parsley
½ pound mozzarella cheese, shredded

1. Preheat the oven to 350°F.

2. In a shallow bowl, beat together the egg and milk. Dip each veal cutlet in the mixture and then dredge in the bread crumbs.

3. Heat ¼ cup of the olive oil in a large skillet over medium heat. Fry each cutlet until golden, about 3 minutes per side. Drain the cutlets on paper towels.

4. Wipe out the skillet. Place it over medium-high heat and add ¼ cup fresh olive oil. Add the eggplant slices and fry for about 3 minutes on each side, adding additional olive oil, as needed. Drain the eggplant on paper towels.

5. Cover the bottom of two 13 × 9-inch baking pans with a ¼-inch layer of the tomato sauce. Lay the cutlets in the pans. Top each cutlet with a slice of the eggplant and a slice of the prosciutto. Pour in the remaining sauce. Sprinkle with the parsley and mozzarella. Bake until the mozzarella has melted and is golden, 30 minutes.

Serves 4

Frank Gambino at work in the firehouse kitchen.

Marcello Sindoni's
STUFFED VEAL CUTLETS

This hearty Southern Italian dish is wonderful with buttered noodles or rice.

¼ *pound boiled ham, finely chopped*
¼ *pound salami, finely chopped*
¼ *pound mortadella, finely chopped*
½ *cup finely chopped Fontina cheese*
⅓ *cup golden raisins, soaked in water to cover for 30 minutes and drained*
¼ *cup pignoli (pine nuts)*
Salt and freshly ground black pepper, to taste
2 eggs
1 cup seasoned (Italian) fine, dried bread crumbs
16 veal cutlets (1 pound total), pounded thin
2 onions, cut into 8 thick hunks each
16 bay leaves, rinsed in water
¼ *cup olive oil*

1. In a large bowl, combine the ham, salami, mortadella, and Fontina cheese. Add the raisins and pignoli and season with salt and pepper. Add 1 of the eggs and stir well.

2. Preheat the broiler.

3. In a small bowl, lightly beat the remaining egg. Place the bread crumbs in a shallow bowl. Lay the cutlets out flat. Divide the stuffing mixture among the cutlets, placing stuffing in the center of each cutlet. Roll up each cutlet, dip thoroughly in the egg, and then dredge in the bread crumbs. Thread the rolled cutlets onto four 12-inch metal skewers, alternating each with a hunk of the onion and a bay leaf, like shish kebabs. Each skewer should hold 4 rolled cutlets, 4 hunks of onion, and 4 bay leaves. End each skewer with a bay leaf.

4. Broil the skewers for 2 minutes on each side.

5. Preheat the oven to 400°F.

6. Transfer the skewers to an ovenproof serving dish, drizzle with the olive oil, and bake in the oven until the meat is cooked through, 10 minutes. Serve hot.

Serves 4

Chef Scaffone's
SCALOPPINE
OF
VEAL PIZZAIOLA

Barbetta, one of the oldest Italian restaurants in the city, was a haven of fine Italian cooking in the earlier part of the century. This recipe, which originally appeared in *Where to Dine in '39,* by Diana Ashley, came from the chef of Barbetta and was copied throughout the city. Although it is currently not on the menu at the restaurant, they feel sure it will be again. It remains a classic of the hearty old school.

PIZZAIOLA SAUCE
¼ cup olive oil
2 onions, chopped
2 green bell peppers, stemmed, seeded, and chopped
2 ribs celery, chopped
1 teaspoon salt
¼ teaspoon freshly ground black pepper
3 cloves garlic, minced
2 cups canned crushed tomatoes
¼ teaspoon dried red pepper flakes
1 tablespoon minced fresh parsley

SCALOPPINE
16 veal tenderloin medallions (about 2 pounds), pounded ¼ inch thick
½ cup all-purpose flour
¼ cup plus 2 tablespoons olive oil
6 tablespoons (¾ stick) butter

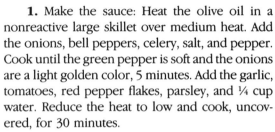

1. Make the sauce: Heat the olive oil in a nonreactive large skillet over medium heat. Add the onions, bell peppers, celery, salt, and pepper. Cook until the green pepper is soft and the onions are a light golden color, 5 minutes. Add the garlic, tomatoes, red pepper flakes, parsley, and ¼ cup water. Reduce the heat to low and cook, uncovered, for 30 minutes.

2. Prepare the scaloppine: Dredge the veal medallions in the flour; set aside on waxed paper. Warm a large sauté pan or skillet over medium heat, add the olive oil and butter, and heat. Add the veal medallions and cook until light golden all over, 1½ minutes per side. Add the pizzaiola sauce and cook for 1 minute more.

Serves 4

Barbetta's on 46th Street for a before-the-theater Italian dinner.

Thorstensson's
DILL KALV

Elisabeth Thorstensson, chef of the Seagram Company's private dining room, says that this dish is "typically Swedish," tasty, and inexpensive. Ms. Thorstensson's mother, who was a teacher, used to cook it on a winter weekend and serve it throughout the week.

1 boneless shoulder of veal (3 to 3½ pounds), tied
1 teaspoon salt
20 black peppercorns
2 ribs celery, trimmed and cut into 2-inch lengths
2 large carrots, peeled, trimmed, and cut into 2-inch lengths
1 onion, chopped
½ cup fresh dill, chopped
3 tablespoons distilled white vinegar
3 tablespoons sugar
3 tablespoons butter
3 tablespoons all-purpose flour
½ teaspoon salt
¼ teaspoon freshly ground black pepper

1. Place the veal in a large heavy pot and add enough cold water to barely cover. Partially cover the pot and bring to a boil. Reduce the heat and simmer for 10 minutes, skimming frequently. Add the salt, peppercorns, celery, carrots, and onion. Cover and simmer until the meat is tender, 60 to 90 minutes. Remove from the heat and let stand, uncovered, until ready to serve.

2. Meanwhile, in a nonreactive saucepan, combine half of the dill with the vinegar and sugar and bring to a boil. Remove from the heat and set aside to steep for 30 minutes. Strain and reserve the liquid.

3. Transfer the meat to a warm platter. Strain the cooking liquid, reserving 2½ cups for the sauce.

4. Melt the butter in a large saucepan over medium heat. Using a whisk, stir in the flour. When blended, add the reserved cooking liquid, stirring constantly. Add the reserved sweet-and-sour dill liquid. Simmer, stirring frequently, until thickened, 2 to 3 minutes. Remove from the heat, whisk in the remaining fresh dill, season with salt and pepper, and serve with the hot sliced veal.

Serves 4 to 6

Thomas Miner's
LEG OF LAMB STUFFED WITH OYSTERS

When creating a colonial era menu for George Washington's birthday, Thomas Miner, chef of the Fraunces Tavern Restaurant, combined two favorites—oysters, which once crowded the bays around New York, and lamb, which once ranged in the briny marshes of lower Manhattan. It is a seriously hearty and savory roast, best served with green beans or other light vegetables. And maybe a little pudding (see the Index for Kibby's Fig Pudding) for dessert.

1 cup fine, dried bread crumbs
2 hard-cooked egg yolks, mashed
3 anchovy fillets, chopped
¼ cup chopped onion
1 teaspoon dried thyme leaves
1 teaspoon dried winter savory
⅛ teaspoon freshly grated nutmeg
Salt and freshly ground black pepper, to taste
12 oysters, shucked
2 raw eggs
4½ pounds boneless leg of lamb, butterflied

1. Preheat the oven to 325°F.

2. Place the bread crumbs, egg yolks, anchovies, onion, thyme, savory, nutmeg, salt and pepper, and oysters in the bowl of a food processor. Pulse a few times to mix the ingredients and mince the oysters. With the motor running, add the raw eggs and process to make a paste.

3. Spread the oyster paste over the inside of the leg of lamb. Roll up the leg and tie it at intervals with butcher's twine. Place the roast in a baking pan. Roast for 2¼ hours. Let the lamb rest for 15 minutes before slicing.

Serves 6 to 8

Fragrant LEG OF LAMB WITH OREGANO POTATOES

Rina Anoussis, owner of The Travel Business, sends hundreds of people all over the globe. But when she cooks, she merely travels back in time to her native Greece for this savory, easy roast. The dish is wonderful served with her husband Takis's Artichokes à la Polita (see Index).

4 pounds potatoes, peeled
4 pounds boneless leg of lamb
4 to 6 cloves garlic, cut into slivers
Salt and freshly ground black pepper, to taste
2 tablespoons fresh oregano
2 tablespoons olive oil
Juice of 2 lemons

1. Preheat the oven to 300°F.

2. Using a melon baller, scoop balls from the

potatoes (or cut into cubes with a knife) and set aside in a bowl of cold water.

3. Cut small slits in the lamb and slip the garlic into the meat. Rub the lamb with salt and pepper, 1 tablespoon of the oregano, and the olive oil. Place the lamb in a roasting pan. Roast for 45 minutes.

4. Remove the potatoes from the cold water. Sprinkle them with salt, the remaining 1 tablespoon oregano, and the lemon juice. Place the potatoes around the lamb in the roasting pan. Roast for 45 minutes, turning the potatoes occasionally and adding water from time to time, if necessary, to ensure that the pan is never dry.

5. Using an instant-read thermometer, check the doneness of the meat. The meat is medium-rare at 145°F, well-done at 165°F. When it is cooked as you like, remove from the oven and let rest for 10 minutes. Slice and serve with the potatoes.

Serves 6

Grandma Sarah's LAMB AND PRUNE CASSEROLE (PRESSURE COOKER METHOD)

Rose Levy Beranbaum, the cookbook author, inherited this recipe from her grandmother. "This unusual combination of lamb and prunes is so succulent and gloriously flavorful that it has always been one of my very favorite recipes. It was originally billed as a stew, but I like to boil down the liquid and juices until just enough remains to glaze the lamb. Grandma simmered the meat in a large pot on top of the stove for several hours, but in the pressure cooker this recipe works to a perfection of melting tenderness in only about 30 minutes." This recipe requires a 6-quart pressure cooker.

3 tablespoons all-purpose flour
1 tablespoon kosher salt, or 2 teaspoons
    table salt
¼ teaspoon freshly ground black
    pepper
Large pinch of cayenne pepper
4 pounds lamb shanks, boned, meat
    cut into 2-inch pieces
4 tablespoons vegetable oil
1 large onion, thinly sliced
2 celery ribs, thinly sliced
1 clove garlic, minced
2 teaspoons fresh thyme or ½ teaspoon
    dried
1 bay leaf
2 cups pitted prunes
6 small red potatoes, cut in half

■━━━━━━━━━━━━■

1. In a plastic or paper bag, combine the flour, salt, black pepper, and cayenne and shake to mix. Add a few pieces of the lamb at a time and toss to coat with the flour mixture until all of the lamb is coated. If any of the flour mixture remains, set it aside.

2. Heat a large heavy skillet, preferably cast iron, until hot. Add 2 tablespoons of the oil and heat until a film appears over the oil. Add only as much lamb as will fit without crowding (overcrowding will cause the meat to steam and turn gray). Brown the lamb on all sides, in batches, over medium-high heat, adding more oil as necessary. It should take about 3 minutes per side. Remove the lamb to a bowl and set aside.

3. In the same pan, sauté the onions and celery until the onions are golden brown; sprinkle on any remaining flour mixture, stir in the garlic, and cook, stirring, for about 30 seconds.

4. Spoon the mixture into the pressure cooker. Top with the lamb. Add the thyme, bay leaf, and 1½ cups water. Bring to full pressure and cook for 20 minutes. Add the prunes and potatoes and cook at full pressure for 10 minutes. The meat should be almost falling-off-the-bone tender and the potatoes firm, but done.

5. Remove the lamb and vegetables to a large serving platter. Bring the gravy to a boil and cook until reduced and thickened, 5 to 10 minutes. Pour over the meat and vegetables, and serve.

Serves 6 to 8

Middle Eastern LAMB

When she was a correspondent for United Press International in the Middle East, author Brooke Kroeger was given this recipe for lamb baked in yogurt by her friend Shirley Rizvi. Brooke has since moved back to New York, where the dish—served with green beans and rice to sop up the yogurt sauce—remains a hit at her dinner parties. You might also enjoy it with Greenmarket Spring Lima Bean and Early Corn Ragout (see Index).

Brooke Kroeger picked up the recipe for this fragrant lamb dish when she lived in the Middle East.

1 leg of lamb (6 to 8 pounds) trimmed, bone in
2 cups plain yogurt
½ teaspoon freshly grated nutmeg
½ teaspoon freshly ground black pepper
½ teaspoon salt
6 cloves garlic, minced
1 small piece (½ inch) fresh ginger, peeled and
    minced
¼ cup olive oil
6 whole cloves
12 to 15 fresh mint leaves

1. In a nonreactive large roasting pan, combine the yogurt, nutmeg, pepper, salt, garlic, ginger, and olive oil. Add the lamb and turn to coat with the mixture. Marinate at room temperature for at least 4 hours, or refrigerate overnight.

2. Preheat the oven to 400°F.

3. Pour off and reserve the marinade. Pat the cloves and the fresh mint leaves on the lamb; baste generously with the marinade. Cover the lamb with a foil tent. Roast, basting every 20 minutes with the marinade, for 1 hour.

4. Reduce the heat to 300°F. Remove the foil and continue roasting the lamb, basting frequently, until it registers an internal temperature of 150 to 155°F for medium, 1½ to 2 hours total.

Serves 8

Spicy LAMB STEW

This recipe from friends originally came from a Jamaican cab driver who happened to pick them up in a snowstorm on a New York night. Oblivious to their audience, the two discussed the contents of the refrigerator in the apartment for which they were headed. When they paid the $4 fare, the driver offered them this approach to the ingredients on hand. It was a superb meal.

2 tablespoons all-purpose flour
1 teaspoon salt
½ teaspoon ground cinnamon
¼ teaspoon black pepper
2 pounds stewing lamb, cut into 1½- to 2-inch
    pieces
3 tablespoons vegetable oil
2 cups canned beef broth
1 bay leaf
2 cups canned tomatoes
1 onion, chopped
½ teaspoon dried oregano
1 pound fresh green beans, trimmed

1. Combine the flour, salt, cinnamon, and pepper. Dust the lamb cubes with the mixture and reserve the excess flour.

2. In a nonreactive heavy casserole, heat the oil over medium-high heat. Working in batches, brown the lamb pieces on all sides, then drain off the excess oil. Return the lamb to the casserole; add 1 cup of the broth and the bay leaf. Cover the pan, reduce the heat, and simmer for 20 minutes. Remove the bay leaf.

3. Drain the tomatoes and add their juice to the stew. Break the tomatoes into small pieces and set aside. Stir the onion, oregano, and green beans into the stew and simmer, covered, until the meat is tender, about 1 hour.

4. Pour ¼ cup of the cooking liquid into a bowl and whisk in the remaining flour to make a paste. Gradually stir the flour paste into the stew. Stir in the tomatoes and season with salt and pepper to taste. Simmer for 10 minutes more.

Serves 6

ing, using the remaining 1 tablespoon olive oil and the remaining 2 shanks. Remove to a plate.

4. Using the same casserole, combine the onions, leeks, garlic, sun-dried tomatoes and their oil, tomatoes, and wine. Cook over medium heat until the onions are soft, 5 to 7 minutes. Add the oregano, pepper, and rosemary. Stand each shank on end in the casserole. The vegetables will not cover the shanks. Bring the mixture to a boil. Bake, uncovered, for 1 hour, adding more wine, if necessary, to keep the meat moist.

5. Turn the shanks over and continue baking for 45 minutes. Watch the sauce carefully near the end so that it does not burn. You want to reduce the sauce to a thickened mass that will coat the meat but not stick to the pot.

6. Remove the casserole from the oven and allow to cool. Remove the meat from the bones and return the meat to the casserole. Reheat the mixture on top of the stove over medium heat, stirring well. Pack equal portions of the ingredients into 6 ramekins or custard cups. Serve, unmolding onto dinner plates.

Serves 6

Deborah Markow's BRAISED LAMB SHANKS

Deborah Markow, who holds a Ph.D. in art history, dresses up lamb shanks by unmolding the meat timbales on a platter and surrounding them with risotto or barley cooked in stock—it makes a delicious winter meal for company. "I got the idea to mold the braised meat from the manner in which deboned meat stews are served in restaurants in Europe. It turns a plebian stew into an elegant dish."

4 lamb shanks (about 1 pound each)
2 tablespoons olive oil
2 tablespoons all-purpose flour
3 onions, chopped
4 leeks, diced and rinsed well
6 cloves garlic, minced
8 sun-dried tomatoes packed in oil
2 tablespoons oil from sun-dried tomatoes
2 cups peeled, seeded, chopped tomatoes
  (fresh or canned)
2 cups dry red wine
½ teaspoon dried oregano
½ teaspoon freshly ground black
  pepper
Pinch of dried rosemary

1. Preheat the oven to 325°F.

2. With a very sharp knife, remove as much of the fat, caul, and external membrane from the lamb shanks as is possible. Release the meat from the narrow end of the shank by cutting the meat one-third of the way down the bone.

3. In a large, heavy, enameled casserole over medium-high heat, heat 1 tablespoon of the olive oil. Dry 2 shanks and lightly dredge with flour. Cook the shanks in the oil until lightly browned on all sides. Remove to a plate. Repeat the brown-

Deborah Markow adds a bit of elegance to her braised meat dish by serving it in timbale molds.

Mama Balducci's
BRODETTO

Balducci's is a New York landmark: Tourists go to gawk at the exotic fruits and vegetables (and point out their prices), and New Yorkers seek out its high-quality food, unavailable in such abundance under almost any other roof. Earlier this century, when the high-end emporium was not much more than a vegetable stand, there was Mama Balducci. Her daughter, Nina Balducci, part of the continuing Balducci success story, offers this dish as one of her mother's best.

4 pounds baby lamb leg, boned, meat trimmed,
    and cut into chunks
1 large onion, chopped
6 plum tomatoes, chopped
3 tablespoons chopped fresh Italian (flat-leaf)
    parsley
2 large fresh basil leaves, chopped
1 tablespoon plus ½ teaspoon salt
2 teaspoons plus 1 large pinch freshly ground
    black pepper
½ cup dry white wine
2 pounds fresh peas, shelled
8 large eggs, beaten
⅔ cup freshly grated Parmesan cheese

■———————————■

   1. In a nonreactive, large, heavy pot, combine the lamb, onion, tomatoes, 2 tablespoons parsley, the basil, 1 tablespoon salt, 2 teaspoons pepper, the wine, and 1 cup water. Simmer, uncovered, over medium-low heat for 1 hour.

   2. Meanwhile, in a small saucepan, blanch the peas in ½ cup boiling water for 30 seconds. Remove from the heat, drain, and set aside to cool.

   3. In a bowl, beat together the eggs, cheese, the remaining 1 tablespoon parsley, ½ teaspoon salt, and pinch of pepper. Stir in the peas; set aside.

   4. Preheat the oven to 350°F.

   5. Place the lamb in a large casserole. Pour

Balducci's, where the merchandise is top quality and compelling.

the egg mixture over it. Bake until the custard is golden brown, 20 to 30 minutes.

   Serves 8

South African
BOBOTIE

Elizabeth Herz was born and raised in South Africa, where her mother cooked with local ingredients (including ostrich eggs). Chicken eggs work just fine, according to Elizabeth, who recommends serving this tender beef custard with chutney, rice, and chopped tomatoes.

2 thick slices country-style white bread, crusts
    removed
1 cup warm milk
2 tablespoons vegetable oil
1 large onion, chopped
2 tablespoons curry paste or powder
1 tablespoon ground coriander
2 pounds minced raw or cooked lamb
1 tablespoon apricot jam
1½ teaspoons salt
1 tablespoon distilled white vinegar
1 egg, whisked
¼ cup raisins
20 roasted whole almonds

CUSTARD
3 eggs
2 tablespoons grated lemon zest
½ teaspoon grated fresh ginger
2 cups milk
Sprinkle of freshly grated nutmeg

1. Preheat the oven to 350°F.

2. In a flat bowl, soak the bread in the warm milk.

3. In a nonreactive heavy skillet, heat the oil over medium heat. Add the onion and sauté until the onion is translucent, 5 minutes. Add the curry and coriander and cook until the spices no longer smell raw, 5 minutes more. Add the lamb and sauté, breaking up the lamb with a large spoon, until cooked or warmed through. Remove the skillet from the heat.

4. Using a slotted spoon, remove the bread from milk and gently squeeze out any excess milk. Add the bread, jam, salt, vinegar, egg, raisins, and almonds to the meat mixture and blend well. The consistency should be the same as for a meat loaf.

5. Oil a 3-quart baking dish or soufflé dish. Add the meat mixture and smooth the surface, gently pressing the mixture into place with your fingertips.

6. Make the custard: Beat the eggs, lemon zest, and ginger with the milk. Strain through a sieve onto the meat. Garnish with nutmeg. Bake until the custard is set, 30 to 45 minutes.

Serves 8 to 10

Elizabeth Herz brings to her New York kitchen the South African dishes she was raised on.

Malca Lothane's
COUSCOUS

Whether running restaurants or coffee shops, Malca Lothane has been one of the most verbose couscous proselytizers in the city. Her recipe shows her dedication to all things Moroccan. It takes some time to assemble, but it's worth it.

⅓ cup dried chick-peas, soaked overnight in water to cover
2 onions, cut into quarters
1 to 1½ pounds lamb shoulder, cut into 2-inch cubes
¼ teaspoon saffron threads or powder
⅛ teaspoon turmeric
2½ tablespoons butter
1 teaspoon salt
½ teaspoon freshly ground black pepper
¼ teaspoon ground cinnamon

GLAZED TOPPING
¼ cup raisins
4 onions, quartered and cut into ¼-inch slices
¼ teaspoon saffron threads
⅛ teaspoon turmeric
¼ teaspoon ground ginger
⅓ cup sugar
1½ tablespoons butter
1 teaspoon ground cinnamon
Salt and freshly ground black pepper, to taste

ASSEMBLY
3 carrots, halved lengthwise and cut into 2-inch pieces
2 small zucchini, halved lengthwise and cut into 2-inch pieces
2 tomatoes, peeled, seeded, and coarsely chopped
2 cups couscous
½ cup whole blanched almonds
Ground cinnamon, for dusting
2 tablespoons minced fresh parsley
2 tablespoons minced cilantro

1. Drain the chick-peas. Return to the pan and cover with fresh cold water. Cover and cook for 1 hour over medium heat. Drain, cool, and remove the skins by submerging the peas in a bowl of cold water and gently rubbing the peas between your fingers. Rinse the chick-peas and set aside.

2. Make the broth: In a large heavy pot, combine the onions, lamb, saffron, turmeric, butter, salt, pepper, cinnamon, and 6 cups water. Bring to a boil. Reduce the heat to medium-low and simmer until the meat is tender, 1 hour.

3. In a nonreactive saucepan, prepare the glaze: Remove 1 cup liquid from the simmering lamb broth. Add the raisins, onions, saffron, turmeric, ginger, sugar, butter, cinnamon, and salt and pepper. Cook, covered, for 1 hour.

4. Remove the cover and continue cooking over moderate heat until the liquid evaporates and the onions look glazed, about 30 minutes. Remove from the heat and set aside, uncovered.

5. Stir the chick-peas, carrots, zucchini, and tomatoes into the broth mixture. Simmer over medium heat for 30 minutes.

6. Meanwhile, prepare the couscous according to package directions.

7. Return the glaze mixture to the heat. Remove the couscous from the pot to a large serving dish and make a well in the center. Strain the meat and vegetables from the broth. Place the meat and vegetables in the couscous well. Cover with the onion glaze, sprinkle the almonds on top, and dust with the cinnamon. Pour enough of the remaining broth over the couscous to moisten. Sprinkle on the parsley and cilantro. Serve immediately.

Serves 5

Sharone's
CURRIED GOAT

Sharone Huey, a personal trainer at the Sports Training Institute, brought this recipe with her from Jamaica. It makes a soulful dish and, when served with a big bowl of boiled rice, easily feeds a crowd. If you can't find goat, lamb makes a delicious substitute.

2½ pounds boneless goat (or lamb) stewing meat, cut in 1½-inch cubes
1 teaspoon salt
½ teaspoon freshly ground black pepper
Dash of cayenne pepper
2 tablespoons curry powder
4 garlic cloves, crushed
4 scallions, trimmed and chopped
2 white onions, chopped
2 tablespoons butter
1 red bell pepper, stemmed, seeded, and minced
1 green bell pepper, stemmed, seeded, and minced
½ cup raisins
½ cup shredded unsweetened coconut
½ cup chopped peanuts

1. In a nonreactive bowl, season the goat meat with the salt, black pepper, cayenne, and 1 tablespoon of the curry powder. Add the garlic, scallions, and onions. Set aside to marinate at room temperature for at least 1 hour.

2. Melt the butter in a large cast-iron skillet over medium heat. Scrape the seasonings off the goat and reserve. Brown the goat, turning in the butter, for 5 minutes. Add the red and green bell peppers and sauté for 3 minutes more. Add 2 cups water and the reserved seasonings. Reduce the heat, cover the pan, and simmer for 40 minutes.

3. Stir in the remaining 1 tablespoon curry

powder, remove from the heat, cover, and set aside for 10 minutes.

4. Place the raisins, coconut, and peanuts in individual bowls. Serve as garnishes with the goat and rice.

Serves 4 to 6

Spice-Rubbed
MIXED GRILL

Architect turned interior designer Charles Morris Mount says his mixed grill was in the works "for about 20 years." Born in Alabama, Mount's father was a politician who often marinated chicken with dried spices overnight in the icebox, then grilled them for company. Mount, who lives on the Upper West Side, explains that "the dry rubbing technique is great. You can do it ahead of time, and it just gets better the longer it marinates. And when you cook it, it's self-basting."

SPICE RUB
½ cup packed dark brown sugar
2 tablespoons ground cumin
2 tablespoons chili powder
1 tablespoon ground cinnamon
1 tablespoon freshly grated nutmeg
1 tablespoon ground mace
½ teaspoon ground cloves
½ teaspoon cayenne pepper
½ tablespoon freshly ground black pepper,
* plus more to taste*

MIXED GRILL
1 pork loin (1½ pounds)
8 lamb rib chops (2 pounds)
8 boneless chicken breast halves
* (3 pounds)*
2 teaspoons salt, plus more to taste

1. Mix all of the spice rub ingredients together in a small bowl. Sprinkle the pork, lamb, and chicken with the 2 teaspoons salt, and then sprinkle all over with the spice rub. Transfer the meats and chicken to a large baking dish, cover, and refrigerate overnight.

2. Preheat the grill until hot. Grill the pork loin until a meat thermometer inserted into the center of the roast registers 150°F, 30 to 40 minutes. Grill the chicken breasts, turning once, until cooked through, about 12 minutes. Grill the lamb chops, turning once, for about 7 minutes for medium rare. Remove the meats and chicken from grill.

3. Cut the pork loin crosswise into ¼-inch-thick slices. Transfer a chicken breast half, a lamb chop, and 2 slices of pork loin to each dinner plate and serve.

Serves 8

At home with Charles Morris Mount.

Esposito's
HOMEMADE ITALIAN SAUSAGE WITH PEPPERS AND ONIONS

Sausage and pepper vendors are as common as traffic lights on midtown street corners and are fixtures at street fairs throughout the five boroughs. This version, from a cousin of the Esposito Pork Store family, is king of that circuit and easy to recreate.

2 pounds sweet or hot Italian sausage links

2 red bell peppers, stemmed, seeded, and cut lengthwise into ¼-inch strips

2 green bell peppers, stemmed, seeded, and cut lengthwise into ¼-inch strips

2 tablespoons olive oil (optional)

4 large Bermuda onions, thinly sliced

4 cloves garlic, coarsely chopped

Salt, to taste

Freshly ground black pepper, to taste

4 hero rolls, sliced lengthwise

1. Fry the sausage in a large skillet over medium-low heat with a few drops water added to prevent the sausage from sticking. As the water evaporates, continue to fry, turning frequently, until the sausage is golden brown, about 15 minutes. Drain on paper towels and keep warm. The sausage can also be barbecued on the grill for about 10 minutes over high heat.

2. Sauté the bell peppers in the sausage fat over medium heat until softened, 5 minutes. Add the olive oil, if needed. Add the onions and garlic, season with salt and pepper, and continue cooking until all of the vegetables are lightly browned, 10 to 15 minutes. Serve with the sausage on the rolls.

Serves 4

John and George, behind the counter at Esposito's in Brookyn.

June Bobb's
GARLIC PORK

Advises Mrs. Bobb, who lives and cooks this delicious dish in Brooklyn, "Be sure to close all your closet doors or your clothes will reek of the wonderful aroma of garlic pork for days. In Guyanese households garlic pork is served with generous slices of homemade bread."

2 cups cider vinegar

6 thick, center-cut pork chops, boned and excess fat removed, each cut into 4 pieces

15 large cloves garlic

10 wiri-wiri chiles (or other small hot red chiles; if they are more than the size of a dime in circumference, use only 5)

¼ cup plus 1 tablespoon dried thyme

Salt, to taste

6 whole cloves

2 tablespoons vegetable oil

1. In a nonreactive medium bowl, mix the vinegar with 2 cups water. Add the pork and mix with a fork so that each piece of pork gets washed in the mixture. With fork or tongs, transfer the pork to a plastic storage container with a tight-fitting lid. Reserve the vinegar mixture.

2. In a blender or food processor, grind together the garlic, chiles, and thyme. Add 1 cup of the vinegar mixture and process for a few seconds. Pour the mixture over the pork and add enough of the remaining vinegar mixture to cover the pork completely. Add the salt and cloves, stir thoroughly, and cover the container tightly with a lid. Refrigerate for 4 days.

3. Heat the oil in a large heavy skillet over medium heat. Remove the pork from the marinade and pat dry with paper towels. Reserve the marinade. Brown the pork in batches in the skillet, about 3 minutes per side. Set each batch aside while browning the remaining pork.

4. Pour ¼ cup marinade (pick out any cloves) into the skillet and reduce by half over high heat, 1 to 2 minutes. Return all the pork to the skillet, stir so the pieces absorb the marinade, and remove from the heat. Serve hot.

Serves 3

David Poisal's
ROAST PORK WITH CORN

Creamed corn lacks sophistication says David Poisal, a maître d' at Claire Restaurant in the Chelsea neighborhood of Manhattan, but it gives panache to this hearty pork roast.

1 pork loin roast (boned and tied), 4 pounds
3 cloves garlic, cut into slivers
3 tablespoons Dijon mustard
Salt and freshly ground black pepper, to taste
2 cups cream-style corn
1 green bell pepper, stemmed, seeded, and diced
1 onion, diced

1. Cut evenly spaced slits in the roast with a small knife and insert the slivers of garlic. Rub the roast with the mustard. Season well with salt and pepper. Cover and let the roast rest at room temperature for 1 hour.

2. Preheat the oven to 350°F.

3. Place the roast in a heavy casserole. Add the corn, bell pepper, and onion. Sprinkle with salt and pepper. Cover the casserole and roast, stirring occasionally, for 1¾ hours. Remove the

cover and continue roasting until the internal temperature of the meat registers 170°F, about 45 minutes.

Serves 6

Staten Island
ROAST PORK

Staten Island resident Frances Kovar uses lots of garlic to perfume her pork roast. The mustard slowly develops a tasty crust over the meat and becomes a deliciously tart contrast to the sweet pork.

1 boneless pork loin roast (2 to 2½ pounds)
½ teaspoon salt
¾ teaspoon dried oregano
¾ teaspoon dried thyme
¼ teaspoon freshly ground black pepper
3 cloves garlic, cut into slivers
2 tablespoons Dijon mustard
1 tablespoon vegetable oil

1. Preheat the oven to 325°F.

2. Cut small slits in the roast. Mix together the salt, oregano, thyme, and pepper. Add the slivered garlic and coat them with the spices. Insert the garlic slivers into the slits in the roast. Rub any remaining spice mixture over the surface of the meat.

3. Combine the mustard and oil. Brush half of the mixture over the meat. Place the meat on a rack in a roasting pan. Insert a meat thermometer and roast, uncovered, for 1 hour.

4. Brush the remaining mustard mixture over the roast. Roast until the thermometer reaches 170°F, 1 hour more.

Serves 4

FESTIVALS

Street fairs, block parties and church suppers are pageants that mark the bends and turns of the seasons in New York City, times when the small towns inside the city bloom.

Some festivals mean hand-lettered signs and home-baked brownies. Others are big business. The city averages twelve hundred street celebrations a year. All are a blend of church and community and petty profiteering that turns residential blocks into carnivals. Some are worthy eating adventures—most

often, when the season dwindles toward winter and they move indoors to church basements and school gyms.

Elsewhere, seasonal celebrations have aromas. A spring festival in the Pacific Northwest, for instance, smells of cherry blossoms and asparagus. Summer progresses from sweet peas to roses and peaches in the Southern Atlantic states and ends in a blast of basil and mint. The bittersweet smell of apples and grapes at a harvest dinner presages smoke from New England chimneys. In New York we have the smell of fried dough to gauge the progress of the year.

The first whiffs from a block party in early spring have filled me with the promise of a kid on the way to the fair. I've danced for Polish "Chrusciki," at the **Ukrainian festival** on the Lower East Side in May and later, stood in line—with open heart and open wallet—for a similar version at the **Czechoslovakian festival** in Astoria.

Oddly, the delicacy begins to lose its ethnic allure when the

Making a food choice can be tough at Our Lady of Pompei Church's Festa Italiana on Carmine Street in Greenwich Village.

UKRAINIAN FESTIVAL 7th Street between Second and Third Avenues, Manhattan. Third weekend in May: Friday 6 P.M. to 9 P.M., Saturday 10 A.M. to 10 P.M., Sunday 1 P.M. to dusk. Marks conversion of the Ukrainian nation to Christianity. Food includes "the three staples": pierogis, stuffed cabbage (see recipe, page 294), and borscht (see recipe, page 60). Also, crafts and folk dancing. Sponsored by St. George's Ukrainian Catholic Church, 33 East 7th Street, (212) 674-1615.

NINTH AVENUE FAIR Ninth Avenue, between 37th and 57th Streets, Manhattan. A mid-May weekend. Eat the world in 20 blocks; international cuisine. Highlights include Italian, Greek (recipe for Greek Stuffed Quail, page 358), and Thai (recipe for Pad Thai, page 247).

CZECHOSLOVAKIAN FESTIVAL Bohemian Hall, 29-19 24th Avenue, Astoria, Queens. Their number-one, best-selling food item is roast duck with caraway seeds. They also feature roast loin of pork, kielbasa, and other Czech and Slovak specialties. Organized by the Bohemian Hall, (718) 274-4925; call for information.

ST. ANTHONY'S FEAST Sullivan Street at West Houston, Manhattan. Usually held the second weekend of June. The feast lasts 10 days and celebrates the patron saint of St. Anthony's Church at 154 Sullivan Street. It is much like San Gennaro, with its Italian prominence, but is smaller in size and frenzy. For more information, contact St. Anthony's Church at (212) 777-2755.

LOWER EAST SIDE JEWISH FESTIVAL East Broadway between Clinton and Essex Streets, Manhattan. Sunday in June, 11 A.M. to 6 P.M. This festival features all-kosher food, including falafel and calzones. Organized by Fred Siegel at Educational Alliance, Inc. (212) 475-6200.

PHILIPPINE INDEPENDENCE STREET FAIR 45th Street between Madison Avenue and Avenue of the Americas, Manhattan. Nearest Sunday between June 12 and June 16, noon to 8 P.M. Singing, dancing, Philippine specialties include barbecued pork, and *pancit* (dish of noodles and chicken; for recipe, see page 246). Organized by Mrs. Nilda Jaynal, chairperson, Philippine Independence Day Committee, (914) 592-8607.

FEAST OF MT. CARMEL Italian East Harlem, Pleasant Avenue and 115th Street, Manhattan. July 11 to 15, 8 to 11 P.M.

Father Peter describes his church's feast as "a meeting of the League of Nations." Twelve different countries are represented at the parish, and one could work down the Isthmus of Panama with churchgoers from Mexico, Ecuador, Peru, and so on.

SEVENTH AVENUE STREET FAIR Seventh Avenue between Prospect Avenue and Ninth Streets, Windsor Terrace, Brooklyn. July 27, 9 A.M. to 9 P.M.

OUR LADY OF MT. CARMEL FEAST East 187th Street, between Cambreleng and Arthur Avenues, the Bronx's Little Italy. July 18th to 28th, 6 to 11 P.M. Italian food, such as sausage and peppers (see recipe, page 307) and cheesesteak, rides and games. Organized by Our Lady of Mt. Carmel Church, 627 East 187th Street; (212) 295-3770.

OUR LADY OF POMPEII FEAST Carmine and Bleecker Streets between Seventh Avenue and Avenue of the Americas, Manhattan. Starts on a Thursday and runs 11 days in July, 11 A.M. to 11:30 P.M. Rides, games, Italian food like zeppoles, sausage, and peppers. Organized by Our Lady of Pompeii Church, 25 Carmine Street; (212) 989-6805.

FIESTA DE SANTIAGO APOSTLE Church of Our Lady of Guadalupe, 229 West 14th Street, between Seventh Avenue and Ninth Avenue, Manhattan; (212) 243-5317. For four days at the end of July, Our Lady of Guadalupe celebrates Spain's patron saint, St. James the Apostle.

QUEENS IRISH STREET FAIR Old Rockaway Beach Boulevard, Far Rockaway, Queens. July 27 and 28, 10 A.M. to 8 P.M.

HARLEM WEEK Daily hours vary, as do locations, but activity can often be found at 139th Street between Lenox and Fifth Avenues and 125th Street, between Adam Clayton Powell Jr. Boulevard and Fifth Avenue, Manhattan. First Monday of August through the third Sunday of August, culminating with Harlem Day on the last day of the festival. Harlem Week is really Harlem Two Weeks, but why quibble? It's a celebration of Harlem's ethnic diversity, with music, lectures, and a smorgasbord of culinary delights. Sponsored by the Uptown Chamber of Commerce, (212) 427-7200. Call for information and schedules.

One of the many chef-vendors at Little Italy's popular San Gennaro feast.

smells drifts from the Ninth Avenue Fair and into my kitchen windows. "Funnel cake?" I sniff. "Venetian Galani?" It's all fried dough.

This creeping sense that the distinct seasons and disparate cultures in New York have ended up in one big corporate Fry-O-Lator deepens into the face of *oreillettes* at **Bastille Day** on Little West 12th Street or, later that month, *buñuelos,* at the **Fiesta de Santiago**. By August, a greasy blast from any street fair can epitomize the sodden and the sordid, broken promises, picked pockets, gained pounds, lost parking spaces.

And then I smell zeppole in late September. The Italian version of the same fried dough rises, thick as the mother-of-all smog, from the **Feast of San Gennaro** and I swoon. I react to the aroma of fried dough carried by a fall breeze like others respond to the autumnal smell of crushed grapes. A simultaneous ending and beginning has a certain allure.

I can't stay away from San Gennaro. It is the autumn equinox on the solar calendar of New York City street fairs. It is the end of fried dough season. It is the beginning of the falafel, Caribbean curried goat, German bratwurst, and Indian saté smells from less-traveled street fairs; it is the harbinger of the scent of Southern fried chicken and greens, chicken paprikás, braised Norwegian lamb rib, and Swedish cakes that begins to pull people into church suppers around the city.

Like witches around a cauldron, New Yorkers dance a denial of the annual ritual. At San Gennaro, the jungle of festooned fire escapes, streets draped with glitter and lights and bawdy neon defies the fading leaves on the trees along Mulberry Street. The hawkers, the concertina music, the carnival-like, rock-concert frenzy of the crowd all seem determined to push away the impending quiet of cool weather and closed windows.

But like summer taunting an inevitable fall, a neighborhood politician sits perched above a tank of water, daring the pitches of his competitors and constituents, at 50 cents a throw.

A week later, any lingering eau de dough is banished by the smell of spitted lamb, turning slowly over charcoal along Atlantic Avenue at its annual bazaar. Early in October, the perfume from dozens of varieties of apples, made into sauce and butters, pies and crisps, at the **Big Apple Festival,** send up an irreversible signal: fall.

Then comes the pungent smell of bratwurst and sauerkraut at the **Glendale-Myrtle Avenue Oktoberfest.** The scent of burned sparklers and firecrackers mingle with ginger and soy on the streets of Chinatown on **Ten-Ten Day,** when the establishment of the Chinese Republic is still (unofficially) celebrated (it's an off-beat, festive day for dim sum or a banquet). Soon the spicy Indian aromas arise from the **Festival of Lights.** Finally, the

FEAST OF ST. ANTHONY Villa Avenue and Van Cortland Avenue, between 204th and 205th Streets, Bedford Park, the Bronx. August 7th to 18th, 3 to 11:30 P.M.

ST. STEPHEN'S DAY St. Stephen of Hungary

Catholic Church, 414 East 82nd, between York and First Avenues, Manhattan. Celebrated on the Sunday closest to August 20. A Hungarian religious feast. Festive holiday dishes may include chicken paprikás (see recipe, page 346) and poppy seed tea cake.

Mass starts at 10:15. Food and music from 1:00 on. For information, contact St. Stephen of Hungary, (212) 861-8500.

FESTA OF ST. ROSALIA Arthur Avenue from 67th Street to 75th Street, Brooklyn. August 30 to September 5. Sponsored by St. Rosalia's Society.

QUEENS ETHNIC FOLK FESTIVAL Held at the Bohemian Hall, 29-19 24th Avenue, Astoria, Queens; (718) 264-4925. First Saturday of September. This festival features music and dance with 9 or 10 ethnic groups performing every year. Since ethnic con-

centration changes every year, it's difficult to predict what one might expect; in recent years they've had a variety of Middle Eastern foods such as falafel (see recipe, page 10) and shish kebabs. Organized by the Ethnic Folk Art Center in Manhattan, (212) 691-9510.

THE GREAT IRISH FAIR Coney Island, Brooklyn. Second weekend of September. Features bands, food, Irish sports like hurling. Organized by the Ancient Order of Hibernians.

Serving up specialties at the Harlem festival, held in August during Harlem Week (left). Street decorations help set the festive tone at the San Gennaro feast (right).

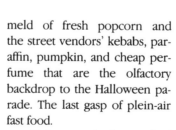

meld of fresh popcorn and the street vendors' kebabs, paraffin, pumpkin, and cheap perfume that are the olfactory backdrop to the Halloween parade. The last gasp of plein-air fast food.

Within a week, slow-cooked suppers in the basements of churches and other community organizations have taken their place. As Kate Simon notes in *New York Places and Pleasures:* "New

York is as great a fiesta town as Oaxaca or Naples; our fiestas are less well-advertised and harder to find, especially through the cold half of the year, when they stay hidden."

Though they often serve some of the homiest ethnic and all-American cooking in the city, church suppers are ad-hoc events. Call ahead. Some charge nominal fees ($5 to $10); most expect that guests will attend

church service and contribute a covered dish to the meals that follow.

I usually begin the season in Harlem, with Southern country-style dinners, move to Brooklyn's Caribbean communities for Thanksgiving, and head for the Hungarian church in Yorkville when the frost sets in.

Shortly after the Christmas tree is lit at Rockefeller Center, The Swedish Seaman's Church down the block serves the traditional, sweet spicy saffrons brod along with buttery cookies and cakes and coffee in its reading room. Sitting to nibble and sip and peruse books on Scandinavian saints, surrounded by whispered Swedish, with snow drifting by the lead-paned windows of the town house, is quin-

tessential small-town winter.

Later in the month, The Norwegian Seaman's Church serves an old-world Christmas dinner. It was a cozy world last year, a dinner of perhaps 70 people, watching each other as if to gauge just how much of Norway and their shared past will survive New York and their disparate presents.

I thought ahead; one does at a feast that marks time. I thought about the Blessing of the Waters at St. Nicholas Greek Orthodox Church in the middle of January, and the lemony chicken soup that is sometimes served to revive the young men after their ceremonial plunge into the Hudson River. I thought about Chinese New Year in February, Greek Easter in Astoria, the smell of *shmura,*

the Orthodox matzoh, that perfumes some streets in Crown Heights around Passover.

The Scandinavian cookie platter was a jolt. There, among the sweet butter cookies were delicate curls of fried dough, sprinkled with powdered sugar. They smelled sweet and full of spring, like a pot of paper whites blooming in midwinter.

Funnel cakes, another popular street fair offering (above left). Ethnic foods help draw New Yorkers to a street fair along Manhattan's Park Avenue (above).

S·T·R·E·E·T F·A·I·R·S

ONE WORLD FESTIVAL 35th Street, between First and Second Avenues, Manhattan. Second week of September. Starts at noon or 1 P.M., lasts all afternoon. Tons of ethnic stuff is featured: food, jewelry, clothes, music, dancing. Organized by the New York Armenian community and Armenian Cathedral of St. Vartan on Second Avenue at 34th to 35th Streets.

SAN GENNARO Mulberry Street from Worth to East Houston Streets, Manhattan. Ten days in September, always scheduled so September 19th (the saint's day) falls during the festival. New York's most popular feast celebrates the Bishop of Benevento, San Gennaro, the patron saint of Naples. There are rides, games, foods. Religious service at Most Precious Blood Church, 113 Baxter Street, on September 19th at 6 P.M. For more information, call the San Gennaro Festival, (212) 226-9546.

ATLANTIC ANTIC Atlantic Avenue, from Flatbush Avenue to the East River, Brooklyn. Last Sunday in September, 10 A.M. to 5 P.M. Since 1974, the Atlantic Antic has been delighting lovers of Middle Eastern food, music, and culture. It features all kinds of Middle Eastern food, including baba ganoush and falafel. Organized by the Atlantic Avenue Association Local Development Corporation, (718) 875-8993.

ST. LUCIA DAY New York's Swedish community rents a hall (usually the Salvation Army Hall on 14th Street) to celebrate the Scandinavian Festival of Lights, December 13. St. Lucia was from Sicily and she wore candles in her hair—hence the lights. The celebration is the unofficial start of the Christmas season. Expect to sing Christmas carols and partake in a celebration. Saffron brod (see recipe, page 108), gingerbread, and coffee are traditional treats eaten on St. Lucia Day. For information, stop by The Swedish Seaman's Church, 5 East 48th Street in early December—their newsletter will explain the upcoming festivities—or call them, (212) 832-8443.

St. James the Apostle is featured at the Fiesta de Santiago Apostle (left); traditional dances are performed during the Ukrainian Festival (above); and food, of course, plays a major part in both (right).

The Birds

To Roast A
FINE BIRD

Buffalo is a wing town. Houston is a leg town. Boston favors breasts. There is an odd congruency between the nature of a given city and its preference in chicken. It comes as no surprise that New York City wants the whole bird.

Anyone who has seen chickens strung like outsized pearls on the rotisserie at a Greek coffee shop, seen the racks of soy-roasted ducks and chickens that hang in Chinatown shop windows, or watched a 4-star chef tenderly trussing a poulet has probably surmised that New York is a whole bird kind of town. The casual browser, however, may not be aware of the divergent philosophies that New Yorkers have about choosing and roasting a bird.

There are chefs who redden with rage at the very mention of the words "free range," others who appear close to apoplexy in the presence of anything other

Savor the chicken escabèche (page 339) from the late chef Felipe Rojas-Lombardi, seen here at The Ballroom. Photo: Harold Naideau

than a kosher bird. Like artists defending their canvases, they champion their choice in chicken. As if they were applying the final strokes to the Mona Lisa, they brush their chicken with seasoning and marinades to create masterpieces that are unveiled in the citadels of chic and tiny storefronts, on pushcarts—and on family dinner tables. Chicken zeal is not confined to the professional kitchen in New York.

POULTRY VALUES

This is a town of firm, though wildly varied chicken principles. Roast chicken, in particular, is a very serious subject. Devotees share a vision of the perfect roast bird: tender, well-perfumed meat under a crackle of skin. But the path to perfection is pitted with deep philosophical discord.

French chefs, like André Soltner, who owns the restaurant Lutèce, tend to espouse the "poussin" point of view. The poussin, a young chicken that weighs about 20 ounces and costs at least that many cents a pound more than most specialty-farmed birds, has a delicate and faintly gamey taste. It is logical, therefore, that Mr. Soltner would wince when the words "garlic," "rosemary," or "chile pepper" are so much as whispered in the vicinity of one of his little chickens. "So overwhelming," he says, pity for the poussin rising in his throat.

American chefs like David Liederman don't suffer such empathy. Mr. Liederman, the restaurant and cookie impresario, takes a kosher chicken stance and maintains that kosher chicken, which is salted and washed

three times by law, absorbs a trace of salt that boosts that bird's flavor. In addition, he seeks only 2½- to 2¾-pound chickens, which are older and generally more flavorful than lesser weight, younger birds. He marinates his kosher chickens in a heady herbaceous mélange and says, "The longer they marinate, the better they taste."

Mr. Liederman's taste parallels current chicken fashion in New York. In the late '80s, when the American Institute for Wine and Food held a testing of four chickens—kosher, Perdue, Bell & Evans, and a free range—56 out of 64 tasters rated the kosher chicken number one. Bell & Evans and Perdue split second place. Nevertheless, many restaurant chefs swear by their pricey, range-fed chicken, which, like the kosher model, is generally lean and has firm, full-flavored flesh. Yet both free range and kosher chickens cost up to three times more a pound than generic supermarket chicken and some people get "cook's block" when faced with such precious fowl. Awe of the bird, they say, can throttle their creativity.

This might explain why the strength of seasoning and the duration of marination both tend to increase as the price of chicken decreases in New York City.

THE BIRD
AS A BLANK CANVAS

In Chinatown—where chicken can be had for about one-quarter the price of chicken at Lutèce—fresh, medium-priced chickens that are relatively fatty and weigh close

to three pounds are marinated in a pungent blend of soy, ginger, and Chinese five-spice powder. Mohammad Rouzi, who has sold Afghan-spiced chicken from a pushcart in Midtown, uses "the cheapest chicken around," which generally means that the chicken has a mild, undistinguished taste and is, for the cook, a neutral canvas. This allows, even necessitates, that Mr. Rouzi slap tomato, onion, garlic, and ground coriander on his chicken in a Jackson Pollock-like fashion.

Facing similar chickens, cooks in the tiny Indian restaurants in Jackson Heights, Queens, choose yogurt and vinegar, garlic, ginger, and spices as their medium.

While their selection and seasoning philosophies vary, the local chicken cognoscenti almost agree about the actual roasting. They believe that a very hot oven and frequent basting are the key to a crisp skin and that the roasted bird should rest, lightly covered, at room temperature before carving. Most are perplexed by Mr. Soltner's tenderizing rite: When the chicken thigh registers 158° to 160°F on a meat thermometer, he drops a teaspoon of water in the roasting pan, closes the

Chef André Soltner of Lutèce.

oven door, turns off the heat, and waits three minutes before removing the bird. "For a soft breast," he explained.

The idea of creating a mini-steam room in the oven sends terror through the hearts of those who worship crisp chicken skin. Even so, most maintain an appreciative, though arm's length tolerance of divergent roasting behavior. People, after all, don't choose their preference in chicken preparation. They are born to a certain roasted chicken: their mother's. To malign another person's chicken is to malign his past. "I can only roast chicken the way I roast chicken," Mr. Soltner says softly.

André Soltner's
ROAST CHICKEN

4 fresh thyme sprigs
5 fresh tarragon sprigs
4 parsley sprigs
2 small onions
2 poussins or small chickens (1 pound each), well
    rinsed and patted dry
2 teaspoons peanut oil
1 teaspoon salt
½ teaspoon freshly ground black pepper
¼ cup dry white wine
¼ cup chicken broth
2 tablespoons minced Italian (flat-leaf) parsley
1 tablespoon butter

1. Place 2 of the thyme sprigs, 2 of the tarragon sprigs, 2 of the parsley sprigs, and 1 onion inside each poussin cavity. Truss the birds. Remove the leaves from the remaining sprig of tarragon and set aside.

2. Preheat the oven to 450°F.

3. On the stove, heat a roasting pan over high heat. Add the peanut oil and brown the poussins on all sides. Sprinkle with salt and pepper and place the pan in the oven. Roast, basting frequently with the pan juices, until a chicken leg registers 155° to 160°F on an instant-reading thermometer, 20 to 25 minutes. Carefully remove the poussins to a serving platter and keep warm.

4. Drain the fat from the roasting pan. Place the pan over medium heat, add the wine, and using a wooden spoon, scrape the pan well. Add the chicken broth, the reserved tarragon leaves, and minced parsley. Simmer for 2 minutes. Remove from the heat and whisk in the butter. Pour the sauce over the poussins and serve immediately.

Serves 2

"We broil them, we roast them, we boil them, we fry them . . . . Heaven knows what we don't do to them. But it doesn't matter. In the very simplicity of the food and its treatment is our right to acclaim ourselves a nation of good eaters."

—OSCAR TSCHIRKY, LEGENDARY MAÎTRE D' OF THE RITZ

TO BUY A GOOD BIRD

Chicken

In New York, Bell & Evans Chicken and Empire Kosher Chicken are superior commercial brands that are widely available. In addition, a handful of local butchers offer top-quality fresh chickens.

BAYARD STREET MEAT MARKET: 57 Bayard Street, near Elizabeth Street; (212) 619-6206.

BALDUCCI'S: 424 Sixth Avenue, between 9th and 10th Streets; (212) 673-2600.

BOBO POULTRY: 287 Broome Street, between Eldridge and Allen Streets; (212) 274-0130.

NEVADA MEAT MARKET: 2012 Broadway, between 68th and 69th Streets; (212) 362-0443.

UNION SQUARE GREENMARKET: At Union Square on Wednesdays, Fridays, and Saturdays all day from 8 A.M. on (get there by noon, the chickens go fast).

WAH CHONG LIVE MEAT MARKET: 248 Bowery at Stanton Street; (212) 226-0968.

Game Birds

During the fall and winter, a wide variety of fresh game birds—squab, guinea hen, quail, and mallard duck—are available in the city. In addition to top-quality chicken and duck, these butchers have the largest selection and highest quality of game birds.

AKRON PRIME MEATS: 1174 Lexington Avenue, near 80th Street; (212) 744-1551.

FITZ & SONS: 944 First Avenue, near 52nd Street; (212) 753-3465.

JEFFERSON MARKET: 455 Sixth Avenue, between 10th and 11th Streets; (212) 675-2277.

IRON GATE PRODUCTS: 424 West 54th Street, between Ninth and Tenth Avenues; (212) 757-2670. This wholesale company sells game birds, foie gras, and caviar on a limited scale to the public. Call ahead.

OTTOMANELLI'S MEAT MARKET: 285 Bleecker Street, near Seventh Avenue; (212) 675-4217.

RAOUL'S BUTCHER SHOP: 179 Prince Street, between Sullivan and Thompson Streets; (212) 674-0708.

THE IRON GAT

PURVEYORS: SEAFOOD·GAME·

Adolfo's
CUBAN ROAST CHICKEN

Fashion designer Adolfo prepares this hearty, family recipe for company dinners.

¾ cup raisins
1 cup boiling water
3 sweet or hot Italian sausages
3½ cups firm, cooked, short-grain white rice
¾ cup pine nuts, toasted
½ cup pimiento-stuffed green olives, halved
*½ cup pitted spicy green olives, sliced, or ½ cup
    chopped olives*
Salt and freshly ground black pepper, to taste
1 tablespoon olive oil
*1 roasting chicken (4½ to 5 pounds), well rinsed
    and patted dry*
2 tablespoons butter
1 teaspoon paprika
*1 cup New York Penicillin (page 47) or canned
    chicken broth*
½ cup medium-dry sherry

1. Preheat the oven to 425°F. Place the raisins in a small bowl and cover with the boiling water. Set aside until cool, about 20 minutes. Drain and place the raisins in a large bowl.

2. In a skillet over medium-low heat, cook the sausages until lightly browned. Remove from the heat and allow to cool, about 20 minutes. Slice into 1-inch rounds. Add to the bowl with the raisins.

3. Stir the rice, pine nuts, both kinds of olives, salt, and pepper into the raisin-sausage mixture. Moisten with the olive oil; stir to mix well. Stuff the chicken loosely with the stuffing; reserve any that does not fit. Truss, then rub the chicken with the butter; sprinkle with the paprika and more black pepper. Roast the chicken for 10 minutes.

4. Add the chicken broth and sherry to the pan, along with the reserved leftover stuffing. Re-

duce the oven temperature to 350°F and roast, basting occasionally, until the juices run clear when the thigh is pricked, about 40 minutes more. Allow the chicken to rest for 10 minutes before carving.

Serves 4

Canal Street
OVEN-ROASTED CHICKEN

The Asian seasonings give a subtle, addictive perfume to this simple roast chicken.

⅓ cup light soy sauce
¼ cup peanut oil
1 tablespoon Oriental sesame oil
1 tablespoon dry sherry
1 clove garlic, crushed
½ teaspoon salt
½ teaspoon finely grated fresh ginger
2 teaspoons five-spice powder
*1 chicken (2½ to 3 pounds), well rinsed and
    patted dry*

Canal Street is the northern border of New York's Chinatown.

1. In a shallow dish large enough to hold the chicken, mix the soy sauce, peanut and sesame oils, and the sherry. Add the garlic, salt, ginger, and five-spice powder. Mix well. Rub the chicken inside and out with the mixture. Cover and marinate in the refrigerator for at least 2 and up to 12 hours. Baste frequently with the marinade.

2. Preheat the oven to 400°F.

3. Transfer the chicken to a roasting pan. Strain the marinade through a sieve; discard the solids and spoon the liquid over the chicken. Roast the chicken, basting frequently, until the juices run clear when the thigh is pricked, 45 to 50 minutes. Allow the chicken to rest for 10 minutes before carving.

Serves 2

A Chinatown shop window often includes an intriguing poultry display.

Chinatown
SOY SAUCE CHICKEN

Once a staple of Chinatown, soy sauce chicken has been eclipsed in recent years by salt-baked birds. But the dish is still a satisfying one, especially served with fried rice and a quick cucumber salad.

1 star anise
¾ cup soy sauce
⅓ cup packed dark brown sugar
¼ cup dry sherry
1 tablespoon honey
3 cloves garlic, minced
3 slices fresh ginger, smashed
1 chicken (3½ to 4 pounds), well rinsed and
*   patted dry*

1. In a nonreactive pot large enough to hold the chicken snugly, gently boil 1 cup water and the star anise, covered, for 20 minutes.

2. In a small bowl, mix the soy sauce, brown sugar, sherry, honey, garlic, and ginger, and add the mixture to the pot. Cover and bring to a boil; then reduce the heat to a simmer and cook for 5 minutes. Add the chicken, laying it on its side, and bring the liquid back to a boil. Cover and turn the heat to low. Simmer, basting frequently, for 15 minutes.

3. Turn the chicken to the other side and simmer, basting frequently, for another 15 minutes.

4. Turn once more, this time breast side up, and cook until golden brown, 15 minutes more. Remove the chicken and let cool to room temperature. Reheat the cooking liquid and spoon out about 2 tablespoons onto each plate before serving the carved chicken.

Serves 4

Homemade
TANDOORI CHICKEN

Kaneez Fatima rocked Muslim tradition when she took over the beehive-shaped tandoor oven at Shaheen Palace in Queens several years ago. The clay ovens, which fire-up to 800°F, have traditionally been the domain of men; in addition, *purdah,* an ancient Muslim custom, bars women from public activity. Nevertheless, as a child in Pakistan, Kaneez Fatima began fashioning breads for tandoori cooking and progressed to marinated vegetables and meats. Today she is a master of the flash-cooking method and she views this expertise as a birthright. "Tandoor, to us, is like a plow to a farmer," she says. "It's our life and soul." This chicken can be roasted in a home oven or grilled over charcoal.

1 chicken (3½ to 4 pounds), skinned,
    well rinsed, patted dry, and
    quartered
1 teaspoon salt
1 cup plain yogurt
1 tablespoon fresh lemon juice
1 tablespoon distilled white vinegar
2 cloves garlic, pounded to a paste
2 teaspoons minced fresh ginger
1½ teaspoons garam masala
    (recipe follows) or tandoori
    seasoning
¼ cup olive oil

1. Using a sharp knife, slash the chicken pieces diagonally along the grain, cutting about ½ inch deep and about ¼ inch apart. Rub the slashes with the salt and set the chicken in a ceramic bowl. In a small bowl, combine the yogurt, lemon juice, vinegar, garlic paste, minced ginger, and garam masala and pour over the chicken. Cover with plastic wrap and marinate in the refrigerator overnight, turning once.

2. One hour before serving, remove the chicken from the refrigerator and preheat the oven to 500°F. It has got to be very, very hot. If using a charcoal grill, light the coals.

3. Remove the chicken from the marinade and drizzle each piece with olive oil. Roast until the juices run clear when a thigh is pricked, 35 to 40 minutes. If grilling, cook, turning the chicken four to five times, until the juices run clear, about 30 minutes.

Serves 2

GARAM MASALA

G aram masala is a blend of Indian spices that is available in many specialty stores. It can be made easily at home.

1½ teaspoons ground coriander seeds
1½ teaspoons ground cardamom
1½ teaspoons ground black pepper
¼ teaspoon ground cloves
½ teaspoon ground bay leaf

Combine the spices thoroughly in a small bowl. Store in a clean glass jar away from the heat.
Scant 2 tablespoons

Igor's ROSEMARY CHICKEN

A rchitect Igor Jozsa compares the art of cooking to painting and architecture. "They are very similar. You have a cultural or historical background and an idea of what you want to achieve; so with an inspiration, you change the elements, working with what's available, until you get what you want." Jozsa lived in Tuscany for several years and says the technique for Rosemary Chicken is typical of the region. "In Tuscany, they cook a similar recipe using a traditional flat ceramic plate with a very heavy cover that presses the meat against the platter. We can use a heavy cast-iron skillet, and as a weight, we can use a slightly smaller cast-iron skillet."

Igor Jozsa suggests weighting down the chicken to achieve crispiness.

6 cloves garlic, crushed
2 tablespoons fresh or dried rosemary
Juice of 4 limes (about ½ cup)
½ cup olive oil
½ teaspoon salt
¼ teaspoon freshly ground black pepper
1 chicken (3½ to 4 pounds), well rinsed, patted
    dry, and quartered
4 rosemary sprigs, for garnish
1 lime, quartered, for garnish

1. In a bowl, combine the garlic, rosemary, lime juice, olive oil, salt, and pepper. Place the quartered chicken in the bowl, turn to coat the pieces, cover with plastic wrap, and marinate in the refrigerator for 3 hours. Turn the chicken quarters once during the marinating time.

2. Heat a cast-iron skillet to hot. Add the chicken pieces and weigh them down with a heavy lid or another cast-iron skillet. Cook until crispy, 15 minutes on each side.

3. Serve the chicken, garnished with a sprig of rosemary and a wedge of lime.

Serves 4

Lillian Hellman's
MASHED POTATO AND SCALLION DRESSING

The late author and playwright used this dressing to stuff her holiday goose—it makes an irresistible sponge, absorbing the fat while the bird roasts.

6 large potatoes, peeled
3 tablespoons butter
1 tablespoon heavy (whipping) cream
1 tablespoon salt
1½ teaspoons freshly ground black pepper
1 bunch scallions, trimmed, white and green
    parts chopped

Boil the potatoes in cold water to cover until they are soft, 30 minutes. Put the potatoes through a potato ricer or mash them. Add the butter, cream, salt, and pepper and mix well. Stir in the scallions.

4 cups, enough to stuff a 9- to 10-pound turkey

WHERE'S THE BIRD?

New York's master stuffers know that everyone has their favored method for roasting a bird in order to get a crisp skin and tender flesh, but not everyone has a great stuffing. So they offer these formulas for filling everything from squab to capon, pheasant, and, of course, turkey.

To make Sarah Shankman's dressing, use the recipe for her corn bread (see below).

Thanksgiving CORN BREAD DRESSING

S ays Sarah Shankman, who grew up south of the Mason-Dixon line but now cooks and writes mysteries in Greenwich Village, "In the South, that which fills a Thanksgiving turkey is called dressing rather than stuffing. This dressing may be used inside a bird, baking the remainder separately. Best, however, is to serve the dressing as a side dish with a roasted chicken."

*½ pound sweet Italian sausage, preferably with
    fennel
Vegetable oil or butter, if needed
½ cup finely chopped green bell pepper
½ cup finely chopped celery
½ cup finely chopped scallions
1 small yellow onion, finely chopped
Sarah Shankman's Corn Bread (page 107), baked
    and cooled
1 teaspoon powdered sage
⅛ teaspoon cayenne pepper, or more to taste
½ teaspoon freshly ground black pepper
2 hard-cooked eggs, coarsely chopped
2 raw eggs
1¼ cups New York Penicillin (page 47) or canned
    chicken broth*

1. Preheat the oven to 350°F. Lightly oil an 8-inch-square baking pan.

2. Remove and discard the casing from the sausage. Crumble and sauté in a cast-iron skillet over medium heat until cooked through, about 5 minutes. Remove the sausage with a slotted spoon, leaving the drippings in the pan. Add up to 1 teaspoon oil or butter as necessary and sauté the bell pepper, celery, scallions, and onion over medium heat until soft, 10 minutes.

3. In a large bowl, crumble the corn bread until there are no big lumps. Add the sausage, vegetables, sage, cayenne, black pepper, and hard-cooked eggs. Combine well. (The recipe can be prepared to this point and refrigerated overnight, if desired.)

4. Beat the raw eggs and add to the mixture, along with the chicken stock. The mixture should be damp but not soupy. Pat, but do not pack, into the prepared baking pan. Bake until set, 40 to 45 minutes.

Serves 8

TO STUFF A FINE BIRD

W hether one "stuffs" or "dresses" a bird is a matter of geographic chauvinism. Generally, in New York, the former nomenclature is preferred, though the precise recipes vary widely. A holiday meal can feature a turkey, capon, chicken, duck, or squab stuffed in the manner of America's Deep South, a four-star restaurant in France, or an Italian country home. Following are the recipes that a disparate group of New Yorkers pull out for a post-Macy's parade dinner. But none need be limited to Thanksgiving and turkey. All the following recipes work well in a winter's capon, duck, guinea hen, chicken, or, in several cases, goose.

Soudiana Bedard's
TURKEY STUFFING

Mary Bedard, whose mother devised the recipe, explains, "This stuffing was originally packed into a five-pound cloth sugar bag and put into the turkey cavity as a penny-wise way of retrieving all the stuffing after roasting the bird." The stuffing is delicious baked on its own, even when there is no turkey. Leftovers can be formed into patties, fried, and served with poached eggs for breakfast.

1 pound pork sausage, removed from
    casing and crumbled
2 pounds ground lean beef
2 to 3 tablespoons poultry seasoning
3 pounds potatoes, peeled and
    quartered
8 tablespoons (1 stick) unsalted
    butter
1 teaspoon salt, or to taste
1 teaspoon freshly ground black pepper,
    or to taste

1. Preheat the oven to 350°F. Grease a 3-quart baking pan or casserole.

2. Crumble the sausage into a skillet and brown over medium heat, breaking up the pieces with a spoon, 7 minutes. Drain and transfer the sausage to a large bowl.

3. Return the skillet to medium heat and add the ground beef. Season the meat with 2 teaspoons of the poultry seasoning and cook, breaking up the pieces with a spoon, until evenly browned, 5 minutes. Drain and add the beef to the sausage.

4. Meanwhile, boil the potatoes in salted water until tender, 20 minutes. Drain and mash the potatoes with the butter. Add the potatoes to the meat mixture. Season the mixture with an additional 1 to 2 tablespoons of poultry seasoning, to

taste. Add the salt and pepper to taste.

5. Transfer the stuffing to the prepared baking pan or casserole. Bake, covered, for 30 minutes. Uncover and continue baking until lightly browned, 15 minutes more.

12 cups

Italian
FIG AND PROSCIUTTO
STUFFING

Fire fighter Sal Vicante got a hankering for turkey with an Italian accent one Thanksgiving. Since then he has used this stuffing in a wide range of birds. "The guys love it," he says.

2 cups dried figs, tough stems removed
1 cup Madeira wine
¼ pound prosciutto, minced
1 cup toasted pecans, chopped
8 tablespoons (1 stick) butter
1 onion, minced
1 cup minced Italian (flat-leaf) parsley leaves
1 cup minced celery ribs and leaves
1 tablespoon salt, or to taste
1½ teaspoons freshly ground black pepper
2 teaspoons dried thyme
1 teaspoon dried rosemary
1 teaspoon dried sage
8 cups cubed stale bread (½-inch cubes), lightly
    toasted
⅓ cup New York Penicillin (page 47) or canned
    chicken broth

1. In a nonreactive saucepan, simmer the figs in the Madeira for 15 minutes. Drain, pat dry, and roughly chop. Place the figs, prosciutto, and pecans in a medium bowl. Set aside.

2. Melt the butter in a skillet over medium heat. Add the onion and sauté until soft, about 5 minutes. Add the parsley, celery, salt, pepper, thyme, rosemary, and sage, and cook for 5 minutes. Place the mixture in a large bowl, add the cubed bread and chicken broth, and toss to combine. Add the fig mixture and toss to combine.

3. When cool, stuff the turkey and bake. Or if you prefer, preheat the oven to 350°F and bake the stuffing in a casserole until lightly browned, 40 minutes.

About 12 cups, enough to stuff a 22-pound turkey

A Doorman's VERY RICH MEAT STUFFING

This is a heart-stopping stuffing. Paddy O'Hearn, a doorman on Upper Park Avenue, devised the recipe after listening to accounts of a dinner that was once cooked by a devotee of Paul Bocuse in his building. Mr. O'Hearn only uses this

Park Avenue—where ideas for good recipes can come from overheard conversations.

to stuff turkey, but that, he says, is more in deference to his cholesterol than a reflection of the recipe. The very rich meat stuffing is also delicious in capon, squab, or chicken.

Giblets from 1 turkey or other poultry
6 thick slices bacon
1 cup rendered chicken fat (see page 342)
3 tablespoons unsalted butter
1 onion, chopped
2 ribs celery, chopped
1 clove garlic, minced
1 cup sliced white mushrooms
¼ pound ground lean beef
¼ pound ground veal
2 links sweet Italian sausage, casings removed
1 veal kidney (about 2 pounds), chopped
9 chicken livers (about 2 pounds), chopped
6 cups stale bread crumbs
1 tablespoon salt, or to taste
1½ teaspoons freshly ground black pepper, or to taste
1 cup minced Italian (flat-leaf) parsley leaves
1 teaspoon dried mint
1 teaspoon dried thyme
1 teaspoon ground allspice
1 teaspoon ground cumin
½ cup Cognac or other brandy
1 cup New York Penicillin (page 47) or canned chicken broth
12 chestnuts, boiled, peeled, and sliced
2 cups pine nuts, toasted

1. Place the giblets and 4 cups of cold water in a saucepan over low heat. Simmer for 1 hour. Strain, reserving the broth; let the giblets cool, then chop.

2. Place the bacon, chicken fat, and butter in a large skillet, and cook for 3 minutes over low heat. Add the onion, celery, and garlic, and cook for 5 minutes. Add the mushrooms, stir well to combine, and cook for 2 minutes. Add the ground beef, ground veal, and sausage, and cook for 5 minutes, stirring with a spoon to break up the pieces of meat. Add the kidney and simmer for 10 minutes. Add the giblets and chicken livers, and cook, stirring gently, for 5 minutes.

3. Place the mixture in a large bowl, add the

bread crumbs, salt, pepper, parsley, mint, thyme, allspice, and cumin, and stir to combine. Add the Cognac and chicken broth and stir. Add the chestnuts and pine nuts and stir well. Adjust the seasonings.

4. When cool, stuff the turkey and roast. Or if you prefer, preheat the oven to 350°F and bake the stuffing, covered, in a casserole for 25 minutes. Uncover and continue baking until lightly browned, 15 minutes.

About 16 cups, enough to stuff a 25-pound turkey with extra for baking in a casserole

Laurie Colwin's
BAKED CHICKEN

For eight years, the late novelist Laurie Colwin made this chicken for every dinner party she hosted. Eventually, she said, her guests "asked me to cool it." Nevertheless, this chicken is what the writer's mission in the kitchen is about: "It's good, simple cooking," she said. People, she claimed, "scream uncontrollably at the idea of baking the chicken for 2½ hours, but this is what makes it crusty and luscious."

Serve it with buttered orzo and Suki's Korean Spinach (see Index).

1 cup Dijon mustard
1 large clove garlic, minced
2 tablespoons fresh thyme, or 1 tablespoon dried
1 teaspoon freshly ground black pepper
⅛ teaspoon ground cinnamon
2 broiling chickens (2½ to 3 pounds each), well rinsed, patted dry, and quartered
3 cups fresh bread crumbs, lightly seasoned with salt and pepper
4 tablespoons (½ stick) unsalted butter
1 tablespoon sweet paprika

1. Preheat the oven to 325°F.

2. In a bowl, combine the mustard, garlic, thyme, pepper, and cinnamon. Coat the chicken pieces with the mustard mixture. Roll each piece in the bread crumbs and arrange in 1 or 2 shallow baking pans.

3. Dot each piece of chicken with some of the butter and sprinkle with the paprika. Bake for 2½ hours.

Serves 4 to 6

A long baking time is what gives writer Laurie Colwin's chicken its special flavor. Photo: Nancy Crampton

Delmonico's
DEVILED CHICKEN

This recipe is adapted from a version that was once served at the legendary restaurant. It is a toothsome dish, easy to make, and the bread crumbs provide a crisp coating.

4 tablespoons (½ stick) unsalted butter, at room temperature
1 tablespoon Dijon mustard
1 tablespoon apple cider vinegar
½ teaspoon salt
1 teaspoon sweet paprika
1 chicken (3½ to 4 pounds), well rinsed, patted dry, and quartered
½ cup fine, dry bread crumbs

1. Combine the butter, mustard, vinegar, salt, and paprika in a small bowl. Rub the mixture all over the chicken and under the skin without detaching it completely. Refrigerate, covered, for 4 to 6 hours.

2. Preheat the oven to 375°F.

3. Place the chicken pieces, skin side up, in a nonreactive roasting pan. Sprinkle with the bread crumbs. Bake until the juices from the thigh run clear, 40 minutes.

Serves 4

Amy's
STUFFED CHICKEN BREASTS

T he filling for this recipe is basically gussied up leftover lasagne filling. The stuffed chicken can be made ahead and kept warm for up to an hour before serving with rice or noodles. The dish, according to its inventor, Amy Graf, is terrific cold.

3 tablespoons olive oil
1 teaspoon minced garlic
1 cup thawed, frozen chopped spinach, squeezed
    dry before measuring
1/4 teaspoon coarse (kosher) salt, plus more to taste
Pinch of freshly ground black pepper, plus more to
    taste
3 tablespoons butter, melted
1/2 teaspoon sweet paprika
1 cup ricotta cheese
1/2 cup grated Swiss cheese
1/2 cup grated Muenster cheese
1/4 cup freshly grated Parmesan cheese
1 egg, lightly beaten
1/4 cup chopped fresh herbs, such as rosemary,
    oregano, basil, and thyme
2 whole chicken breasts (2 1/2 pounds total), skin
    intact and split

1. Warm the olive oil in a nonreactive skillet over medium heat. Add the garlic and sauté for 30 seconds. Add the spinach, salt, and pepper and cook until the spinach softens, about 3 minutes.

2. Preheat the oven to 375°F. Line a baking sheet with foil and set aside.

3. In a small bowl, combine the butter with the paprika; season with salt and pepper to taste. Set aside.

4. In a medium bowl, combine the spinach mixture with the cheeses, beaten egg, and herbs. With your fingers, carefully stuff the cheese mixture under the skin of the chicken breasts. Baste the chicken breasts with the butter mixture. Bake until the skin bubbles and browns, 30 to 40 minutes.

Serves 4

Betty's
FRIED CHICKEN

B etty Ciarrochi's unusual variation was the winner of the annual fried chicken contest at the Mississippi Picnic in Central Park.

8 tablespoons (1 stick) butter, at room
    temperature
1 chicken (3 to 3 1/2 pounds), well rinsed, patted
    dry, and cut into 8 pieces
1/2 cup milk
2 eggs, lightly beaten
2 teaspoons Tabasco sauce
2 cups all-purpose flour
1/2 teaspoon salt
1/2 teaspoon freshly ground black pepper
1 cup corn oil

1. Spread the softened butter under the skin of the chicken pieces.

2. Combine the milk, eggs, and Tabasco in a mixing bowl. In a brown paper bag, combine the flour, salt, and pepper.

3. Heat the oil over high heat in a large heavy skillet. Dip each piece of chicken in the milk and egg mixture, then place it in the paper bag and shake until thoroughly coated with the flour. Shake off the excess and place the chicken in the hot oil.

4. Reduce the heat to medium and cook slowly, turning the chicken pieces 3 or 4 times, until dark brown and thoroughly cooked, about 35 minutes.

Serves 2 to 4

LIZ SMITH'S FRIED CHICKEN

The Texas-born society columnist tells it in her own words:

"One of the most important things about fried chicken is the chicken itself. I'd say avoid Mr. Perdue like the plague. Go to some kosher butcher if possible and try to buy a small fryer. Most people don't know what a fryer is any-more—a very young chicken. Today there are giant chickens being sold and they do not make very good fried chicken.

"This is why some fried chicken fanciers have given up and only fry wings. At least a wing has some resemblance to being small enough to fry.

"Wash your chicken. Salt and pepper it. (I don't think shaking the salt and pepper in a paper bag quite works, so I lay mine out and do it, turn it over and do it again. Salt and pepper are very important to good fried chicken.)

"Shake the salted-pep-pered chicken with flour in a brown paper sack.

"I do not deep-fry chicken. But some deep-fried chicken is excellent, so I'm not against it. It's just another way. The important thing is for the grease to be very, very hot. I'd say have three-fourths of an inch of grease in the pan or skillet.

"Put pieces so they do not touch. Let them brown on one side and turn them. I always keep checking, which purists say is not the thing to do. When it looks right, it's right. Drain on another brown paper bag. (Better than a paper towel.)

"I know lots of people put spices, Tabasco, milk, crumbs, and other stuff on chicken. But I don't. However, I like almost all kinds of fried chicken. I even like Kentucky Fried Chicken though never in my life did I have anything resembling it down South.

"Fried chicken must not be pink inside. The most important thing about eating it is to forget your diet."

All fried chicken makers, like bar-becuers, have their own special secrets. Popular syndicated columnist Liz Smith shares hers. Photo: Courtesy of Liz Smith

VERNON: THE KING OF JERK

Jerk-style Jamaican barbecue is more prevalent than McDonald's along East 233rd Street in the Bronx, and Allan Vernon is known there as Vernon, the King of Jerk.

Vernon, who moved to New York City from Jamaica 20 years ago, is circumspect about his title. He says he didn't get to be king just by owning two of the best jerk houses in the city. He has a vision. "I see my jerk sauce on the shelves of every grocery store in the land," Mr. Vernon said.

When his countrymen hear him talk like that, they suggest that Mr. Vernon might rather be president than king. But they like to hear his Horatio Alger tale. It began in 1972, when Mr. Vernon was working as a carpenter on a building in Harlem. His ambition burning hot as a Caribbean sunset, he studied the panorama of his adopted city and tried to gauge what was missing. He decided that there was a "lack of jerk."

FILLING THE GAP

New York had approximations of Texas barbecue, Carolina low-country barbecue, Korean barbecue, and Szechwan barbecue. But no one had blended Jamaican peppers, herbs, and spices to make a proper jerk marinade for beef, chicken, porgy, or red snapper. No one had tried to figure out how to combine oven baking and charcoal grilling to approximate the slow, steamy way the jerk-style barbecue is cooked in shallow pits in Jamaica.

The origin of the name jerk is obscure, but it is thought to derive from a word used by the Arawak Indians for sun-dried beef, *charqui* or jerky, later revised by African runaways and their descendants in Jamaica.

Mr. Vernon moved in to fill New York's jerk gap. In 1982, he opened Vernon's Jerk Paradise, a fluorescent-lighted carry-out counter that features jerk-style Jamaican barbecue at 987 East 233rd Street. This was "the first stage of the dream," Mr. Vernon said, "letting people know who you are and what you can do."

Since opening day, Caribbean people who live in the neighborhood have dropped by at the first pang of jerk deprivation. For those who live in Brooklyn, Queens, Connecticut, and New Jersey, a jerk fix requires planning. They save their appetites, listen to reggae music, and look at snapshots from back home before driving to the Bronx. By the time they are in aroma range of Jamaican barbecue, they are in a frenzy of homesickness. The King of Jerk, a benign despot, soothes them.

MORE POWER TO THE KING

No one does jerk like Mr. Vernon. And once he had "a foot in the American dream," he says, it seemed only natural that he "move on up." He opened a second jerk dispensary, a fancier restaurant also called Vernon's Jerk Paradise, at 252 West 29th Street in Manhattan. Patrick Ewing came in, along with half the Knicks, who shoot hoops just four blocks north. Bill Cosby began requesting Vernon's jerk for cast lunches on the set of his television show.

It is as if Mr. Vernon had dug a pit, lighted a barbecue, and sent an irresistible fog of jerk over Chelsea. Some 2,000 people have signed the guest book in his pink dining room.

Mr. Vernon has earned his crown and doesn't wear it lightly. As he sees it, he is obliged to maintain a pure jerk state of mind: "Good jerk requires patience," he says. It takes forbearance to find the blend of peppers and smoke that makes

Vernon and a plate of his Jerk Style Chicken.

a barbecue "hot and smooth without choking you." He also has the obligation to warn his customers about a consequence of eating jerk. On his menu, he posted a caveat: "Caution, this food will make you greedy."

Faster than he can jerk a chicken, Mr. Vernon made a deal with a spaghetti-sauce factory in New Haven. Now, one day a month he drives his white Dodge van up to the Bronx Terminal Market, loads it up with peppers and fresh spices, and drives to New Haven. Within an hour of his arrival his deep mahogany sauce replaces the red tomato sauce in the cooking vats in the New Haven plant.

In 12 hours Mr. Vernon can pump several hundred gallons of his jerk sauce into jars the size and shape of mayonnaise jars. The label has a picture of Mr. Vernon smiling and flanked by two Jamaican peppers. "I'm proud of my sauce," he says. "Other people have figured out how to combine Jamaican spices. But I am the only one who makes an all-purpose sauce, a seasoning, a condiment.

Behind the bar of his restaurant on 29th Street, Mr. Vernon, who typically wears Missoni-like sweaters and a gold horseshoe ring, exudes the calm of Someone Who Would Be Heinz. He was featured in "Mo Hotta, Mo Betta," a newsletter devoted to chili pepper products. His sauce is sold by greengrocers in the Bronx, Brooklyn, and Queens, and even Zabar's and Grace's Market Place, the Manhattan food emporiums, stock it.

When business is slow, he polishes the jars of sauce that he keeps at the bar to sell. He can't decide which side of the jar looks better, the one that has his picture or the one that tells his tale: "Vernon's Jerk Sauce. Pioneers in jerk-style cooking since 1982."

NORAH'S FRIED CHICKEN

The following fried chicken philosophy appeared in *What's Cooking at Columbia,* a slender, faculty cookbook that was published by Columbia University Press in 1942.

"Wash, wipe and salt the pieces of chicken. Mix pepper into a tablespoon of flour. Roll chicken in flour and put in a frying pan in which is melting fat about the size of a medium-sized banana. Use bacon and other drippings if possible. The fat should be only warm when the chicken goes in. Put in the undesirable pieces first and fry till the chicken is a golden brown. This should be done under a cover and over a low flame. Give about half an hour to frying the whole chicken. As the pieces brown, put them in a kettle, with the odds and ends at the bottom. Add 1½ cups water to the grease in the pan and boil for a moment. Pour the liquid over the chicken in the kettle and place on an asbestos mat over the flame. Cover the pot, and after the contents begin to steam, reduce the heat to the lowest possible flame. Steam this way for at least an hour and a half (2 hours is not too long, especially if the chicken is not very tender). Water may be added if necessary."

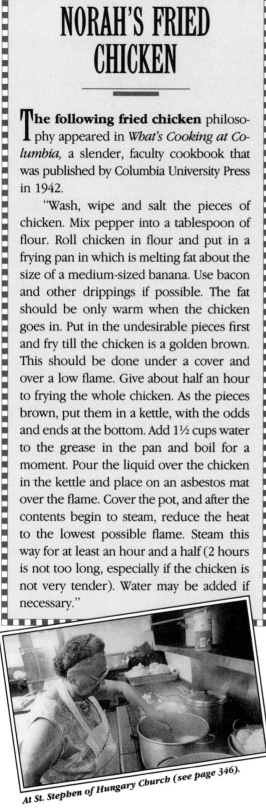

At St. Stephen of Hungary Church (see page 346).

Yvonne "Lola" Bell serves up her fried chicken, Island-style.

Caribbean FRIED CHICKEN

Yvonne "Lola" Bell, gospel singer and chef, was inspired by this dish to create the Fried Chicken Music Video, the first fried chicken video ever recorded. Caribbean chicken is seasoned in layers. She said it was important to follow the directions very carefully; otherwise the spices will not "harmonize."

1 fryer chicken (3½ to 4 pounds), well rinsed, patted dry, and cut into 8 pieces
Juice of 1 lemon
3 cloves garlic, minced
3 tablespoons sweet Hungarian paprika
2 tablespoons freshly ground black pepper
1 tablespoon plus a dash of cayenne pepper
2 teaspoons salt
2 tablespoons dark soy sauce
2 tablespoons Louisiana hot sauce, such as Red Devil
3 cups all-purpose flour
2 cups solid vegetable shortening

1. In a large bowl, soak the chicken in the lemon juice, making sure all of the pieces are coated. Set aside for 15 to 30 minutes.

2. Remove the chicken pieces one at a time and rub all over with the garlic. Place the pieces on a flat suface and cover with waxed paper. In a small bowl, combine the paprika, black pepper, 1 tablespoon of the cayenne pepper, and salt. In another bowl, combine the soy sauce and hot sauce. Dip the chicken in the spice mixture, coating both sides, then lightly coat with the soy sauce mixture.

3. Place the flour in a heavy paper bag and add a dash of cayenne pepper. Add 2 pieces of chicken and shake to coat well. Continue with the remaining chicken, placing the floured pieces on waxed paper.

4. Melt the shortening in a large cast-iron frying pan over high heat. When a speck of flour sizzles actively on contact, add the chicken pieces to the pan and fry until golden brown on both sides and the juices run clear when a thigh is pricked, about 25 minutes. Drain on paper towels.

Serves 4

Vernon's Jerk Style
JAMAICAN CHICKEN

This pungent Jamaican sauce can be used to marinate pork butts, beef round roasts, porgies, red snapper, as well as chicken. Says Vernon, "You can even use my sauce like ketchup. One guy pours it on his scrambled eggs." The sauce keeps well in the refrigerator tightly covered.

For Vernon's Jerk Snapper recipe see the Index; for more on Allan Vernon, see pages 334 and 335.

JERK SAUCE
1¼ pounds large white onions, quartered
½ pound fresh Jamaican chiles (also called Scotch bonnets), cored and quartered (see Note)
4 ounces fresh ginger, peeled
¼ cup ground allspice
¼ cup fresh thyme leaves
3 tablespoons freshly ground black pepper
1 cup white wine vinegar
1 cup dark soy sauce

1 chicken (4 to 6 pounds), well rinsed, patted dry, and cut into 6 pieces

1. Pulverize the onions, chiles, and ginger in a blender or food processor. Transfer the mixture to a large bowl and stir in the allspice, thyme, black pepper, vinegar, and soy sauce.

2. Coat the chicken with the sauce. Cover and marinate in the refrigerator for 24 hours, turning once.

3. Preheat the oven to 350°F. Place a meat thermometer in one of the thigh pieces. Place a shallow pan of boiling water on the oven floor. Put the chicken on a rack and place in a roasting pan. Roast, basting frequently with the sauce, until three-quarters cooked (120°F on the meat thermometer), 30 to 45 minutes. Remove the chicken from the oven. Remove the meat thermometer.

4. Preheat a broiler or grill.

5. Baste the chicken with more jerk sauce. Sear the chicken for 5 minutes under a preheated broiler or over a very hot charcoal fire. Remove from the heat and let sit for 15 minutes before eating.

Serves 6

Note: Be sure to wear rubber gloves when handling these very hot peppers. If you don't, you could irritate and burn your skin.

Robert Pearson's
BARBECUED CHOPPED CHICKEN

Robert Pearson described this dish as a natural "by-product" of barbecue, the strings and chunks left after a whole chicken has been barbecued. Because of the size of the scraps, they really absorb the sauce, and the dish can be concocted hours before serving. Try it accompanied by Green Market Spring Lima Bean and Early Corn Ragout (see Index). For more about Robert Pearson, see The New York Barbecue Summit in the Meat chapter.

SAUCE
6 tablespoons (¾ stick) butter
6 tablespoons vegetable oil
3 onions, finely diced
1½ lemons, juiced, rinds reserved
6 cups ketchup
1½ cups red wine vinegar
½ cup plus 1 tablespoon Worcestershire sauce
¾ cup packed dark brown sugar
1½ teaspoons cayenne pepper
2 tablespoons salt
2 tablespoons dry mustard

CHICKEN
5 pounds chicken pieces
1 onion, quartered
2 tablespoons corn oil
¼ cup cider vinegar
1 tablespoon salt
1 tablespoon freshly ground black pepper
1 tablespoon pasilla chili powder

1. Make the sauce: Melt the butter with the oil in a nonreactive large sauté pan over medium heat. Add the onions and cook until lightly browned. Stir in all of the remaining sauce ingredients, including the lemon rinds, and simmer for 20 minutes. Remove from the heat and discard the rinds. If you desire a very smooth sauce, purée the mixture in a blender or food processor. You should have 2½ quarts.

2. Prepare a charcoal grill for grilling.

3. Prepare the chicken: In a large bowl, combine the chicken with 4 cups of the barbecue sauce. Rub the sauce all over chicken, coating well.

4. Place the chicken skin side down on the grill and grill for 15 minutes. Turn and grill for 15 minutes more. Remove the pieces to a platter as they are done and set aside until cool enough to handle. Pull the chicken from the bones in bite-size pieces. Discard the bones. (The skin may be saved if you want a very rich sauce. Set it aside for now.)

5. Purée the onion in a food processor or blender. (If you want to use the chicken skin, purée it with the onion.) Warm the oil in a large sauté pan over medium heat. When hot, add the onion purée and cook, stirring frequently, until translucent. Stir in the vinegar, salt, pepper, chili powder, and the remaining 6 cups barbecue sauce. Stir in the cooked chicken and simmer over low heat until the sauce thickens, 30 minutes.

Serves 4 to 6

Felipe's
CHICKEN ESCABECHE

The late, well-known chef at Manhattan's The Ballroom, Felipe Rojas-Lombardi, was a native of Peru, but after more than 20 years in America he called himself "a New Yorker by heart." Escabèche, which can be made with rabbit, fish, or game, was brought to South America by the Spanish Moors. Native South Americans added their own touches of peppers and the fiery achiote oil. New Yorkers just love the taste.

1 chicken (3½ to 4 pounds), well rinsed, patted dry, and cut into small serving pieces

2½ tablespoons coarse (kosher) salt

¼ cup achiote oil (recipe follows)

12 large cloves garlic, peeled

12 small onions (about 1½ inches in diameter), peeled, with a small X cut into the root end

3 fresh serrano chiles, seeded and cut into julienne

4 bay leaves

½ teaspoon cayenne pepper

12 to 15 fresh thyme sprigs, or 1 tablespoon dried

4 carrots, peeled and cut into 2½-inch-long sticks

4 cups red wine vinegar

2 cups dry red wine

4 ribs celery, cut diagonally into ½-inch slices

2 red bell peppers, stemmed, seeded, and cut into julienne

2 green bell peppers, stemmed, seeded, and cut into julienne

1. Sprinkle the chicken parts with 1½ teaspoons of the coarse salt.

2. Heat the achiote oil in an earthenware casserole or large skillet. Add the chicken pieces and sauté over medium-low heat until golden brown on all sides, 4 minutes per side. Remove the chicken from the skillet and set aside.

3. Add the garlic and onions to the remaining achiote oil in the skillet. Cook over low heat until the onions are soft and golden, about 10 minutes. Add the serrano chiles, bay leaves, cayenne, the remaining 2 tablespoons salt, the thyme, and carrots and cook for 5 minutes. Stir in the vinegar and red wine and bring to a boil. Lower the heat and simmer, uncovered, for 15 minutes.

4. Add the celery and red and green bell peppers and continue cooking for 10 to 15 min-

utes. Return the chicken pieces to the casserole, cover, remove the pan from the heat, and set aside to cool to room temperature. Serve right from the casserole. Garnish with fresh thyme sprigs, if available.

Serves 4 to 6

Felipe Rojas-Lombardi at The Ballroom's tapas bar. Photo: Harold Naideau.

ACHIOTE OIL

1 cup olive oil or vegetable oil

½ cup annatto seeds

1 dried serrano chile, crumbled

1 bay leaf

1. Combine the oil, annatto seeds, serrano chile, and bay leaf in a saucepan. Let sit at room temperature, stirring now and then, for 30 minutes.

2. Place the saucepan over low heat, and while

stirring, gently bring the oil to a boil. Remove from the heat and set aside to cool thoroughly, stirring now and then.

3. Strain the oil through a fine sieve or several layers of cheesecloth. Discard the seeds, bay leaf, and chile; the oil will be a bright red-orange color. It can be kept, tightly covered, in the refrigerator for up to 1 year.

Makes 1 cup

Yvonne's
POLLO ENCEBOLLADO
(CHICKEN WITH ONIONS)

This soulful braised chicken is a family recipe from Yvonne Ortiz and is delicious served with rice. It is also an irresistible leftover.

1 cup olive oil
3 cups sliced onions
1 chicken (3 to 4 pounds), well rinsed, patted dry, and cut into 8 pieces
¼ cup distilled white vinegar
10 whole peppercorns
10 whole allspice
2 to 3 bay leaves
½ cup pimiento-stuffed olives
Salt and freshly ground black pepper, to taste

1. In a nonreactive large skillet, heat ¼ cup of the oil over medium heat. Add the onions and sauté until soft, 7 minutes. Add the chicken and cook until browned all over, 3 minutes per side.

2. In a small bowl, whisk together the remaining ¾ cup oil and the vinegar. Add to the skillet, along with all of the remaining ingredients, and stir to combine. Add just enough water to

cover. Cook until the chicken is opaque at the bone and the sauce thickens slightly, 30 minutes.

Serves 4

CHICKEN ADOBO
The Philippines

Reynaldo Alejandro, former curator of the expansive culinary collection at the New York Public Library, says, "Adobo is the national dish of the Philippines. It is a generic term for food cooked in vinegar, garlic, and soy, and the amount of the ingredients, as well as the different spices, vary all over the island. This is my family's recipe."

8 chicken thighs
½ cup distilled white vinegar
½ cup light soy sauce
3 bay leaves
½ teaspoon freshly ground black pepper
4 cloves garlic, minced
1 tablespoon vegetable oil

1. In a nonreactive saucepan, combine the chicken thighs, vinegar, soy sauce, bay leaves, pepper, and 2 teaspoons of the minced garlic. Place over high heat and bring to a boil. Reduce the heat and simmer, uncovered and turning often, until the chicken is tender, about 25 minutes.

2. Set the chicken aside. Strain the cooking liquid and skim to remove the fat. Set aside.

3. Return the saucepan to high heat and add the vegetable oil and remaining garlic. When the oil is hot, add the chicken and fry until browned on each side, 3 minutes per side. Add the reserved cooking liquid and simmer for 5 to 10 minutes.

4. Remove the chicken pieces to a serving dish. Pour the sauce over the chicken and serve.

Serves 4

SCHMALTZ AND GRIBENESS

Stan Zimmerman isn't afraid of the warriors for good health. Let them storm New York with their olive oil and their butter substitutes and parsimonious nonstick frying pans! Let them wage psychological warfare in the name of clean arteries! Just let them try to keep people from Sammy's Famous Roumanian Steak House, the preserve of high fat and Dracula-defying portions of garlic that Mr. Zimmerman opened in a Lower East Side basement in 1975.

"My customers know what they are doing," Mr. Zimmerman said. "When they book a table here, they book a bed at St. Vincent's Hospital at the same time." To date, he said, no one has died in the dining room.

But Mr. Zimmerman acknowledges that there could be long-term effects from dining regularly at Sammy's, at 157 Chrystie Street (at Delancey Street), a place that is decorated with hundreds of snapshots of guests and their business cards as well as posters that describe the qualifications of a Jewish mother. "The food's heavy," Mr. Zimmerman said. "My waiters work out at Jack LaLanne. That's the only way they can carry the plates."

In fact, the frequent lifting of forkfuls of Sammy's fried kreplach or kishka could be enough to bring on carpal tunnel syndrome. The stuffed cabbage is the size of a medium-range torpedo, and the Roumanian tenderloin steak looks like something Fred Flintstone and a few of his Stone Age buddies might enjoy.

Schmaltz—rendered animal fat, which in this country is generally made from chicken—accounts for the heft of many of the dishes. Gribeness, the cracklings left over in making schmaltz, add their share. And while he knows that good health warriors would wag a frantic finger at those ingredients, Mr. Zimmerman is about as eager to lighten the schmaltz in his cooking as most French chefs are to abandon butter.

In fact, to Mr. Zimmerman, schmaltz is butter. "When it's cold, schmaltz is smooth and satiny," he said. "When it's room temperature, it's like melted butter," he added, nodding toward the syrup pitchers full of rich yellow fat that are placed on the tables at Sammy's. "Delicious on bread or, listen to this, with gribeness and chopped liver and black radish and a little chopped onion, which is what I refer to as a Jewish Caesar salad, because waiters make it at the table."

Mr. Zimmerman contends that his pro-schmaltz position is a populist stand. "I've seen a table of four go through two pitchers of schmaltz," he said. I had one movie star, no names please, ask me to mail it to Hollywood, he missed a good schmaltz so much. I was honored. I didn't charge."

The possibility of schmaltz deprivation can drive people to do terrible things. "I had one lady, a very rich lady, put the pitcher in her thousand-dollar handbag," he said. "I was honored. I wrapped it up for her."

Schmaltz is easy to prepare, will keep for about a month if well refrigerated, and can be used to smooth out chopped liver, or for frying latkes or kishka or even chicken, liver, or steak.

But as far as Mr. Zimmerman is concerned, schmaltz is nostalgia. And where is it written that a small dose of nostalgia has no health benefits of its own? Who can possibly arbitrate the issue of nostalgia versus nutrition?

Mr. Zimmerman concedes that schmaltz might be a special-occasion kind of indulgence. Particularly, he said, around the holidays.

"It's dietetic," he said. "Eat schmaltz and you won't be eating again for a couple of days."

Schmaltz and GRIBENESS

U se schmaltz for frying and sautéing or as a spread. It's wonderful spread on fresh rye bread with a sprinkling of salt. Gribeness can be used to garnish mashed potatoes and salads or eaten as finger food.

2 pounds chicken fat and skin
1 large onion, grated
2 teaspoons salt

1. Cut the chicken skin in ¼-inch strips and dice the fat. Place the skin and fat in a large heavy skillet, add 1 cup water, and simmer over medium heat until the water evaporates, 35 to 45 minutes.

2. Add the onion to the pan and continue cooking over medium heat until the onion is soft and golden and the skin is medium brown, about 5 minutes.

3. Strain the mixture: The liquid is the schmaltz. Add the salt to the solid part (the skin and onion), which is the gribeness. Both should be stored in tightly covered containers in the refrigerator. They will keep for up to a month.

About 2 cups each of schmaltz and gribeness

John Schumacher's CHICKEN MARENGO

T his pungent fricassee was a winner at an early March of Dimes Gourmet Gala in New York City and remains a favorite on the Upper East Side dinner party circuit. Serve over steamed or boiled rice.

¼ cup all-purpose flour
3 tablespoons minced fresh tarragon, or 1
*   tablespoon dried*
Salt and freshly ground black pepper, to taste
1 chicken (4 pounds), well rinsed, patted dry, and
*   cut into 8 pieces*
⅓ cup olive oil
⅓ cup (5⅓ tablespoons) butter
1 cup dry white wine
2 cloves garlic, minced
1 large can (28 ounces) Italian-style peeled plum
*   tomatoes*
¼ pound mushrooms, sliced
1 tablespoon minced fresh parsley

1. Preheat the oven to 350°F.

2. In a shallow bowl, mix together the flour, tarragon, and salt and pepper to taste. Coat each piece of chicken with the mixture and set aside. Reserve any remaining flour mixture.

3. Heat the olive oil and butter in a non-reactive large skillet over medium-high heat. When the fats are very hot but not smoking, add the chicken pieces a few at a time, making sure not to crowd the pan. Brown evenly on all sides, 3 minutes per side. Drain on paper towels or a paper bag.

4. Pour off any excess fat from the skillet. Add the reserved flour mixture to the skillet and stir with a wooden spoon over medium heat until smooth and light brown. Slowly whisk in the wine and cook until the mixture thickens slightly and coats the back of a spoon, 15 minutes.

5. Place the chicken in a nonreactive large casserole. Pour the sauce over. Add the garlic and tomatoes and stir to combine. Bake, uncovered, for 50 minutes.

6. Add the mushrooms and parsley, adjust the seasonings, and bake for 10 minutes more.
Serves 4

George and Jenifer Lang at the Café des Artistes. Photo: Stephen Ellison.

The Lang's
CHICKEN & KOHLRABI FRICASSEE

Jenifer and George Lang, who own the popular Café des Artistes, began with an old-fashioned Hungarian recipe and, over the years, this hearty, finely honed fricassee evolved. Because it can be made ahead of time, it is a natural winter company dish.

DUMPLINGS
1 pound skinless, boneless chicken breasts
2 tablespoons fresh dill leaves
1 teaspoon salt
Freshly ground black pepper, to taste
2 egg whites
2 cups heavy (whipping) cream

CHICKEN
8 tablespoons (1 stick) butter
⅔ cup all-purpose flour
6 cups New York Penicillin (page 47) or other homemade chicken stock
2 cups dry white wine
Salt and freshly ground black pepper, to taste
3 young kohlrabi, peeled and sliced ½ inch thick
1 pound baby carrots, peeled and trimmed, or 1 pound regular carrots, peeled and cut into ½-inch diagonal pieces
2 chickens (3 pounds each), well rinsed, patted dry, and cut into 8 pieces each

TO FINISH
3 quarts New York Penicillin (page 47) or other homemade chicken stock
⅓ cup sugar
Juice of 2 lemons

1. Make the dumplings: Place the chicken breasts, dill, salt, and pepper in a food processor. Process until finely minced, about 30 seconds. Add the egg whites and process again. With the machine running, slowly pour the heavy cream through the feed tube. As soon as the cream is added, turn off the machine. Transfer the mixture to a bowl; cover and chill for at least 4 hours, preferably overnight.

2. Make the fricassee: Melt the butter in a nonreactive, very heavy, deep, large pot over medium heat. Stir in the flour and cook, stirring constantly with a wooden spoon, until the roux turns a pale-blond color, about 5 minutes.

3. Pour in the 6 cups chicken stock and the wine, and bring to a boil, whisking constantly. Add a generous amount of salt and pepper, and reduce the heat to low. Simmer, stirring occasionally, for 10 minutes.

4. Parboil the kohlrabi and carrots together

in a large pot of boiling salted water for 6 minutes. Drain, then rinse with cold water to stop the vegetables from cooking further.

5. Add the cut-up chicken pieces to the large heavy pot and mix in the parboiled vegetables. Cover the pot with a tight-fitting lid and simmer for 45 minutes.

6. Meanwhile, remove the dumpling batter from the refrigerator. Place the 3 quarts of chicken stock in a large wide pot and bring to a boil over medium-high heat. Reduce the heat to a simmer. Using 2 large soup spoons, make small egg-shaped dumplings from the batter and drop them into the stock. Keep at a simmer, lowering the heat if necessary to prevent it from boiling. Cook the dumplings until cooked through, 8 to 10 minutes. Remove with a slotted spoon and drain for a few seconds on a clean cloth towel or napkin.

7. Remove the fricassee from the heat. Add the dumplings and cover the pot.

8. In a heavy skillet, heat the sugar until it melts and caramelizes, turning a golden brown color. As soon as it caramelizes, remove the pan from the heat and stir in the lemon juice. Remove about 2½ cups of stock from the fricassee and add it to the skillet. Stir over medium heat until well blended, about 30 seconds.

9. Skim off any excess fat from the fricassee. Drizzle the sauce over the fricassee, stir, and return to the stove top to heat just to a simmer. Serve.
Serves 8

Esposito's
CHICKEN FRICASSEE

At Esposito & Sons Pork Store and Meat Market, the butchers sell pork, beef, chicken, and game at old-time prices, but they give away recipes for free. This simple, one-pot dish from John Esposito has been a favorite among the customers for years.

Even when used in small amounts, fine Hungarian sweet paprika adds a special touch.

½ cup all-purpose flour
1 tablespoon salt
½ teaspoon freshly ground black pepper
½ teaspoon sweet paprika
1 chicken (3½ to 4 pounds), well rinsed, patted
    dry, and cut into 8 pieces
¼ cup vegetable oil
1 small onion, thinly sliced
1 rib celery, thinly sliced
1 cup dry white wine

1. Combine the flour, salt, pepper, and paprika in a plastic or paper bag. Add the chicken and shake well to coat. Place the chicken pieces on waxed paper and reserve the remaining flour mixture.

2. In a nonreactive 12-inch skillet, warm the oil over medium-high heat. Add the chicken pieces and cook until browned all over. Add the onion, celery, and wine and bring to a boil. Reduce the heat to low, cover, and simmer until fork-tender, about 2½ hours.

3. Remove the chicken to a warm platter. In a small cup, mix together 1 tablespoon of the reserved flour mixture with ¼ cup water until smooth. Stir into the skillet and cook over medium heat, stirring constantly, until the mixture thickens. Pour the sauce over the chicken and serve.
Serves 4

Upper Manhattan
ARROZ CON POLLO

There are as many versions of arroz con pollo, says Carmen Luisa Reyes, as there are Puerto Ricans who moved to Upper Manhattan. This version is particularly soulful and, with just a salad before and a flan afterwards, it makes a sturdy meal.

STOCK
3 to 4 pounds chicken parts (wings, thighs, legs,
*   necks, backs, and gizzards), well rinsed, patted*
*   dry, and excess fat trimmed*
½ green bell pepper, stemmed, seeded, and cut in
*   2 pieces*
4 ajieito chiles
6 cilantro stems
1 teaspoon salt

RICE MIXTURE
1 small onion, quartered
½ green bell pepper, stemmed, seeded, and cut in
*   2 pieces*
4 ajieito chiles, seeds removed under running
*   water*
3 cloves garlic, peeled
6 cilantro stems
3 tablespoons corn oil
1 cup tomato sauce
4 cups medium-grain white rice, rinsed and
*   drained*
Salt, to taste

1. Prepare the stock: Combine the chicken pieces, bell pepper, ajieitos, and cilantro with 4 cups cold water in a nonreactive heavy stockpot. Cover and cook over high heat for 10 minutes. Add the salt, reduce the heat to a simmer, and cook for 10 minutes more. Discard the necks, gizzards, and backs.

2. Prepare the rice mixture: In a blender or food processor, combine the onion, bell pepper, ajieitos, garlic, cilantro, and ¼ cup water. Purée until smooth. Warm the oil in a nonreactive, large, heavy pot over medium heat. Add the contents of the blender and the tomato sauce, and bring to a boil. Reduce the heat to a simmer.

3. Remove the stock from the heat and strain it into the sauce pot. Add the chicken pieces to the pot and stir well. Stir in the rice and increase the heat to high. Cook, uncovered, until the rice absorbs most of the liquid, about 15 minutes.

4. Cover the pan, reduce the heat to low, and cook the rice for about 10 minutes more. Watch the pot, giving the mixture a stir or two if it seems to be sticking. Add salt to taste.
Serves 4

Pearl's
CHICKEN CACCIATORA

Mrs. Pearl Colton, who lives in the Bronx, is extremely protective about her cacciatora. People ask her for the recipe, but she doesn't give it freely. Her mother used to make it for her when she was single, saving the sauce to serve with pasta at another meal.

8 tablespoons (1 stick) butter
2 large onions, diced
2 green bell peppers, stemmed, seeded, and diced
1 chicken (3½ to 4 pounds), well rinsed, patted
*   dry, and cut into 8 pieces*
1 clove garlic, minced
1 can (16 ounces) stewed tomatoes (about 2 cups)
1 can (15 ounces) tomato sauce (1¾ to 2 cups)
2 bay leaves
1 teaspoon crushed dried oregano
1 teaspoon salt
½ teaspoon celery seeds
¼ teaspoon freshly ground black pepper
½ cup dry red wine

1. Melt the butter in a nonreactive, large, deep skillet over medium heat. Add the onions and bell peppers and cook until the onions are translucent and the peppers are soft, 5 minutes. Use a slotted spoon to remove the vegetables to a bowl. Add the chicken and brown on all sides, 3 minutes per side.

2. Return the vegetables to the pan, add the garlic, and cook for 1 minute. Add the stewed tomatoes, tomato sauce, bay leaves, oregano, salt, celery seeds, and pepper and stir well. Cover, reduce the heat to low, and simmer until the chicken is cooked through and the sauce is thick, 35 to 40 minutes.

3. Slowly pour the wine into the skillet and stir to combine. Cook for 2 minutes more and serve.

Serves 4

THE SAVVY SHOPPER

SAVVY SHOPPER

Top-quality **Hungarian paprika,** noodles, and dumplings can be purchased at **PAPRIKAS WEISS,** 1546 SECOND AVENUE, BETWEEN 80TH AND 81ST STREETS; (212) 288-6117. The store also handles mail orders.

Edward Weiss at Paprikas Weiss.

Mrs. Hathansel's
CHICKEN PAPRIKAS

Members of The Mother's Club at St. Stephen of Hungary Catholic Church on East 82nd Street begin cooking on Saturday for the dinners they serve after Sunday mass. Sometimes they cook once a month; other times the group of six to twelve women cut and dice, stew and braise every week in the basement of the church. They always charge $6 for the hefty meals they serve at long folding tables to over a hundred parishioners and guests. Especially in the winter, Sunday dinner at St. Stephen's Hungarian Church is an antidote to the Manhattan brunch scene and offers a rib-sticking taste of the Old World.

While The Mother's Club may make several different soups and a goulash, braised ribs and stewed fish, and hot slaw and big vats of dumplings, they always make chicken paprikás. This version was made one spring afternoon by Julia Hedrik and friends, though she refused all credit. "Mrs. Hathansel taught me how to make it," she said, referring to the president of The Mother's Club. "You could say she is the Major-Mother around here, and everybody's paprikás descends from hers."

2 tablespoons pork fat or fatback
1 chicken (3½ to 4 pounds), well rinsed,
*   patted dry, and cut into 8 pieces*
Salt and freshly ground black pepper,
*   to taste*
1 large white onion, chopped
1 red bell pepper, stemmed, seeded,
*   and minced*
½ fresh tomato, chopped
2 to 3 teaspoons sweet Hungarian
*   paprika*
1½ tablespoons all-purpose flour
1 cup New York Penicillin (page 47)
*   or canned chicken broth, or more*
*   as needed*
1 cup sour cream

The Mother's Club at St. Stephen's prepares post-mass meals. The money raised is donated to favorite church causes.

1. Melt the pork fat in a nonreactive large pot over medium heat. Add the chicken pieces, sprinkle them lightly with salt and pepper, and brown for about 5 minutes on each side. Remove the chicken and reserve.

2. Add the onion and bell pepper to the pot, lower the heat, and sauté until soft, about 5 minutes. Stir in the tomato and 2 teaspoons of the paprika and continue to cook over low heat for 5 minutes.

3. Add the flour to the pot, scraping and stirring well to combine, and cook until the flour begins to turn golden. Add the chicken broth and stir very well. Add the chicken, cover, and simmer, stirring occasionally and adding more chicken broth if necessary, until the chicken begins to fall off the bone.

4. Adjust the seasonings with additional salt, pepper, and paprika to taste. Add the sour cream and stir well. Serve with egg noodles or spaetzle.

Serves 4

Haitian
CHICKEN IN A POT

Nicole Buisson, a manicurist in Manhattan, was taught to make this dish by her mother while growing up in Haiti and now cooks it for her daughter and son before going to work in the morning. It is a soulful, one-pot dish that is best served with rice.

1 chicken (3½ to 4 pounds), well rinsed, patted dry, quartered, and drumsticks separated from the thighs
4 cups New York Penicillin (page 47) or canned chicken broth
1 teaspoon white wine vinegar
1 onion, sliced
4 cloves garlic
½ teaspoon minced fresh chile (or dried red pepper flakes)
½ teaspoon freshly ground black pepper
½ teaspoon salt
6 whole cloves
1 teaspoon dried thyme
1 bay leaf
1 cup broccoli florets
1 cup cauliflower florets
1 cup diced carrots

1. In a large ovenproof casserole, combine the chicken pieces, chicken broth, vinegar, onion, garlic, chile, black pepper, salt, cloves, thyme, and bay leaf. Bring to a boil over medium heat. Reduce the heat and simmer for 15 minutes.

2. Preheat the oven to 350°F.

3. Cover the casserole, place in the oven, and bake for 1 hour.

4. Stir in the broccoli, cauliflower, and carrots. Cover and bake until the vegetables are tender, about 20 minutes. Adjust the seasonings with additional salt and pepper.

Serves 4

THE CURATOR OF COUNTRY CAPTAIN

Names regularly become name-brands in the New York food world. Mothers might weep, but generally they do it all the way to the bank. Nathan Handwerker, for instance, made his peace (and a significant fortune) by allowing "Hot Dog" to replace his family name. To the public ear, the name David Liederman isn't half as sweet as "David's Cookies"; "Eli" has mainly become a first name to "Bread."

It would be fair to call Cecily Brownstone, Cecily Country Captain, but the former food columnist and one of the human cornerstones of authentic cooking in New York demurs the use of her name. On the other hand, she wouldn't mind being known as the Curator of Country Captain Chicken. For nearly four decades, she has valiantly exposed the myths about the dish and served as a one-woman preservation society for a particular version of curried chicken.

"I first heard about Country Captain in the 1950s, but it's been around since at least the eighteenth century," said Ms. Brownstone, who, along with her collection of 60,000 cookbooks, has lived in Greenwich Village for more than five decades.

OH CAPTAIN, MY CAPTAIN

During her tenure the dish has gone in and out of style in New York. One era idolized the dish's exotica, another loved its simplicity. Each wave of Country Captain Chicken vogue was rife with misinterpretations of the recipe which, to Ms. Brownstone, boils down to misrepresentation of Country Captain, a sort of character assassination that simply burns her up.

"Using a breast, can you imagine," she said in a telephone interview. "I don't want to give names, I really don't want to get into that, but can you imagine that someone actually used cream? That's right, cream. And they called it Country Captain! It's very discouraging. It really is."

Heaven knows, Ms. Brownstone tried to keep the record—and the recipe—straight.

As early as 1960, when she was writing for the Associated Press and was the ad hoc matriarch of James Beard's culinary saloon in Greenwich Village, Miss Brownstone investigated the origins of Country Captain. At that time, the dish was widely regarded as a specialty of the southern United States, but Miss Brownstone blew the lid off that assumption. Searching cookbooks she found the earliest reference to the dish in *Miss Leslie's New Cookery Book,* which was published in 1857. Within days, Miss Brownstone had published her initial Country Captain exposé.

The dish, according to Miss Leslie is "an East Indian Dish and a very easy preparation of curry." Miss Leslie said that the term "Country Captain" signifies "a captain of native troops (or 'Sepoys') in the pay of England; their own country being India, they are there called generally the country troops." Miss Leslie speculated that the dish was "introduced at English tables by a Sepoy officer." Ms. Brownstone accepted her thesis.

The game stall at the Fulton Market in early Country Captain days.

THE PREFERRED VERSION

Nevertheless, as time passed, Miss Brownstone began to prefer the Country Captain Chicken of Alexander Filippini, who was the chef of Delmonico's in the early twentieth century, to that of Miss Leslie's. The former called for browning the chicken with peppers and onions and adding almonds and currants; the latter called for onions ("boiled and sliced") and curry powder, suggesting "It will be a great improvement to put in, at the beginning, three or four tablespoonfuls of finely grated coconut."

It is not surprising that Ms. Brownstone prefers Mr. Filippini's version—it tastes better. Ms. Brownstone published the recipe in hundreds of newspapers and was unflagging in getting it included "for the record" in dozens of cookbooks. When she saw fake Captains in restaurants or in cookbooks, she took the matter up with whoever was in charge. The late James Beard was a significant ally in her crusade. Teaching her recipe in his cooking school, he indoctrinated a generation of chefs with the formula for the real Captain. Another friend, Irma Rombauer, aided the Captain cause by including the recipe in *The Joy of Cooking*.

Still, it seemed that to know the Captain was to want to change the Captain.

"For years, every variation upset me," said Ms. Brownstone, who also noted that her response has mellowed in recent years. The Country Captain recipe in the 1990 *Fannie Farmer* calls for a touch of orange juice, and instead of screeching, Ms. Brownstone, who is now "older than is polite to talk about," merely sighs.

"I guess you could say that I am more accepting," she said. But she is quick to add, "I would like to get all this confusion cleared up once and for all, dear, and would be happy to fax over the original recipe as well as some history of the dish as soon as I am finished with my lunch."

Cecily Brownstone's
ORIGINAL COUNTRY CAPTAIN CHICKEN

Here is *the* recipe from Ms. Brownstone, hot off the fax. Serve with steamed rice.

¼ cup all-purpose flour
1 teaspoon salt
¼ teaspoon freshly ground black pepper
1 broiler chicken (3½ to 4 pounds), well rinsed, patted dry, and cut into 12 pieces
4 tablespoons (½ stick) butter
1 onion, finely diced
1 green bell pepper, finely diced
1 clove garlic, crushed
1½ teaspoons curry powder
½ teaspoon dried thyme leaves
1 can (16 ounces) stewed tomatoes
3 tablespoons currants
⅓ cup blanched almonds, toasted

1. Combine the flour, salt, and pepper in a large bowl. Coat the chicken pieces in flour and place on waxed paper.

2. Preheat the oven to 350°F.

3. Melt the butter in a nonreactive, ovenproof, large skillet over medium heat. Add the chicken and cook until evenly browned on all sides, 3 minutes per side. Remove with a slotted spoon and set aside.

4. Reduce the heat under the skillet to low and add the onion, bell pepper, garlic, curry powder, and thyme. Add the tomatoes and stir to scrape up any bits from the bottom of the pan.

5. Return the chicken to the skillet. Bake, uncovered, for 25 minutes. Add the currants and cook until the chicken is cooked through, 5 minutes more. If the sauce gets too thick, thin with ¼ cup water. Sprinkle with the almonds and serve.

Serves 4

Peter Rose's
BUTTER CHICKEN

This update of a traditional, New Netherland chicken by scholar and cookbook author Peter Rose is a delicate dish that should be served with boiled potatoes and a mixture of snow peas and regular peas. The recipe originally appeared in Ms. Rose's book, *The Sensible Cook*.

3 pounds chicken legs, thighs, and breasts,
    well rinsed and patted dry
1 blade mace, or a pinch of ground
    mace
1 teaspoon salt
4 tablespoons (½ stick) butter
2 tablespoons minced fresh parsley
1 tablespoon fresh lemon juice
Grated zest of 1 lemon
Freshly ground black pepper,
    to taste
½ cup heavy (whipping) cream
1 lemon, thinly sliced, for garnish

1. In a heavy saucepan, combine the chicken, mace, and salt. Cover with cold water and bring to a boil. Poach until just barely cooked through, about 15 minutes.

2. Remove the pan from the heat and set the chicken aside to cool. Reserve 1 cup of the chicken broth. Remove the meat from the bones and cut into bite-size pieces.

3. In a nonreactive large skillet, melt the butter over medium heat. Add the parsley, lemon juice, lemon zest, and pepper and simmer until the sauce reduces, about 15 minutes.

4. Add the cream and cook, without boiling, until the sauce is hot and thick. Add the chicken and cook until warmed through. Garnish with the lemon slices.

Serves 4

The Russian Tea Room.
Photo courtesy of The Russian Tea Room

The Russian Tea Room's
CHICKEN KIEV

After a meal of borscht, chicken Kiev, and Russian cream, the great pianist Van Cliburn proclaimed to a post-concert dinner party, "Well, it's delicious, and certainly better than anything I've tasted in Russia!" This recipe is adapted from one that appeared in *The Russian Tea Room Cookbook,* by Faith Stewart-Gordon and Nika Hazelton. For best results with this Russian classic, cut the chicken breasts from three (3½ pound) chickens and leave the wing bones attached to the breasts. Serve over a bed of hot cooked rice with buttered vegetables on the side.

12 tablespoons (1½ sticks) butter, chilled
3 whole chicken breasts with wing bones attached,
*   well rinsed, patted dry, halved, skinned, and*
*   boned*
¾ teaspoon salt
¾ teaspoon freshly ground black pepper
3 tablespoons all-purpose flour
2 eggs, beaten
⅔ to 1 cup fine dry bread crumbs
Vegetable oil, for deep-frying

1. Cut the butter into 6 equal pieces. Place each piece in the center of a square of waxed paper, cover with another piece of waxed paper, and with your hands roll each piece of butter into a 3-inch-long log about ¾ inch thick. Place the butter logs in the freezer for 30 to 40 minutes.

2. Cut the wing tip and middle wing joint from each split chicken breast, leaving only the short bone that is attached to the meat like a handle. Scrape the skin and meat off this bone. With a cleaver or heavy knife, trim the joint neatly. Carefully cut this bone almost, but not entirely, loose from the breast half to which it is attached;

the bone should hang from a thread of meat and sinew and be easy to twist. Lay the breast, smooth side down, on a cutting board and trim off the fat and gristle. With a small sharp knife and the help of your fingers, carefully pull off the small "tender" attached to each breast half. Lay the tender and the breast, smooth side down, on a sheet of waxed paper and cover both with another sheet of waxed paper, allowing the bones and the part of the meat to which it is attached to stick out. With the flat side of a cleaver, mallet, or rolling pin, pound the meat to a thickness of ⅛ inch. (Each pounded breast half will be about 8 inches long and 5 inches wide; each pounded tender will be about 7 inches long and 2 inches wide.) Pound the meat as thin as possible at the edges; the thinner the edges, the easier it will be to seal firmly to prevent the butter from oozing out during cooking. Be careful not to tear the meat or to detach it from the bone.

3. To assemble the kiev, gently peel off the waxed paper from each breast half and tender. Sprinkle 1 side of each breast and tender evenly with ⅛ teaspoon each salt and pepper. Place 1 portion of the frozen butter in the center of each breast half. Fold the wide side of the breast half lengthwise over the butter; repeat with the other side. Fold the boneless end up over the butter. Twist the wing bone around and push the bone into the butter, leaving only the ½-inch tip of the wing bone visible. Wrap the tender like a shawl around the bone and press it down tightly to adhere to the breast. It is essential to seal the butter tightly inside the meat, or it will ooze out during cooking.

4. Coat each cutlet on all sides with the flour, shaking off the excess. Dip each cutlet lightly into the beaten eggs, shaking off the excess, and then roll in bread crumbs, coating evenly. Place the cutlets in a single layer on a platter and refrigerate for 1 to 2 hours.

5. Heat 3 to 4 inches of the oil in a large heavy saucepan or deep-fat fryer until it registers 360°F on a deep-frying thermometer, or until a 1-inch bread cube dropped into the hot oil turns golden in slightly less than 1 minute. Add 2 of the cutlets and fry in the hot oil until golden brown, about 5 minutes. The cutlets should not touch each other during frying; turn them twice. Use tongs or 2 spoons for turning and removing the cutlets from the hot oil; this will prevent your from piercing

them. Drain the cutlets on paper towels and transfer to a heated serving dish. Keep warm in a low oven (150° to 175°F) until all of the cutlets are ready. Serve immediately.

Serves 6

Michael's
CHAMPAGNE CHICKEN

Michael Esposito, a butcher in Manhattan's Hell's Kitchen neighborhood, advises: "Never use any wine for cooking that you would not drink on its own!" Since this recipe uses less than 1 cup of Champagne, drink the rest with dinner for a luxurious treat. Esposito recommends serving Champagne Chicken with rice or couscous.

½ cup all-purpose flour
½ teaspoon salt, plus more to taste
¼ teaspoon freshly ground black pepper, plus
    more to taste
2 whole boneless chicken breasts, well rinsed,
    patted dry, halved, and trimmed
3 tablespoons unsalted butter, margarine, or light
    oil
Juice of 1 lime
½ cup Champagne
½ pound mushrooms, sliced
¼ teaspoon freshly grated nutmeg

---

1. In a shallow bowl, combine the flour, salt, and pepper. Dredge the chicken in the mixture; set the breasts aside on a clean plate.

2. Warm a nonreactive 10-inch skillet over medium heat. Add the butter and when hot, sauté the chicken until lightly browned on all sides, 3 minutes per side. Remove the chicken to a plate.

3. Add the lime juice and Champagne to the

skillet and stir to scrape up the bits from the bottom of the pan. Let the sauce simmer over medium-low heat until the alcohol burns off. Add the mushrooms and nutmeg and cook until the mushrooms soften and the sauce reduces by one-quarter to one-third, 5 minutes.

4. Return the chicken to the skillet and cook over medium heat until the chicken is cooked through, 5 to 8 minutes more. Correct the seasonings with more salt and pepper, then serve.

Serves 4

"21" Club
CHICKEN HASH

Since opening as a speakeasy during the Prohibition, the "21" Club has served chicken hash. At that time, the dish epitomized elegance up and down the Eastern seaboard. Over the years, chicken hash fell from the domain of chic and plenty, landing in tin cans on grocery store shelves and steam table vats and, ultimately, out of favor. Except at "21." On several occasions a well-intended manager or chef has tried to update the dish, or—horror of all horrors—attempted to replace it with something more au courant. Such attempts have been swiftly suppressed by patrons, who view chicken hash as a "grandfathered dish," safe from the vicissitudes of public taste, and certainly, an indelible part of the "21" mystique. Serve it over toast, waffles, baked potatoes, or wild rice, or incorporate it into an omelet or crêpe.

BECHAMEL SAUCE
2 cups milk
2 tablespoons butter
2 tablespoons all-purpose flour
¼ teaspoon freshly ground white pepper
Salt, to taste
Dash of Tabasco sauce
Dash of Worcestershire sauce

HASH
½ cup light cream
¼ cup dry sherry
2 cups diced cooked chicken breast
2 egg yolks

1. Preheat the oven to 300°F.

2. Make the béchamel sauce: Scald the milk in a heavy saucepan over medium-high heat. Remove from the heat and set aside.

3. Melt the butter in a heavy ovenproof saucepan over medium heat. Whisk in the flour and cook, whisking, for 2 minutes. Gradually stir in the hot milk and continue to whisk until the mixture thickens, 15 minutes. Remove from the heat; season with the pepper, salt, Tabasco, and Worcestershire sauce.

4. Cover the saucepan and place it in the oven. Bake until very thick yet fluffy, 1½ hours. Strain the sauce and correct the seasonings. You should have 1 cup sauce.

5. Make the hash: In a nonreactive saucepan over medium heat, whisk the béchamel sauce with the cream until fluffy. Add the sherry and mix well. Reduce the heat to low and stir in the chicken. Cook until heated through, 5 minutes. Correct the seasonings. Stir in the egg yolks.

6. Serve the hash hot over one of the foods listed above.

Serves 4

Welcome to "21." Photo courtesy of "21" Club.

Hot and Sour CHICKEN WITH RED PEPPERS

Food maven Elaine Louie suggests serving this feisty chicken with boiled rice and fresh peas.

SAUCE
1 tablespoon cornstarch
½ cup New York Penicillin (page 47) or canned chicken broth
3 tablespoons soy sauce
2 tablespoons dry sherry
3 tablespoons white wine vinegar
½ teaspoon sugar

STIR-FRY
2 skinless, boneless chicken breasts (about 1½ pounds), cut into 1-inch cubes
1 egg white
1 tablespoon dry sherry
1 teaspoon salt
1 tablespoon cornstarch
¼ cup vegetable oil
1 slice (¼ inch thick) fresh ginger, minced
2 teaspoons dried red pepper flakes, or more to taste
1½ tablespoons commercial black bean sauce

Elaine Louie in her kitchen.

1. Make the sauce: Dissolve the cornstarch in the chicken broth in a small bowl. Stir in the soy sauce, sherry, vinegar, and sugar; set aside.

2. For the stir-fry: Mix the chicken, egg white, sherry, salt, and cornstarch together in a bowl.

3. Heat the oil in a wok or skillet until very hot. Add the chicken and stir-fry until the pieces turn white but are still raw inside, about 30 seconds. Remove the chicken with a slotted spoon

and set aside. Add the ginger and red pepper flakes to the wok and stir. Add the chicken and stir-fry for 2 minutes. Add the black bean sauce and the reserved sauce and stir-fry until the sauces mingle and thicken, about 1 minute.

Serves 4

Sev Meoun's CAMBODIAN CHICKEN SALAD

This bright-tasting, exotic chicken and noodle salad makes a delicious summer meal, served warm or cold.

½ bundle bean threads (cellophane noodles)
3 tablespoons nuoc nam (Oriental fish sauce)
2 tablespoons rice wine vinegar
1 tablespoon sugar
2 cloves garlic, minced
1¾ cups shredded cooked chicken
½ pound Chinese cabbage, shredded
1 carrot, peeled and shredded
1 cucumber, peeled, seeded, and shredded
1 small onion, thinly sliced
2 tablespoons finely chopped fresh mint leaves
2 tablespoons chopped unsalted peanuts

1. Place the cellophane noodles in a large pot of boiling water. Simmer for 2 minutes; remove from the heat. Let the noodles sit in the hot water until tender, about 7 minutes. Drain and set aside.

2. In a small bowl, combine the fish sauce, vinegar, sugar, and garlic.

3. In a large mixing bowl, combine the cooked chicken, cabbage, carrot, cucumber, onion, and cellophane noodles. Add the vinegar mixture and toss well. Add the mint and peanuts, toss well, and serve.

Serves 4 to 6

Cookbook author Julie Sahni.

Fragrant Cornish Hens
IN PINE NUT SAUCE

This recipe from well-known cook and food writer Julie Sahni is a stunning example of the elusive flavors in Indian cuisine. Sweet and savory combine to create a dish that is both fragrant and totally satisfying.

½ cup pine nuts
2 teaspoons ground fennel
2 tablespoons ground coriander
1 teaspoon ground cardamom
½ teaspoon cayenne pepper
1 teaspoon saffron threads, crushed
2 small Cornish hens, well rinsed, patted
*   dry, and split in half*
¼ cup plus 1 tablespoon light vegetable
*   oil*
1 onion, minced
1 tablespoon minced garlic
2 tablespoons minced fresh ginger
1 tomato, puréed, or ⅓ cup canned
*   tomato purée*
1 teaspoon coarse (kosher) salt, or
*   to taste*
1 green bell pepper, stemmed, seeded,
*   and cut into 1-inch pieces*
1 red bell pepper, stemmed, seeded,
*   and cut into 1-inch pieces*
2 tablespoons heavy (whipping) cream or milk, or
*   more as needed*

1. In a small heavy skillet, toast 3 tablespoons of the pine nuts over medium heat until light brown, 3 minutes. Remove, allow to cool, and reserve for garnish. Grind the remaining ¼ cup plus 1 tablespoon pine nuts into a powder with an electric grinder or a mortar and pestle.

2. Combine the ground pine nuts, fennel, coriander, cardamom, cayenne, and saffron in a bowl; set aside.

3. Remove the skin and any visible fat from the Cornish hens and pat dry. Warm 1 tablespoon of the oil until very hot in a nonreactive skillet over high heat. Add the hens and brown over medium-high heat, turning often, for 4 minutes. Remove the hens to a plate and set aside.

4. Add the remaining ¼ cup oil and the minced onion to the pan. Cook over high heat until lightly colored, stirring often, about 4 minutes. Add the garlic and ginger, reduce the heat to medium-high, and cook for 2 minutes. Stir in spice-nut mixture and cook for 1 minute. Stir in the tomato, salt, and 1 cup water.

5. Add the hens to the pan and bring the mixture to a boil. Reduce the heat, cover, and cook at a gentle simmer, basting often, until the hens are fork-tender, about 30 minutes.

6. Add the bell peppers and cook until the peppers are soft but not mushy, 5 minutes. Add 2 tablespoons cream, or more as necessary, to thin and glaze the sauce. Arrange the hens on a heated platter, surround with the peppers, and sprinkle with the toasted pine nuts.

Serves 4

CHURCH SUPPERS

Always remember to call ahead, not only to confirm dates, times, and availability, but also to confirm that suppers are open to the public. Some churches have covered dish dinners and all attending are expected to bring something. Others sell tickets.

Manhattan

Cost is between $5 and $6, depending on what they serve.

BAPTIST TEMPLE CHURCH: 20 West 116th Street; (212) 996-0334. *Sunday Dinner, after service: Church representative describes dinner as "typical black church food," such as fried chicken and collard greens. Not every week, call first.

*Thanksgiving Dinner: traditional Afro-American dishes
*Sunday Dinner, 1 to 2:30. Among the foods commonly served are fried fish, chicken, shrimp, salad, and greens.

Preparing food for a congregation or fundraiser means cooking in large quanties. Here, preparing a fund raising meal, are members of The Mother's Club of St. Stephen of Hungary Catholic Church at 414 East 82nd Street, (212) 861-8500.

ROCKY MT. BAPTIST CHURCH: 37-41 Hillside Avenue, Inwood; (212) 941-1253.

Brooklyn

LAFAYETTE AVE-NUE PRESBYTER-IAN CHURCH: 85 South Oxford Street; (718) 625-7515.
*Maundy Thursday
*Thanksgiving
Lafayette Avenue Church is multiethnic; located in Fort Greene, the congregation is black, West Indian, Native American, and white. Their dinners are traditionally American-type meals, but you may find a special island or Southern dish.

BAY RIDGE UNITED CHURCH: 636 Bay Ridge Parkway; (718) 836-4978.
*150th Anniversary Dinner was November 11, 1990.
*Fellowship dinners: Scottish Night—April or May; Italian Night—Friday after Columbus Day.

CHRIST CHURCH OF BAY RIDGE: 7301 Ridge Boulevard; (718) 745-3698.
*Five weeks of Lenten Suppers
*Oktoberfest; embracing the German population of the Church, which also includes Scandinavians and other Europeans. Christ Church's Oktoberfest celebrates with German food and music.

UNION CHURCH OF BAY RIDGE: 8101 Ridge Boulevard; (718) 745-0348.
*Lenten Suppers; they

have a diverse ethnic congregation and the suppers reflect that—everything from Italian to Scandinavian.

FLATBUSH CHURCH OF THE REDEEMER: 494 East 23rd Street; (718) 434-0131.
*They have potluck dinners, often on Sunday evenings, with "spice" from the many Caribbean immigrants in the area.

GOOD SHEPHERD LUTHERAN CHURCH: 7420 4th Avenue; (718) 745-8520.
*Lenten Suppers, evenings during Easter season. Scandinavian, German, and Eastern European churchgoers share festive dishes.

ST. MARY'S EPISCOPAL CHURCH: 230 Classon Avenue; (718) 622-3262.
*Lenten Suppers
*Thanksgiving; the traditional turkey, yams, and trimmings are brought by parishioners of the church, which is primarily West Indian.
*Picnics, brunches, benefit dinners throughout the year

VANDERVEER PARK UNITED METHODIST CHURCH: East 31st Street and Glenwood Road; (718) 434-3745.
*Thanksgiving; the traditional turkey, plus yams, and other West Indian specialties.
*Other dinners throughout the year. Call for more information. Meals at Vanderveer have a Caribbean flavor.

Summer
GRILLED QUAIL

Candice Odell and Julian Shapiro, computer wizards who live in Brooklyn, favor this grilled quail for summer dinner parties.

MARINADE AND QUAIL
⅓ cup olive oil
2 cloves garlic, crushed
1 shallot, minced
¾ teaspoon herbes de Provence
1 tablespoon fresh lemon juice
Salt and freshly ground black pepper, to taste
4 quails (¾ pound each), butterflied, well rinsed, and patted dry

DRESSING
3 tablespoons walnut oil
2 tablespoons olive oil
2 tablespoons sherry vinegar
Salt and freshly ground black pepper, to taste

BREAD AND SALAD
8 baguette slices
8 cups mixed greens, including lettuce, arugula, mâche, and radicchio, well rinsed, spun dry, and torn into bite-size pieces
2 endives, trimmed and cut into julienne

Candice Odell and Julian Shapiro with son Raphael.

1. Marinate the quail: In a large nonreactive bowl, combine all of the marinade ingredients through the pepper. Rub on the quails. Refrigerate, turning occasionally, for 6 hours.

2. Make the dressing: In a bowl, whisk together the ingredients for the dressing.

3. Prepare charcoal for grilling.

4. Remove the quails from the marinade and grill the quails, skin side down, for 3 minutes. Turn and grill for 3 minutes more. Brush the baguette slices with the quail marinade and grill until toasted, 1 minute per side. Transfer the quail and toasts to separate plates and keep warm.

5. Toss the salad greens with the dressing; divide among 4 dinner plates. Place 1 quail in the center of each salad and drizzle any meat juices that have drained from the birds over the quail. Serve with a toast round on 2 opposite sides of each plate.

Serves 4

Greek Stuffed
QUAIL

Every year at the Ninth Avenue Food Fair, this delicious quail is made and sold. Try to get freshly made Greek feta, as it makes all the difference in the world. It is important to cook off the alcohol so that the acidity does not overwhelm the flavor of the quail.

Salt and freshly ground black pepper, to taste
8 quails (¾ pound each), well rinsed and patted dry
1¾ cups fresh Greek feta cheese, crumbled
½ cup finely chopped fresh parsley
2 teaspoons dried oregano, crushed
4 to 6 tablespoons unsalted butter, melted
⅓ cup retsina (Greek resinated white wine)
1 cup New York Penicillin (page 47) or canned chicken broth

1. Preheat the oven to 450°F.

2. Lightly salt and pepper the quails. In a small bowl, combine the feta, parsley, oregano, and additional pepper to taste. Stuff the mixture into the quails and truss.

3. In a skillet, heat 2 tablespoons of the melted butter over medium-high heat. Add the quail and gently brown on each side, about 5 minutes.

4. Arrange the quails, breast side down, on a rack over a baking pan and let them rest for 5 minutes. Brush with the remaining melted butter and roast until the juices run clear when a thigh is pricked and the skin is golden brown, 15 to 20 minutes.

5. Meanwhile, pour out the excess butter from the skillet used to brown the quails. Set the pan over high heat until it begins to sizzle. Add the wine and cook until the alcohol burns off and the wine reduces to a glaze over the bottom of the pan, 5 minutes. Pour in the chicken broth and boil until reduced by half, about 5 minutes more.

6. Remove the birds from the rack and set aside to rest. Pour the pan juices into the sauce. Remove the trussing from the quails and serve them with the sauce.

Serves 4

Ali Fathalla's
QUAIL STUFFED WITH CURRIED COUSCOUS

Ali Fathalla, the chef of Ca'Nova restaurant, really loves this dish because it "shows off" the best of his native Egyptian cuisine. Mr. Fathalla learned this recipe from his father, who was a fantastic cook. He has adapted this dish for lighter eating. Words to the wise: Undercook the couscous at the first stage because it will cook again in the bird; there is nothing worse than soggy couscous.

5 tablespoons olive oil
2 cloves garlic, minced
Salt and freshly ground black pepper,
    to taste
8 quails (¾ pound each), boned (see Note),
    well rinsed, and patted dry
1 cup New York Penicillin (page 47)
    or canned chicken broth
¼ cup chopped onion
2 tablespoons very finely diced carrot
2 tablespoons very finely diced
    zucchini
½ teaspoon ground coriander
½ teaspoon curry powder
Pinch of saffron (optional)
½ pound quick-cooking couscous
2 tablespoons chopped fresh parsley
1 tablespoon chopped cilantro

━━━━━━━━━━━━

1. Preheat the oven to 400°F.

2. In a medium bowl, mix together 2 tablespoons of the olive oil, half of the garlic, ½ teaspoon salt, and ¼ teaspoon pepper. Rub the quail with the marinade, then set aside for at least 30 minutes at room temperature, or cover and refrigerate overnight.

3. Meanwhile, bring the broth to a boil in a small saucepan.

4. While the broth is heating, warm 1 tablespoon of the olive oil in a large skillet over medium heat. When hot, add the onion, carrot, zucchini, and the remaining minced garlic. Sauté until the vegetables soften, 10 minutes. Add the coriander, curry, and saffron. Stir in the couscous and the hot stock. Cover and remove from the heat. Let sit for 10 minutes.

5. Uncover the skillet, break up the couscous with a fork, and stir in the parsley and cilantro. Season to taste with salt and pepper. Let cool.

6. Remove the quail from the marinade. Stuff each cavity with 2 tablespoons of the couscous mixture. Truss the quail; arrange them in a large baking pan. Roast the quail until the thigh juices run clear when pierced with a fork, 6 to 8 minutes.

Serves 4

Note: Ask your butcher to bone these tiny birds for you.

EILEEN SAYS EVERYTHING IS PEKING DUCKIE

Peking duck, the classic recipe and dining ritual from China's Imperial City, rests somewhere between the Christmas goose and the Sabbath chicken in cultural significance and would seem to be the kind of dish imbued with emotion and symbolism. But Eileen Yin-Fei Lo, who is possibly the Peking Duck Master of the Western Universe, is singularly unsentimental about the dish.

"Don't touch my duckie," she barked recently as her husband, Fred Ferretti, tried to help her unload groceries from the back of the family station wagon. "You break my duckie, I break you," said Eileen Yin-Fei Lo, who stands slightly less than five feet tall and slightly higher than Mr. Ferretti's ample waist. She explained that, after selecting a fresh duck, the single most critical factor in getting a crisp-skinned creature is unmarred skin.

Otherwise "the duck won't dry so good," she said. In her book, there is nothing worse than a damp duck, and Mrs. Yin-Fei Lo is an expert on avoiding this condition. First, she explains, she buys a good duck, with head and feet intact, and cleans it in many rinses of water. "Just open the bill under the faucet and woosh," she says, "around 15 minutes, clean duck."

KITCHEN HANG-UP

Next, she pats the duck dry and, using a length of butcher's twine about 8 inches long, fashions a noose for the duck and hangs it over the sink for 15 minutes.

"When my kids were little they would say 'eeeck,'" said Mrs. Yin-Fei Lo. "I would say, 'No eeck, Peking duck.'" Children are not the only ones who are squeamish at the sight of a swinging duck. At the China Institute, where Mrs. Yin-Fei Lo teaches cooking, grown-ups occasionally ask her why she insists on using a duck with neck and head intact.

"Are you crazy? How else you going to hang the duck?" she clucks.

Her favorite part of the Peking process appears to be using the bicycle pump. Eagerly she places the air pump under the duck, inserts the nozzle into the small incision she has made in the neck, places her size 3½ foot on the pump, and starts thumping like a rock 'n' roll drummer on his favorite cymbal.

"I hope it's crispy, I hope it's crispy, I hope it's crispy," she says, thump, thump, thumping air between the skin and the flesh to ensure that it will be.

A LITTLE OFF THE BOTTOM AND SIDES

Afterwards, Mrs. Yin-Fei Lo uses a cleaver to whack off the first two joints of each of the duck's wings and feet. She inserts a 7-inch chopstick from wing-to-wing under the skin of the duck's back, which lifts the skin and sets the wings in a crucifixion-like pose. Holding the duck by the noose, Mrs. Yin-Fei Lo scalds it to tighten the skin. After coating it with a vinegar and honey mix, she returns the duck to the gallows, aims a household fan at it, and smiles as the bird drifts in the breeze.

The weather, she says, can play tricks on you, but on a dry breezy day, it takes about 10 hours to fan-dry a duck at home. "Just do it in a cool place" is Mrs. Yin-Fei Lo's response to questions about sanitation. After the drying, the duck is roasted for about 40 minutes and cooled for 40 minutes, during which time Mrs. Yin-Fei Lo stands on her tiptoes, rolling and frying the pancakes that accompany the delicacy, and addresses the issue of how viable a dinner of Peking duck is in today's busy households.

"So what the big deal?" she said. "You clean and pump and dry the night before, and the next day you cook," she said.

In addition, the Peking process appears to build a certain kind of self-confidence.

"I warn you not to touch my duck," growled Mrs. Yin-Fei Lo. She paused for a moment, studied her husband's quick retreat, flipped another Peking pancake, and said: "Usually people do what I say when I make a duckie."

At a Chinatown market with Eileen Yin-Fei Lo.

Eileen Yin-Fei Lo's
PEKING DUCK

DUCK
1 duck (5 pounds), including the head, wings, and feet
7 cups boiling water
3 tablespoons distilled white vinegar
3 tablespoons maltose or honey

PANCAKES
1¾ cups bread flour, plus an additional ½ cup for dusting
¾ cup boiling water
1½ teaspoons Oriental sesame oil
2 tablespoons vegetable oil (optional)

SAUCE
¼ cup hoisin sauce
½ teaspoon sugar
½ teaspoon Oriental sesame oil
½ teaspoon Shao Hsing rice wine or dry sherry

ASSEMBLY
12 scallions, white part only, trimmed to 2-inch pieces, stalk ends slivered into fringes

1. Prepare the duck: Clean the duck inside and out, removing all membranes and fat. Rinse thoroughly with cold water. Allow the water to drain. Tie off the neck of the duck with a piece of string and insert the nozzle of an air pump into the neck opening. Inflate with the pump until the skin separates from the flesh.

2. Gently remove the pump nozzle. With a cleaver remove the first 2 joints of each of the duck's wings and feet. Gently insert a 7-inch stick or chopstick under the skin, from wing through the back to wing, to lift the skin away from the body and promote even drying.

3. Hold the duck with one hand and use the other hand to ladle 4 cups of the boiling water onto the skin of the duck. The entire outside must

Most **Chinese restaurants** need a day's notice to prepare a Peking duck dinner. Variations abound and the quality of the dish varies, but these restaurants serve some of the more reliable versions:

GOLDEN UNICORN: 18 East Broadway at Catherine Street; (212) 941-0911.

HUNAN GARDEN: 1 Mott Street; (212) 732-7270.

SHUN LEE PALACE EAST: 155 East 55th Street, between Lexington and Third Avenues; (212) 371-8844.

SHUN LEE WEST LINCOLN CENTER: 43 West 65th Street, off Central Park West; (212) 595-8895.

Eileen Yin-Fei Lo's marketing takes her past windows filled with Chinese-style poultry and ribs.

be scalded. It is advisable to hang the duck on a hook over the sink to ease preparation. The skin will darken and tighten when scalded. Hang the duck for 30 minutes, allowing the skin to dry; on humid days this process may take longer.

4. In a wok, mix together the remaining 3 cups boiling water with the vinegar and maltose or honey and bring to a boil. Ladle the coating onto the skin of the hanging duck, making sure the skin is thoroughly coated. Allow 10 to 12 hours of drying time.

5. Make the pancakes: Place the flour in a large bowl. Slowly add the boiling water and mix with chopsticks or a wooden spoon, stirring in one direction only. When the flour absorbs the water and is cool enough to handle, turn out the dough onto a lightly floured board and knead until smooth, about 2 minutes. Wrap the dough in plastic and set aside for 30 minutes.

6. Roll the dough with your hands into a 12-inch-long rope. Divide the dough into 12 equal pieces. Dust a work surface with flour and flatten each piece with the palm of your hand, dusting on additional flour if the dough is sticky. Working with 2 pieces at a time, gently wipe the top of 1 with sesame oil and place the other flattened piece on top. Roll out into a 7-inch circle.

7. Heat a seasoned wok over low heat for 1 minute. If your wok isn't seasoned, lightly oil with some of the vegetable oil before heating. Put the pancake in the wok and cook until the pancake begins to bubble, 1 minute. Carefully flip and cook until a few light brown spots appear. Remove the pancake from the wok and carefully peel the 2 layers apart with your fingers. You will have 2 pancakes, each browned lightly on one side and white on the other. Continue with the remaining rounds of dough, stacking the cooked pancakes on top of each other and keeping them covered with foil. Add more vegetable oil if needed.

8. Preheat the oven to 450°F for 30 minutes.

9. While the oven is heating, make the sauce: In a small bowl, mix together the hoisin sauce, sugar, sesame oil, and rice wine. Set aside.

10. Place a large roasting pan filled with 1½ inches of water on the bottom shelf of the oven. Then position an oven rack over the pan and place the duck, breast side down, directly on the rack. Roast the duck for 10 minutes. Reduce the heat to 425°F, turn the duck over, and roast for 10 minutes. If the duck begins to burn, reduce the temperature to 400°F. Roast the duck, turning frequently to ensure that the head and tail do not burn, another 45 minutes. The duck is ready when the skin is a deep brown color and crispy. Remove from the oven and allow to cool for 3 minutes.

11. Slice the skin off the duck in scallop-like pieces. Slice the meat similarly. Spread 1 teaspoon of the hoisin sauce mixture on the white side of the pancake, then add 1 scallion brush, 2 pieces of meat, and 2 pieces of skin. Roll up and eat.

Serves 4 to 6

STORE-BOUGHT PEKING DUCK

In Chinatown, Peking duck is one of the big draws.

To buy a fresh Peking duck with head and feet attached, call either of these Chinatown butchers 48 hours ahead:

UNITED MEAT MARKET: 84 Mulberry Street, between Canal and Bayard Streets; (212) 962-6440.

CHEUN HING POULTRY MARKET: 123B Mott Street near Hester Street; (212) 966-0771.

DUCK
In Pecan Glaze

Inspiration struck real estate developer Mitchell Mailman in the middle of dessert. "I've always loved butterscotch," he explains. "I was eating out, and I ordered an ice cream with a sauce I thought would be butterscotchy. It wasn't what I thought, but I liked it and figured it would taste great as a sauce for duck."

1 duck (3½ to 4 pounds), well rinsed and patted dry
8 tablespoons (1 stick) unsalted butter
½ cup broken pecans (pieces about the size of raisins)
¼ cup bourbon
½ cup maple syrup

1. Preheat the oven to 375°F.

2. To prepare the duck for roasting, rinse the cavity, trim away any loose skin, remove any visible fat, and prick the skin extensively with a fork. Place the duck, breast side up, on a rack in a roasting pan. Roast the duck, periodically draining any liquid that collects in the cavity by tilting the duck upward and allowing the juices to drip into the roasting pan.

3. Meanwhile, melt the butter in a nonreactive skillet over medium heat. Add the nuts and sauté 1 minute to brown slightly. Be careful not to burn and blacken the nuts. Lower the heat, add the bourbon and syrup, and simmer, stirring frequently, until reduced by half. Remove from the heat and set aside.

4. After the duck has roasted for 1 hour, strain the nut glaze. Reserve the pecans separately. Cover the duck skin with dampened cheesecloth and spoon the glaze onto the cloth to moisten it. Continue to roast for about 1 hour more, glazing the duck frequently until you have about ¼ cup sauce left.

5. Once the duck is completely cooked (180°F on a meat thermometer), preheat the broiler.

6. Remove the cheesecloth from the duck and cover the skin with the pecan pieces and remaining glaze. Place the duck under the broiler and broil with the oven door open just long enough to glaze the skin. The pecans should not turn black. Let the duck rest for 5 to 10 minutes before serving.

Serves 4

Joyce Foray's
ROAST DUCK
WITH
CARAWAY

This recipe, handed down from Joyce Foray's Czechoslovakian grandmother, is a favorite at the Bohemian Hall in Astoria, where Foray (by profession, a bookkeeper) cooks for the popular Czech festivals. At home, Foray serves

At Astoria's Bohemian Hall, where the festival turn-outs are huge, Joyce Foray satisfies the hungry crowds with a family favorite.

this duck with Czech-style sauerkraut and bread dumplings.

*1 duck (about 5 pounds), well rinsed,
    patted dry, and trimmed of excess
    fat and skin*
1 tablespoon salt
2 tablespoons caraway seeds

1. Salt the duck inside and out. Cover and refrigerate overnight.

2. Preheat the oven to 425°F.

3. Line the floor or bottom rack of the oven with aluminum foil. Fill a large baking pan with water and place it on the oven floor or bottom rack. Clean another oven rack and place in the middle position. With a fork, prick the duck all over. Rub the caraway seeds over the duck. Set the duck on the oven rack. Roast, turning frequently, until the thigh juices run clear when pricked with a sharp knife, about 2 hours. Let the duck rest for 5 to 10 minutes before carving.

Serves 4

Louie's
RED-COOKED DUCK

This wonderfully seasoned duck is delicious with boiled rice. It makes a good centerpiece for a meal flanked by a clear soup and a light dessert. The leftover shredded duck can be made into soup by combining the duck, Chinese mushrooms, any reserved duck juice, chicken broth, Chinese noodles, and minced scallions.

1 duck (5 pounds), well rinsed, patted dry,
    and excess fat trimmed
1 cup soy sauce
1 star anise
¼ cup sugar
2 thin slices fresh ginger
2 scallions, cut into 2-inch lengths
16 dried Chinese mushrooms, soaked
    in warm water for 20 minutes, stems
    removed, caps squeezed to remove
    excess water

1. Bring a large pot of water to a boil. Blanch the duck for 2 minutes. In a separate nonreactive pot that will hold the duck snugly, combine 3 cups water, the soy sauce, star anise, sugar, ginger, and scallions. Add the duck and bring the liquid to a boil. Cover and reduce the heat to a simmer. Cook for 1 hour 50 minutes, turning the duck several times and basting to achieve an even, reddish-brown color.

2. Add the mushrooms and cook for 10 minutes more.

3. Remove the duck and mushrooms to a serving dish. Either chop the duck into small pieces or serve it whole, using chopsticks to pluck off the meat.

Serves 4

Hunting Lodge
WILD DUCK

Lighting designer Howard Brandston gets good use out of this recipe during the annual respite he and his friends enjoy at a hunting lodge in Manitoba, Canada. He uses this recipe for wild duck, but if wild ducks are unavailable, you can substitute regular duck; just increase the cooking time.

This dish goes nicely with wild rice.

4 large (4½- to 5½-pound) ducks
    (mallards or canvasbacks), backs and
    rib bones removed by the butcher,
    well rinsed and patted dry
1½ cups dry red wine
1½ cups dry red wine
⅓ cup soy sauce
¼ cup olive oil
2 tablespoons balsamic vinegar
3 tablespoons dried sage
¼ cup garlic powder
3 tablespoons dried basil
2 teaspoons dried red pepper flakes
1 teaspoon coarsely ground black pepper
½ teaspoon dried tarragon
2 bay leaves, crushed

1. Cut the partially boned ducks in half.

2. Combine all of the remaining ingredients in a nonreactive large roasting pan. Add the ducks, cover, and marinate in the refrigerator for 24 to 36 hours, turning once during this time.

3. Prepare charcoal for grilling.

4. Grill the ducks 8 to 10 minutes on each side.

5. Preheat the oven to 400°F.

6. After grilling, arrange the ducks in a large baking pan. Bake in the oven until rare, 45 to 50 minutes.

Serves 8

From River, Sea and the Fulton Market

A Day Dawns AT FULTON

Like an ancient lobster locked in battle on the dark ocean floor, the Fulton Fish Market persists—an economic dinosaur, a social anomaly.

The South Street Seaport development whittled away at its right claw, the condominiums at Peck Slip dented its side. Pier 17 claimed the city's last landing dock in Manhattan, scarring the market's feelers. But five days a week, in the hours before the sun rises over lower Manhattan, the 170-year-old fish exchange at the base of the East River defends its diminishing turf.

Wholesale volume has dipped 25 percent in the past decade. Still, more than 90 million tons of fish are traded annually in the Fulton Fish Market proper—the city-owned, quarter-acre garage lined with trading stalls east of the elevated East River Drive—and in the privately owned wholesale marts just west on South Street.

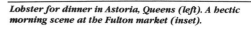

Lobster for dinner in Astoria, Queens (left). A hectic morning scene at the Fulton market (inset).

Boats no longer unload near the market. The 450 species of fish sold are trucked or flown in. But, the Fulton Fish Market is still king: the highest-volume wholesale seafood mart in the country. And the deals are still person-to-person, handshake-by-handshake, cash-to-pocket.

3:30 A.M. Squishing through the little bit of ocean that seeps from bushel baskets of mussels, from burlap bags of little-neck clams, and from wooden fish crates layered with flat fish head-to-tail, and crunching the packing ice underfoot, The Buyers move through Fulton Market.

"All right, who's next?" The Sellers slosh across their cement-floored stalls. Brown rubber boots laced mid-shin, they brush the underside of their low-lying plywood display planks. Tiny, silver-skinned hake from Canada; piles of smelts; blushing center-cut swordfish, piece weight scrawled in blurred purple marker across its thick, gray hide; lustrous silver Dover sole; sturdy mud-colored skate; fragile, deep coral shad roe near the splayed white-flesh shad. All less than 24 hours old, the fish glisten under the fluorescent lights and the beaming, tin-shaded incan-descent lamps that swing from the market's airplane-hangar-high ceiling.

"Watch your back. Watch your back." Above the steady, iron-lunged purr of the caravan of 18-wheelers that idles out front, The Movers shout their warning. Stocking-capped heads bowed to the puddles, to the pebble-like snails underfoot, they push hand trucks between The Buyers and The Sellers. "Your back." They yell above the peep-peep-peep of the orange Toyota forklifts that unload the seafood—trucked from piers in New Bedford and Province-town, from Elizabeth City, North Carolina, and the Great Lakes; flown in from Norway, Costa Rica, Panama, and the Philippines—and lower it to the floor of Manhattan's fish exchange.

"Move it, big guy." The journeymen push fat 40-pound cotton bags of scallops and waxed boxes of baby-finger-size orange-pink shrimp. Off the semis and onto the sellers' floor. Off the floor, onto the buyers' vans.

"$3.50 on the cod… $7 on the

sword. . . ." It's the Fulton Fraternity rap.

"Can't do it." Buyers shake their heads, moving from wholesaler to wholesaler.

"Some lousy market today," says Marvin Paige, who owns Claire restaurant in Manhattan. "Nothin' here," says Steve Cohen, buyer (of some 4,000 pounds of fish a day) for the Grand Central Oyster Bar and Restaurant.

Trimming fish steaks.

4 A.M. The Buyers are gulping watery coffee from white Styrofoam cups and comparing notes. So far there's no bluefish, no medium fluke; the Boston mackerel is junky, there's no Spanish mackerel. And, sorrowful shakes of the head all around, prices are high.

"Weather's bad," says Seymour Samuels, "nothin's cheap." The market, according to Samuels, since 1945 co-owner of Blue Ribbon Fish, has changed. Demand has skyrocketed. The nation's fisheries have diminished. Fish are being flown in from all over. "It's a world market now," says Samuels. Gently he unwraps a Styrofoam air-shipping crate. Inside are small, Mediterranean bass. "In Portugal it is called *roballo,* in Italy it is called *branzini,* in France it is called *loup de mere,*" says Samuels. "Here we call it $8.75."

"Very beautiful," nods Gilbert Le Coze, owner of Manhattan's Le Bernardin. Which means sold. Samuels nods. He marks three boxes. Le Coze pulls a folded envelope from the pocket of his blue down jacket. He makes a note. The Buyer and Seller shake hands.

Peter Ashkenasy and Marvin Paige discuss the day's offerings.

4:45 A.M. The Movers lean against their hand trucks near the bonfires under the East River Drive. They feed shipping pallets, fish crates, and corrugated boxes into the flames, warm their hands, and suck in the fishy, diesel-fumed air.

In the tiny room at the rear of Blue Ribbon Fish, The Buyers are tallying their purchases and making lists for their drivers. "I got all the hake, the monk, and the red snapper," Greg Heller, a retailer from Philadelphia yells into the phone. "Halibut, you can forget."

"Mr. Newmann's down there cryin' over the halibut," says Steve Cohen. Robert Newmann, co-owner of the city's Rosedale Fish market, takes high prices personally. He's shopped Fulton Fish for 49 years and he takes a lot of the market personally. "It's the last piece of civilization in this town," he says. "We know each other; maybe not each other's names, but we know who we are. We're polite. We're family."

Grand Central
OYSTER BAR AND RESTAURANT

In the late nineteenth century, oyster bars and restaurants crowded Canal Street, serving huge platters of bivalves and pots of oyster stew. Since 1913, the Oyster Bar and Restaurant in Manhattan's Grand Central Terminal has maintained the tradition. At the bar, a battery of cooks shuck 10 to 12 varieties of the city's freshest oysters, toss them in pans, and turn out the restaurant's signature oyster stew and pan roast. Both of these recipes are adapted from *The Grand Central Oyster Bar and Restaurant Seafood Cookbook*.

2. Whisk together the Tabasco, sauce, Worcestershire sauce, celery salt, and the remaining 1 tablespoon clam juice in a nonreactive small saucepan over high heat. Whisk in the heavy cream and continue whisking until the mixture comes to a boil. Add the warm oysters and their cooking liquids and stir gently for 1 minute.

3. Place the toast in a wide soup bowl. Pour the pan roast over the toast and sprinkle with a dash of paprika. Serve immediately.

Serves 1

The Grand Central Oyster Bar and Restaurant.

OYSTER PAN ROAST

1 tablespoon butter
6 to 8 large oysters, freshly shucked, liquor strained and reserved
3 tablespoons bottled clam juice
1 tablespoon Tabasco sauce
1 tablespoon Worcestershire sauce
Dash of celery salt
½ cup heavy (whipping) cream
1 slice white bread, toasted
Dash of sweet paprika

1. Melt the butter in a nonreactive skillet over high heat. Reduce the heat to medium and add the oysters, their liquor, and 2 tablespoons of the bottled clam juice. Cook until the oysters just begin to curl around the edges, 2 minutes. Remove from the heat.

OYSTER STEW

1 tablespoon butter
9 medium oysters, freshly shucked, liquor strained and reserved
1 tablespoon bottled clam juice
1 tablespoon Worcestershire sauce
½ cup half-and-half
½ teaspoon celery salt
¼ teaspoon sweet paprika

1. Melt ½ tablespoon of the butter in a nonreactive saucepan over medium heat. Add the oysters, their liquor, the clam juice, Worcestershire sauce, half-and-half, and celery salt and stir gently until the mixture comes to a boil.

2. Ladle the stew into a warmed bowl; top with the remaining ½ tablespoon butter and a sprinkle of paprika.

Serves 1

Mrs. Wilkenson's
SCALLOPED OYSTERS

Adapted from her 1846 housekeeping diary, on file at The New-York Historical Society.

1 cup fresh bread crumbs, dried overnight
1½ tablespoons minced fresh parsley
½ teaspoon freshly grated nutmeg
⅛ teaspoon cayenne pepper
8 tablespoons (1 stick) butter, cut into small pieces
4 dozen oysters, freshly shucked, liquor strained and reserved

1. Preheat the oven to 350°F.

2. In a large bowl, combine the bread crumbs, parsley, nutmeg, and cayenne.

3. Dot the bottom of a 10-inch, round casserole with one-third of the butter. Place a layer of oysters, sprinkle with some of the bread crumbs, and dot with half of the remaining butter. Repeat, ending with a slightly heavier layer of bread crumbs and the remaining butter. Bake until cooked through (it will not brown), 10 to 15 minutes. Serve, drizzled with the reserved liquor.

Serves 4

OLD NEW YORK

" 'Oysters: Oysters here's your beauties of Oysters: Here's your fine, fat, salt Oysters.'

"To serve the citizens through the course of the day and in the evening, this man, with his cart loaded with oysters, is heard from street to street, crying as above.

"This very delicious and wholesome shellfish is caught in various places, but in the greatest plenty, and largest size, at Blue-Point, which lies near the middle of Long-Island, on the south side.... They sell from twelve cents, to two dollars per hundred. There are many oyster stands in the city, where black men are ready with some of the finest oysters, which they open and serve out raw from one to three cents apiece...."

—CRIES OF NEW YORK, 1808–1814
SAMUEL WOOD

From the 1840s, The Oyster Man by Nicolino Calyo. Courtesy of The Museum of the City of New York

Gilbert Le Coze's
SHELLFISH STEW

Monsieur Le Coze, the impresario of Le Bernardin, created this recipe in his Paris restaurant and serves it still in New York. The variety and freshness of the seafood are most important in this dish and are what sends him to the Fulton Fish Market every morning. The dish can be served as a first course or as a meal.

1¼ pounds small cultured mussels, preferably Rope
32 littleneck clams
32 Manila clams
12 bay scallops in the shell
12 oysters (Belon, Cotuit, or similar)
½ pound (2 sticks) unsalted butter, at room temperature
2 cloves garlic, finely minced
2 shallots, finely minced
4 tablespoons minced fresh parsley
½ cup dry white wine
12 ripe tomatoes, chopped, with juices reserved
1½ cups heavy (whipping) cream
Juice of 1 lemon
Salt and freshly ground black pepper, to taste

Gilbert Le Coze with his sister, Maguy, co-owners of Le Bernardin. Photo courtesy of Le Bernardin

1. Scrub the shellfish under running water. Beard the mussels. Set aside on ice or in the refrigerator.

2. Preheat the oven to 425°F.

3. In a medium bowl, cream the butter until smooth. Add the garlic, shallots, 2 tablespoons of the parsley, and the white wine and mix until smooth. Set aside.

4. Purée the tomatoes with their juices in a food processor or blender. Strain out seeds and skins. Bring the tomato purée to a boil in a non-reactive medium saucepan over medium-high heat. Reduce the heat to low. Whisk in the heavy cream and simmer for 4 minutes. Add the butter mixture and simmer gently.

5. Place 2 cups water in a large stockpot. Add the mussels, all of the clams, and the scallops, cover, and steam over medium heat until the shellfish just open, 3 to 5 minutes. Discard any that don't open. Remove from the heat.

6. Shuck the oysters. Arrange them, on their half shells, on a baking sheet. Bake in the oven until slightly warmed through, 3 to 4 minutes.

7. Divide the shellfish and oysters equally among 4 large deep plates. Sprinkle the lemon juice and the remaining 2 tablespoons parsley over the shellfish.

8. Strain the shellfish cooking liquid into the hot tomato sauce. Add salt and pepper to taste, stir, and spoon the sauce over the shellfish.

Serves 4

Harriet's
STEAMED MUSSELS

Harriet Orlando of Brooklyn serves this dish in a huge bowl with plenty of extra crackers, bread, or pasta for sopping up the sauce. It is very spicy; if you prefer a milder dish, use less red pepper. Says Harriet, "These mussels are always a big hit."

6 cloves garlic, chopped
¼ cup olive oil
3 pounds mussels, well scrubbed and bearded
2 tablespoons chopped fresh parsley
1 teaspoon dried red pepper flakes
⅓ cup dry white wine
4 biscuits with pepper (or common crackers or oysters crackers), optional

Out in the backyard with Harriet Orlando.

1. In a nonreactive large pot, sauté the garlic in the olive oil over medium heat until softened, 5 minutes. Add the mussels, 1 tablespoon of the parsley, the red pepper flakes, and wine. Cover tightly and steam over medium heat until the mussels open, 3 to 5 minutes. Remove the mussels from the broth, discarding any that haven't opened. Strain the broth through a fine-mesh sieve lined with cheesecloth and reserve.

2. Place 1 biscuit in each of 4 soup dishes. Spoon the mussels and broth over the biscuits. Garnish with the remaining 1 tablespoon parsley.

Serves 4

Horatio Street
STEAMED MUSSELS

Writers of the 1920s, '30s and '40s often make reference to Bohemian dinners in Greenwich Village holes-in-the-wall that featured lots of philosophizing, cocktails, and cigarettes, and, often, a big pot of mussels in the middle of the table. This version recalls the stories of those days and is adapted from a spiral-bound community cookbook, *The Horatio Street Festival of Foods Cookbook.*

8 slices baguette
7 tablespoons olive oil
¼ cup finely chopped onion
2 cloves garlic, finely minced
1 cup fresh peeled, chopped tomatoes
1 cup dry white wine
4 dozen fresh mussels, well scrubbed, bearded, and drained
2 tablespoons finely chopped fresh parsley
1 tablespoon finely chopped fresh basil

1. Preheat the broiler.

2. Brush both sides of the baguette slices with 2 tablespoons of the olive oil and place on a broiling tray. Toast until lightly brown on both sides. Set aside.

3. Warm the remaining 5 tablespoons olive oil in a nonreactive large pot over medium heat. Add the onion and garlic and cook, stirring frequently, until the vegetables are softened, about 5 minutes. Add the tomatoes and wine, increase the heat to high, and add the mussels. Cover the pot and steam until the mussels open, 3 to 5 minutes. Discard any mussels that haven't opened. Sprinkle with the parsley and basil. Arrange 1 or 2 pieces of toast in the bottom of each soup bowl. Spoon the mussels and broth into bowls and serve.

Serves 4

Jerry Giorgio's
STUFFED MUSSELS

Detective Jerry Giorgio, who solved the notorious late 1970s murder of the violin player whose body was found at the bottom of an air shaft, has been an officer with the New York City Police Department for over 30 years, with homicide for 20. This recipe was created by his mother, who lived in Greenwich Village. Detective Giorgio serves the mussels with a bowl of fusilli topped with the remaining tomato sauce.

2 pounds mussels, well scrubbed and bearded
¼ cup olive oil
2 cloves garlic, peeled
6 cups tomato sauce
12 fresh basil leaves
1 teaspoon salt
½ teaspoon freshly ground black pepper
2 cups seasoned fine, dried bread crumbs
1 bunch fresh parsley, chopped
1 cup freshly grated Parmesan cheese

1. In a large pot, bring ½ cup water to a boil. Add the mussels, cover, and steam until the mussels are barely open, 3 to 5 minutes. Remove the mussels from the broth, discarding any that haven't opened. Strain the broth through a fine-mesh sieve lined with cheesecloth and set aside. Cool the mussels separately from the broth.

2. In a nonreactive large saucepan, warm the olive oil and garlic over medium heat until the garlic begins to brown, 5 to 7 minutes. Add the tomato sauce, basil, salt, and pepper and simmer the sauce, uncovered, to blend the flavors, 30 minutes.

3. In a bowl, combine the bread crumbs, parsley, and Parmesan. Slowly drizzle in enough of the reserved mussel broth to make a mixture the consistency of oatmeal. Add the remaining mussel broth to the tomato sauce.

4. Using a teaspoon, spoon some of the stuffing over the mussel into each half of the shell. Using string or thread, tie each mussel shut. Add the tied stuffed mussels to the tomato sauce. Cover and simmer for 15 minutes. Carefully remove the strings (making sure none slipped into the sauce) and serve in wide soup bowls.

Serves 6

Gage & Tollner's
CLAM BELLIES

Gage & Tollner opened in 1879 in downtown Brooklyn, at the height of New York's oyster house era. Originally an oyster house, the restaurant offered clams and oysters cooked 20 different ways. "Soft clams," large steamers from Ipswich, Massachusetts, served broiled or fried, were the most popular item. Sometime after the turn of the century, soft clams were renamed "clam bellies," which is how they are ordered at Gage & Tollner today.

12 large steamer clams, well scrubbed and opened
1 large egg, beaten
2 tablespoons milk
Dash of Tabasco sauce
½ cup cracker meal
¼ teaspoon salt
2 cups vegetable oil, for deep-frying (for fried clam bellies)
6 tablespoons (¾ stick) butter, melted (for broiled clam bellies)

FOR SERVING FRIED CLAM BELLIES
4 lemon wedges

FOR SERVING BROILED CLAM BELLIES
8 toast points (see Note)
4 lemon wedges
4 parsley sprigs

1. Separate the clam bellies from the muscles; discard the muscles. In a medium bowl, combine the egg, milk, and Tabasco. In a separate bowl, combine the cracker meal and salt. Dip each clam in the egg mixture, then roll in the crumbs and set aside on waxed paper. Continue breading the remaining clams.

2. For fried clam bellies: Place the oil in a large, heavy, deep pan. Set over high heat until a crumb placed in oil bubbles vigorously or the oil registers 350°F on a deep-frying thermometer. Carefully lower the breaded clams into the hot oil with a slotted spoon. Cook a few at a time, without crowding, and fry until golden, about 3 minutes. Remove the clams with a slotted spoon, and drain on paper towels or a brown paper bag. Serve with lemon wedges.

3. For broiled clam bellies: Preheat the broiler.

4. Place the clams on a broiler tray. Drizzle the melted butter over the clams and broil, shaking the pan occasionally, until evenly browned on all sides, 3 to 4 minutes. Serve on toast points, brushed with additional melted butter. Garnish with lemon wedges and parsley.

Serves 2 as an appetizer

Note: For toast points, trim the crusts from 2 slices of white bread. Cut each slice diagonally into 4 triangles, toast, and drizzle with melted butter.

Singer's STUFFED LOBSTER

From Joan Singer, "Since we live in Sheepshead Bay, my husband and I enjoy eating a good lobster. But eating in our neighborhood's famous seafood restaurants can become an enormous expense, so we decided to make lobster at home. Our lobster can be cooked under the broiler or, covered, on a charcoal grill. Once you've tried this recipe, you'll never eat anyone else's again."

8 tablespoons (1 stick) butter, melted
2 cups fine, dried bread crumbs
¼ pound bay scallops
¼ pound small shrimp, peeled and deveined
1 teaspoon salt
½ teaspoon freshly ground black pepper
Dash of Tabasco sauce
1 lobster (2 to 3 pounds), split in half lengthwise from head to tail, sand sac and intestines removed
4 to 10 large lettuce leaves, if broiling

■————————————————■

1. Preheat the broiler or prepare a grill. Move the broiler tray as far from the heat source as possible.

2. In a mixing bowl, combine the butter, bread crumbs, scallops, shrimp, salt, pepper, and Tabasco sauce.

3. Place the lobster, top shell down, on a broiling pan and fill the cavity with the stuffing. If broiling, cover the lobster with half of the lettuce leaves to prevent burning. Broil or grill (place the cover on the grill) for 10 minutes. Replace the burned lettuce leaves with fresh leaves. Continue to broil until the lobster meat is white, another 10 minutes. Remove the lettuce and dig in!

Serves 2

Joan Singer with her husband Herb.

Anne Rosenzweig's
LOBSTER CLUB SANDWICH

When she established herself as one of the country's premier women chefs in the 1980s, Anne Rosenzweig created this haute version of the old-fashioned ladies-lunch fare. It became a classic. And according to its creator, one must definitely remove the white gloves before eating: "Mayonnaise and tomato juice must dribble down your arms as you eat this."

BRIOCHE
1¼ pounds (5 sticks) unsalted butter
1 cup sugar
1 tablespoon salt
6 cups all-purpose flour
2 cups milk
1 ounce cake yeast, or 1½ packages
  active dry yeast
10 large eggs, beaten

LEMON MAYONNAISE (see Note)
2 egg yolks
1½ teaspoons Dijon mustard, at room
  temperature
¼ cup freshly squeezed lemon juice, at room
  temperature
1½ cups soy oil
1 tablespoon plus 1 teaspoon grated
  lemon zest
Salt and freshly ground black pepper,
  to taste

ASSEMBLY
2 cups crisp cold greens, such as romaine,
  frisée, red leaf lettuce
2 fresh ripe tomatoes, sliced (cold)
16 slices apple-smoked or double-smoked
  bacon, fried crisp
1 pound cooked, cold lobster tail meat,
  sliced on the bias ½ inch thick

1. Make the brioche: Cream together the butter, sugar, and salt in a large bowl. Add the flour and beat until the mixture resembles small peas.

2. In a small saucepan, heat the milk to lukewarm. Remove from the heat and stir in the yeast. Set aside until foamy, 5 to 10 minutes. (If the yeast doesn't foam, start over with fresh milk and yeast.)

3. Add the yeast mixture to the flour mixture and stir well. Add the beaten eggs. If you have a mixer with a dough hook, process at low speed for 10 minutes. If you are mixing by hand, beat until the dough has a sheen and pulls away from the sides of the bowl into a rough ball. Add more flour if the dough is too sticky. Remove to a clean bowl, cover, and set aside in a warm place to rise until doubled in bulk, 3 hours.

4. Punch down the dough. Cover and refrigerate until doubled in bulk, overnight.

5. Preheat the oven to 350°F.

6. Remove the dough from the bowl and allow to soften for about 15 minutes. With a sharp knife, cut the dough into 4 pieces. Roll out each piece into a cigar shape on a lightly floured board. Wind each brioche into a tight coil and press the seam closed with your fingertips. Bake on baking tiles or a baking sheet until the bottoms sound hollow when tapped, 50 minutes. Cool on a wire rack.

7. Make the lemon mayonnaise: In a small bowl, whisk together the egg yolks, mustard, and lemon juice until thick. Add the oil drop by drop, whisking constantly, until the mayonnaise begins to emulsify. At this point the remaining oil can be added in a thin stream, until the mayonnaise is thick. Fold in the lemon zest and season with salt and pepper. Cover and refrigerate for at least 1 hour, or un-

Anne Rosenzweig in the kitchen at Arcadia, pre the arrival of daughter, Lulu.

til you are ready to proceed with the rest of the recipe.

8. Assemble the sandwiches: Slice each brioche lengthwise into 4 even slices. Toast lightly. Spread mayonnaise on each toasted slice. Layer each bottom slice with the lettuce, then the tomato, bacon, and lobster. Top with a slice of toast and repeat the layering 2 more times to make 4 triple-decker sandwiches.

Serves 4

Note: This fresh mayonnaise includes raw egg yolks and, therefore, should be made with farm-fresh, salmonella-free, refrigerated eggs.

Rosanna Wong's
STEAMED LOBSTER WITH GINGER AND SCALLIONS

It is difficult to perfume a lobster with anything better than ginger and scallions and difficult to find a better version than this family recipe from Rosanna Wong.

2 tablespoons shredded or finely chopped fresh
  ginger
1 tablespoon dry white wine or sherry
1 teaspoon Oriental sesame oil
1½ teaspoons light soy sauce
1 teaspoon sugar
¼ teaspoon salt
Pinch of freshly ground white pepper
2 lobsters (1½ pounds each), hacked into small
  chunks
1 lemon, sliced into rounds
3 scallions, trimmed, cut in half lengthwise, and
  cut into 2-inch pieces

1. In a nonreactive bowl, combine the ginger, wine, oil, soy sauce, sugar, salt, and pepper. Add the lobster, toss to coat thoroughly with the marinade, and set aside to marinate for 10 minutes.

2. Bring 2 cups water to a boil in a large pot. Add the lobster and its marinade, the lemon slices, and half of the scallions. Cover and steam until the meat is white and the shell is pink, 10 to 15 minutes. Garnish with the remaining scallions.

Serves 2

Mammy's
SHRIMP AND RICE CREOLE

From Mammy's Restaurant, which before closing in the mid-1950s was on Montague Street in Brooklyn. This recipe is adapted from one that originally appeared in *Ford Treasury of Favorite Recipes from Famous Eating Places*.

2 tablespoons vegetable oil
1 onion, minced
1 green bell pepper, stemmed, seeded, and minced
1 clove garlic
2 cups canned whole tomatoes
1 teaspoon filé powder
Salt and freshly ground black pepper, to taste
1 cup fine, dried bread crumbs
3 tablespoons butter, melted
½ pound shrimp, peeled and deveined
2 cups cooked long-grain rice

1. Heat the oil in a nonreactive large skillet over medium heat. Add the onion and bell pepper and cook until the onion is translucent and the pepper is soft, 5 minutes. Add the garlic and sauté for 1 minute. Stir in the tomatoes, filé powder, and salt and pepper to taste. Reduce the heat to low, partially cover, and cook for 1 hour.

2. Preheat the oven to 375°F.

3. In a medium bowl, combine the bread crumbs and butter. Stir to mix and set aside.

4. Increase the heat under the skillet to medium. Add the shrimp and cook until they are just pink, about 3 minutes. Remove from the heat.

5. Transfer the shrimp and sauce to a 2-quart ovenproof casserole. Stir in the rice and top with the bread crumbs. Bake until bubbly and the bread crumbs are browned, 30 minutes.

Serves 4

Camarones Y Langosta
ENCHILADA

Bob Medina, an avid home cook, who oversees the thousands of files of newspaper clips that are accrued daily at *The New York Times,* serves this Latin-American ragout in a corn or flour tortilla to company.

5 cloves garlic
1 tablespoon salt
2 lobster tails
1 tablespoon olive oil
2 pounds large shrimp, peeled and deveined
1 can (16 ounces) tomato sauce
½ cup ketchup
1 large onion, chopped
½ large green bell pepper, stemmed, seeded, and chopped
10 pimiento-stuffed olives
3 bay leaves
1 tablespoon minced fresh parsley
½ teaspoon dried oregano
½ teaspoon dried red pepper flakes
½ teaspoon freshly ground black pepper
½ teaspoon chili powder
½ cup dry white wine

1. In a mortar with a pestle, mash the garlic and salt together. Set aside.

2. Bring 2 cups water to a boil in a saucepan. Add the lobster tails and boil until the shells turn bright red, 5 minutes. Remove the lobster and reserve ½ cup of the cooking liquid.

3. In a nonreactive large casserole, warm the oil over medium heat. Add the shrimp and cook until they turn pink, 3 to 5 minutes. Remove to a bowl with a slotted spoon. To the casserole, add the garlic-salt paste and stir well. Add the tomato sauce and ketchup and simmer for 2 minutes. Add the onion, bell pepper, olives, bay leaves, parsley, oregano, red pepper flakes, black pepper, and chili powder and simmer for 2 minutes. Stir in the reserved lobster water and the wine and simmer gently for 30 minutes.

4. Shell the lobster meat and add it and the shrimp to the casserole. Cook until heated through, 3 minutes. Serve in large bowls, with bread or tortillas to sop up the delicious juices.

Serves 6

Bob Medina enjoys a frothy New York favorite, cappuccino.

Ed Bradley's
SHRIMP CREOLE

Ed Bradley, of CBS's "60-Minutes," uses Matouk's Hot Sauce in this recipe, which he prepares for company. The sauce is a fiery blend of papaya and hot peppers from Trinidad and is sold in some West Indian and Indian shops, including Kalustyan, 123 Lexington Avenue, New York, NY 10016, where it is available by mail.

6 tablespoons (¾ stick) unsalted butter
3 onions, finely chopped
3 cloves garlic, finely minced
3 ribs celery, finely chopped
3 green bell peppers, stemmed, seeded, and
    chopped
2 jalapeño chiles, seeded and minced
Salt and freshly ground black pepper, to taste
4 tomatoes, cubed
¼ cup finely minced fresh parsley
1 bay leaf
3 tablespoons Matouk's Hot Sauce, or more to
    taste (see recipe introduction)
2 pounds medium shrimp, peeled and deveined
3 to 4 cups cooked long-grain rice, for serving
Lemon wedges, for serving

1. In a nonreactive large saucepan over medium heat, melt 2 tablespoons of the butter. Add the onions and garlic and sauté, without browning, until the onions are translucent, 5 minutes. Add the celery, bell peppers, and jalapeños and season with salt and pepper to taste. Cook, stirring often, until crisp-tender but not soggy, about 4 minutes. Stir in the tomatoes, parsley, and bay leaf, then cover and bring to a boil. Reduce the heat and simmer for 10 minutes.

2. Stir in the Matouk's Hot Sauce. Remove the bay leaf and set the pan aside.

3. Melt the remaining 4 tablespoons butter in a nonreactive large skillet over high heat. Add the shrimp and sauté until they turn pink, about 3 minutes. Pour the tomato mixture over the shrimp, stir well, and bring just to a boil. Remove from the heat immediately. Serve over rice with lemon wedges.

Serves 6

Cook up Ed Bradley's spicy creole—it takes far less than 60 minutes. Photo courtesy of CBS

Stir-Fried
SHRIMP WITH SCALLIONS

Elaine Louie recommends cooking this dish in two batches in an ordinary-size wok. Overloading a wok will cause the food to steam rather than fry. Serve this with boiled rice and cucumber salad. This recipe was adapted from *Chinese Home Cooking,* a pamphlet written by Elaine Louie and Julia Chang Bloch and published by The Organization of Chinese American Women.

2 tablespoons soy sauce
2 tablespoons Scotch whiskey or dry sherry
2 teaspoons sugar
4 tablespoons vegetable oil
6 slices fresh ginger (¼ inch thick), lightly smashed
2 bunches scallions, or 1 bunch Chinese or
    Western chives, trimmed and cut into 2-inch
    lengths
2 pounds medium shrimp, rinsed and patted dry
Cooked rice, for serving

1. In a small bowl, mix together the soy, whiskey, and sugar. Set aside.

2. In a wok, heat 2 tablespoons of the oil until very hot. Add 3 of the ginger slices and stir-fry for 1 minute. Add half of the scallions, half of the shrimp, and half of the soy mixture and stir-fry rapidly until the shrimp turn pink, 3 to 5 minutes. Remove to a warm platter, discarding the ginger.

3. Return the wok to the heat and warm the remaining 2 tablespoons oil until very hot. Add the remaining ginger, shrimp, scallions, and soy mixture and stir-fry as before. Add to the previously cooked shrimp and mix. Serve over cooked rice.

Serves 4 to 6

BREADED SHRIMP
In Green Paste

Zubin Mehta, the former music director of the New York Philharmonic, finds chile peppers as indispensable as a baton in his life. He grew up eating Parsi Indian food in Bombay and when his career moved him through Europe, the Middle East, and the United States, he found that he had to take drastic measures to ensure palatable meals: He totes his own chiles.

Gentlemen before him have packed elegant snuff or pill boxes, but Mr. Mehta carries a jeweled silver case of hot cayenne, tabasco, Scotch bonnet, and bird chile peppers in his pocket.

"Unlike jalapeños, these varieties dry the best," he explained. He is, therefore, always prepared to spice up a restaurant meal or cook an impromptu meal in the home of friends.

1 cup loosely packed cilantro leaves and tender stems
½ cup fresh mint leaves
½ cup grated fresh coconut
¼ cup freshly squeezed lemon juice
5 cloves garlic
8 fresh hot green chiles, stemmed
1 tablespoon sugar
Salt, to taste
1½ pounds jumbo shrimp, peeled, tails left on
Vegetable oil, for shallow-frying
2 large eggs, lightly beaten
3 cups fine, dried bread crumbs

1. Combine the cilantro, mint, coconut, lemon juice, garlic, chiles, sugar, and salt in a food processor or blender. Process into a paste; set aside.

2. Butterfly and devein the shrimp. To prevent them from curling during cooking, thread a toothpick along the length of each shrimp. Place the shrimp in a dish, add the green paste, and toss to coat thoroughly.

3. Heat

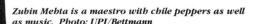

Zubin Mehta is a maestro with chile peppers as well as music. Photo: UPI/Bettmann

the oil to a depth of ½ inch in a large heavy skillet over medium-high heat. Dip the shrimp first in beaten egg and then in bread crumbs. Slip them into the hot oil, in batches if necessary, and cook, turning, until cooked through and the bread crumbs are golden, 3 minutes. Drain on paper towels before serving.

Serves 4

Hell's Kitchen
GREEK SHRIMP WITH FETA

This dish was a favored call at the old Paradise restaurant on 41st Street. The recipe is adapted from *Secrets from New York's Best Restaurants*, by Earlyne S. Levitas and Lydia Moss.

3 tablespoons olive oil
2½ cups chopped onions
¼ cup finely chopped fresh parsley
1 clove garlic, minced
½ teaspoon sugar
*3 cups chopped fresh plum tomatoes
   (about 1½ pounds)*
*1 cup dry white wine, preferably retsina (Greek
   resinated wine)*
1½ pounds shrimp, peeled and deveined
1 cup crumbled feta cheese

1. Preheat the oven to 425°F.

2. Warm the oil in a nonreactive large skillet over medium heat. Add the onions and sauté until light golden brown, 7 minutes. Add the parsley, garlic, and sugar and stir to mix. Add the tomatoes and cook until they soften and their liquid is absorbed, about 20 minutes.

3. Add the wine to the skillet and cook until the liquid is absorbed. Add the shrimp and cook, stirring constantly, for 30 seconds. Remove from the heat.

4. Pour the shrimp and sauce into a 2-quart casserole. Top with the feta cheese. Bake until the cheese melts, 5 minutes.

Serves 4

Dina Merrill's
ROSEMARY SHRIMP

This simple, herbaceous dish is wonderful for company, especially served with rice or salad.

2 cloves garlic, minced
*2 tablespoons minced fresh rosemary, or 1
   tablespoon dried*
¼ cup dry white wine
2 tablespoons freshly squeezed lemon juice
Salt and freshly ground black pepper, to taste
⅓ cup olive oil
1 pound medium shrimp, in their shells
2 lemons, quartered, for garnish
Rosemary sprigs, for garnish
*4 pita breads, cut into triangles and toasted, for
   serving*

1. In a small bowl, combine the garlic, rosemary, wine, lemon juice, salt, and pepper. Set aside.

2. In a nonreactive large skillet, warm the oil over high heat until it is hot. Add the shrimp and cook, stirring frequently, until the shrimp turn pink, about 3 minutes. Stir in the rosemary mixture. Remove from the heat.

3. Transfer the shrimp and sauce to a 2-quart baking dish large enough to hold the shrimp in one layer. Cover and marinate in the refrigerator overnight.

4. Arrange the shrimp on a platter, garnishing with the lemon wedges and rosemary. Serve at room temperature with toasted pita. Everyone gets to dig in and peel their own.

Serves 4

FERNANDO LARA, MARINE MURALIST

Fernando Lara approaches the display window at the Citarella Fish Company in Manhattan like a latter-day Diego Rivera. Instead of an artist's smock, he wears a black rubber apron. He wears a New York Mets cap rather than a beret and, instead of paint, his palette includes gray sole and white scallops, deep rose salmon fillets, orange stone crab claws, and blue-black mussels.

Every morning the diminutive artist, who was born in Mexico City, regards the empty window at 2135 Broadway (75th Street) with the eagerness and fear of a muralist in front of a blank wall.

His compositions stop pedestrians. Some, like the 10-by-4-foot American flag that he fashioned with stripes of shrimp and squid and squid-head stars, have a patriotic motif. Others, like the whole salmon wearing a sombrero, drinking a can of beer, and swinging in a hammock, are a response to the weather.

The windows change daily and all are intricate, exuberant mosaics that celebrate fish, stop traffic, and take Mr. Lara about six hours a day to create. It is his full-time job.

ICE-COLD CANVAS

"I come in at 6 A.M. to make my canvas," he said, adding that it takes about an hour to pack a hundred pounds of ice into the slanting display area. "I have to get a good surface that doesn't melt all day."

Before he lays the first stroke of fish, Mr. Lara tapes sheets of paper across the window glass. Artists need privacy, he explained. Next, he uses a slat from a fish crate to judiciously measure his canvas and then marks the center with a toothpick.

"I must be exactly at the center," he said,

positioning the store's sign there. Mr. Lara scrutinizes its placement, adds a flounce of lettuce, and proceeds.

A REGULAR VAN GOGH

On a recent smoldering day, Mr. Lara was thinking about sunflowers.

"I was so worried about the window when I walked home from the subway" said Mr. Lara, who lives in Astoria, Queens. "Then I see some sunflowers and I know," he said, his voice fading in awe of the inspiration.

He began to build a sunflower mosaic by fanning 32 slices of gray sole around the outer rim of the ring.

It took nearly an hour to fix the sole fillets in position. He used toothpicks as nails, tapping them gently into place with the handle of the fish knife he held, in contemplative moments, like a brush. He accented the sole with orange stone crab claws, arranged a concentric fan of salmon steaks, and created a white line by tucking squid bodies around the edges. He uses about 500 toothpicks a day.

Mr. Lara suffers over his decisions. Do New England or New Zealand mussels provide a better contrast to the flounder fillets in the center of his flower? Should he try making a leaf out of seaweed? But these are the kind of troubles he dreamed about having when he first came to New York in 1979.

"I worked as a busboy in the Mexican restaurant across the street, and I looked over at the window and dreamed," he said. He was captivated, though he had never studied art or fish. In 1983, he got closer, taking a job as a fish cutter at Citarella. He then spent four years getting to know his medium.

Mr. Lara estimates that he uses an average of $800 worth of fish a day (it is never sold later). And although John Corbo, Citarella's manager, said Mr. Lara has "no limit, no budget," he admitted that, "We do get a little nervous when we see him moving toward the $14 a pound gray sole."

But the store is committed to the work of its in-house artist.

"The display is a statement of who we are," Mr. Corbo said. "The window makes people notice the store." And no one has made fish store windows as noticeable as Mr. Lara.

ONCE AN UNDERSTUDY, NOW A STAR

He got his chance one day in 1983 when his predecessor called in sick. "I was afraid, because we were friends, and he made the window and I wanted the window very much," Mr. Lara said.

Artist Fernando Lara creating a masterpiece in the window of Citarella.

But after the Lara premiere, his predecessor retired. "He said he never liked to make the window, and he could see I loved to make the window," Mr. Lara said. "I love to make the window. The window is my life."

Mr. Lara has made over 2,000 windows to date. He has never repeated a design, and he is fond of showing the portfolio with pictures of his favorite windows.

"Working in New York is tough," he said, referring not to urban decay but to "so many artists who look at your work." He is proud that other artists write to him, that tour buses stop in front of his window. But fame hasn't mitigated his creative angst. "I think of the window, of tomorrow, of another window," he said.

Just past noon, he peels the paper off another day's window with the flourish of an artist unveiling a canvas. He beams. Then he nods to his friend, Isidro Lopez, the chef of Citarella. It is time for lunch.

"I don't cook fish," Mr. Lara whispers. "I do the window."

Malachi McCormick's SCALLOP PIE

Malachi McCormick's recipe is topped with an Irish touch.

Malachi McCormick crafts handmade books, translates Irish poetry, and writes cookbooks in his home on Staten Island. This favorite family recipe makes a soulful one-pot dinner. The potato furrows formed by fork tines are an Irish culinary trademark.

1 pound boiling potatoes,
    peeled and cut into chunks
3 cloves garlic, peeled
5 tablespoons butter
½ cup minced scallions
1 pound small white mushrooms, cleaned and
    trimmed
2 tablespoons all-purpose flour
1 cup light cream
¼ cup sweet sherry
2 pounds bay scallops
About 3 tablespoons milk (optional)
2 tablespoons chopped fresh parsley

---

1. Place the potatoes in a pan, cover with cold water, and bring to a boil over high heat. Reduce the heat to a simmer and cook until tender, about 30 minutes.

2. Meanwhile, mince 2½ of the garlic cloves. In a nonreactive heavy saucepan, melt 3 tablespoons of the butter. Add the minced garlic and sauté for 2 minutes. Add the scallions and mushrooms and sauté to soften, 3 minutes. Sprinkle the flour over the mixture and stir well. Slowly add the cream, stirring constantly, and bring to a boil. Add the sherry and scallops and immediately remove from the heat.

3. Preheat the oven to 350°F.

4. Remove the potatoes from the heat and drain. Add 1 tablespoon of the butter. Mince the remaining ½ garlic clove and add it to the potatoes. Mash the potatoes until fluffy, adding the remaining 1 tablespoon butter and a few tablespoons of milk if the potatoes are too dry.

5. Pour the scallop mixture into an 8-inch deep-dish pie plate. Spoon the potatoes on top of the scallops and spread evenly with a fork. Use the tines of the fork to draw furrows into the top. Bake until the tips of the furrows are golden brown, 20 minutes. Garnish with the parsley and serve.

Serves 6 to 8

BAY SCALLOPS with Ginger and Jalapeño

"Here's something I did for breakfast, though it works as well for lunch or dinner, and anyone can make it," said Jason Epstein, editorial director of Random House. "The only problem is that you need fresh local bay scallops, which are hard to find these days. Serve the scallops on a toasted baguette."

3 tablespoons peanut oil
3 cloves garlic, minced
1½ teaspoons minced jalapeño chile
4 scallions, greens trimmed to 3 inches and split
3 thin slices fresh ginger
Salt and freshly ground black pepper, to taste
1½ pounds bay scallops
2 tablespoons chopped fresh Italian (flat-leaf)
    parsley

Warm the oil in a nonstick skillet over medium heat. Add the garlic and jalapeño and cook to soften, 30 seconds. Add the scallions, ginger, salt, and pepper. Add the scallops, increase the heat to high, and cook, stirring constantly, until the scallops are just cooked through, 2 to 3 minutes. Remove to a warmed platter and garnish with the parsley.

Serves 4

Isidro Lopez's
CARIBBEAN SQUID

Serve this squid dish from Chef Lopez of Citarella Fish Company with rice and a crisp lettuce salad.

2 tablespoons olive oil
1 clove garlic, minced
¼ jalapeño chile, minced
1 small onion, minced
1 yellow bell pepper, stemmed, seeded, and minced
1 red bell pepper, stemmed, seeded, and minced
2 pounds cleaned squid
2 tablespoons tomato paste
1 cup dry white wine
¼ cup minced fresh cilantro leaves
Salt and freshly ground black pepper, to taste

1. In a nonreactive large skillet, warm the oil over medium heat. Add the garlic, jalapeño, and onion and sauté until the onion is soft, about 5 minutes. Add the bell peppers and sauté for 3 minutes.

2. Meanwhile, cut the bodies (mantles) of the cleaned squid into ½-inch rings. Add the rings and tentacles to the bell peppers and toss for 5 minutes. Stir in the tomato paste and wine and cook for 5 minutes. Add the cilantro and salt and pepper. Serve warm.

Serves 4 to 6

Lidia Bastianich's
OVEN-BAKED SQUID

Growing up in northern Italy, Lidia Bastianich remembers cleaning squid (the boredom of it) and eating squid (the endless variation of it). Now she cooks this simple squid dish at Felidia, her Italian restaurant on Manhattan's East Side. It is tough to beat and the recipe is adapted from her book, *La Cucina di Lidia*.

Lidia Bastianich at Felidia's in Manhattan.

8 cleaned small squid (4 to 6 ounces each)
4 cloves garlic, peeled
¼ cup olive oil
Salt and freshly ground black pepper, to taste
¼ cup bottled clam juice
¼ cup chopped fresh parsley

1. Preheat the oven to 375°F.

2. Arrange the squid in a single layer in a heavy flameproof baking pan. Add the garlic, olive oil, and salt and pepper and stir to mix. Cover the pan with aluminum foil. Bake for 20 minutes.

3. Remove the foil, turn the squid, and add the clam juice. Bake, uncovered and turning occasionally, until the squid are tender, 10 to 15 minutes. Test for doneness with a fork or skewer; it will slide out easily when the squid is done.

4. Transfer the pan to the stovetop and cook over high heat until the sauce is syrupy. Remove the squid to a serving platter. Strain the sauce, add the parsley, and spoon over the squid.

Serves 4

SHADDING
ON THE HUDSON

American shad is a member of the herring family, which may partially account for the fish's slow rise in status in New York. Herring was common food in the Netherlands, and from March to early May, the fish used to clog the Hudson in New Amsterdam as well.

"Many varieties of fish were caught on the Hudson," writes Lila Perl in *Red Flannel Hash and Shoo-Fly Pie,* "but shad was so plentiful that only the poorer classes were not ashamed to be caught eating them."

The salted shad of New Amsterdam, writes Ms. Perl, "were considered the equivalent of the common salt herrings of Holland."

ARMY CHOW

According to a cargo list at The New-York Historical Society, thousands of barrels of salted shad were shipped to American troops during the Revolution. In an article in the *New York Observer,* John and Karen Hess write that the fish was called "elft, the eleventh fish, by the early Dutch settlers in New York. It was on the eleventh of March each year that the first shad were caught and cooked on a plank—a method learned from the Indians."

Nevertheless, the fish remained in low culinary esteem. In "Immigrant Voices," a 1991 reading from the archives at Ellis Island, one steerage passenger recalls: "On the boat they gave us food. They charged plenty. I still have that herring taste in my mouth. Herring, Herring, Herring."

Presumably, the aftertaste continued to prejudice the palate against native shad because the public appetite for shad began to whet only when the local stocks began to dwindle.

In the mid-nineteenth century, restaurant menus began touting baked, broiled, and pan-fried shad. The curse of the fish is its bones, which are as fragile as they are plentiful. By the mid-nineteenth century, housekeeping manuals had begun to deal efficiently with that problem, with recipes for "potted shad" in which thick shad steaks are lightly pickled, which dissolves the bones. Some home cooks also recommended covering the whole gutted fish with wine and baking it for 20

Mouth of the Moodna on the Hudson, an engraving by G.W. Wellstood.

hours in a 250°F oven, which they claimed melted the delicate bones. I'd call the bones soft, and edible.

By the early 1900s, shad roe had become a frenzied seasonal ritual in New York. According to newspaper accounts, restaurateurs and chefs from private clubs regularly came to fisticuffs competing for the plump pairs of roe that were sold at the Fulton Market.

By that time, according to Bob Gabriolson, whose family has shadded for five generations on the Hudson, the seasonal runs were getting smaller every year. Now, the catch is less than 10 percent of what it was 50 years ago.

IN SPRING, A NEW YORKER'S FANCY TURNS TO SHAD

Today, shad, the fish, is revered. Shad, the roe, practically has a cult following. Shad is a perfect example of the basic perversity of the New York appetite. We crave what is hard for us to get.

Shad roe can be broiled or baked, though most aficionados prefer it pan-fried. The late Mildred Cassiday, who cooked seafood at Sweets near Fulton Landing, once told me that the secret to perfect pan-fried shad roe is to lightly blanch and cool the roe before pan-frying it. This makes the roe sturdier and less likely to break in the pan. Her technique was used to adapt a bacon and shad roe dish that was served one spring at the Century Club, as well the adaptation of shad roe with butter, lemon, and capers that was served at the Harvard Club (see the accompanying recipes).

Century Club's
SHAD ROE

2 pairs of shad roe
½ cup milk seasoned with a dash of Tabasco sauce
4 slices thick-cut bacon, rind removed
½ cup all-purpose flour seasoned with ¼ teaspoon salt and ⅛ teaspoon pepper
1 cup dry white wine
2 tablespoons Madeira wine
Juice from ¼ lemon
1 tablespoon unsalted butter, chilled
¼ teaspoon salt
⅛ teaspoon freshly ground black pepper

1. Bring enough water to cover the roe to a boil in a large shallow pot. Reduce the heat to a simmer and carefully slide the roe into the water. Remove the pot from the heat, cover, and set aside for 5 minutes.

2. Place the seasoned milk in a shallow pot large enough to hold the roe. Carefully remove the shad roe from the water, slide them into the milk, cover, and refrigerate for 30 minutes.

3. Fry the bacon in a nonreactive large skillet over medium heat. Meanwhile, remove the shad roe from the milk and lightly dredge it in the seasoned flour. When the bacon is nearly crisp, remove it, drain, and reserve. Increase the heat under the skillet to high. When the bacon fat is sizzling, sauté the shad roe on each side until crisp, about 4 minutes per side. Remove.

4. Combine the white wine and Madeira. Pour off half the bacon fat. Return the pan to low heat and pour the wine mixture into the pan. Cook, scraping and stirring, for 3 minutes; remove from the heat. Add the lemon juice and whisk in the cold butter to thicken the sauce. Season with salt and pepper to taste. Drizzle the sauce over the shad and serve, garnished with the bacon slices.

Serves 2

Harvard Club
SHAD ROE

The Harvard Club, with flags flying.

2 pairs of shad roe
1 cup milk
6 tablespoons (¾ stick) unsalted sweet butter
1 cup all-purpose flour seasoned lightly
    with salt and pepper
½ cup dry white wine
Juice of 1 lemon
1 tablespoon drained capers, rinsed
¼ teaspoon salt
⅛ teaspoon freshly ground black pepper
3 tablespoons minced fresh parsley

1. Bring enough water to cover the roe to a boil in a large shallow pot. Reduce the heat to a simmer and carefully slide the roe into the water. Remove the pot from the heat, cover, and set aside for 5 minutes.

2. Place the milk in a shallow pot large enough to hold the roe. Carefully remove the shad roe from the water, slide them into the milk, cover,

and cool in the refrigerator for 30 minutes.

3. Warm 3 tablespoons of the butter in a non-reactive large sauté pan over medium heat. Dredge the shad roe in the flour. Sauté the shad in the butter until golden, about 4 minutes on each side. Remove from the pan and set aside.

4. Return the pan to medium heat and add the white wine. Cook, stirring and scraping, for 3 minutes. Stir in the lemon juice, capers, salt, and pepper; remove from the heat. Thinly slice the remaining 3 tablespoons butter. Whisk the butter, bit by bit, into the sauce. Stir in the parsley. Drizzle the sauce over the shad roe and serve.

Serves 2

Mrs. A. D. Duane's
POTTED SHAD

Now in the collection of The New-York Historical Society, Mrs. A. D. Duane's recipe book was scribbled between 1859 and 1874. Her formula for potted shad reads:

"After the shad has been washed in cold water, you must cut off the head, fins, and tail. You then cut the shad in pieces about the size of your hand. Take a stone pot (an ordinary butter pot) and sprinkle about a handful of kitchen salt in it, a teaspoon of black pepper, two tablespoons of ground allspice, one tablespoon of whole allspice, and one of whole cloves. You then put on top of this a layer of the fish, then a layer of the salt, pepper, etc., and so on until all your fish is in. Be sure and put the salt, etc., on top of the last layer of fish. Pour in vinegar until the fish is entirely covered. Tie a piece of brown paper over the top of the pot, make a paste of flour and water and paste the paper down on the jar as to make it air tight. Put it in the oven about 9 o'clock in the evening and let it remain there until the next morning, when the servant makes up her fire. Put it in the cellar to cool."

The following recipe accommodates today's scarcity of stone pots, servants, and wood-fired ovens.

1 tablespoon coarse (kosher) salt
1 tablespoon freshly ground black
    pepper
2 tablespoons ground allspice
1 tablespoon whole cloves
1 shad (2½ to 3 pounds), skinned,
    cleaned, head, tail, and
    main bones removed
2 cups cider vinegar

1. Preheat the oven to 200°F.

2. In a small bowl, combine the salt, pepper, allspice, and cloves. Stir to mix and set aside. Cut the shad into thick steaks.

3. Use a small, heavy, ovenproof casserole that will allow you to tightly pack the fish. Sprinkle some of the spice mixture in the bottom of the casserole. Place a layer of fish on top of that. Continue layering the spice mixture and fish, making sure some of the spices are left for the top. Combine the vinegar with 2 cups water and pour over the fish to cover. Cover the pot tightly with a lid.

4. Place in the oven and bake for 6 hours. Cool in the refrigerator, then remove from the marinade and serve.

Serves 4

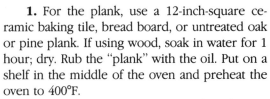

New York
PLANKED STUFFED
SHAD

This recipe is based on a description that appeared in *The Beginning and Growth of the*

Hotel and Club Life of New York, a steward's manual that is dated 1904 and is in the collection of The Museum of the City of New York. Serve it with boiled new potatoes.

1 tablespoon vegetable oil
1 shad (4 pounds), split and gutted,
    head, tail, and fins intact
2 teaspoons salt
1 teaspoon freshly ground black
    pepper
1 teaspoon freshly grated nutmeg
2 leeks
4 tablespoons (½ stick) butter,
    melted
1 lemon, quartered
2 cups fine, dried bread crumbs
¼ cup chopped fresh parsley
Lemon wedges, for serving

1. For the plank, use a 12-inch-square ceramic baking tile, bread board, or untreated oak or pine plank. If using wood, soak in water for 1 hour; dry. Rub the "plank" with the oil. Put on a shelf in the middle of the oven and preheat the oven to 400°F.

2. Rinse the fish. Mix together the salt, pepper, and nutmeg and sprinkle three-quarters of the mixture on the inside and outside of the fish; set the rest aside.

3. Split the leeks in half lengthwise, then widthwise; rinse completely. Put in a shallow pot, cover with cold water, and cook over medium heat until tender, about 15 minutes. Drain the leeks. Pour 1 tablespoon of the butter over the leeks, add the juice of ¼ lemon, and sprinkle with the remaining salt mixture.

4. Reduce the oven heat to 375°F. Put the leeks inside the shad and sprinkle the leeks with the bread crumbs and parsley. Close the fish, then baste it with the remaining melted butter and the juice from the remaining ¾ lemon. Place the fish on the plank. Bake until the fish is cooked through, 40 minutes. Serve with lemon wedges alongside.

Serves 6

TINY CRAB CAKES
with Green Onion Sauce

This recipe was developed by François Keller and cooked for the first American Chefs' tribute to James Beard, held at Rockefeller Plaza to benefit Citymeals-On-Wheels. It makes a wonderful hors d'oeuvre.

CRAB CAKES
1 pound lump crabmeat, picked over
¾ cup fine, dried bread crumbs
1 hard-cooked egg, minced
¼ cup minced onion
¼ cup minced red bell pepper
¼ cup minced green bell pepper
2 large eggs, lightly beaten
1½ teaspoons salt
1 teaspoon dry mustard
⅛ teaspoon cayenne pepper
Freshly ground black pepper,
  to taste

GREEN SAUCE
1 cup mayonnaise
¼ cup plus 3 tablespoons heavy cream
  or milk
1 hard-cooked egg, finely minced
¼ teaspoon Tabasco sauce
1 teaspoon Worcestershire sauce
2 teaspoons freshly squeezed lemon
  juice
¼ teaspoon dry mustard
¾ teaspoon salt
⅛ teaspoon freshly ground black pepper
¼ teaspoon sugar
3 tablespoons finely chopped scallions
  (green and white parts)

ASSEMBLY
1 cup fine, dried bread crumbs
4 to 6 tablespoons butter

1. Make the crab cakes: Mix together all of the crab cake ingredients. Cover and refrigerate the mixture until firm, about 1½ hours.

2. Meanwhile, make the green sauce: In a mixing bowl, whisk together all the green sauce ingredients. Cover and refrigerate for 1 hour before serving.

3. To assemble the dish: Shape the crab mixture into 24 small cakes or balls. Coat each crab cake with the bread crumbs.

4. Melt 4 tablespoons butter in a large heavy skillet over medium heat. Sauté the crab cakes in batches until brown on all sides, 5 minutes per side. Add more butter, if needed, to complete sautéing the crab cakes. Serve with the green sauce.

Makes 24 small crab cakes

FILLET OF SOLE MARGUERY
à la Diamond Jim

From *On the Town in New York from 1776 to the Present* by Michael and Ariane Batterberry: "[Charles] Rector [of Rector's], like Louis Sherry, would go to any extreme to please a favored patron, even to the point of taking his own son out of college and packing him off to Paris as a kitchen apprentice for two years. Diamond Jim Brady became obsessed by filet of sole Marguery while in France, and could not rest until the dish could be duplicated for him in New York. George Rector, the son of Charles, was then studying law in a rather desultory manner at Cornell. He had spent many summer months in the paternal sculleries and hankered to cook despite it . . . George eventually talked his way into the Parisian cathedral of haute cuisine, the Café Marguery, and by dint of diligent sipping, sniffing, and snooping, solved the riddle. Chef Marguery, rather than boxing his pla-giarist's ears, loaned him out to the Palais des Champs-Elysées as a chef for a state dinner to King Oscar of Sweden. For his triumph, George was decorated by the French government with the Cordon Bleu. Returning to New York, he was met at the dock by Brady, who, chubby little hands cupped to quivering jowls, could be heard bellowing above the crowd, 'Did you get the recipe?' "

2 *flounders (1 to 1½ pounds each), filleted, bones, skin, and heads reserved*
1 *pound inexpensive fish, such as tilefish, bass, or pike, cleaned and cut into small pieces*
½ *cup thinly sliced carrots*
1 *small leek, split, well rinsed, and chopped*
3 *parsley sprigs*
10 *black peppercorns*
1 *small bay leaf*
1 *thyme sprig*
Salt and freshly ground black pepper, to taste
12 *oysters, shucked and poached*
12 *medium shrimp, boiled, peeled, and cleaned*
¼ *cup dry white wine*
8 *tablespoons (1 stick) unsalted butter*
4 *egg yolks, beaten*

The very dapper financier, James Buchanan Brady, aka "Diamond Jim." Photo: The Bettmann Archive

1. In a large heavy saucepan or stockpot, combine the flounder bones, skin, and heads, along with the inexpensive fish pieces, carrots, leek, parsley, peppercorns, bay leaf, thyme, and 6 cups cold water. Bring to a boil over high heat. Reduce the heat to a simmer and cook until the liquid is reduced to about 2 cups, 30 to 40 minutes.

2. Preheat the oven to 325°F.

3. Remove the fish stock from the heat and pour through a fine strainer; discard the solids.

4. Butter a medium-size nonreactive baking pan. Place the flounder fillets in the pan and pour on 1 cup of the strained fish stock. Season with salt and pepper. Bake until the fish is cooked through, 15 to 20 minutes.

5. Remove the pan from the oven and use a spatula to carefully remove the fillets to a warmed ovenproof platter. Garnish the platter with the oysters and shrimp. Reserve the baking pan.

6. Preheat the broiler.

7. Pour the remaining fish stock into the re-served baking pan and set over low heat on the stovetop. Scrape the bottom and sides of the pan and simmer until the liquid is reduced to 3 or 4 tablespoons. Strain the reduced stock into the top of a double boiler. Add the wine and butter and cook over gently steaming hot water, stirring fre-quently, until the butter melts. Add the egg yolks and stir until the sauce thickens, 3 to 5 minutes.

8. Remove from the heat and pour over the fish, oysters, and shrimp. Place the platter under the broiler and broil until the fish is lightly browned, 3 to 5 minutes.

Serves 6

Canal Street
PAN-FRIED SOLE

Cooking a whole fish can be difficult, since even under the tenderest of care a cooked fish tends to crumble. For best results, use a large slotted spoon to move your fish. This dish should be crispy and yet juicy, so high oil temperature is essential. However, every time you place the fish in the oil, the oil temperature falls. This is why you will cook the fish in two stages at controlled temperatures. The first cooking sets the outside "crust." The following frying cooks the fish to crispy perfection.

FISH

1 gray sole (1½ pounds), cleaned, cut in half widthwise, head removed, rinsed in salted water
½ teaspoon salt
1 teaspoon soy sauce
1½ teaspoons cornstarch
5 cups vegetable oil, such as peanut
2 scallions, white part only, shredded

SAUCE

2 tablespoons vegetable oil
1 teaspoon shredded fresh ginger
2 tablespoons soy sauce
½ teaspoon dry sherry
½ teaspoon sugar
Dash of finely ground white pepper
1 cilantro sprig

1. Prepare the fish: Rub the pieces of the fish with the salt, soy sauce, and then the cornstarch.
2. Pour the oil into a 14-inch wok; the oil must be at least 2 inches below the rim of the wok. Heat until the oil reaches 350°F on a deep-frying thermometer; it will be smoking. Carefully lower 1 piece of the fish into the oil and cook for 15 seconds. Immediately remove to a plate. Return

the oil to 350°F and cook the second piece of fish for 15 seconds. Remove to a plate. Bring the oil to 400°F and recook the first piece for 1 minute. Remove. Bring the oil back to 400°F and fry the second piece for 1 minute. The fish is done when the tiny bones on the fish are crispy enough to eat. Remove the pieces to a platter, reassembling them into a fish shape. Scatter the scallions on top of the fish.
3. Prepare the sauce: Drain the oil from the wok. Heat the 2 tablespoons fresh oil over medium-high heat until very hot. Add the ginger and stir-fry until fragrant, 10 seconds. Pour the oil and ginger over the scallions.
4. Return the wok to medium-high heat and add the soy sauce, sherry, sugar, and pepper. Bring to a boil. Remove from the heat and pour over the fish. Garnish with the cilantro.
Serves 2

Along Canal Street in Chinatown.

STEAMED GRAY SOLE
with Black Bean Sauce

As a teenager on Manhattan's Upper West Side, Eddie Schoenfeld attended the Ethical Culture School by day, but at night he made a study of Chinese food, becoming in his time a connoisseur, and one of the few non-Chinese people in New York to rise through the ranks in local Chinese restaurant kitchens and, eventually, own Chinese restaurants. The following two dishes are ones that he prepares for his sons in their Brooklyn home.

It's important to have the correct equipment for this dish. You will need a 14-inch wok and a 12-inch steamer.

1 gray sole (1½ pounds), cleaned,
   head removed
2 tablespoons Japanese soy sauce
1½ tablespoons fermented black beans,
   flattened with a cleaver and then
   coarsely chopped
1 tablespoon Chinese rice wine
1 teaspoon Chinese dark soy sauce
½ teaspoon sugar
1 scallion, trimmed and cut into ⅓-inch
   pieces
1 quarter-size slice fresh ginger, peeled
   and finely minced
1 clove garlic, finely minced
Pinch of finely ground white pepper
Pinch of MSG (optional)

■————————————————————■

1. Rinse the fish in lightly salted water. Drain and pat dry. Set aside on a plate that will easily fit into your steamer.

2. To make the sauce, combine all of the remaining ingredients in a nonreactive bowl. Spoon the sauce over the fish.

3. Fill a wok half full of water. Top with a steamer. Bring the water to a boil over high heat. Carefully lower the plate into the steamer, cover, and steam until the fish flesh pulls away from the main bone, 5 to 10 minutes.

Serves 2

St. Luke's
SOLE IN YOGURT

This dish is easy and satisfying. The recipe originally appeared in *St. Luke's Cookbook,* a small community cookbook that was compiled by parents of the pupils in the private school.

2 pounds flounder fillets, rinsed and
   patted dry
Salt and freshly ground white pepper,
   to taste
1 cup plain yogurt
½ cup mayonnaise
1 tablespoon freshly squeezed lemon juice
½ teaspoon curry powder
3 tablespoons butter
½ pound white mushrooms, trimmed
   and sliced
½ pound seedless green grapes

■————————————————————■

1. Preheat the oven to 350°F.

2. Sprinkle the fish with salt and pepper. In a bowl, combine the yogurt, mayonnaise, lemon juice, and curry powder. Spread the mixture over one side of the fillets. Starting at the thinner end, roll up and secure each fillet with a toothpick (or tie with string). Place the rolls in a medium-size nonreactive baking dish and top with any leftover yogurt mixture.

3. Melt the butter in a skillet over medium heat. Add the mushrooms and cook until softened, about 5 minutes. Add the grapes and stir for 1 minute to heat through. Pour over the fish.

4. Bake, covered with aluminum foil, until the fish is cooked through, 30 minutes.

Serves 4 to 6

Marvin's
FISH AND LEEKS

Former Department of Health Assistant Commissioner Marvin Bogner says, "Here's my recipe for what I call 'a fish dish for people who don't like fish.'" Bogner, a free-lance consultant, bemoans the fact that "most Americans think fish has to be odoriferous." This simple fish is mellowed by leeks, a vegetable Bogner calls "the perfect foil for any fish dish."

Marvin Bogner collects the makings of his popular fish dish.

LEEKS
4 tablespoons (½ stick) butter
1 cup heavy (whipping) cream
1 cup dry vermouth
Salt and freshly ground black pepper, to taste
4 leeks, split, well rinsed, and cut into julienne

FISH
1 cup dry vermouth
2 ribs celery with leaves, broken in half
2 carrots, peeled and sliced
2 bay leaves
4 fillets (about 2 pounds) firm white fish, such as sole or turbot, about ½ inch thick
¼ cup diced, seeded tomatoes
2 tablespoons unsalted butter

1. Prepare the leeks: In a nonreactive sauté pan, heat the butter, cream, and vermouth, stirring frequently until smooth. Add salt and pepper and then the leeks. Cook over low heat until tender, about 20 minutes.

2. Meanwhile, prepare the fish: In a nonreactive, wide, deep saucepan over medium-high heat, combine 6 cups water with the vermouth, celery, carrots, and bay leaves. Bring to a boil. Reduce the heat to a simmer, add the fish, and poach until cooked through, 3 to 5 minutes.

3. In a nonreactive small saucepan over medium heat, cook the tomatoes in the butter until warm, about 3 minutes.

4. To serve, divide the leeks and their sauce among 4 dinner plates. Carefully slice the poached fish fillets into ½ inch strips and place atop the leeks. Top with the tomatoes. Serve immediately.

Serves 4

Portuguese
BACALHAU A "PEQUENINA"

When asked to describe some personal memories of this dish, Maria da Encarnacao, who works at the Portuguese tourist office in Manhattan, seemed reluctant and offered, instead, to look at an encyclopedia. When she was a child, her family's maid used to make it for the holidays. Her own brood loves it. Maria likes to cook it on a long weekend and serve it throughout the week.

Maria da Encarnacao in her kitchen.

1½ pounds dried boneless salt cod
3 pounds potatoes, peeled and cut
    into thick rounds
Salt, to taste
1¼ cups olive oil
2 large onions, diced
3 cloves garlic, crushed
6 egg yolks
Freshly ground black pepper,
    to taste
2 tablespoons minced fresh parsley
2 tablespoons minced fresh cilantro

1. Soak the dried salt cod for 24 hours in plenty of cold water. Change the water 3 or 4 times.

2. Preheat the oven to 375°F. Oil a deep 2-quart ovenproof casserole.

3. Drain the fish. Place the salt cod in a pan and cover with fresh cold water. Bring to a boil. Lower the heat and simmer gently until the cod flakes when prodded with a fork, about 7 minutes. Drain again and set aside to cool until it can be handled. Coarsely flake the fish.

4. While the cod is cooking, dry the potatoes and sprinkle them with salt. Heat a large, cast-iron frying pan, add 1 cup of the olive oil, and fry the potatoes in batches until they are golden and tender, 10 to 15 minutes. Drain the potatoes on paper towels and set aside. Reserve the frying oil.

5. Arrange the fried potatoes and boiled cod in alternating layers in the prepared casserole, beginning and ending with potatoes.

6. In a small saucepan, heat the remaining ¼ cup olive oil over medium heat. Add the onions and garlic and cook until soft but not brown, 5 minutes. Remove from the heat and set aside.

7. In a small mixing bowl, very lightly beat the egg yolks. Slowly add the onion mixture and the reserved frying oil, stirring constantly. Season the sauce with salt and pepper to taste.

8. Pour the sauce over the layered cod and potatoes and bake until heated through, 10 to 15 minutes. Serve at once, sprinkled with the parsley and cilantro.

Serves 6

Bill Thomas'
TUNA ROCKEFELLER

Bill Thomas, president of the New York City Emerald Society, makes this dish for fellow fire fighters, who swear it's better than the oyster version. It is one of the best uses of canned tuna around.

1 pound fresh spinach, well rinsed
½ pound sliced bacon
½ cup fine, dried bread crumbs
1 cup sour cream
1 teaspoon salt
½ teaspoon freshly ground black pepper
Juice of 1 lemon
2 cans (7 ounces each) white tuna,
    drained and flaked
4 tablespoons freshly grated
    Parmesan cheese

1. Preheat the oven to 350°F. Butter an 8-inch square baking dish or ovenproof casserole.

2. Steam the spinach until wilted, 2 minutes. Drain and purée in a food processor or blender. Set aside.

3. Fry the bacon in a large skillet until crisp. Drain and crumble.

4. In a bowl, combine the spinach purée, bacon, bread crumbs, sour cream, salt, pepper, lemon juice, tuna, and 2 tablespoons of the Parmesan. Stir until well mixed. Place the mixture in the buttered baking dish; sprinkle with the remaining 2 tablespoons Parmesan. Bake until the bread crumbs are lightly browned, 20 minutes.

Serves 6

Ser Meoun's
AMOK

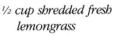

A firm, white-fleshed fish is best for this traditional Cambodian dish. Ser Meoun recommends serving amok with steamed rice. Galangal is a variety of gingerroot, mudfish is another name for sea bream, and kachai are slender and short tuberous roots used in fish dishes.

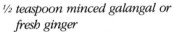

Ser Meoun is able to prepare traditional Cambodian dishes in her New York home.

*½ cup shredded fresh
    lemongrass*
3 cloves garlic
*1 tablespoon sweet
    paprika*
*1 teaspoon dried
    kachai*
*½ teaspoon minced galangal or
    fresh ginger*
*1 tablespoon mudfish (a condiment found in
    Asian food shops; optional)*
1 cup unsweetened coconut milk
1 teaspoon salt
1 tablespoon sugar
1 large egg
*1 pound white fish fillet, such as bass or cod, cut
    in thin strips*
*8 leaves bok choy, Chinese cabbage, or large
    spinach leaves*

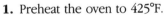

1. Preheat the oven to 425°F.

2. Combine the lemongrass, garlic, paprika, kachai, galangal, mudfish, coconut milk, salt, sugar, and egg in a blender or food processor. Process until liquified. Place the strips of fish in a bowl, cover with the liquified seasonings, and stir for about 3 minutes.

3. Rinse the cabbage leaves. Line 4 small

ovenproof bowls or ramekins with the leaves. Spoon the fish mixture on top. Fold the cabbage leaves over the mixture. Bake until cooked through, 8 to 10 minutes.
Serves 2

Gina Zarrilli's
WHOLE RED SNAPPER WITH COUSCOUS

The inspiration for this dish came to Gina in Morocco. Moroccan cuisine is famous for its delicate and seductive interplay of scent and taste. The sauce in this recipe does not overwhelm the other spritely flavors, rather, it provides a wonderful foil for the couscous.

FISH STOCK
*1½ pounds inexpensive fish parts,
    including bones and heads*
½ cup thinly sliced carrots
*1 small leek, split, well rinsed,
    and chopped*
3 fresh parsley sprigs
10 black peppercorns
1 small bay leaf
2 fresh thyme sprigs

SNAPPER
*2 red snappers (2 pounds each),
    cleaned and boned, heads and
    tails intact*
2 tablespoons butter
1 orange, sliced (8 slices)
2 fresh rosemary sprigs
¼ cup dry white wine
2 shallots, peeled and chopped
Juice of 1 lemon
Juice of 1 orange
Pinch of saffron
Salt and freshly ground white pepper and salt

COUSCOUS

1 pound precooked couscous
4 tablespoons olive oil
2 teaspoons ground cumin
1 teaspoon ground coriander
½ teaspoon turmeric
Salt, to taste
1 small red onion, grated
1 red bell pepper, stemmed, seeded,
*   and chopped*
2 tablespoons finely chopped parsley
2 tablespoons coarsely chopped cilantro

SAFFRON SAUCE

1 cup dry white wine
2 teaspoons saffron threads
4 shallots, chopped
1 red bell pepper, stemmed, seeded,
*   and cut into julienne*
½ cup heavy (whipping) cream
Salt, to taste
Juice of ½ lemon

---

1. Make the fish stock: In a heavy soup or stockpot, combine the fish parts, carrots, leek, parsley, peppercorns, bay leaf, and thyme with 2½ quarts cold water. Bring to a boil over high heat. Reduce the heat so the stock just barely simmers and cook for 30 minutes. Strain and discard the solids; set the stock aside.

2. Prepare the snapper: Rinse the fish under cold water and pat dry. Cut the butter into small pieces and divide them equally between the fish, spreading the pieces out in each cavity. Stuff both fish with the orange slices and rosemary.

3. In a nonreactive baking dish that will allow the fish to lay flat, combine the wine, shallots, lemon juice, orange juice, saffron, salt, and pepper. Place the fish in the pan, cover, and set aside to marinate for 30 minutes. Turn the snapper over and marinate the other side for 30 minutes more.

4. Meanwhile, preheat the oven to 250°F.

5. Prepare the couscous: Place the couscous in a large strainer or colander. Run cold water over it until it is thoroughly wet. Let drain. Place the couscous in an ovenproof bowl and bake until it is dried out and clumpy, 20 minutes. Separate the grains with 2 forks (or your fingers once the grains have cooled a bit) until there are no lumps.

6. In a large bowl, combine 2 tablespoons of the olive oil, the cumin, coriander, turmeric, and salt. Mix well and add the red onion and bell pepper. Stir in the parsley and cilantro. Add the couscous and mix well; adjust the seasonings, if necessary. Drizzle with the remaining 2 tablespoons olive oil; set aside.

7. Make the saffron sauce: In a nonreactive heavy saucepan, combine 2 cups of the fish stock with the wine, saffron, and shallots. Bring to a boil. Reduce the heat to a high simmer and cook until the stock is reduced by half, 10 to 15 minutes. Add the red bell pepper, and then carefully stir in the cream. Reduce the heat to a slow simmer and reduce again by half. Add salt to taste and the lemon juice. Reduce the heat to warm and cover.

8. Preheat the oven to 350°F.

9. To cook the fish: Pour off the fish marinade but leave the orange slices and rosemary in the fish. Add enough fresh fish stock to moisten the bottom of the pan. Cover the pan with foil and bake until the fish is just done (opaque), about 25 minutes.

10. Meanwhile, place the couscous in the oven to warm. When the fish is done and the couscous is warm, remove from the oven.

11. With a spatula remove the fish to a platter. Strain the pan juices and add them to the sauce. Carefully separate the fillets and spoon about 1 cup of the couscous on top of the fillets. Reheat the sauce until hot and adjust the seasoning if necessary. Spoon the sauce around the fish.

Serves 4

Moroccan flavors make Gina Zarrilli's snapper dish luscious.

Frank Germanotta offers a perfect dish to share with friends.

BLUEFISH BAKED WITH
Apples & Potatoes

Frank Germanotta, an art director at Estée Lauder, contrasts the color of this dish with a red cabbage slaw on the side. "This dish is easy, and you can do all of the prep work ahead of time, so it's great for entertaining."

4 potatoes, cut into ¼-inch slices
4 firm, tart cooking apples, peeled, cored,
*   and cut into ⅛-inch slices*
1 tablespoon minced shallots
2 cloves garlic, minced
⅓ cup olive oil
6 bluefish fillets (6 to 8 ounces each)
1 cup coarse, mild mustard
1½ cups dry white wine
Chopped fresh parsley, for garnish

1. Preheat the oven to 350°F.

2. Place the potatoes, apples, shallots, garlic, and half of the olive oil in a nonreactive roasting pan and toss well to combine. Bake until the vegetables are tender, 15 minutes.

3. Meanwhile, rub the bluefish fillets with the remaining olive oil and the mustard.

4. Place the bluefish fillets on top of the bed

of roasted apples and potatoes and pour the wine over it all. Bake until the fish is cooked through, 10 to 15 minutes. Sprinkle with parsley before serving.

Serves 6

Vernon's
JERK SNAPPER

It is tough to beat this Jamaican way of barbecuing fish, especially on a hot summer night. This recipe was supplied by New York's jerk king supreme. For more about Vernon, see page 334.

¾ cup Jamaican Jerk Sauce, prepared through
*   step 1 (see page 337 and note below)*
1 onion, coarsely chopped
1 fresh thyme sprig
1 scallion, trimmed
1 Scotch bonnet or jalapeño chile, stem removed
1 cup port wine or sherry (optional)
4 red snappers (1 to 1½ pounds each), cleaned
*   and boned, heads and tails intact*

1. In a blender or food processor, combine the jerk sauce, onion, thyme leaves, scallion, chile, port, and 2 cups water. Process until smooth. Pour the mixture into a shallow, nonreactive baking pan. Add the fish, cover, and marinate in the refrigerator for 2 hours, turning once after 1 hour.

2. Prepare a grill or preheat the broiler.

3. Remove the fish from the marinade and place on a fish grid. Grill or broil until the fish flakes easily with a fork, 5 to 8 minutes per side.

Serves 4

Note: The ingredients for Jerk Sauce make up more than you'll need for this dish. Keep the extra, covered, in the refrigerator and use it within a few days on other fish or poultry dishes.

Zarela's
RED SNAPPER HASH

Zarela Martinez, doyenne of Zarela's Mexican restaurant, created this irresistible dish after tasting a similar version in Tampico. It can be served by itself as a first course, or with tortillas or rice as a meal.

Zarela Martínez combines chiles and snapper for a dish with real pizzazz.

8 tablespoons (1 stick) unsalted butter
6 large cloves garlic, finely minced
10 scallions with green tops, trimmed and minced
3 ripe tomatoes, peeled and chopped
2 fresh jalapeño or serrano chiles, trimmed but not seeded, finely chopped
1½ teaspoons ground cinnamon
1 teaspoon ground cumin
½ teaspoon ground cloves
½ teaspoon salt
2½ pounds red snapper fillets, cut in half crosswise, skinned, small bones removed with tweezers

---

1. In a nonreactive, large, heavy (preferably nonstick) skillet, melt 4 tablespoons of the butter over medium heat. When the foam subsides, add half of the garlic, reduce the heat to medium-low, and sauté, stirring constantly, for 1 minute. Add the scallions and increase the heat to medium. Sauté, stirring frequently, for 1 minute. Add the tomatoes, chiles, spices, and salt and sauté until the flavors are well blended, about 2 minutes.

2. Add the fish to the skillet, arranging the fillets in 1 layer over the tomato mixture. Adjust the heat to maintain a low simmer and cook the fish until the flesh just begins to turn opaque,

about 1 minute. Carefully turn the fillets over with a spatula and cook on the other side for 1 minute. The fish will still be somewhat rare on the inside. Turn off the heat and allow the fish to cool in the sauce. When the fish has cooled, break it apart with your fingers.

3. In a nonreactive large skillet, melt the remaining 4 tablespoons butter. Add the remaining garlic and cook for 30 seconds. Add the fish hash and sauté over high heat until heated through, 3 minutes. Serve the fish hash immediately.

Serves 6

SALMON
à la Basilique

Bianca Jagger won the first prize at a March of Dimes Gourmet Gala with this salmon dish. "I love the lightness and the flavor of this dish and cook it often for guests," said Bianca. "It's best served with a mound of lightly steamed vegetables and some rice."

1 whole salmon (about 3 pounds), head and tail intact, cleaned
4 cups loosely packed coarsely chopped fresh basil leaves
2 tablespoons olive oil
½ cup finely grated onion
Salt and freshly ground black pepper, to taste

---

1. Stuff the salmon cavity with the basil; drizzle the olive oil on top. Sprinkle on the onion, salt, and pepper. Wrap the salmon in foil and let rest in the refrigerator for 2 hours.

2. Preheat the oven to 425°F.

3. Bake the salmon until flaky but still moist, 35 to 40 minutes.

Serves 4 to 5

Betti's
SCALLOP OF SALMON WITH RED AND GREEN SAUCE

From Betti Zucker: "I make lots of basil paste in the summer when fresh basil is plentiful, because it will keep for at least six months in the refrigerator as long as you cover the purée with olive oil and keep it in a covered container. I often call the red sauce 'red magic' because it's easy, quick, and so versatile." You can use it as a side for poultry, lamb, beef, or fish, or as an hors d'oeuvre on grilled French bread, or as a filling in an omelet.

BASIL PUREE
½ cup packed fresh basil leaves, well rinsed
*   and dried*
2 to 4 tablespoons olive oil

RED PEPPER SAUCE
3 tablespoons olive oil
1 jar (12 ounces) roasted red peppers,
*   drained, dried, and chopped*
2 cloves garlic, minced
1 can (28 ounces) imported whole
*   Italian plum tomatoes*
2 teaspoons fresh thyme leaves, crushed
*   between your fingers*
Salt and freshly ground black pepper,
*   to taste*

FISH
2 salmon fillets, preferably from the
*   tail end (2 to 2½ pounds total weight),*
*   skinned and small bones removed*
*   with a tweezer*
2 tablespoons olive oil
¼ teaspoon salt
½ teaspoon freshly ground white pepper
2 cloves garlic, minced

1. Make the basil purée: Place the basil in a food processor and turn the machine on. Drizzle in the oil and process until a thick shiny paste forms. Stop the machine once or twice, if necessary, to scrape the sides of the bowl. (It's best to serve this at room temperature or cold because heating the purée destroys its delicate flavor.) Set aside.

2. Make the red pepper sauce: In a non-reactive large skillet, heat the olive oil. Add the red peppers, garlic, and tomatoes, crushing each one between your fingers. (Reserve the tomato liquid in case the sauce is too dry.) Add the thyme and cook, stirring occasionally, until the liquid reduces and the sauce thickens, 15 to 20 minutes. Add the reserved tomato liquid, if necessary, and season with salt and pepper. Keep warm while preparing the fish.

3. Meanwhile, preheat the broiler.

4. Prepare the fish: Cut the salmon crosswise into pieces about 2 inches wide. Line a baking sheet with aluminum foil and rub the olive oil over the foil. Place the salmon on the foil and season with the salt and pepper. Broil until the salmon flakes easily but is barely cooked in the center, about 3 minutes. Don't overcook.

5. Stir the garlic into the red pepper sauce. Serve the salmon with the warmed red pepper sauce around the fish and the basil purée drizzled on top.
Serves 4

Preparing dainty soft-shelled crabs for epicure-an New Yorkers, 1889.
Courtesy of The New-York Historical Society

"There were some truly exceptional tastes to be tasted, too, especially in seafoods. Nothing in the world could beat a soft-shelled crab from Chesapeake Bay, eaten preferably inside a crusty roll on a street corner downtown. Incomparable oyster stews were prepared at the Grand Central Oyster Bar by Viktor Yesenky and his 36 oystermen. Louis Massan's waterside restaurant on Fulton Street, beside the fish market, offered its customers (sitting at communal tables) five kinds of roe, tongue of cod, sturgeon's liver, squid stew, and the cheeks of cod and salmon."

—JAN MORRIS, MANHATTAN '45

Barbara Scott-Goodman's
SALMON STEAKS VINAIGRETTE

Barbara Scott-Goodman swears by this simple salmon dish that can be prepared on a charcoal grill or under the broiler. It is delicious served with rice and fresh boiled peas.

1 tablespoon white wine vinegar
Juice of 2 oranges (about 1 cup)
Juice of 2 limes (about ¼ cup)
4 cloves garlic, sliced
¼ cup olive oil
¼ cup finely chopped cilantro
Salt and freshly ground black pepper, to taste
4 salmon steaks (about 6 to 8 ounces each)

1. In a mixing bowl, combine the vinegar, orange and lime juices, and garlic. Whisk in the olive oil. Stir in the cilantro and salt and pepper.

2. Place the salmon steaks in a shallow nonreactive container. Pour the vinaigrette over the salmon and marinate for 30 to 60 minutes, turning once.

3. Preheat the broiler.

4. Broil the steaks until cooked through, 5 to 6 minutes per side. Serve with 1 tablespoon of the vinaigrette drizzled over each steak.

Serves 4

A TRIP DOWN MENU LANE

Menus of New York City restaurants past can cause a certain kind of vertigo. They're artifacts of people who could afford to dine out, elegant footprints in the march towards modernity. Old menus lead the culinary cartographer through Edens of plenty and around cul de sacs of extinct provisions, up Everests of exuberant cooking and across deserts of culinary humdrum. Soon, the time traveler senses a certain circularity in the path from a 1776 Tavern Bill of Fare to Le Menu Bistro today.

The collection of 25,000 historical menus at The New York Public Library and the 15,000 menus at The New-York Historical Society show a progression of available ingredients, the incorporation of immigrant cooking, and the flashes of individual genius that have shaped the tastes of *le tout* New York—and often America. But these influences bow to the psychosocial pendulum that sweeps back and forth across the bills of fare.

"The cycle goes simple to fancy, simple to fancy, and back again," said Reynaldo Alejandro, author of *Classic Menu Design*. The shift is as rhythmic as the tides. When there is peace and public confidence and the money rushes in, it usually carries a gilded age of cuisine. When prosperity ebbs, it leaves a hankering for the simple, good-old-days in its wake.

Consider the duck. In the earliest New York City menus, it was roasted, canvasback duck, a no-nonsense preparation that endured from Colonial times

The Shakspeare on lower Manhattan's Nassau Street is typical of an early New York tavern.

until the robber barons invaded the city and *aiguillettes de canards,* sculpted slivers of sautéed duck, reigned. Then along came Long Island Duckling, often à la orange, always crisp-baked and served without question—until duck breast, sautéed rare and fanned out in thin slices appeared in the late 1970s.

Since the recent days of duck breasts and berries, there has been a moment of duck carpaccio, a whisper of duck sausage, but neither fussy dish could forestall the inevitable. On a recent menu of The Four Seasons in Manhattan, duck is roasted again, whole, with apples. Le Cirque serves the whole duck, stewed. "When people are comfortable, they experiment and indulge," said Sirio Maccioni. "When people have something on their minds, like now, they

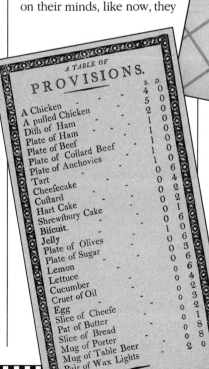

order more conservatively."

Colonial New Yorkers had a lot on their minds and their tavern menus showed it. There were the fish species that migrated through the local waters—bluefish, mackerel, alewives, sturgeon, and shad—the oysters that ringed the waterlines throughout New York Bay, pork from the pigs that roamed and foraged in the streets, canvasback ducks, and a bounty of local game. *Snert,* a Dutch meat and pea porridge (see recipe, page 69), oyster stew (see recipe, page 370), and turtle soup appeared on the bills of fare; saddles of mutton, venison, or beef were roasted until they slid from the bone. Meals were cheap, communal, and eaten in a hurry.

An early tavern menu (left) with prices in shillings and pence lists charges even for table candles. A current menu from Le Cirque (above).

"Don't fall for the romance of early New York life," said Michael Batterberry, who, along with Ariane Batterberry, wrote *On the Town in New York*. "Those were rough times: people wanted comfort, not challenge."

The culinary status quo wasn't really shaken until the mid-1800s. Earlier in the century, dining developed in tandem with the growing city. Local menus show the rise in hotel dining (which travelogues consistently describe as somber and functional), and as greater distance grew between home and the office, short-order houses served pandemonious midday meals to businessmen. There was a slight shift in ingredients—grouse,

quail, venison, and bear were pushed aside by pork, capon, and beef; deep sea fish edged out freshwater varieties—but the cooking techniques remained the same. And oysters and turtle were still everyman's chow. Taverns courted gentleman with their turtle barbecue. The Batterberry's cite a 1802 advertisement from Hatfield's Tavern: "A mammoth turtle will be cooked in the best style on Wednesday next," it read. "The lovers of good cooking will be gratified."

Dr. Nan Rothschild, an archeologist at Barnard College and author of *New York Neighborhoods,* said that the change in the local pantry is a barometer of the evolution of the city. By 1800, the

CARTE
DU
RESTURANT FRANÇAIS, DES
Frères DELMONICO,
CORNER OF
Beaver, William and _____ Streets,"
NEW-YORK.

POTAGES.	s.	d.	SOUPS.
Consommé			Broth
Potage Julienné			Vegetable Soup
" au vermicelli			Vermicelli do
" au macaroni			Macaroni do
" au pain			Bread do
" aux choux			Cabbage do
" au riz			Rice do
" aux huîtres			Oysters do
" à la purée			Purée do
" Conti			Conti do
" de tortue			Turtle do
" de santé			Diet do

HORS D'ŒUVRES.

SIDE DISHES.

Saucisses	Sausages
" à la Chipolata	Chipolata sausages
Saucisson de Lyon	Lyons sausage
Boudin noir	Black Pudding
Thon mariné	Pickled tunny fish
Salade de Laitue	Salad of lettuce
" de chicorée	" of endive

quaint harbor community of 4,000 houses on the tip of lower

A lunchroom in Manhattan, 1888 (facing page), with nary a woman in sight; a menu from the mid-18th century (facing page), when hotel dining was popular; the beautiful Delmonico's; and a page from their famous 11-page menu.

Manhattan had swollen to a city of 60,000. From the urban archeological digs that she has conducted, Dr. Rothschild has added up food clues. "As the village became a city there was less backyard farming, hunting, and fishing and an increase of professional food purveyors," she said. By the mid-1800s, when the city was flush from banking and industry, professionalism had spread to food preparation. And the pendulum started to swing.

Delmonico's opened and beamed an irresistible *haute valence*. The earliest surviving menu, an 1838 sample at The New-York Historical Society, is eleven pages long and is written in French and English. There are twelve soups, including *potage tortue verte l'Anglaise,* thank you. Beef, veal, mutton, lamb, and poultry were each offered in dozens of different ways. There were nearly fifty varieties of seafood. Duck was sautéed with olives; there was wild duck "salame." *Le tout* New York, at least *le tout* male New York, swarmed in to order twelve-course dinners. Nice ladies still dined only in hotel dining rooms. Nevertheless, in 1848, George C. Foster, a reporter with the *Herald Tribune,* marveled at the city's emerging restaurants. "No where else, either in Europe or America, does anything like it

E. HURD'S OYSTER and **DINING SALOON,**
UNDER THE
WAVERLY HOUSE, Cor. of Atlantic & Furman-st.

BILL OF FARE.
BREAKFAST AND SUPPER.

(menu of breakfast, supper, dinner, and dessert items with prices)

exist. It is the culmination, the consummation, the concentration of Americanism; with all its activity, perseverance, energy and practicality in their highest states of development. In this view, the eating-houses of New York rise

to the dignity of a national institution." And while it was widely imitated, Delmonico's remained the benchmark of lavish dining.

"Delmonico's is credited with introducing haute cuisine to America," said Michael Batterberry. "They certainly introduced socio-gustatorial snobbery." By the 1890s, when money was easy, fussy sautéed dishes had eclipsed roasts and stews on the menu at Delmonico's and other hoity-toity eateries like Rector's. Pricey food art reached its apogee by mid-century in *pièces montées,* ornate sugar confections. In early March 1885, wrote Susan Williams in *Savory Suppers and Fashionable Feasts,* thirty men took three days to prepare a pretheater dinner for ten in the large banquet halls of the Waldorf. The society columnist at a Rochester newspaper was appalled at the "exhibition of 19th century extravagance that makes your hair stand on end."

The restaurant pendulum hovered on the high side for nearly fifty years. There were occasional quivers toward the plain and simple. The Civil War brought a spate of conservatism and nostalgia, said Jean Ashton, former director of the library at The New-York Historical Society. "Dutch kitchens were the thing," she said. "It was a way of hearkening back to simpler times." Low-down oyster saloons flourished on Canal Street. Affordable oyster houses and steak houses, like Sweets, Gage & Tollner, Keens Chop House,

and Peter Luger opened, but even their simple fare was offered in lavish profusion. The original menu of Gage & Tollner, which is in the personal collection of the restaurant's current owner, offers six soups, eight fish, dozens of meat dishes, and two dozen varieties of oysters prepared in twenty different ways.

The New York of Diamond Jim Brady was the epicenter of conspicuous consumption—and a place that opened its arms to ethnic exotica. "In less prosperous times, immigrant populations more or less remained isolated in enclaves," said Mrs. Ashton. "During the show-off years, we see ethnic dishes being assimilated on main street menus."

Even before Delmonico's opened, a stream of French émigrés loosed by the revolution in that country had splashed into New York. Some opened tiny bistros and introduced peasant-style dishes; the richer and more cultured (in this case, the majority) gave splendid dinner parties that kindled the taste for French cuisine that Delmonico's sated. According to Barry Moreno, the librarian at Ellis Island, the French remained the dominant force in the Catholic church of New York until the 1820s, when they were outnumbered by Germans. Despite their numbers, however, German cooking remained the province of "Little Germany," and offhand offerings of New York *biergartens* until 1881. The opening of Luchow's that year legitimized German cooking.

Oyster saloon offerings were plentiful and varied in the mid-1800s (facing page). The Harrison Grey Fiske dinner in 1900—heavy-duty dining (above). Dinnertime elegance at the St. Regis (below). Tiny bistros opened with the arrival of French émigrés (right).

Soon after, sauerbraten, schnitzel, and spaetzle popped up on hotel menus; German bakers were king in the city.

By the 1860s, some of the Cantonese immigrants who'd prospected during the California gold rush settled on the old Doyers farm by the Bowery. Today, Chinatown is still contained within the five-block area bounded by Canal, Mulberry, and the Bowery; and until the turn of the century, their cooking stayed in Chinatown. In the early 1890s, newspapermen from nearby Park Row discovered Chinatown's tiny, cheap eateries and in 1895 chow mein made the leap from Chinatown to a banquet menu at the Waldorf Hotel. "This kind of incorporation always seems to happen during eras of big spending," said Mr. Alejandro.

In the 1880s, according to Mr. Moreno, "the Italians came in droves." But they didn't take over in droves: "In general, these were poor immigrants," said Mr. Moreno. They were primarily Catholic, but "they didn't have the education or money to take much control of the church or to open restaurants for that matter." The first wave of Italian immigrants settled in Little Italy, south of Greenwich Village where they sold sausages and peppers (see recipe, page 307), zeppole, and clams from sidewalk stands. By the turn of the century, Italian émigrés had established a fiefdom in New York's corner fruit stands.

The city continued to gar-

The Gartenhaus was a German beer garden in Yorkville.

ner talented refugees, capable of producing their homeland in microcosm. After the Spanish-American War, Hispanic refugees from the Caribbean, primarily Cuba and Puerto Rico, streamed into the city. They added cuchifritos to the menu of New York street food and eventually opened Hispanic holes-in-the-wall in Spanish Harlem, where flavorful dishes like arroz con pollo (see recipe, page

Pell Street in Chinatown, 1926.

47), gefilte fish (see recipe, page 40), herring with horseradish sauce, poppy seed pastries, and strudel—was launched. Goulash (see a variation—*szekely*—page 58) and chicken paprikás (see recipe, page 346) appeared on menus in the late 1890s, seemingly the first Eastern European dishes to make the jump from the wobbly café tables on the Lower East Side to the white tablecloth restaurants further uptown.

A magnanimous nod from the elite during boom years seems to clear a path toward foreign fare in less prosperous times. After World War I and Prohibition, "haute cuisine lay in tatters," said Delmon-

ico's chef Charles Ranhofer. In his cookbook, *The Epicurean,* he writes that dwindling numbers of customers and the loss of revenue from liquor resulted in "curtailment in the kitchen," and "menus became less elaborate." Twelve-course meals were whittled down to a succession of ten, a shaving that he repeated in most economic downswings, ultimately yielding the three-course meals of today. Speakeasies like the "21" Club and Sardi's appeared, but Robert Kreindler, one of the founders of "21," later described the clubby pace they set as "luxury dining, not gourmet dining." (The recipe for the "21" Club chicken hash is on page 353 and their burger is on page 292.)

After the boom years, fancy restaurants served up old-fashioned French and American food. Tearooms, like the Kirby Allen on Madison near 67th Street,

345) were served.

By the 1880s, noted Mr. Moreno, thousands of Yiddish-speaking Jews had fled Russia, Poland, Austria, Hungary, and Romania and settled on the Lower East Side between the Bowery and the river. According to Michael Batterberry, some Jewish housewives were known as good cooks and some converted their front parlors into dining rooms, and a taste for home-style, Eastern European cooking—borscht (see recipe, page 60), boiled beef, chicken soup (see recipe, page

Little Italy in the late 1800s.

proliferated serving modestly priced, all-American, home cooking. The Colony opened quietly in 1922, but its excellent French/Italian fare was a sleeper for five years. Meanwhile, immigration restrictions enacted in the 1920s stemmed the ethnic tide for nearly forty years. But the tiny, hole-in-the-wall restaurants that had opened during the boom years to serve émigrés, Bohemians, and a blue-collar crowd, became the darlings of New York society.

German and Hungarian immigrants moved on up to Yorkville, and storefronts with Prussian, Bavarian, and Viennese cooking flourished, according to Henry Marx, editor of *Auf Bau,* the German-lanugage newspaper of New York. The Russian Revolution sent both deposed royalty and gypsies to New York; Ukrainian cafés opened on the Lower East Side (for a Ukrainian blini and caviar recipe, see page 33, for pierogi, see page 251). In the 1920s, the Russian Tea Room opened (for the restaurant's Chicken Kiev recipe, see page 351). Italian restaurants with red-and-white checkered tablecloths, Chianti bottle lamps, and Neapolitan cooking abounded.

In Harlem, where jazz clubs beckoned, chicken was called "yardbird," spaghetti was known as "strings," and Patsy's, said to be the home of the first coal-fired brick pizza oven in New York, opened (for the New York–style pizza recipe, see page 99). Greek eateries dotted Ninth Avenue. Radiating from Pier 88 on West

Inside the once popular Luchow's of 14th Street (above).
A current menu from The "21" Club (left).

48th Street, where the French ocean liners berthed, tiny bistros started serving 50-cent lunches of onion soup, frog's legs, and beef daube. New York, writes the Batterberrys, had become "a kaleidoscopic city where age might wither, but customs never staled. New York was the only place on earth renowned equally for its osso bucco, ratatouille, Swedish pancakes, Russian Babka, paella, weiner schnitzel and matzoh balls."

By 1939, when peace and prosperity reigned and an appetite for fancy food returned, a wide range of "ethnic" restaurants had become mainstream. *Where to Dine in '39,* a guide

The '21' Club Dinner

Cold Appetizers

the Half Shell 14.50
...cktail 16.50
...Cocktail 17.50
...vlax 17.50   Beluga Caviar Service 70.00 per ounce
...to Salad 14.50   Parma Prosciutto with Melon 15.50
    Irish Smoked Salmon with Horseradish Crisps 17.50
    Endive, Walnut and Roquefort Cheese Salad 12.00

Asparagus Vinaigrette 15.00
Artichoke Vinaigrette 12.00
Caesar Salad 12.00
Salad of Mixed Greens 9.00
Endive, Radicchio and Arugula Salad 11.00

Hot Appetizers

...ald 15.00   Wild Mushroom Ravioli in Duck Consomme 15.50
...i 16.00   Maryland Crab Cake with Horseradish Cream 18.50
    Spinach Salad with Hot Bacon Vinaigrette 12.00

Barbequed Filet of Pork
on Jalapeno-Corn Bun 16.00
Pasta with Shrimp, Scallops,
Tomato & Basil 15.00

Soups
8.50

Gazpacho
    Senegalaise
        Cold Potato and Leek
Black Bean
Lobster Bisque

Entrees

...rilled Vegetables, Toasted Whole Grain Foccacia and Tomato-Pesto Vinaigrette 24.00
    Seafood Ravioli with Lobster Consomme and Vegetable Confetti 27.00
Grilled Sea Bass Filet with Vegetable Couscous and Roasted Eggplant 33.00
Roast Tandoor Style Chicken with Chickpea Salad and Cucumber Raita 26.00
    Tropical Fruit Plate with our own Raspberry Granite 23.00
CULINARY SELECTIONS DESIGNED FOR THE CALORIE AND CHOLESTEROL CONSCIOUS

Mixed Green Salad with
Wheat Berries, Sprouts and Tomato
9.00

Entrees

Cold Poached Salmon, Cucumber Salad 32.00
Tarragon Vinaigrette 36.00
...ak 37.00   Pan Roasted Lobster, Black Bean Vinaigrette...   Whole Maine...
    Wood Grilled Atlantic Halibut with Red Wine...
...euniere 38.00   ...eared Red Snapper, Tomatoes, Oli...
    Grilled S...
...and Spinach Gnocc...   ...Duck with Plum Sauce...
...en Grape "Verjus"   ...Vegetable Cous...
... Style 38.00   ...Spiced Lamb "Firecrackers" 39.00
...t Crispy Shall...   ...Ribeye or Sirloin 39.00
...ld Mushroom...   ...rhouse (for two only please)
... 29.00

'21'
Chicken H...

Steak Tartare 29.00

Vegetable...
8.00
...le   Fried Zucchini Stri...
    Creamed Spin...
...er or Soup served as entree...   Hash Browns

by Diana Ashley, lists 24 French restaurants, 12 German, 11 Italian, 5 Spanish, 4 each of Swedish, Russian, and Chinese, and a smattering of Armenian, East Indian, English, and Jewish spots. That year, the French Pavilion at the World's Fair brought eighty cooks and chefs to the city and many, like Pierre Franey, returned two years later to work at Le Pavillon.

"New Yorkers had gotten a taste for the French," said Mr. Franey. "Now they could pay for the very best." The lavish restaurant set a style that still echoes in dishes like pike quenelles with lobster sauce, Veal Oscar, and stuffed vegetable *garni*. Le Pavillon also embraced ethnic dishes and remade them in the restaurant's upscale image. Russian coulibiac of salmon and Greek moussaka were two of the most popular items on the menu. Good times in dining were rolling again.

They rolled into the '60s. With the exception of the addition of beef Wellington, local

Welcoming in 1936 at The "21" Club: stage star Ernest Truex, his wife, and tablemate Alex Clark.

menus didn't vary from Le Pavillon-esque haute. But the restaurant's showy service took off like an out-of-control silver-domed roast trolley through fancy New York restaurants. There was carving and flaming at every table. Tableside Caesar Salads were rampant (for a recipe, see page 171). In the ebullient, post-war city, Chinese fleeing the Communist regime in their homeland opened adventuresome Shanghai, Hunan, and Peking restaurants next to old-school Cantonese. Japanese restaurants sprouted up. The dining pendulum took a swing to the right in the early winds of the Vietnam War in an "epidemic of these reactionary British pubs," said Mr. Batterberry.

In historical perspective, the dining doldrums of the 1960s and '70s may end up being a waver rather than a sweep of the pendulum. As the economy strengthened, so did the cooking. By the mid-'70s, Northern Italian cooking had breathed new life into the city's Italian eating scene and added more dollars to dinner checks. On local French menus, béchamel and velouté sauces had been eclipsed by beurre blanc. Restaurants like the Quilted Giraffe and Hubert's ushered in the gilded age of nouvelle cooking. They, and their imitators, were partial to Japanese presentation and intrigued by the fiery, pungent flavors that a flood of Pakistani, Indo-Chinese, African, and Caribbean immigrants were bringing to New York.

For all its innovative dishes, like the omnipresent duck breast with raspberries, nouvelle cuisine looped back in time. A 1982 menu from An American Place describes a salad of "wild greens, cress, herbs and flowers." In seventeenth-century New Amsterdam, wrote Peter Rose in *The Sensible Cook,* "salads fragrant with fresh herbs and sprinkled enticingly with blue borage and orange calendula flowers," were often served at the beginning of the meal.

The pendulum began to tremble even before Wall Street did in 1987. Building on the precepts of nouvelle cooking, stars of the New York restaurant scene became obsessed with Americana.

There were no Dutch kitchens, but there were johnny-

cakes at An American Place and the baked Alaska that was invented at Delmonico's to celebrate the Union's forty-ninth state, was flaming again at The Rainbow Room, which along with Gage & Tollner (Gage & Tollner's recipe for their famous clam bellies is on page 374) and the "21" Club, was revived.

Updated versions of the cheap holes in the wall of the 1920s and '30s have returned in the form of the ubiquitous bistro and the modern trattoria. Some Indo-Chinese émigrés have opened Thai restaurants; others have opened soup shops where big bowls of broth and noodles make a $3 meal (see Su Chow Soup, page 49). Jamaican vendors have moved their jerked chicken, pork, and beef from pushcarts and fast-food stands to sit-down restaurants. (See Vernon's Jerked Chicken recipe on page 337.) Afghan émigrés are beginning to move from sidewalk stands into storefront restaurants. The aroma of shish kebab and falafel from Arabic vendors has begun to permeate sidewalks and street fairs.

Boom-year restaurants like Hubert's, Jam's, and 150 Wooster have closed. Other restaurants are chasing the pendulum again.

Most of the menus of the top dining rooms in New York City today could be photocopies of each other. Innovators are playing it safe, at least for the duration. There are shanks and mashed potatoes everywhere. People who know menus are not surprised.

"Like an old club member at the bar, New York restaurants keep repeating themselves," said Mr. Batterberry, who is currently updating *On the Town in New York*. He is philosophical about dining days to come. "Any country that goes from Carter to Reagan to Bush is going to have some manic mood swings in the kitchen," he said. If current menu trends proceed in a logical, historical pattern, he expects to achieve a longtime goal.

"I've every reason to believe that I will eventually taste a roasted canvasback duck," he said.

"All-U-Kan-Eat" at a bargain luncheonette, 1910 (facing page). All-You-Can-Eat at today's pushcarts, (below).

A Little Something Sweet

Ebinger's
BLACKOUT CAKE

For those who grew up in Brooklyn, when Brooklyn was the world, there is no sweeter sound than the Ebinger's brand name. No other word can pull such heartstrings, signal such salivation.

Blackout Cake! Othello! Lemon Cupcakes! Crumb Buns! Proust can keep his madeleine. Give Brooklynites anything Ebinger's. The family bakery opened on Flatbush Avenue in 1898 and eventually became a string of 54. Anybody who lived in Brooklyn lived close to an Ebinger's. The unstinting quality and consistency of its 200 German-style pastries made them shrines.

When Ebinger's went bankrupt in 1972, it wasn't just the end of an era; it was also the end of a certain kind of innocence.

Then, in 1982, Lou Guerra, a Brooklyn baker, tried to revive the label (and, he said, the original recipes) in a storefront bakery on Fort Hamilton Parkway. But he said his efforts sputtered financially until 1989, when John Edwards, who grew up near the Snyder Avenue Ebinger's, bought the business and mounted his own cam-

John Edwards and the highly esteemed Blackout Cake (left). The less highly esteemed Ebinger's truck (inset).

paign to stoke the Ebinger's flame. He quietly began to manufacture commercial versions of Ebinger's pastries, packing them into The Boxes and shipping them to supermarkets.

COULD IT BE?

When they appeared, sightings of The Box kindled a certain kind of hope.

"Ahhh," moaned Marion Lindner, now in her sixties, who grew up near the Flatbush Avenue Ebinger's. "My youth."

"Now this, this is cake," said David Frischt, in his mid fifties, who grew up near the Bedford Avenue Ebinger's. "At least, God willing, it is still cake."

But can the cakes, once handmade for a 24-hour shelf life, be adapted to the realities of mass production, stay fresh for a week, and still be Ebinger's cakes?

This may seem like a simple epicurean conundrum. But those of the Ebinger's faith know that it is more. The second (or, some say, third) coming of the Brooklyn brand name may be a triumph of quality. Or it could be another victory for that old pair of tricksters, denial and desire.

People who once believed in the contents of The Box will want to believe. It doesn't matter what the current baker says. "These are *not,* I repeat *not* the Ebinger's cakes I grew up on," Mr. Edwards asserted. "I intend to establish a commercial line that is close to the old-time flavor. Then I can establish an all-natural gourmet line and make the real old-time cakes."

But locally The Box response is impervious to his disclaimer, untouched by his rational business plans.

"It's embryonic recall," explained Dan Kaplan, a Manhattan lawyer in his sixties who grew up near the Avenue M Ebinger's. "You have to put a cage around me to keep me away from The Boxes."

He is not alone. "They come in and start pointing and jumping up and down," said Louis Colon, manager of the Sloan's Supermarket at 255 Ninth Avenue (24th Street) in Manhattan. "At first we couldn't keep enough of that cake on the shelves."

"It isn't just cake!" wailed Mr. Kaplan. "Ebinger's was a way of life. The Boxes! The stores! You could eat off the floors! The Ebinger's girls!"

IT TAKES A CERTAIN MATURITY

Dr. Annie Hauck-Lawson, mid thirties, an assistant professor of nutrition sciences at Brooklyn College who grew up near the 7th Avenue Ebinger's in Brooklyn's Park Slope, said the median age of the Ebinger's girls was about 80, but they could slice and box a cake faster than a woman a quarter their age. And that was just one facet of the Ebinger's mystique. ("The Boxes!" she said. "Perfectly tied with this red and white striped string!")

Having studied Brooklyn's eating patterns for her Ph.D. dissertation, Dr. Hauck-Lawson concluded: "The borough is such an ethnic mix and Ebinger's was one commonality. Everybody could walk to an Ebinger's, and what could be wrong with fabulous cake?"

The combination of accessibility and unstinting quality created a "legendary bakery," said Lyn Stallworth, co-author of *The Brooklyn Cookbook.*

Her book details the Ebinger's initiation of one Elizabeth White: "From the way they were talking, in a mixture of awe and greed, I knew this was not just a cake—it was almost like Percival describing the Holy Grail," Ms. White recalled in the book.

A display like this brings joy to all New Yorkers who get teary at the mention of Ebinger's.

"Later, when I had my first taste of blackout cake, I understood."

The Brooklyn Cookbook also records reverberations from the fall of Ebinger's. It quotes another Brooklynite, Leonard S. Elman, as saying, "Brooklynites are united in the belief that their lives were impoverished when Ebinger's closed its doors for the last time." Like many Ebingerists, he kept a cake in his freezer for nearly a year after the closing. Eating it, he said, made him feel as if he were drinking his last bottle of 1926 Lafite.

For others, eating the last crumbs of a long-frozen Ebinger's was like losing a foul ball caught at Ebbets Field. On August 27, 1972, *The New York Times* noted that Ebinger's had closed the previous day, going "the way of the Navy Yard, the Dodgers and Luna Park." An ill-timed overexpansion was cited as the cause of death.

A LOSS OF FAITH

It was like losing God. "My life ended when Ebinger's closed," said Dick Forman, in his mid-fifties and a physicist with the Mitre Corporation in McLean, Virginia, who grew up near the Avenue U Ebinger's store.

He and scores of other New York Ebingerists undertook personal projects to resurrect their favorite cakes.

Blackout Cake—three layers of devil's food cake sandwiching a dark chocolate pudding, with chocolate frosting, and sprinkled with chocolate cake crumbs—was a holy quest. "Catholics have a Pope," said Mr. Kaplan. Ebingerists, it seems, had Blackout Cake and they wanted it back.

Mr. Forman compiled what he knew to be true of the cake and bedeviled food magazines and baking experts for advice. "No one could help. They said it was a *commercial* recipe. What do they know?"

The closest he came to an authentic Ebinger's blackout cake, he said, was by using "Betty Crocker brownie mix—the one with the little packet of Hershey's chocolate."

"You replace the Hershey's with Fox's U-Bet Chocolate Syrup and decrease the eggs from two to one, and you hit that point between brownie and blackout," he said. Still, something was missing.

Mr. Forman tracked down one of the Ebinger scions, who told him that her father had a special cocoa formulated for the cake. Feeling that he lacked the expertise to move forward into cocoa formulations, Mr. Forman gave his blackout file—the archive, he calls it—to Rose Levy Beranbaum, author of *The Cake Bible*.

Another old-time New York favorite—Fox's U-Bet Chocolate Flavored Syrup.

AN EXPERT'S OPINION

"Dozens of people have asked for help with blackout cake," Ms. Beranbaum said. "They think I will be the answer to their prayers, but I don't think so." The cake itself is not impossible to re-create, she said, but the memories may be. "I have the definite feeling that in the case of blackout cake, the memories are better than the cake ever was," she said.

Blasphemy! Ebingerists have an almost theological belief that the original bakery's line of pastries resonated perfectly to the New York sweet tooth: they were huge, inexpensive, and not cloying.

In addition, Mr. Kaplan said, the cake was synonymous with "a time, a quality, a connection."

In the long years since the fall of Ebinger's, there has been intermittent hope for the searchers. In 1982, Lou Guerra, a baker, revived the name and opened an Ebinger's on Fort Hamilton Parkway and 63rd Street in the Bay Ridge section of Brooklyn. He had discovered that "the Ebinger's name was in the public domain," he told a reporter at the time. Moreover, his father, Guy Guerra, also a baker, claimed to have been given the Ebinger's recipes by Arthur Ebinger, the son of the founding Ebinger.

Whatever their origin, the recipes yielded cakes that made Ebingerists weak at the knees. "Authenticity Not In Doubt," *The New York Times* said in 1982. Customers started lining up at the bakery at 7:30 in the morning, Lou Guerra told a reporter. "The way people are buying cake, you'd think they'd all been on diets for the past 10 years," he said.

LIFE EXTENSION

Nevertheless, the 24-hour shelf life of an Ebinger's cake couldn't be reconciled with the economic realities of modern life. When Mr. Edwards took over, he adjusted the recipes and moved into supermarkets. "I repeat, the recipes have been adjusted for a longer shelf life," Mr. Edwards said. "These are not, I repeat, not the cakes I grew up on."

"The Boxes! At A & P!" Mr. Kaplan said. "Are they trying to commercialize my childhood?" Still, as surely as a man given a chance to live life's best moments over would, he is drawn to The Boxes. So far, he hasn't dared to taste.

Manny Krantz, on the other hand, couldn't wait. The retired tailor, now in his seventies, who grew up near the Avenue U Ebinger's in the Sheepshead Bay section of Brooklyn, fidgeted not so long ago in the checkout line of the Sloan's on Ninth Avenue. Although a courtly gentleman, he finally succumbed to the contents of The Box in his shopping cart. He even used his fingers.

"It's not quite the same," said Mr. Krantz. But his memory was immediately overwhelmed by an intense desire to believe. He was more willing to doubt himself than the contents of The Box, and he quickly amended his response. "Of course, I am not quite the same anymore either."

All-Chocolate BLACKOUT CAKE

Using three different formulas from different Ebinger's incarnations, I developed this recipe for the home cook. This—and eleven other versions—were tested for taste, texture, and nostalgia by a panel of twelve Ebingerites.

CAKE
½ cup unsweetened Dutch-process cocoa
    powder
2 tablespoons boiling water
2 ounces unsweetened chocolate, chopped
¾ cup milk
1 cup (2 sticks) unsalted butter, softened
    slightly
2 cups sugar
4 large eggs, separated
2 teaspoons vanilla extract
2 cups all-purpose flour
1 teaspoon baking powder
1 teaspoon baking soda
1 teaspoon salt

FILLING (see Note)
1 tablespoon plus 1¾ teaspoons unsweetened
    Dutch-process cocoa powder
2 cups boiling water
¾ cup plus 1 tablespoon plus ½ teaspoon
    sugar
1 ounce bittersweet chocolate, chopped
2 tablespoons cornstarch dissolved in
    1 tablespoon cold water
¼ teaspoon salt
1 teaspoon vanilla extract
2 tablespoons unsalted butter

FROSTING
12 ounces semisweet chocolate, chopped
12 tablespoons (1½ sticks) unsalted butter
½ cup hot water
1 tablespoon light corn syrup
1 tablespoon vanilla extract

1. Preheat the oven to 375°F. Butter and lightly flour two 8-inch round cake pans.

2. Make the cake: Place the cocoa in a small bowl and whisk in the boiling water to form a paste.

3. Combine the chocolate and milk in a small saucepan over medium heat. Stir frequently until the chocolate melts, about 3 minutes. Remove from the heat. Whisk a small amount of the hot chocolate milk into the cocoa paste to warm it. Whisk the cocoa mixture into the milk mixture. Return the pan to medium heat and stir for 1 minute. Remove and set aside to cool until tepid.

4. In the bowl of a mixer, cream the butter and sugar together. Beat in the egg yolks, one at a time, and add the vanilla. Slowly stir in the chocolate mixture.

5. Combine the flour, baking powder, baking soda, and salt. Using a spatula or a wooden spoon, slowly add the flour mixture to the chocolate mixture. Fold in until just mixed.

6. In another bowl, whisk the egg whites until soft peaks form. Using a rubber spatula, gently fold the egg whites into the batter. Divide the batter between the prepared pans. Bake until a toothpick inserted in the center of a cake comes out clean, 45 minutes. Cool the cakes in the pans on a rack for 15 minutes. Gently remove the cakes from the pans and continue to cool.

7. While the cake is baking, make the filling: Combine the cocoa and boiling water in a small saucepan over low heat. Stir in the sugar and chocolate. Add the dissolved cornstarch paste and salt to the pan and bring to a boil, stirring constantly. Boil for 1 minute. Remove the pan from the heat and whisk in the vanilla and butter. Transfer the mixture to a bowl, cover, and refrigerate until cool.

8. Make the frosting: Melt the chocolate in a double boiler over hot, not simmering, water, stirring until smooth. Remove the top of the double boiler from the heat and whisk in the butter, 1 tablespoon at a time. Return the top to the heat, if necessary, to melt the butter.

9. Whisk in the hot water all at once and whisk until smooth. Whisk in the corn syrup and vanilla. Cover and refrigerate for up to 15 minutes prior to using.

10. Assemble the cake: Use a sharp serrated knife to slice each cake layer horizontally in half to form 4 layers. Set 1 layer aside. Place 1 layer on a cake round or plate. Generously swath the layer with one-third of the filling. Add the second layer and repeat. Set the third layer on top. Quickly apply a layer of frosting to the top and the sides of the cake. Refrigerate for 10 minutes.

11. Meanwhile, crumble the remaining cake layer. Apply the remaining frosting to the cake. Sprinkle it liberally with the cake crumbs. Serve the cake within 24 hours. Store in a cool place.

Serves 8 to 10

Note: Please note that these ingredients make a very runny filling that pleased the 12 devout Ebingerists who taste-tested different versions of this cake. Those who desire a less syrupy consistency can stir in an additional 1 to 2 tablespoons cornstarch.

Fallen
CHOCOLATE SOUFFLE CAKE

For best results, David Waltuck, the chef/owner of Chanterelle restaurant, recommends using Valrhona dark bittersweet Guanaja 70 percent chocolate (available at Dean & DeLuca and other gourmet stores or through mail order, see Index). If you can't get it, Lindt and Tobler make good bittersweet or extra-bittersweet chocolate. In a pinch, use semisweet chocolate and reduce the sugar to ½ cup.

1 pound bittersweet or semisweet chocolate,
  broken into pieces
1 cup (2 sticks) unsalted butter
9 large eggs, separated
¾ cup granulated sugar
Unsweetened cocoa powder, for dusting
Confectioners' sugar, for dusting

1. Preheat the oven to 300°F. Line the bottom of a 9-inch springform pan with parchment paper. Lightly butter and flour the paper.

2. Melt the chocolate and butter in a double boiler or metal bowl set over barely simmering water. Stir to combine, remove from the heat, and set aside to cool.

3. In a bowl, combine the egg yolks with all but 1 teaspoon of the sugar and beat at high speed until the mixture is light and forms a ribbon when the beaters are lifted from the bowl.

4. In a separate bowl, combine the egg whites with the reserved teaspoon sugar. Beat until the egg whites form soft peaks. Fold one-third of the chocolate mixture into a bowl with one-third of the yolk mixture. Fold in one-third of the egg whites. Repeat two more times so that all of the ingredients are incorporated.

5. Pour the batter into the prepared pan. Bake for 30 minutes. Do not overcook; the center of the cake should still be soft. Let the cake cool to room temperature for 3 hours; do not remove from the pan sooner or the cake will fall apart.

6. Remove the sides of the springform pan and dust the cake with cocoa, then confectioners' sugar, and then cocoa and sugar again. Cover and refrigerate overnight. Before serving, let the cake warm to room temperature. Dust again with cocoa and confectioners' sugar.

Serves 8 to 10

Sally Deitz's OUTRAGEOUS CHOCOLATE CAKE

E xplains Sally Deitz, "This recipe was given by an Austrian countess to a friend while they were students at Mt. Holyoke. It is flourless and dense and always draws rave reviews."

Use chunks of the best chocolate for Sally Deitz's rich mousse cake.

CAKE
8 ounces semisweet chocolate (the best you can find), chopped
8 large eggs, separated
2 tablespoons sugar
1 teaspoon vanilla extract

TOPPING
8 ounces semisweet chocolate, chopped
8 large eggs, separated
2 tablespoons sugar
1 teaspoon vanilla extract

1. Preheat the oven to 350°F. Butter and sugar a 9-inch springform pan.

2. Make the cake: Melt the chocolate in a double boiler over hot, not simmering, water. Remove from the heat.

3. In a mixing bowl, combine the egg whites, sugar, and vanilla. Beat until stiff, but not dry, peaks form.

4. In a large bowl, whisk the egg yolks until thick. Add the melted chocolate and combine. Fold in the egg whites.

5. Pour the mixture into the prepared springform pan. Bake until just firm in the center when gently shaken, 12 to 15 minutes. Place the pan on a rack to cool to room temperature. Expect the cake to fall.

6. Make the topping: Repeat steps 2, 3, and 4. Spread the unbaked chocolate mousse on top of the baked mousse in the springform pan. Chill for at least 12 hours. Serve with whipped cream.

Serves 16 to 20

TO BUY FINE CHOCOLATES

Larry Burdick makes extraordinary truffles and chocolates for a number of New York restaurants as well as by special order; (212) 996-2149.

DEAN & DELUCA: 560 Broadway at Prince Street; (212) 431-1691. Their Espresso Bar at the Paramount Hotel (235 West 46th Street; (212) 869-6890) carries an extensive selection of Manon chocolates.

ECONOMY CANDY: 131 Essex Street at Rivington Street; (212) 254-1531. For old-time penny candies and hard candies as well as well-priced dried fruits, nuts, and not-so-fine chocolate.

FRASER MORRIS: 931 Madison Avenue at 74th Street; (212) 988-6700; and 1264 Third Avenue, between 72nd and 73rd Streets; (212) 288-7717. Sells fine candies and giant strawberries dipped in chocolate. Prices are high and so is the quality.

LE CHOCOLATIER MANON: (212) 995-9490. Call for the current availability of their buttercreams, pralines, truffles—a dizzying array of fabulous, elegant chocolates.

LI-LAC CHOCOLATES: 120 Christopher Street, between Bleecker and Hudson Streets; (212) 242-7374. Good-quality old-time chocolates in nostalgic shapes like the Statue of Liberty and city skyscrapers.

PLUMBRIDGE CONFECTIONS: 30 East 67th Street, between Madison and Park Avenues; (212) 744-6640. Fine chocolates, spiced and mocha nuts, and addictive candied citrus peels.

TEUSCHER CHOCOLATES OF SWITZERLAND: 25 East 61st Street at Madison Avenue; (212) 751-8462; and 620 Fifth Avenue, between 49th and 50th Streets; (212) 246-4416. Superb chocolates; the champagne truffles are legendary.

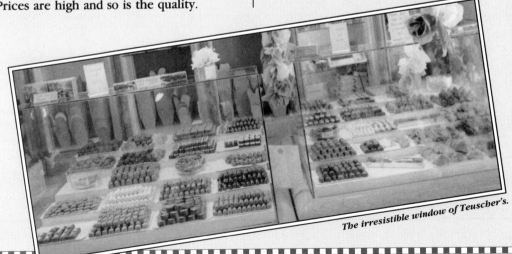

The irresistible window of Teuscher's.

Miss Milton's
LOVELY
FUDGE PIE

For more than 30 years Serendipity at 225 East 60th Street has been delighting sweet tooths. According to legend, this pie was special enough to win over Marilyn Monroe, who sometimes had it shipped to her on movie locations.

½ cup (1 stick) unsalted butter, softened
½ cup sugar
3 large eggs, separated
½ cup all-purpose flour
2 ounces (2 squares) unsweetened chocolate, melted and cooled
1 tablespoon vanilla extract
¼ cup strawberry preserves
1 cup heavy (whipping) cream, whipped until soft peaks form

1. Preheat the oven to 325°F. Butter and flour an 8-inch pie plate.

2. In a mixing bowl, cream the butter with the sugar by hand or machine. Lightly beat the egg yolks and add to the butter-sugar mixture. Add the flour, chocolate, and vanilla and mix well.

3. In another bowl, beat the egg whites until stiff but not dry. Fold into the batter.

4. Spread about one-fourth of the batter evenly over the bottom of the pie pan. Spread the preserves on top, spreading not quite to the edges. Cover with the remaining batter.

5. Bake until the surface of the pie feels firm but the texture feels soft, about 30 minutes. Do not overbake. Set the pie on a rack to cool to room temperature. Serve with whipped cream.

Serves 6

The renowned Wonder Wheel is still a Coney Island favorite.

Coney Island
FUDGE

A bite of this fudge will bring back memories of childhood summers at Coney Island—the Cyclone, the Wonder Wheel, the cool sand under the boardwalk, the fudge.

1 cup light cream
4 ounces semisweet chocolate, chopped
2 cups sugar
½ teaspoon salt
2 tablespoons unsalted butter
1 teaspoon vanilla extract
½ pound walnuts or pecans, chopped

1. Combine the cream, chocolate, and sugar in a heavy saucepan over low heat. Cook, stirring constantly, until the chocolate melts and the mixture is smooth. Add the salt and let the mixture come to a boil. Turn down the heat to very low and cook without stirring until the mixture reaches the soft-ball stage, 236°F on candy thermometer.

2. Remove the pan from the heat. Add the butter and vanilla, but do not stir. Let the mixture cool until lukewarm (110°F). Then beat the fudge with a wooden spoon until creamy. Add the nuts and mix well. Transfer the fudge to a buttered 8-inch-square baking pan. Cover and chill. When firm, cut into small squares.

Serves 10

Regina CAKE

For holiday time or any time, Meryle Evans' chocolate-frosted cake.

Historian Meryle Evans says, "Regina Cake has been a family favorite for special occasions for three generations. It was named in honor of my grandmother's cook, Regina. The cake is the tried and true 1-2-3-4 that can still be found on cake flour boxes, but the filling is unusual. It is mocha and matzoh meal, and we have always theorized that Regina used the meal in place of nuts when she had none in the house. I've done the reverse and suggested nuts as a substitute for the matzoh meal if it is not available."

CAKE
1 cup (2 sticks) unsalted butter or
*   margarine, softened*
2 cups granulated sugar
4 large eggs
3 cups cake flour
1 tablespoon baking powder
½ teaspoon salt
1 cup milk
1 teaspoon vanilla extract

FILLING
½ cup (1 stick) unsalted butter,
*   softened*
1 cup confectioners' sugar
1 cup matzoh meal or finely chopped
*   almonds*
1 large egg
3 to 4 tablespoons strong black
*   coffee*

FROSTING
1 cup unsweetened cocoa powder
2 cups confectioners' sugar
¾ cup strong black coffee
3 tablespoons unsalted butter
1 teaspoon vanilla extract
½ teaspoon almond extract
1 cup flaked coconut (optional)

1. Preheat the oven to 350°F. Generously butter and flour three 9-inch round cake pans.

2. Make the cake: In a mixing bowl, cream the butter. Gradually add the sugar and beat until light and fluffy. Beat in the eggs, 1 at a time.

3. Sift together the cake flour, baking powder, and salt. Add the dry ingredients alternately with the milk to the creamed mixture, incorporating well after each addition. Stir in the vanilla.

4. Divide the batter among the prepared cake pans. Bake until a toothpick inserted in the center comes out clean and the cake shrinks from the side of the pan, 25 to 30 minutes. Cool the cakes in the pans on wire racks for 5 minutes. Remove from the pans and let cool completely before filling and frosting.

5. Make the filling: In a mixing bowl, beat the butter with the sugar until well blended. Mix in the matzoh meal; beat in the egg. Add the coffee and mix well. The filling may look curdled, but cover and chill until ready to use and it will combine well.

6. Make the frosting: Combine the cocoa and sugar in a medium saucepan. Add the coffee and butter and cook over low heat, stirring constantly, until smooth and thick, about 10 minutes. Remove from the heat and stir in the vanilla and the almond extracts.

7. To assemble: Place 1 layer of the cake on a serving plate. Cover with half of the filling. Add the second layer and spread with the remaining filling. Top with the third layer. Spread the frosting on the top and sides of the cake while the frosting is still warm. If the frosting hardens too quickly, place the saucepan over low heat and soften slightly, stirring constantly. Sprinkle the cake with the coconut, if desired.

Serves 8 to 10

Estelle Parsons'
WALNUT TORTE

This rich, subtle cake took first prize in a New York City March of Dimes Gourmet Gala—for good reason!

TORTE
2½ cups finely ground walnuts
¾ cup granulated sugar
7 egg whites

FILLING
½ cup plus 1 tablespoon sugar
3 egg yolks
3 tablespoons strong black coffee, at room temperature
½ cup walnuts, coarsely chopped
Confectioners' sugar, for dusting

---

1. Preheat the oven to 400°F. Butter and flour three 9-inch round cake pans.

2. Make the torte: Combine the ground walnuts and sugar in a large bowl. In a separate bowl, preferably copper, whisk the egg whites until stiff. Fold into the walnut-sugar mixture and stir gently to combine. Divide the batter evenly among the prepared cake pans. Bake until delicately browned on top, 15 minutes. Cook on wire racks.

3. Make the filling: Warm ½ cup of the sugar, the egg yolks, and coffee in a heavy saucepan over low heat. Cook, stirring, until the mixture thickens enough to coat the back of a spoon, about 10 minutes. Do not allow the custard to boil. Remove from the heat and strain. Press plastic wrap directly on top and refrigerate to chill slightly.

4. In a small bowl, stir together the chopped walnuts and the remaining 1 tablespoon sugar until the sugar turns brown. Fold the nut mixture into the filling.

5. To assemble: Place 1 layer of cake on a serving plate. Cover with half of the filling. Add the second layer and spread with the remaining filling. Top with the third layer and sprinkle with confectioner's sugar.

Serves 6 to 8

Selma Frishling's
PASSOVER NUT CAKE

When Selma Frishling, a retired schoolteacher, was growing up, Passover cake came around once a year, and Selma was ready. "My mother was very patient. I did whatever she'd let me do when she made this cake," Frishling recalls. "We always ate it plain, without filling or frosting, accompanied by a cup of tea."

12 large eggs, separated
1⅓ cups sugar
Juice and grated zest of 3 lemons
¾ cup matzoh meal
4 cups ground walnuts (about 1 pound shelled nuts)
1 teaspoon ground cinnamon

---

1. Preheat the oven to 350°F. Butter a 13 × 9-inch cake pan.

2. In a nonreactive large mixing bowl, beat the egg yolks until frothy. Add the sugar, lemon juice, and lemon zest and continue beating until thick and fluffy.

3. In a separate bowl, beat the egg whites until stiff but not dry. Using a rubber spatula, fold the egg whites into the egg yolk mixture. Combine the matzoh meal, ground walnuts, and cinnamon. Fold them into the mixture.

4. Pour the batter into the prepared pan. Bake until the top is golden and firm, 50 to 60 minutes.

Serves 8 to 10

A FINE AND FANCY CAKE

Actors are waiters, dancers are aerobics teachers, and some artists sculpt cakes in New York City. They don't make ordinary layer cakes with piped flowers and sugary Victorian swags, these bakers can make cakes that are a perfect replica of Grand Central Station or the Statue of Liberty. They can paint a beloved vista on top of a cake that can serve 50, reproduce certain anatomical parts, or create a bust of the family cat. For a showstopping centerpiece for a birthday or other special occasion, here is a list of the city's most creative cake masters.

OLIVE ALPERT: 9511 Shore Road, Brooklyn, NY 11209; (718) 833-3092.

ELLEN BAUMWOLL, BIJOUX-DOUX: 304 Mulberry Street, New York, NY 10012; (212) 226-0948.

MARGARET BRAUN: 94 Greenwich Avenue, New York, NY 10013; (212) 929-1582

RICK ELLIS: One University Place, Apt. #20C, New York, NY 10003; (212) 228-3624.

CHERYL KLEINMAN, CHERYL KLEINMAN CAKES: 32 Downing Street, Apt. #3D, New York, NY 10014; (212) 242-6195.

ANDREA LANZI, SANT AMBROEUS: 1000 Madison Avenue, New York, NY 10021; (212) 570-2211.

PATTI PAGE, BAKED IDEAS: 450 Broadway, New York, NY 10013; (212) 925-9097.

COLETTE PETERS: 186 Clinton Avenue, Apt. #6, Brooklyn, NY 11203; (718) 605-4577.

CLIFF SIMON, CAKES BY CLIFF: 529 East 6th Street, New York, NY 10009; (212) 777-9253.

Cheryl Kleinman of Cheryl Kleinman Cakes.

Seija Goldstein with her daughter Jennie.

Aunt Olga's
CARDAMOM CAKE

The Finnish traditional coffee table, according to Seija Goldstein, is a gracious assortment of home-baked goodies laid out with coffee for afternoon guests. Goldstein's Aunt Olga, who lives in Finland, taught her how to make this cardamom-scented confection.

Unseasoned, fine, dried bread crumbs, for the pan
2 large eggs
1 scant cup granulated sugar
1¼ teaspoons ground cardamom
1¼ teaspoons baking powder
Pinch of salt
1¼ cups all-purpose flour
1 cup heavy (whipping) cream
Confectioners' sugar, for dusting

1. Preheat the oven to 350°F. Butter an 8 × 4-inch loaf pan and dust with plain bread crumbs.

2. In a mixing bowl, beat the eggs and granulated sugar until light.

3. Combine the cardamom, baking powder, salt, and flour. Alternately blend the flour mixture and heavy cream into the egg and sugar mixture until all is added. Pour the batter into the prepared cake pan. Bake until a toothpick inserted into the center of the cake comes out clean, 50 to 60 minutes. Cool on a wire rack. Remove from the pan and dust with confectioners' sugar before serving in thin slices.

Serves 6 to 8

Evelyn's
SAND TORTE

Evelyn Levin grew up in Queens where her German mother taught her to make this fine, subtle cake.

½ cup (1 stick) unsalted butter, softened
1 cup sugar
1 teaspoon grated lemon zest
2 large eggs
1½ cups all-purpose flour
1½ teaspoons baking powder
½ cup freshly squeezed orange juice

1. Preheat the oven to 350°F. Butter an 8 × 4-inch loaf pan.

2. In a mixing bowl, cream the butter and sugar together until light and fluffy. Add the lemon zest and eggs and beat to combine well.

3. In a separate bowl, combine the flour and the baking powder. Alternately add ½ cup of the flour mixture and about 3 tablespoons of the orange juice to the butter mixture, mixing well between additions, until all the flour and juice are added and the batter is smooth. Pour the batter into the loaf pan. Bake until a toothpick inserted in the center of the cake comes out clean, 40 to 50 minutes. Cool on a wire rack, then remove the cake from the pan and wrap in plastic wrap. This cake is best if made the day before serving.

Serves 6 to 8

George Washington's CARROT TEA CAKE

This cake was served on the occasion of British Evacuation Day on November 25, 1783, at the Fraunces Tavern, in what now is the South Street Seaport area. George Washington was in attendance, and this tea cake was named in his honor. The recipe has been adapted from *The 13 Colonies Cookbook* by Mary Donovan, Amy Hatrack, and others.

2 cups all-purpose flour
1 tablespoon ground cinnamon
2 teaspoons baking soda
1 teaspoon salt
¾ cup corn oil
2 cups granulated sugar
4 large eggs, beaten
2 cups finely grated carrots
1 teaspoon confectioners' sugar

---

1. Preheat the oven to 350°F. Generously oil a 9-inch springform pan or a Bundt pan (if using a Bundt, be careful to grease it thoroughly).

Fraunces Tavern as it looked in 1889. Courtesy of The New York Public Library Picture Collection.

2. In a medium bowl, combine the flour, cinnamon, baking soda, and salt. Stir well and set aside.

3. In a large bowl, combine the oil, granulated sugar, eggs, and carrots and mix well. Add the flour mixture and stir until smooth. Pour the batter into the prepared pan. Bake until moist yet firm to the touch, 1 hour. Cool in the pan, then remove and dust with the confectioners' sugar.

Serves 8 to 10

Cranberry-Nut COFFEE CAKE

Marilyn Froim, a retired schoolteacher who lives in Brooklyn, favors this family recipe for "the delicious combination of flavors." Her family traditionally eats it around Thanksgiving, when cranberries are plentiful.

½ cup (1 stick) unsalted butter or margarine, softened
1 cup sugar
2 large eggs
1 teaspoon almond extract
2 cups all-purpose flour
1 teaspoon baking powder
1 teaspoon baking soda
½ teaspoon salt
1 cup plain yogurt or sour cream
1 cup walnut pieces
1 cup whole-berry cranberry sauce, preferably homemade

---

1. Preheat the oven to 350°F. Butter and flour a 10-inch tube pan.

2. In a nonreactive large bowl, beat the butter and sugar until blended. Add the eggs and almond extract and beat well.

3. Sift together the flour, baking powder,

baking soda, and salt. Beat into the creamed mixture alternately with the yogurt. Add half of the walnuts and stir to combine.

4. Spread half of the batter evenly over the bottom of the pan. Spread half of the cranberry sauce over the batter. Spoon in the remaining batter. Top with the remaining sauce and nuts.

5. Bake the cake until a tester inserted in the center comes out clean, 50 to 55 minutes. Cool on a rack for 5 minutes in the pan. Remove from the pan and finish cooling on a rack.

Serves 8 to 10

1. Preheat the oven to 350°F. Lightly butter a tube or Bundt pan.

2. In a large bowl, cream the shortening until fluffy. Add the sugar and egg and stir until smooth. Stir in the soup. Add all of the dry ingredients and stir until smooth and well combined. Pour the batter into the prepared pan. Bake until a toothpick inserted in the center of the cake comes out clean, 40 to 45 minutes.

3. Remove from the oven and allow to cool in the pan. Unmold and sprinkle the confectioners' sugar on top.

Serves 8 to 10

Doris Hosking's
TOMATO SOUP CAKE

Tomato soup cake has a moist density similar to carrot or pumpkin cake, as well as a subtle and, for most, unidentifiable tartness. Few can guess the secret ingredient! Leftovers, if there are any, will keep well for up to a week.

½ cup solid vegetable shortening
1 cup granulated sugar
1 large egg
1 can (10¾ ounces)
    condensed tomato soup
2 cups all-purpose flour
1½ teaspoons baking soda
1 teaspoon ground cinnamon
1 teaspoon freshly grated
    nutmeg
½ teaspoon ground cloves
Pinch of salt
½ cup chopped walnuts
½ cup raisins (optional)
Confectioners' sugar, for
    dusting

Aunt Phil's
BROWN SUGAR CAKE

Elizabeth Benjamin, who lives in the East Village, got this recipe from her Aunt Phil and makes it for dinner and breakfast or tea.

4 large eggs
1 pound light brown sugar (about 2 cups)
1½ teaspoons vanilla extract
1¾ cups sifted all-purpose flour
½ cup chopped dates
⅛ teaspoon salt

1. Preheat the oven to 350°F.

2. Combine the eggs and sugar in a double boiler over hot, not simmering, water and cook, stirring frequently with a wooden spoon, until thick enough to coat the back of the spoon, about 20 minutes.

3. Stir in the vanilla, flour, dates, and salt. Pour the batter into an ungreased 13 × 9-inch baking pan. Bake until a toothpick inserted in the center of the cake comes out clean, 20 minutes. Cool in the pan, then cut into squares and serve.

Serves 6 to 8

ON TOP OF THE CARROT CAKE HILL

Renee Allen Mancino, the proprietor of Carrot Top Pastries, may bake the best carrot cake in the world.

In less than 10 years, she has expanded her original home-oven operation to a two-cafe, one-commercial-bakery empire. She bakes cakes for dozens of Manhattan's finest restaurants and fancy food stores, as well as for Stevie Wonder, Archbishop Desmond Tutu, Richard Pryor, and hundreds of other celebrities.

Once, all she had for transporting her supplies was a shopping cart; now she drives a black BMW M3. She is not unimpressed by her success, but she doesn't take it personally either. She sees herself as a straightforward product of the American dream.

"I'm just your basic Buckeye in the big city," said Mrs. Mancino, who grew up in Cleveland and moved to New York City in 1970 to study mortuary science. Certain Ohioans, she said, are born with the daring it takes to leave home on a lifelong quest to "find your family in you." She is now in her 40s and that process has been inextricably linked to carrot cake and certain aspects of her character. "I learned everything the hard way, but once I learned it, baby, I never forgot," she said.

EARLY TRAINING

The lessons began in adolescence. "I was bad," she said. "I was so bad my mother and grandmother, who were good Christian ladies, by the way, taught me how to bake to try to keep me at home and out of trouble."

Their efforts were not immediately rewarded. At 15, Renee Allen was sentenced to a year's residency in a reform school for truancy. "I came out of that place a straight-A student,

determined to go to medical school," Mrs. Mancino recalled. At her grandmother's funeral, she realized her specialty: forensic medicine.

She moved to New York where, in short order, she studied mortuary sciences, joined the Black Muslims, married badly, had a baby, and was widowed. Her husband's death left her with a baby girl to support in Inwood. She began baking carrot cakes.

She sent her earliest efforts—gratis—to a Black Muslim who was in jail upstate. Word got around. Within a year, she was baking 1,200 loaf-shaped cakes with buttercream frosting each week. "Prisoners could call Wednesday," she said. "I'd write orders all day."

And then she went to work. "I'd take my .38 gun and my shopping cart, go pick up my supplies at Pathmark, and come home and bake," she said. The cakes were picked up on Saturdays by a group of families on their way to visit prisoners upstate.

She studied on Sundays. In 1977, she was accepted by Columbia University's Medical School. After a summer of baking to earn both her tuition and a Montessori school tuition for her daughter, Tanyika, she took a Florida vacation. Two days before she was to enter medical school, the car in which she was a passenger crashed; she went through the windshield. Her memory has never completely recovered.

"I forgot everything I wanted to be," she said. "Medical school? Are you kidding? I couldn't even remember my name."

She did remember that she had a daughter. Gradually, she said, she recalled other things: "Embalming, certain facts about chemistry, how to make carrot cake."

She re-established her pastry-prison franchise and began delivering cakes to fancy food stores and restaurants also.

SOMETIMES THINGS WORK OUT JUST FINE

In 1980 she married Robert Mancino, a New York City police officer. While he was on patrol, he found her a place for a store, on Broadway at 214th Street. In an effort to expand their market to the other end of Manhattan, the couple built a mobile bakery on the back of a flatbed truck and drove it to Wall Street every day for two years. Seven years ago, they opened a second cafe and bakery on Broadway at 164th Street.

Mrs. Mancino has learned a lot about carrot cake—for instance, Canadian carrots are too bitter, and carrots from California are best; carrots grated too far ahead of time don't give a cake proper moisture; vegetable oil bakes more evenly in the batter than butter.

Mrs. Mancino has learned a lot about herself, too. "They say God protects babies and fools," she said. "I fall under that clause."

After 17 years as a Muslim, Mrs. Mancino is a Christian again. Her daughter has graduated from college. Her husband has built her a new house. She has a six-foot boa constrictor named CleoPatrick. And more cake orders than she can handle.

Mrs. Mancino believes in just desserts. One afternoon, wearing a tan jumpsuit and lizard pumps, a rope of nine-centimeter pearls around her neck, and a Marine cap perched on her hair, she furiously repainted the front of her store, brushing away the graffiti that a new generation of incorrigibles had left.

"People are bad for lack of knowing what makes them good," she said.

And then she stood back to admire the nine-foot orange fluorescent carrot that hangs in her doorway. She glanced across the street to the Riverdale Funeral Home, smiled contentedly, and said, "I feel real comfortable here."

Renee Mancino of Carrot Top Pastries.

Carrot Top
CAKE

A supreme carrot cake from Renee Mancino.

At Carrot Top, the carrot cake is number 1, but it's hard to pass up hot apple pie.

CAKE
1 cup vegetable oil
2 cups granulated
   sugar
3 cups freshly
   grated carrots
   (about 7
   carrots)
1 cup walnuts,
   coarsely
   chopped
2 cups all-
   purpose flour
1 tablespoon
   baking powder
1 teaspoon
   ground
   cinnamon
1 teaspoon
   freshly grated
   nutmeg
½ teaspoon salt
4 large eggs

FROSTING
4 tablespoons
   (½ stick)
   unsalted
   butter,
   softened
¼ cup solid
   vegetable
   shortening
12 ounces (1½ large packages) cream cheese,
   softened
2 tablespoons milk
1 tablespoon vanilla extract
1½ cups confectioners' sugar

1. Preheat the oven to 350°F. Oil an 11 × 9-inch sheet cake pan.

2. Make the cake: In a large bowl, combine the oil, granulated sugar, carrots, walnuts, flour, baking powder, cinnamon, nutmeg, and salt and stir to combine. Add the eggs and mix well. Pour the batter into the prepared pan. Bake until the cake is springy to the touch, 45 minutes. Cool in the pan on a wire rack.

3. Make the frosting: Cream together the butter, shortening, and cream cheese with a wooden spoon or hand mixer in a medium bowl. Add the milk and vanilla. Add the confectioners' sugar and stir until smooth. When the cake is cool, frost.

Serves 8 to 10

Ray Kraft's
SAUERKRAUT SURPRISE CAKE

Sauerkraut is another ingredient that gives moistness and mysterious underpinnings to a cake. This recipe is adapted from one that appeared in *A Culinary Collection from the Metropolitan Museum of Art*, edited by Linda Gillies.

CAKE
½ cup (1 stick) unsalted butter,
   softened
1½ cups granulated sugar
3 large eggs
1 teaspoon vanilla extract
2 cups all-purpose flour
1 teaspoon baking powder
1 teaspoon baking soda
¼ teaspoon salt
1 cup unsweetened cocoa
   powder
1 cup sauerkraut (fresh or bagged,
   not canned), well rinsed, drained,
   and chopped

FROSTING
4 ounces semisweet chocolate, chopped
2 ounces (2 squares) unsweetened chocolate, chopped
4 tablespoons (½ stick) unsalted butter
½ cup sour cream
1 teaspoon vanilla extract
¼ teaspoon salt
2 cups confectioners' sugar, sifted

1. Make the cake: Preheat the oven to 350°F. Butter and flour a Bundt cake pan.

2. In a large bowl, cream the butter and sugar until fluffy. Beat in the eggs, 1 at a time, then add the vanilla.

3. Sift together the flour, baking powder, baking soda, salt, and cocoa. Slowly beat the dry ingredients into the creamed mixture, alternating with 1 cup water. Stir in the sauerkraut. Pour the batter into the prepared pan. Bake for 35 to 40 minutes.

4. Cool completely in the pan.

5. Make the frosting: In the top of a double boiler over simmering water, melt both types of chocolate with the butter over low heat. Remove from the heat. Stir in the sour cream, vanilla, and salt. Gradually add the confectioners' sugar, beating until the frosting is spreadable.

6. When the cake is completely cool, carefully remove it from the pan and frost all over.

Serves 8 to 10

Kate's Café au lait
CHEESECAKE WITH A MOCHA CRUST

Cookbook editor Kate Slate makes this rich mocha cheesecake in her Upper West Side apartment.

Kate Slate's crust combines chocolate wafers with espresso for a touch of mocha.

CRUST
1 box (8½ ounces) chocolate wafer cookies
¼ cup sugar
1 teaspoon ground cinnamon
1 tablespoon plus 1 teaspoon powdered instant espresso coffee
Pinch of salt
6 tablespoons (¾ stick) unsalted butter, melted

FILLING
1½ pounds (3 large packages) cream cheese, softened
⅔ cup sugar
2 teaspoons powdered instant espresso coffee
½ teaspoon salt
3 large eggs
3 cups sour cream
1½ tablespoons Kahlua or dark rum
1 teaspoon vanilla extract
2 tablespoons unsalted butter, melted

1. Preheat the oven to 350°F. Butter a 9-inch springform pan.

2. Make the crust: In a food processor or blender, grind the cookies into moderately fine-textured crumbs. Add the sugar, cinnamon, powdered espresso, and salt and process briefly to blend. Transfer to a bowl, pour the butter over the crumbs, and toss with a fork to moisten evenly. Gently press the crumbs evenly over the bottom and sides of the prepared pan.

3. Make the filling: In a food processor, combine the cream cheese, sugar, powdered espresso, salt, and eggs. Blend until smooth, scraping down the sides of the container as necessary. Add the sour cream, Kahlua, vanilla, and butter and blend.

4. Pour the filling into the cookie-crumb shell. Bake in the center of the oven for 45 minutes.

5. Turn off the oven, prop the oven door open slightly, and allow the cake to rest in the oven for 1 hour more.

6. Cool the cheesecake to room temperature on a rack. Cover and refrigerate for at least 8 hours before serving.

Serves 10 to 12

Lindy's
NEW YORK–STYLE CHEESECAKE

1 cup plus 3 tablespoons all-purpose flour

2 cups sugar

2½ teaspoons grated lemon zest

½ teaspoon vanilla extract

3 egg yolks

½ cup (1 stick) unsalted butter, softened

2½ pounds (5 large packages) cream cheese, softened

1½ teaspoons grated orange zest

5 whole eggs

¼ cup heavy (whipping) cream

1. In a bowl, combine 1 cup of the flour with ¼ cup of the sugar, 1 teaspoon of the lemon zest, and ¼ teaspoon of the vanilla. Form a well in the center and add 1 egg yolk and all of the butter. Work with a fork to make a dough. Add up to 2 tablespoons of water, if necessary, to make a pliable dough. Form into a ball, cover with plastic wrap, and refrigerate for 1 hour.

2. Preheat the oven to 400°F. Butter the sides and bottom of a 9-inch springform pan.

3. In the bowl of a mixer, combine the cream cheese, the remaining 1¾ cups sugar, 3 tablespoons flour, 1½ teaspoons lemon zest, and all of the orange zest and beat well. Add the 5 whole eggs, the remaining 2 egg yolks, and the remaining ¼ teaspoon vanilla and beat well. Add the heavy cream and beat well.

4. Roll out one-third of the chilled dough on a floured surface; the dough will be very moist and fragile. Roll it out in pieces and evenly press them, with your hands, into the bottom of the prepared pan. Don't worry if it looks like it is

The counter at Junior's, where cheesecake (see recipe, facing page) is king.

going to fall apart. Bake until golden, 15 minutes, and cool in the pan on a wire rack.

5. Roll out the remaining dough in pieces and evenly shape them to fit the sides of the pan, a piece at a time. Make sure that there are no holes in the crust and try to keep the edges neat.

6. Increase the oven temperature to 550°F. Pour the cream cheese mixture into the crust. Bake for 12 to 15 minutes. Reduce the heat to 200°F and continue baking for 1 hour. Turn off the heat and keep the oven door open wide. Let the cake cool in the oven for 30 minutes.

Serves 8 to 10

Junior's CHEESECAKE

¼ cup graham cracker crumbs
¾ cup plus 2 tablespoons sugar
3 tablespoons sifted cornstarch
30 ounces (3¾ large packages) cream cheese, softened
1 large egg
½ cup heavy (whipping) cream
¾ teaspoon vanilla extract

1. Preheat the oven to 350°F. Generously butter the bottom and sides of an 8-inch springform pan. Lightly coat the bottom of the pan with the graham cracker crumbs and refrigerate the pan.

2. In a large bowl, combine the sugar and the cornstarch. Beat in the cream cheese. Beat in the egg. Slowly drizzle in the heavy cream, beating constantly. Add the vanilla and stir well. Pour the mixture into the prepared pan. Bake until the top is golden, 40 to 45 minutes. Cool in the pan on a wire rack for 3 hours.

Serves 8 to 10

Sarah Challinor Smith's CHEESECAKE

CRUST
1½ cups pulverized graham crackers
⅓ cup sugar
½ cup melted butter

FILLING
1½ pounds (3 large packages) cream cheese, softened
½ cup sugar
4 large eggs
⅛ teaspoon salt
1½ teaspoons vanilla extract

TOPPING
2 cups sour cream
¼ cup sugar
1 teaspoon vanilla extract

1. Preheat the oven to 350°F. Butter the bottom and sides of a 9-inch springform pan.

2. Make the crust: Combine the graham cracker meal, sugar, and butter in a bowl. Mix well. Press the mixture into the prepared pan and place in the freezer until firm, 5 minutes.

3. Make the filling: Using a mixer or food processor, combine the cream cheese, sugar, eggs, salt, and vanilla until smooth. Pour into the chilled crust and bake until the cake begins to turn gold, 50 to 60 minutes. Cool the cake slightly in the pan on a wire rack. Leave the oven on.

4. Meanwhile, make the topping: Stir together the sour cream, sugar, and vanilla. When the cake is cool, spread the topping over it and bake for an additional 15 minutes. Cover with plastic wrap and refrigerate overnight before serving.

Serves 6 to 8

NEW YORK CHEESECAKE

Just as the city cannot claim to have invented steak, New York can't claim to be the birthplace of cheesecake. But historic detail has never stopped New Yorkers.

To them, it doesn't matter that fresh cheesecakes have been baked in Europe since at least 1440. When researching her facsimile edition of Mary Randolph's 1824 book *The Virginia House-wife,* for instance, Karen Hess found recipes for Lemon Cheesecake and Cheese-Cake Pudding, from as early as 1736. At that time, the denizens of New Amsterdam were eating things like Dutch "sweet seed cakes" and pumpkin cornmeal pancakes.

New Yorkers wave a dismissive hand to these facts and say that cheesecake wasn't really cheesecake until it was cheesecake

Does that sign in the window say "Kids Eat Free?" Think of all that cheesecake!

in New York. This explains the New York cheesecake appellation and offers a view of one of the city's specialties: appropriation.

WHAT WE MEAN WHEN WE SAY CHEESECAKE

In the case of New York Cheesecake, an Eastern European-style cake made from pot and cream cheeses was claimed as the city's own. (Don't tell that to someone who grew up near Arthur Avenue in the Bronx or in Bensonhurst in Brooklyn, where cheesecake is Italian-style, made with ricotta. But that is another story and recipes follow.)

Early versions of the cake were probably heavy. In *Bronx Primitive,* her memoir of growing up in the Bronx, Kate Simon recalls the "cementlike cheesecakes" that her mother made on Fridays. The confection moved from homes to restaurants. By 1940, cheesecake was the main call at Lindy's, the fabled theater-district restaurant that actors and actresses jammed for late-night dessert.

The Guys & Dolls razzle-dazzle that surrounds Lindy's cheesecake may not be the only reason that Lindy's became synonymous with New York cheesecake. Between homes like the Simon's and restaurants like Lindy's, the Eastern European cake experienced an unbeatable lightness of being. The recipe for Lindy's smooth cake (page 434) has appeared in numerous cookbooks—and at least one part of the formula is said to derive from the great Appropriation Tradition.

COOKIE VS. GRAHAM CRACKER CRUSTS

Albert Dunayer, whose New Jersey bakery produces dozens of private-label cheesecakes, including, for a time, Lindy's, claims that the fabled cake, like all early New York cheesecakes, originally had a thick, cookie crumb crust, not a dusting of graham cracker crumbs. Mr. Dunayer says that he pioneered the graham cracker crust.

"People didn't eat that heavy cookie crust," said Mr. Dunayer, who owns A&D Cheesecake in East Brunswick, New Jersey, "I couldn't stand to see the waste." His "creation" springs from the New York Cheesecake tradition—it is a more refined version of the Junior's Cheesecake graham cracker crust (page 435) that Mr. Dunayer grew up on in Brooklyn.

Since there are so few variables in a good cheesecake, nuance is wildly debated. For instance, Junior's, the delicatessen that opened on Flatbush Avenue in 1929, stands by its rich, smooth cake with the graham cracker crust. The thick crust denomination has its followers: Walter Rosen, son of Junior's founder, orders four tons of cream cheese a week to feed his customers and to fill his mail orders (call 1-800-826-CAKE).

In addition to his own "Linda's Cheesecake," Mr. Dunayer makes 30,000 to 40,000 pounds of private-label cakes a day and says that flavors—swirls of cherry or pineapple, for instance—have supplanted the fruit slicks that blanketed cheesecake in the days of Broadway Danny Rose. Several home cooks, however, say this cosmetic change is an appropriation and ensuing exag-

geration of older and more subtle cheesecake perfuming devices that harken back at least to Mary Randolph's days.

"Vanilla, all you need is the slightest touch of vanilla and, so help me, your in-laws will be calling you from England to arrange their visits around when you bake cheesecake," said Sarah Challinor Smith, who lives on Manhattan's Upper East Side. "Mine do," she added, admitting that while her sour cream–topped cake is not technically original (or local), it is "from a friend, she lives in Boston, I've made this enough to call it my own and I live in New York."

Across town, Kate Slate stands by a mocha addition to her cheesecake and is equally discreet about its origins. "Maybe I was inspired by a recipe in a magazine," she said mysteriously.

To them, the use of ricotta is anathema. "The idea is smooth," gasped Mrs. Smith. But, of course, the old-time makers of cookie-style crusts must have shuddered at the arrival of graham cracker crusts. And to most New York Italians, the ineffability of a ricotta pie makes it clearly superior to cream cheese–based cake.

Many see a ricotta component in the future of New York Cheesecake.

"Ricotta has that sweet, dairy flavor," said Scott Bromley, a Manhattan designer who was converted to ricotta pies when perusing design shows in Milan. Moreover, he points out that the traditional Italian Easter pie, made with ricotta and wheat berries, has endured and been imitated for nearly 2,000 years—in fact, people fight for places in the lines at the Brooklyn and Queens bakeries that make the cake.

After all, "New Yorkers upgrade everything constantly," he said. "Especially their image."

The fate of the ricotta cheesecake's pie crust—currently a cookie-like model—remains to be seen.

Scott Bromley's
RICOTTA PIE

CRUST
2¼ cups all-purpose flour
½ cup sugar
⅛ teaspoon salt
½ cup (1 stick) unsalted butter, chilled and cut
    into small pieces
1 whole large egg
1 large egg yolk
2 teaspoons grated lemon zest
⅓ cup ice water

FILLING
1 pound fresh whole-milk ricotta
½ cup sugar
1 tablespoon all-purpose flour
4 large eggs, separated
¼ cup heavy cream
¼ cup sour cream
1 teaspoon vanilla extract
2 tablespoons Marsala wine
¼ teaspoon salt

1. Make the crust: In a bowl, combine the flour, sugar, and salt. Use a fork or pastry blender to work in the butter, until the mixture resembles coarse meal. Stir in the whole egg and egg yolk. Add the lemon zest and drizzle in the ice water 1 tablespoon at a time, adding just enough for the dough to come together into a ball. Knead briefly on a lightly floured board until smooth. Cover the dough with plastic wrap and refrigerate while making the filling.

2. Preheat the oven to 350°F. Butter a 9½-inch tart pan.

3. Make the filling: Using a food processor or mixer, beat the ricotta until smooth. Add the sugar and flour and beat until smooth. Using a wooden spoon, stir in the egg yolks, heavy cream, sour cream, vanilla, Marsala, and salt.

4. In a separate bowl, beat the egg whites

until soft peaks form. Fold the egg whites into the batter.

5. On a lightly floured surface, roll out the dough until it's ¼ inch thick. Press into the prepared tart pan. Pour in the filling. Bake until golden, 50 to 60 minutes. Turn off the oven, open the oven door, and leave cake inside for an additional 30 minutes.

Serves 8 to 10

Cathy's
WHEAT BERRY PIE

This dense pie is a winner with people who prefer less sweet desserts.

WHEAT BERRIES
¼ pound whole wheat berries
1 cup milk
2 tablespoons unsalted butter
1 cup granulated sugar
¼ teaspoon ground cinnamon
¼ teaspoon grated lemon zest

CRUST
1¾ cups all-purpose flour
½ cup granulated sugar
½ teaspoon baking powder
Pinch of salt
Pinch of ground cinnamon
½ cup (1 stick) unsalted butter, chilled and cut
    into small pieces
2 egg yolks
¼ cup Marsala, rum, or dry sherry, chilled

FILLING
1 pound whole-milk ricotta cheese
3 large eggs
¼ cup chopped citron (optional)
Confectioners' sugar, for dusting (optional)

1. Prepare the wheat berries: Soak the wheat berries in plenty of cold water for 2 days and nights, changing the water daily. Drain well.

2. Boil the wheat berries in 4 cups water for 15 minutes; the grain will crack and soften. Drain the berries and return them to a clean saucepan. Add the milk, butter, sugar, cinnamon, and lemon zest and bring to a boil. Reduce the heat to low and simmer until the wheat berries absorb the milk, about 1 hour.

3. Preheat the oven to 325°F. Butter a 10-inch springform pan.

4. Meanwhile, make the crust: Sift together the flour, sugar, baking powder, salt, and cinnamon. Cut in the butter with a pastry blender or 2 forks until the mixture is the consistency of cornmeal. Add the egg yolks and mix well. Gradually add the wine; the dough will be crumbly.

5. Squeeze the dough together to make a rough ball. Roll it out to a 12-inch circle between 2 sheets of waxed paper. Press the dough into the prepared pan. Roll out the scraps of dough that remain and cut into lattice strips. Prebake the pie shell for 10 minutes; remove from the oven and set aside to cool.

6. Make the filling: In a bowl, beat the ricotta until smooth. Beat in the eggs, 1 at a time, then stir in the wheat berry mixture and citron, if using. Pour the filling into the pie shell and cover with a lattice of pastry strips. Bake until a knife inserted into the center comes out clean, about 50 minutes. Sprinkle with confectioners' sugar, if desired.

Serves 6 to 8

Beth Polazzo and a plate of chewy, freshly-baked brownies.

½ cup all-purpose flour
1 teaspoon baking powder
½ teaspoon salt
¼ cup solid vegetable shortening
1 cup packed light brown sugar
1 large egg
½ teaspoon vanilla extract
½ cup chopped walnuts
½ cup semisweet chocolate chips

Beth Polazzo's
BUTTERSCOTCH BROWNIES

This is a sleeper: Beth Polazzo's butterscotch brownies are not gorgeous to look at, but they are so toothsome that it is impossible to eat just one.

1. Preheat the oven to 350°F. Butter an 8-inch-square baking pan and lightly dust it with flour.

2. In a mixing bowl, combine the flour, baking powder, and salt and set aside.

3. Melt the shortening in a saucepan over medium heat. Stir in the brown sugar. Remove from the heat and set aside to cool for 5 minutes.

4. Quickly stir in the egg. Add the flour mixture and stir. Add the vanilla, walnuts, and chocolate chips, stirring between each addition. Spread the mixture in the prepared pan. Bake until a toothpick inserted in the center of the brownies comes out clean, 25 minutes.

5. While still warm, cut into 16 pieces.

Makes 16 brownies

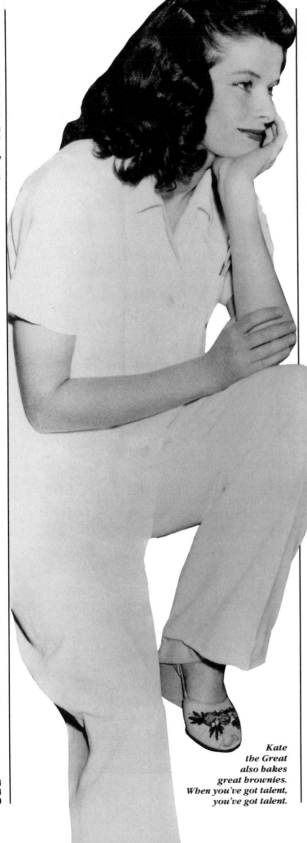

Kate the Great also bakes great brownies. When you've got talent, you've got talent.

Katharine Hepburn's
BROWNIES

About 20 years ago, gossip columnist Liz Smith got her friend Katharine Hepburn's brownie recipe and published it in the *New York Post*. Among brownie intelligentsia, this chewy, dense model is as legendary as the actress who penned its formula.

2 ounces (2 squares) unsweetened chocolate
½ cup (1 stick) unsalted butter
1 cup sugar
2 large eggs, lightly beaten
½ teaspoon vanilla extract
¼ cup all-purpose flour
¼ teaspoon salt
  1 cup coarsely chopped walnuts

1. Preheat the oven to 325°F. Butter and flour an 8-inch-square baking pan.

2. Melt the chocolate with the butter in a saucepan over low heat. Remove from the heat and stir in the sugar. Stir in the eggs and vanilla and mix until smooth. Add the flour, salt, and nuts and stir until smooth. Pour into the prepared pan. Bake until a toothpick inserted in the center of the brownies comes out clean, 40 minutes.

Makes 16 brownies

Susan Mulcahy's
HELLO DOLLYS

Susan got this recipe from her mother, Jean. The bars are drop-dead rich and addictive.

½ cup (1 stick) unsalted butter
1 cup honey graham cracker crumbs
1⅓ cups shredded sweetened coconut
1 cup chocolate chips
1 cup walnuts or pecans, chopped
1 can (14 ounces) sweetened condensed milk

1. Preheat the oven to 350°F.

2. Melt the butter. Pour it into the bottom of an 8-inch-square baking pan. Sprinkle the crumbs over the butter. Sprinkle the coconut over the crumbs. Sprinkle the chocolate chips over the coconut. Sprinkle the nuts over the chocolate chips. Drizzle the condensed milk over all of the other ingredients. Do not mix, just layer the ingredients.

3. Bake until a toothpick inserted in the center of the Dollys comes out clean, 30 to 35 minutes. Cool well in the pan. Cut into 2-inch squares. Store in the refrigerator, wrapped in plastic wrap, for 1 to 2 days before serving. These freeze well.

Makes 16 squares

Robert Weinstein's
NIGHT BEFORE THE DIET BARS

These bars are so sinfully rich, start by serving small slices and let 'em ask for more. They will. They will!

12 ounces (1½ large packages) cream cheese, softened
2 cups sugar
4 large eggs
1 cup all-purpose flour
1 teaspoon vanilla extract
3 ounces (3 squares) unsweetened chocolate, melted and cooled
1 cup coarsely chopped walnuts
1 cup milk chocolate chips

1. Preheat the oven to 325°F. Butter a 9-inch-square cake pan.

2. In a large bowl, beat the cream cheese and sugar until light and fluffy. Beat in the eggs, 1 at a time. Add the flour and vanilla. Pour one-third of the mixture into a small bowl and set aside.

3. Add the melted chocolate to the large bowl and mix well. Pour the batter into the prepared pan. Pour the contents of the small bowl on top of the chocolate layer and top with the walnuts and chocolate chips. Bake until a toothpick inserted in the center comes out clean, about 1 hour.

Makes 18 bars

Zabar's
BLACK AND WHITE COOKIES

Black and white cookies are found in almost every deli in New York. Zabar's version are to deli black and white cookies what pâté is to chopped liver. Faintly redolent of lemons, these cakelike rounds, glazed with half chocolate, half sugar glaze, are a yin-yang sensation.

COOKIES
1¾ cups granulated sugar
1 cup (2 sticks) unsalted butter, softened
4 large eggs
1 cup milk
½ teaspoon vanilla extract
¼ teaspoon lemon extract
2½ cups cake flour
2½ cups all-purpose flour
1 teaspoon baking powder
½ teaspoon salt

FROSTING
4 cups confectioners' sugar
⅓ to ½ cup boiling water
1 ounce bittersweet chocolate

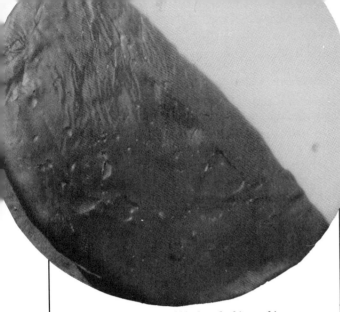

The traditional oversized black and white cookie.

1. Preheat the oven to 375°F. Butter 2 baking sheets and set aside.

2. Make the cookies: In a large mixing bowl, combine the sugar and butter and mix by machine or hand until fluffy. Add the eggs, milk, and vanilla and lemon extracts and mix until smooth.

3. In a medium bowl, combine the flours, baking powder, and salt and stir until mixed. Add the dry ingredients to the wet in batches, stirring well to combine. Using a soup spoon, drop spoonfuls of the dough 2 inches apart on the prepared baking sheets. Bake until the edges begin to brown, 20 to 30 minutes. Allow to cool completely.

4. Make the frosting: Place the confectioners' sugar in a large bowl. Gradually add enough of the boiling water to the sugar, stirring constantly, until mixture is thick and spreadable.

5. Remove half of the frosting to the top half of a double boiler set over simmering water and add the chocolate. Warm the mixture, stirring, until the chocolate is melted and the frosting is smooth. Remove from the heat. With a brush, coat half the cookie with chocolate frosting and the other half with white frosting.

Makes 2 dozen cookies

Don't miss the pistachio-filled pastry at Poseidon on Ninth Avenue.

SOME VERY GOOD BAKERIES

Sixty years ago, when Alexander M. Selinger opened his first bakery in New York City, there were fine bakeries on every street corner. "Everyone finished their cakes by hand, it was an art." But over the years, Mr. Selinger, who owns the Eclair Bakeries, went to dozens of his competitors' funerals and going-out-of-business sales. "I went to hire the bakers, it was a dying art," he said. There are still a handful of traditional pastry shops in the city where cakes are handmade and special orders are accepted:

ALBA: 7001 18th Avenue, Queens; (718) 232-2122. The best Italian bakery in the city. Cannoli are hand-filled to order; the zuppa Inglese and Sicilian cassata—sponge cake layered with ricotta and citron and burnished with bittersweet glaze—are worth the trip. The bakery also makes traditional Italian holiday cakes.

BONTÉ PATISSERIE: 1316 Third Avenue, between 75th and 76th Streets; (212) 535-2360. A wonderful French bakery that makes some of the best fruit tarts in the city.

COLETTE FRENCH PASTRY: 1136 Third Avenue, between 66th and 67th Streets; (212) 988-2605. Makes French-style cakes and fruit tarts with delicate cream filling and an extraordinary chestnut bavaroise.

DUMAS PATISSERIE: 1330 Lexington Avenue, between 88th and 89th Streets; (212) 369-3900. Bakes fine-quality tarts and croissants, as well as puff pastry for home use, and makes French-style sorbet.

ECLAIR: 141 West 72nd Street, between Columbus and Broadway, (212) 873-7700; Grand Central Terminal, Lower Level, (212) 684-8877; At the Basement in Macy's, Herald Square, (212) 564-7166; 984 54th Street, at First Avenue, (212) 759-5355. A good, old-time bakery with a repertoire of over 200 cakes, distantly Eastern European inspired, all adapted to American tastes. This bakery is a sweet throwback.

LUNG MOON BAKERY: 83 Mulberry Street at Canal Street; (212) 349-4945. Makes the best Chinese moon cakes, coconut buns, and custard tarts in Chinatown.

RIGO HUNGARIAN VIENNESE PASTRY: 318 East 78th Street, between First and Second Avenues; (212) 988-0052. Makes fine Viennese-style cakes, strudels, and chocolate-chestnut hearts.

SANT AMBROEUS: 1000 Madison Avenue, between 77th and 78th Streets; (212) 570-2211. Exquisite (and exorbitantly priced) Italian pastry.

WILLIAM GREENBERG: 1377 Third Avenue, between 78th and 79th Streets, (212) 861-1340; 1100 Madison Avenue, between 82nd and 83rd Streets, (212) 744-0304. American-style pies, fruit crisps, brownies, schnecken (see recipe, page 448), and cookies are pricey and worth every penny.

Aunt Hetty's POPPY SEED COOKIES

These tender, faintly sweet, faintly nutty cookies are a deliciously subtle addition to coffee, tea, or sweet wine. They are also good with ice cream.

3½ cups all-purpose flour
2¼ teaspoons baking powder
Scant ½ cup poppy seeds
¾ cup (1½ sticks) unsalted butter or margarine,
*   softened*
1 cup sugar
3 large eggs
1 tablespoon vanilla extract

---

1. Preheat the oven to 350°F. Lightly butter 2 baking sheets.

2. In a bowl, combine the flour, baking powder, and poppy seeds; set aside.

3. In a mixing bowl, cream together the butter and sugar until light and fluffy. Add the eggs and vanilla and beat at low speed until smooth.

4. With the mixer still running on low, gradually add the dry ingredients. Scrape down the sides of the bowl, then mix for an additional minute.

5. Roll the dough, about 1 teaspoon at a time, into little balls about ½ inch thick. Place them 2 inches apart on the prepared baking sheets. Flatten the balls with the palm of your hand to make rounds about ¼ inch high. Dip your palm in cold water if necessary to prevent it from sticking to the cookies.

6. Bake until golden brown, about 20 minutes. Transfer the warm cookies to wire racks and let cool completely. Stored in an airtight container, the cookies will stay fresh for at least 2 weeks.

Makes 7 to 8 dozen cookies

Zoë Morsette's OATMEAL MACAROONS

Zoë Morsette, who lives in Long Island City, says, "This is a favorite cookie that my Norwegian-American mother brought east from Minnesota. I believe that she found the recipe in a Lutheran churchwomen's cookbook in Duluth."

1 cup granulated sugar
1 cup packed light brown sugar
1 cup solid vegetable shortening, melted
2 large eggs, beaten
1 cup shredded sweetened
*   coconut*
1 teaspoon vanilla extract
1 teaspoon baking
*   soda*
½ teaspoon salt
1 cup all-purpose flour
4 cups rolled oats

Zoë Morsette's macaroons probably have Norwegian roots.

1. Preheat the oven to 375°F. Butter 2 baking sheets.

2. In a large bowl, blend both sugars, the melted shortening, and eggs. Stir in the coconut and vanilla.

3. In a separate bowl, mix the soda, salt, and flour. Combine both mixtures. Add the rolled oats, 1 cup at a time, and mix until the batter is very stiff. Drop the batter by teaspoonfuls 2 inches apart on the prepared baking sheets. Bake until lightly browned, 12 to 14 minutes.

Makes 6 dozen cookies

"Moon" Cookies A LA GR'MA NETTIE

This simple recipe, which Eric Asimov inherited from his grandmother, is wonderful with coffee or after dinner with other sweets.

1 cup sugar
3 cups all-purpose flour
2 teaspoons baking powder
Pinch of salt
2 large eggs
½ cup vegetable oil
2 teaspoons grated lemon zest
½ cup poppy seeds

1. Preheat the oven to 350°F. Butter 2 baking sheets.

2. In a large bowl, mix together the sugar, flour, baking powder, and salt. Make a well in the center, add the eggs, oil, lemon zest, poppy seeds, and ½ cup water and mix well until smooth. Gather up the dough into 2 balls.

3. Roll out half of the dough on a floured board until ½ inch thick. Cut out cookies with a cookie cutter or the floured rim of a glass. Place

them 2 inches apart on the prepared baking sheets. Repeat with the remaining ball of dough, then gather up all the scraps and reroll, cutting out as many more cookies as possible. Bake the cookies until brown, about 15 minutes.

Makes about 2 dozen cookies

David's Cookies, buttery, fresh, fragrant, and hard to pass by.

Delicious BUTTERSCOTCH CHOCOLATE CHUNK COOKIES

David "the Cookie King" Leiderman says of his cookies: "these are easy to make and absolutely delicious. They develop a butterscotch flavor as they bake and are extremely fragile."

1 cup (2 sticks) unsalted butter, softened
1 cup packed light brown sugar
½ teaspoon salt
½ teaspoon vanilla extract
1 large egg
1¾ cups unbleached all-purpose flour
8 ounces imported bittersweet chocolate, roughly
   chopped

1. Preheat the oven to 350°F. Generously butter a baking sheet.

2. Combine the butter, brown sugar, salt, vanilla, and egg in a large bowl. Using an electric mixer or by hand, beat the ingredients to make a smooth batter. Add the flour and chocolate and stir until no traces of flour remain.

3. Drop the batter by heaping tablespoonfuls on the prepared baking sheet, spacing the cookies 2 inches apart. Bake until the edges of the cookies are barely brown, 6 to 8 minutes. Remove and let cool on a wire rack.

Makes 20 cookies

Starr Niego's
RUGELACH

This recipe was given to Mrs. Niego's great-great-grandmother by a lady named Mrs. Korngut, who lived next door in their apartment building at Second Avenue and 13th Street.

DOUGH
1 cup (2 sticks) unsalted butter, chilled
8 ounces (1 large package) cream cheese, chilled
2 tablespoons sugar
2 cups all-purpose flour, sifted
2 egg yolks
1 teaspoon vanilla extract

FILLING
¼ cup apricot jam
¼ cup raspberry jam
Juice of ½ lemon
½ cup walnuts, finely chopped
¾ cup raisins

1. Make the dough: In a mixing bowl, combine the butter, cream cheese, sugar, and flour with your fingertips.

2. In a separate bowl, combine the egg yolks and vanilla. Add to the flour mixture and mix well until smooth. Form the dough into a ball, wrap in plastic, and chill overnight.

3. Preheat the oven to 425°F. Butter 2 baking sheets and refrigerate.

4. Make the filling: In a small bowl, combine the apricot and raspberry jams with the lemon juice and mix well. Roll out the dough on a floured board into a rectangle about ¼ inch thick. Cut the rectangle into 3 strips. Cut the dough strips into 4-inch triangles. Each strip should make about 12.

5. Using a pastry brush, brush each triangle with the jam mixture. Sprinkle each with some of the chopped nuts and then with some of the raisins. Beginning at the base, roll up each triangle and bend it into a crescent shape. Place, tip down and 2 inches apart, on the prepared baking sheet. Bake until lightly browned, 10 to 15 minutes. Cool on a wire rack and store in a covered container.

Makes about 3 dozen cookies

Gertrude Greenberg's
SCHNECKEN

William Greenberg learned to make schnecken from his Aunt Gertrude. He still makes it in his namesake shops and he's adapted the recipe for home kitchens.

BUNS

3 packages active dry yeast

½ cup lukewarm (105° to 110°F)
 water

1½ cups (3 sticks) lightly salted butter,
 softened

½ cup granulated sugar

3 egg yolks

1½ teaspoons distilled white vinegar

1 cup sour cream

5½ cups all-purpose flour

FILLING

½ cup (1 stick) unsalted butter, softened

1 cup packed light brown sugar

48 pecan pieces (about ¼ pound)

1 tablespoon ground cinnamon

2 cups plump black raisins

1 teaspoon ground cinnamon, for sprinkling

---

*Everyone should be lucky enough to have a bakery as good
as William Greenberg's close by.*

1. Make the buns: Dissolve the yeast in the lukewarm water and set aside.

2. In a large bowl, cream together the butter and granulated sugar. Add the egg yolks. Blend in the vinegar and sour cream. Add the dissolved yeast and then the flour and mix very well. The dough should be heavy, but not pasty. Turn out the dough onto a floured board and knead for 10 minutes. Divide the dough in half, shape each half into a ball, wrap each ball in plastic, and refrigerate for at least 6 hours or up to 3 days.

3. Preheat the oven to 425°F. Lightly butter 24 muffin cups.

4. Make the filling: In a mixing bowl, cream the butter with half of the brown sugar. Place 1 teaspoon of this mixture in the bottom of each buttered muffin cup. Set 2 pecan pieces in each.

5. Remove the dough from the refrigerator.

Roll out each half on a floured board into a rectangle 18 inches wide, 10 inches long, and about ¼ inch thick.

6. Sprinkle each sheet of dough with the remaining ½ cup brown sugar, the 1 tablespoon cinnamon, and the raisins. Roll up the dough as you would a jelly roll and cut into 1½-inch slices. (Each sheet should yield 12 slices.)

7. Place each slice of dough in a muffin cup, with one of the spiral sides up. Bake until browned and fragrant, 20 minutes. Let cool briefly, then carefully turn out, making sure the topping comes with the schnecken. Sprinkle with a little additional cinnamon. Serve at room temperature.

Makes 2 dozen schnecken

Le Cirque's
CRÈME BRÛLÉE

Sirio Maccioni began dreaming crème brûlée in 1982. While dining in Spain, he ate a crema with a caramelized sugar topping so thick that you had to break it with a small hammer and he imagined a version with a thinner, elegant caramel crackle. This version, tailored to be tapped with the most elegant silver spoon, is now imitated around the country.

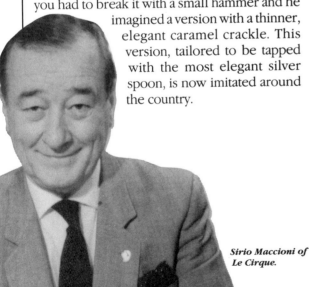

Sirio Maccioni of Le Cirque.

4 cups heavy (whipping) cream
1 vanilla bean, split lengthwise
Pinch of salt
8 large egg yolks
¾ cup plus 2 tablespoons granulated sugar
8 tablespoons packed light brown sugar

1. Preheat the oven to 300°F. Place eight ¾-cup ramekins in a roasting pan.

2. In a saucepan over low heat, combine the cream, vanilla bean, and salt. Warm for 5 minutes.

3. In a large bowl, combine the egg yolks and granulated sugar. Pour in the hot cream and stir gently to combine. Strain the custard into a pitcher and skim off any bubbles.

4. Pour the custard into the ramekins, filling them up to the rim. Place the roasting pan in the oven and carefully pour warm water into the pan until it reaches halfway up the sides of the ramekins. Loosely cover the pan with aluminum foil. Bake until set, 1¼ hours.

5. Remove the ramekins from the water bath and allow to cool. Cover individually and refrigerate for at least 3 hours or up to 2 days.

6. When ready to serve, preheat the broiler.

7. Uncover the ramekins and place them on a baking sheet. Top each with 1 tablespoon of the brown sugar and, using a metal spatula or knife, spread the sugar evenly over the custards. Broil the custards until the sugar caramelizes, 30 seconds to 2 minutes. Serve immediately or refrigerate for up to 4 hours.

Serves 8

Lisa Chernick's
MEXICAN FLAN

Lisa Chernick learned to make this flan when she worked as a cook at Benny's Burritos during the scorching summer of 1988. For some reason, whenever the weather gets especially furnace-like, Chernick gets the itch to flan. "The secret," she divulges, "is to reduce the milk as long as you have the patience to stand nearby stirring it. I've made it starting with 6 cups, and it's really creamy."

VANILLA SUGAR
1 vanilla bean
1¼ cups sugar

FLAN
4 cups whole milk
3 whole eggs
4 egg yolks
Pinch of salt

Outside Benny's Burritos.

1. Make the vanilla sugar: Place the vanilla bean in a small jar or bottle. Cover completely with the sugar, bending the bean, if necessary, to keep it submerged in the sugar. Cover and store for at least 1 week before using.

2. Make the flan: Remove the vanilla bean from the sugar and cut it in half lengthwise. Combine the milk and vanilla bean halves in a heavy saucepan and bring to a boil over medium heat. Reduce the heat to a simmer and cook, stirring occasionally, until the milk reduces to 3 cups, about 40 minutes. Remove from the heat and allow to cool to lukewarm.

3. Meanwhile, combine ¾ cup water with ¾ cup of the vanilla sugar in a small saucepan and bring to a boil over medium-high heat. Reduce the heat slightly so the mixture does not boil over or splatter and cook until the syrup is deep golden brown, 10 to 15 minutes. Immediately remove from the heat. Quickly pour the mixture into a 10 × 6-inch baking dish, tilting the dish to coat the sides and bottom completely with the caramelized sugar. (Wear potholders so you don't burn yourself while you do this, and whatever you do, don't attempt to taste the caramel while it's this hot. It's like lava.) Set the pan aside.

4. Preheat the oven to 325°F.

5. In a medium-size bowl, stir together the eggs, egg yolks, the remaining ½ cup of the vanilla sugar, and the salt. In a steady stream, slowly pour

the lukewarm milk through a strainer into the egg mixture, whisking constantly. (If you've lured a friend over with the promise of flan, have him or her either hold the strainer or whisk the mixtures together at this point. It's pretty tough to do it alone.)

6. Place the caramel-coated baking dish in a roasting pan that is at least 2 inches bigger all the way around. Pour the flan mixture into the caramel-coated dish. Carefully pour room-temperature water into the roasting pan until it reaches halfway up the sides of the baking dish. Cover the pan with aluminum foil and carefully place the pans in the oven, making sure not to spill water into the flan. Bake for 50 minutes.

7. Remove the foil and continue to bake until a knife inserted in the middle comes out clean and the flan is firm to the touch, 10 minutes more. Let cool to room temperature. Cover and refrigerate.

Serves 12

Malvina's
COFFEE MACAROON
CREAM

Malvina C. Kinard has a terrific memory. "This recipe is from my early childhood in Montgomery, Alabama—80 years ago!" she recalls. It's a welcome addition to the more traditional Passover macaroon fare.

1½ tablespoons (1¼ envelopes) unflavored gelatin
¼ cup cold water
2 cups strong, hot coffee
⅓ cup sugar
½ teaspoon almond extract
1½ cups heavy (whipping) cream
1 cup macaroon crumbs

1. In a mixing bowl, dissolve the gelatin in the cold water. Add the hot coffee, sugar, and almond extract and stir to dissolve the sugar and gelatin. Cover and refrigerate until the mixture begins to set, 1 to 1½ hours.

2. Meanwhile, whip the cream until it forms soft peaks. Cover and refrigerate.

3. When the coffee mixture has begun to set, remove it from the refrigerator. Fold in the whipped cream and macaroon crumbs. Spoon into 6 or 7 dessert cups or wineglasses and refrigerate for about 6 hours.

Serves 6 to 7

In early New York, children sold cherries door to door, according to Samuel Woods' *Cries of New York,* originally published in 1808, with a later edition in 1814. The book offers this poem to go with the scene.

> "The children are quite blithe
>   and merry,
>   When summer brings the
>   crimson cherry.
> This season kindly then imparts
>   Its maydukes and its sweet
>   ox-hearts,
>   With common black,
>   and red ones too,
>   And various kinds
>   of lovely hue,
>   How anxious then
>   each youth and maid
> Survey the fruit, so
>   well display'd;
> And, while they are
>   thus carried round,
>   They long to stop,
>   and buy a pound.
>   While their kind
>   friends, their
>   wishes meet,
> And give them much de-
> sired treat."

Sensational CHOCOLATE FONDUE

Like necessity, clever marketing has been the mother of many a fine dish in New York City. When brainstorming a promotion campaign for Swiss products in the United States, Beverly Allen of Allen Associates merged the traditional fondue with the country's Toblerone chocolate. Chocolate fondue was officially baptised on July 4th, 1964, at the now defunct Chalet Suisse, where it was an overnight sensation. Bittersweet chocolate can be used by those who prefer a less sweet taste.

FONDUE
10 ounces Toblerone chocolate (3 bars), broken
*   into separate triangles*
½ cup heavy (whipping) cream
2 tablespoons kirsch, cognac, Cointreau, rum, or
*   any other flavored liqueur or brandy*

FOR DIPPING
Any combination of these, or whatever else you
*   dream up:*
Angel food cake, cut into 1-inch chunks
Ladyfingers, cut into 1-inch chunks
Profiteroles, cut into 1-inch chunks
Orange or tangerine slices
Strawberries
Pineapple chunks
Banana slices

---

1. In a saucepan, fondue pot, or chafing dish over low heat, combine the chocolate, cream, and liquor and stir until the chocolate melts and the mixture is smooth.

2. Keeping the mixture very warm, preferably in a fondue pot over a low flame, spear a piece of cake or fruit and dunk it into the chocolate mixture. Eat immediately.

Serves 6

FOX'S U-BET CHOCOLATE FLAVORED SYRUP

Sometime between 1910 and 1920, the ultimate Fox's U-Bet Chocolate Flavored Syrup was invented in a basement in the Brownsville section of Brooklyn. "I honestly don't remember when," said David Fox, the third-generation owner of the company that is still located in Brownsville. He also doesn't remember whose picture is on the yellow-and-red label of the company's glass syrup bottles, but he doesn't tamper with it. "We leave the recipe and the packaging alone," he said.

He does, however, remember how the syrup got its name. Herman Fox, his grandfather, caught a bad case of wildcatting fever "sometime in the 1920s." He left his hometown for Texas and returned oil-less, but with a new addition to his vocabulary. Fellow drillers, it seems, were big on the friendly phrase, "You bet." When he stamped the phrase on his label, Fox hit pay dirt.

The syrup is now available in major metropolitan areas across the United States. Its milk chocolate tones—"and Brooklyn water, that's the secret ingredient," said Mr. Fox—have made it an indispensable, unalterable ingredient in the Egg Cream—an eggless, creamless drink that evokes the idiosyncratic luncheonettes and soda fountains that once crowded the city's street corners.

Today, egg creams are back in vogue. And their precise formulation is again a subject of dinner table conversation. Aficionados agree that the forceful jet spray of an old-fashioned seltzer bottle is necessary to create the drink's distinctive foam. And, as one egg cream cultist, Mel Brooks, said, "You got to get Fox's U-Bet Syrup. If you use any other syrup the egg cream will be too bitter or too mild."

David Fox's
CLASSIC BROOKLYN EGG CREAM

1 cup milk
¼ cup seltzer
2 tablespoons Fox's U-Bet
Chocolate Flavored Syrup

Pour the milk into a 12-ounce chilled glass. Spritz in the seltzer until a white head reaches the top of the glass. Spoon in the syrup with a little wrist action.
Serves 1

David Fox and New York's own U-Bet Chocolate Flavored Syrup. An egg cream isn't an egg cream without it.

Schrafft's
HOT FUDGE SAUCE

Opening in 1906, Schrafft's Ice Cream Parlor grew to become a string of 39 family restaurants. New Yorkers call this the empire that hot fudge sauce built, and the original recipes for the hot fudge and hot butterscotch are prized.

1 tablespoon unsweetened cocoa
   powder
1 cup sugar
¾ cup heavy (whipping) cream
¼ cup light corn syrup
2 tablespoons unsalted butter
2 ounces unsweetened chocolate,
   chopped
1 teaspoon vanilla extract
Pinch of salt
Few drops of malt vinegar

---

1. In a heavy medium saucepan, whisk together the cocoa, sugar, and ¼ cup of the heavy cream until smooth. Stir in the corn syrup, butter, chocolate, and the remaining ½ cup heavy cream and bring to a boil over medium heat. Do not stir while the mixture heats. Keep over medium heat until the mixture registers 236°F on a candy thermometer, about 3 minutes.

2. Remove from the heat and stir in the vanilla, salt, and vinegar. The sauce will thicken upon cooling or when poured over ice cream.

Makes 1½ cups

Schrafft's
BUTTERSCOTCH SAUCE

The second of the two Schrafft's favorites.

1 cup packed light brown sugar
½ cup light corn syrup
6 tablespoons (¾ stick) unsalted butter
⅛ teaspoon salt
½ cup heavy (whipping) cream
½ teaspoon vanilla extract

---

1. In a heavy medium saucepan, combine the brown sugar, corn syrup, butter, and salt. Bring to a boil, stirring constantly, over medium heat. Cook for 1 minute.

2. Turn off the heat and stir in the cream. Then stir in the vanilla. The butterscotch sauce can be served hot, warm, or cold. To reheat, stir over low heat. If the sauce separates upon standing, whisk until smooth.

Makes 1¾ cups

Schrafft's on Broadway in the 1920s.
Photo courtesy of Schrafft's

Fresh cherries make the best clafouti.

well in the center and set aside.

4. Drain the fruit and reserve the liquid. Pour the liquid into a blender and add the remaining ⅓ cup sugar, the milk, eggs, vanilla, and salt. Blend until smooth. Pour the mixture into the well in the flour and stir gently until smooth and well blended.

5. Spread the fruit evenly over the bottom of the prepared pie plate. Pour the batter over the fruit. Bake for 5 minutes. Lower the heat to 350°F and bake until the clafouti is puffy and golden brown, 45 to 50 minutes. A sharp knife should come clean when inserted in the middle. Cool on a wire rack.

6. The clafouti should be warm, but not necessarily hot, when served. It will sink as it cools. Sprinkle the top with confectioners' sugar just before serving.

Serves 6 to 8

VARIATIONS:

Apple: Use 1¼ pounds peeled, cored apples, sliced ¼ inch thick. Sauté in 6 tablespoons butter until browned, then macerate in ¼ cup dark rum, cognac, or Calvados, ⅛ teaspoon ground cinnamon, and ⅓ cup sugar for 30 minutes. Proceed with the recipe as directed.

Pear: Use 1¼ pounds peeled, cored, and sliced pears. Sauté in 4 tablespoons butter until golden, then macerate in ¼ cup red or white wine, kirsch, or cognac and ⅓ cup sugar. One-half cup blanched, pulverized almonds may be added to the batter with 1 teaspoon almond extract. Omit the vanilla. Proceed with the recipe as directed.

Katherine's
CLAFOUTI

Today, half a dozen types of cherries can be found at the greenmarkets in late June. Katherine Alford, a cooking instructor at Peter Kump's New York Cooking School, thinks there is no finer use for them than in a traditional French clafouti, a simple, elegant, and satisfying dessert. In other seasons, different fruit can be substituted and hints for their use follow.

3 cups pitted black cherries (frozen or canned cherries can be used but should be drained well)
¼ cup kirsch or cognac
⅔ cup granulated sugar
⅔ cup all-purpose flour
1 cup milk
3 large eggs
1 tablespoon vanilla extract
⅛ teaspoon salt
Confectioners' sugar, for garnish

1. In a nonreactive bowl, macerate the cherries with the kirsch and ⅓ cup of the sugar for 1 hour.

2. Preheat the oven to 425°F. Butter an 8- or 9-inch pie plate.

3. Place the flour in a medium bowl. Make a

Old-Fashioned
APPLE DUMPLINGS

A handwritten recipe in an 1827 housekeeping manual at The New-York Historical Society instructs:

"Pare some sour apples and take out the cores. Make a crust and roll out pieces each large enough to roll an apple in. Flour a cloth and tie each apple in separately after it is rolled up in the crust—boil them until the apple is soft. Throw them into a pan of cold water, which makes the cloth cleave off from the dumpling. Serve them with molasses or sugar and cinnamon, or a pudding sauce. It is a nice way to cook them, to put them in a deep pan, half fill it with water and bake them in an oven. This stews the dumpling on the bottom and bakes the top crust. Of course baked dumplings do not require to be tied in a cloth. Crust for dumplings may be made of lard or butter. It may be made of biscuit dough—and the very best and most wholesome crust is made of boiling potatoes; pound them fine, add some salt and knead in flour till it is stiff as bread dough."

Here is a tasty adaptation:

1 pound boiling potatoes, peeled and diced
⅓ cup molasses
½ cup sugar
1 tablespoon ground cinnamon
2 Granny Smith apples, halved and cored
1 cup all-purpose flour
1 large egg yolk
Pinch of salt
3 tablespoons unsalted butter

1. In a large heavy pot, cover the potatoes with cold water and cook over medium heat until tender, about 20 minutes. Remove from the heat, drain, and set aside to cool to room temperature.

2. Meanwhile, warm the molasses and 1 cup water in a small saucepan until smooth. Remove from the heat.

3. Preheat the oven to 350°F.

4. In a small bowl, combine the sugar and cinnamon. Roll the apple halves through the sugar, coating evenly on all sides. Reserve the remaining spiced sugar. There will be quite a bit left. Place the apples, cut side down, in the center of an 8-inch-square baking pan. Pour the molasses mixture around them.

5. With a ricer or masher, mash the potatoes until smooth. Add the flour, egg yolk, and salt

and mix until the dough is stiff. Reserve 2 tablespoons of the cinnamon sugar and add the rest to the potato dough. Knead on a lightly floured board until smooth and no longer sticky, 5 minutes, adding more flour if necessary. Roll out the dough so that it will just cover the apples. It will be about ½ inch thick. Place the dough over the apples and sprinkle on the reserved cinnamon sugar. Dot with the butter. Bake until the dough is golden and the apples are soft when pricked with a knife, about 50 minutes.

Serves 4

Denny's VERY SPECIAL SOUFFLE

Dr. Denton Cox, who has been perfecting his delicious soufflé for several decades, says, "Sprinkling the top of this soufflé with confectioners' sugar before baking produces a very thin crust with the texture of a macaroon."

5 large eggs, separated
1⅓ cups superfine sugar
½ teaspoon vanilla extract
⅓ cup Bénédictine liqueur
4 large egg whites
¼ teaspoon salt
Confectioners' sugar, for garnish

Denton Cox's soufflé makes a wonderful ending to a special dinner.

1. Preheat the oven to 375°F. Place a high collar of aluminum foil around the top of a 2-quart soufflé dish and secure it with string or tape. Butter the soufflé dish and the inside of the ring of foil. Dust the buttered area with confectioners' sugar.

2. In a mixing bowl, beat the egg yolks with half of the sugar until the mixture is very smooth and a pale creamy yellow color. Beat in the vanilla and Bénédictine.

3. In a bowl, preferably copper, beat all 9 of the egg whites with the salt until soft peaks form. Gradually add the remaining sugar and continue beating until the egg whites form stiff, glossy peaks. Fold one-fourth of the egg whites into the egg yolk mixture to lighten it. Then very gently fold the egg yolk mixture into the egg whites.

4. Pour the batter into the soufflé dish and sprinkle the top with sifted confectioners' sugar. Bake until the top is light golden brown, 25 to 30 minutes. The center of the soufflé should be almost runny. Serve immediately.

Serves 6

Kibby's
FIG PUDDING

This heirloom recipe is simple, festive, and the perfect ending to a winter meal.

1¼ cups chopped dried figs
3 large eggs, separated
¾ cup sugar
¾ cup chopped walnuts
¼ cup all-purpose flour
1 teaspoon baking powder
Whipped cream, for serving

1. Preheat the oven to 350°F. Butter an 8-inch-square baking pan.

2. Place the figs in a bowl and cover with hot water. Set aside to soften, 1 hour.

3. In a large bowl, combine the egg whites with ¼ cup of the sugar and beat until stiff, but not dry, peaks form.

4. In another large bowl, combine the egg yolks with ¼ cup of the sugar and whisk until thick and light. Drain the figs well and add to the egg yolks along with the nuts.

5. In a fourth bowl, combine the flour, baking powder, and the remaining ¼ cup sugar.

6. Fold the egg whites into the egg yolk mixture. Fold in the flour mixture and mix gently. Pour the mixture into the prepared pan. Bake until golden brown, 30 to 40 minutes. Check after 20 minutes to make sure the top isn't browning too quickly. If it is, cover with aluminum foil for the last 10 to 15 minutes of baking. Serve warm or at room temperature with whipped cream.

Serves 8

OLD NEW YORK

"A black man, pushing a wheel-barrow before him, cries aloud, 'Butter-mileck.' This sells at three cents the quart. It is a wholesome and safe drink in summer; and with bread, or wheat flour, boiled and sweetened with sugar or molasses, makes a very agreeable diet; and the good housewife, by hanging it, mixed with sour milk, over slow fire, turns it to a curd; and, with the addition of a little butter, salt and sometimes sage, makes what is called pot-cheese. It is made into round balls, and brought to market for sale; and it is good food."

—*Cries of New York,* 1808–1814
Samuel Woods

Karen Bradley's
FRESH FRUIT ICE

This easy and excellent dessert can be served alone or with fresh strawberries, said Ms. Bradley, who is the director of personnel at New York University. Since the fruits used are available all year round, fresh fruit ice can help you pretend it's August in February (turning up the heat in the apartment helps too).

Juice of 3 oranges
Juice of 3 lemons
3 bananas
2 cups sugar
2 cups cold water

1. In a mixing bowl, combine the orange juice, lemon juice, and bananas, mashing the bananas well. Stir in the sugar and cold water. Pour the mixture into 3 ice cube trays and place in the freezer until half frozen (almost solid), about 1 hour.

2. Remove the trays from the freezer. Transfer the ice mixture to a food processor and process until smooth. Return the mixture to the ice cube trays. Freeze until solid, 1 hour more.

Serves 6 to 8

Try Karen Bradley's light, fruity ice as a refreshing ending to any meal.

Noona's
GRANITA DI CAFFE

Emma Capasso made this refreshing granita for her family when they lived in the Bronx. It is a wonderful improvisation for someone who doesn't have an ice cream freezer.

2 tablespoons sugar
1 tablespoon sambuca or anisette
2 cups brewed, hot espresso coffee
Whipped cream, for garnish

1. Add the sugar and liqueur to the hot coffee and stir to dissolve the sugar. Cool in the refrigerator.

2. When cool, pour the mixture in a shallow container and set in the freezer for 2 hours. Every 8 to 10 minutes thereafter, stir the mixture to break up the large ice crystals. When it resembles crushed ice, spoon the granita into parfait glasses, top with a dollop of fresh whipped cream, and serve.

Serves 4 to 6

Mousse
D'HIVER

This white chocolate mousse was invented by Ruth Morrison for a promotion of white chocolate in the late 1970s.

6 ounces Toblerone white chocolate,
 broken into small pieces
⅓ cup milk
¼ teaspoon fresh lemon juice
2 egg whites
1 cup heavy (whipping) cream

1. Melt the chocolate in the top of a double boiler over simmering water. Stir occasionally until the chocolate melts and is smooth. Remove from the heat, whisk in the milk, and set aside to cool to room temperature.

2. In a large bowl, beat the lemon juice and egg whites until stiff. Gently fold the whites into the cooled chocolate mixture.

3. Whip the cream until it forms soft peaks. Fold the cream into the chocolate mixture. Divide the mousse among 4 stemmed glasses. Cover and refrigerate for at least 2 hours before serving. If desired, garnish with whipped cream, candied cherry halves, or fan-shaped cookies.

Serves 4

Izetta Leonard's
BREAD PUDDING

I zetta Leonard, who lives in Brooklyn, recommends eating this bread pudding with ice cream. Leftovers reheat nicely in the microwave.

1 cup milk
1 large egg
1 cup sugar
1½ cups raisins
2 ripe bananas, mashed
1½ cups all-purpose flour
2 tablespoons ground cinnamon
½ teaspoon freshly grated nutmeg
2 cups bite-size pieces of crustless, stale bread

When the bananas are good and ripe and the bread is dry and stale, that's the time to whip up Izetta Leonard's tasty pudding.

1. Preheat the oven to 350°F. Butter an 8-inch-square baking pan.

2. In a small bowl, mix together the milk, egg, sugar, raisins, and bananas.

3. In a large bowl, stir together the flour, cinnamon, nutmeg, and bread. Pour the liquid ingredients into the dry and stir until well mixed.

4. Pour the batter into the prepared pan. Bake until a toothpick inserted into the center of the pudding comes out clean, about 45 minutes. Serve warm.

Serves 8

Ruth's
NOODLE PUDDING

R uth Weinstein remembers her mother making this noodle pudding "when we had company." Weinstein serves this as a side dish or dessert all year round. "It's one of those dishes the kids are always begging for. It's very easy and it comes out perfect every time."

1 pound medium-width egg noodles
1 pound pot cheese or cottage cheese
1 pound farmer's cheese, broken into pieces
1 cup sugar
5 large eggs, lightly beaten
2 cups sour cream
¼ teaspoon salt
1 cup milk
1 cup golden raisins
1 teaspoon vanilla extract
½ cup (1 stick) unsalted butter
¼ teaspoon ground cinnamon

1. Preheat the oven to 350°F.

2. Cook the noodles until tender according to the package instructions. Drain.

3. In a large mixing bowl, combine the noodles, pot cheese, farmer's cheese, sugar, eggs, sour cream, salt, milk, raisins, and vanilla.

4. Place the butter in a large baking pan (15½ × 10 × 2½ inches) and heat in the oven until the butter melts.

5. Remove the pan from the oven, pour in the noodle mixture, and sprinkle the cinnamon over the top. Bake until firm and the top is golden, 1 hour. Allow to cool in the pan before cutting.

Serves 12 or more

Ruth Epstein's NESSELRODE PUDDING/PIE

Early New York cooking manuals refer to Nesselrode desserts with the frequency that people today speak of running out for a pint of Häagen-Dazs. Manhattanite Ruth Epstein developed this recipe, which is worth the time it takes.

1 tablespoon (1 envelope) unflavored gelatin
3 tablespoons dark rum
1 tablespoon cold water
1½ cups heavy (whipping) cream
½ cup milk
Pinch of salt
¼ cup plus 2 tablespoons sugar
2 eggs, separated
2 cups Nesselrode, drained (see Note)
1 prebaked 9-inch pie shell, if serving as a pie
    (Crust ingredients and steps 1 to 3, page 465)
1 ounce semisweet chocolate, grated, for garnish

1. In a small bowl, dissolve the gelatin in the rum and cold water; set aside to soften.

2. In a saucepan, scald the cream and milk. Remove from the heat and set aside to allow the mixture to cool slightly.

3. In the top of a double boiler off the heat, whisk together the salt, 2 tablespoons of the sugar, and the egg yolks. In a steady stream, add the milk and cream to the mixture, stirring constantly. Set the top of the double boiler over simmering water and cook, stirring constantly, until the mixture is thick, 10 minutes. Do not let the mixture boil. Remove from the heat and stir in the gelatin mixture. Set aside.

4. In a bowl, preferably copper, beat the egg whites with the remaining ¼ cup sugar until stiff peaks form. Fold the Nesselrode into the egg whites, then fold the mixture into the reserved gelatin mixture. Cover and refrigerate for 5 minutes.

5. Turn the mixture into the pie shell or spoon into 8 parfait glasses. Chill until firm. Garnish the pie or puddings with chocolate shavings.

Serves 8

Note: To make Nesselrode, combine the following ingredients in a nonreactive container. Let macerate for at least 4 days or up to 2 weeks.

⅔ cup Marsala wine, warmed
⅔ cup golden raisins
⅔ cup dried currants
3 tablespoons minced candied red cherries
3 tablespoons minced candied orange peel
3 tablespoons minced candied citron
⅔ cup chopped chestnuts

Hannah Davis'
BAKED APPLE CRUNCH

Mrs. Hannah Davis is often referred to as "the first widow of the Revolution," as she was the wife of Captain Isaac Davis, the Acton, Massachusetts gunsmith who commanded the Acton Minutemen. On April 19, 1775, Captain Davis was felled by the first redcoat shots at Concord. Mrs. Norden, a descendant of Mrs. Davis, brought the recipe to the Fraunces Tavern, where it enjoys a devoted following.

FILLING
2 pounds Granny Smith apples (about 8 apples),
    peeled, cored, and sliced
½ cup granulated sugar
1 teaspoon ground cinnamon
1 teaspoon freshly grated nutmeg
1 teaspoon ground cloves

CRUNCH
½ cup all-purpose flour
¼ cup granulated sugar
3 tablespoons unsalted butter
1 teaspoon vanilla extract
2 tablespoons confectioners' sugar, for garnish
    (optional)

1. Preheat the oven to 350°F.

2. Make the filling: In a large bowl, combine the apples, sugar, and spices. Stir to coat the apples thoroughly. Spoon the filling into a 9-inch pie plate or round casserole and set aside.

3. Make the crunch: In a medium bowl, combine the flour, sugar, butter, and vanilla. Work the mixture between your fingers and crumble on top of the apple filling. Bake on the middle shelf in the oven until golden, 1 hour. Garnish with the confectioners' sugar, if desired.

Serves 6 to 8

Elias Shammas'
MIDDLE EASTERN BAKED APPLES

Warm and soft, with spices out of a nursery rhyme, traditional baked apples evoke memories of childhood comfort foods. These baked apples are a more grown-up version, with the additions of nuts and currants, but they will still soothe the soul on a cold winter night.

New York apples for a Middle Eastern dish.

5 tablespoons unsalted
    butter, softened
¼ cup sugar
¼ cup honey
½ cup shelled pistachio
    nuts
½ cup pine nuts
½ cup chopped walnuts
½ cup currants
½ teaspoon ground
    cloves
½ teaspoon ground cinnamon
1½ teaspoons rosewater
6 medium to large Golden Delicious
    apples, cored
Vanilla ice cream or whipped cream, for serving

Elias Shammas serves his comforting baked apples while they are still warm.

1. Preheat the oven to 350°F. Butter an 8-inch-square baking dish.

2. In a mixing bowl, cream 4 tablespoons of the butter with the sugar and honey. Add all of the nuts, the currants, cloves, cinnamon, and rosewater. Chop all of the ingredients together until the mixture resembles a paste.

3. Stuff each apple with the nut mixture and stand, stem end down, in the baking dish. Rub the skin of each apple with the remaining 1 tablespoon butter and sprinkle any remaining nut mixture over the apples.

4. Bake until the apples are soft, 25 to 30 minutes. Serve warm, with vanilla ice cream or whipped cream.

Serves 6

Martin Jacobs'
APPLE PANCAKE

Photographer Martin Jacobs makes this giant flourless apple pancake for dessert and for breakfast. It is soul warming any time of the day.

2 large eggs, separated
1½ teaspoons sugar
Pinch of salt
2 tablespoons unsalted butter
¼ cup plus 2 tablespoons chunky
    applesauce, warmed
Ground cinnamon, for sprinkling
2 tablespoons sour cream

1. In a mixing bowl, beat the egg whites until they reach soft peaks. Add the sugar and beat a few strokes more.

2. In a separate bowl, beat the egg yolks with the salt. Fold the whites into the yolks and gently mix.

3. Melt the butter in a 10-inch nonstick skillet over medium heat. Pour in the egg mixture and cook until the bottom is light brown, 1 minute. Turn the pancake, spoon ¼ cup of the applesauce over half of the pancake, and cook until the second side is light brown, about 30 seconds. Fold over like an omelet and cook for 30 seconds.

4. Slide the pancake onto a plate and top with the remaining 2 tablespoons applesauce, a dusting of cinnamon, and the sour cream.

Serves 1

The Algonquin's
FAMOUS
APPLE PIE

The famed "round table" (and just about everyone else who frequented the midtown hotel lobby) had a soft spot for apple pie. This version was served for decades, and the recipe is adapted from *Feeding the Lions: An Algonquin Cookbook,* by Frank Case.

CRUST

2 cups all-purpose flour

1 tablespoon sugar

1 teaspoon salt

½ cup (1 stick) unsalted butter, chilled and cut
    into small pieces

½ cup solid vegetable shortening

½ cup ice water

FILLING

8 apples, peeled, cored, and thinly sliced

1 tablespoon grated lemon zest

⅔ cup sugar

1 teaspoon ground cinnamon

⅛ teaspoon freshly grated nutmeg

3 tablespoons butter, cut into small pieces

Sugar and flour, for dusting the top
    of the pie

The lobby of the Algonquin. Photo courtesy of the Algonquin

1. Make the crust: In a large bowl, stir together the flour, sugar, and salt. With a pastry
blender or 2 forks, cut the butter and shortening
into the flour mixture until it resembles small
peas. Add the ice water, a little at a time, and mix
as little as possible until the crust comes together
into a rough ball. Remove from the bowl, divide
into 2 balls, cover with plastic wrap, and refrigerate for 30 minutes.

2. Preheat the oven to 450°F.

3. Roll out one ball of dough into a 13-inch

circle ¼ inch thick. Fit the dough in a 9-inch pie
plate and trim, leaving ½ inch of pastry around
the edges.

4. Add the filling: Fill the pie shell with the
apples and sprinkle on the lemon zest. In a small
bowl, stir together the sugar, cinnamon, and nutmeg. Sprinkle over the apples. Dot the apples with
2 tablespoons of the butter.

5. Roll out the remaining piece of dough into
a 13-inch circle ¼ inch thick. Perforate the dough
in several places with the tines of a fork. Lay the
top crust on top of the apple filling and trim and
crimp the edges.

6. Dot the top of the crust with the remaining
1 tablespoon butter. Sprinkle lightly with sugar
and flour. Bake the pie for 15 minutes. Reduce
the heat to 350°F and bake until the pastry is golden,
30 minutes more. Serve warm or cold.

Serves 6 to 8

Kay's
TARTE TATIN

K ay LeRoy slaved over this recipe until it was
just right. "It was worth it," she explains, "for
it is extremely delicious." You must use an ovenproof dish since the oven heat is so high. For
best results, use cast iron.

CRUST

2 cups all-purpose flour

1 teaspoon salt

½ cup solid vegetable shortening, chilled

5 to 7 tablespoons ice water

FILLING

¾ cup plus 2 tablespoons (1¾ sticks) unsalted
    butter, softened

1¼ cups granulated sugar

3 tablespoons packed dark brown sugar

6 large Red Delicious apples, peeled and cored

Whipped cream, for serving

1. Preheat the oven to 425°F.

2. Make the crust: Sift the flour and salt twice into a chilled bowl. Cut in the shortening with a pastry blender until the mixture resembles coarse meal. Sprinkle in the ice water 1 tablespoon at a time until the pastry comes together in a ball, pressing lightly. Do not knead. Cover with plastic wrap and refrigerate for 1 hour. Roll out the dough on a lightly floured board ⅛ inch thick.

3. Make the filling: In a deep, round, 10-inch copper pan or ovenproof dish, combine ¾ cup (1½ sticks) of the butter, ¼ cup of the granulated sugar, and 1 tablespoon of the dark brown sugar and mix well. Spread the mixture around the sides and bottom of the pan, making sure that the bottom has a thick even coating.

4. Slice the apples about ¼ inch thick. Arrange them in even layers, overlapping in rose petal fashion, in the pan. The layer of apples should reach the rim of the pan.

5. Melt the remaining 2 tablespoons butter with the remaining 2 tablespoons dark brown sugar. Drizzle over the apples. Cover with the pastry and trim and press it to the edge of the pan. Make a small slit in the middle for the steam to escape.

6. Bake the tarte tatin until the pastry is lightly browned, 30 minutes. Remove from the oven and increase the heat to 475°F. Cover the pan with aluminum foil. Return the tarte to the oven and bake until the liquid around the apples has changed from runny yellow to a dark sticky amber, 45 to 60 minutes.

7. Remove the tarte from the oven and let cool on a rack for 5 minutes. Invert a large plate over the top of the dish and reverse to turn out the tarte.

8. In a heavy saucepan, slowly melt the remaining 1 cup granulated sugar over low heat, stirring occasionally. When the sugar melts and turns dark amber, remove it from the heat. Using a large wooden fork or wooden spatula, drip the caramelized sugar onto the surface of the tart. Serve warm, with whipped cream.

Serves 6 to 8

Sally Darr's
GOLDEN DELICIOUS APPLE TART

When she ran La Tulipe, the tiny bastion of French cooking on West 13th Street, self-trained chef Sally Darr perfected this recipe. It is such a delicate balance of pastry and apples that it became the most requested dish in her repertoire. Serve with vanilla ice cream or lightly sweetened fresh whipped cream.

CRUST
1 cup all-purpose flour
1 tablespoon sugar
Pinch of salt
*½ cup (1 stick) unsalted butter, chilled and
    thinly sliced*
3 to 4 tablespoons ice water

FILLING AND GLAZE
*7 Golden Delicious or Cortland
    apples*
⅓ cup sugar
*½ cup (1 stick) unsalted butter,
    thinly sliced*
¼ cup apricot preserves
1 tablespoon dark rum

1. Make the crust: In a medium bowl, combine the flour, sugar, and salt. Add the butter and cut in with a pastry blender or 2 forks until the mixture resembles small pebbles. Stir in just enough of the ice water for the dough to come together into a rough ball.

2. Turn out the dough onto a lightly floured surface and push it with the heels of your hands into a 6 × 4-inch rectangle. Fold up the bottom one-third of the rectangle, then fold the top one-third down, like you are folding a letter. Turn the dough 90 degrees and repeat, rolling out the dough to a 6×4-inch rectangle and folding. Cover the dough with plastic wrap and chill for 1 hour in the refrigerator.

3. Remove the dough from the refrigerator and set aside for 10 minutes to soften slightly, so it is easy to handle. Roll out the dough into a 13-inch circle. Fit the dough into a 10½-inch tart pan with a removable bottom. Press the dough gently into place, prick the bottom with a fork, and cover with plastic wrap. Chill for 1 hour.

4. Preheat the oven to 425°F.

5. Prepare the filling and glaze: Remove the pastry from the refrigerator. Core, peel, and halve the apples. With the flat side of the apple down, cut crosswise into thin slices. Fan the slices in concentric circles, with the wider part of the fan in toward the center. Reserving 1 sliced apple half, continue, leaving the center of the tart empty. Arrange the remaining apple half (about 6 apple slices) in the center of the tart. Sprinkle the apples with the sugar and dot with the butter. Bake until the crust is brown and the apples lightly caramelized, about 1 hour.

6. Remove the tart from the oven and carefully remove the sides of the pan. Slide the tart onto a rack to cool to room temperature.

7. In a nonreactive saucepan, melt the apricot preserves with the rum until the mixture is smooth, 5 minutes. Strain the glaze through a fine sieve and brush over the tart.

Serves 8

Warm Caramelized BANANA TART

Nancy Hiller "adores" bananas. She keeps anywhere from 10 to 20 of them on her kitchen counter at all times. This dessert is a conglomeration of bananas and other foods she loves—macadamia nuts, chocolate, and sweet, tender dough. It has become a signature dish at the Union Square Cafe, where it was conceived and nurtured.

CRUST
1 cup (2 sticks) unsalted butter, chilled
½ cup sugar
1 teaspoon vanilla extract
1 large egg
1 large egg yolk
2 cups all-purpose flour

MACADAMIA CRUNCH
½ cup unsalted macadamia nuts
½ cup sugar
1 tablespoon plus 1 teaspoon light corn syrup
2 tablespoons unsalted butter, cut into small pieces

CHOCOLATE SAUCE
4 ounces bittersweet chocolate, such as Valrhona, chopped
¼ cup heavy (whipping) cream

ASSEMBLY
6 to 8 very ripe bananas
2 tablespoons Sugar-in-the-Raw
6 scoops best-quality vanilla bean ice cream

1. Make the dough for the crust: In a large mixing bowl, cream the butter. Add the sugar and mix until fluffy. Add the vanilla and mix. Add the egg and the egg yolks, 1 at a time, mixing to incorporate between additions and scraping down the bowl often. Do not overbeat. Gradually add the flour, mixing until the dough pulls away from the sides of the bowl and comes together into a rough ball. Remove from the bowl, cover with plastic wrap, and refrigerate for at least 2 hours or as long as overnight.

2. Preheat the oven to 350°F.

3. Make the macadamia crunch: Place the nuts on a baking sheet. Toast in the oven until lightly browned, about 10 minutes. Remove and cool. Coarsely chop by hand. Lightly butter a baking sheet and keep it handy.

4. In a small heavy saucepan, combine the sugar and corn syrup and stir in 1 tablespoon water. Cook over low heat until the mixture registers 111°F on a candy thermometer. Add the butter and stir until melted. Continue cooking until the mixture registers 311°F on a candy thermometer, 15 minutes. Immediately remove from the heat. Stir in the nuts and pour the mixture in a thin layer on the buttered baking sheet. Allow to cool and harden fully. Coarsely chop.

5. Preheat the oven to 300°F.

6. Remove the dough from the refrigerator and allow to soften, about 30 minutes. On a lightly floured board, roll out the dough ¼ inch thick. Place the bottom of a 9-inch tart pan over the dough and trace around the edges with a small knife. Place the dough in the tart pan; press lightly to fit the bottom only. Do not make sides; it should be like a disk. Bake until light golden brown. Cool on a wire rack.

7. Meanwhile, make the chocolate sauce: In the top of a double boiler over simmering water, combine the chocolate and cream. Cook, stirring frequently, until melted and creamy. Remove from the heat. If the mixture is too thick, add a few drops of water to reach the desired thinness. Cover and keep warm.

8. Preheat the broiler.

9. Peel the bananas; slice diagonally ¼ inch thick. Arrange the banana slices on the pastry disk, overlapping each other in concentric circles, covering the dough completely. Sprinkle the Sugar-in-the-Raw liberally over the bananas. Broil until the sugar caramelizes, 3 to 5 minutes.

10. Remove the tart from the pan and place on a serving platter. Drizzle 1 tablespoon of the chocolate sauce on each serving plate. Place a slice of the tart on the plate, top with a scoop of ice cream, and sprinkle the macadamia crunch over the top.

Serves 6

The mural at the Union Square Cafe.

William Kontos'
GREEK DINER BANANA CREAM PIE

William Kontos proudly offers up a heaping banana cream pie.

The diners and coffee shops that New York's Greek immigrants run are rarely lacking glass-doored, revolving pastry display cases where mile-high pies float like cumulus clouds. This banana cream pie comes from the Georgia Diner in Queens.

CRUST
2 cups all-purpose flour
1 teaspoon granulated sugar
¼ teaspoon salt
½ cup plus 2 tablespoons (1¼ sticks) butter,
    chilled and cut into small pieces
About ½ cup ice water

BANANA CREAM
4 cups heavy (whipping) cream
2 teaspoons confectioners' sugar
2 envelopes unflavored gelatin
½ cup lukewarm milk
2 eggs, lightly beaten
2 tablespoons banana extract
2 bananas

TOPPING
2 cups heavy (whipping) cream
¼ cup confectioners' sugar
1 teaspoon vanilla extract

1. Preheat the oven to 375°F.

2. Make the crust: In a medium bowl, combine the flour, granulated sugar, and salt. Using a pastry blender or 2 forks, cut the butter into the flour until the mixture resembles coarse meal. Stir in the ice water a little at a time, adding only enough so that the mixture pulls away from the sides of the bowl into a rough ball.

3. Turn out the dough onto a floured board and knead for a few seconds. Roll out into an 11-inch circle. Fit the dough into a 9-inch pie plate. Prick the bottom with a fork and crimp the edges. Line the dough with waxed paper and weight it down with pie weights or dried beans. Bake until golden brown, about 30 minutes. Remove from the oven and remove the waxed paper and pie weights. Set aside to cool.

4. Make the banana cream: In a small bowl, stir together the heavy cream and confectioners' sugar; set aside.

5. In a medium bowl, mix the gelatin in 1 tablespoon water. Stir in the lukewarm milk and stir constantly until dissolved. Stir in the eggs. Stir in the heavy cream mixture and the banana extract.

6. Peel and slice the bananas. Line the bottom of the pie crust with the banana slices, overlapping slightly. Pour the cream mixture over.

7. Make the topping: In a large bowl, whip the heavy cream with the confectioners' sugar and vanilla until stiff peaks form. Spoon over the pie. Refrigerate until firm, at least 4 hours.

Serves 6 to 8

Palm Room's BUTTERSCOTCH PIE

This satiny pie is based on a recipe that originally appeared in *Where to Dine in '39*, by Diana Ashley.

PIE
1/4 cup cornstarch
2 tablespoons butter
1 cup packed light brown sugar
2 large eggs, separated
1/2 cup rye whiskey
2 tablespoons confectioners' sugar
1 prebaked 9-inch pie shell (Crust ingredients and steps 1 to 3, page 465)

WHISKEY SAUCE
1 tablespoon cornstarch
2 tablespoons sugar
1 teaspoon freshly grated nutmeg
1 tablespoon butter
1 1/4 cups boiling water
1 egg yolk, beaten
1/4 cup rye whiskey

1. Preheat the oven to 350°F.
2. Make the pie filling: In the top of a double boiler, combine the cornstarch and 1 1/2 cups water. Stir well and add the butter and brown sugar. Whisk together the egg yolks and add them, stirring well. Place the double boiler over lightly simmering water and cook, stirring frequently, until the filling coats the back of a spoon, 15 minutes. Remove from the heat and set aside to cool for 5 minutes.
3. Stir the whiskey into the filling. Pour the filling into the prebaked pie shell and set aside.
4. In a large, preferably copper, bowl, beat the egg whites with the confectioners' sugar until

stiff peaks form. Spoon onto the pie filling, taking care that the meringue covers the filling completely and touches the crust all around. Bake until the meringue is browned, 20 to 30 minutes.
5. While the pie is baking, make the whiskey sauce: In a nonreactive small saucepan, combine the cornstarch and 1/3 cup water. Cook, stirring, until smooth. Add the sugar, nutmeg, and butter and blend well. Add the boiling water and cook, stirring frequently, over low heat until thickened, about 10 minutes. Remove from the heat, add the egg yolk and whiskey, and stir well. Serve with the pie.

Serves 6 to 8

Rhoda's LEMON MERINGUE PIE

Mrs. Rhoda Harris says she likes a tart pie. "This one doesn't call for as much sugar as most lemon meringues." She makes this sunny family favorite with a lard short crust for special spring occasions like Easter, but you can use the buttery crust with the Greek Diner Banana Cream Pie, if you wish.

FILLING
3/4 cup sugar
1 1/2 cups cold water
1/3 cup freshly squeezed lemon juice
Grated zest of 1 lemon
1/4 cup cornstarch
1 tablespoon butter
Pinch of salt
2 large egg yolks
1 prebaked 9-inch pie crust (Crust ingredients and steps 1 to 3, page 465)

MERINGUE
2 large egg whites
⅓ cup sugar
Pinch of cream of tartar

1. Preheat the oven to 350°F.

2. Make the filling: In a nonreactive saucepan over medium heat, stir together the sugar, cold water, lemon juice, lemon zest, cornstarch, butter, and salt. Bring to a boil and continue to stir until the filling is thick enough to lightly coat the back of a spoon, 2 to 3 minutes. Remove from the heat.

3. In a large bowl, lightly beat the egg yolks until they are fluffy. Whisking constantly, pour the hot mixture into the yolks and mix well. Allow the filling to cool for a few minutes. Pour the filling into the prebaked, warm pie shell. Set aside.

4. Make the meringue: Whisk the egg whites until frothy. Slowly pour in the sugar and cream of tartar and continue to beat until the whites stand in stiff peaks. Pile the meringue on the pie, making sure it touches the pie crust all around and completely covers the pie. Bake until the meringue is golden brown, 20 to 30 minutes. Let the pie cool completely before serving.

Serves 6 to 8

Pat Riley's
MOCHA ANGEL PIE

Pat Riley's Mocha Angel Pie, like all meringue pies, should not be attempted on a humid day. The egg whites will droop and the meringue will sweat and take on an unappetizing chewy texture.

CRUST
3 large egg whites
¼ teaspoon cream of tartar
Dash of salt
¾ cup sugar
½ cup chopped nuts, such as pecans and walnuts (optional)

Pat Riley's pie has a nutty meringue crust.

FILLING
6 ounces semisweet chocolate
6 ounces bittersweet chocolate
1 tablespoon instant coffee powder
¼ cup boiling water
1¼ cups heavy (whipping) cream
1 teaspoon vanilla extract

1. Preheat the oven to 275°F. Butter an 8- or 9-inch pie pan.

2. Make the crust: In a large bowl, beat the egg whites until they form soft peaks. Add the cream of tartar and salt, and gradually beat in the sugar and nuts. Spread two-thirds of the mixture over the bottom of the prepared pie pan. Drop the remaining mixture in mounds along the rim. Bake until the meringue is crisp and bisque-colored, about 1 hour. Remove from the oven and let cool, away from drafts, on a wire rack.

3. Make the filling: In the top of a double boiler, melt the chocolates over hot, not simmering water. Dissolve the instant coffee in the boiling water. Stir the mixture into the chocolate. Remove from the heat and set aside to cool for 15 minutes.

4. In a large bowl, whip the cream with the vanilla until stiff. Fold the cooled chocolate mixture into the whipped cream. Pour the filling into the pie shell and refrigerate until firm, at least 3 hours.

Serves 6 to 8

Frances'
DIFFERENT SWEET POTATO PIE

Frances Thomas Someum, a native of Jamaica, owns a luncheonette in Restoration Plaza, Brooklyn. This is a delicious dessert with unusual flavors for a sweet potato pie.

6 large sweet potatoes
1 cup (2 sticks) unsalted butter,
    melted
3 large eggs, beaten
1 cup loosely packed light brown sugar
1 teaspoon vanilla extract
1 teaspoon lemon extract, or
    1 teaspoon finely grated lemon zest
    and 1 tablespoon finely grated orange zest
1 tablespoon ground cinnamon
1 teaspoon freshly grated nutmeg
½ cup sweetened shredded coconut
Pinch of salt
1 small can (6 ounces) evaporated milk
3 unbaked 9-inch pie crusts (Crust ingredients
    and steps 1 to 3, through crimping the edges,
    page 465)

1. Preheat the oven to 375°F.

2. Place the sweet potatoes in a large pot, cover with cold water, and boil until the potatoes are soft, 15 minutes. Drain, cool, and peel. Put the potatoes through a food mill or mash with a potato masher.

3. In a large mixing bowl, combine the mashed sweet potatoes with the butter, eggs, brown sugar, vanilla and lemon extracts, spices, coconut, salt, and evaporated milk. Mix thoroughly.

4. Divide the sweet potato filling among the 3 pie crusts. Bake until the centers of the pies are firm and the crust is golden, 40 to 45 minutes.

Makes 3 pies, each serving 6 to 8

The Pink Teacup in Greenwich Village.

42 GROVE

"Sweet Potatoes. Carolina Potatoes. Here's your sweet Carolinas," cried the vendors who plied the streets of New York. The potatoes were carted 'round the city and sold for 75 to 150 cents per bushel, according to Samuel Woods in his book, *The Cries of New York 1808–1814*. Says Woods, "These, as well as other potatoes, turnips & etc. are measured by heaping the bushel. They are kept ready boiled in many places by the huxter women, who sit in the streets and in victualling houses."

The Pink Teacup's
SWEET POTATO PIE

For decades, this pie has drawn the denizens of Greenwich Village nights to the Pink Teacup at 42 Grove Street where it is served.

2 pounds sweet potatoes, peeled
½ cup (1 stick) butter, softened
1 teaspoon ground cinnamon
¼ teaspoon ground ginger
¼ teaspoon freshly grated nutmeg
½ teaspoon salt
1 cup packed light brown sugar
2 tablespoons granulated sugar
3 large eggs, separated
½ cup freshly squeezed orange juice
1 tablespoon grated orange zest
½ cup evaporated milk
1 unbaked 9-inch pie crust (Crust ingredients and steps 1 to 3, through crimping the edges, page 465)
Whipped cream, for serving (optional)

1. Preheat the oven to 450°F.

2. Boil the sweet potatoes in plenty of cold water over medium heat until soft, 15 minutes. Drain.

3. In a large bowl, mash the sweet potatoes. Add the butter, cinnamon, ginger, nutmeg, salt, and sugars and beat until well mixed. Beat the egg yolks until light. Add them to the mixture along with the orange juice, orange zest, and evaporated milk. Mix well.

4. In a mixing bowl, beat the egg whites until stiff. Fold them into the filling. Pour the mixture into the pie shell. Bake for 10 minutes. Reduce the oven temperature to 350°F and continue baking until the filling puffs up and is firm in the middle, 30 minutes more. Cool the pie on a rack. Serve with whipped cream, if desired.

Serves 6 to 8

MAIL ORDER

ANGELICA'S
147 First Avenue, New York, NY 10003; (212) 677-1549, (212) 529-4335.
Organic flours and grains, herbs, spices, herbal remedies. They will ship if you're more than 100 miles away and have a minimum order of $50. No credit cards.

APHRODISIA
282 Bleecker Street, New York, NY 10014; (212) 986-6440.
Culinary and medicinal herbs; catalog available.

BALDUCCI'S
Mail Order Division, 11-02 Queens Plaza South, Long Island City, NY 11101; (800) 822-1444, (800) 247-2450 (NY State only).

Imported goods, emphasis on Italian products. They accept AMEX, MC, and Visa. Send $3 plus a self-addressed stamped envelope for their catalog. Minimum order of $20.

BARNEY GREENGRASS
541 Amsterdam Avenue, New York, NY 10024; (212) 724-4707.
Smoked fish, other old-style deli favorites. No credit cards.

CAVIARTERIA
29 East 60th Street, New York, NY 10022; (212) 759-7410, (800) 4-CAVIAR.
Smoked fish, caviar, foie gras,

smoked roe, fresh truffles from December to February. They accept AMEX, MC, and Visa. Free catalog.

CHEESE OF ALL NATIONS
153 Chambers Street, New York, NY 10007; (212) 732-0752.
Huge selection of cheeses, gift packaging. They accept AMEX, MC, and Visa. Catalog available.

D'ARTAGNAN
399-419 St. Paul Avenue, Jersey City, NJ 07306; (201) 792-0748, (800) DARTAGN.
Fresh foie gras, moulard ducks, country pâté, fresh chickens, venison, turkey, and game birds; overnight shipping and all products guaranteed. They accept AMEX, MC, and Visa. Free catalog. Minimum order outside of Manhattan is $100.

DEAN & DELUCA

Mail Order Department, 560 Broadway, New York, NY 10012; (212) 431-1691, (800) 221-7714. No catalog, but they will ship their products, everything from soup to nuts. They stock Valrhona bittersweet chocolate. They accept AMEX, MC, and Visa. Minimum shipping cost is $3.

ECONOMY CANDY

108 Rivington Street, New York, NY 10002; (212) 254-1531. Hard candies, nuts, dried fruits, candied peels, almond paste, condiments, much more. They accept AMEX, MC, and Visa; $25 minimum. Free catalog.

GRAND CENTRAL OYSTER BAR AND RESTAURANT

Grand Central Station, Lower Level, New York, NY 10016; (212) 490-6650. They will ship smoked salmon, sturgeon, and trout overnight. They accept AMEX, MC, and Visa. Free catalog.

H & H BAGELS WEST

2239 Broadway, New York, NY 10024; (212) 595-8000. Fresh bagels. They accept AMEX, MC, and Visa. Modest catalog available. Minimum order is two dozen.

IDEAL CHEESE

1205 Second Avenue, New York, NY 10021; (212) 688-7579. Extensive high-quality cheeses from around the world—goat, low-calorie, classics; next day air shipping. They accept AMEX, MC, and Visa. Free catalog and price list.

IRON GATE PRODUCTS

520 Barretto Street, Bronx, NY 10474; (212) 378-7800. Caviar and smoked fish shipped overnight. They accept AMEX. Free catalog.

JUNIOR'S

386 Flatbush Avenue Extension, Brooklyn, NY 11201; (718) 852-5257, (800) 826-CAKE. Delivers New York Cheesecake overnight anywhere in the United States. They accept AMEX, MC, Visa, and DC. Junior's will not ship if temperature is 80 degrees or above.

KATAGIRI

224 East 59th Street, New York, NY 10022; (212) 755-3566. Japanese ingredients; free catalog. AMEX, MC, and Visa accepted. Minimum charge is $25.

Facing page (left to right): Jars of fruits and nuts at Angelica's; focaccia from Balducci's; caviar-to-go from Caviarteria; Barney Greengrass' tempting offer for Long Island weekends. This page: Multitudinous choices at Economy Candy.

KATZ'S DELI

205 East Houston Street, New York, NY 10009; (212) 254-2246. For going on 50 years this delicatessen has had a sign that reads "Send a salami to your boy in the Army" posted in their storefront. They also ship excellent pastrami, corned beef, gefilte fish, and knishes. They accept AMEX.

LOBEL'S PRIME MEATS

1096 Madison Avenue, New York, NY 10028; (212) 737-1372. One of the city's best meat markets will ship its goods, including pricey "hot" Wyoming hamburgers at over $11 a pound. They accept AMEX, MC, and Visa.

MAISON GLASS

11 East 58th Street, New York, NY 10022; (212) 755-3316. Caviar, smoked fish, gift baskets. They accept AMEX, Visa, MC, DC, and Optima. The minimum charge is $15.

MANGANARO FOODS

488 Ninth Avenue, New York, NY 10018; (212) 563-5331. Imported Italian goods, fresh cheese, sausages, and bread. They accept AMEX, MC, Visa, and DC. Free catalog. Minimum charge is $20.

MANON LE CHOCOLATIER

Located on the 7th floor of Bergdorf Goodman, 57th Street and Fifth Avenue, New York, NY 10019; (212) 995-9490; call (212) 753-7300 ext. 8069 for mail order.
They accept AMEX, MC, and Visa.

McNULTY'S TEA & COFFEE

109 Christopher Street, New York, NY 10014; (212) 242-5351, (800) 356-5200.
Free catalog. AMEX, MC, and Visa accepted.

PAPRIKAS WEISS

1546 Second Avenue, New York, NY 10028; (212) 288-6117. Hungarian specialties, spices, herbs, many imported European items; seasonal catalog. They accept AMEX, MC, and Visa.

PETROSSIAN

182 West 58th Street, New York, NY 10019; (212) 245-2217, (800) 828-9241.

Caviar, smoked salmon, other fine goods. They accept AMEX, MC, and Visa. Free catalog. They have various minimum charges for delivery in and outside of Manhattan.

PORTO RICO

201 Bleecker Street, New York, NY 10012; (212) 477-5421.

Coffee and tea, machines, sales twice a year. They accept AMEX, Visa, MC, and DC.

SCHAPRIA COFFEE COMPANY

117 West 10th Street, New York, NY 10011; (212) 675-3733.

Coffee and tea since 1903; same day shipping. They accept MC and Visa. Free catalog. Minimum charge is $10.

SILVER PALATE

274 Columbus Avenue, New York, NY 10023; (212) 799-6340.

Preserves, dessert sauces, savory sauces, and condiments. They accept AMEX, MC, and Visa.

SPICE AND SWEET MAHAL

135 Lexington Avenue, New York, NY 10016; (212) 683-0900.

Indian and other Asian ingredients, spices. No credit cards.

TODARO BROTHERS

555 Second Avenue, New York, NY 10016; (212) 679-7766.

Italian items such as oils and cheeses. They accept AMEX, MC, and Visa. The minimum charge for credit cards is $45 for AMEX and $35 for MC and Visa.

ZABAR'S

2245 Broadway, New York, NY 10024; (212) 496-1234.

Kitchen equipment, large inventory of foods, especially hard-to-find ethnic ingredients; free catalog. They accept AMEX, MC, and Visa.

The book *Chinese Home Cooking* is available from the Organization of Chinese American Women, 1300 N Street N.W., Washington, DC, 20005. The cost, including postage and handling, is $11.95. The recipes in this cookbook come from New York Chinese-American home cooks.

Facing page (left to right): A sign at Katz's; a few of Manganaro's olive oil choices; Edward Weiss at Paprikas Weiss. This page: Out in front of Spice & Sweet Mahal; the fish at Todaro's; the cheeses at Zabar's.

BIBLIOGRAPHY

Adams, Charlotte. *The Four Seasons Cookbook.* New York: Crescent Books, 1971.

Adamson, Helen Lyon. *Grandmother in the Kitchen: A Cook's Tour of American Household Recipes from the Early 1800s to the Late 1890s.* New York: Crown, 1965.

Alejandro, Reynaldo. *Classic Menu Design: From the Collection of The New York Public Library.* Glen Cove, New York: PBC International, Inc., 1988.

Ashley, Diana. *Where to Dine in '39.* New York: Crown, 1939.

Baron, Stanley. *Brewed in America.* Boston: Little, Brown & Co. Inc., 1962.

Bastianich, Lydia, and Jacobs, Jay. *La Cucina di Lidia.* New York: Doubleday, 1990.

Batterberry, Michael and Ariane. *On the Town in New York from 1776 to the Present.* New York: Charles Scribner's Sons, 1973.

Beck, Bruce. *The Official Fulton Fish Market Cookbook.* New York: E.P. Dutton, 1989.

Blot, Pierre. *The Handbook of Practical Cookery for Ladies and Professional Cooks.* New York: D. Appleton and Co., 1867.

_____. *How to Eat and How to Cook It.* New York: D. Appleton and Co., 1863.

Bodkin, B.A. *New York City Folklore.* New York: Random House Inc., 1956.

Boorstin, Daniel J. *The Americans: The Colonial Experience.* New York: Random House Inc., 1958.

Botsford, Harry. *New York's One Hundred Best Restaurants.* Portland, Maine: Bond Wheelright, 1955.

Braunstein, Susan L., and Joselit, Jenna Weissman, eds. *Getting Comfortable in New York: The American Jewish Home, 1880-1950.* New York: The Jewish Museum, 1990.

Brody, Iles. *The Colony: Portrait of a Restaurant and Its Famous Recipes.* New York: Greenberg, 1945.

The Calhoun School. *The Educated Palate.* New York: The Calhoun School Parents Association, 1988.

Case, Frank. *Feeding the Lions: An Algonquin Cookbook.* New York: The Greystone Press, 1942.

Chantiles, Vilma Liacouras. *The Ethnic Food Market Guide and Cookbook.* New York: Dodd, Mead, 1984.

Chapell, George S. *The Restaurants of New York.* New York: Greenberg, 1925.

Charles Street Association Cookbook. New York: Charles Street Association, 1976.

Claiborne, Craig. *The New York Times International Cookbook.* New York: Harper & Row, 1971.

Dana, Robert, W. *Where to Eat in New York.* New York: Current Books, 1948.

Dell'Orto, Seline. *The Manganaro Italian Family Cookbook.* Dallas: Taylor, 1989.

Diat, Louis. *Cooking à la Ritz.* Philadelphia: J.B. Lippincott Co., 1941.

Dickson, Paul. *The Great American Ice Cream Book.* New York: Atheneum, 1973.

Donovan, Mary, Hatrack, Amy, and Shull, Frances. *The Thirteen Colonies Cookbook.* New York: Praeger, 1975.

Editors of American Heritage. *The American Heritage Cookbook and Illustrated History of American Eating and Drinking.* New York: American Heritage Publishing Company, 1964.

Federal Writers' Project of the Works Progress Administration. *New York Panorama.* New York: Pantheon, 1984.

Flexner, Stuart Berg. *Listening to America.* New York: Simon & Schuster, 1982.

Frigand, Lisa, ed. *The Ninth Avenue International Cookbook and Shopping Guide.* New York: Richard Basini Associates, 1976.

Gillies, Linda, ed. *A Culinary Collection from The Metropolitan Museum of Art.* New York: The Metropolitan Museum of Art, 1973.

The Grand Central Oyster Bar & Restaurant Seafood Cookbook. New York: Crown, 1977.

Greene, Gael. *Bite.* New York: W.W. Norton & Co., 1971.

Hamilton, Dr. Alexander. *Hamilton's Itinerarium.* W.K. Bixby, printer, 1907.

Hooker, Richard J. *Food and Drink in America.* Indianapolis: Bobbs-Merrill, 1981.

The Horatio Street Festival of Foods Cookbook. New York: The Horatio Street Association, 1978.

The Hotel and Restaurant Management Department of New York City Technical College. *The City Tech Cookbook.* Olathe, Kansas: Cookbook Publishers, Inc., 1988.

Jacobs, Jay. *New York à la Carte.* New York: McGraw Hill, 1978.

James, Rian. *Dining in New York.* New York: John Day Co., 1930.

Jones, Evan. *American Food: The Gastronomic Story.* New York: Random House Inc., 1974.

Kalm, Peter. *Peter Kalm's Travels into North America.* New York: Wilson-Erickson Inc., 1937.

Kennedy, Nancy, ed. *Ford Treasury of Favorite Recipes from Famous Eating Places.* New York: Golden Press, 1959.

Kirkland, Alexander. *Rector's Naughty 90's Cookbook.* Garden City, New York: Doubleday, 1949.

Langdon, Philip. *Orange Roofs and Golden Arches.* New York: Alfred Knopf, 1986.

Leeds, Mark. *Ethnic New York.* Lincolnwood, Illinois: Passport Books, 1991.

Levitas, Earlyne S., and Moss, Lydia. *Secrets from New York's Best Restaurants.* Atlanta: Secrets, 1975.

Lo, Eileen Yin-Fei. *The Chinese Banquet Cookbook.* New York: Crown, 1985.

_____. *The Dim Sum Book: Classic Recipes from the Chinese Teahouse.* New York: Crown, 1982.

Louie, Elaine, and Bloch, Julia Chang. *Chinese Home Cooking.* Washington, D.C: Organization of Chinese American Women, 1985.

Macall, Lawton. *Knife and Fork in New York.* New York: Robert M. McBride and Company, 1948.

Macoy, Robert. *The Centennial Guide to New York City and Its Environs.* New York: Nathan Cohen Books, 1975.

Mariani, John F. *The Dictionary of American Food and Drink.* New York: Ticknor and Fields, 1983.

McAllister, Ward. *Society As I Have Found It.* New York: Cassell, 1890.

Middleton, Scudder. *Dining, Wining and Dancing in New York.* New York: Dodge, 1938.

Mitchell, Jan. *Luchow's German Cookbook.* Garden City, New York: Doubleday, 1952.

Moritz, Mrs. C.F., and Kahn, Miss Adele. *The Twentieth Century Cookbook.* New York: G.W. Dillingham Co., 1898.

Perl, Lila. *Red-Flannel Hash and Shoo-Fly Pie: American Regional Foods and Festivals.* Cleveland: World Publishing Company, 1965.

Ranhofer, Charles. *The Epicurean.* New York: C. Ranhofer, 1900.

Rector, George. *Dining in New York with Rector.* New York: Prentice Hall, 1939.

Rimmer, Leopold. *History of Old New York and the House of Delmonico's.* 1898.

Root, Waverley, and de Rochemont, Richard. *Eating in America: A History.* New York: Ecco Press, 1976.

Rose, Peter, ed. and trans. *The Sensible Cook: Dutch Foodways in the Old and the New World.* Syracuse, New York: Syracuse University Press, 1989.

Ross, George. *Tips on Tables.* New York: Covici, Friede, 1934.

Rothschild, Nan A. *New York City Neighborhoods: The 18th Century*. San Diego: Academic Press, 1990.

Sala, George Augustus. *America Revisited*. London: Vizetelly and Co., 1883.

Sardi, Vincent, Jr. *Curtain Up at Sardi's*. New York: Random House Inc., 1957.

Sax, Irene. *Cook's Marketplace New York*. San Francisco: 101 Productions, 1984.

Simon, Kate. *Bronx Primitive*. New York: Harper & Row, 1982.

_____. *Fifth Avenue: A Very Social History*. New York: Harcourt Brace Jovanovich, Inc. 1978.

Sineno, John. *The Firefighter's Cookbook*. New York: Vintage Books, 1986.

Slomon, Evelyne. *The Pizza Book*. New York: Times Books, 1984.

Stallworth, Lyn, and Kennedy, Rod, Jr. *The Brooklyn Cookbook*. New York: Alfred A.Knopf, Inc., 1991.

Stern, Michael and Jane. *American Gourmet*. New York: HarperCollins, 1991.

Stewards Manual 1904. New York: Stewards Association of New York City, 1904.

Stewart-Gordon, Faith, and Hazelton, Nika. *The Russian Tea Room Cookbook*. New York: Putnam, 1981.

St. Luke's Cook Book. New York: St. Luke's School, 1975.

Stokes, I.N. Phelps. *The Iconography of Manhattan Island*. New York: Robert H. Dodd, 1915.

Thomas, Lately. *Delmonico's, A Century of Splendor*. Boston: Houghton Mifflin, 1967.

Thorne, John. *Down East Chowder*. Boston: Jackdaw Press, 1982.

_____. *The English Muffin*. Boston: Jackdaw Press, 1980.

Weiss, Edward, with Buchan, Ruth. *The Paprikas Weiss Hungarian Cookbook*. New York: Gramercy Publishing Company, 1979.

What's Cooking at Columbia. New York: Columbia University Press, 1942.

Where and How to Dine in New York. New York: Lewis, Scribners' & Co., 1903.

Williams, Susan. *Savory Suppers and Fashionable Feasts*. New York: Pantheon, 1985.

Wilson, Charles Morrow. *Empire in Green and Gold: The Story of the Banana Trade*. New York: Henry Holt and Co., 1947.

Winkler, Max. *The Longchamps Cookbook*. New York: Harper & Brothers, 1954.

Woods, Samuel. *Cries of New York, Reprint of Samuel Woods' ed. of 1808 with additional cries from his later ed. of 1814*. New York: Harbor Press, 1931.

Worden, Helen. *The Real New York*. Indianapolis: Bobbs-Merrill, 1932.

Wright, Mabel Osgood. *My New York*. New York: Macmillan, 1930.

CREDITS

The following pieces originally appeared in an adapted form in *The New York Times* and are reprinted by permission:
Page 15: "A Taste of the Tropics," May 2, 1990. Page 36: "New York's Artesian Springs," July 10, 1991. Page 76: "Manhattan Clam Chowder," January 24, 1990. Page 80: "The Brotherhood of Brick Oven Bakers," April 4, 1990. Page 232: "Salvatore 'Mr. Wab' Medici of East Harlem, November 13, 1991. Page 228: "Bumper Crops in Bensonhurst," September 9, 1991. Page 261: "The New York Barbecue Summit," May 22, 1991. Page 280: "New York Steak," January 2, 1991. Page 334: "Vernon, the King of Jerk,"

July 11, 1990. Page 382: "Fernando Lara, Marine Muralist," August 7, 1991. Page 415: "Ebinger's," June 5, 1991. Page 430: "On Top of the Carrot Hill Cake," November 7, 1990.

The following pieces originally appeared in an adapted form in *The New York Times Magazine* and are reprinted by permission: Page 45: "A New York Panacea," March, 1991. Page 319: "To Roast a Fine Bird," May 5, 1991. Page 348: "The Curator of Country Captain," April 12, 1991. "Food Walks" appeared in *New York, New York, The New York Times Magazine, Part 2,* Fall 1989.

The following pieces originally appeared in an adapted form in *New York Newsday* and are reprinted by permission: Page 100: "Stalking the Perfect Pizza Pie," May, 1989. Page 367: "A Day Dawn's at Fulton," February, 1989.

Thank you to the following for permission to adapt and reprint previously published recipes: Page 99: "Evelyne Slomon's Perfect Pizza Pie." From *The Pizza Book* by Evelyne Slomon. Copyright © 1984 by Evelyne Slomon. Reprinted by permission of Times Books, a division of Random House, Inc.
Page 168: "Peter Rose's Dutch Cabbage Salad" and page 350: "Peter Rose's Butter Chicken," from *The Sensible Cook: Dutch Foodways in The Old and New World* by Peter Rose. Copyright © 1989 by Peter Rose. Reprinted by permission of Peter Rose.
Page 277: "Brisket with Sweet Potatoes and Prunes." From *Cooking Under Pressure* by Lorna J. Sass. Copyright © 1989 by Lorna J. Sass. Reprinted by permission of William Morrow Company.
Page 338: "Chicken Escabèche." From *The Art of South American Cooking* by Felipe Rojas-Lombardi. Copyright © 1991 by Felipe Rojas-Lombardi. Reprinted by permission of HarperCollins Publisher.
Page 351: "The Russian Tea Room's Chicken Kiev." From *The Russian Tea Room Cookbook* by Faith Stewart-Gordon and Nika Hazelton. Copyright © 1981 by Faith Gordon-Stewart and Nika Hazelton. Reprinted by permission of Elaine Markson Agency.
Page 370: "Oyster Pan Roast" and "Oyster Stew." From *The Grand Central Oyster Bar and Restaurant Seafood Cookbook* by Jerome Brody. Copyright © 1977 by Jerome Brody. Reprinted by permission of Crown Publishers, Inc.
Page 385: "Lidia Bastianich's Oven-Baked Squid." From *La Cucina di Lidia* by Lidia Bastianich and Jay Jacobs. Copyright © 1990 by Lidia Bastianich and Jay Jacobs. Used by permission of Doubleday, a division of Bantam Doubleday Dell Publishing Group, Inc.

ADDITIONAL PHOTO CREDITS
Festivals
Page 317: St. James, courtesy of Larry Murphy; dancers, courtesy of St. George's Ukrainian Catholic Church.

A Chronology of Significant Culinary Events in New York City
Page 191: Peter Minuit, The Bettmann Archive. Pages 192-193: Old Brewery, The Bettmann Archive; oyster stand, courtesy of The Museum of the City of New York. Pages 194-195: Tom Carvel courtesy of Carvel Ice Cream Bakery; ice cream cone courtesy of The New York Public Library Picture Collection; tropical fruits courtesy of The New-York Historical Society. Pages 196-197: root beer seller and tea water courtesy of The New York Public Library Picture Collection. Pages 198-199: luncheon courtesy of The New York Public Library Picture Collection; Modern School, UPI/Bettmann. Pages 200-201: students, UPI/Bettmann; A&P menus courtesy of A&P. Pages 202-203: Nathan's courtesy of Nathan's Famous. Pages 204-205: fish stands and Dr. Kennion courtesy of The New York Public Library Picture Collection; Automat, The Bettmann Archive. Pages 206-207: gumball machine, Sheilah Scully and the Postermat; J.H. Kellogg courtesy of Kellogg Co. Pages 208-209: Waldorf courtesy of The New York Library Picture Collection. Pages 210-211: Goya courtesy of Goya Foods, Inc.; Unisphere, UPI/Bettmann Newsphotos; Brent family courtesy of Florida Photographic Collection.

A Trip Down Menu Lane
Page 402-403: Shakspeare, The Bettmann Archive; tavern menu courtesy of The New-York Historical Society; Le Cirque menu courtesy of Le Cirque. Page 404-405: hotel menu courtesy of The New York Public Library; Delmonico's, UPI/Bettmann. Page 407: Fiske dinner courtesy of The Byron Collection, Museum of the City of New York; St. Regis courtesy of The New York Public Library Picture Collection. Page 408-409: Pell Street and the Gartenhaus, The Bettmann Archive. Page 410-411: Luchow's and Ernest Truex, UPI/Bettmann; "21" Club courtesy of The "21" Club. Page 412: All-U-Kan, The Bettmann Archive.

COVER PHOTO IDS

Front cover:

Top: Renee Mancino (page 430)

Middle: Sirio Maccioni (page 226)

Bottom: Vera Mallis (page 291)

Back cover:

Top: Murray Trachtenberg, general manager of the Carnegie Deli

Middle: Vernon's Jerk Style Chicken (page 337)

Bottom: Molly O'Neill

Spine: Nipa Kitpanichvises (page 257)

Inside Front and Back Covers

(by the number):

❶ Dorothy Cann, president of the French Culinary Institute, and graduates (page 125).

❷ Beth Polazzo with, from left to right, husband David, son Matt holding Norton the dog, and friend Adam Stofsky (page 439).

❸ George Howell, owner of Havana Dry Beverages (page 36).

❹ Jean-Georges Vongerichten, chef at Jo-Jo (page 185).

❺ Steve Goldfinger (page 61).

❻ Cheryl Kleinman of Cheryl Kleinman Cakes (page 426).

❼ Daisann McLane (page 137).

❽ Faina Merzylak (page 251).

❾ Barbara Scott-Goodman (page 68) with daughters Alexandra (left) and Isabelle (center).

❿ Allan Vernon, the "King of Jerk" (page 334).

⓫ Thomas Verdillo, owner of Tommaso's (page 144).

⓬ Francesco Antonucci, chef at Remi (page 256).

⓭ Loretta Butler (page 64).

⓮ Frances Edelman of the Polish Tearoom, with husband Harry (page 259).

⓯ Jacques Williams (page 16).

⓰ Izetta Leonard (page 457).

⓱ Andrea Girard (page 30).

⓲ Andrea Hellrigl, chef at Palio (page 102).

⓳ Yvonne "Lola" Bell (page 336).

⓴ Margot Mustich (center) with daughter Emma and grandmother-in-law Catherine DiStasio (page 27) .

㉑ Millie Chan (page 11).